Administ

Administrative Law

Administrative Law

Fourth Edition

Timothy Endicott

Fellow in Law, Balliol College,
Professor of Legal Philosophy, University of Oxford

OXFORD
UNIVERSITY PRESS

OXFORD
UNIVERSITY PRESS

Great Clarendon Street, Oxford, OX2 6DP,
United Kingdom

Oxford University Press is a department of the University of Oxford.
It furthers the University's objective of excellence in research, scholarship,
and education by publishing worldwide. Oxford is a registered trade mark of
Oxford University Press in the UK and in certain other countries

First edition 2009
Second edition 2011
Third edition 2015

Impression: 1

Published in the United States of America by Oxford University Press
198 Madison Avenue, New York, NY 10016, United States of America

British Library Cataloguing in Publication Data
Data available

Library of Congress Control Number: 2018942141

ISBN 978–0–19–880473–4

Printed in Great Britain by
Bell & Bain Ltd., Glasgow

For Peter Endicott

Outline contents

Detailed contents

Judicial review and the rest of administrative law

Some teachers treat administrative law as a course on judicial review. Others focus on other legal institutions and processes, on the ground that judicial review plays a limited role in the actual day-to-day resolution of disputes, and in control of government action. I hope that this book will be useful for both purposes. The law of judicial review is very complex, and important in itself, but the main role of the account of judicial review in this book is to help you to learn the principles of responsible government that are crucial to every area of administrative law. This approach is useful because of one very remarkable feature of judicial review: that the judges have largely created their own powers to control the government, and they continue to develop those powers. Ombudsmen, tribunals, auditors, commissions, and the many other agencies that oversee administration need to develop and elaborate their own roles; the judges have largely invented their own role.

In the course of doing so, the judges have laboured to articulate the constitutional principles of administrative law in their reasons for decisions. If you are interested in how judges create powers and responsibilities for themselves, how they can do justice with vigilance and creativity, and when their creativity amounts to arrogance instead, then you will love administrative law.

The book points out more than once that judicial review is not the most important technique for preventing abuse of public power, or for holding government to account. But the judges' attempts to craft and to justify their role are extremely useful for understanding other accountability techniques. So, for example, the chapter on ombudsmen includes a discussion of judicial review of the reports of ombudsmen, because I think that you can understand both ombudsmen and the courts better if you understand why judicial review of ombudsmen is almost entirely pointless.

Controversy

This book does not tell you the consensus among lawyers. On many surprisingly basic questions of administrative law, there is no consensus. The constitutional principles of administrative law generate deep controversies about some of the simplest practical questions in administrative law. It would be impossible to state the law without saying anything controversial, so I have not tried to avoid stating controversial views; I have tried to make it obvious when I am doing so.

You will see the fundamental disagreements at every turn; when the judges are not disagreeing with each other, you may find the text disagreeing with all of them. I try to point out the controversies, and to help you to reach (and to defend) your own view of the law. I am sure that you will disagree with some of what you read in this book (or in other books, or in the cases). The good news is that you will be able to find the resources, in the cases and legislation discussed in this book, to support an argument in favour of your point of view.

The fourth edition

The book aims to help you to achieve a sound grasp of the basic principles, and not to serve as a commentary on recent developments. But it is worth explaining why the changes in this edition are substantial. The reason is not Brexit, which has not yet changed administrative law at all; the Note on Brexit that follows this Preface explains why, and explains the implications that we can foresee for administrative law after the UK's proposed withdrawal, which is expected to occur in March 2019.

The primary reason for changes in this edition is that, in the three years since the publication of the third edition, the United Kingdom Supreme Court has been extraordinarily prolific in making innovative administrative law decisions. Those decisions have, in particular, expanded the role that the courts were already taking in imposing transparency on government. Litigation over consultations has been put to novel uses in campaigns against the government's austerity policies, particularly in *R (Moseley) v Haringey LBC* [2014] UKSC 56. That decision has given the courts a new role in deciding the issues that ought to be raised in a consultation (see 1.6.1). The courts' role in holding government agencies to their undertakings, through the doctrine of legitimate expectations, has similarly been augmented in *Mandalia v Home Secretary* [2015] UKSC 59 and *R (Lee-Hirons) v Secretary of State for Justice* [2016] UKSC 46, through a new doctrine that a public authority may not lawfully depart from a policy that favoured the claimant, unless it has good reason.

Notice the common thread in these developments: each opens a new avenue for challenging policy making and implementation (on the ground that it involved inadequate consultation, or that it was inconsistent with the defendant's own policy). Yet each serves as a reminder of the limited role of the courts in controlling government. Claimants resort to these indirect avenues when their real complaint concerns the content of government policy decisions, and the courts will not interfere simply on the ground that the defendant made the wrong decision. That deferential approach has limits, and the courts can interfere with the substance of a discretionary decision on grounds that are outlined in 2.3 and elaborated in Chapter 8. In a recent series of famous cases, the Justices have thought out loud about replacing or augmenting those doctrines with a general doctrine of proportionality—although there is no ground for such a change (see 8.3), and no sign that they will actually try to make it (see the discussion of *Pham v Home Secretary* [2015] UKSC 19, *Keyu v Foreign Secretary* [2015] UKSC 69, and *Youssef v Foreign Secretary* [2016] UKSC 3 in 8.3). This edition also adds discussion of the important Supreme Court decisions in *R (UNISON) v Lord Chancellor* [2017] UKSC 51 and *R (Evans) v Attorney General* [2015] UKSC 21, each of which broke new ground in the measures that the judges are prepared to take to impose their understanding of the rule of law on the government.

But it would be a mistake to think that the judges are always expanding their own role in the governance of the United Kingdom. In *Poshteh v Kensington and Chelsea Royal LBC* [2017] UKSC 36, the Supreme Court restrained the judges' role in the determination of social security benefits, in defiance of the Strasbourg Court's more aggressive approach. And in a challenge to the government's 'bedroom tax' in *R (SG) v Secretary of State for Work and Pensions* [2015] UKSC 16, the Supreme Court refused to use the protection against discrimination in Art 14 of the European Convention on Human Rights to remodel social security provision. In *Michael v Chief Constable of South Wales* [2015] UKSC 2, the Court restrained the use of tort liability to hold public authorities accountable for failings, holding by a 5–2 majority that the police were not liable in negligence for a careless failure to rescue a woman who sought their help, even where they had a public law duty to help her.

So the courts have not taken over public administration. Yet it is certainly true that litigation has become a standard element in the policy-making process. David Cameron's government responded by proposing a series of measures to protect public authorities from judicial review, in the Criminal Justice and Courts Act 2015 (restricting oral hearings on permission to seek judicial review (10.3.2), requiring claimants to face more of the costs of litigation and to disclose their financial resources (11.3), and requiring courts to refuse relief in judicial review where the outcome for the claimant would have been the same if the decision had been made lawfully (10.4.7)). The 2015 legislation is important for the purpose of the book because it gives the reader the opportunity to assess the purpose of judicial review of government action, and its fitness for that purpose. Judicial review often functions as an artificial and unsatisfactory secondary battlefield for political causes, rather than as a bulwark of the rule of law. But there is no really just and effective way for the government to prevent unjustified challenges against itself, and there is value in the development of the law by independent courts. The small changes to the litigation process that the government was able to get through Parliament are not going to resolve the tension in the judicialization of public decision making; that will require self-control on the part of the judges, and wise use of the discretions that they have under the 2015 legislation.

Thanks...

I started this book because I thought that students of English law should know about *habeas corpus*, and because I wanted to publish some of what I learned from giving tutorials in Balliol College. I have tried to say 'thank you' to my students by explaining some of the basic equipment that judges and lawyers take for granted (rights, precedent, distinguishing, process and substance, presumptions, exceptions, floodgates arguments, subjective and objective tests ... see the Index).

Several Balliol students have served as research assistants. Rosie Davidson helped me to start the book, and I am very grateful to her and to Brydie Bethell, Isabella Costelloe, Hannah Crowther, Laura Findley, Hayley Hooper, Melody Ihuoma, Craig Looker, Conor McLaughlin, Rhiannon Painter, Margaret Price, Angela Rainey, and Fiona Ryan. Emer Murphy made an extraordinarily helpful contribution to the work on the first edition, and did a large part of the work for the online resources (including writing some of the case summaries on the website).

I have benefited from encouragement and advice and criticism from Nick Barber, Olivia Bargery, Anthony Bradley, Anthony J Bellia Jr, Sir Ross Cranston, Margaret Lee Grimm, Hayley Hooper, Angus Johnston, Aileen Kavanagh, Jeff King, David Phillip Jones, Donal Nolan, Owen Rees, Marc Rimmer, Sir Philip Sales, Joanna Simon, and Lord Toulson. Michael Spence saved me from mistakes and managed to encourage me at the same time. Anne Davies gave me priceless guidance on Chapter 15. I have benefited from the opportunity to discuss some of the issues of this book with John Finnis.

For the fourth edition, Karen Tsang provided research assistance with terrific diligence and flair. She gave expert advice on a variety of large and small recent developments, including important Supreme Court decisions, and the implications of the Criminal Justice and Courts Act 2015. She also gave detailed suggestions on updating Chapter 15, compiled the data for Figures 10.1 and 12.1, and tested every web link in the book.

I also benefited from the very able research assistance of Paulina Fishman on what counts as a 'public authority' for the purposes of the Human Rights Act (see (15.5.3)). I am very grateful to Ruth Dixon for advice on statistics on judicial review and on tribunals for Figure 12.1, and for explaining to me the challenges involved in understanding them. Peter Endicott updated the Index, and improved it in the process.

I am grateful to the Law Faculty in Oxford for funding for research assistance, and to Oxford University Press for good advice, support, and patience. Particular thanks to my editor, Carol Barbersmith, for her advice and for keeping me to a resolution not to lengthen the book. For moral support, my thanks to Naomi and Peter Endicott, Orville and Julianne Endicott, Michael Spence, and Dan Edwards.

Note on Brexit

As this book goes into production—one year to the day before the United Kingdom is scheduled to withdraw from the European Union, on 29 March 2019—the European Union (Withdrawal) Bill (Bill 2017–19) has been approved by the House of Commons, and is being debated in the House of Lords. The legislation is to provide a framework for UK law after Brexit. The House of Lords will debate over 300 proposed amendments; any that they approve will then be considered by the House of Commons. The legislation may or may not receive Royal Assent by the summer of 2018.

It is not clear what form the legislation will finally take, and Parliament is legislating without knowing what final agreement—if any—the UK government will reach with the EU. In the Commons, the EU Withdrawal Bill was amended to require a new act of Parliament to approve the final EU–UK agreement (this is the only point on which the government lost a vote during the House of Commons debates over the Bill). The resulting uncertainties are deep. The purpose of this note is not to speculate on how Brexit will affect administrative law, but to explain why it matters, and to promise to keep you up to date by way of the companion website for this book.

The great repeal—and the complications

The Bill starts out, 'The European Communities Act 1972 is repealed on exit day.' By itself, that repeal would vaporize large parts of the UK's international trade law, employment law, consumer protection law, environmental law, energy law, competition law, data protection law, pharmaceutical regulation—all of the many regulatory regimes in the UK that have been developed through EU law since the 1970s. That body of law includes 'EU-derived' legislation made by the UK government under the 1972 Act, and EU law that is currently directly effective in the UK according to the 1972 Act. The EU Withdrawal Bill provides that the content of all that law will continue in effect after exit day, just as on the day before, as 'retained EU law'.

It may seem simple to retain EU law (translated into domestic law as of exit day), with scope for Parliament to change the rules in the future as it may decide. But there are huge complications. First, since EU law works within a system of EU institutions, much retained EU law will need to be amended with effect from exit day, in order for it to make sense outside the EU system. The volume of changes that will need to be made is too much for Parliament itself to deliberate over them. The obvious solution is to confer lawmaking power on government departments to make the necessary changes. Those powers will include 'Henry VIII' powers to amend acts of Parliament. The separation of powers between legislature and executive would be damaged in the process, if the executive were given legislative power that it cannot exercise responsibly. The government is proposing to create those powers only for a limited time, and only for the purpose of making technical changes to resolve transitional difficulties arising from the translation of so much EU law into domestic law.

The second complication concerns the implications for devolution. The Scottish Parliament, the Northern Ireland Assembly, and the National Assembly for Wales cannot currently legislate contrary to EU law; complex decisions have yet to be made as to their future role in matters that are currently within EU competence.

A third complication concerns the interpretation of retained EU law after exit day. EU law will change and develop, in particular through interpretive decisions of the Court of Justice of the EU (CJEU). The impact—if any—of CJEU decisions in the UK after exit day needs to be determined. The final EU–UK agreement may have complicated implications for that question, because an agreement on trade may make it necessary for UK to law to be harmonized with EU law in some ways, such as concerning manufacturing standards for consumer products.

The future of administrative law

Brexit will not change UK administrative law until exit day (that is why Brexit has had no repercussions for the fourth edition of this book). At that point there will be significant changes, which will create new challenges for courts and legislatures. Certain elements in the changes to administrative law are already foreseeable. Rather than directly regulating governance in the UK, EU administrative law will become a source of analogies and potential models for the development of UK law (like US or Canadian law). The Charter of Fundamental Rights of the EU (see 3.11, pp 113–4) will presumably no longer have effect in the UK. The role of 'general principles of EU law' (see 1.7, pp 37–9) in interpreting retained EU law is unresolved. We can expect that the UK will not be liable to compensate British citizens under the *Francovich* doctrine (see 14.7, pp 573–4) for loss caused by breach of retained EU law. It is not clear whether any element of the EU law on the control of public contracting (see 15.4.4, pp 601–2) will survive the translation of EU law into domestic law. In its final form, the withdrawal legislation can be expected to provide for novel forms of parliamentary scrutiny of the use of the delegated powers that will facilitate the translation of EU law into UK domestic law; the judges can be expected to be creative in adding their own forms of scrutiny.

Many important and difficult questions need to be resolved in the coming months and years, through negotiation between the EU and the UK, and between the UK government and the devolved administrations, and through legislation. The most important concern trade in goods and services, cooperation in security and the administration of justice, movement of people (in particular, the rights of British citizens currently residing in other EU countries, and the rights of citizens of other EU countries currently residing in the UK), cooperation in regulation of fisheries and protection of the environment, the implications for Scottish devolution, and the problem of how to create a border across the island of Ireland between the EU and a non-EU state.

In that context, the implications for administrative law are relatively manageable. But you will have to watch this space to learn the actual results. The EU Withdrawal Act, once it is enacted, will shape the future course of administrative law. The future will also be shaped by the courts' interpretation of that Act, and by their approach to claims for judicial review of the delegated legislation that will be made to complete the translation of EU law to domestic law (even where the delegated legislation is approved in Parliament: see 7.3.4, pp 266–8).

For updates, see: http://www.oup.com/uk/endicott4e/brexit.

How to use the book

A 'look for' section at the beginning of each chapter outlines the key ideas that you should aim to understand as you work your way through the chapter.

> **LOOK FOR • • •**
>
> - The purpose of judicial review: is it to police action? To right injustices to claimants?
>
> - The relation between standing (the entitlemen purposes of judicial review.
>
> - The increasing potential for political campaign

'From the mists of time' boxes can be found within the text. They point out some of the deep and under-appreciated links between administrative law in the twenty-first century and in past centuries.

> ┌─ **FROM THE MISTS OF TIME** ─────
>
> Under Henry VIII, Commissioners of Sewers wen vide public services, such as drainage ditches, ar for the expense. The Privy Council ordered the tained in the courts against the Commissioners William Blackstone, in his *Commentaries on the Lc* 3. ch 6. looked back on the early development of

Pop quizzes are interspersed throughout the text. They give you the opportunity to put your critical thinking to work on particular problems.

> ● *Pop quiz* ●
>
> Who established the sovereignty of Parliament? Lorc 'It is a construct of the common law. The judges cre any authority for that? Can the judges, as Lord Steyn the principle?

A 'take-home message' at the end of each chapter lets you check that you have understood the main points.

> **TAKE-HOME MESSAGE • • •**
>
> - The real objective of administrative law is good ment that makes for a good community). But adn ernment indirectly, by providing techniques for a
>
> - Administrative law can promote responsible gc stitutional principles: a general, unspecific princ

A list of reading can be found at the end of each chapter. It points you towards key cases and other legal materials that you should read to understand the material covered, and lists a manageable amount of secondary reading selected from the vast literature on administrative law.

> **READING • • •**
>
> R (Abbasi) v Foreign Secretary [2002] EWCA Civ 159&
> A and X v Home Secretary [2004] UKHL 56
> Rahmatullah v Foreign Secretary [2012] UKSC 48
> R (Lumba) v Secretary of State for the Home Departn
> R (Moseley) v Haringey LBC [2014] UKSC 56
> R (Evans) v Attorney General [2015] UKSC 21

Critical questions are offered at the end of each chapter. These have a similar function to the pop quizzes, but allow for a broader overview of the material covered in the chapter.

> **CRITICAL QUESTIONS • • •**
>
> 1 Why do you suppose that *habeas corpus* is use didn't the Belmarsh detainees ask for *habeas* [2004] UKHL 56?
>
> 2 Suppose that the government detains peopl says, in *habeas corpus* proceedings, that there

The Glossary at the end of the book explains legal and administrative jargon.

> ## Glossary
>
> The Index shows where you can find further explanation of the
>
> **Abuse of power:** A use of public power that is blam some person, or is very damaging to the public int from merely using it wrongly. Abuse of power is ge

A simple approach to learning the law

Administrative law is extremely complex—so you should take a simple approach to learning it. I recommend that you read the cases in the list of suggested reading at the end of each chapter while you are working on the material in each chapter. Then use the academic readings in the list when revising for an exam or writing an essay. And at that point, it may also be useful to read more of the cases discussed in the chapter. The simple approach allows you to master the principles of the subject first without being overwhelmed by the cases, and then it allows you to put the principles to work when you read the additional cases. My main advice is to get stuck in to the leading cases, so that you can decide whether you agree with the arguments of the book. Understanding a small number of leading cases in depth is much more useful for learning the law, and for doing well in exams, than knowing a little about a great number of cases.

Case citations

Square brackets pinpoint the *paragraphs* in case reports or other documents that have numbered paragraphs. If paragraphs in a report are not numbered, the pinpoint for a quotation is given by page number. Citations are not repeated when it is obvious what source is referred to.

For simplicity, I have used the neutral citation as the only form of citation for recent cases. Here is what to do if you are using the book in a library and you want to read the cases in the law reports. Go to the Law Reports (in most cases, the Appeal Cases) for the right year, and look in the list of contents for the party names. The neutral citation is included at the top of the report, and paragraphs of the reasons are numbered in the reports. Use the same method for the All England Reports. The Weekly Law Reports include the neutral citation in the contents list.

Guide to the online resources

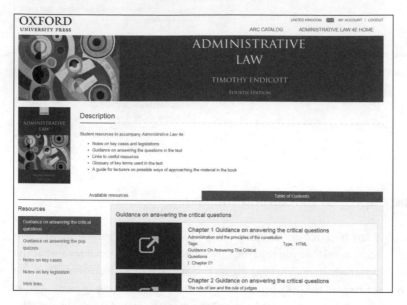

http://www.oup.com/uk/endicott4e/

This book is accompanied by the following online resources:

- Notes on key cases and legislations—these are not the same as headnotes, and their purpose is not to save you from reading the case. The purpose is to alert you to the importance of the case for administrative law, so that you can read the case for a purpose. Links to reports of important judgments and legislation cited in the book are also included.

- Guidance on answering the questions in the text—no substitute for the work that you will need to do in reading the cases and in making your own arguments. The suggestions are only meant to help you to get into that work.

- Links to useful resources—links to the many judicial and administrative institutions in England and Europe that explain their functions and processes on their websites.

- Glossary of key terms used in the text.

- A guide for lecturers on possible ways of approaching the material in the book.

Table of cases

Cases are listed by the name of the claimant.

Abbreviations

ex p	*ex parte*
BC	Borough Council
CC	County Council
DC	District Council
DPP	Director of Public Prosecutions
LBC	London Borough Council
MBC	Metropolitan Borough Council
QBD	Queen's Bench Division (a branch of the High Court; the part of the Queen's Bench Division that decides judicial review cases has been called the 'Administrative Court' since reforms to the Civil Procedure Rules 1998)

Other Jurisdictions

Canada

New Zealand

United States

Court of Justice of the European Union

Table of legislation

Secondary legislation

International Treaties and Conventions

Part I
Introduction

1 Administration and the principles of the constitution

Administrative law includes a complex variety of processes and doctrines that confer and control public power. This chapter outlines the underlying constitutional principles.

LOOK FOR • • •

- **Good administration**: what it is, and how it is related to constitutional principles.

- The fundamental constitutional principle of **responsible government**, and the **system principles** that promote it.

- **Accountability**: what it is, and how the law can promote it.

- **Arbitrary government** and the **rule of law**.

- The different roles of different institutions in restraining arbitrary government.

- The particular responsibilities of the courts: the **principle of legality**, and the requirement of **due process**.

- The **principle of relativity**: the requirements of constitutional principles depend on the context in which they are applied.

> ❛ The King hath no prerogative, but that which the law of the land allows him. ❜
> **Case of Proclamations (1611) 12 Co Rep 74 (Sir Edward Coke)**

> ❛ . . . the King was greatly offended, and said, that then he should be under the law, which was treason to affirm, as he said; to which I said, that Bracton saith, That the King ought not to be under any man but under God and the law. ❜
> **Prohibitions del Roy (1607) 77 ER 1342, 12 Co Rep 63 (Sir Edward Coke)**

1.1 Arbitrary government and the core of administrative law

After the invasion of Afghanistan at the end of 2001, US forces captured more than 600 men suspected of links to Al Qaeda. They were imprisoned in Guantánamo Bay, a US naval base in Cuba. The point of keeping the men outside the United States was to avoid *habeas corpus*, the ancient remedy for arbitrary detention that the Americans inherited from English law. The Bush administration knew that, if the men were imprisoned on US soil, they would be able to ask the courts to decide whether their imprisonment was lawful. The President wanted to be able to detain the men as long as he chose, in conditions that he chose, with no recourse except what he chose to give them.

The families of the detainees claimed that the men should have access to an independent legal process. They also claimed that some of the detainees were innocent visitors to Afghanistan and Pakistan, sold to the US forces by villagers for bounty money. In November 2002, the mother of Feroz Abbasi, a British detainee in Guantánamo Bay, asked the English courts to declare that the Foreign Secretary had a duty to take steps to get the government of the United States to release him.

In *R (Abbasi) v Foreign Secretary* [2002] EWCA Civ 1598 [65], the Court of Appeal concluded that Abbasi's detention was **arbitrary**:

> ❛ . . . in apparent contravention of fundamental principles recognised by both jurisdictions and by international law, Mr Abbasi is at present arbitrarily detained in a "legal black-hole". ❜

It was strong language for judges. By calling the detention 'arbitrary', they were saying that the US government was claiming an uncontrolled power that lends itself to abuse. The detainees were being held on the say-so of the President, when the decision ought to be controlled by law. But although the English judges in Abbasi's case frankly condemned the detention, they refused to tell the Foreign Secretary what to say to the Americans; they held that the best way to conduct relations with another country over Abbasi's situation did not depend simply on whether that country was detaining him arbitrarily, but involved considerations that judges could not assess.

Meanwhile, the families' claims were going through the US federal courts. The Bush administration argued that the courts should not listen to complaints by a foreigner detained outside the United States. The justices of the US Supreme Court were deeply divided; in 2008, more than six years after the detentions began, they finally held 5–4 that the US Constitution required that the detainees in Guantánamo Bay should be able to challenge their detention in the US federal courts through *habeas corpus*.[1]

1.1.1 The story of *habeas corpus*

What if the British government were to try to create an enclave abroad, like Guantánamo Bay, for uncontrolled executive detention? The whole long history of *habeas corpus* from the twelfth century to the twenty-first century gave no definite answer to this question. The phrase *habeas corpus* ('produce the body') was used in a variety of early judicial writs (directions from a court issued in the name of the King), designed to get a person into the court to give evidence, or to respond to a claim. In the 1300s, the judges developed one such writ into an order to an official to explain why a person was being detained. If the official did not give a lawful reason for the detention, the court would order the detainee released.

The writ read as a command of the King, as follows:

> ' We command you to produce before us the body of ____, with the day and the reason of his detention, to undergo and receive whatever our court then and there may order concerning him. ' [2]

This writ, invented by judges, gives a power to judges: power to order the release of a person who was being detained unlawfully. They still have that power today—so long as there is jurisdiction to hear the claim.

The late medieval English judges were able to invent *habeas corpus* because they could issue writs in the King's name. Their role as the King's judges gave them a far-reaching power of constitutional invention. But the fact that they were the King's judges also endangered their independence. In *Darnel's Case* (1627) 3 Howell's St Tr 1, the judges refused to issue *habeas corpus* for detentions ordered by the King himself. It can't have helped that the King had just dismissed an uncooperative Lord Chief Justice, and replaced him with a supporter. It would take an Act of Parliament—the Habeas Corpus Act 1640—to extend *habeas corpus* to control detention ordered by the King. Since 1640, the courts have been able to review the lawfulness of detention by the government.

The courts invented the power, and Parliament extended it, without anyone ever defining its extent. As a result, judges have a very wide discretion to decide their own jurisdiction. In the eighteenth century, Lord Mansfield was uncertain whether *habeas corpus* was available to control detentions overseas, saying that where the judges 'cannot judge of the cause, or give relief upon it, they would not think proper to interpose'.

---

[1] *Boumediene v Bush* 553 US 723 (2008).

[2] John H Baker, *An Introduction to English Legal History* (4th edn, Butterworths, 2002), 552.

But they *would* listen to a claim, 'where a writ of *habeas corpus* out of this Court would be the properest and most effectual remedy' (*R v Cowle* (1759) 2 Burr 834, 860; see 5.1 for discussion of *R v Cowle*).

Administrative law gives judges the job of deciding what judges can do. Lord Mansfield had the right attitude. The judges should be ready to use their constitution-making power to provide a remedy, where they can act properly and effectively to right injustices by other public officials. But if they cannot 'judge of the cause', or if they cannot give an appropriate remedy, judges should not interfere with other people's decisions.

In *Rahmatullah v Foreign Secretary* [2012] UKSC 48, the general question of *habeas corpus* for overseas detentions finally came before the English courts. Yet you will not find any argument on the issue that had convulsed the US Supreme Court: can *habeas corpus* be issued in respect of the detention of an alien, outside the country? This point unites the UK judges: the decisions at every step in the *Rahmatullah* litigation (in the Divisional Court,[3] and twice in the Court of Appeal, and then on appeal to the Supreme Court) took it for granted that *habeas corpus* is available when an alien is detained abroad. In the 700-year history of *habeas corpus* there was no authority for that general proposition before *Rahmatullah*.[4]

An even more remarkable feature of *Rahmatullah* is that the court issued *habeas corpus* when the British government was not even detaining the claimant. Yunus Rahmatullah was being held by the Americans at Bagram airbase in Afghanistan, where—unlike in Guantánamo Bay—the US courts did not allow detainees to ask for *habeas corpus*.[5] The British had captured him in Iraq in 2004, and handed him over to the Americans. The US authorities took him to Afghanistan. In 2003, the UK and the United States had agreed that detainees transferred to the United States would be returned on request from the UK. But it was unclear whether that agreement was superseded by a later one that did not provide for such returns of detainees, and it was perfectly clear that neither agreement was legally enforceable.

The Divisional Court refused to issue *habeas corpus*, on the ground that the defendant did not have control over the detention. But the Court of Appeal allowed Rahmatullah's appeal and issued the writ, on the basis that it was unclear whether the UK government could assert control over the detention, and that issuing the writ would be one way to find out. In response to the writ, the UK government requested Rahmatullah's return from the United States, and the US government responded with a diplomatic letter. The letter spoke at some length without saying anything. Then the letter just stopped, without having answered the request for Rahmatullah's release.

---

[3] A 'divisional court' is a court of first instance (i.e., a court that holds an initial hearing rather than an appeal) that has more than one member; many first-instance judicial review decisions, as in *Rahmatullah*, are made by a divisional court of two or three judges.

[4] Although the judges in *Abbasi* [15], had suggested that it would be surprising if *habeas corpus* were not available in such circumstances.

[5] *Al Maqaleh v Hagel* (No 12–5404) US Court of Appeals for the District of Columbia, 24 December 2013.

Rahmatullah's lawyers went back to the Court of Appeal, asking the Court to require the UK government to demand a straight answer from the Americans. But the Court held that it was now clear, in light of the US response, that the UK government was not in a position to assert control over the detention. On a further appeal, the UK Supreme Court decided that the Court of Appeal had been right to issue the writ, and also to conclude, after seeing the US response, that it had become clear that the UK government was not in control of the detention. Baroness Hale and Lord Carnwath dissented vigorously; they thought that the Court should require the UK government to go back to the Americans and assert the UK's right to the return of Rahmatullah under the 2003 agreement.

In all these cases—the US Guantánamo Bay cases, and *Abbasi*, and *Cowle*, and *Rahmatullah*—the judges' job was not only to decide the government's legal powers; the judges also had to decide their own legal powers. Lord Mansfield's approach is a good guide to that latter job. The power of executive officials to detain people cries out for control by an independent decision maker: not only because of the risk of malicious abuse, but also because even decent and committed officials should have to account to others for the justice of imprisoning someone. An uncontrolled power to detain people is an arbitrary power. If the judges can judge of the cause of imprisonment, and give an effectual remedy, they do a good job of deciding their own powers when they insist on doing so.

By that criterion, the English judges did well to invent *habeas corpus*, and the Habeas Corpus Act 1640, extending *habeas corpus* to detention by the Crown, was a wise measure. The US Supreme Court was right to extend *habeas corpus* to Guantánamo Bay, if it could do so without interfering irresponsibly with the US government's efforts to prevent terrorist attacks. And the Court did well not to extend *habeas corpus* to detentions in Afghanistan if it could not properly consider the issues or give a good remedy for detentions in a war zone. Conversely, if they could control detention in Afghanistan without interfering irresponsibly with the war effort, the judges failed to seize an opportunity to control arbitrary power.

In *Abbasi*, the judges would have been prepared to order Abbasi's release if he had been held by the UK government, but they were quite reasonably not prepared to order the UK government to demand his release from another country. Even though they could see that the US government was acting arbitrarily,[6] they could not 'judge of the cause' as to whether the UK government should start a dispute about it with the Americans. So they could not hold that the decision not to do so was arbitrary.

What about *Rahmatullah*? It was a step forward for the UK Supreme Court to establish—by treating it as something taken for granted—that *habeas corpus* can be used to challenge detention outside the UK. And Rahmatullah certainly was being detained arbitrarily by the Americans. But the UK judges had no reason, at any point, for thinking that the writ of *habeas corpus* would provide an effectual remedy. Imagine

---

6   A US detainee review panel had decided there was no ground for detention (*Rahmatullah*, [5]), but the US government had still not released him, and there was no legal process available to him in the United States to seek an independent remedy against his detention.

asking the US government, 'Can the UK government assert control over the detention of an Al Qaeda suspect in your detention centre in Afghanistan?' It should have been obvious all along, even to non-diplomats, that the Americans would not agree that the UK could control Rahmatullah's detention. There is really no answer to the plain speaking of Lord Justice Laws, in the Divisional Court in *Rahmatullah*, that it was 'impossible to say that the Secretary of State is in a position in effect to direct the claimant's delivery. The claimant is not within his power or control' (*Rahmatullah v Foreign Secretary* [2011] EWHC 2008 [34]).

In Lord Mansfield's terms, the judges were in no position to give an effectual remedy. As a process designed to secure the release of Rahmatullah from custody, the litigation in *Rahmatullah* was entirely pointless. But, as you will often find in administrative law, claimants may find a value in pursuing litigation even when they have no prospect of getting the result for which they are asking (see 11.2.1, p 419).

And, as you approach administrative law, it is worth remembering the willingness of senior judges—the three judges in the Court of Appeal, and all seven justices in the UK Supreme Court in *Rahmatullah*—to issue the writ, and to push *habeas corpus* somewhat beyond its rationale. It was their way of asserting their commitment to the courts' responsibility for opposing arbitrary government.

1.1.2 The European Convention on Human Rights

In the twenty-first century, the judges' creative role in deciding the scope of their own power is not restricted to the development of the common law. The European Convention on Human Rights (ECHR; see Chapter 3) gives a similarly creative role to the European Court of Human Rights in Strasbourg, and the Human Rights Act 1998 gives the UK judges a role in deciding the extent of their own power.

If terrorism suspects were detained in a British Guantánamo Bay, the European Convention on Human Rights would apply. In the Strasbourg Court, or in the English courts under the Human Rights Act (see 3.3), they could assert 'the right to liberty' that is guaranteed by Art 5, which provides a restrictive list of legal grounds on which a person may be detained.[7]

● *Pop quiz* ●

Why do you suppose Rahmatullah's lawyers sought *habeas corpus*, instead of bringing a claim based on Art 5 under the Human Rights Act?

In *A and X v Home Secretary* [2004] UKHL 56, nine men were detained without trial, on suspicion of involvement in international terrorism. The men were held in Belmarsh Prison. The media called it 'Britain's Guantánamo Bay', but it was very different: Belmarsh is in south London, not on foreign soil. The Belmarsh detainees had access

---

[7]   See *Al-Skeini v United Kingdom* (2011) 53 EHRR 18, extending Convention rights to British operations in Iraq.

to review hearings from the start (although not to the ordinary process of the courts). What's more, they could have left the country. They were foreign nationals, whom the British government could not lawfully deport.[8] Unable to deport them, and not wanting to release them in the UK, the British government decided to derogate from the right to liberty in Art 5 of the Convention (that is, it decided to make an exception to it). Parliament authorized detention without trial of people in that situation, in the Anti-terrorism, Crime and Security Act 2001 s 23.

The European Convention provides for derogations from Art 5, but only 'in time of war or other public emergency threatening the life of the nation', and only 'to the extent strictly required by the exigencies of the situation' (Art 15). The Home Secretary thought that the situation strictly required indefinite detention without trial. The Law Lords decided 8–1 that the detentions were not strictly required; Lord Hoffmann did not even think that the emergency was a threat to the life of the nation. Lord Walker alone thought that the judges ought to defer to the Home Secretary's judgment as to whether the situation required the detentions. The majority thought that they could hold that the detentions were unnecessary, without interfering illegitimately with the Home Secretary's work.

The history of *habeas corpus* gives the judges power to determine the extent of their own jurisdiction. They exercise similar control over their own power in giving effect to the European Convention on Human Rights, because they have authority to decide the extent to which they should go along with decisions of the government. If the judges are to use these far-reaching powers responsibly, they must use them in a way that shows respect for the constitutional role of the Home Secretary—that is, with **comity** (see 1.5.3) toward the Home Secretary. In the Guantánamo Bay litigation, the dissenting US Supreme Court justices thought that they had to defer to the Commander-in-Chief's judgment as to how to run a campaign that he called a 'war' (*Boumediene v Bush* 553 US 723 (2008) (Scalia J)); the majority would not defer. In *Abbasi*, the Court of Appeal deferred to the Foreign Secretary's judgment as to whether to demand the release of detainees from Guantánamo Bay. In *A and X*, the UK Supreme Court would not defer to the Home Secretary's judgment as to whether it is necessary to detain people indefinitely.

1.1.3 What is arbitrary government?

Arbitrary government is conduct that ought to be controlled by another public authority, but is not. A decision-making arrangement does not count as arbitrary government if there is a good reason for leaving the decision maker free to act as he or she sees fit. So, for example, Parliament's power to levy an income tax is not an example of arbitrary government, even though no other institution has legal power

---

8   They would have faced inhuman or degrading treatment if they had been deported to their own countries, and the European Court of Human Rights has held that deportation in that situation would violate the right, under Art 3 of the Convention, not to be subjected to torture or to inhuman or degrading treatment (*Chahal v United Kingdom* (1996) 23 EHRR 413—see 3.6, p 93).

to control it. Parliament's exercise of power needs to be controlled by the people, and control by any other institution would not make the decision less arbitrary. But a decision-making arrangement is arbitrary if it needs to be controlled by other institutions, but it is not. That would be a failure in the rule of law. And a particular decision is arbitrary if legal institutions can identify it as a departure from responsible government.

- **Arbitrary government is government that is contrary to the rule of law.**
- **The power of a public institution or official is arbitrary (and therefore contrary to the rule of law) if a technique for control of the power by another institution or person is needed, but is lacking.**

If the US President or the British Home Secretary could order people to be detained indefinitely without judicial process, that would give them an arbitrary power. The courts should not leave it to the government to decide whether imprisonment is necessary in a case like *Boumediene*, or *A and X*. But why did the Court of Appeal in the *Abbasi* case leave it to the government to decide whether to demand Abbasi's release by a foreign power? The judges held that the considerations at stake in the Foreign Secretary's decision included the answers to questions such as whether the UK ought to stand shoulder to shoulder with the United States in combating terrorism, and if so, whether demanding the return of British detainees would damage the alliance, and how it would affect relations with other countries besides the United States. The Court of Appeal held that those questions are not **justiciable** (see 7.3.1, p 254)—that is, they are not suitable for judges to decide.

There were two crucial issues in *Rahmatullah, Abbasi,* and *A and X*: the first was whether there were considerations at stake that the courts could not assess; the second was whether the interests of the claimant needed to be protected by the court in spite of any such issues. If the British government is detaining suspects, as in *A and X*, the decision may affect relations with other countries in ways on which the court cannot pass judgment. But the court can still identify indefinite detention as arbitrary, regardless of the other issues at stake. A court is able to decide whether the Home Secretary is acting arbitrarily if he or she imprisons people, but a court cannot determine whether the Foreign Secretary is acting arbitrarily if he or she refuses to make demands to a foreign government.

Some of the most important executive decisions are simply not controlled by law (such as the decision to put a Bill before Parliament), or are barely controlled by law (such as the decision to wage war, or to sign treaties). Even if they are exercised capriciously and without regard to the relevant considerations, they are not arbitrary in the sense that is contrary to the rule of law. When the government decides to put a Bill before Parliament, the law courts are not capable of determining whether the government is responding to the relevant considerations, without damaging the constitutional functions of the executive and of the legislature. That would be a breach of the **comity** that courts owe toward other public authorities.

The core of administrative law is the provision of processes independent of the government, for the prevention of government action that can be identified as arbitrary with no breach of comity. That is, the core task of administrative law is to impose the rule of law on public authorities.

FROM THE MISTS OF TIME

Under Henry VIII, Commissioners of Sewers were given statutory power to provide public services, such as drainage ditches, and power to charge landowners for the expense. The Privy Council ordered that no actions should be entertained in the courts against the Commissioners of Sewers. Two centuries later, William Blackstone, in his *Commentaries on the Laws of England (1765–1769)*, Book 3, ch 6, looked back on the early development of judicial review as follows:

' The pretense for such arbitrary measures [that is the Privy Council's orders preventing claims against the Commissioners] was no other than the tyrant's plea, of the necessity of unlimited powers in works of evident utility to the public, "the supreme reason above all reasons, which is the salvation of the king's lands and people." But now it is clearly held, that this (as well as all other inferior jurisdictions) is subject to the discretionary coercion of his majesty's court of king's bench. '

● *Pop quiz* ●

The 'tyrant's plea' was an argument of **comity**—that is, an argument that judicial interference with the executive would damage the ability of the executive to carry out its constitutional function. If courts ought to act with comity toward the executive, what was wrong with that argument?

1.2 Administration

'Administrative' is used in a very broad sense in administrative law. Administration is more than just the operation of government departments and the carrying out of government programmes. The **executive** includes all agencies of central government, but does not include the courts or Parliament.[9] **Administration** includes all of the conduct of the executive except conduct in Parliament, such as presenting Bills to the House of Commons or the House of Lords.

Administrative law also controls local authorities, which have executive and legislative functions assigned to them by Parliament. It also controls decision makers that are more or less independent from the government, such as the Crown Prosecution Service (see 7.3.6, p 270). And it controls decision makers such as

---

[9] What about private agencies doing work for the government? See Chapter 15.

tribunals (see Chapter 12) and ombudsmen (see Chapter 13) that are themselves independent, and are themselves responsible for controlling administrative decision making.

'Government' and 'the government'

Government is organized action on behalf of a political community. The phrase 'the government' can be used very widely to include all of the agencies engaged in government, but it is usually used for the political leadership of the executive in an independent state. So in the UK, 'the government' usually refers to the ministers of the Crown: that is, the Prime Minister and the ministers whom the Queen appoints on the advice of the Prime Minister.

'Administrative law' also includes the legal control of much decision making that is not administrative at all, and which is not done by the executive. It controls the operation of the courts that are traditionally called '**inferior courts**'—courts that have been created by statutes that specify their jurisdiction. (I will call them 'courts of specific jurisdiction'; the High Court, by contrast, has a general inherent jurisdiction over the administration of justice.)

The sturdy skeleton of twenty-first-century administrative law was created between the twelfth and the seventeenth centuries, as the judges in the Court of King's Bench developed techniques for monopolizing the administration of justice. After the King's special courts disappeared in the Glorious Revolution of 1688, the King's Bench exercised supervisory jurisdiction over all other public authorities except Parliament and the courts of equity, in a process that has come to be called '**judicial review**'. For centuries more, it was still thought that the prerogatives of the Crown could not be controlled by the judges. After the seventeenth century, prerogatives came to be exercised on the advice of the ministers of the Crown. 'On the advice of' the ministers means, in effect, *by* the ministers, and it was long thought that the ministers' responsibility to Parliament was the only constitutional control on prerogative. But in a line of cases running from the 1980s into the twenty-first century,[10] the judges have asserted jurisdiction to decide the lawfulness of *any* exercise of government power, including an exercise of the prerogative of the Crown, where the issues at stake are suitable for a court to determine.

So the 'administrative' in 'administrative law' refers, roughly, to all public action that is not taken in the High Court or in Parliament. And in the twenty-first century the judges use techniques that they developed in the Middle Ages to control almost all such action, including the government's responses to terrorism.

---

[10] From *Council of Civil Service Unions v Minister for the Civil Service* [1985] AC 374 (the *GCHQ* case—see 7.3.1, p 254) to *R (Miller) v Secretary of State for Exiting the European Union* [2017] UKSC 5 (see 7.3.1, p 260).

1.3 The principle of relativity

There is no single way in which the law should control administrative decisions, because of the vast and complex variety of those decisions. Good rules of administrative law are related to the nature of the decision in question. The way in which the law ought to control a decision—if at all—depends on:

- the type of power being exercised;

- the nature of the body (the expertise of its members and the degree to which they are independent of government, etc.);

- the processes by which it acts;

- the sorts of considerations that need to be taken into account if the power is to be exercised with integrity;

- the way the decision affects particular people

—and more. The variety of these features of decisions has two important consequences. First, it has led to the development of a complex assortment of institutions and legal processes for controlling the exercise of public powers, and for giving redress against complaints about administrative action. Second, it means that any particular legal process for the control of government must operate with attention to the diversity of forms of public power that may be under control. As a result, it is very hard to generalize about the rules that ought to govern the courts' general jurisdiction to control various types of government decision, and to supervise the other institutions (such as tribunals and ombudsmen) that control the exercise of government power.

The requirements of administrative law, and the processes that it provides, must *not* depend on the whims of the government, or on the likes and dislikes of the judges. But they must depend on the context—on the nature of the body that makes an administrative decision, and on the type of decision, and on the nature of the impact it has on people who want to complain about it, and on the circumstances in which it is made. The law should not impose the same forms of control on a power to conduct relations with other countries that it imposes on a power to detain people.

Lord Steyn said, in *R (Daly) v Home Secretary* [2001] 2 AC 532, 548, that: 'In law context is everything.' In *R (Persey) v Environment Secretary* [2002] EWHC 371 [43], Simon Brown LJ called that 'the most quoted dictum in all of administrative law'. But Lord Steyn must have been speaking ironically: context is *not* everything. Contexts are the sets of circumstances in which everything plays out. The basic reasons for the rules of administrative law are, for the most part, very general constitutional principles. They are just as sound in other countries, and in the European Union (see, e.g., 8.7, p 311). For the most part, they have been recognized for centuries. Administrative law has undergone significant transformations in each of the past seven decades. Some basic features of the constitution have changed radically since the Middle Ages. Yet the common strands are remarkable.

Relativity (that is, the way in which administrative law varies with the context) is very important, but don't let that make you think that there are no constitutional principles: the principles are fundamental. The rest of this chapter outlines the principles; the rest of the book will explain how their application by various institutions, through various processes, depends on the contexts in which official power is exercised.

1.4 The principles of the constitution

Principles are abstract, basic rules—starting points for reasoning about what is to be done. A principle is a *constitutional* principle if:

- it regulates what constitutions regulate (that is, the framework of government); and

- it does so in the way that constitutions regulate things (that is, by putting issues beyond the agenda of day-to-day politics).

Freedom of expression is a principle of the UK's constitution. What makes it so? First of all, the principle regulates the framework of government, since it protects people's ability to criticize the government, and it promotes accountability.[11] But what takes political censorship off the agenda in day-to-day politics? Not just the fact that the UK has signed the European Convention on Human Rights (which provides that 'Everyone has the right to freedom of expression' –Art 10), or that the Human Rights Act 1998 gives certain forms of legal effect to the Convention, or that it would be a tort for the government to close down a printing press by force for criticizing the government. An international convention, a statute, and a rule of the common law cannot by themselves make it into a constitutional principle, because Parliament can repeal its statutes and change the common law, and the British constitution does not require the government to abide by its international conventions. A constitutional principle cannot be repealed by a statute, and it must bind the government. Our unwritten constitution has no principles at all, unless the institutions of government adhere to them to some extent. But then, a country with a written constitution is the same: the institutions of government must adhere to the principles set out in the document to some extent, or the document is only a sham.

Freedom of expression is a principle of the British constitution because the authorities that have power under the constitution regulate themselves and each other, to some considerable extent, in a way that is guided by the principle. To identify a principle of a country's constitution, you must find support for it in the constitutional institutions' conduct. You must be able to say that it is *their* principle. Yet a country can have a constitutional principle even if there is a great deal of conduct that is contrary to

....
[11] Freedom of speech protects much more than only speech criticizing the government; it is not *just* a constitutional principle.

the principle. So, for example, the separation of powers was already a British constitutional principle even when the Home Secretary had the legal power to decide how long prisoners on life sentences would stay in prison (a power that violated the principle— see 3.1, pp 74–75).

Parliamentary sovereignty (a law-making power that is not limited by law) is a principle of our constitution. Does that mean that the constitution has no other principles, because nothing is put off the ordinary political agenda? No. It only means that Parliament has lawful power to decide to what extent English law adheres to the principles of the constitution. Parliament has the power to infringe freedom of speech, or to empower others to do so.[12] If it were to do so, it would act against a constitutional principle. If Parliament infringes freedom of speech so extravagantly that the framework of our government is no longer generally committed to freedom of speech, then freedom of speech will no longer be a principle of the constitution at all.

Why have constitutional principles? The point of regulating the framework of government in a way that puts some issues off the political agenda is to support good government.

1.4.1 Good government

Government is organized action on behalf of the community. *Good* government does what government can to make it a good community. Justice is the pre-eminent principle of good government, but its principles also include efficiency and compassion. They include everything that is necessary for government to serve a community well.

Administrative law cannot secure all that. It has a crucial role in securing good government, but its role is strictly limited. Administrative law only supports good government indirectly, by doing what the law can effectively do to secure *responsible government*. The first constitutional principle of administrative law is that good government requires responsible government.

1.4.2 Responsible government

Responsible government responds to the considerations that make for good government. So, for example, instead of pursuing the personal benefit of the rulers, responsible government responds to the needs of the community (for everything from good roads, to social security, to integrity in foreign relations). Responsible government means, primarily, that government action is taken in the interest of the governed (and not for the personal advantage of the officials). But it is only *primarily* in the interest of the governed, because responsible government does not abuse strangers to serve the interests of the governed. If military attacks on other countries and unjust policies

---

[12] Doing so might infringe the European Convention on Human Rights; that would violate Britain's treaty obligations and would give judges a power under the Human Rights Act 1998 to declare that Parliament had acted incompatibly with the Convention, but Parliament's action would still have force in English law. See Chapter 3.

towards refugees would benefit the people of this country, that does not mean that our officials are acting responsibly if they take those actions and adopt those policies. Responsible government, while acting in the interests of the governed, also responds to the community's duties of justice to visitors and to outsiders. Even then, you might say, it is still responding to the interests of the governed in a sense, since they need a way in which their community can act with justice.

What is the difference between responsible government and good government? The added ingredient in good government is success. Responsible government aims in good faith to serve the community well; good government serves the community well. Irresponsible government is arbitrary government. Administrative law only indirectly promotes good government; it directly promotes responsible government, by standing against arbitrary government.

> **Responsible government** is reasonable government (see 7.1.3, p 244, on what
> reasonableness is).

The constitutional principles of administrative law justify much of the law that is stated in this book. They also give good grounds for criticizing some important aspects of the law, and they explain its limitations. This chapter outlines two basic, interwoven groups of principles: **system principles** (principles governing the relations between parts of the system of government); and **principles of accountability** (principles that promote responsible government by requiring public authorities to account for their conduct).[13] Both types of principle are against arbitrary government, so they indirectly promote good government. The two types are interwoven for various reasons: partly because adhering to the system principles makes government more accountable, and partly because non-legal forms of accountability can support that especially famous system principle, the rule of law.

1.5 System principles

1.5.1 The separation of powers

Like any good constitution, the British constitution allocates power to various distinct state institutions. It is very important (especially for administrative law) that the point of the separation of powers is not merely to spread power around among various bodies, but to create *two particular branches of government*—the courts and the legislature—that are distinct from the executive branch. It is not just that power needs to be spread out; the separation of powers gives distinctively *different* powers to the legislative, judicial, and executive branches of government.

---

[13]   Further principles, of less generality, are explained throughout the book; they mostly represent facets of the broad principles outlined here. Note, also, that many general substantive principles of the law are relevant to administrative law. For example, the principle of freedom of speech, discussed in 1.4, affects the way in which administrative law should regulate the use of public power.

The executive is the primary branch of government. The functions of the executive are open-ended, while the core judicial function (passing judgment on legal claims) and the core legislative functions (passing judgment on legislative proposals and, in our constitution, determining who shall form a government, and scrutinizing and endorsing or removing the government) are more specific and limited functions of government. The courts and the legislature can close for vacations, but the executive cannot.[14] The executive manages the police and the military; neither the courts nor the legislature handle guns. It is the executive that gives effect to the decisions of the courts and the legislature. So it is the executive that is chiefly responsible for the rule of law. In the UK, Parliament can change the constitution, and the courts can determine the law of the constitution, but it is the government that must uphold the constitution. And all of the powers of the separate branches of the state are inherited from the unified power of the **Crown**.

The Crown

At the time of the Norman Conquest in 1066, the **Crown** was a symbol for the person of the monarch, who really did exercise the executive, judicial, and legislative power of the state. Today, the Crown is a symbol for a symbol. It is a symbol for the Queen, who is herself a symbol for the power of the state. That power is exercised by the government. Ministers exercise executive authority in the name of the Queen, the judges are called the 'Queen's judges', and legislation is said to be passed by 'the Queen in Parliament'.

Even in countries with written constitutions, like the United States and South Africa, the executive is the primary branch of government. While these countries adopted constitutions approved through deliberation in assemblies, it took executive acts to set up the processes and to convene the assemblies.[15]

Why are powers separated into these three particular functions (judicial, legislative, and executive)? In any process of constitution formation, the executive has reasons to allocate powers to special institutions that are more or less independent of the executive and to which the executive will be accountable.

- **Responsible government needs an effective agency for making clear, open, prospective, stable, general rules for the community.** So, in the *Case of Proclamations* (1611) 12 Co Rep 74, Sir Edward Coke held that the Crown has no prerogative to change the common law or statute, or to create new offences.

---

[14] But the courts cannot *altogether* close down: for example, it is important for the rule of law that you should be able to find a judge in the vacation, or in the middle of the night, to issue a writ of *habeas corpus*. This was first achieved in the Habeas Corpus Act 1679.

[15] We can actually put England in the same category: after the Glorious Revolution in 1688, William of Orange summoned an irregular Parliament that declared him to be King and passed the Bill of Rights.

- **Responsible government needs an independent and effective agency to resolve disputes over the rules.** So, in *Prohibitions del Roy* (1607) 12 Co Rep 63, Coke held that the King could not decide cases personally in the courts. Coke explained it on the basis that the 'artificial reason and judgment of law' take special training, but he was being polite: if the King were trained as a lawyer, it would still be inappropriate for him to sit as a judge. The reason is the constitutional need to prevent the executive from certain sorts of abuse of power. The constitution does so by authorizing independent judges to determine the requirements of the law.

Each branch needs to be well organized for its own tasks. That means, incidentally, that *all three* branches must carry out executive, legislative, and judicial tasks (see Table 1.1).

Powers need to be separated *within* branches, and not just between branches. This is one reason for the complexity of administration. In the executive branch, it is extremely important that police and prosecutors are able to operate independently of the government, to prevent corruption and simply to insulate decisions from party politics (see 7.3.6, p 269). Some agencies act at arm's length from government with various forms of accountability to ministers (see Chapter 15), while departments act at the direction of ministers. The chambers of the legislature need speakers who can exercise executive power on behalf of the chamber. The courts need judges and administrators to carry out the legislative work of making rules and the executive work of allocating judges to cases, and so on.

Table 1.1 Examples of the varied functions within branches of the state

	Executive functions	Judicial functions	Legislative functions
Executive branch	...	Deciding some complaints against government departments	Delegated legislation; legislation under the prerogative
Judicial branch	Keeping order in the court and managing facilities	...	Making rules governing procedures and the costs of litigation
Legislative branch	Keeping order in Parliament; administering the process for voting on Bills	Deciding disputes over contempt and breach of privilege	...

The separation of powers has an importance to the constitution that is wider than its role in controlling the executive. What role does it have in administrative law? It has two roles: first, some administrative decision-making power needs to be separated from the government. Separation of powers *within* the executive branch of government was a crucial feature of the statutory creation of a multitude of quasi-independent tribunals in the twentieth century, to resolve complaints against decisions made by the growing welfare state (see Chapter 12). The new system of tribunals established by the

Tribunals, Courts and Enforcement Act 2007 has enhanced their independence and made them more like courts, so that tribunals today function as a part of the judicial branch of government, rather than the executive branch.

Second, the separation of powers requires good decisions as to the limits of administrative power. It is a reason for taking certain decisions away from executive officials and giving them to judges, so that the decisions are no longer governed by administrative law. The most dramatic example is the judges' use of the Human Rights Act 1998 to declare that it was incompatible with the European Convention on Human Rights for the Home Secretary to decide the minimum period of time to be spent in prison by a prisoner on a life sentence, before he or she could be considered for parole (see 2.5.1, p 55). The executive should not have powers that ought to be exercised by judges. And the executive should not have excessive legislative power, either (see the Note on Brexit, p xxi).

1.5.2 Subsidiarity

Subsidiarity is familiar to students of EU law, because of the special role it has played both in political debates about European integration, and in the legal development of the effect of EU law in member states. The principle is that government power ought to be assigned at the right level. Larger, more remote organizations should not take over tasks that can be carried out more effectively and justly at a level that is closer to the people whom the organizations ought to serve. So, for example, subsidiarity explains the dominant role that the European Union plays in international trade among member states, and the peripheral role that it plays in criminal law and family law.

But subsidiarity is not simply a European principle. It explains the special tasks of local authorities. And it is a principle of law in general: the law's role in regulating your action and mine ought to be subsidiary to our own responsibility for our lives, rather than treating us like slaves. As a constitutional principle, subsidiarity promotes responsible government. It is a guide to allocating power to the institutions that can exercise it most responsibly.

> **Margin of appreciation**
> The principle of subsidiarity can be seen at work in the leeway that the European Court of Human Rights in Strasbourg allows to the authorities of contracting states, in passing judgment on what the Convention rights require in the context of a particular country (see 3.7, p 101).

1.5.3 Comity

Separation of powers and subsidiarity are principles of power allocation; **comity** is the respect that a public authority ought to show for the way another public authority exercises its power. You might say that it is respect for the separation of powers, and for subsidiarity.

It is not enough to have separate branches of the state; we also need each public authority to act in a way that is compatible with the allocation of power to other public authorities.

Article 9 of the Bill of Rights 1689 is a requirement of comity: 'That the freedom of speech and debates or proceedings in Parliament ought not to be impeached or questioned in any court or place out of Parliament.' The courts would be interfering with the constitutional function of Parliament if they were to allow lawsuits for defamation against MPs for what they say in the House of Commons. The irony is that it is no better for someone to tell damaging lies about you in the House of Commons than it is anywhere else. The Bill of Rights thus prevents certain injustices from being remedied by the courts. That is not as shocking as it sounds, because although everyone has a right not to be defamed, no one has a right to a *remedy against* defamation that would interfere with the representation of the people. Comity always has this ironic effect: it prevents one institution from doing justice, in order to preserve the capacity of another institution for good government.

Comity is a crucially important principle of administrative law, because of the judges' remarkable ability to invent powers for themselves. They have a general, inherent jurisdiction over the administration of justice, which we saw in the story of *habeas corpus*. Why shouldn't they use that jurisdiction to replace all administrative decisions with their own decisions? The answer is complex, but parts of it are obvious: judges would not necessarily be better than administrative authorities at making administrative decisions (and they might be worse); they do not represent the people (which may be very important for some administrative decisions); and their processes are good for resolving legal disputes, but are not designed for accomplishing the massively diverse purposes of administration. And, most obvious of all, the constitution forbids it. Comity is a principle of the constitution, because the framework of government is regulated by the principle that a public authority (such as a court) ought to respect the constitutional functions of other public authorities.

> **A judicially enforceable rule that official action is unlawful if it is contrary to good government would transform a court into a governing council. That would violate the principle of comity.**

1.5.4 The rule of law

A community is not ruled by law unless:

- the life of the community is governed by clear, open, stable, prospective, general standards;

- government officials adhere to those standards; and

- there are independent tribunals (that is, courts) that regulate the conduct of the other institutions.

Two facets of the ideal of government by law are easily overlooked, and they are especially important for administrative law: first, the **rule of law** requires not only standards, but also processes; second, the rule of law does *not* require that *everything* be controlled by clear, open, stable, prospective, general standards, or by legal processes. The rule of law only requires that the law control decisions to the extent that it will improve government. We cannot decide whether the community attains the ideal unless we know which aspects of the conduct of government must be regulated by law.

The importance of process

The rule of law requires not just a set of standards, but also a set of processes. The processes must be designed to give effect to the standards, but that is not their only purpose. The processes must also serve the same purpose that the standards serve—that is, to support responsible government. Consider the change in setting a minimum period of imprisonment for life prisoners, which used to be decided by politicians and is now decided by judges (see 2.5.1, p 55). The change is a step towards the rule of law, but not because life sentences are now governed by rules. The standards that judges use in determining the minimum period of imprisonment are no more definite than the standards that the Home Secretary used to use. But the new process is less arbitrary, because the decision is made by someone who, unlike the Home Secretary, is under no political pressure to respond to public opinion as to what should happen to a particular murderer. In this respect, the life of our community is no longer ruled by politics.

What is to be ruled by law?

For a community to attain the **rule of law** (and to escape arbitrary government), the law must control some executive functions of government—but not all. Which functions need to be controlled by law, and how?

Why does the rule of law demand that judges decide the time that life prisoners spend in prison, when it does not demand that judges decide government expenditure, or appoint ministers, or set the rate of income tax? The point of the rule of law is to prevent arbitrary government.[16] The rule of law only requires a decision to be controlled by legal standards or processes if that will help to prevent arbitrary government.

As Lord Steyn put it: 'In our system of law the sentencing of persons convicted of crimes is classically regarded as a judicial rather than executive task' (*R v Home Secretary, ex p Anderson* [2002] UKHL 46 [39]). A sentencing decision on the mere say-so of the Home Secretary is arbitrary, but the appointment of a minister on the mere say-so of the Prime Minister is not arbitrary. Not that it is all right for the Prime Minister to make bad appointments! But legal control of the decision cannot improve the appointment of ministers.

---

[16] The rule of law is also opposed to *anarchy*, which means that effective executive decision making (and, e.g., the capacity to respond to emergencies without being prevented by legalities) is itself a requirement of the rule of law.

> Notice that the requirements of the rule of law are defined by the **principle of relativity** (see 1.3). Whether the law ought to regulate the use of a particular administrative power depends on the type of power, who exercises it, the considerations on which it ought to act, and the way in which the decision affects people.

The separation of powers and the rule of law are linked, and the link is very important to administrative law. Attaining the rule of law requires that *some* official decisions be controlled by legal standards and processes; we cannot decide which decisions those are without a clear understanding of the rationale for the separation of powers. The executive branch must accept judicial decisions; conversely, the law should not give legal institutions forms of control over the executive that they cannot exercise with comity towards the executive.

The judges' role in achieving the rule of law is more limited than it is sometimes thought to be. Yet they still have a critically important role, because the rule of law is a *reflexive* ideal: it requires the system to regulate itself. The judges' independence and effective power enable them to provide the self-regulation that a system of government needs if it is to attain the rule of law. And for the same reason the rule of law demands that the judges craft and abide by rules for their own conduct that will distinguish their actions from their arbitrary say-so. So, for example, *habeas corpus* gives judges a wide discretionary power, since it provides for a detainee to undergo 'whatever our court then and there may order concerning him'. But it gives the judges no power to release a detainee who is lawfully imprisoned or to allow unlawful imprisonment.

The rule of law is not necessarily improved when judges interfere with administrative decisions. *More judicial control* of official action, and *more legal regulation* of the life of the community, do not necessarily bring the community closer to the ideal. In fact, excessive interference with administration at the whim of judges will actually detract from the rule of law (see Chapter 2). That is why comity is a requirement of the rule of law.

1.5.5 Principles allied to the rule of law

The principle of legality

An obvious, central requirement of the rule of law is that public officials should be bound by the law. No administrative authority has discretion to violate the law, or to suspend it. One aspect of this principle was enacted in Art 1 of the Bill of Rights 1689: '... the pretended power of suspending the laws or the execution of laws by regal authority without consent of Parliament is illegal'. The rule applies even to national defence: the government has a very wide discretionary power under the royal prerogative to defend the UK, but it cannot do so by raising taxes, or using land, or conscripting people, unless Parliament authorizes it by statute.

And this principle of legality has a much broader application that is of great importance in the law of judicial review. First, if a statute sets out to protect administrative action from judicial review, judges will bend over backwards to apply the legislation restrictively, so that they can still prevent abuse of power (or even so that they can simply quash a decision that is incompatible with their interpretation of legislation—see 2.7.1, p 67). Second, and more generally, the courts will read down general grants of administrative power so that the power must be used in a way that is compatible with certain basic legal values. It is a 'familiar and well-established' principle that 'general words . . . should not be read as authorising the doing of acts which adversely affect the basic principles on which the law of the United Kingdom is based' (*Jackson v Attorney General* [2005] UKHL 56 [28]).

Which values do those basic principles protect? This is an aspect of the question of what must be ruled by law and what can best be left to executive decision. There is no authoritative catalogue of legally protected values, and the result is that judicial review is dynamic: it is up to the judges to decide which basic values should be protected against the general powers of public authorities. The foremost examples involve the value of **access to justice**: it is the sphere in which the judges feel most able to interfere with a general executive power. In *R (UNISON) v Lord Chancellor* [2017] UKSC 51, the Lord Chancellor had introduced fees of up to £1,200 for an employee to bring a claim in an employment tribunal. The purposes were both to transfer a large part of the cost of the tribunals system from taxpayers to claimants, and also to give claimants an incentive not to pursue weak claims. But an incentive not to pursue a weak claim is also an incentive not to pursue a strong claim. The number of claims plummeted after the fees were imposed, from more than 190,000 in 2012–13 to fewer than 90,000 in 2016–17. In the *UNISON* case, the unanimous Supreme Court held that the fees were unlawful. The reason was that, although Parliament had given the Lord Chancellor discretion to set fees, he could not lawfully use that power to set fees that had the effect of preventing access to justice [119]. Lord Reed based his reasons for the Court on the rule of law ([67]–[68]). Access to courts and tribunals is essential for the law to have effect: 'the possibility of claims being brought by employees whose rights are infringed must exist, if employment relationships are to be based on respect for those rights' [72]. The judges will not ordinarily overturn exercises of administrative discretions to determine the cost of public services (see 7.3.2); the explanation for the decision in *UNISON* is that they see tribunals as a very special kind of public service. Access to justice is a common law right that the courts are prepared to protect, through the principle of legality.

Access to justice has figured in all the key cases in which the principle of legality has been developed. Because prisoners may need access to their solicitors, and even to journalists, in order to pursue a campaign to remedy a miscarriage of justice, it has been held unlawful for the Home Secretary to use a general power to regulate prisons in a way that interferes disproportionately with a prisoner's correspondence with a solicitor (*R (Daly) v Home Secretary* [2001] UKHL 26; see 8.3), or to impose a blanket ban on journalists using interviews with prisoners (*R v Home Secretary, ex p Simms* [2000] 2 AC 115 (HL)). In *Simms*, Lord Hoffmann said that the courts presume that 'even the most general words were intended to be subject to the basic rights of the individual' (at 131).

Even though there is no authoritative catalogue, it is clear that the principle of legality protects other values besides access to the courts. English law has always had a special regard for property rights, and general powers to interfere with property have been controlled since the Commissioners of Sewers cases of the 1500s (see 7.1). We can add freedom of expression to the list of protected values (not only in a case like *Simms* in which freedom of expression affects access to the courts, but generally), but with a proviso: the protection that the judges give to it varies widely depending on the other interests at stake in an administrative decision that controls the media (*R v Home Secretary, ex p Brind* [1991] 1 AC 696). That is an instance of the principle of relativity: varying forms of protection are given to different legally protected interests in varying circumstances. And the principle of legality does not protect all important interests. It does not, for example, protect the right to vote. In *Moohan v Lord Advocate* [2014] UKSC 67, the majority of the Supreme Court held that the common law does not recognize 'a right of universal and equal suffrage from which any derogation must be provided for by law and must be proportionate' [34].

One aspect of the principle of legality has been 'expressly enacted', as Lord Hoffmann put it, in the Human Rights Act 1998 s 3(1):

> ' So far as it is possible to do so, primary legislation and subordinate legislation must be read and given effect in a way which is compatible with the Convention rights. '[17]

That applies to legislation granting general administrative powers, so that they cannot be used to violate Convention rights, unless the legislation authorizes it. But there are two differences between the principle of legality and the effect of s 3 of the Human Rights Act 1998. First, there *is* an authoritative catalogue of the protected values for the purpose of the Human Rights Act: they are the values protected by the Convention rights (see Chapter 3). Second, the courts have found it 'possible', under s 3 of the Human Rights Act, to interpret a statute as having an effect that is actually contrary to what was enacted (see 3.3.1, p 80). In this respect, the principle of legality is different. Lord Phillips said in *Ahmed v HM Treasury* [2010] UKSC 2 [117]: 'I do not consider that the principle of legality permits a court to disregard an unambiguous expression of Parliament's intention. To this extent its reach is less than that of section 3 of the Human Rights Act.'

On the role of the principle of legality in judicial review, see 8.1, p 278.

Due process

All governmental decisions ought to be made by processes that put the relevant considerations effectively before the decision makers. Very often, the only way in which to achieve that goal is to give people affected by the decision an opportunity

---

[17]   *R v Home Secretary, ex p Simms* [2000] 2 AC 115, 132.

to participate in the process. If a public authority is deciding whether you committed murder, you ought to be able to participate in the process in ways that would be superfluous or damaging if a public authority were deciding whether to build a new school in your town. The role that you ought to have in the process varies radically, depending on the nature of the decision, and the way in which it affects you, and whether the decision maker needs your input in order to grasp the relevant considerations. There is no general right to any form of participation in administrative decisions, but there is a common law right to a form of participation that is due, in the circumstances.

FROM THE MISTS OF TIME

Due process (see Chapter 4) is an ancient English idea. The Americans inherited it from the time of the Plantagenets, and wrote it into their Bill of Rights: the Fifth Amendment provides that 'No person shall be ... deprived of life, liberty, or property, without due process of law.'

By the Middle Ages, it was already an accepted legal principle that a person should be given the form of participation in a decision-making process that is due—that is, appropriate in the context. In the Petition of Right 1628, Parliament reminded King Charles that Parliament had guaranteed 'due process of law' nearly 300 years earlier:

> ' And in the eight-and-twentieth year of the reign of King Edward III, it was declared and enacted by authority of parliament, that no man, of what estate or condition that he be, should be put out of his land or tenements, nor taken, nor imprisoned, nor disinherited nor put to death without being brought to answer by due process of law. '[18]

There is an especially close relation between due process and the principle of legality. Courts protect legally recognized values not only by reading down general powers, but also by conferring special procedural protections on persons when a decision affects a basic legal value. For example, where a statute undeniably gives a public authority power to destroy property, the courts hold that the common law requirement of due process requires the public authority to give a hearing to the person who owns the property (see 4.1, p 122).

As a result of the close relationship between due process and the principle of legality, the law of due process gives us a deeper understanding of the values that both principles protect. For example, we can find a catalogue of legally protected values in the statute of 1354: decisions were not to be made without considering representations from the persons affected, if they stood to lose their title, land tenure, personal liberty, inheritance, or their life. Compare the values protected in various ways 700 years later,

---

[18] ' ... nul homme, de quel estate ou condicion q'il soit, ne soit oste de titre ne de tenure, ne pris, n'emprisone, ne desherite, ne mis a la mort, saunz estre mesne en repons par due process de lei' 28 Ed III c 3 (1354).

by the European Convention on Human Rights: life; freedom from torture[19] and from slavery; personal liberty; freedom from retrospective punishment; privacy; family life; freedom of religion, expression, and association; marriage; freedom from discrimination; and (in the Protocols to the Convention) property; education; free elections; freedom of movement; and freedom from expulsion. The Protocols also prohibit the death penalty.

What about the Bill of Rights 1689?

The catalogue of protected values in the Bill of Rights was a response to abuses of executive power under the Stuart Kings, and its focus was not on protecting the freedom of individuals, but on protecting Parliament from the King. It prohibited suspension of laws by the executive, taxation without approval by Parliament, prosecutions of people who bring petitions to the Crown, and the raising of a standing army. It protected the bearing of arms by Protestants, free elections, free speech in Parliament, freedom from excessive bail, freedom from cruel and unusual punishment, the proper use of juries, and frequent Parliaments. It was mostly a Bill of Parliament's authority, and the rights of Members of Parliament.

Legal certainty

In *R v Bolton* (1841) 1 QB 66, the parish claimed that Bolton was occupying one of its houses as a pauper (that is, rent-free), and threw him out; he claimed that he had been paying rent for the house, so that he had a right to stay there. The magistrates decided against him on this question of fact, and in judicial review the Court of Queen's Bench refused to hear evidence that the magistrates had got the facts wrong. Lord Denman CJ said: 'It is of much more importance to hold the rule of law straight than, from a feeling of the supposed hardship of any particular decision, to interpose relief at the expense of introducing a precedent full of inconvenience and uncertainty in the decision of future cases.'

English judges today lack Lord Denman's relish for leaving an injustice unremedied. Instead, they would rather run the risk of downplaying the value of legal certainty—'the principle that parties should know where they stand' (*R (Thomas) v Central Criminal Court* [2006] EWHC 2138 [20]). Legal certainty is one of the general principles of EU law developed by the Court of Justice of the European Union

---

[19] Torture was inflicted before the Civil War on warrants issued by authority of the King. In *A & others v Home Secretary* [2005] UKHL 71 [12], Lord Bingham said that the common lawyers had regarded torture as 'totally repugnant to the fundamental principles of English law' and 'repugnant to reason, justice, and humanity'. Lord Bingham said that no warrant authorizing torture had been issued since 1640. The House of Lords unanimously held in *A & others* that the common law allows no admission of evidence obtained by torture.

(CJEU).[20] It is especially important in the European Court of Human Rights,[21] because the Convention could be read to give the Court an open-ended power to revisit administrative decisions in a way that would have shocked Lord Denman. For example, the requirement of hearings by an independent tribunal in Art 6 of the Convention could have been read to require a vast range of administrative decisions to be made by judges, rather than by administrative agencies. But the courts have rejected that approach (see 5.3). In *R (Beeson) v Dorset County Council* [2002] EWCA Civ 1812 [15], Laws LJ said that the courts should not use Art 6 to undermine 'the imperative of legal certainty'. Lord Hoffmann added, 'Amen to that, I say', in *Runa Begum v Tower Hamlets LBC* [2003] UKHL 5 [59].

The more power the judges are given to generate uncertainty, the more attention they need to pay to the principle of legal certainty. It is not generally in tension with other values, and it is not generally an overriding value. But it *is* enough to generate a **presumption of non-interference** (see 7.1.1, p 238)—that is, a rule that a decision made by a body to whom a power has been allocated is not to be interfered with merely because a different decision ought to have been made. There has to be some justification for undoing what has been done. In the High Court, such a justification is a 'ground of judicial review'; that is, a basis on which the Court can hold a decision to be unlawful, and can give the claimant a remedy.

1.5.6 What happened to justice?

Think of Mr Bolton, thrown out of his house and told by the Lord Chief Justice that it is more important to hold the rule of law straight than to do justice in a way that might create uncertainty. And let's suppose for the moment that the parish council's decision was unjust (we don't know, because the court never heard the matter). Should the court have done justice in the case, or held to the rule of law?

It is an injustice for a government agency to fail in its duty to act with due regard for the public interest and for the private interests that are at stake in public decisions. But not all injustices are controlled by law. And they cannot all be put right by judges. Every police officer, housing officer, teacher, politician—and, in one way or another, every one of our 5.4 million public-sector employees—has a responsibility for justice. So have decision-making institutions such as school boards and local councils. The role of the law in controlling all of that is extremely important *and* strictly limited. Its importance can lead people to discount the limits or to forget them. The role of courts is *even more strictly limited* than the role of the law, because there are so many other legal techniques for controlling administration, and resort to the courts is meant to be a last resort (see 2.7, p 64).

....

[20] See, e.g., Case C-61/05 *Commission v Portugal* [2006] 3 CMLR 36; Case C-310/04 *Spain v Council* [2006] ECR I-7285 [141].

[21] See *Evans v United Kingdom* (2006) 43 EHRR 21.

Imagine if the Prime Minister were to choose a crony as Chancellor of the Exchequer, instead of a person who could do the job much better. That would be an injustice to the whole nation, but the rule of law does not require a legal remedy for it. In fact, **comity** would forbid the High Court to interfere with the appointment. If a politician who had been overlooked were to go to the High Court and ask the judges to quash the Prime Minister's decision on the ground that the decision was unjust, the court should not even give permission for the claimant to seek judicial review. Even in the face of an allegation of injustice, the courts' role is limited by its responsibility for the rule of law. It would be a breach of comity, and not an assertion of the rule of law, for judges to review the decision. This limitation on the courts' role allows judges to remedy many injustices, but not all. The judges have no general jurisdiction to impose justice on other public officials.

So, in Mr Bolton's case, the Court was right to refuse to consider the magistrates' decision if it would have been a breach of comity to question their decision on the facts. But if the Court could have reviewed the decision without damaging the magistrates' ability to do their job, then the Court missed an opportunity to do justice according to law. And today the courts would take a different approach from that of Lord Denman: they would hear the claim, but would quash the magistrates' finding of fact only if it was patently untenable (see 9.2.3). Even today, the courts' role in helping someone like Mr Bolton is not to replace the administrative decision with their own decision.

HOW TO RECONCILE JUSTICE AND THE RULE OF LAW

Comity is a system principle that requires constitutional institutions *not* to act on principles of justice! But the reasons for the principle of comity are themselves reasons of justice: it will promote just government under the constitution if the institutions allow each other to function without undue interference. And interference with a decision can be inappropriate even if the decision itself was unjust. Comity is a requirement of responsible government.

1.6 Accountability

An accountable government faces up to people. Accountability is a fundamental requirement for responsible government, because public officials cannot be trusted to act responsibly if they don't have to face up to anyone.

The principle of accountability is unspecific. Its reach is much broader than law: the most constitutionally important accountability techniques are the political techniques of democracy. At the national level, democracy is secured through the combination of:

- elections to Parliament;

- the constitutional rule that entrusts the government to the party with the confidence of the House of Commons;

- the rule that ministers of the Crown must answer questions in Parliament;

- the practice of debating policy in Parliament, as well as deliberating over legislation; and

- the rule that the power of the Crown is to be exercised on the advice of the ministers.

Democracy is also secured at different levels, through different democratic mechanisms, in the European Union,[22] through devolved law-making institutions and administrations in Scotland, Wales, and Northern Ireland, and in local government. At all of these levels of government, the law regulates elections and gives legal effect to legislative decisions. But effective government accountability depends on much more than just law. It depends on party politics, on participation by voters, on independent and critical media, and on the commitment and integrity of MPs and other representatives. The role of the media gives a healthy reminder of the limited role of law in the accountability of the government: the law needs to protect the media from political censorship, but the government will not be held to account unless journalists actually do their job, and the commercial forces that shape the media allow them to communicate effectively.

Accountability needs to take diverse forms in a complex twenty-first-century state. Parliament imposes certain forms of political accountability on government, and the courts impose certain forms of legal accountability on government, but accountability has to reach far beyond the courts and Parliament. Auditors hold public authorities to account for their financial conduct, and their decisions may be backed by massive financial penalties for officials involved in corruption. Other accountability techniques such as ombudsmen and inquiries (see Chapter 13) are effective because they create publicity that has crucial political effects. Public authorities ought to be accountable in a wide variety of ways to a wide variety of people and institutions—to the police, to school inspectors, to a variety of tribunals, to the voters, to the media, to the courts, to the EU institutions, to the states that are party to the Geneva Conventions, to the United Nations . . . .

This book is about a limited set of accountability techniques: the legal ones. Legal accountability is imposed by laws that give one institution or public official legal power to call another to account. It encompasses a relatively restricted, yet still vast, array of accountability techniques. Legal accountability is neither more nor less important than other forms of accountability. It is often thought that Parliament is failing to provide proper political accountability, and that the courts have had to step into the breach, through judicial review. But that depressing view of parliamentary control of

---

22 Those mechanisms are not found chiefly in the role of the European Parliament (it is not the legislature; it shares legislative power with the Commission and the Council). Democracy in the European Union depends on democratic processes in the member states, whose representatives make up the Council; member states also nominate Commissioners (subject to approval by the European Parliament).

the executive is actually irrelevant to public law. Parliament and the courts have very different supervisory functions over the government (see 2.5.3, p 58), and neither can take the place of the other. The political and legal processes serve as complementary accountability techniques.

Securing accountability

Special problems of legal accountability arise when the government makes deals with private companies to provide public services. Chapter 15 deals with the ways in which legal accountability can be disrupted by contracting out.

1.6.1 Open government: a new constitutional principle?

In *Local Government Board v Arlidge* [1915] AC 120, the House of Lords refused to order a government department to disclose advice it had received from a planning inspector. Lord Shaw said that a court order of disclosure would be inconsistent 'with efficiency, with practice, and with the true theory of complete parliamentary responsibility for departmental action' (137). In 1947, Lord Greene approved of the *Arlidge* approach, saying that 'the idea that a Minister can be compelled to disclose to anybody information . . . which he has obtained as a purely administrative person, is alien to our whole conception of government in this country' (*B Johnson & Co v Minister of Health* [1947] 2 All ER 395, 401).[23] Our 'whole conception of government' has changed dramatically since the 1940s. The result is a massive gain in accountability, because a minister becomes more accountable if he or she has to disclose the information on which a governmental decision is based. The change has largely been the result of legislation.

The **Freedom of Information Act 2000** (which came into full effect in 2005) provides a right to *some* government information. Before that, no one outside Parliament had any general right to demand information from the government, although there have long been various ways of getting information from government. The following are the main examples from before the freedom-of-information era. They are still very important:

- public authorities have legal duties to give reasons for some decisions (see Chapter 6);

- in litigation, parties can get disclosure of information relevant to their claims or defences (including from public authorities);

- since the Exchequer and Audit Departments Act 1866, there has been a statutory system of public reporting to Parliament of financial information about the operation of government—the audit and reporting functions are now carried out independently of government by the National Audit Office, under the National Audit Act 1983; and

---

[23] He approved of the approach of the House of Lords in *Arlidge*.

- Parliament's scrutiny role means that an MP can demand non-confidential information from the government if it would not be too expensive to obtain, and its disclosure would not be prejudicial to national security.

By contrast, the new right to information is general—that is, you do not need a reason to ask for it. You have a right to any information *unless* it fits within a list of grounds for withholding information, set out in the Act (ss 21–44).

More than 40,000 freedom-of-information requests are made each year to the bodies subject to the Act, which include not just central government departments but the National Health Service, local government, police, and schools and universities. Information requested is withheld in full or in part in more than one-third of requests.[24] Most refusals of disclosure have been based on the exemptions for personal or confidential information, or for information on investigations by public authorities. But many requests have been refused on the basis of an exemption that is especially interesting for our purposes: a public authority can withhold information on 'the formulation or development of government policy' (s 35(1)(a)). For example, in 2017, as part of its campaign against the Conservative government's approach to the Brexit negotiations, the trade union Unite made a freedom-of-information request to the Department for Environment, Food and Rural Affairs (Defra) to find out what estimate had been made as to how much food prices would rise in the lead-up to Brexit and afterwards. Defra withheld the information, citing s 35 and saying that 'a public authority needs a safe space to formulate policy effectively'.[25] That safe space is just what the House of Lords thought, in the *Arlidge* case in 1915, was required for good government. The space is not very safe today: application of the policy exemption has become a battlefield on which the new principle of open government is being worked out. And it is being worked out in a highly judicialized framework, which the government cannot control. On the Brexit food prices issue, the union can complain to the Information Commissioner, who can issue a notice requiring disclosure. The union and Defra can appeal against the Information Commissioner's decision to the First-tier Tribunal—see 12.1, p 448—with the possibility of further appeals to the Upper Tribunal, and then to the Court of Appeal and the Supreme Court.

Tony Blair's government, introducing the legislation in 1999, was aware that this judicial framework would take control over information out of the hands of government. So at the end of the 2000 Act they added a major fall-back exemption: under s 53(2), even after a decision has been made under the Act that information is subject to disclosure, a minister can issue a certificate 'stating that he has on reasonable grounds formed the opinion' that non-disclosure is not contrary to the Act. That provision was intended to enable the government to veto disclosure. But the Supreme Court vetoed the veto in *R (Evans) v Attorney General* [2015] UKSC 21. Rob Evans, a *Guardian* journalist made Freedom of Information Act requests to seven government departments, asking to see all of Prince Charles's letters to them. The government refused disclosure;

....
[24] See Cabinet Office, 'FOI Statistics Bulletin 2016 Annual', 20 April 2017.

[25] http://www.unitetheunion.org/news/government-suppressing-brexit-food-price-report/.

the Information Commissioner upheld that decision, but the Upper Tribunal allowed Evans's appeal. Then the Attorney General issued a certificate under s 53(2) of the 2000 Act, preventing disclosure of the letters in spite of the Upper Tribunal's decision that they were disclosable under the Act.

The case divided the Supreme Court Justices over the constitutional principles of administrative law. The majority did not say that the Act was invalid; they used the principle of legality to restrict the power that it gave to government.[26] Lord Neuberger for the majority cited the rule of law [51], and the 'fundamental' principle 'that a decision of a judicial body should be final and binding and should not be capable of being overturned by a member of the executive' [115]. Lord Hughes said:

> ' The rule of law is of the first importance. But it is an integral part of the rule of law that courts give effect to Parliamentary intention. The rule of law is not the same as a rule that courts must always prevail, no matter what the statute says. ' [154]

And Lord Wilson said that 'parliamentary sovereignty, emblematic of our democracy', is 'among the most precious' of constitutional principles [168].

In support of the decision, Lord Neuberger cited Lord Hoffmann's account of the principle of legality in *Simms* (see earlier, pp 23–24). But in *Simms*, Lord Hoffmann was applying the principle to protect 'the basic rights of the individual' (at 131; see *Evans* [56]). In the Freedom of Information Act, Parliament created a vast new right of access to government information, and qualified that new openness by giving the government an override. The Supreme Court treated that legislative purpose as if it were contrary to the basic rights of the individual (as it would be if, e.g., Parliament gave the government an override over the writ of *habeas corpus*!). The result is contrary to what Parliament enacted. It treats the new principle of open government as if it were a fundamental right, like the right to liberty.

Fall-out for the monarchy?

As a result of the Supreme Court's decision in Evans, you can now see Prince Charles's correspondence with government departments online.[27] The monarchy did not suffer the blow to its public image that the government had presumably been trying to avoid; Prince Charles's letter of 21 October 2004, to the Minister for the Environment reflects the tone of much of the correspondence:

' . . . I particularly hope that the illegal fishing of the Patagonian Toothfish will be high on your list of priorities because until that trade is stopped, there is

---

26 For practical purposes, the government can use the power only when only there are 'serious flaws in the determination of the . . .Tribunal which could not be the subject matter of an appeal and could not be brought before a higher tribunal or court' [77], a situation that will presumably never arise.

27 https://www.gov.uk/government/collections/prince-of-wales-correspondence-with-government-departments.

> little hope for the poor old albatross, for which I shall continue to campaign . . . .
> Yours most sincerely, Charles. '
>
> Meanwhile, the government proposed legislation, which Parliament passed, to amend the Freedom of Information Act to create an absolute exemption for communications from the heir to the Throne.[28]

The Freedom of Information Act is the most important element in a general trend towards open government. It is supported by the **Public Interest Disclosure Act 1998**, which protects 'whistleblowers' from victimization by their employers if they disclose information about malpractice by public bodies. And the courts have taken important further initiatives. In *Kennedy v Charity Commission* [2014] UKSC 20, a journalist challenged a refusal by the Charity Commission to disclose information about its inquiry into the activities of a charity founded by the MP George Galloway. The Freedom of Information Act did not help the journalist: s 32 exempts judicial proceedings and inquiries from the duty to disclose. But the Supreme Court held that there is 'a common law presumption in favour of openness' in Charity Commission inquiries, because of the public interest in scrutiny both of the activities of charities and of the working of the Commission itself (Lord Mance [47]). The Charity Commission and other bodies conducting inquiries have a discretion to release information, and journalists can now use judicial review to ask the judges to overturn a decision to withhold information that is of public interest, unless there are 'persuasive countervailing considerations to outweigh the strong prima facie case that the information should be disclosed' [56].

....

The European Court of Human Rights catches up

Kennedy was decided by developing a common law presumption of open government, and the Court did not find a right of access to government information in the ECHR. But then in 2016, the European Court of Human Rights invented a limited form of freedom-of-information law under the ECHR, in a landmark decision holding that the right of freedom of expression in Art 10 of the ECHR may require disclosure 'where access to the information is instrumental for the individual's exercise of his or her right to freedom of expression'—*Magyar Helsinki Bizottság v Hungary* (Application no 18030/11) 8 November 2016 [156].

....

The Supreme Court took another major step to make government more transparent in *R (Lumba) v Home Secretary* [2011] UKSC 12, imposing a legal duty on the government to publish certain administrative policies. The claimants were immigrants to the UK who had been sentenced to prison for criminal offences; on their release from prison, the Home Office had to decide whether to detain them under its statutory powers for

....

[28] Constitutional Reform and Governance Act 2010 Sch 7 para 3.

the purpose of extradition. Lord Dyson wrote that 'The rule of law calls for a transparent statement by the executive of the circumstances in which the broad statutory criteria will be exercised' [34]. *Lumba* is a novel and ground-breaking development in the law; it goes beyond access to information, because it requires public authorities not only to publicize existing policies, but to create transparent policies for the exercise of some powers. But the decision needs to be read in its context, in accordance with the **principle of relativity**: the new duty in *Lumba* is not a general duty to establish open policies, but a duty to do so for the application of 'broad statutory criteria' in the exercise of powers that affect a person as acutely as the exercise of an executive power of detention. Cranston J pointed this out in *Hossain v Home Secretary* [2016] EWHC 1331 [137]: *Lumba* was 'concerned with the statutory power of executive detention and directed at excluding the vice of arbitrariness from its exercise'.

The new legal requirements of openness in *Evans*, *Kennedy*, and *Lumba* are the most innovative judicial steps towards open government. Further very important steps have been taken in developing the law of due process in administration (see Chapters 4 and 6). Those steps have included an increase in the availability of oral hearings, duties of disclosure of information before a hearing, and enhanced duties to give reasons for decisions. And since the 1970s, the doctrine of legitimate expectations (see 8.4) has made it much more difficult for the government to make secret changes in its policies and practices. In the leading case of *R v Home Secretary, ex p Doody* [1994] 1 AC 531, 561, Lord Mustill identified a general trend: 'I find in the more recent cases on judicial review a perceptible trend towards an insistence on greater openness, or if one prefers the contemporary jargon "transparency", in the making of administrative decisions.'

What's more, judicial review itself has become an aspect of the trend. Public interest litigation (bringing a claim to pursue a campaign in the public interest rather than to obtain personal benefit) has turned the Administrative Court into a new kind of forum in which political activists can hold the government to account (see 11.2). And remarkably, the courts have given permission to seek judicial review to claimants who have no prospect of success, when they raise issues that the courts consider to be so important that they deserve an airing (such as the government's refusal to hold a public inquiry into its decision to invade Iraq: *R (Gentle) v Prime Minister* [2006] EWCA Civ 1078—see 10.3.2, p 387).

Public interest immunity

Until *Conway v Rimmer* [1968] AC 910, public authorities had a 'Crown privilege' to withhold documents in litigation (see *Duncan v Cammell Laird and Co Ltd* [1942] AC 624). It was a legally uncontrolled power (like the privilege of private parties not to disclose correspondence with their solicitors). In *Conway*, the House of Lords held that the courts' responsibility for the administration of justice required them to decide whether there was a public interest in secrecy that was sufficiently urgent to justify non-disclosure. The decision in *Conway* increased disclosure in litigation, and was a landmark in dismantling government secrecy.

Consultation

Government has also become more open through the expanded use of public consultation in policy making. It is a trend that successive governments have embraced, in order to achieve public confidence in the policy process and broader acceptance of decisions. Yet there is a serious tension (and successive governments have been ambivalent about consultation), because consultation facilitates opposition to the plans that public authorities are trying to pursue.

The government has a set of non-binding 'Consultation Principles', which aim to achieve proportionality between the nature of the policy or proposal and the form of the consultation. The government revised the Principles in 2016 to 'reduce the risk of "consultation fatigue" by making sure we consult only on issues that are genuinely undecided'.[29] But meanwhile, the courts have expanded legal control of consultations, imposing rules that public authorities cannot control. The landmark case is *R (Moseley) v Haringey LBC* [2014] UKSC 56. The local council defendant had proposed to cope with central government funding cuts by reducing benefit payments. The council had a statutory duty to consult persons with an interest in the proposal; the Supreme Court held that the consultation was unlawful because the authority was legally required to invite comments on alternatives that the authority would rather not have discussed.

There is 'no general common law duty to consult persons who may be affected' by a public decision (*Moseley* [35]).[30] Consultation is, for the most part, a form of openness that the government brings upon itself. But the courts have made their auxiliary role in supervising consultations into a real nuisance for public authorities. The Supreme Court held in *Moseley* that when a statute imposes a duty to consult, the 'Sedley criteria'[31] apply:

1. 'consultation must be at a time when proposals are still at a formative stage;

2. the proposer must give sufficient reasons for any proposal to permit of intelligent consideration and response;

3. adequate time must be given for consideration and response; and

4. the product of consultation must be conscientiously taken into account in finalising any statutory proposals' (*Moseley* [25]).

Lord Wilson held that the details of the duty to consult were determined by the 'common law duty of procedural fairness' (*Moseley* [23]; see 4.4.2), and a majority

---

[29] http://www.gov.uk/government/publications/consultation-principles-guidance.

[30] Although Lord Reed went on to say, 'A duty of consultation will however exist in circumstances where there is a legitimate expectation of such consultation, usually arising from an interest which is held to be sufficient to found such an expectation, or from some promise or practice of consultation' [35]. Cf. *R (Rotherham MBC) v Secretary of State for Business, Innovation and Skills* [2015] UKSC 6 [69]: 'a failure to consult can of itself render a decision unlawful, but that will, at least normally, only be where there is a specific obligation or commitment to consult'.

[31] Named for Sir Stephen Sedley, who had introduced them in argument while he was a barrister: *R v Brent LBC ex p Gunning* (1985) 84 LGR 168.

agreed with him. Lord Reed disagreed, and held that the purpose of the consultation in *Moseley* was 'not to ensure procedural fairness in the treatment of persons whose legally protected interests may be adversely affected, as the common law seeks to do', but resulted from Parliament's decision 'to ensure public participation in the local authority's decision-making process' [38]. On either approach, identifying alternatives to the authority's proposal was 'necessary in order for the consultees to express meaningful views on the proposal' [40]. But the majority endorsement of Lord Wilson's approach has important implications for the extent of duties to consult: it suggests that the courts ought to require consultation wherever they determine that fairness requires it.

Previously, the common law requirement of procedural fairness had been held to yield a duty to consult only (1) where a decision affects the claimant very personally (such as a decision to close a day care centre for people with disabilities: see *R (LH) v Shropshire Council* [2014] EWCA Civ 404; cf. *R v North and East Devon Health Authority, ex p Coughlan* [2000] 3 All ER 850), or (2) where a public authority has promised it, or has developed a regular practice of consultation (see *R (Niazi) v Home Secretary* [2008] EWCA Civ 755). After *Moseley*, there will be more scope to argue that common law procedural fairness requires consultation in order for a public policy decision to be made lawfully (see *Moseley* [24]).

Consultation generates litigation where, as in *Moseley*, complaining that a consultation was unfair creates a way of taking the government to court, when someone with a burning complaint about the outcome has no prospect of persuading a court to interfere with the substance of the decision. The classic administrative mistake is to make the decision before the end of the so-called consultation. That will be held to be procedurally unfair (*R (Parents for Legal Action Ltd) v Northumberland County Council* [2006] EWHC 1081). But the courts will not overturn a decision just because there was a defect in the consultation, if the purpose of the consultation has been accomplished. And if a public authority makes a decision without carrying out a legal duty to consult, the courts will not require the authority to reverse the resulting decision if that would be disproportionately costly. In *Moseley*, the Supreme Court issued a declaration that the consultation had been unlawful, but refused to order the local authority to carry out a new consultation exercise, since its plan for its finances had been in operation for two years.

Consultation in Europe

The European Commission has Guidelines on Stakeholder Consultation for policy initiatives and proposals. They are much more elaborate than the UK government's guidelines; the principles of the scheme are 'participation, openness and accountability, effectiveness and coherence'. The Guidelines generally allow twelve weeks for internet-based feedback from the public.[32]

---

[32] See https://ec.europa.eu/info/files/better-regulation-guidelines-stakeholder-consultation_en.

Is openness a new constitutional principle?

Openness in government is not altogether new, and it is not unrestricted. To get things in perspective, keep in mind the forms of openness that the government has had to live with for centuries. The most important is the power of MPs to ask questions of ministers in Parliament. The openness of the courts themselves is an important aspect of open government, and it is much older than the scrutinizing role of MPs. The independence of police and prosecutors and auditors is more recent, but it pre-dates the twentieth century.

And various forms of public inquiry are ancient. Since 1276, coroners—independent judicial investigators—have had a statutory duty to investigate 'the deaths of persons slain, drowned, or suddenly dead' (see *R (Amin) v Home Secretary* [2004] 1 AC 653 [16]), and even that statutory rule only confirmed the common law of the time. Public inquiries have been required for decisions on land use planning for generations—both for government projects and for the approval of private projects. In hearing the many challenges from opponents of planning decisions, the judges have enhanced procedural rights in inquiries.

And in some respects, the role of judicial review in promoting open decision making goes back centuries. In *Bentley's Case* (1748) Fort 202, the Court of King's Bench held that the University of Cambridge had to comply with natural justice by giving a doctor a hearing before depriving him of his degree. Fortescue J cited a decision of 1470 by the Chancellor and Judges 'that it is required by the law of nature that every person, before he can be punish'd, ought to be present' (206). For more than 500 years, it has been unlawful (unless specially authorized by statute) for the government to use administrative means to make a secret decision to punish anyone for anything.

Open government is only partly new. But the principle that *administrative information in general* is to be open (subject to exemptions) really is a new principle, which has only developed in the twenty-first century. It is of constitutional importance. The value of transparency is partly that it can contribute to political control of government (by giving the opposition the opportunity to embarrass the government, and by letting MPs know what questions to ask in Parliament). It can also contribute to the rule of law (by exposing unlawful official conduct, and by giving a potential claimant useful information in deciding whether to bring a legal claim against a public authority). But it has a more basic importance, because it makes the government face up to people: it is in itself an accountability technique.

1.7 Europe and the principles of the constitution

A breach of EU law is unlawful in UK law.[33] The European Communities Act 1972 s 2(1) provides that all rights with direct effect under the EU treaties shall have effect in UK law; s 2(2) authorizes the government to make regulations in UK law to implement

---

[33] European Communities Act 1972 s 2; see *Bourgoin SA v Ministry of Agriculture, Fisheries and Food* [1986] QB 716. See the Note on Brexit, p xxi, for discussion of the implications of the proposed withdrawal of the UK from the European Union.

the UK's obligations in EU law, and s 2(4) provides that 'any enactment passed or to be passed, shall be construed and have effect subject to [s 2(1) and s 2(2)]'. In *R v Transport Secretary, ex p Factortame (No 2)* [1991] 1 AC 603, the House of Lords held that: 'Under the terms of the Act of 1972 it has always been clear that it was the duty of a United Kingdom court, when delivering final judgment, to override any rule of national law found to be in conflict with any directly enforceable rule of Community law' (Lord Bridge, 659). That rule even includes a 'rule of national law' that has been made by Act of Parliament.

Acting incompatibly with EU law is, therefore, unlawful, and a ground of judicial review. And under the *Factortame* doctrine, EU law can be used for a purpose that administrative law cannot achieve: to ask the courts to hold that an act of Parliament has no effect.

EU law has a deep significance for administrative law because of the resources it offers for challenging the actions of the UK government. And it has a broader significance, too, because of the techniques that the CJEU uses in controlling the actions of the EU institutions. The European Union has borrowed freely from the traditions of member states, and has developed new devices and doctrines aimed at enhancing the effectiveness of EU law, while imposing the rule of law on the EU institutions. In this book, you will find those devices and doctrines in sections on some of the topics at the frontiers of administrative law—human rights law (see 3.11 on the Charter of Fundamental Rights of the European Union), the doctrine of proportionality (see 8.3), the protection of legitimate expectations (see 8.4), the role of ombudsmen (Chapter 13), and the very un-English doctrine of state liability to compensate for loss caused by unlawful state conduct (see 13.7, p 496). These developments have become integral parts of the practice of administrative law in this country; they originate in the administrative law doctrine of the CJEU.

The administrative law of the EU institutions is a creature of the treaties, and of the decisions of the CJEU. The CJEU reviews the legality of some acts of the institutions (the European Parliament, the Council, the Commission, and the European Central Bank). Article 263 of the Treaty on the Functioning of the European Union (TFEU) provides that 'the Court of Justice shall declare the act concerned to be void' if a claimant succeeds in showing that any of the following grounds apply:

- 'lack of competence';

- 'infringement of an essential procedural requirement';

- 'infringement of the Treaties or of any rule of law relating to their application'; or

- 'misuse of powers'.

These grounds reflect the same concern for the rule of law that underlies the English law of judicial review. 'Essential procedural requirements' are the demands of due process. Lack of competence (called 'jurisdiction' in English law) and infringement of any rule of law are grounds of review for the same reason in EU law as in English law: the judges are given jurisdiction to impose the law on the other EU institutions.

The really interesting problems of judicial review in the CJEU are remarkably similar to those in the English courts. 'Misuse of powers' gives the CJEU an opportunity to craft for itself the same sort of far-reaching supervision of *some* discretionary acts of public agencies that the English courts have crafted. And in its case law the CJEU has developed 'general principles of EU law' that enhance its supervisory jurisdiction: they include the protection of fundamental rights, proportionality, and protection of legitimate expectations. Under Art 230, decisions that breach those general principles will be held to have been a misuse of a power, or to have infringed a rule of law.

There are really crucial differences between the work of the CJEU and the work of the English courts: the CJEU determines the validity of legislative instruments made by European institutions, and (very importantly) those instruments are all meant to be passed for the accomplishment of limited objectives specified in the treaties. But one similarity with English judicial review is really striking: the case law of the CJEU reveals the same tension over the requirements of comity. This one basic question of constitutional principle poses challenges under EU law as it does under the common law of public administration: how can a court promote responsible government, while acting with due respect for the allocation of power to another institution?

When we look at the doctrines of legitimate expectations and proportionality (in which English judicial review has been particularly influenced by the analogies with EU law), we will look closely at one important case on judicial review of reforms to the Common Agricultural Policy, in order to see how the CJEU copes with the same problems of comity and accountability that English courts face.[34]

European laws

Don't confuse EU law with the law of the European Convention on Human Rights. Both are European, but if you use the term 'European law' at all, it is best kept for EU law (which used to be called 'Community law'). The ECHR is the creature of a separate treaty organization, the Council of Europe (see 3.2). There are twenty-eight member states of the EU; forty-seven states have signed up to the European Convention.

1.8 Conclusion: 'the properest and most effectual remedy'

The main task for law makers and judges in developing administrative law is to fashion what Lord Mansfield called 'the properest and most effectual remedy' against irresponsible government.[35] Over the past eight centuries, judges have developed a variety of techniques for controlling administrative decisions. Over the past century, Parliament and the government have created an enormous array of new institutions

---

[34] Case C-310/04 *Spain v Council* [2006] ECR I-07285 (see 8.7).

[35] *R v Cowle* (1759) 2 Burr 834, 856.

and processes for the same purpose. The most effectual remedy depends on the type of government action, and the context in which it is taken.

For judges (in courts and in tribunals), for ombudsmen, and for other people who have the opportunity to right injustices in public administration, giving a proper and effectual remedy means doing justice while acting with comity toward other public authorities. That is why the new techniques of administrative law vary in their application: they are tailored to the complexity of modern administration. The courts retain (in fact, they have enhanced) their role of intervening in administration, but, as in Lord Mansfield's day, their job is to do so only when their techniques for controlling government provide the 'properest' remedy. So there is no general rule determining when judges should or should not substitute their own judgment for that of an administrative official: it depends on the circumstances.

Administrative law cannot guarantee good government. It cannot even guarantee responsible government. But it does have a core role of curtailing exercises of public power that can be identified as arbitrary by institutions given power to oversee official action. By restraining the arbitrary use of power, administrative law can give effect to the constitutional principles that support responsible government: system principles, and principles of accountability. The core role of administrative law is to impose the rule of law on the executive.

Administrative law can improve administration in various ways that go beyond that core role. So, for example, ombudsmen can promote good administration directly, by investigating complaints of bad administration (see Chapter 13). But, like judicial review, that can only succeed if the ombudsmen who are interfering with an administrative decision do so with respect for the role of the public authorities in question. Comity is a general principle that applies to ombudsmen and tribunals as well as to judicial review. And it applies to the role of courts in hearing ordinary claims for compensation against public authorities in tort and contract (see Chapters 14 and 15).

Judicial review is of limited importance as a process for resolving complaints against public authorities (see 2.7). But two features of the judges' work are important for learning administrative law. First, the judges give reasons for their conclusions as to what the law requires. The courts have tried to articulate the principles of public law in a way that no other public institution has the capacity or the authority to do. Reading and understanding the judges' explanations for their decisions is the central element in learning administrative law.

Second (and most remarkably), unlike any other institution the courts have authority to determine the nature and the scope of their own power. That is why we began with the story of *habeas corpus*, which is perhaps the most dramatic instance of the judges' constitution-making power. In judicial review, the judges not only have to resolve a dispute between two parties; they are public authorities who have to work out the extent of their own power to interfere with the work of other public authorities. Judges do not have the luxury of simply quashing a decision if there was something wrong with it. When they interfere with another public authority's use of its power, they are crafting standards for the control of *their own* power. And even if a decision was unlawful, the common law gives them a discretionary power to decide whether to interfere (see 10.4.6, pp 396–400).

The special importance of comity in that process means that the study of judicial review is a good way in which to approach the general problem of administrative law. Chapter 2 introduces that problem: how can one public authority interfere with another in a way that promotes responsible government?

TAKE-HOME MESSAGE ● ● ●

- The real objective of administrative law is **good government** (that is, just government that makes for a good community). But administrative law promotes good government indirectly, by providing techniques for achieving **responsible government**.

- Administrative law can promote responsible government by giving effect to constitutional principles: a general, unspecific principle of **accountability**, and system principles (principles that govern the role of government decisions in a system of institutions). The main system principles are **the separation of powers**, **subsidiarity**, **comity**, the **rule of law** (which includes the principles of legality and **due process**), access to justice, and legal certainty.

- Those are general principles, but their application is shaped by the **principle of relativity:** the requirements of general constitutional principles depend on the type of decision that needs to be controlled and on the context in which it is made.

- The core task of administrative law is to impose the **rule of law** on public authorities. It does so by preventing arbitrary government action, and by securing the legal rights of persons with a complaint against a public authority.

- **Comity** is a principle that ought to constrain the courts in imposing the rule of law on other public authorities. That is, they should do so with respect for the capacity of another public authority to do its job.

CRITICAL QUESTIONS ● ● ●

1 Why do you suppose that *habeas corpus* is used very little in Britain today? Why didn't the Belmarsh detainees ask for *habeas corpus* in *A and X v Home Secretary* [2004] UKHL 56?

2 Suppose that the government detains people without statutory authority and says, in *habeas corpus* proceedings, that there is reason to think that they are terrorists, that the reason for the suspicion is not something that can be put to the court in evidence, and that the court should not interfere because the freeing of the people in question would create a catastrophic danger to the United Kingdom. What should the court do?

3 Are tribunals (Chapter 12) and ombudsmen (Chapter 13) part of the executive branch of government, or the judicial branch?

4   Should one public authority ever *abandon* comity towards another public authority?

5   Could there be responsible government in an absolute monarchy?

6   Who should decide what is to be ruled by law?

READING • • •
R (Abbasi) v Foreign Secretary [2002] EWCA Civ 1598
A and X v Home Secretary [2004] UKHL 56
Rahmatullah v Foreign Secretary [2012] UKSC 48
R (Lumba) v Secretary of State for the Home Department [2011] UKSC 12
R (Moseley) v Haringey LBC [2014] UKSC 56
R (Evans) v Attorney General [2015] UKSC 21
R (UNISON) v Lord Chancellor [2017] UKSC 51

On the rule of law:
Tom Bingham, *The Rule of Law* (Penguin 2011)
On accountability:
Anne Davies, *Accountability: A Public Law Analysis of Government by Contract* (OUP 2001) ch 4, 'Accountability Mechanisms'
Elizabeth Fisher, 'Transparency and Administrative Law' (2010) 63 CLP 272
On *habeas corpus*:
Timothy Endicott, '*Habeas Corpus* and Guantánamo Bay: A View from Abroad' (2009) 54 American J of Jurisprudence 1
Judith Farbey, Robert Sharpe, and Simon Atrill, *The Law of Habeas Corpus* (OUP 2011)

 The following online resources accompany this chapter: **summaries** of key cases and legislation; **updates** on the law; **guidance** for answering the pop quizzes and questions; and **links** to legislation, cases, and useful websites.

2 The rule of law and the rule of judges

At common law, the judges will hold administrative conduct to be unlawful on any of three grounds: error of law, lack of due process, and improper exercise of discretionary power. Chapters 4–9 address those grounds in detail. This chapter raises the basic question of how the three grounds of judicial review are supported by constitutional principle. Each ground must be moderated by the principle of comity.

LOOK FOR • • •

- The question that the public authority must answer in order to do its job.

- The court's approach to that question: will the court impose its own answer, or review the public authority's decision on some other ground?

- **Deference** by judges to administrative authorities, and the limits of deference.

- The difference—and the connections—between the rule of law and the rule of judges.

- The **core rationale** for judicial review.

> ' It may be misfortune for the applicant that the court . . . cannot begin to evaluate the comparative worth of research in clinical dentistry; but it is a fact of life. '
>
> *R v Higher Education Funding Council, ex p Institute of Dental Surgery*
> [1994] 1 WLR 242, 262 (Sedley J)

2.1 *Walker*: an introduction to the grounds of judicial review

In May 1995, a Serbian tank fired a shell at the accommodation block in Bosnia where British members of the United Nations Peacekeeping Force were staying. Trevor Walker was one of the peacekeepers sleeping in the compound. The shell injured his right leg so badly that it had to be amputated above the knee.

Walker applied for compensation under a criminal injuries compensation scheme that the Ministry of Defence had introduced in 1979. The scheme was not enacted in a statute and did not create any legal right to compensation; the Ministry merely decided, and announced, that the Army Board would make payments to members of the Armed Forces injured abroad in crimes of violence. The Ministry published special guidelines for peacekeepers in Bosnia, which stated that compensation was *not* available if a peacekeeper was injured as a result of 'military activity by warring factions'.

The Ministry rejected Sergeant Walker's application for compensation, on the ground that the attack on the accommodation block was military activity by a warring faction. Sergeant Walker applied for judicial review of the decision, and his application was rejected by a High Court judge. The Court of Appeal and (in a split decision) the House of Lords upheld the decision to dismiss his challenge (*R v Ministry of Defence, ex p Walker* [2000] 1 WLR 806).

Think of the question of *whether Sergeant Walker should receive compensation*. If the Law Lords rejected his appeal only because they agreed with the Ministry on *that* question, then the court in judicial review simply replaces the administrative decision with the decision that the judges would have made. That is not what the Law Lords claimed to do in *Walker*. Instead, they claimed to apply the three traditional grounds for judicial review. Understanding those grounds means understanding the difference between the rule of law and the rule of judges.

Remember the restriction on compensation: there was to be no compensation for injuries caused by 'military activity of warring factions'. Walker claimed:

(1) that the Ministry misinterpreted the restriction, so that the decision was based on an **error of law**;

(2) that it had been '**irrational**' for the Ministry to introduce the restriction at all; and

(3) that the restriction had been introduced by an **unfair process**.

These three complaints in *Walker* illustrate the three general grounds of judicial review.

Note on styles of cause

Why wasn't *Walker* called *Walker v Ministry of Defence*? The answer is that Sergeant Walker had no cause of action—that is, he could assert no legal right to a remedy in an ordinary claim. So he could not bring an ordinary claim, but he was able to bring an application for judicial review (since the Civil Procedure Rules 1998, it has been called a 'claim for judicial review'), to ask the High Court to review the lawfulness of the decisions of the Ministry of Defence. The case is styled *R v Ministry of Defence, ex p Walker* because the idea is that the Crown initiates the proceeding (on the application of Walker) to ask the court to review decisions of the Ministry of Defence to decide whether they were lawful. The court was not asked whether Sergeant Walker had a right to compensation, but whether the Ministry misinterpreted its own rules, or used its discretion unlawfully in making its rules, or made the rules by a process that was unfair to Sergeant Walker. On the differences between a claim for judicial review and an ordinary claim, see 10.3.

Since the Civil Procedure Rules 1998 came into force, the courts have stopped using '*ex parte*', and started using 'on the application of': for example, *R (on the application of Begum) v Denbigh High School* [2005] EWCA Civ 199.[1] The reason is that the initial application for permission to seek judicial review is no longer heard *ex parte* (that is, without the defendant being involved in the process). But the new style of cause maintains the medieval heritage: the Queen, in an exercise of her ancient prerogative to administer justice, brings the claim for judicial review on behalf of the claimant, in order to ask her judges to determine the lawfulness of official conduct.

These are not just technicalities; they reflect a feature of judicial review that has great practical importance: a claimant in judicial review *does not need to assert any right to a remedy*.

2.2 Error of law

Walker's lawyers said that the attack that injured him was a crime, and that it could not count as 'military activity' if it was criminal. Lord Slynn said that the issue was 'whether the Ministry of Defence has correctly interpreted the scheme . . . or whether its decision involves an error of law' (*Walker*, 810). Along with the majority, he decided against Walker on this point because 'in my opinion the exclusion from compensation as a matter of interpretation covers the injury to Sergeant Walker' (812).

Lord Hobhouse dissented because he interpreted the scheme differently (at 819): 'My Lords, Sergeant Walker is right to say that applying the Government's own criteria his case falls on the right side of the line and he should be compensated. . . . The attack was a criminal act not an act of war.'

---

[1] The citation of cases is abbreviated in this book by omitting 'on the application of'.

When a public authority applies a scheme of standards to a case in order to decide whether to confer benefits or to impose burdens on a person, judicial review is available to correct an error in the agency's understanding of those standards. So the judges in *Walker* asked: how are the guidelines for the scheme to be interpreted? The majority agreed with the Ministry's interpretation of the guidelines, and Lord Hobhouse dissented because he agreed with Walker's interpretation.

This ground of judicial review is remarkable. It is unlike the approach that judges in other common law countries take to interpretations of the law by public authorities (see 9.1.8, p 335). In England, the judges will not merely ask if other authorities' interpretations are unreasonable or arbitrary; a decision will be quashed if it runs contrary to the judges' own interpretation of the standards the agency is applying. In English law, judges are to show no deference to other public authorities on questions of law.

Deference

Judges and academics use the word 'deference' in various ways—they sometimes use it to mean a spineless attitude. Everyone agrees that judges shouldn't be spineless. Here, 'deference' is used instead for the attitude of a judge who treats a decision with respect because of the fact that it was made by another public authority. Some judges have been reluctant to use the term 'deference' in this way (see 7.2.4, p 252).

The fact that another public authority made the decision can require the judges to keep their hands off the decision altogether (as, e.g., when the Queen appoints a cabinet minister), or to scrutinize the decision and the reasons for it very closely (as they used to do when the Home Secretary set tariffs of imprisonment—see 2.5.1, p 55). So in accord with the **principle of relativity** (see 1.3), judges can and do defer *more* or *less* to other public authorities, depending on the type of decision (see 7.1.2, p 241).

Chapter 9 explains the doctrine of review for error of law, and why administrative authorities still have some leeway in applying their rules. On a question of **how to interpret** the standards that other public authorities apply, the judges will impose their own view. As long as those standards are correctly interpreted, though, the judges may defer to other public authorities on particular questions of **how to apply** them to the facts of a case (the difference between interpreting and applying standards is explained in 9.3). The judges are *not* meant to impose their own conclusion on the question of how to apply a scheme of standards to the particular case.

Was Walker's injury caused by military activity of warring factions? *That* was a question for the Ministry and not for the court. But if the Ministry decided it on the basis of a misinterpretation of the rule, then the court would strike down the decision.

The role of the courts in imposing their own interpretations on administrative authorities is not very well defined, and it is pulled in two different directions, as the judges describe their own role in modest or immodest ways. On the one hand, judges sometimes say that they will quash a decision because the law has been incorrectly *applied in the case*, and not only on the ground that it has been misinterpreted. So Lord Hobhouse said in *Walker*: 'If the ministry fails correctly to interpret and apply the terms of the scheme, the decisions it takes are open to judicial review' (817). Taken literally, those statements would make the administrative decision in a case like *Walker* merely provisional—to be replaced by the decision of a judge.

On the other hand, judges often suggest that review for error of law leaves flexibility for public authorities to answer a question of law one way or another. Because the ground of review is *error* of law, the court has to decide that the public authority interpreted the law wrongly (and not merely differently from the way in which the judges would have interpreted it) before there is ground for judicial review. And sometimes the judges suggest that they cannot hold that a public authority has erred in law, unless there was something *very* wrong with their interpretation of the law. As Lord Slynn put it (813):

> If I had come to the view that this phrase was imprecise enough for several meanings to be adopted, then I would not accept that the minister's interpretation of it was such as to be "so aberrant that it cannot be classed as rational" [2]

On the question of how to apply the law to the case, the judges often make it clear that they really won't impose their own view. The public authority's decision can go either way without being quashed on judicial review, as long as it is reasonable. Consider Lord Hoffmann's reason for rejecting Walker's argument on error of law (*Walker*, 815):

> He was fired upon by a Serbian tank. I do not see how it can be said that the ministry could not reasonably take the view that this was military activity by a warring faction.

This statement suggests that, in order to succeed, Walker would have had to persuade the judges that 'the ministry could not reasonably take the view' that it took—either because the Ministry misinterpreted the rules, or because the Ministry could not reasonably apply the rules (correctly interpreted) to his case in the way that it did. Essentially, in judicial review the judges require correct interpretation and reasonable application of the rules. Chapter 9 explains the ways in which the judges give effect to those requirements.

....

[2] *R v Monopolies and Mergers Commission, ex p South Yorkshire Transport Ltd* [1993] 1 WLR 23, 32 (Lord Muskill). On the *South Yorkshire Transport* case, see 9.3.1, pp 353–355.

> **Isn't it odd that there were no legal rights at stake in *Walker*?**
> Lord Slynn asked 'whether the Ministry of Defence has correctly interpreted the scheme . . . or whether its decision involves an error of law'. But the Ministry was not interpreting the *law*; it was only interpreting a scheme of payments made *ex gratia* (that is, given as a favour, not as a right). The judges did not even comment on this remarkable fact about *Walker*, which shows two respects in which the judges' approach to judicial review is very broad: they will review a decision that does not affect the legal position of the claimant in any way, and they will quash a decision for 'error of law' if it is based on a misinterpretation of rules that create no legal rights and, in fact, have no legal status at all—apart from the legal status that they gain from the judges' willingness to control their application.

2.3 Improper use of discretionary power

Sergeant Walker also argued that if the restriction *did* apply, the Ministry never should have adopted it in the first place. But this argument was different: he could not simply claim that the Ministry had made an error in adopting the restriction, because error in the use of a discretionary power *is not a ground of judicial review*. The Ministry had no legal duty to create a particular sort of compensation scheme, or to create a scheme at all. So when the Ministry decided to offer compensation, the terms on which it would do so were up to the Ministry. It had **discretion** (see 7.2, p 247). The courts had no legal power to choose the terms on which compensation ought to be awarded. But the courts did have legal power to *control* the choice that the Ministry made if there was a shortcoming in the Ministry's decision that made it unlawful. The courts are meant to decide whether the exercise of a discretionary power was lawful, without taking away the discretion.

Lord Slynn explained this ground of review in *Walker* by saying that: 'It is not for the courts to consider whether the scheme with its exclusion is a good scheme or a bad scheme, unless it can be said that the exclusion is irrational or so unreasonable that no reasonable minister could have adopted it' (812). That is the traditional approach to supervising the exercise of discretionary powers, and it gave Sergeant Walker a difficult test to meet. He argued that the restriction was 'irrational' because troops in Northern Ireland were entitled to compensation if they were injured by a terrorist attack, and, he argued, there was no rational basis for distinguishing between their situation and his. But Lord Slynn said 'the line may be fine, but to adopt it as a general rule cannot be said to have no rational base despite what seemed to me to be common features between the two situations' (812).

So the judges' approach to discretion, to *some* extent, is to keep their hands off it. They won't interfere merely because they would have made a different decision, and they will not generally interfere on the ground that the public authority made the wrong decision. So Lord Hoffmann suggested that the Ministry of Defence used its discretion in the wrong way—and there *still* was no ground for interfering with its decision: 'Speaking entirely for myself, I find the distinction a fine one . . . in neither Northern Ireland nor Bosnia were the British soldiers engaged in warfare. . . . But I cannot say that the distinction drawn by the ministry is irrational. That is too high a hurdle to surmount' (816).

What does it take to surmount that high hurdle? It takes a special flaw in the exercise of discretion—a flaw that allows judges to say that the decision was improper *even though* the public authority had a discretion. Sometimes this notion of a specially flawed exercise of discretion is summed up as an 'unreasonable' exercise of discretion. But as Lord Greene pointed out in the famous case of *Associated Provincial Picture Houses Ltd v Wednesbury Corporation* [1948] 1 KB 223 (CA), this word 'unreasonable' has to be treated carefully, in a way that is consistent with the lawful discretionary power of the public authority. Lord Greene explained the special defects that justify interference with discretionary power, by saying that an administrative decision maker must 'direct himself properly in law' (that is, there must be no error of law). And in addition, the decision maker must:

- 'call his own attention to the matters which he is bound to consider'; and

- 'exclude from his consideration matters which are irrelevant to what he has to consider' (229).

Doing otherwise is acting 'unreasonably' in the sense that justifies judicial interference with a decision. Then Lord Greene added (229):

> Similarly, there may be something so absurd that no sensible person could ever dream that it lay within the powers of the authority. Warrington LJ in *Short v Poole Corporation* [1926] Ch 66 gave the example of the red-haired teacher, dismissed because she had red hair. That is unreasonable in one sense. In another sense it is taking into consideration extraneous matters. It is so unreasonable that it might almost be described as being done in bad faith; and, in fact, all these things run into one another.

The 'something so absurd' ground of review is often called '*Wednesbury* unreasonableness'. Remember that the principle that the court may overturn a decision if it is *Wednesbury* unreasonable is just one of the various grounds of review that Lord Greene mentioned, which are often collectively called 'the *Wednesbury* principles'. He explained *Wednesbury* unreasonableness in three different ways. To be unreasonable in this sense, the exercise of a discretionary power must be *so* unreasonable that:

- 'no sensible person could ever dream that it lay within the powers of the authority' (*Wednesbury*, 229);

- 'it might almost be described as being done in bad faith' (229); or

- 'no reasonable authority could ever have come to it' (230).

He added that 'to prove a case of that kind would require something overwhelming' (230). Lord Greene was responding to the argument that unreasonable exercises of discretion are unlawful—and he did not simply accept that argument. He held that certain *extraordinarily* unreasonable decisions are to be struck down in judicial review.

This means that there is no general rule that unreasonable actions of public authorities are unlawful.

What is reasonableness?

To act reasonably is to be guided by reasons that ought to guide your action (see 7.1.3). Some of the reasons on which public decisions ought to be based can best be identified and assessed by the public authorities to whom a decision-making responsibility was assigned, rather than by the judges (who are responsible for the rule of law, and not for good government in general). An action is unreasonable in the special, restricted sense that provides a ground of judicial review if it is not guided by reasons *that the law authorizes judges to insist on*.

Only certain sorts of unreasonableness are grounds for judicial review. The reason is **comity** (see 1.5.3, p 19). No one should ever make an unreasonable decision, but a rule that judges should quash any unreasonable decision would give the judges a role in the work of other public authorities that would not actually improve administration; it would instead shift administrative decision making into the courts. It is not generally the judges' job to decide which administrative decisions would be reasonable. Before there is ground for judicial interference, an action has to be unreasonable in a way that enables the judges, from their detached perspective on the court, to see that no person *in the position of the public authority in question* can seriously defend the action as the authority's legitimate use of a lawful power.

Lord Greene's speech is the most influential statement of the judicial control of discretionary power in English legal history. In Chapters 7 and 8, we will see the ways in which the law has developed since Lord Greene's decision, and why (in spite of many premature announcements of the death of *Wednesbury*) his statement is still an integral part of the law today. The crucial points to keep in mind are (1) that the case involved a challenge to a local authority licensing decision and does not give a general code for the control of all discretionary powers of public authorities; and (2) that '*Wednesbury* unreasonableness' was only *one* of the grounds of judicial review listed in *Wednesbury*, which also include the doctrine of relevance and the rule against bad faith.

Twenty years after the *Wednesbury* decision, in *Padfield v Minister of Agriculture* [1968] AC 997, Lord Reid added another item to the list of special flaws that call for a discretionary decision to be quashed by the judges. It was a remarkable case in which the House of Lords quashed a decision that a politician had made for political purposes (see 8.2, p 282). The *Padfield* addition was that a statutory power can only be used 'to promote the policy and objects of the Act'—and that determining those purposes 'is always a matter of law for the court' (Lord Reid, 1030).

Padfield was a striking and creative decision (and controversial: Lord Morris dissented vehemently). And yet it relied on two very old principles that, presumably, Lord Greene was taking for granted in his speech in *Wednesbury*—that a person who has a discretion must **genuinely consider exercising it** (see 8.1.2, p 279), and that it must be used **for the 'objects' of the statute** and not for the public authority's extraneous purposes: 'The question whether a judge, or a public officer, to whom a power is given . . . is bound to use it upon any particular occasion, or in any particular manner, must be solved . . . from the context, from the particular provisions, or from the general scope and objects of the enactment conferring the power' (*Julius v Bishop of Oxford* (1880) LR 5 AC 214, 235 (Lord Selborne)).

Special flaws in a discretionary decision may justify judicial interference.

- **Genuine exercise**: a public authority must not refuse to consider exercising a power, or merely pretend to exercise it.
- **Relevance**: matters that are irrelevant must not form the basis of the decision, and matters that the authority is bound to consider must be considered.
- **Proper purposes**: the authority must not use the power for purposes that are incompatible with the reasons for which it was given the power.
- The judges will quash a decision that is '**so absurd**' that no sensible person could ever dream that it lay within the powers of the authority'.
- The judges will quash a decision that is made in **bad faith**. (See Chapters 7 and 8.)

As Lord Greene pointed out, these grounds of review tend to run into one another. More precisely, acting for improper purposes, *Wednesbury* unreasonableness, and bad faith *are all instances of acting on irrelevant considerations*. If a public authority uses a power for some object that the legislation excludes, it is acting on irrelevant considerations. And without acting on irrelevant considerations, a public authority cannot do 'something so absurd that no sensible person could ever dream that it lay within the powers of the authority'. And acting in bad faith is simply an extreme instance of acting on irrelevant considerations: the fact that an action may hurt your enemies may seem appealing to you, but it is irrelevant to your exercise of a public power.

So the common threads in all of these grounds of judicial review of discretionary action are (1) the rule that a public authority must act on relevant and not on irrelevant considerations; and (2) the judicial determination to identify a hands-off way of controlling the considerations on which public authorities must act.

Now return to *Walker*, and consider whether he had a good argument that the Ministry of Defence had used its discretion unlawfully. The Ministry had discretion as to whether to set up a scheme, and if so, as to what restrictions to impose. So the court could only quash the decision if the *Wednesbury* principles authorized the court to do so. What were the considerations on the basis of which the Ministry introduced the restriction? The Ministry had decided that the original restriction (ruling out compensation for injuries from acts of violence 'committed by an enemy' in war) was too generous, since the peacekeeping role in Bosnia exposed the troops not to enemies of the UK, but to two hostile factions. The consideration that the scheme should not be too generous was a relevant consideration, and because of the Ministry's discretion on the question of how generous it should be, the court deferred to the Ministry.

Statute and prerogative

Does it matter that the powers in *Padfield* and *Wednesbury* were statutory powers, rather than prerogative powers? It seemed to make a difference when those cases were decided, because it was not until *Council of Civil Service Unions v Minister for the Civil Service* [1985] AC 374 (see 7.3.1, p 254) that the House of Lords unequivocally held that the courts could review the exercise of the prerogative on the same broad grounds as the exercise of statutory powers. Today, the grounds of judicial review are essentially the same for the exercise of prerogative power as for the exercise of statutory powers. But in *R (Miller) v Secretary of State for Exiting the European Union* [2017] UKSC 5 [55], the majority of the Supreme Court remarked, obiter, that the exercise of the government's prerogative power to make or unmake treaties 'is not reviewable by the courts'. No doubt they said that because the proper exercise of the treaty power is very commonly based on considerations of international relations that judges cannot assess (see 7.3.1). But imagine it were established before the court that a Prime Minister had signed a treaty in order to secure a bribe. Then the judges would be able to identify the decision as an abuse of power without passing judgment on international relations, and there is nothing in the separation of powers between court and executive that would make it inappropriate for a court to hold such conduct to be an abuse of the prerogative, and therefore unlawful.

● *Pop quiz* ●

What was the source of the power that the Ministry of Defence exercised in creating the criminal injuries compensation scheme?

2.4 Due process

Sergeant Walker did not persuade the House of Lords that the Ministry had misinterpreted the restriction, or that it was an abuse of power for the Ministry to adopt the restriction. But he also challenged the *process* by which the Ministry had adopted the restriction.

The criminal injuries compensation scheme had been introduced with fanfare. The Ministry announced it to service commanders, to let Armed Forces personnel know that a generous new benefit was being created for them. When the Ministry decided to *restrict* the scheme in 1994 by excluding compensation for injuries caused by military activity of warring factions, the Minister announced the change in the House of Commons with no fanfare. It was not announced directly to soldiers or to their commanders. Sergeant Walker argued that this process was unfair. He claimed that he had a **legitimate expectation** (see 8.4) that he would be compensated under the scheme as it had originally been announced, and that it was unfair to disappoint that expectation without having first communicated the new restriction to the services as openly as the original scheme was communicated.

Walker was arguing that the Ministry's conduct was unlawful because it was procedurally unfair. A decision is unfair if it wrongly neglects the interests of someone affected by the decision. The substance of the decision here was *the new restriction*. The procedure that Walker complained of was *adopting the restriction without communicating with services personnel*. The decision was *substantively* unfair if it was unfair for the Minister to restrict the scheme; it was *procedurally* unfair if it was unfair for the Minister to do so without announcing it to services personnel.

Decisions cannot be quashed for substantive unfairness in general. Unfairness is a form of unreasonableness, and we have seen that unreasonableness is not a general ground of judicial review. To ask a court to quash a substantively unfair decision, it is necessary to use the standards for the control of discretion (the special, restricted forms of reasonableness) that are addressed in Chapter 8. Public authorities should not make decisions that wrongly neglect the interest of an affected person, but that does not mean that judges should replace the administration's assessment of people's interests with their own assessment. That is the basic reason for the restrained standards of control of discretionary power outlined in 2.3.

Procedural unfairness, by contrast, is a ground of judicial review, and a relatively clear and uncontroversial ground—although in Chapter 4 we will see fierce controversies about just what counts as unfair. Procedures are steps that a public authority takes in the course of making and announcing decisions, to communicate with people affected, or with people who might have information to contribute or opinions that ought to be taken into account. *Fair* procedures give the persons affected an appropriate role in the process. Think of the decision to convict an accused person of murder. To treat the accused fairly, a criminal court needs to make sure that the accused is told what allegations he or she is facing and with what offence he or she is charged. The accused needs to be present when the prosecution makes its case, and needs to have an opportunity to respond to the evidence by challenging it and by introducing contrary evidence of his or her own. And if the accused is not able to do that, he or she needs help from someone who is competent to do it. In English criminal law, those requirements take the remarkable form of a jury trial with elaborate rules of indictment, disclosure before trial, a right to lead evidence and to choose whether to testify, a right to cross-examine prosecution witnesses, and a right to be represented by counsel and to have legal aid.

Associated with these demands of fairness is the requirement that the decision maker not be biased. In an English murder trial, that requirement is met by rules preventing a biased juror from participating in the decision and preventing a biased judge from presiding over the trial.

Fairness to a person affected by a decision is not the only reason for the law to impose procedural requirements. Good procedure in a murder trial is important to the public, too. It promotes good decisions, and makes the process open to the public, in a way that helps to hold the criminal justice system accountable.

Administrative decisions are all more or less radically different from the decision to convict a defendant of murder. And the procedures that are necessary for good decision making differ correspondingly. They depend on the nature of the decision, and on the relevant considerations (see 4.4). Administrative law only requires *due* process, and not the equivalent of a murder trial, to test every action a public authority takes. The interests in participation, in openness, and in fairness call for different procedures in different decision-making regimes.

So we can return to *Walker* with an understanding of the special role for judicial review on grounds of due process: a court that is concerned not to usurp the Ministry's discretion to decide the terms of the compensation scheme can still require the Ministry to use fair *procedures* in making its decisions. And Lord Slynn said that 'it would have been better if the ministry had given a degree of publicity of the change similar to that given to the original proposal' (814). If judges can impose procedural requirements without usurping the public authority's role, and if they thought it would have been better for the Ministry to announce the change to services personnel, why didn't Walker succeed on this ground of judicial review? Why didn't the House of Lords hold that the Ministry's procedure was unlawful?

The answer is that the requirement of due process does not mean that a court will interfere simply because the process could have been better. Lord Hoffmann said: 'I do not think that your Lordships are concerned to decide in general terms whether it would have been better administration to make the announcement in a different way' (815). The Law Lords' conclusion was that the process was not unfair to Sergeant Walker. He did not know the 1980 policy, and he had not been told that his case would be treated under it. There is no doubt that the Ministry would have been acting in a more open and accountable fashion if it had publicized the new restriction as widely as it had publicized the new scheme. But judicial review is not a general technique for improving administrative process.

2.5 Constitutional principles and judicial review

The **system principles** of the constitution (see 1.5) ought to govern judicial review—in particular, parliamentary sovereignty, the separation of powers, comity among public authorities, and the rule of law. What is the link between grounds of judicial review and constitutional principles? **Parliamentary sovereignty** requires that judges pass judgment on the lawfulness of administrative decisions if Parliament directs them to do so (and requires them not to do so if Parliament has directed them not to do so). The **separation of powers** requires judges not to take over powers of the administration, and judges can promote the separation of powers by holding it unlawful for administrative authorities to act contrary to statute or to the common law. **Comity** requires judges to support the ability of administrative authorities to do their job.

The most important principle behind judicial review is the **rule of law**, and its demands are related to the demands of all of the other system principles. The rule of law requires that public authorities adhere to consistent, open, prospective, non-arbitrary standards, and it *also* requires decision-making processes that distinguish govern-ment action from the mere arbitrary whim of the people in power. But given that pub-lic authorities ought to act in those ways, why should courts interfere? Why not leave administrative agencies to construct and follow their own consistent, open, prospec-tive, non-arbitrary standards, and to devise their own processes?

Here is an easy answer, which may seem plausible: law is for the judges, you may think, so that any question of the standards that administrative agencies ought to fol-low is a question for judges. The main point of this chapter is that it would be a mistake to think this. Judicial review *can* promote the rule of law. But we are not necessarily closer to the rule of law just because a question—even a question of law—is decided by a judge, rather than another public official.

2.5.1 How judicial review can promote the rule of law: the imprisonment of murderers

Replacing the decision of one official with the decision of another does not neces-sarily promote the rule of law. But it *can* do so. We can find the best examples in the courts' claims to have imposed the rule of law on the imprisonment of murderers. Parliament gave the Home Secretary power to decide how long to imprison under-age murderers (detained 'at Her Majesty's pleasure': Children and Young Persons Act 1933 s 53(1)), and in the case of adults the power to decide the 'tariff', or period to be served for the purposes of retribution and deterrence before consideration for parole (Crime (Sentences) Act 1997 s 29). In the 1990s, the judges, who openly opposed what amounted to a sentencing decision by a politician, imposed a variety of restrictions on its exercise. Each restriction promoted the rule of law. They held that:

- the Home Secretary could not impose a secret tariff (*R v Home Secretary, ex p Doody* [1994] AC 531);

- the prisoner had a right to make representations (*Doody*);

- the prisoner had a right to be given reasons for the decision (*Doody*);

- the tariff could not ordinarily be increased retrospectively (*R v Home Secretary, ex p Pierson* [1998] AC 539); and

- it was unlawful for the Home Secretary to base his decision on public clamour in favour of a harsh sentence for a particular offender (*R v Home Secretary, ex p Venables and Thompson* [1998] AC 407).[3]

The European Convention on Human Rights went further than the common law could go, in imposing the rule of law on the Home Secretary. First, the European Court of Human Rights declared that detention of child murderers at Her Majesty's pleasure is contrary to the guarantee of an independent tribunal in the European Convention

---

[3]   For discussion of the *Venables* case, see 3.1, p 74.

on Human Rights Art 6 (*V v United Kingdom* (2000) 30 EHRR 121).[4] Then, after the Human Rights Act 1998 came into effect, the House of Lords held that it is incompatible with Art 6 for the Home Secretary to decide the tariff for an adult murderer (*R v Home Secretary, ex p Anderson* [2002] 3 WLR 1800). The government responded to *Anderson* by asking Parliament to amend the legislation, and the power to set the tariff was given to the judges.

Why say that these developments in English law promote the rule of law, rather than merely the rule of judges? Because each of them, in varying ways, stands in the way of **arbitrary** (see 1.1.3, p 9) decisions about imprisonment. The judges did what they could to insulate the Home Secretary's decision from the pressures from the media that are liable to motivate a Cabinet minister. And taking the power away from the Home Secretary under the Human Rights Act detached it from those pressures. The result is that what happens to a murderer is ruled by a process of decision making that can be distinguished from a whim of the Home Secretary.

The rule against secret tariffs and the prohibition on retrospective increases promote the rule-of-law values of openness and prospectivity; the right to make representations promotes the rule of law by requiring the decision maker to face up to the factual claims and the arguments of the offender. The right to reasons supports that function of representations. A requirement of reasons increases openness, and also opposes arbitrary decisions, through the pressure it puts on the decision maker who has no rationale to offer. And the control on the considerations on which the Home Secretary may act promotes the rule of law by insulating the decision, to some extent, from political influence.

Note that there are more straightforward ways in which sentencing could be ruled by law: a statutory tariff, like the tariff of twenty-five years before parole in Canada for first-degree murder (Criminal Code s 745), would achieve legal control of the sentencing decision much more simply and effectively than all of the subtle judicial developments in the English cases.

The idea that the English judicial and legislative developments and the Canadian legislative tariffs promote the rule of law depends on an assumption. The assumption is that the period an offender spends in prison is the sort of decision that ought to be controlled by law. There are many sorts of decision that the judges will not review on the grounds they used in the life sentence cases and to which Art 6 of the European Convention has no application: decisions about government expenditure, the appointment of ministers, and the disposition of the Armed Forces are the obvious examples. Why should the law control the time that life prisoners spend in prison in a way in which it does not control decisions about government expenditure, or the appointment of a minister, or the disposition of the Armed Forces? A good understanding of the rule of law requires an understanding of which governmental decisions need to be

---

[4]   To carry out the UK's treaty obligation to comply with declarations of the European Court of Human Rights, the Home Secretary immediately announced that he would exercise his statutory power in Venables' and Thompson's cases and in future cases on the basis of the recommendation of the Lord Chief Justice.

controlled by artificial and cumbersome legal processes, in order to achieve responsible government. For the appointment of ministers, we can achieve responsible government through parliamentary controls on the Prime Minister and through general elections; judicial review of the decision would add nothing. In fact, judicial interference would *detract* from responsible government. To achieve responsible government in the imprisonment of murderers, on the other hand, the control that Parliament and the electorate can exert on government would not be enough. It would be arbitrary to subject a particular murderer's life to political forces. We need the decision to be made by an independent tribunal.

We saw that although all administrative decisions should be reasonable, a *legal* requirement of reasonableness would require courts to decide (to some extent) what reasons are good reasons (see 1.5.3, p 19). The courts have no general jurisdiction to do that, and it would be a breach of comity for them to invent one for themselves. Yet it is *not* a breach of comity for them to invent for themselves powers to control administration, where (1) they are capable of controlling a decision without damaging another public authority's capacity to carry out its tasks; and (2) the alternative is to leave a public authority free to engage in arbitrary government. The invention of *habeas corpus* (see 1.1.1, p 5) is perhaps the oldest example of the use of the judges' creative role, and in the twenty-first century the courts retain a dynamic jurisdiction to decide what new forms of judicial control are required for responsible government. Like any governmental power, the courts' jurisdiction will itself be a tool for arbitrary government, if the judges do not use it responsibly.

● *Pop quiz* ●

Judges, unlike administrative officials, are **independent** (see 5.3). Does that mean that replacing another public authority's decision with the decision of a judge generally promotes the rule of law?

2.5.2 Judicial deference to administrative authorities

In *Walker*, why were the judges reviewing the compensation decision at all, when the rules of the scheme had always said that 'whether or not to make such a payment, and if so, the amount, shall be wholly within the discretion of the Army Board'? On the one hand, it seems that the courts should respect the fact that a decision has been committed to another public authority (whether the power is conferred by a statute or, as in *Walker*, by a prerogative act by the government). On the other hand, a very wide grant of power should not be turned into a tool for abuse. These two principles are in tension, but they do not contradict each other. In *Walker*, Lord Hoffmann pointed out that the scheme gave discretion to the Army Board, and simply added: 'But the discretion may not be exercised arbitrarily' (815). The central challenge for judges in judicial review is to prevent other public authorities from using their powers arbitrarily—which the judges need to do in order to impose the rule of law—without imposing their own judgment as to how other public authorities should use their discretionary powers. This means that judges must very often defer to other public authorities—to some extent—on the question of how to use a power. To **defer** to (e.g.) the Ministry on (e.g.) the question of whether injuries caused by military activity of warring factions should be excluded from the compensation scheme is to treat *the fact that the Ministry decided that those injuries are to be excluded* as a reason why they should be excluded.

Courts cannot do everything. They have a **supervisory jurisdiction** over public bodies such as the Ministry of Defence, but they are not a defence agency. They have a supervisory jurisdiction over the Higher Education Funding Council, but they are not a higher education funding agency. So, in *R v Higher Education Funding Council, ex p Institute of Dental Surgery* [1994] 1 WLR 242, the Court of Appeal refused to evaluate the worth of research in dentistry; it could not decide whether the Council's funding decision was based on a sound evaluation, so it would not interfere with it. The Court deferred to the Funding Council on the question of how to evaluate dentistry research. This may seem tragic, because if the Funding Council misjudged the worth of the claimant's research, the Court's deference leaves the claimant with no remedy for an injustice. But it is not tragic: it just reflects the fact that courts cannot be expected to achieve perfect justice. The funding of higher education would not be better governed if the judges were to forget this.

How far should the courts defer to an administrative decision? Sometimes very radically, sometimes not at all, and more or less depending on the type of decision, the body that is making it, and the context in which it is made. This feature of judicial review explains why courts will quash administrative decisions for certain forms of unreasonableness, but *not* for unreasonableness in general. Much of Chapters 7 and 8 are concerned with the considerations requiring greater or lesser deference by courts to the judgment of public authorities whose decisions they are reviewing.

2.5.3 Isn't it Parliament's job to control the executive?

There is a myth in modern British constitutional lore: that the courts have had to control the government because Parliament has been failing to do so. According to this myth, the electoral system tends to create strong majorities, and the party whips control the backbenchers through threats and promises, with the result that the House of Commons is under the control of the executive, instead of the executive being under the control of Parliament. Judicial review did not develop as a substitute for proper parliamentary control, and it can never act as a substitute:

(1) judicial review is *ancient*, much older than the tradition of parliamentary supervision of administration; and

(2) judicial review and parliamentary control of administration are *complementary*.

The roots of the courts' authority to control administration are medieval. And by the seventeenth century the courts were asserting that authority in a very creative way. It was only after the seventeenth century that Parliament was able to exercise any reliable and creative control over the government. It is certainly more than 300 years since English judges doubted their power to supervise the legality of executive action (although they have dramatically revised their views as to what makes executive action unlawful).

FROM THE MISTS OF TIME

Nearly 400 years ago, the Chief Justice, Sir Edward Coke, could claim that 'to this Court of King's Bench belongs authority, not only to correct errors in judicial proceedings, but other errors and misdemeanors extra-judicial, tending to the breach of peace, or oppression of subjects, or to the raising of faction, controversy, debate or any manner of misgovernment' (*Bagg's Case* (1615) 11 Co Rep 94 (Coke CJ)). That was putting it too high, because it has never been the judges' job to correct 'any manner of misgovernment'; to do that, they would have to decide (e.g.) the value of research on dentistry for themselves, instead of leaving that to the Higher Education Funding Council. Coke's statement has to be read as subject to the requirements of **comity**.

Lord Chief Justice Holt put it less extravagantly in *Groenvelt v Burwell* (1700) 1 Ld Raym 454, holding that 'by the common law', 'this court will examine if other courts [including statutory authorities such as, in the case, the censors of the College of Physicians of London] exceed their jurisdiction'.

The judges who developed judicial review were not making up for Parliament's failings. Judges and MPs have different capacities and different opportunities to supervise the executive. Judges have special competence for controlling certain forms of misgovernment (unlawful uses of power), and Parliament has special competence for controlling other forms of misgovernment (the pursuit of policies that are contrary to the national interest).

Parliament has control over administration, first, because the Prime Minister is the leader of the party that has the confidence of the House of Commons, and he or she needs to conduct the administration in a way that helps to sustain that confidence. More specifically, too, the practice of Parliament allows MPs to ask questions of ministers concerning administration in departments and executive agencies for which they are directly or indirectly responsible. The possibility of asking embarrassing questions in the House of Commons supports a practice of written questions from MPs to departments, which helps the MP to get a response to complaints on behalf of constituents. Since the 1960s, MPs have been able to refer complaints to the Parliamentary Commissioner for Administration (PCA), or 'Parliamentary Ombudsman' (see Chapter 13). And the work of the Parliamentary Ombudsman is supported by the Public Administration Select Committee of the House of Commons, which receives reports from the Ombudsman and makes recommendations to the House.

Apart from the role of individual MPs in responding to complaints, since the late 1970s select committees of MPs have had the task of overseeing the administration of departments. There are now nineteen departmental select committees. They are made up of backbench MPs, and they help Parliament to control the executive by examining policy, expenditure, and administration in each of the main government departments and their associated agencies. Even though each committee has a government majority, the committees provide a technique for general scrutiny of administration that is more effective than debates in the House of Commons itself. Select committees do for the House of Commons what it cannot do in a debate among all 650 MPs, by taking written and oral evidence. The committees can summon witnesses to give evidence or to produce documents. A select committee report can generate political pressure in the House of Commons, and the onus of responding to a report can itself change government policy.

Judicial review of the lawfulness of executive action is very different. If it is done right, it is consistent with parliamentary control of the government. The work of the select committees and debates in the House of Commons impose an important control on administration in the public interest (or at least they *can* do so, depending on political pressures), but they do not provide effective redress for the complaints of particular persons about administrative action.

While courts can only interfere with the government on legal grounds, Parliament can hold the government to account on *any* grounds. Courts only promote good government indirectly; Parliament can do so directly. Parliament can also insist on the rule of law. A complaint of unlawful administrative action *could* (like any complaint of bad government) be good material for questions in the House of Commons, or even grounds for a vote of no confidence. Or it could play a role in a parliamentary election campaign. But elections and debates in the House of Commons are not remotely as well designed as a claim in the High Court for responding to a particular person's complaint, for identifying the facts, or for deciding a dispute as to what counts as unlawful.

Consider *R v Bolton* (1841) 1 QB 66 (see 1.5.5, p 26), in which Mr Bolton's council threw him out of his house. He could have complained to his MP, who could have raised the matter in the House of Commons; the government could have taken executive action to help Mr Bolton in response to clamour in the House, or Parliament could have passed a statute retrospectively benefiting him and imposing new duties on the parish council (or new duties on the courts to control the parish council). All that is fanciful, though, as a way of dealing with a particular person's complaint—especially in the case of a pauper thrown out of a council house. When a particular personal problem ends up being discussed in Parliament, it is because of some particular media frenzy that may have nothing to do with the justice of the case. Parliament is not an effective forum for securing justice according to law for particular individuals. The courts have access problems as well (the expense of legal services is the most significant). But once Mr Bolton is in court, he has an opportunity to make an argument to a person independent of government, and the public authority is put in the predicament of having to meet his argument with a lawful justification of its action. That arrangement is a necessary technique for imposing the rule of law on the executive, even if Parliament is doing its job well. Administrative law does not make up for any modern failure by Parliament to carry out its responsibility; Parliament never did the things that we need the courts to do.

And on the other hand, judicial review can never be a remedy for inadequate parliamentary control. Parliament controls the executive in the national interest, as a representative assembly. Legal institutions impose the rule of law on the executive, and hear particular cases. So if Parliament is not doing its job well, the legal institutions *cannot* solve that problem. Judges do not have any techniques to fill a constitutional vacuum left by spineless backbenchers, excessive party discipline, or a weak opposition.

2.6 The twentieth-century judicial adventure

The story so far is that the judges are prepared to pass judgment on other public authorities' interpretation of the law, to impose due process on them, and to quash a decision that they can identify as an abuse of power. This dynamic pattern of judicial law making is compatible with the role of Parliament in the constitution, and it can potentially be justified by the constitutional principle of the rule of law. Whether it is actually justified always depends on whether the judges exercise their power with comity toward other public authorities, which requires the judges to defer to the initial decision maker on many questions, sometimes very radically. But if the judges find a lack of **due process**, or if they can identify a decision, from their rather isolated point of view in the court, as an **abuse of power**, they do not need to defer to another public authority's opinion that it was the right thing to do.

In the development of their role, the judges repeatedly need to assess what deference is due to other public authorities on particular questions; they make a mistake if they think that they must *generally* defer to administrative decision makers, or if they think that they can *generally* decide for themselves the grounds on which administrative decision makers should act.

In the first half of the twentieth century, the courts developed a tendency towards general deference to administrative authorities. After World War II, the courts went through a remarkable period of expansion and new articulation of the grounds of judicial review that was so far-reaching that it has seemed to many lawyers as if administrative law was invented in the second half of the twentieth century. It should already be apparent that many of the most dramatic judicial inventions are centuries old. But the developments in the decades after World War II are remarkable, and even a partial list will give you a picture both of the capacity of the courts to develop new rules of administrative law and also of the state of the law in the twenty-first century.

Timeline of the twentieth-century judicial adventure

- *Ridge v Baldwin* [1964] AC 40: an administrative authority can be subject to the law of due process, even where it does not have a duty to act judicially (see 4.3.2, p 130).
- *Conway v Rimmer* [1968] AC 910: instead of having a 'Crown privilege' against disclosing documents in litigation, the government must ask a court to decide

whether public documents should be withheld from a party in litigation for reasons of the public interest ('public interest immunity'—see 1.6.1, p 34).

- *Anisminic v Foreign Compensation Commission* [1969] 2 AC 147: the courts will avoid giving effect to a statute providing that an administrative decision is not to be challenged in court. (Note that this is *not* the way the House of Lords described what it was doing in *Anisminic*! See 9.1.3, p 323.)

- *O'Reilly v Mackman* [1983] 2 AC 237: any decision based on an error of law will be quashed (see 9.1.2, p 321).

- *Council of Civil Service Unions v Minister for the Civil Service* [1985] AC 374: the three general grounds of judicial review apply to an exercise of prerogative power.

- *Gillick v West Norfolk and Wisbech Area Health Authority* [1986] AC 112: judicial review extends to guidance circulars issued by a department of state without any specific authority and without any legal effect. (Compare the application of the three grounds of judicial review to a decision with no legal consequences, in *Walker*.)

- *R v Panel on Take-overs and Mergers, ex p Datafin Plc* [1987] 1 QB 815 (CA): judicial review can be available against a body that is not a government agency; in fact, the body need not even be a legal person (see 15.5.1, p 605).

- *M v Home Office* [1993] 3 WLR 433: the courts can award injunctions against ministers of the Crown, and declare them to have acted in contempt of court.

- *R v Home Secretary, ex p Doody* [1994] 1 AC 531: cases on disclosure and duties to give reasons have developed a general trend toward openness in the making of administrative decisions.

In the control of discretionary powers, there has been a marked move away from general deference to administrative authorities, towards deferring only for specific reasons. The *Wednesbury* principles can be traced back for centuries before the 1940s (see 7.1, p 234). But after the 1940s the courts gave them further articulation, and in the course of doing so they extended them. That movement includes the *Padfield* case, and the prisoner cases discussed in 2.5.1. It also includes the following.

- *Inland Revenue Commissioners v Rossminster* [1980] AC 952: the House of Lords held that *Liversidge v Anderson* [1942] AC 206 was wrongly decided (see Lord Diplock, *Rossminster*, at 1011). In *Liversidge*, a majority of the House of Lords had decided that the courts had to defer radically to the Home Secretary's judgment as to whether there is good reason for a detention under a statutory power.

- The development of a doctrine of **legitimate expectation** that, to some degree, protects substantive interests (and not only interests in consultation or a hearing) against changes to or deviations from government policy (see 8.4).

- *R v Home Secretary, ex p Ahmed and Patel* [1998] INLR 570: the signing of a treaty can create a legitimate expectation that government will act in conformity to the treaty.[5]

---

5   The effect is limited because a minister can lawfully adopt and act on a contrary policy.

- *R v Home Secretary, ex p Simms* [2000] 2 AC 115: the courts have articulated the **principle of legality**, which is a rule that powers conferred in general terms by a statute do not empower public authorities to act contrary to certain legally protected values.

The courts' control of discretionary powers has also been extended since the 1940s through tort liabilities of public authorities (see Chapter 14). This development is complex and does not amount to a general doctrine that judges will award compensation whenever a claimant suffers loss because a public authority used its power unlawfully. The judges have (with notable exceptions) been very cautious not to turn causes of action in tort into tools by which claimants can get courts to decide what administrative decisions ought to have been taken (see 14.2, p 532).

FROM THE MISTS OF TIME

The judges sometimes seem to think that judicial review was invented in the twentieth-century adventure. So, in the *Page* case, Lord Browne-Wilkinson referred to 'the great development that has recently taken place in the law of judicial review whereby the courts have asserted a general jurisdiction to review the decisions of tribunals and inferior courts' (*R v Lord Chancellor, ex p Page* [1993] AC 682, 700). The tradition of general judicial supervision was already old when *Keighley's Case* (1609) 10 Co Rep 139 imposed judicial control over the Commissioners of Sewers, who had been given legal power by a statute that said nothing about judicial control. The *Keighley* decision implicitly asserted a general jurisdiction to review the decisions of tribunals and inferior courts.

In fact, English judicial history is unified across the centuries by *excessive* judicial claims of responsibility for controlling administrative decision making. (On why the claim in the *Page* case is excessive, see 9.1.6, p 327.)

Since 1998, this judicial creativity has not diminished; the barristers' (and therefore the judges') energy has turned to the development of claims based on the Human Rights Act 1998. Chapter 3 discusses ways in which grounds of judicial review are affected by the European Convention on Human Rights and by EU law.

In addition to their role in developing the grounds of judicial review, the judges have reformed the *process* for seeking judicial review (see Chapter 10), and in particular they have taken a very relaxed approach to **standing** (see Chapter 11). These judicial reforms have facilitated 'public interest litigation', turning judicial review into an instrument for political campaign groups to ask the courts to make decisions that they cannot persuade the government to make.

Much of this book is concerned with the good achievements and the drawbacks of the judicial adventure, and with the ways in which the judges are building on it in the twenty-first century. The most *important* achievement has been an array of very wide-ranging and far-reaching improvements in the fairness and openness of administrative decision-making processes. The more *dramatic* achievement has been a judicial willingness to stand against abuse of power even in very political contexts that would have been considered out of bounds for judges in the 1940s. The drawbacks include the creation of a massively expensive litigation industry in the pursuit of pointless complaints against administrative decisions on grounds that the courts are not well equipped to apply. And occasionally the drawbacks include a form of judicial imperialism as the judges succumb to the temptation constantly offered to them by claimants' barristers, to replace administrative decisions with decisions that the judges think would have been better.

With these dramatic advantages and drawbacks, judicial review gives us a way of understanding the constitutional principles of administrative law. The judges' supervisory jurisdiction is an important feature of English administrative law, and it is the most useful way into the subject. The irony is that we can only understand its place in the constitution if we see that judicial review actually plays a very *limited* role in controlling administrative action.

2.7 Judicial review isn't everything

Other techniques for controlling administrative decisions are much more important than judicial review to millions of people: most important of all are discussion and negotiation with public authorities themselves over their decisions and policies and plans. And, during the same period in which the judges have reinvigorated judicial review, Parliament has enhanced old techniques and instituted new techniques for resolution of disputes and for supervision of administration, which have restructured the law and practice of administration:

- administrative **tribunals** were reconstructed into a highly judicialized system by the Tribunals, Courts and Enforcement Act 2007 (Chapter 12);

- **ombudsmen** schemes have been created to investigate complaints of maladministration in some departments of central government and local government (Parliamentary Commissioner for Administration Act 1967 and Local Government Act 1974) (Chapter 13);

- the system of supervision of administration by **parliamentary select committees** in the House of Commons has been enhanced; and

- **audits** scrutinizing the economy, efficiency, and effectiveness of central government spending are carried out by the National Audit Office, and the Local Audit and Accountability Act 2014 imposed a privatized scheme of audits for local authorities (see 15.4.3, pp 600–601).

Ombudsmen and auditors have capacity for forms of investigation that courts cannot carry out. Ombudsmen, unlike courts, can uphold a complaint even where there has been no unlawful decision. Their reports can get results for a complainant that are more flexible than the courts' remedies, and they are better equipped than courts to recommend general improvements in administrative practice. Auditors have a systematic role that courts could never fulfill, in holding government departments and other public bodies to account for their finances. Parliamentary committees have a role in representative politics that enables them to hold public administration to account for matters of policy on which judges would need to defer. Judges are restricted to identifying *unlawful* procedures. Ombudsmen, parliamentary committees, and auditors can recommend *better* procedures.

As for adjudication of legal claims, far more cases are resolved in tribunals than in courts. And if a claim reaches a court, it is far more likely to do so in a statutory appeal from a tribunal or directly from a government decision[6] than in a claim for judicial review. Tribunals can operate more informally than courts, and their judges may have specialized expertise that High Court judges do not have.

For these reasons, and others to be explained in Chapters 12, 13, 14, and 15, other forms of recourse are *much* more important, for people who have a complaint about government, than judicial review. A lawyer who only knew about judicial review would be severely unprepared to assist clients with complaints against government.

The alternatives to judicial review are not merely used more often than judicial review; their role is essential to the principles of the subject. You cannot understand judicial review itself if you think it is the primary form of legal control of administrative action. It is not even the *secondary* technique. It is a last resort. As Lord Scarman put it: '[A] remedy by way of judicial review is not to be made available where an alternative remedy exists. This is a proposition of great importance. Judicial review is a collateral challenge: it is not an appeal' (*R v Inland Revenue Commissioners, ex p Preston* [1985] AC 835, 852). In the *Preston* case, the House of Lords held that judicial review should not generally be used when a statutory appeal process was available. The same applies if the public authority has an internal complaints process (*R (S) v Hampshire County Council* [2009] EWHC 2537). And likewise, you cannot seek judicial review if you have a right to pursue your complaint in the tribunals system (see Chapter 12).

This approach to judicial review has survived the judicial adventure of the twentieth century, and in fact it has been taken further since the Civil Procedure Rules 1998 gave the courts more flexible authority and encouragement to control and to reduce litigation. In *R (Cowl) v Plymouth City Council* [2001] EWCA Civ 1935, [1] and [25], Lord Woolf, whose report on civil procedure led to the 1998 reforms, emphasized the 'paramount importance' of avoiding litigation through alternative dispute resolution, and warned against 'over-judicialising' complaints against public authorities. The Court of Appeal refused permission for judicial review, told the parties to negotiate about the future instead of arguing about the past, and included the resulting agreement between the parties in its final decision. That important decision simply rejects

---

6   To give one important example, the Housing Act 1996 s 204 gives a right of appeal to a county court on a point of law from an internal review of decisions as to what housing is suitable for homeless people. See *Runa Begum v Tower Hamlets LBC* [2003] UKHL 5.

the idea that all complaints of unlawful conduct are to be heard by a court. For all the importance of judicial review, it remains a last resort.

It may seem tempting to think that because the rule of law is a fundamental constitutional principle, the judges *must* be prepared to pass judgment on any allegation of official unlawfulness, so that the government will be held to the law. As surprising as it may seem, that would be a serious mistake. Whether judicial review should be allowed in any case is itself a question of due process. If there is another way in which to resolve a dispute with the government, due process does not require judicial review.

FROM THE MISTS OF TIME

In *R v Barker* (1762) 3 Burr 1265, 1267 (see 11.1.1, p 410), Lord Mansfield held that: 'A *mandamus* . . . ought to be used upon all occasions where the law has established no specific remedy, and where in justice and good government there ought to be one.' Note the last part of that decision: a *mandamus* (today, a mandatory order requiring a public authority to exercise a legal power) *will not be issued* unless justice and good government require the order to be made.

Chapter 10 addresses the judicial review process. For now, it is worth outlining some of the restrictions on judicial review, to put it in its place as an extraordinary process.

Restrictions on judicial review

- No one has a right to seek judicial review; a claimant must first ask the court for **permission**.[7]
- The claimant must proceed within a very restrictive three-month **time limit** for claims for judicial review. Even more stringent time limits are imposed by statute in some particular fields.
- The claimant will not be given **standing** (Chapter 11) to bring a claim for judicial review unless a court decides that he or she has a 'sufficient interest' in the matter of the claim.
- The courts have **discretion in remedies**: even if they find that a decision was unlawful, they do not need to quash it if there are good grounds for giving it effect (see 10.4.6, p 396).
- **An unlawful process is not in itself a reason for quashing a decision**. So, for example, if a hearing does not meet lawful requirements, the decision will not be quashed if the irregularity was not substantial enough to make it unfair (*NJ v Essex County Council* [2006] EWCA Civ 545).
- **Power to remit**: if the judges find that a decision was unlawful, they have very wide power under the Civil Procedure Rules to send the matter back to the initial decision maker for it to make a lawful decision.

---

[7]   Note that an ordinary claim, such as a claim in tort, is different: a claimant has a right to bring a claim, although a court can strike it out on the defendant's application if the claim does not present an arguable right of action. See Chapter 14.

In spite of these basic restrictions on judicial review, the government has sometimes wanted to set up bodies whose decisions cannot be challenged in the courts. But when Parliament has enacted provisions designed for that purpose (called 'privative clauses' or 'ouster clauses'), the courts have offered no cooperation at all.

2.7.1 Ouster clauses

At the beginning of the twentieth-century judicial adventure, it was not obvious that the courts had jurisdiction to give judicial review if a statute stated that the decision of an administrative body was 'final'. But in *Pyx Granite Co Ltd v Ministry of Housing and Local Government* [1960] AC 260, it was clarified. Viscount Simonds said: 'It is a principle not by any means to be whittled down that the subject's recourse to Her Majesty's courts for the determination of his rights is not to be excluded except by clear words' (286). The decision was right, because the fact that an administrative decision is final does not mean that the courts should not interfere when it has been made unlawfully. But Viscount Simonds's statement of the principle comes dangerously close to suggesting that it is the courts' job to determine all questions of right—when it is actually their job to ensure that authorities that have power to determine questions of right do so with due process and do not abuse their power.

Far from being whittled down, Viscount Simonds's principle became overextended in the following years. Lord Steyn suggested, in *Jackson v Attorney General* [2005] UKHL 56, [102], that the courts might disregard an attempt *by Parliament* 'to abolish judicial review or the ordinary role of the courts'. It sounds like an assertion of the rule of law against arbitrary decision making by Parliament itself. But if you try to imagine the scenario in which Parliament departs so radically from the British political tradition, you will not be imagining a scenario in which the judges will still be free to impose the rule of law.

In the real world, though, the courts will actually refuse—to some extent—to go along with Parliament's decisions about ousting judicial review. In *Anisminic v Foreign Compensation Commission* [1969] 2 AC 147 (HL), Parliament had provided that:

> ' The determination by the Commission of any application made to them under this Act shall not be called in question in any court of law. '[8]

Yet the House of Lords, in a deeply divided decision, quashed the Commission's determination of an application made to them under that Act. The majority's ground was that the Commission had misinterpreted the legislation in such a way that its decision did not count as a genuine determination for the purpose of the statute. The Court was not allowed to call a determination into question, so the majority in the House of Lords decided that it *wasn't* a determination!

---

[8]   Foreign Compensation Act 1950 s 4(4).

Anisminic is the paradigm example of a judicial tendency to exaggerate the importance of judicial review. If the minority in the House of Lords had prevailed in the
case, the result would simply have been that foreign compensation would have been
governed by the Commission's interpretation of the legislation (an interpretation with
which one of the Law Lords agreed), rather than by the interpretation of the majority of the judges. It would still have been possible for courts to interfere—in spite of
the ouster clause—with an abuse of power by the administrative decision maker (see
9.1.4, p 324).

The very sceptical approach that judges take to ouster clauses has a long tradition.
William Blackstone wrote in the 1760s that because administrative tribunals derogate
'from the general jurisdiction of the courts of common law', they 'cannot be extended
farther than the express letter of their privileges will most explicitly warrant'.[9] One
way in which things have changed since the 1760s is that it would now be a mistake
to think of tribunals as derogating from the common law courts' jurisdiction. When
a new administrative scheme is created (e.g., to award compensation from a foreign
compensation fund, or to provide social security, or to award criminal injuries compensation to soldiers), Parliament is taking nothing away from the common law courts
if it creates a new tribunal to operate the scheme, or to resolve disputes over its operation. We will see in Chapter 12 that one central feature of the tribunals system is that
finally, after centuries, English law has escaped from the presumption that the ordinary courts are the default forum to determine all legal disputes. Administrative tribunals do not necessarily take away anything at all from the role of the courts, and the
role that the courts can play in controlling administrative tribunals should be worked
out by asking what they can do to improve decision making—and not by presupposing
that the rule of law requires them to interfere with a decision that derogates from their
jurisdiction.[10]

And even after *Anisminic*, we do not have a general rule that Parliament cannot oust
judicial review of an administrative tribunal. In *R (Privacy International) v Investigatory
Powers Tribunal* [2017] EWCA Civ 1868, an advocacy group sought judicial review of
a decision of the Investigatory Powers Tribunal; the Court of Appeal held that judicial
review was prevented by an ouster clause providing that 'determinations, awards and
other decisions of the Tribunal (including decisions as to whether they have jurisdiction) shall not be subject to appeal or be liable to be questioned in any court'.[11]

The judges in both the Divisional Court and the Court of Appeal distinguished
Anisminic partly on the ground that the ouster clause in *Privacy International* was
'unambiguous', because it expressly applied to 'decisions as to whether they have

---

[9]   *Commentaries on the Laws of England* (1769), Book iii, ch 6.

[10] Note the strategy in the tribunals system, which is—wisely—*not* to try to insulate the tribunals
system from the ordinary courts by means of an ouster clause, but to allow statutory appeals to
the Court of Appeal (see 12.4.9, p 466).

[11] Regulation of Investigatory Powers Act 2000 s 67(8); the Investigatory Powers Act 2016 s 242
provided for appeals from decisions of the Tribunal.

jurisdiction' [48]. Perhaps more importantly, the Court of Appeal focused on the Tribunal's role as an independent judicial tribunal conducting closed procedures to hear complaints that government had acted unlawfully in the interception of communications, surveillance, and covert intelligence. The special role of the Investigatory Powers Tribunal (IPT) meant that judicial review would be a way for claimants to try to circumvent 'the elaborate regime put in place to allow the IPT to determine claims against the intelligence services in a closed procedure' [43]. Sales LJ held, as a result, that 'construing' the ouster clause to allow judicial review would 'subvert' Parliament's intention [44].

Sales LJ held in *Privacy International* that 'the restrictive approach to interpretation of ouster clauses which is illustrated by *Anisminic* is an example of the application of the principle of legality' [21]. The principle of legality is essential to the rule of law (see 1.5.5, p 22); it also creates a standing temptation for courts to exaggerate their own responsibility for the administration of justice. The majority of the House of Lords succumbed to the temptation in *Anisminic*; the Court of Appeal resisted the temptation in *Privacy International*. The courts *do* have a general jurisdiction to control the lawfulness of decisions by other public authorities, but the decision-making power of other public authorities is not a derogation from any general jurisdiction of the courts to decide all legal disputes. The creation of any jurisdiction creates a risk of abuse of power. And the court does have a responsibility for restraining abuse of power, to the extent that it can lawfully do so. The courts should do whatever they can lawfully do to prevent other public authorities from turning an ouster clause into a cloak for abuse of power. But if Parliament has decided that determinations of a commission or tribunal are not to be questioned in court, there is no justification for judges quashing a determination of the body on the ground that it was based on a misinterpretation of the rules that it must apply. Yet we will see in Chapter 9 that the law of English judicial review requires judges to do just that. In developing that rule, the English judges have gone beyond their responsibility to impose the rule of law and have imposed the rule of judges.

And there is one rule-of-law consideration that always weighs *against* judicial review: the interest in the finality of proceedings. Litigation actually works against the rule of law, because it suspends the legal effect of decisions and reduces legal certainty (see 1.5.5, p 26). The availability of litigation over the lawfulness of an executive decision always leaves matters up in the air and makes it impossible, for a time, to take an official decision at face value. And litigation often creates incidental risks that the relevant information will no longer be available, or will be misunderstood, in the judicial hearing. As the European Court of Human Rights held in *Pullar v United Kingdom* (1996) 22 EHRR 391 [32], it is 'an important element of the rule of law' that 'the verdicts of a tribunal should be final and binding unless set aside by a superior court on the basis of irregularity or unfairness'.[12] In cases of 'irregularity or unfairness', as the

----

12 Cited in *Montgomery v HM Advocate* [2003] 1 AC 641 (PC), 669. The comment concerned a judicial tribunal, but the same reasoning applies to administrative decision makers.

Strasbourg Court called it, judicial review *is* essential to the rule of law, in spite of the drawbacks of litigation. To justify judicial review, we cannot simply say that the rule of law must subject everything to the rule of courts. We need to find special reasons of constitutional principle that make the litigation a proportionate response to the claim.

● *Pop quiz* ●

Who established the sovereignty of Parliament? Lord Steyn said in *Jackson* [102], 'It is a construct of the common law. The judges created this principle.' Is there any authority for that? Can the judges, as Lord Steyn suggests, change or abolish the principle?

2.8 Conclusion: the core rationale for judicial review

The core rationale for judicial review may seem to be that if an administrative action is unlawful, courts must step in to impose the law. That is an easy mistake to make, because judges are absolutely essential to justice and the rule of law—not just judges, but independent, creative judges. The judges' capacity is limited, however, and so their constitutional role is limited too. They 'cannot begin to evaluate the comparative worth of research in clinical dentistry' (*R v Higher Education Funding Council, ex p Institute of Dental Surgery* [1994] 1 WLR 242), for example. Where fidelity to the law requires an administrative authority to evaluate research in clinical dentistry, the judges are not well equipped to improve the authority's fidelity to law.

The core rationale for judicial review

Where there is no other process for imposing the rule of law, independent judges should support the rule of law by interfering with another public authority's decisions (*if* the judges can do so effectively and without damaging the public authority's capacity to do its own job), to impose due process, and to oppose arbitrary government.

Control of administrative action by law goes well beyond the core rationale for judicial review. For example, the law sets up ombudsmen to *improve* administration directly, and it establishes tribunals with expert membership to resolve disputes with public authorities, and auditors to improve economic efficiency in administration. But the core rationale for judicial review identifies a central set of tasks for judges—tasks that they are justified in taking on themselves (as they took upon themselves the *habeas corpus* jurisdiction in the Middle Ages). If the courts leave behind the limited role that is supported by that rationale, they may or may not make better decisions than the administrators, but they will not be imposing the rule of law.

Every aspect of administrative law involves processes by which one public authority exercises some form of legal control over the conduct or decisions of another. The central problems for administrative law are as follows.

- What processes ought to be available for the control of one public authority's decision by another public authority?

- On what grounds ought the second public authority to interfere with a decision of the first public authority?

- How can that interference be reconciled with the comity that one public authority owes towards another?

All of these problems are addressed (articulately, with remarkable results) in the law of judicial review, and that is why Chapters 4–9 unpack the grounds of judicial review outlined in this chapter.

TAKE-HOME MESSAGE • • •

- Respect for **parliamentary sovereignty** requires judges to interfere with other public authorities on any grounds on which Parliament enacts that they should do so.

- Respect for the **rule of law** justifies judges in imposing due process on other public authorities in their decision making (Chapter 4). Because the rule of law is opposed to the arbitrary use of power, the rule of law also justifies judges in developing a doctrine of review for abuse of power (Chapter 7).

- The rule of law also requires judges to control the way in which administrative authorities **interpret** the law. But the judges' duty to impose the rule of law on the administration does not justify the doctrine of review for error of law (see Chapter 9).

- Where judges are able to identify a decision as unreasonable while acting with respect for the decision-making advantages of the initial decision maker (that is, with comity), there is ground for judicial review. But **the judges have no general jurisdiction to decide what would be reasonable**.

- **Comity** requires judges to supervise decisions of other public authorities in a way that shows respect for their role, and which reflects the reasons why the power to make those decisions was given to a body that is not a court.

CRITICAL QUESTIONS • • •

1 **What is the purpose of judicial review: is it to police the lawfulness of administrative action? To right injustices to claimants?**

2 **Can you explain the difference between review for error of law and review for the proper use of discretionary power?**

3   Can you find examples of judges explicitly basing their decisions in judicial review on the rule of law?

4   Do judges play a political role in judicial review? Should they do so?

5   Can you think of *any* grounds on which a court ought to be prepared to review a decision by the Prime Minister to recommend the appointment of a particular person as a minister of the Crown?

6   Would judicial review become unnecessary if Parliament were better at scrutinizing the executive?

READING • • •

Associated Provincial Picture Houses Ltd v Wednesbury Corporation [1948] 1 KB 223 (CA)

R v Ministry of Defence, ex p Walker [2000] 1 WLR 806 (HL)

John Laws, *The Common Law Constitution* (CUP 2014)

Stephen Sedley, *Lions under the Throne: Essays on the History of English Public Law* (CUP 2015)

Lord Sumption, 'The Limits of Law' in Nicholas Barber, Richard Ekins, and Paul Yowell, *Lord Sumption and the Limits of the Law* (Bloomsbury 2016) 15–26

The following online resources accompany this chapter: **summaries** of key cases and legislation; **updates** on the law; **guidance** for answering the pop quizzes and questions; and **links** to legislation, cases, and useful websites.

3 Human rights law

The **European Convention on Human Rights (ECHR)** is a remarkable treaty that not only guaranteed certain rights, but also established an international court, the European Court of Human Rights in Strasbourg. The **Human Rights Act 1998** gives English judges *dramatic*, but *limited*, techniques for vindicating the Convention rights, and requires them to take into account the judgments of the Strasbourg Court. The Charter of Fundamental Rights of the European Union protects similar rights to the ECHR, but does so with direct effect in UK law. This chapter surveys what the judges in the European Court of Human Rights in Strasbourg, in the Court of Justice of the EU in Luxembourg, and in the English courts have made of the power they have been given to develop human rights law, and to develop their own role in the law and politics of human rights.

LOOK FOR • • •

- The content and the structure of the **Convention rights**.

- The ways in which those rights are protected in the English common law of administration, and through the **Human Rights Act 1998**.

- Tests of **proportionality** required by the Convention, and the extraordinary role that they give to judges.

- The interaction between the Strasbourg Court, the Court of Justice of the EU, and the English courts.

> ' The importance of the Human Rights Act is unquestionable. It does not however supersede the protection of human rights under the common law or statute. . . . Human rights continue to be protected by our domestic law, interpreted and developed in accordance with the Act when appropriate. '
>
> *R (Osborn) v Parole Board* [2013] UKSC 61 [57] (Lord Reed)

> ' The Convention respects the general principle of the separation of powers between the executive and the courts, including the principle that there remain some areas which are essentially matters for the executive and not the courts. '
>
> *R (Gentle) v Prime Minister* [2006] EWCA Civ 1689 [75]

3.1 *Venables and Thompson*: the difference the Convention makes

When they were ten and eleven years old, Jon Venables and Robert Thompson killed Jamie Bulger, who was two years old. After the boys were convicted of murder, the Home Secretary had a statutory power to set a tariff (the time they would spend in prison before they could be considered for release—see 2.5.1, p 55). The Bulger family and others campaigned for a long tariff. The Home Secretary received thousands of letters, a petition signed by 278,300 people, and 21,281 coupons clipped out of *The Sun*, in favour of imprisoning the boys for the rest of their lives. The coupons read: 'Dear Home Secretary, I agree with Ralph and Denise Bulger that the boys who killed their son James should stay in jail for LIFE.' The coupons followed a campaign under headlines such as '80,000 call TV to say Bulger killers must rot in jail' (*R v Home Secretary, ex p Venables and Thompson* [1998] AC 407, 525). The Home Secretary set a tariff of fifteen years, rather than the eight years that the trial judge had recommended. And because the Home Secretary wanted the world to know that he was responding to the popular clamour, he announced that one of his reasons for that long tariff was 'the public concern about this case, which was evidenced by the petitions and other correspondence'.

When Venables and Thompson challenged the tariff decision in judicial review, a controversy over the separation of powers divided the House of Lords. The majority held that it was unlawful for the Home Secretary to take the coupons into account. Lord Steyn said (at 526):

> ' In fixing a tariff the Home Secretary is carrying out, contrary to the constitutional principle of separation of powers, a classic judicial function. . . . Parliament must be assumed to have entrusted the power to the Home Secretary on the supposition that, like a sentencing judge, the Home Secretary would not act contrary to

> fundamental principles governing the administration of justice. Plainly a sentencing judge must ignore a newspaper campaign designed to encourage him to increase a particular sentence. It would be an abdication of the rule of law for a judge to take into account such matters. '

Lord Lloyd dissented (at 517), arguing that:

> ' It is to the Home Secretary that Parliament has entrusted the task of maintaining public confidence in the criminal justice system, and as part of that task gauging public concern in relation to a particular case when deciding on the earliest release date. I do not regard it as the function of the courts to tell him how to perform that task. '

The judges had to work out whether the principles of the separation of powers and the rule of law (see 1.5.1, p 16, and 1.5.4, p 20, respectively) *prohibited* the Home Secretary from acting on the basis of public clamour—or whether Parliament had deliberately given him the power *because* politicians respond to popular opinion. It was not the judges' job to prevent him from doing the job that Parliament gave him. But did Parliament give him the job of deciding like a judge? Or the job of deciding like a politician? The question raised an especially controversial problem of **comity** (see 1.5.3, p 19), because the courts had to decide whether the Home Secretary—a politician—could act on political considerations.

How much simpler it became when the lawyers for Venables and Thomson took their case to the European Court of Human Rights in Strasbourg. In two sentences, the Court observed that Art 6 of the European Convention on Human Rights guarantees a fair hearing by an independent tribunal, and held that 'independent' means independent *of the executive*. Since the Home Secretary is a member of the executive, the Strasbourg Court declared that the boys' right under Art 6 had been violated (*V v United Kingdom* (2000) 30 EHRR 121).

Why was the Strasbourg decision so much simpler? The Strasbourg Court did not need to invent a justification for controlling another public authority's power. By signing the Convention, the United Kingdom had given the Strasbourg Court the task of deciding whether the boys' rights had been violated. Today, in limited ways, the Human Rights Act 1998 gives English courts the same task.

Some problems of comity are solved when the law gives judges the job of enforcing fundamental rights. Their task is prescribed by law when a Convention right has been violated. Yet deciding *whether* a Convention right has been violated often requires a court to work out and to justify its own role in protecting fundamental rights. Really difficult problems of comity emerge in litigation over Convention rights, when courts need to decide whether to defer to other public authorities in deciding the content of the rights.

We need to deal with those problems throughout this book; in this chapter, we start with a sketch of the institutions that give effect to the Convention rights, the processes by which they do so, and the content of the rights themselves.

3.2 The European Convention, the Strasbourg Court, and the English courts

In 1950, Britain signed the European Convention on Human Rights. In 1966, Britain allowed petitions by individuals to the European Court of Human Rights in Strasbourg. The Convention empowers the Strasbourg Court to interpret and to apply the Convention in deciding complaints either by another contracting state, or by a person who claims to have been the victim of a violation of a Convention right by a contracting state (Arts 32–34). Judgments of the Strasbourg Court bind the state against which a complaint is made (Art 46). But they are not directly binding in English law. They are binding in *international* law, which requires states to abide by treaty obligations. The British government has a mostly (but not completely: see 3.10, p 110) consistent practice of complying with its treaty obligations. But those obligations cannot be enforced in an English court.

The Convention had no direct effect in English law before the Human Rights Act 1998 came into force in October 2000, but the British government consistently responded to declarations of the Strasbourg Court by providing a remedy. So, for example, as soon as the European Court of Human Rights declared that Venables' and Thomson's right under Art 6 had been violated, the Home Secretary announced that he would ask the Lord Chief Justice to decide the tariff, and the Lord Chief Justice reinstated the eight-year tariff set by the trial judge. If the Home Secretary had not done that, the United Kingdom would have been in violation of its treaty obligation. But Venables and Thompson would not have been able to ask an English court to do anything about it.

Even before the Human Rights Act, though, the Convention had an indirect effect in English administrative law: Lord Bingham said that 'the Convention exerted a persuasive and pervasive influence on judicial decision making in this country, affecting the interpretation of ambiguous statutory provisions, guiding the exercise of discretions, bearing on the development of the common law' (*R v Lyons* [2003] 1 AC 976 [13]). The judges used it indirectly, when deciding what actions counted as an abuse of discretion. But *R v Ministry of Defence, ex p Smith* [1996] QB 517 shows how limited that effect was: Convention rights provided a background to applying the ordinary principles of judicial review (see 7.1.3, p 245) and did not provide a different ground of review.

Jeanette Smith was discharged from the Royal Air Force under a policy that homosexuals could not serve in the Armed Forces, regardless of their conduct. She claimed that the policy infringed her right to respect for her private and family life under Art 8 of the Convention. But the Human Rights Act was years in the future, and she could not argue in the English courts that the policy was unlawful on the ground that it infringed a Convention right. In judicial review, she used Art 8 as a ground for arguing that the policy was an unlawful use of discretion under the ordinary English doctrines of control of discretionary power.

Simon Brown LJ said that the protection of fundamental rights *is* a responsibility of the courts, but that they could only interfere 'if it were plain beyond sensible argument that no conceivable damage could be done to the armed services' if the policy were overturned (*R v Ministry of Defence, ex p Smith* [1996] QB 517, 541):

> ❛ If the Convention for the Protection of Human Rights and Fundamental Freedoms were part of our law and we were accordingly entitled to ask whether the policy answers a pressing social need and whether the restriction on human rights involved can be shown proportionate to the benefits then clearly the primary judgment (subject only to a limited "margin of appreciation") would be for us and not others: the constitutional balance would shift. ❜

That is, the questions for an English court in 1996 remained the traditional questions discussed in Chapter 2: whether the Ministry of Defence had acted on relevant considerations, and whether the decision was one that a reasonable decision maker could make. *Smith* made it clear that the courts would not turn Convention rights into legal limits on administrative action. That was up to Parliament.

Jeanette Smith took her complaint to Strasbourg, and it was upheld: the Court held that the blanket ban on homosexuals serving in the military violated Art 8. The Court reached that decision by addressing the question that the English courts had declined to address: whether the impact of the policy on the private interests protected by Art 8 was **disproportionate** to the benefits that the Ministry of Defence was trying to achieve. The Court emphasized that the English law of judicial review had prevented the English courts from considering 'whether the interference with the applicants' rights answered a pressing social need or was proportionate to the national security and public order aims pursued' (*Smith v United Kingdom* (2000) 29 EHRR 493 [138]).

The *Venables and Thompson* and *Smith* cases show the two crucial respects in which the work of the Strasbourg Court differs from the protection of fundamental rights in the common law:

(1) At common law, the courts control the exercise of a statutory power in ways that promote the rule of law and the separation of powers, but the courts cannot take the power away, even if it conflicts with those principles (*Venables and Thompson*).

(2) At common law, fundamental rights are relevant to the legal control of a statutory or prerogative power only *if* the fact that such rights were violated is a reason to hold that an action was unlawful under the *Wednesbury* principles (*Smith*).

Under the Convention:

(1) no infringement of rights can be justified on the ground that the legislature of a state authorized it;

(2) the Strasbourg Court decides whether the impact of the action of a public authority on the interests protected by Convention rights is *proportionate to the pursuit of legitimate purposes.*

Until 2000, those special effects of the Convention could only be pursued by a complaint to the Strasbourg Court. The Human Rights Act has indeed shifted the constitutional balance, through four quite specific devices.

3.3 The four techniques of the Human Rights Act 1998

The Human Rights Act does not incorporate the Convention into English law; rather, it uses four techniques to give specific effects to some[1] of the Convention rights:

- a new technique for reading and giving effect to statutes (s 3);

- a new ground on which administrative action can be unlawful (s 6);

- a new power to give a remedy in relation to acts that are unlawful under s 6, including an award of damages if 'necessary to afford just satisfaction' (s 8) (see 14.6); and

- a new fast-track method for the government to amend statutes that the judges declare to be incompatible with Convention rights (ss 4, 10).

Under s 6, 'it is unlawful for a public authority to act in a way which is incompatible with a Convention right'—except that it is not unlawful to do so if the public authority 'was acting so as to give effect' to an incompatible provision in primary legislation. If the public authority was acting so as to give effect to primary legislation, its action is lawful, but the court can declare that the primary legislation is incompatible with Convention rights under s 4 of the Human Rights Act.[2]

Under s 3, 'so far as it is possible', primary and subordinate legislation 'must be read and given effect in a way which is compatible with Convention rights'. If that is *not* possible, the court can declare that the primary legislation is incompatible with a Convention right (s 4).

A declaration of incompatibility does not affect the validity or change the legal effect of the provision that has been declared incompatible with a Convention right (s 4(6)). From the judges' point of view, it 'acts primarily as a signal to Parliament that it needs to consider amending' the legislation (*Benkharbouche v Embassy of the Republic of Sudan* [2015] EWCA Civ 33 (Lord Dyson [72])). But it also triggers a new amendment procedure (s 10), by which the government can make a remedial order. A remedial order

---

[1]   The duty of contracting states under Art 1 to 'secure to everyone within their jurisdiction the rights and freedoms defined in Section I of this Convention' was omitted, as was the Art 13 right to an effective remedy; in both cases, the drafters of the Human Rights Act wanted to control the techniques that were being created, rather than authorize judges to give effect to the Convention on its own terms. This is one reason why it is misleading to say that the Act 'incorporated' the Convention into English law.

[2]   'Primary legislation' includes not only Acts of Parliament, but also Orders in Council under the prerogative (s 21(1)). So those exercises of executive authority cannot be quashed under s 6, even though they are subject to judicial review on common law grounds.

can amend a statute if each House of Parliament approves it by a resolution—a process that is simpler and faster than the passage of a new statute. So a declaration of incompatibility makes it easy for the government to change the legislation. And it has the effect of imposing an obscure sort of political onus on the government to do so—although the Human Rights Act itself does *not* say that the government must change the legislation.

A declaration of incompatibility is a discretionary remedy. Even if legislation is incompatible with the Convention, the court may decline to issue a declaration of incompatibility where one has already been issued in previous litigation, or where the particular claimant seeking a declaration has not been deprived of a Convention right (*R (Chester) v Secretary of State for Justice* [2013] UKSC 63).

A popular misconception

When the courts declare that a statute is incompatible with the Convention, as in *A and X v Home Secretary* [2004] UKHL 56 (see 1.1.2, p 8), politicians and reporters often say that the courts have struck down or overturned the statute. That is a misconception. The Act leaves it to Parliament to decide *whether to change* a statute, after a court declares that it is incompatible with a Convention right.

This blind spot in the media corresponds to a very strong expectation that has developed in British politics: the expectation that, when the British courts declare that a statute is incompatible with a Convention right, the government will present a remedial measure to Parliament, and Parliament will approve it. In fact, there is nothing in UK law to require any remedial measure even to be considered. But the developing political expectation that it will happen is bolstered by a sobering fact: if the government does not respond to a declaration of incompatibility by changing the statute, the complainant can still go to the Strasbourg Court. And the government will be bound in international law to honour any declaration that is made in Strasbourg.

After the Human Rights Act, in *R (Anderson) v Home Secretary* [2002] UKHL 46, the House of Lords did the same thing for adult murderers that the Strasbourg Court had done for child murderers in *V v United Kingdom*. Once the House of Lords accepted that deciding the tariff for a life prisoner was a sentencing function, the case was as straightforward in the English courts as Venables' and Thompson's case had been in the Strasbourg Court: Art 6 requires an independent tribunal for sentencing decisions, and the Home Secretary is not an independent tribunal.[3] The House of Lords issued a declaration of incompatibility under s 4 of the Human Rights Act, and the government introduced a remedial order to change the legislation so that judges would determine the tariff.

Anderson is a good example of the effect that the Human Rights Act has on English public law. But, as we will see in 3.3.1 and 3.3.2, it also shows the effect that the Act

---

[3]   The fate of a life prisoner *after* the tariff is still governed by an administrative process carried out by the Parole Board, with representations made by the Home Office and the prisoner (see 4.5, p 137).

does *not* have. Anderson's lawyers asked the Law Lords to use s 3 or s 6 to fix the incompatibility themselves, rather than leave it to the government and Parliament to fix the incompatibility through a remedial measure. That approach would have restructured UK law, and the House of Lords refused to do it. And yet we will see that, in the right circumstances, the judges *will* actually use s 3 to give legislation an effect that is contrary to what Parliament enacted.

A cure for the American disease?

The US courts can quash an Act of Congress that violates the US Bill of Rights. The only democratic technique for overruling the judges is a constitutional amendment, and amending the Constitution is very difficult (US Constitution Art V). In Canada, the courts can quash statutes that violate the Charter of Rights. But the federal and provincial legislatures can put a statute beyond the judges' reach by expressly providing that it is to have effect notwithstanding the Charter.

In formulating the Human Rights Act 1998, the Labour government was keen not to give judges the power to quash statutes at all (and the English judges did not generally want that role).

But note . . .

(1) The less direct techniques of the Human Rights Act do not free the judges from making the policy judgments that US and Canadian judges must make, because the issues that underlie a decision in the UK to declare that a statute is incompatible with the Convention rights are similar to the issues that underlie a decision in the United States or Canada to quash a statute. The UK judges' role is *no less political* than the role of the US and Canadian Supreme Courts. But the power of the US Congress is more restricted than the power of Parliament, because the legal effect of the judges' decisions is different.

(2) Section 3 of the Act has no parallel in the United States or Canada; as we will see in 3.3.1, it actually enables the English courts to take a more creative approach to interpretation than the US and Canadian judges.

3.3.1 Section 3: the art of the possible

> **3. Interpretation of legislation**
>
> (1) So far as it is possible to do so, primary legislation and subordinate legislation must be read and given effect in a way which is compatible with the Convention rights. . . . '

A claimant challenging action under a statute will generally want to use s 3, if possible, and ask the court to give the legislation an effect that is compatible with the

Convention. That result may be much better for the claimant than a declaration of incompatibility, which does not affect the operation of the legislation or the lawfulness of action taken under it. The government may prefer that result, too. If the court can remove an apparent incompatibility by interpreting it away, the government will not need to make a remedial measure. A declaration of incompatibility means that the government controls the form of any change in the law (subject to approval by each House of Parliament), but the government may not want that control. The courts have said repeatedly that a declaration of incompatibility is 'a measure of last resort' (e.g., Lord Steyn in *R v A (No 2)* [2001] UKHL 25 [44], and *Ghaidan v Godin-Mendoza* [2004] UKHL 30 [39]), and that s 3 is 'the principal remedial measure' (*Ghaidan* [39]).

So when a statute seems to be incompatible with a Convention right, both parties *and* the court may be in favour of finding a way to give the statute an effect that conforms to the Convention rights. But the courts are to do so only so far as 'it is possible'. Claimants often ask courts to push the boundaries of the possible, and public authorities may ask the courts to push the boundaries too, as an alternative to a declaration of incompatibility.[4] Where are the boundaries?

Judges still have to 'read and give effect' to legislation. Legislation does not have effect *subject to* Convention rights, as legislation has effect subject to rules of EU law.[5] Section 3 'does not affect the validity, continuing operation or enforcement of any incompatible primary legislation' (s 3(2)(b)). So this may seem easy: if a statute can be read in more than one way, then a court must choose a Convention-compatible reading, if there is one. If the statute is clearly incompatible with a Convention right, then it is impossible to read it and to give effect to it in a way that is compatible with the Convention (and the court can only declare that it is incompatible).

But it is not actually that simple. The judges have decided that s 3 must have some more far-reaching effect than that. The Act did not need to do anything merely to let the judges resolve ambiguities in a Convention-compatible manner, for they could do that already.[6] It is common ground both that s 3 changes the effect of legislation *and* that it does not give the judges a licence to ignore a statute. But because the Human Rights Act does not say what change it is making, it is unclear what would count as ignoring a statute.

At first, the judges showed restraint. Consider *Anderson*, an important early case on s 3. The Home Secretary had a statutory power to set a tariff of imprisonment for murderers. But Art 6 requires a hearing by an independent tribunal. The Law Lords made a declaration of incompatibility under s 4. Why couldn't they have held that it was possible to give effect to the Act in a way that is compatible with Art 6? The Act did

---

[4] In *R (H) v London North and East Region Mental Health Review Tribunal* [2001] EWCA Civ 415 and *Ghaidan v Godin-Mendoza* [2004] UKHL 30, the government's counsel argued that the statutes in question should be interpreted so as to make them comply—so that a declaration of incompatibility would not be necessary.

[5] See 1.7, p 37.

[6] See, e.g., Lord Steyn in *R v A (No 2)* [2002] 1 AC 45, [44], and Lord Millett in *Ghaidan* [60].

not require the Home Secretary to use his power to impose a longer tariff than the trial judge or the Lord Chief Justice had recommended. So you might think that s 3 of the Human Rights Act required the court to read and give effect to the Act as allowing the Home Secretary to set a tariff that an independent tribunal (that is, the trial court) had recommended. Then the prisoner would have no Art 6 complaint, yet the legislation would not be contradicted.

The Law Lords all rejected that approach: it 'would not be judicial interpretation but judicial vandalism' (Lord Bingham, *Anderson* [30]); 'It would not be interpretation but interpolation inconsistent with the plain legislative intent' (Lord Steyn [59]); it would be 'to engage in the amendment of a statute and not in its interpretation' (Lord Hutton [81]). Their conclusion was that it is not possible to give effect to an act conferring a power on the Home Secretary *as if* it allowed the Home Secretary to impose the tariff recommended by the judges.

That is the restrained approach: it holds on to the distinction between interpreting what Parliament has enacted and giving effect to a statute *as if* Parliament had enacted something else. But then what is the point of s 3, and what effect does it have on legislation? In *Ghaidan*, the House of Lords gave a revolutionary answer. Section 3 may result in a change in the effect of legislation as long as the change is not fundamental, and it is the judges' job to decide what the change is to be and what was fundamental to the legislation.

The 'fundamental features' approach

Since 1920, legislation has protected a widow from being thrown out of her home if her late husband had a protected tenancy. Widowers gained similar protection by legislation in 1980, and unmarried survivors of cohabiting heterosexual partners gained it in 1988 (*Ghaidan* [14]). Juan Godin-Mendoza claimed the same protection when his same-sex partner died. He claimed a statutory right to succeed to the tenancy as a surviving spouse under the 1988 amendment to the Rent Act 1977. The legislation counted a person 'living with the original tenant as his or her wife or husband' as a spouse [4]. The House of Lords held that treating survivors of long-term homosexual partnerships less favourably than survivors of long-term heterosexual partnerships infringed their rights under Arts 8 and 14 of the Convention.

But Godin-Mendoza was not living with the original tenant as his wife or husband.[7] So he was not a 'spouse' under the statute. When the House of Lords held that it was contrary to his Convention rights for his relationship to be treated differently from a heterosexual relationship, you might think that the result would be a declaration of incompatibility under s 4. But the House of Lords revolutionized s 3 by using it to give the Rent Act an effect that was compatible with its conclusion on Godin-Mendoza's

---

[7]   The House of Lords had decided that a person does not live with his or her homosexual partner 'as his or her wife or husband' in *Fitzpatrick v Sterling Housing Association Ltd* [2001] 1 AC 27, a case in which the original tenant had died before the Human Rights Act came into effect.

Convention rights—an effect that was incompatible with the legislation as Parliament had enacted it.

How could the Lords give Godin-Mendoza statutory protection if the statute only provided protection for a person living with the original tenant as his or her wife or husband? Lord Steyn built on his earlier decision in *R v A (No 2)* [2002] 1 AC 45, in which, he said, the House of Lords had 'rejected linguistic arguments in favour of a broader approach' (*Ghaidan* [47]–[48]).[8] He suggested that 'linguistic arguments' are picky and technical and should not stand in the way of 'bringing rights home' [46]. Similarly, Lord Rodger insisted on 'concentrating on matters of substance, rather than on matters of mere language' [123]. But legislation is nothing but the authoritative decision of the legislature to enact the mere language of a Bill into law. The task of judges in interpretation has always been to decide the effect of that decision in the context in which it is taken. The opposition to 'linguistic arguments' should not obscure the fact that the House of Lords decided in *Ghaidan* to use s 3 to depart from what Parliament had decided. Lord Nicholls said, 'to an extent bounded only by what is "possible", a court can modify the meaning, and hence the effect, of primary and secondary legislation' [32]. As Lord Rodger put it, 'where the court finds it possible to read a provision in a way which is compatible with Convention rights, such a reading may involve a considerable departure from the actual words' [119]. He might just as well have said 'a considerable departure from the Act'. In *Sheldrake v DPP* [2005] 1 AC 264 [28], Lord Bingham held that the s 3 interpretive obligation 'may require the court to depart from the legislative intention of Parliament'; Lord Reed has put it that the obligation in s 3 of the Human Rights Act does not even arise, unless the legislature's intention 'cannot be given effect compatibly with the Convention rights' (*S v L* [2012] UKSC 30 [15]).

Once the courts will treat a statute as if it means something different from what it means, where will it all end? The *Ghaidan* answer is that the courts should not 'adopt a meaning' that is inconsistent with 'a fundamental feature of legislation' [33], or 'an important feature expressed clearly in the legislation' [34], or its 'essential principles' [121], or its 'substance' [123], or a 'cardinal principle' [128]. The effect given to the legislation must 'go with the grain of the legislation' [121]; it must not 'remove the very core and essence, the "pith and substance" of the measure that Parliament had enacted' [111].

Lord Bingham said in *Sheldrake v DPP* [2005] 1 AC 264 that the 'limit beyond which a Convention-compliant interpretation is not possible' is illustrated by the decision in *Anderson*, but cannot really be defined. The various judicial statements that the limit is reached when an interpretation would go against the 'thrust' or the 'grain' or the 'pith and substance', he said, should not 'supplant the simple test enacted in the Act: "So far as it is possible to do so . . ."' [28].[9]

---

[8] A statute excluded evidence of the sexual conduct of the alleged victim in a rape trial, unless the similarity between the conduct in the evidence and the facts of the alleged offence '*cannot reasonably be explained as a coincidence*'. In *R v A (No 2)*, the House of Lords gave effect to that provision so as to allow evidence that is '*so relevant to the issue of consent that to exclude it would endanger the fairness of the trial* under article 6 of the Convention' (emphasis added; see *Ghaidan* [46]).

[9] Lord Bingham's summary was adopted in *R v Waya* [2012] UKSC 51 [14].

Since the limit is nowhere explained more definitely than that, the *Ghaidan* approach has the potential to make the effect of statutes very unclear, and to give the courts an unprecedented responsibility for deciding what is possible—and what is impossible. This approach still does not give the Convention the overriding effect on legislation that EU law has. But it gives the courts a vaguely defined power to give a statute an effect that is incompatible with what Parliament enacted.

And because public authorities will often prefer a novel 'interpretation' to a declaration of incompatibility, s 3 can generate really striking, unargued changes in the effect of a statute. The decision in *R (Hammond) v Home Secretary* [2005] UKHL 69 [5], treated a statutory provision that a life prisoner's tariff 'is to be determined by a single judge of the High Court *without an oral hearing*' (emphasis added) as giving the judge a discretion to *require an oral hearing* where fairness required it (Criminal Justice Act 2003 Sch 22 para 11(1)). The Home Secretary accepted that the provision ought to be read that way if it would otherwise be incompatible with the Convention, and because the Home Secretary took that position, the Law Lords treated it as an issue that they did not need to decide (Lord Bingham [17]). Lord Hoffmann said: 'Neither side challenged this proposition and your Lordships are therefore not asked to decide whether such a bold exercise in "interpretation" is permissible' [29]. So if the government does not contest it, a statute can actually be given an effect that is entirely contrary to what Parliament enacted, with no consideration of the issue by the judges.

Yet the judges still like to say, as they did in *Anderson*, that they are interpreting legislation and not amending it. Lord Rodger insisted in *Ghaidan*, at [113], that the majority decision did not cross 'the boundary between interpretation and amendment':

> ‘ When the court spells out the words that are to be implied, it may look as if it is "amending" the legislation, but that is not the case. If the court implies words that are consistent with the scheme of the legislation but necessary to make it compatible with Convention rights, it is simply performing the duty which Parliament has imposed on it and on others. ’ 10

But if courts are performing a duty that Parliament has imposed on them when they take the *Ghaidan* approach, that does not mean that the courts are not amending statutes. The *Ghaidan* approach has precisely the same effect as a rule that the courts may amend legislation to make it compatible with the Convention, as long as the amendment is not fundamental. According to *Ghaidan*, it really does not matter whether a proposed 'interpretation' is patently contrary to an Act of Parliament, as long as it does not go against something fundamental or important or cardinal in the legislation. And the courts are to judge what is fundamental.

---

10   *Ghaidan* [121]. By contrast, in *R (GC) v Commissioner of Police of the Metropolis* [2011] UKSC 21 [115], Lord Rodger dissented from a decision of the Supreme Court that, in his view, 'crossed the line from interpreting to amending the legislation'.

Section 3 does not *say* that courts should amend statutes. So have the courts illegitimately taken on themselves a legislative power to amend statutes, rather than to interpret them? Lord Millett, dissenting in *Ghaidan*, evidently thought so: '[A]ny change in a fundamental constitutional principle', he said, 'should be the consequence of deliberate legislative action and not judicial activism, however well meaning' [57]. But it is possible to say the following in favour of the approach that the judges took to using s 3 to modify statutes in *Ghaidan*: its effect is *limited*, and there are *considerations in favour* of treating the Human Rights Act as authorizing the amendment of statutes by the courts.

Limits on the effect of *Ghaidan*

(1) Under the *Ghaidan* doctrine, judges cannot change a statute as they see fit; they can only change a statute so as to make it compatible with Convention rights.

(2) *Ghaidan* limits the judges' power to change statutes not only through the 'fundamental features' doctrine, but also by insisting that even where no fundamental feature is at stake, s 3 cannot be used to solve a problem of incompatibility with Convention rights, if doing so would require courts 'to make decisions for which they are not equipped' (*Ghaidan* [33]).

(3) *Ghaidan* has a limited impact, because if the courts were to issue a declaration of incompatibility instead, the government would promptly make a remedial measure to conform to the court's declaration. Given the strong political tradition of taking such measures in response to declarations of incompatibility, the *Ghaidan* approach may simply achieve the same change in the law as a remedial measure, without taking parliamentary time.[11]

(4) The *Ghaidan* approach does not stop Parliament from legislating contrary to Convention rights if it chooses to do so: 'If Parliament disagrees with an interpretation by the courts under section 3(1), it is free to override it by amending the legislation and expressly reinstating the incompatibility' (Lord Steyn, *Ghaidan* [43]). The judges would have to give effect to such new legislation according to its terms, but they would be able to issue a declaration of incompatibility.

Considerations in favour of changing the effect of a statute under s 3

Parliament implied in s 3 that the effect of statutes was to change *somehow*, and did not say how. So Parliament invited the judicial activism that Lord Millett opposed in *Ghaidan*.

The 'so far as it is possible' technique in s 3 is borrowed from EU law, and by that borrowing the Human Rights Act implicitly authorizes some sort of change in the effect of statutes. Under the European Communities Act 1972 s 2, the English courts

---

[11] But note that the *Ghaidan* approach can make all the difference for a particular claimant: in *Ghaidan* itself, the dispute was between two private parties, and a remedial measure would not have helped Godin-Mendoza.

have long been construing legislation so as to make it consistent with EU law, 'however wide a departure from the *prima facie* meaning of the language of the provision might be needed in order to achieve consistency' (*Garland v British Rail Engineering* [1983] 2 AC 751, 771 (Lord Diplock)). In order to achieve consistency with the EC Treaty (*Pickstone v Freemans* [1989] AC 66) or a directive (*Litster v Forth Dry Dock & Engineering* [1990] 1 AC 546), the House of Lords was willing to give the legislation an effect that 'may involve some departure from the strict and literal application of the words which the legislature has elected to use' (*Litster*, Lord Oliver, 559).

Then, in a landmark 1990 decision, the European Court of Justice (ECJ) held that EU directives must affect the interpretation of the law of member states in this dramatic fashion, even if the member state law was adopted before the directive was issued. A national court interpreting national law 'is required to do so, *as far as possible*, in the light of the wording and the purpose of the directive' (Case C-106/89 *Marleasing SA v La Comercial Internacional de Alimentación SA* [1990] ECR I-4135 [8], emphasis added).[12] The idea was that the EC Treaty required all of the authorities of member states, including the courts, 'to ensure the fulfilment' of a directive. Similarly, the Human Rights Act was designed to include the English courts in the project of securing the Convention rights, by giving them a new authority (and duty) to 'read and give effect' to primary legislation in a way that is compatible with Convention rights. The power to change the effect of statutes under *Ghaidan* is supported by the fact that the Human Rights Act borrows this 'so far as it is possible' idea from *Marleasing*.

We can summarize the effect of s 3 on administrative law by saying that Parliament did not tell the courts what they can do to make statutes compatible with the Convention rights; Parliament told the courts to do what they can. The phrase 'so far as it is possible to do so' in s 3 is best understood to mean 'so far as it can be done without undermining the control over changes to statutes that the Human Rights Act reserves to the government and to Parliament through s 3(2) and s 4'. So you cannot work out how statutes are to be interpreted without answering a question about the separation of powers between judges and Parliament. And the judges have authority to decide the effect of s 3, so the Human Rights Act gives them an ill-defined (but not unlimited) power to change the effect of statutes.

3.3.2 Section 6: the effect of 'effect'

> **' 6. Acts of public authorities**
>
> (1) It is unlawful for a public authority to act in a way which is incompatible with a Convention right.

---

12 Lord Steyn comments on the *Marleasing* case in *Ghaidan v Godin-Mendoza* [2004] UKHL 30 [45].

> (2) Subsection (1) does not apply to an act if—
>
> (a) as the result of one or more provisions of primary legislation, the authority could not have acted differently; or
>
> (b) in the case of one or more provisions of, or made under, primary legislation which cannot be read or given effect in a way which is compatible with the Convention rights, the authority was acting so as to give effect to or enforce those provisions. . . . '

The problem in the *Anderson* case (see 3.3, p 79) was that Parliament had given the Home Secretary a power that must be carried out by an independent tribunal (under Art 6 of the Convention). If, as Anderson asked them to do, the Law Lords had ordered the Home Secretary to set the tariff recommended by a judge instead of acting on his own judgment, they would have been rejecting Parliament's decision. As Lord Hutton said, 'in forming his own view whether to accept the recommendation of the judiciary as to tariff or to fix a longer tariff period and when to refer a case to the Parole Board, the Home Secretary is acting in accordance with the intention of Parliament' (*Anderson* [82]). So the Home Secretary's decision fell within s 6(2)(b) and was not unlawful, and the House of Lords issued a declaration of incompatibility, instead of quashing the Home Secretary's decision.

In *R (Hooper) v Work and Pensions Secretary* [2005] UKHL 29, an Act of Parliament provided pension benefits to widows, but not to widowers. The Court of Appeal held that the Work and Pensions Secretary had a duty under the Human Rights Act s 6 to make similar payments to widowers too, because it was contrary to Art 14 of the Convention to discriminate between widows and widowers. The House of Lords reversed the decision, holding by a majority that s 6(2) 'gives primacy to Parliamentary sovereignty over the Convention rights' (Lord Hope [78]). If Parliament established a discriminatory scheme of benefits for widows, the minister could not avoid that act of law making by paying out benefits to widowers. The Human Rights Act allows the courts to issue a declaration of incompatibility in such a case, but s 6(2) prevents the courts from holding the administrative action unlawful.

Impact on judicial review

How does the Human Rights Act s 6 affect the three common law grounds of judicial review?

- **Due process:** Art 6 of the Convention has a distinctive requirement of independence for some decisions (see 5.3, p 178), and has had a special impact on the law of bias (Chapter 5). Yet the procedural requirements of Art 6 are very often the same as the common law requirements of due process, and the courts have emphasized that the common law is still the starting point for questions of administrative process (see 3.9, p 108).

The Human Rights Act has changed the law of due process mainly by allowing the courts to issue a declaration of incompatibility, where (as in *Anderson*) a process established by statute is held to contravene Art 6 of the Convention.

- **Error of law**: the Act does not change the doctrine of review for error of law in any way at all. But it does change the law. By s 3, if it is possible to interpret a statute in a way that makes it compatible with Convention rights, then it is an error of law for a public authority (including a court) to interpret the statute incompatibly. The effect is to extend the pattern of the past forty years (since *Anisminic v Foreign Compensation Commission* [1969] 2 AC 147), by giving the courts an even more open-ended and creative way of determining the standards that bind public authorities (see Chapter 9).

- **Control of discretionary powers**: perhaps the most important way in which the Act has affected administrative law is by adding a new form of proportionality that is distinct from the *Wednesbury* principles. But it is important to remember (1) that the Act has no direct effect on an administrative decision that does not violate a Convention right;[13] (2) that, under the *Wednesbury* principles, many acts of public authorities that infringe the Convention requirement of proportionality were already unlawful (see, e.g., *R v Home Secretary, ex p Simms* [2000] 2 AC 115); and (3) that judicial interference with public authorities under the Act will turn out to be more or less restrained, to the extent that judges defer to public authorities (executive authorities and Parliament) in making judgments of proportionality (see 3.7.1).

3.4 Human rights, Convention rights, and the rule of law

You have a right if others owe you a duty to promote or to respect your interests regardless (to some extent) of (some) other considerations. Your right is a *human* right if you have it simply because you are a human being. The right not to be tortured and the right to life are human rights: just because you are a human being, everyone always owes you a duty not to torture you or to murder you, regardless of what they could achieve by doing so. Of course, you have human rights no matter what the law says. You have a *legal* right when *the law requires* others to promote or to respect your interests regardless (to some extent) of (some) other considerations. The effect of protecting the right not to be killed or tortured in Arts 2 and 3 of the Convention is to give those rights a

---

[13] See 8.3, on whether the Human Rights Act may have a more far-reaching indirect effect, by encouraging the courts to develop new, more generally applicable tests of proportionality through the common law.

particular legal effect, with associated processes for remedying violations, and to give courts the authority to decide what those rights require.

Consider the main provisions of the Convention, and you may find it odd to call some of them 'human rights'. Most of them do not enshrine ways in which everyone ought to treat people merely because they are human. Most of the rights enshrine ways of protecting people from arbitrary acts of state power in a community with a legal system. Articles 5, 6, and 7 promote crucial requirements of the **rule of law**: they prohibit arbitrary executive detention, require fair procedures in the determination of criminal charges and civil rights, and prohibit retrospective criminal penalties. The Convention could more accurately have been called 'the European Convention on the Rule of Law'. The same is true of the Universal Declaration of Human Rights, adopted by the United Nations in 1948, which served as a model for the European Convention. Many of the provisions of the Universal Declaration set out principles for a good legal system, rather than universal human rights.[14] Lord Steyn said that 'the rule of law . . . underlies all human rights instruments' (*R (Ullah) v Special Adjudicator* [2004] UKHL 26 [43]). As Lord Hope of Craighead said in *Montgomery v HM Advocate* [2003] 1 AC 641, 673, 'the rule of law lies at the heart of the Convention'.

> **The Preamble to the European Convention on Human Rights** states that the governments of contracting states entered into it 'as the governments of European countries which are like-minded and have a common heritage of political traditions, ideals, freedom and the rule of law'. In *Golder v United Kingdom* (1979–80) 1 EHRR 524 [34], the Strasbourg Court held that it is 'natural' to bear in mind this commitment to the rule of law 'when interpreting the terms of Art 6(1) according to their context and in the light of the object and purpose of the Convention'.

3.4.1 Fundamental freedoms: beyond the rule of law

But the Convention does protect more than just the rule of law. The **fundamental freedoms** in the Convention include not only the freedom from arbitrary detention (Art 5), but also the 'political freedoms' of thought and religion, expression, and association (Arts 9, 10, and 11). Like the rule-of-law provisions, these three Articles promote a certain sort of community, rather than merely guaranteeing rights that everyone has in virtue of being human. Similarly, the Articles protecting private and family life and marriage (Arts 8 and 12) regulate relations in a community, rather than merely protecting persons from inhuman treatment or protecting the rule of law. Article 8, in particular, regulates those relations in ways that are quite new to English law.

So the Convention protects certain human rights, and protects the rule of law, and protects fundamental freedoms. All that unifies the Convention rights is the fact

---

[14] See http://www.un.org/Overview/rights.html.

that they represent the Council of Europe's judgment concerning rights that not only should be protected in law, but also should be put outside the ordinary law-making processes in the countries that were signing up to the Convention, and should be interpreted and applied by an international tribunal. This background is important for administrative law, because it explains the tensions that arise in Convention litigation both in the Strasbourg Court and in English courts under the Human Rights Act. The Convention puts the Strasbourg Court in charge of deciding how, for example, privacy and freedom of expression ought to be protected in the contracting states. But crucial community interests are at stake in deciding when it is legitimate to interfere with people's privacy, or their freedom of expression. The assessment of those interests involves the sort of reasoning that is a central task of government officials and legislatures. The court, then, needs to decide how, if at all, to defer to the judgment of other officials on those issues. Deference in certain respects is essential. The need for deference, ironically, arises from the fact that the Convention requires the Strasbourg Court to assess whether the value of an administrative decision in the public interest is proportionate to its impact on the interests that the Convention protects. The Human Rights Act requires English courts to make the same assessments of proportionality. So it requires the English courts to decide how, if at all, to defer to the judgment of other officials on the value of an administrative decision.

3.5 The special role of Article 6: proportionate process

> **' Article 6—Right to a fair trial**
>
> 1. In the determination of his civil rights and obligations or of any criminal charge against him, everyone is entitled to a fair and public hearing within a reasonable time by an independent and impartial tribunal established by law. . . . **'**

Article 6 of the Convention has the potential to remodel administrative law. Unlike the rest of the Convention rights, it affects all administrative decision making that determines 'civil rights and obligations'. The Strasbourg Court has interpreted that phrase broadly enough to apply to a vast range of administrative decisions (see 5.3.1, p 180). In all such decisions, 'everyone is entitled to a fair and public hearing within a reasonable time by an independent and impartial tribunal established by law'.

In *R (Alconbury Developments Ltd) v Environment Secretary* [2001] UKHL 23, the Divisional Court had made a dramatic declaration that the UK system of land use planning was incompatible with Art 6, because it authorized the Environment Secretary to make decisions that affect rights to the ownership or use of land. The Town and Country Planning Act 1990 gave the Secretary of State power to 'call in' a planning application—that is, to decide whether to approve an application, instead of leaving the decision to the local planning authority. The purpose of the legislation was to enable central government to give effect to its planning policy; the claimants argued that this provision deprived them of their right to have their civil rights determined by an independent and impartial tribunal.

Alconbury shows the potential for courts to use Art 6 to overhaul the administration of government, by taking such decisions out of the hands of administrative authorities and assigning them to independent authorities such as courts. Think about the impact of that approach: the Divisional Court's decision would have meant that the whole business of deciding on planning permission and compulsory purchase would no longer be a matter for elected officials, but for judges.[15] But in a landmark display of judicial restraint under the Human Rights Act 1998, the House of Lords overturned the Divisional Court's decision in *Alconbury*, holding that it is not unfair for a minister to have an overriding power in planning decisions, and that the Art 6 right is satisfied by the availability of judicial review.

How is that possible, when Art 6 requires an independent hearing? Once the court held that planning decisions determined 'civil rights and obligations', you might think that would be the end of it, just as *Venables and Thompson* and *Anderson* were straightforward because the Home Secretary is not independent. The Environment Secretary is not independent, either. The Divisional Court certainly thought that was the end of it: a politician is not independent, so it must be incompatible with the Convention for him or her to determine civil rights and obligations.

It might seem (as the Divisional Court's decision implied) that *Alconbury* is no different from *Anderson*. But in fact there is a very important difference, which illustrates the principle of relativity (see 1.3). As Lord Brown has put it, 'so far as administrative or disciplinary tribunals are concerned, there is compliance with article 6 so long as the requisite guarantees (of an independent and impartial tribunal, a fair and public hearing and the like) are provided, if not at the initial decision-making stage, then on a subsequent review or appeal (by a tribunal with the jurisdiction to undertake a sufficient merits hearing)' (*R (Hammond) v Home Secretary* [2005] UKHL 69, [41]). The decision under review in *Anderson* was not the decision of an administrative or disciplinary tribunal; it was a sentencing decision. A defendant convicted of an offence needs to be protected from the agenda that a Home Secretary may have to respond to public clamour about a particular case; a developer hoping to build a shopping mall cannot expect to be protected from the government's agenda—or from public views—concerning the use of land.

The difference between *Anderson* and *Alconbury* is the difference between a sentencing decision and a decision about the use of land. There is a right to an independent hearing in both cases. But the right to an independent hearing is fulfilled in *different* ways depending on the nature of the matter being determined. The right to an independent hearing in the land use planning regime is fulfilled if an independent court has jurisdiction to review the planning decision, on standards sufficient to guarantee the procedural fairness of the way in which Alconbury was treated. Anderson's case is different because in sentencing, only an independent *initial* decision can guarantee procedural

---

15   For an overview of the planning process, see 5.5, p 189.

fairness—and protect the rule of law. The effect of Art 6 is to implement a principle of proportionality in administrative processes, which is very closely aligned with the principle of proportionality that has emerged in the common law doctrine of due process (see Chapters 4 and 5).

Independence under Article 6

As the nature of a decision determining civil rights becomes more and more of the type the judiciary normally deals with (involving fundamental rights and liberties), the requirements of Art 6(1) become more stringent and an independent tribunal is more likely to be required as the primary decision maker.

As the nature of a decision on civil rights becomes more and more of the type the government normally deals with (involving public policy and the community's interests), the requirements of Art 6(1) become less stringent and judicial review by an independent tribunal is more likely to satisfy Art 6.

In order for a community to be ruled by law, it is not necessary for every aspect of government action to be controlled by legal processes, or for every dispute to be resolved by a court. What is essential for the rule of law is that a dispute should be resolved by an independent decision maker when that is what it takes to prevent arbitrary government (see 1.1.3, p 9).

The result of *Alconbury* is that, even under the Human Rights Act, the law's procedural requirements will be kept in proportion to the subject matter of the decision. And as we will see in Chapter 4, the common law of due process itself requires (subject to any statute providing otherwise) that same form of proportionality. Article 6 will not revolutionize administrative law, even after the Human Rights Act. But *Anderson* shows that it will lead to major changes in particular areas, where statutes establish processes that the courts hold to be incompatible with Art 6.

What to remember about *Alconbury*

(1) The House of Lords was willing to interpret Convention rights by using the principles of the common law. So, for example, to Lord Clyde it was very important that the minister was not *judex in sua causa* ('a judge in his own cause'), but was acting in the public interest [142].

(2) The Law Lords put the intrusive reach of judicial review at its strongest, to support their conclusion that judicial review satisfied Art 6. So the decision includes some very expansive statements of the grounds of judicial review (see, e.g., Lord Slynn [51]–[53]). The Law Lords said that it was not necessary to make judicial review more intrusive to meet the requirements of Art 6.

3.6 Proportionality and the structure of Convention rights

The Convention rights protect fundamental interests—in freedom and privacy, and so on. But the protection is *limited*, because it can be perfectly legitimate to interfere with someone's freedom or privacy. For example, it is quite right for the police to be able to break into a house to stop an assault. It is right to limit freedom of speech through criminal laws against communicating state secrets to an enemy, or through tort liability for publishing damaging lies about other people. But a power for the police to go into any house for any reason they choose would violate Art 8. And laws on state secrets that are too restrictive (or laws on defamation that make it too dangerous to publish critical opinions) would violate Art 10. Laws and official decisions that are *too* burdensome for some purpose are **disproportionate**.

The need to make judgments of proportionality can arise in applying *all of* the Convention rights. The Art 3 right not to be subject to torture allows no justification at all for torture, yet judgments of proportionality are needed in applying the **positive duties** that the Strasbourg Court has interpreted Art 3 as imposing (e.g., to investigate complaints of police brutality). Once the courts use the Convention to impose positive duties on the state to promote the interests protected by Convention rights, they create remarkable challenges for themselves in deciding what is proportionate.

Positive duties

The effect of the Convention rights has developed further than the representatives of the states could have foreseen when they designed the Convention. Article 2 says that 'Everyone's right to life shall be protected by law'. The Strasbourg Court has interpreted it to impose positive duties on states, 'not only to refrain from the intentional and unlawful taking of life ("Thou shalt not kill") but also to take appropriate steps to safeguard the lives of those within its jurisdiction' (*Van Colle v Chief Constable of Hertfordshire* [2008] UKHL 50 [28] (Lord Bingham)). There are other positive duties—for example:

- Art 3: to protect children from inhuman treatment (*Z v United Kingdom* (2001) 34 EHRR 97);

- Art 10: to protect people working in the media from violence (*Ozgur Gundem v Turkey* (2001) 31 EHRR 49);

- Art 3: not to deport a person to a country where there is a serious risk that he will suffer inhuman treatment (*Chahal v United Kingdom* (1996) 23 EHRR 413);[16]

---

[16] The Strasbourg Court treats this duty as absolute, and not subject to proportionality. And if such a person cannot be deported, he or she cannot be kept in detention either. Unless the government has a prospect of lawfully deporting the person or prosecuting him or her, the person must be released (*A and X v Home Secretary* [2004] UKHL 56).

- Art 6: not to deport a person to a country where there is a serious risk that he will undergo a trial in which evidence will be admitted that was obtained through torture (*Othman (AKA Abu Qatada) v Secretary of State for the Home Department* [2013] EWCA Civ 277);

- Art 2: to take proportionate steps to protect military personnel from risk of death, and to compensate families when that duty is not fulfilled (*Smith v Ministry of Defence* [2013] UKSC 41).

An unfair trial is never compatible with the Convention, no matter what objective the state is pursuing. But *what counts as fair* depends on proportionality between procedures and the purposes for which they are provided. So the Strasbourg Court has held that 'the right of access to the courts is not absolute but may be subject to limitations . . . a limitation will not be compatible with Art 6 para. 1 if it does not pursue a legitimate aim and if there is not a reasonable relationship of proportionality between the means employed and the aim sought to be achieved' (*Ashingdane v United Kingdom* (1985) 7 EHRR 528 [57]).

The role of proportionality is easiest to see in Arts 8–11, which protect privacy and family life, freedom of religion, freedom of expression, and freedom of assembly (I will call those freedoms the '**Convention freedoms**'). The Convention freedoms are protected by **qualified rights**—that is, rights that are subject to express provisos.

● *Pop quiz* ●
Which Convention rights are unqualified?

Each of Arts 8–11 has two parts: a presumptive right, and a set of grounds on which the presumptive right is qualified. The structure is as follows:

Right to X (e.g., to Freedom of Expression)

1. Everyone has the right to X.
2. There shall be no interference by a public authority with the exercise of this right except such as is in accordance with the law and is **necessary in a democratic society** in the interests of {**A, B, or C**}.

'Interference by a public authority with the exercise' of the right is an awkward way of saying 'restriction of the freedom that the right protects'. Article 10(2) of the Convention contemplates that a restriction on freedom of expression may be legitimate if it is:

> ' . . . necessary . . . in the interests of national security, territorial integrity or public safety, for the prevention of disorder or crime, for the protection of health or morals, for the protection of the reputation or rights of others, for preventing the disclosure of information received in confidence, or for maintaining the authority and impartiality of the judiciary. '

Those provisos in Arts 8–11 are the **public interest limitations**[17] on Convention freedoms. What limitations are *necessary* to protect such undefined interests of society and of other individuals? The Strasbourg Court developed the doctrine of proportionality to deal with that question. Perhaps the drafters of the Convention used the word 'necessary' simply to underscore that the rights are fundamentally important.[18] The judges' response has been to soften the test of necessity into a requirement that an interference with an interest protected by the Convention must be **proportionate** to the action's effect in pursuing an objective that the Convention acknowledges as legitimate.

Proportionality is a relation between two things. In the application of Convention rights, those two things are (1) the value of pursuing a legitimate state purpose by some course of action; and (2) some resulting detriment to an interest that is protected by a Convention right. So a judgment of proportionality starts with (or takes for granted):

- a legitimate interest (of the community or of individuals) that an action would promote; and

- detriment that the action would cause to an interest that a Convention right protects.

The public interest limitations on Convention freedoms recognize interests that can justify some detriment to the interests that the Convention freedoms protect. An action is proportionate if it does not cause *too much* detriment to a protected interest of an individual (that is, detriment that is out of proportion to the value of pursuing the objective).

The English courts' approach to proportionality has been based on the Canadian Supreme Court's approach to the limits on the rights protected by the Canadian Charter of Rights and Freedoms, a constitutional bill of rights adopted in 1982.[19] The Charter guarantees the rights and freedoms that it sets out 'subject only to such reasonable limits prescribed by law as can be demonstrably justified in a free and democratic society' (s 1). Early in the development of Charter case law, Chief Justice Dickson set out the following components of the proportionality test in the Supreme Court of Canada:

Four components of proportionality

(1) The objective of the measures in question must be 'of sufficient importance to warrant overriding a constitutionally protected right'.

(2) The measures 'must be rationally connected to the objective'.

(3) The measures must impair the right 'as little as possible'.

---

[17] Note, however, that they include limitations based not only on the public interest, but also on the interests of other individuals.

[18] Not all Convention rights use necessity as a test for limits: the protection for property in Art 1 of the First Protocol allows that a person may be deprived of possessions 'in the public interest and subject to the conditions provided for by law and by the general principles of international law'.

[19] In *Bank Mellat v Her Majesty's Treasury (No 2)* [2013] UKSC 39 [68], Lord Reed traced proportionality reasoning to the Canadian jurisprudence and beyond—to German constitutional law, Thomas Aquinas, and Aristotle's *Ethics*.

> (4) [t]here must be a proportionality between the effects of the measures which are responsible for limiting the Charter right or freedom and the objective'—*R v Oakes* [1986] 1 SCR 103 [70].

If the restriction of a freedom does not promote the objective, or if the objective can be promoted as well without restricting the freedom (or without restricting it as much), then the objective does not justify the restriction of the freedom. The judges are already engaged in a far-reaching assessment of government policy making when they pass judgment on whether a measure is rationally connected to its objective, or whether the public authority could have used another measure that would have less impact on the protected interest.[20] But in the fourth component—which really *is* the proportionality test—the judges simply balance the interest that the public authority was trying to advance against the interests of the claimant and others. It means that even if a measure promotes a legitimate objective, and the objective cannot be achieved with less restriction of a freedom, the measure is still held to be unjustifiable (and therefore an infringement of the right) if it restricts the freedom *too much*.

In the early English case law on the Human Rights Act, the fourth component was omitted from Lord Steyn's classic discussion of the proportionality test in *R (Daly) v Home Secretary* [2001] UKHL 26 [27]. In *International Transport Roth v Home Secretary* [2002] EWCA Civ 158 [52], Simon Brown LJ added another requirement that he said was 'implicit in the concept of proportionality':

> '... that not merely must the impairment of the individual's rights be no more than necessary for the attainment of the public policy objective sought, but also that it must not impose an excessive burden on the individual concerned. '

That is the fourth component. Lord Bingham insisted on adding it to the list of considerations in *Huang v Secretary of State for the Home Department* [2007] 2 AC 167 [19]. The result has become a list of four questions, well established in the Supreme Court decisions. The simplest wording of the list is in *R (Quila) v Home Secretary* [2011] UKSC 45 [45] (Lord Wilson):

> ' a) is the legislative objective sufficiently important to justify limiting a fundamental right?
> b) are the measures which have been designed to meet it rationally connected to it?
> c) are they no more than are necessary to accomplish it? and

---

[20] For a prominent example of a UK case decided on those two grounds, see *R (Tigere) v Secretary of State for Business, Innovation and Skills* [2015] UKSC 57 [35]–[38]. Even in *Tigere*, the Supreme Court went on to consider the fourth component of balance between private and public interests.

> d) do they strike a fair balance between the rights of the individual and the inter-
> ests of the community? ' [21]

In *Bank Mellat v Her Majesty's Treasury (No 2)* [2013] UKSC 39 [20], Lord Sumption
adopted Lord Wilson's wording from *Quila*, and also agreed with Lord Reed, who
stated the fourth question as whether 'the impact of the rights infringement is disproportionate to the likely benefits of the impugned measure' (*Bank Mellat* [74]; approved
by Lord Mance in *R (Nicklinson) v Ministry of Justice* [2014] UKSC 38 [171]).

Justifiable infringements of rights?

Judges and commentators very regularly talk as if an infringement of a
Convention right is justified, where the benefits of the impugned measure are
sufficient.[22] It is a widely shared mistake.

The Convention does not say that the right to, for example, freedom of expression may be infringed; it says that the exercise of the freedom may be subjected
to restrictions (Art 10(2)). If you are convicted of treason for selling state secrets, or
if you are held liable in defamation for slandering someone, your right under Art
10 is not infringed, because Art 10(2) *allows* the exercise of freedom of expression
to be restricted. The right of freedom of expression is a right to a restricted freedom, which does not include selling state secrets or slandering people.

Lord Wilson, Lord Sumption, and Lord Reed adopted the same way of speaking when they said that the question in proportionality reasoning is whether 'a fair
balance has been struck between the rights of the individual and the interests of
the community' (*Bank Mellat* [20]), or whether 'the impact of the rights infringement is disproportionate to the likely benefits' (*Bank Mellat* [76]). These statements
imply—mistakenly—that it is legitimate to infringe the rights of an individual for
the benefit of the community. It is *always contrary to the Convention* for a public
authority to infringe a Convention right. The question in proportionality reasoning
is not whether a fair balance has been struck between the rights of the individual
and the interests of the community. The question is whether a fair balance has
been struck between the interests of the individual and the interests of the community. If so, the right has not been infringed.

---

[21] See also *Tigere* [33].

[22] Examples can be found in Lord Bingham's speech in *R (Daly) v Home Secretary* [2001] 2 AC
532 [17]. Compare Lord Hoffmann: 'Even if there had been an infringement of Shabina's rights
under article 9, I would ... have been of opinion that the infringement was justified under article
9.2' (*R (Begum) v Denbigh High School* [2005] EWCA Civ 199, [58]). In fact, a restriction on
Shabina Begum's *freedom* was justified under Art 9(2), so that there *was no infringement* of the
right.

3.6.1 The fourth component in EU law

The same component appears in explanations of proportionality in the Court of Justice of the European Union (CJEU). Article 5.4 of the Treaty on the Functioning of the European Union (TFEU) provides that, 'Under the principle of proportionality, the content and form of Union action shall not exceed what is necessary to achieve the objectives of the Treaties'. The CJEU has crafted a principle of proportionality to give effect to that requirement, just as the Strasbourg Court has crafted its principle of proportionality to deal with the public interest limitations on Convention rights. In a long line of CJEU cases, the doctrine of proportionality has been taken more or less verbatim from the decision in Case 265/87 *Schräder v Hauptzollamt Gronau* [1989] ECR 2237 [21], which stated the fourth component by saying that burdens imposed 'must not be disproportionate to the aims pursued'.[23]

In Convention rights litigation under the Human Rights Act, the fourth component in proportionality reasoning brings a revolution to English administrative law. The revolution is that, in order to determine the lawfulness of acts of public authorities that restrict the Convention freedoms, the English courts must *assess the aims* for which the public authorities act, and weigh the value of pursuing those aims in a particular way, against the impact on interests protected by the Convention (see Figure 3.1).

Notice two features of proportionality reasoning that give judges a potentially intrusive role.

1. It requires them to pass judgment on the value of pursuing a public objective in a particular way.
2. There are no scales! That is, there are no units in which the two sides can both be measured. So there is nothing like a precise answer to the proportionality question of *how much* interference with an interest is too much. That gives judges a resultant discretion (see 7.2.1, p 247).

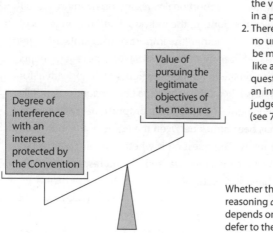

Whether these features of proportionality reasoning *actually* give judges an intrusive role depends on the extent to which the judges defer to the assessments of administrative officials.

Figure 3.1 The proportionality question: how do the scales come down?

---

[23] On the general scope of the principle, see *R (FEDESA) v Minister of Agriculture, Fisheries and Food* [1991] 1 CMLR 507 (Queen's Bench) [13], and see the discussion of proportionality in the CJEU in 8.7.

3.6.2 Proportionality in action: immigration control and Article 8

We can see how far-reaching the judicial role can be if we consider how proportionality reasoning unfolds in the most delicate and contentious area of Convention rights litigation in the twenty-first century: immigration control. The Convention provides no right for persons to choose where to live. But the right to respect for family life in Art 8 has become a very common recourse for would-be immigrants. Whether seeking asylum or applying for ordinary immigration, candidates may spend long enough in the country that they develop family ties, if they did not already have family in the United Kingdom. In this case, refusal of leave to remain in the country will be detrimental to their family life. The House of Lords held, in *R (Huang) v Home Secretary* [2007] UKHL 11 [20], that the Immigration and Asylum Tribunal must ask the following question:

> '... whether the refusal of leave to enter or remain, in circumstances where the life of the family cannot reasonably be expected to be enjoyed elsewhere, taking full account of all considerations weighing in favour of the refusal, prejudices the family life of the applicant in a manner sufficiently serious to amount to a breach of the fundamental right protected by article 8. '

This question does not provide the Tribunal with a *test* of proportionality; the Tribunal judges have no guide to their decision; they have to decide whether the impact on a claimant's family life is *too serious*, in light of public purposes that are unspecified. The House of Lords drew attention to the fourth component, holding that the judges need to balance the interests of society with the interests of claimants (*Huang* [19]). The question is not just whether the burden on the claimant is necessary to achieve a legitimate objective; even if it is, the Tribunal must still ask whether the detriment to an interest protected by the Convention is too serious.

In *Huang*, the House of Lords did not specify the 'considerations weighing in favour of the refusal' of leave to remain in the United Kingdom. If the question is whether refusal would be *proportionate* and a claimant shows that refusal would cause some detriment to his or her family life, what state purpose could make the refusal legitimate in spite of the detriment? Part 2 of Art 8 recognizes that an interference with family life may be justifiable 'in the interests of national security, public safety or the economic well-being of the country, for the prevention of disorder or crime, for the protection of health or morals, or for the protection of the rights and freedoms of others'. It is possible to imagine that immigration control might be useful in more than one of those interests. But the judges have no information as to how it promotes those interests, and the government's agenda in trying to limit immigration is unclear.

In principle, the doctrine of proportionality requires judges to assess for themselves the value of pursuing public purposes in the way that a public authority has done or proposes to do, and to balance that value against the impact of a decision on the claimant. That is the significant change from common law judicial review of executive action.

In practice, in the immigration cases, the judicial role is even more extraordinary, because judges have no way of assessing the public interests at stake. None of the cases give any clear statement of the public interest that can justify deportation, so the supposed balancing act is done merely by asking how bad the impact of deportation would be.

In *Huang*, the Immigration and Asylum Tribunal tried to cope with the wide-open question by holding that deportation of an illegal immigrant will only infringe Art 8 in *exceptional* cases. Lord Bingham had held, in *R (Razgar) v Home Secretary* [2004] UKHL 27 [20], that: 'Decisions taken pursuant to the lawful operation of immigration control will be proportionate in all save a small minority of exceptional cases, identifiable only on a case by case basis.' But in the House of Lords in *Huang*, in writing the unanimous opinion for the Law Lords, Lord Bingham wrote of his own opinion in *Razgar* in the third person: 'He was there expressing an expectation, shared with the Immigration Appeal Tribunal, that the number of claimants not covered by the rules and supplementary directions but entitled to succeed under article 8 would be a very small minority. That is still his expectation. But he was not purporting to lay down a legal test' [20]. There really is no legal test, except that the interests of any child involved 'must be a primary consideration, although not always the only primary consideration', and the judge must decide whether all the considerations in favour of deportation outweigh all the personal interests at stake (*Zoumbas v Secretary of State for the Home Department* [2013] UKSC 74 [10]). The effect of deportation on a person's family life must not be too serious in light of the public interest—whatever that may be—in immigration control.

A consistent line has emerged: in immigration control, the decision maker in question needs to ask whether, in light of the public interests at stake, the impact of the proposed action would have too serious an impact on the claimant's family life. In these cases, given the judges' interpretation of Art 8 of the Convention, the Human Rights Act assigns to judges the whole job of achieving just state action, case by case, in a particularized assessment of each claimant's circumstances. Proportionality reasoning hands that aspect of British government over to judges. But there are still limits to the judges' role. In 3.7, we will see one reason why the judges of the Strasbourg Court are not going to take over the government of this country in general: they apply a 'margin of appreciation' to state action. And in 3.9 we will see that the transfer of power to UK judges in the Human Rights Act has been more limited than you might think. The judges already had substantial power over government through human rights protections in UK law before the Human Rights Act. And under the Human Rights Act, the role of judges is limited by the scope of the Convention rights, and by various forms of deference to Parliament and to administrative decision makers.

The remarkable reach of Art 8

Anything that is against a person's interests can affect his or her private and family life. The Strasbourg Court has held that Art 8 'protects a right to personal development' (*Pretty v United Kingdom* (2002) 35 EHRR 1, [61]). A state that has respect for private and family life will not just refrain from interfering with people in certain ways; it will take all sorts of positive measures to help families and individuals, and to promote their personal development. Does Art 8 impose a positive duty to take any step that is good for an individual, unless doing so would have a disproportionate impact on the interests of the public or of other individuals?

No. Article 8 does not authorize courts to decide what measures the state should take out of respect for private and family life, but only to interfere when the state shows disrespect. The courts have to distinguish between protecting the right to respect for persons (which is their role) and requiring the state to do the right things to promote personal development (which is not the courts' role). The results can seem random. On the one hand, 'the Court of Human Rights has always drawn back from imposing on states the obligation to provide a home, or indeed any other form of financial support' (*Anufrijeva v Southwark LBC* [2003] EWCA Civ 1406 [19]; cf. *Harrow LBC v Qazi* [2003] UKHL 43).[24] On the other hand, it was held in *R (Bernard) v LBC* [2002] EWHC 2282 [32], that people entitled to local authority support under the National Assistance Act 1948 s 21 (because they need special care because of age, illness, disability, or other circumstances) 'are a particularly vulnerable group. Positive measures have to be taken (by way of community care facilities) to enable them to enjoy, so far as possible, a normal private and family life'.

3.7 Subsidiarity and the margin of appreciation

The Strasbourg Court gives a **margin of appreciation** to public authorities in states that are parties to the Convention. The margin of appreciation is a leeway for public authorities to act as they see fit, to some extent, on questions as to the extent of Convention rights (*Handyside v United Kingdom* (1976) 1 EHRR 737; *Smith v United Kingdom* (2000) 29 EHRR 493). This form of deference may seem strange, because a court of human rights is meant to give remedies against violations of rights, and not to decide whether a contracting state has acted reasonably in deciding what counts as a violation. But the Convention freedoms are subject to the public interest limitations. The application of those limitations may legitimately vary, since public interests in, for example, national security and the prevention of disorder may make some restriction on a Convention freedom necessary in one country that is unnecessary in another. Applying the Convention rights means deciding what limitations are legitimate in particular communities. Some things are illegitimate in *any* community (such as torture), but some forms of defamation law may be legitimate in one country and illegitimate in another.

As the Strasbourg Court put it in *Sahin v Turkey* (2005) 41 EHRR 8 [100], 'the national authorities are in principle better placed than an international court to evaluate local

---

24 But 'where the welfare of children is at stake, article 8 may require the provision of welfare support in a manner which enables family life to continue' (*Anufrijeva* [43]). And Art 3 may require welfare support, if it would amount to inhumane treatment to leave someone without such support (*Anufrijeva* [35]).

needs and conditions'.[25] Leyla Sahin insisted on wearing an Islamic headscarf, which was against the rules of her medical school. When she was excluded from lectures, she complained to the Strasbourg Court. The issue was whether the medical school's dress code was necessary for protecting the rights and freedoms of others. The Strasbourg Court deferred to the judgment of the Turkish authorities on that question, holding that 'the role of the Convention machinery is essentially subsidiary' [100]. **Subsidiarity** explains the division of powers between different levels of government (see 1.5.2, p 19). A public decision should be made by an institution at the level at which it can most effectively be made—and that means at a level close to the person it affects, unless there is some reason why a more remote set of institutions can pursue a just purpose more effectively. Not all decisions about life in Europe can be made by the Strasbourg Court. Its role is subsidiary to the responsibility of the contracting states to respect fundamental rights.

An international court would not be playing that subsidiary role if it were to impose its own judgments on all questions as to the effect of the public interest limitations. A court in Strasbourg (with judges drawn from forty-seven different countries) does not have the appreciation of conditions in a particular contracting state that would enable it to make sound judgments on all questions of whether government action is protected by the public interest limitations. Its role is to interfere when the state authorities make judgments that pass beyond the margin of appreciation: judgments that interfere with Convention interests in a way that is so clearly illegitimate that the Strasbourg Court must interfere in order to carry out its subsidiary role. So the margin of appreciation ought to temper proportionality reasoning under the Convention. The Strasbourg Court should not interfere unless government action can be seen to be *clearly* disproportionate, from the Court's detached point of view.

In 1979, Richard Handyside was convicted under the Obscene Publications Act 1959 of publishing material 'such as to tend to deprave and corrupt' children who were likely to read it. He had published *The Little Red Schoolbook*, a Danish sex education manual intended for schoolchildren from the age of twelve. When he challenged his conviction in the Strasbourg Court as a violation of Art 10, the Strasbourg Court did not simply decide for itself whether banning *The Little Red Schoolbook* was necessary for the protection of morals. Its role was to ensure that the English courts acted within the margin of appreciation. The Court based that view of its role on the principle of subsidiarity—'The Convention leaves to each Contracting State, in the first place, the task of securing the rights and liberties it enshrines' (*Handyside* [48])—the reason for the principle being that:

> ' By reason of their direct and continuous contact with the vital forces of their countries, State authorities are in principle in a better position than the international judge to give an opinion on the exact content of these requirements as well as on the "necessity" of a "restriction" or "penalty" intended to meet them. '

---

[25] The same views were upheld by the Grand Chamber of the Court in *Sahin v Turkey* (2007) 44 EHRR 5 [121].

This reasoning led to the conclusion that the Strasbourg Court has a *supervisory* jurisdiction, rather than an original jurisdiction to decide how freedom of expression should or should not be restricted. Its responsibility is to *review* decisions rather than to replace them (*Handyside* [50]): '... it is in no way the Court's task to take the place of the competent national courts but rather to review under Article 10 the decisions they delivered in the exercise of their power of appreciation'.[26]

In 2013, the Council of Europe amended the Convention to refer to the principle of subsidiarity, the doctrine of a margin of appreciation, and the supervisory role of the Strasbourg Court (Protocol 15 to the Convention):

> Affirming that the High Contracting Parties, in accordance with the principle of subsidiarity, have the primary responsibility to secure the rights and freedoms defined in this Convention and the Protocols thereto, and that in doing so they enjoy a margin of appreciation, subject to the supervisory jurisdiction of the European Court of Human Rights established by this Convention ...

The margin of appreciation ought to be limited, or it would undermine the rationale for application of the Convention by an international court. And there are limits. The Strasbourg Court will decide 'whether the reasons given by the national authorities to justify the actual measures of "interference" they take are relevant and sufficient' (*Handyside* [50]). By contrast, in judicial review of administrative conduct under the *Wednesbury* doctrine, English judges will decide whether a public authority's reasons for an exercise of discretion are relevant, but *not* whether they are *sufficient* to justify the decision (see 8.2, p 282). So the Strasbourg Court uses a more intensive form of review of interferences with fundamental interests, in spite of the margin of appreciation. Richard Handyside lost his claim because the Strasbourg Court decided that 'the competent English judges were entitled, in the exercise of their discretion, to think at the relevant time that the Schoolbook would have pernicious effects on the morals of many of the children and adolescents who would read it' [52]. The Strasbourg Court does not directly decide whether freedom of expression should be interfered with in a particular way. It defers to English authorities (including the English courts) by asking whether *their* reasons for interfering with freedom of expression are legitimate. But the deference is limited by the requirement that there must be *sufficient* reason—that is, the reason for interfering with a Convention interest must be proportionate to the pursuit of a purpose that the Convention recognizes as legitimate.

How wide is the margin of appreciation?

The answer to this crucial question is very obscure, and very controversial. Consider the *Hirst* case (see 3.10): a majority of a Grand Chamber of the

---

[26] For reaffirmation of the Strasbourg Court's 'supervisory' role, see *Animal Defenders International v United Kingdom* Application No 48876/08 (2013) 57 EHRR 21: Judgment of the Court [100]; Concurring opinion of Judge Bratza [17]; Dissenting Opinion of Judge Tulkens [6].

Strasbourg Court held that the UK's ban on voting by prisoners was 'outside any acceptable margin of appreciation, however wide that margin might be' (*Hirst v UK (No 2)* (2006) 42 EHRR 41 [82]). In the UK Supreme Court, Lord Sumption and Lord Hughes thought that the issue was 'a classic matter for political and legislative judgment, and that the United Kingdom rule is well within any reasonable assessment of a Convention state's margin of appreciation' (*R (Chester) v Secretary of State for Justice* [2013] UKSC 63 [137]). If the Strasbourg Court and the UK courts disagree on this point, the Strasbourg Court rules, and Lord Sumption and Lord Hughes agreed with the rest of the justices that the Supreme Court should go along with the Strasbourg decision.

3.7.1 Is there a margin of appreciation in the UK courts?

The UK courts do not have same the reasons that the Strasbourg Court has for deference to national authorities. They *are* national authorities. This does not mean that English courts will not defer to Parliament or to administrative authorities in giving effect to the Convention rights. There can also be reasons of **comity** (see 1.5.3, p 19) for UK judges to defer to those other public authorities in making judgments of proportionality between public and private interests. The UK courts should and do defer, for example, to an English school authority on the question of whether a dress code is a proportionate restriction of freedom of religion (*R (Begum) v Denbigh High School Governors* [2006] UKHL 15—see 8.3.1, p 289). So it is not just Strasbourg judges who need to defer; English judges need to do so too.

But perhaps they do not need to do so to the same extent as the Strasbourg Court? In *Re G (Adoption: Unmarried Couple)* [2008] UKHL 38 [120] Baroness Hale said that, 'if the matter is within the margin of appreciation which Strasbourg would allow to us, then we have to form our own judgment'. By 'us', she meant 'the courts'. She did not say what regard, if any, the courts should show for the judgment of Parliament or of administrative authorities. And Lord Hoffmann deliberately left that question open. He said that, when a claim falls within the margin of appreciation allowed by the Strasbourg Court, 'The margin of appreciation is there for division between the three branches of government according to our principles of the separation of powers. There is no principle by which it is automatically appropriated by the legislative branch' [37]. Presumably, there is no principle by which it is automatically appropriated by the judicial branch, either. But as Lord Hoffmann implies, it is the courts that have to decide whose judgment should count.

In *R (Nicklinson) v Ministry of Justice* [2014] UKSC 38, the Supreme Court Justices addressed the role of judicial deference within the margin of appreciation—and disagreed deeply. The claimants wanted to be able to commit suicide, but suffered from disabilities that would make it impossible for them to do so without assistance. The Suicide Act 1961[27] makes it an offence to assist another person to commit suicide. The claimants sought a declaration that the legislation was incompatible with Art 8 of the Convention.

---

[27]   Amended by the Coroners and Justice Act 2009.

According to the Strasbourg Court, contracting states have a wide margin of appreciation in dealing with assisted suicide,[28] and the UK laws were within that margin. Although the private life of persons who seek assistance to commit suicide is affected by the legislation, it is 'primarily for states to assess the risk and the likely incidence of abuse if the general prohibition on assisted suicides were relaxed or exceptions were to be created'.[29]

In *Nicklinson*, the Supreme Court declined, by a 7–2 majority, to hold the prohibition on assisted suicide to be incompatible with the Convention right to respect for private and family life in Art 8. Three of the majority justices and both of the dissenters held that where the Strasbourg Court had allowed the UK a margin of appreciation, the UK courts should simply ask whether there was an infringement of the right. Lord Neuberger put it that, in such a case, the Strasbourg Court has found neither that there was an infringement of the right, nor that there was no infringement, and 'the national courts therefore must decide the issue for themselves, with relatively unconstraining guidance from the Strasbourg court, albeit bearing in mind the constitutional proprieties' [70].

What are the constitutional proprieties? Lord Reed agreed that the court must decide whether the legislation was compatible with the Convention right. But he pointed out that it might depend on issues that 'are by their nature more suitable for determination by Government or Parliament than by the courts'. On those issues, the court ought to proceed 'by giving weight to the determination of those issues by the primary decision-maker' [296]. Lord Sumption held that 'The question whether relaxing or qualifying the current absolute prohibition on assisted suicide would involve unacceptable risks to vulnerable people is in my view a classic example of the kind of issue which should be decided by Parliament' [230]. Lord Hughes and Lord Clarke agreed [267] and [290]. Lord Neuberger and Lord Wilson thought that the courts ought to wait for Parliament to address the issue, although they suggested that the courts would have to do something if Parliament did not address it 'satisfactorily' [118] and [197]. Lord Mance agreed with Lord Neuberger, although he held that the legislature's judgment on the issues was 'entitled to considerable weight' [189]. And Lord Neuberger said that the courts 'would normally be very cautious' before holding that a Convention right was being infringed, where the Strasbourg Court held that the issue was within the margin of appreciation [75]. Lord Kerr and Baroness Hale dissented, and concluded, without deferring to Parliament's judgment, that the Suicide Act was incompatible with Art 8.

Deference by judges to Parliament and to administrative authorities plays, and ought to play, a crucial role in human rights law: see 8.3.1. But the judges disagree deeply about the extent to which they ought to defer to Parliament on the public interest limitations on Convention rights. *Nicklinson* illustrates how unclear and how controversial the constitutional proprieties are, and how much they remain open for decision from case to case.

---

[28] *Haas v Switzerland* (2011) 53 EHRR 33; *Koch v Germany* (2013) 56 EHRR 6.

[29] *Pretty v United Kingdom* (2002) 35 EHRR 1 [74].

But, by confirming *Re G*, the Supreme Court in *Nicklinson* did at least make it clear that the English courts will be prepared to find a violation of a Convention right in a case in which the Strasbourg Court would hold that the action in question was within the margin of appreciation. As Lord Reed put it in *Bank Mellat v Her Majesty's Treasury (No 2)* [2013] UKSC 39 [71]:

> ' ... the concept of the margin of appreciation ... does not apply in the same way at the national level, where the degree of restraint practised by courts in applying the principle of proportionality, and the extent to which they will respect the judgment of the primary decision maker, will depend on the context, and will in part reflect national traditions and institutional culture. '

Asymmetries in the transnational structure of the European Convention

It must seem to the government as if human rights adjudication is stacked in favour of claimants.

- Claimants who lose in Strasbourg, on the ground that the state's action is within the margin of appreciation, can ask a UK court to hold that their Convention right was violated—

- but if a public authority loses in Strasbourg on the ground that its action is outside a margin of appreciation, it will ordinarily (see 3.8) lose in the English courts as a result.

- Claimants who lose on any point in the UK courts can go to Strasbourg—

- but if a public authority loses in the UK courts, there is no way for it to go to Strasbourg to seek a declaration that it had actually acted compatibly with the Convention.

These asymmetries are reminders that the Strasbourg Court is *not* a court of appeal with jurisdiction to hear appeals from the decisions of UK courts.

3.8 Taking Strasbourg decisions into account

The Human Rights Act s 2(1)(a) requires English courts to 'take into account' decisions of the Strasbourg Court. It does not say that the courts must follow Strasbourg. But the judges know that if they hold against a claimant when the Strasbourg Court would hold in his or her favour, the claimant can go to the Strasbourg Court and ask it to follow its own case law. And then the UK will be bound in international law to give effect to the decision of the Strasbourg Court.[30]

---

30   See *Home Secretary v AF* [2009] UKHL 28, Lord Hoffmann [70].

Very early on, the judges developed a view that they should generally go along with Strasbourg's interpretation of the Convention rights. In *R (Alconbury) v Environment Secretary* [2001] UKHL 23 [26], Lord Slynn said: 'In the absence of some special circumstances it seems to me that the court should follow any clear and constant jurisprudence of the European Court of Human Rights.' Lord Bingham gave a reason for this approach: he thought that, because the Convention is an international treaty, it should have a uniform interpretation (that is, the Strasbourg Court's interpretation) in all the contracting states.

> ' . . . the Convention is an international instrument, the correct interpretation of which can be authoritatively expounded only by the Strasbourg court. . . . The duty of national courts is to keep pace with the Strasbourg jurisprudence as it evolves over time: no more, but certainly no less. ' [31]

After *Re G* and *Nicklinson*, it is clear that the UK courts may find an infringement where the Strasbourg Court considers the matter to fall within the margin of appreciation. But that does not mean that the courts have departed from *Ullah*. as Lord Neuberger pointed out in *Nicklinson*, the *Ullah* principle applies where 'the Strasbourg court would intend that its conclusions and reasoning be applicable to all member states' (*Nicklinson* [69]). That means, outside the margin of appreciation.

Another limitation on the *Ullah* principle is that there may be no Strasbourg jurisprudence on a controversial question of interpretation of the Convention rights, and then the UK courts just have to give their best interpretation.[32] Or it can be unclear what view the Strasbourg Court has taken. Judgments by particular Chambers in Strasbourg (panels of seven judges) can conflict with each other, and the Grand Chamber can depart from a Chamber decision. In *Poshteh v Kensington and Chelsea Royal LBC* [2017] UKSC 36 [37], the Supreme Court refused to follow a Chamber's unanimous decision that the question of whether a homeless person should be housed under the Housing Act 1996 was a question of a 'civil right' for the purpose of Art 6 of the Convention (see 5.3.1).[33] The Supreme Court held that 'we should await a full consideration by a Grand Chamber before considering whether (and if so how) to modify our own position' (Lord Carnwath [37]). It is, evidently, conceivable that the Court might not go along with a Grand Chamber decision, either. But as Lord Mance held in the *Chester* case, if a Grand Chamber of 17 judges has clearly addressed an issue, 'It would have then to involve some truly fundamental principle of our law

---

[31] *R (Ullah) v Special Adjudicator* [2004] UKHL 26 [20].

[32] See *Surrey County Council v P* [2014] AC 896, Lord Kerr [86]; *R (Keyu) v Secretary of State for Foreign and Commonwealth Affairs* [2015] UKSC 69, Baroness Hale [291].

[33] The Chamber decision was *Ali v United Kingdom* (2015) 63 EHRR 20, in which the Strasbourg Court had decided contrary to the UK Supreme Court's decision on the scope of Art 6 in *Ali v Birmingham City Council* [2010] 2 AC 39. See 5.3.1.

or some most egregious oversight or misunderstanding before it could be appropriate for this Court to contemplate an outright refusal to follow Strasbourg authority' [27].

The *Ullah* principle is somewhat unstable, because the UK judges will always resist it when they see a serious drawback in a Strasbourg decision. For a well-organized assault on the doctrine, see Lord Wilson's account of a 'retreat from *Ullah*' in *Moohan v Lord Advocate* [2014] UKSC 67 [104]–[105]. Yet Lord Bingham's approach has survived the Supreme Court's landmark decisions in *Nicklinson* and in *Chester*.[34] As Baroness Hale put it in *R (Keyu) v Secretary of State for Foreign and Commonwealth Affairs* [2015] UKSC 69 [291], 'if it is clear that the claimant would win in Strasbourg, then he will normally win in the courts of this country . . . if it is clear that the claimant would lose in Strasbourg, then he will normally lose here too'. The instability will most likely be worked out by the making of exceptions (which *Alconbury* allowed for), rather than by abandoning the principle altogether.

● Pop quiz ●

Can you reconcile the rule that the UK courts will ordinarily follow the Strasbourg Court's interpretations with the decision in *Nicklinson* that the UK court may find a violation of a right where the Strasbourg Court has decided that the issue is within the margin of appreciation?

All courts deciding Convention rights issues must take into account Strasbourg decisions, but the county courts, the High Court, and the Court of Appeal must abide by a precedent of a higher UK court even if it is clearly incompatible with a later decision of the Strasbourg Court (*Kay v Lambeth LBC* [2006] UKHL 10 [43]; *R (Kaiyam) v Secretary of State for Justice* [2013] EWCA Civ 1587). Although the Court of Appeal is ordinarily bound by its own precedents, the House of Lords held in *R (RJM) v Secretary of State for Work and Pensions* [2008] UKHL 63 that it may (but is not required to) depart from its own earlier decision if it is incompatible with a later Strasbourg decision. But the UK Supreme Court will ordinarily depart from its own earlier decision if it is incompatible with a later Strasbourg decision, to bring its case law into line with the decision of the Strasbourg Court (*R (GC) v Commissioner of Police of the Metropolis* [2011] UKSC 21).

3.9 Summary: the common law and the Human Rights Act

Remember *R v Ministry of Defence, ex p Walker* [2000] 1 WLR 806, from Chapter 2. The Human Rights Act would have been of no use at all to Trevor Walker, even if it had been in force when he was denied an award under the Army's criminal injuries compensation scheme. Like many decisions of public authorities, the decision that he complained about did not affect any interest that the Convention protects.

---

[34]   See Lord Sumption's formulation of the principle in *R (Chester) v Secretary of State for Justice* [2013] UKSC 63 [121].

● *Pop quiz* ●

Wasn't Walker's private and family life affected by the denial of criminal injuries compensation? If so, would Art 8 of the Convention be engaged, so that he might have a remedy under the Human Rights Act?

The Human Rights Act gives English judges a new responsibility under s 6 to quash administrative decisions that interfere disproportionately with certain fundamental interests of persons. But that role is limited, and in several ways the role of courts in common law judicial review is more adventurous. The old law of judicial control of discretionary powers gives judges a much more wide-ranging jurisdiction to control government action than the Human Rights Act gives them.

Remember, too, that UK courts were already doing much of what the Human Rights Act says that they should do: as Lord Hoffmann has put it, s 3 'expressly enacts' the principle of legality that was already part of our law (*R v Home Secretary, ex p Simms* [2000] 2 AC 115, 132). The Justices of the Supreme Court have repeatedly insisted that the Convention is not the starting point for human rights in UK law. In *Osborn v Parole Board* [2013] UKSC 61 [63], Lord Reed held that it would be an error 'to suppose that because an issue falls within the ambit of a Convention guarantee, it follows that the legal analysis of the problem should begin and end with the Strasbourg case law'. And he called the role of the Strasbourg Court 'fundamentally subsidiary' ([56], citing *Hatton v United Kingdom* (2003) 37 EHRR 611 [97]).

In *Osborn*, the common law of due process was all that the claimant needed (see 4.11, p 151), and arguing the case on the basis of Art 6 of the Convention added nothing. Lord Reed said, 'The importance of the Act is unquestionable. It does not however supersede the protection of human rights under the common law or statute.' The Act *does* provide 'a number of additional tools enabling the courts and government to develop the law' [57], and it 'requires the courts to take account of the judgments of the European court'. The most important of the tools are not to be found in s 6 (which makes administrative action contrary to Convention rights unlawful), but in s 3 on interpretation, and s 4 on declarations of incompatibility.

And there is one aspect of the judges' new responsibility under the Human Rights Act that challenges the principles of judicial control of administration that we encountered in Chapter 2. It is the judges' role in assessing the value of a public authority's policy objective, in order to determine whether it is legitimate for the authority to pursue the objective in a particular way, at a particular cost to the claimant's privacy or freedom.

English law has had deferential proportionality requirements for centuries. Under the *Wednesbury* principles, it is generally unlawful for a public authority to act in a way that is *so disproportionately* detrimental to a person's privacy or freedom that no reasonable public authority would act that way. Lord Ackner pointed this out in *R v Home Secretary, ex p Brind* [1991] AC 696, 762–3, but he also concluded that there was no basis to apply the doctrine of proportionality that had been developed by the Strasbourg Court 'unless and until Parliament incorporates the Convention into domestic law'. The Human Rights Act has not *incorporated* the Convention into domestic law, but under s 6 the Strasbourg form of proportionality has indeed become a control on those administrative decisions that affect the interests protected in the Convention.

Judicial review under the *Wednesbury* principles is certainly different from judicial application of Convention rights under the Human Rights Act s 6. It may seem that the difference is that the *Wednesbury* doctrine requires that judges defer to other public authorities and that s 6 requires them *not* to defer in deciding what counts as a violation of a Convention right. But the situation is more complicated. Proportionality reasoning can give judges a reason to defer; the reason is that a public authority other than a judge may be better able to assess the public interests that sometimes justify a restriction of freedom, or an intrusion into privacy. This important form of deference is discussed in 8.3, 'Proportionality and deference'.

● *Pop quiz* ●
Are Convention rights constitutional rights?

3.10 A permanent political crisis over human rights law?

In 2005, John Hirst, a man convicted of manslaughter and sentenced to life in prison, challenged the Representation of the People Act 1983, which prevented him from voting in elections while in prison. Article 1 of the first Protocol to the Convention provides that: 'The High Contracting Parties undertake to hold free elections at reasonable intervals by secret ballot, under conditions which will ensure the free expression of the opinion of the people in the choice of the legislature.' Hirst argued that the Convention implied that he had a right to vote, which the legislation violated. He lost a claim for a declaration of incompatibility in the Administrative Court (*Hirst v Attorney General* [2001] EWHC 239 (Admin)), on the ground that although a right to vote is to be inferred from Art 3 of the Protocol, the court should defer to Parliament's evident decision, in the Representation of the People Act, that depriving prisoners of the vote was compatible with that right. Hirst went to Strasbourg, and a Grand Chamber held by a 12–5 majority that the UK's blanket ban on voting by prisoners contravened the Convention. The majority held that although 'the margin of appreciation is wide, it is not all-embracing' (*Hirst v UK (No 2)* (2006) 42 EHRR 41 [82]):

> ' Such a general, automatic and indiscriminate restriction on a vitally important Convention right must be seen as falling outside any acceptable margin of appreciation, however wide that margin might be, and as being incompatible with Article 3 of Protocol No. 1. '

The five dissenting judges said that the majority's reaffirmation of a wide margin of appreciation was inconsistent with their decision, and concluded, at [5], that:

> ' . . . the sensitive political assessments involved call for caution. Unless restrictions impair the very essence of the right to vote or are arbitrary, national legislation on voting rights should be declared incompatible with Article 3 only if weighty reasons justify such a finding. '

The majority in the Strasbourg Court expressly declined to give any indication as to what restrictions on voting by prisoners it might hold to be compatible with the Convention [84]. The British government under Tony Blair and Gordon Brown did not take action to comply with the decision. In 2010, the Conservative–Liberal Democrat coalition government started discussing possible steps to comply, and the mere discussion led to widespread opposition across mainstream politics in the UK: in February 2011, MPs in the House of Commons voted 234–22 in a non-binding motion in favour of keeping the ban. The government published a draft Bill in 2012, but it included the possibility of keeping the existing ban. In 2018, more than a decade after the *Hirst* decision, the UK has done nothing to comply with the legal obligation of parties to the Convention 'to abide by the final judgment of the Court in any case to which they are parties' (Art 46).

The crisis over voting by prisoners has created the first serious political opposition to the Convention and to the role of the Strasbourg Court (even though the role of Art 8 in immigration—see 3.6.2, p 99—and the positive duties imposed by the judges—see 3.6, p 93—have much more significant impact on government). What prospect is there for resolution of the crisis? The judges of the Strasbourg Court are very evidently aware of the risk to the Court's effectiveness, and they have made some serious gestures toward compromise. In *Scoppola v Italy (No 3)* (2012) 56 EHRR 663, a Grand Chamber reaffirmed the *Hirst* holding that a blanket ban on voting by prisoners is outside the margin of appreciation, but upheld an Italian scheme preventing voting by prisoners sentenced to three years' imprisonment or more. *Scoppola* was an olive branch to the British government. But given the present state of British politics, it would be very difficult for any political party to advocate voting by any prisoners at all.

Meanwhile, in *Greens and MT v UK* (2010) 53 EHRR 710 [98], the Strasbourg Court refused to order the UK to compensate prisoners who have been denied the vote since the *Hirst* decision, holding that, in order to give just satisfaction for the violation of their rights, it was enough for the Court to declare that their rights had been violated.[35] The Court went on to say that the UK 'must introduce legislative proposals . . . within six months' to comply with *Hirst* (*Greens and MT* [115]). That was in April 2011. In August 2014, another Chamber of the Court heard new claims for compensation, and held 5–2 that there was a violation of the Convention (following *Hirst* and *Greens and MT*), but again refused to award compensation (*Firth v UK* [2014] ECHR 874).[36]

The disagreement between the Strasbourg Court and the British politicians is not over whether the UK should respect human rights; it is over whether the human rights of prisoners are violated by a blanket ban on voting. The unavoidable upshot of signing the European Convention is that the Strasbourg Court rules on that issue. In spite

---

[35] On 'just satisfaction' under the European Convention, see 14.6.

[36] In *R (Chester) v Secretary of State for Justice* [2013] UKSC 63, the UK Supreme Court held that it ought to abide by the Strasbourg Grand Chamber decisions in *Hirst* and *Scoppola*, but declined to issue a declaration of incompatibility, on the grounds that a Scottish court had already issued one and that the claimant, having been sentenced for murder, would clearly fall within restrictions on voting that the Strasbourg Court would accept.

of the judges' gestures, there is no prospect whatever for a resolution of the tension between the judges' views and the politicians' views.

Similar tensions between judges and the legislature and the executive are standing features of public life in the United States, Canada, India, South Africa, and many other countries that have justiciable constitutional bills of rights. The governments of all those countries have a uniform practice of accepting the decisions of the judges. The British government has consistently shown that it will not accept the decision of the Strasbourg judges on this one issue. The issue of voting rights for prisoners involves a breakdown in the rule of law in the United Kingdom, in the sense that a government supposedly committed to abiding by its obligations in international law is patently refusing to do so.

In the UK, unlike in the United States, Canada, India, and South Africa, the judges in question are judges of an international court (of a kind that the United States, Canada, India, and South Africa would never agree to). One resolution to the crisis in the UK would be for the UK to withdraw from the Convention. Proponents of that step argue that the UK would only be standing up against foreign judges' misguided views as to what human rights people have—but it would look like the UK standing against human rights, and it would affect the country's stature and role in international politics. The Conservative party has seriously considered the possibility of withdrawing from the ECHR. But the Conservative government is not going to do anything at all about the ECHR, until the process of Brexit is completed.[37]

An extraordinary court

There are forty-seven contracting states in the Council of Europe, and therefore forty-seven judges on the Strasbourg Court. The population of the twenty-five smallest countries adds up to less than the population of the UK; they have twenty-five judges, and the UK has one. There is one judge from Russia and one from Germany; also one from San Marino and one from Monaco. Russia and Germany have 3,000 times the population of San Marino and Monaco.

The Parliamentary Assembly of the Council of Europe appoints judges, but does so from a list of three candidates nominated by the government of each country. There is an ongoing process of discussion of reforms of the Convention and the Court, but we should not expect any change in this extraordinary judicial structure, because all nations would need to agree to a change.

The judicial structure was not designed to secure appointments of the continent's leading judges, but to give representation to each contracting state. The large benches (seven judges in a Chamber, and seventeen in a Grand Chamber for important cases) are a resulting technique designed to get useful expertise into the Court's deliberations and to increase public confidence in decisions.

---

[37] See https://www.conservatives.com/manifesto, stating that the UK would remain within the ECHR for the current Parliament.

The role of judges in Strasbourg under the Convention, and of English judges under the Human Rights Act, shares one crucial common thread with the role of the English judges in common law judicial review: the judges need to act with comity (see 1.5.3, p 19) toward other public authorities. The need to make judgments of proportionality in applying the qualified rights creates a potential failure in the separation of powers (see 1.5.1), because it invites judges to answer questions that the legislature or the executive are better equipped to answer. The doctrine of a margin of appreciation in the Strasbourg Court and the emerging doctrine of deference in the UK courts are the judges' answers to that problem.

It is equally essential for politicians and officials to act with comity toward the courts. And their predicament is that comity towards the courts means going along with what the courts say, even on deeply controversial issues on which the politicians disagree with the judges. And as long as the UK is a party to the Convention, that applies to the decisions of the Strasbourg Court just as much as to the decisions of the English courts. The judges of the Strasbourg Court have a jurisdiction that the UK has conferred on them.

3.11 The Charter of Fundamental Rights of the European Union

The European Union proclaimed its Charter of Fundamental Rights in 2000 in Nice, but it only took legal effect under the Treaty of Lisbon in 2009.[38] Article 51 of the Charter provides that it is addressed to the EU member states 'only when they are implementing Union law'. The Charter is meant to enshrine rights that were already part of EU law, but the fact of writing them down and giving them effect under the Treaty means that advocates and judges will treat them as grounds for new claims. For that very reason, Poland and the UK negotiated a special Protocol, which the politicians saw as an opt-out from the Charter. The Seventh Protocol to the Treaty of Lisbon provides that: 'The Charter does not extend the ability of the Court of Justice of the European Union, or any court or tribunal of Poland or of the United Kingdom, to find that the laws, regulations or administrative provisions, practices or action of Poland or of the United Kingdom are inconsistent with the fundamental rights, freedoms and principles that it reaffirms' (Art 1).

But in *C-411/10 R (NS) v Secretary of State for the Home Department* [2012] 2 CMLR 9 [120], the CJEU held that the special Protocol had no effect:

> ' [The] protocol ... does not intend to exempt the Republic of Poland or the United Kingdom from the obligations to comply with the provisions of the Charter or to prevent a court of one of those member states from ensuring compliance with those provisions. '

....

[38] See http://ec.europa.eu/justice/fundamental-rights/index_en.htm.

Decisions of the CJEU are binding in UK law under the European Communities Act 1972. So after *NS*, a UK court must ensure compliance with the Charter, in spite of the Protocol. According to Mostyn J in *R (AB) v Home Secretary* [2013] EWHC 3453 [14]: 'The constitutional significance of this decision can hardly be overstated.' Because the EU Charter includes the rights in the European Convention, the effect of *NS* is to bring about a new form of incorporation of EU human rights law into UK law. Consider *Benkharbouche v Foreign Secretary Affairs* [2017] UKSC 62. The claimants were Moroccan nationals who worked as cleaners and cooks for the Libyan and Sudanese embassies in London. The State Immunity Act 1978 provided that foreign states are immune from proceedings for breach of UK employment law. The Supreme Court held that, in the claimants' cases, those provisions were incompatible with the guarantee of a fair hearing in the determination of civil rights and obligations in Art 6 of the Convention [76]. The Court issued a declaration of incompatibility under the Human Rights Act. But for the same reasons that it violated Art 6 of the Convention, the state immunity also violated the right to an effective remedy before a tribunal for breach of EU law, under Art 47 of the EU Charter of Fundamental Rights. And for that violation, the claimants got more than a declaration of incompatibility: 'a conflict between EU law and English domestic law must be resolved in favour of the former, and the latter must be disapplied' [78]. The claimants could not win their claims under domestic law for unfair dismissal and to be paid the national minimum wage; under the Human Rights Act, they only got a declaration of incompatibility. But for the breach of their rights under EU law, the claimants got direct, immediately effective remedies in the UK courts.

There are also rights in the EU Charter that are not in the European Convention, such as the 'right to the protection of personal data' in Art 8 (which was at issue in the *AB* case). The UK's Data Retention and Investigatory Powers Act 2014 authorized the Home Secretary to require electronic communication service providers to retain data on emails in the interests of national security; in a reference from the High Court, the CJEU held that the legislation violates Art 8 of the EU Charter. As long as the UK is a member state of the EU, the EU Charter will continue to be a dynamic resource for litigants asking the courts to hold that acts of Parliament have no effect.[39]

TAKE-HOME MESSAGE ● ● ●

- The European Convention on Human Rights has not been incorporated in English law; the Human Rights Act 1998 gives **specified, limited legal effects** to the rights protected in the Convention.

- The Human Rights Act:
  - changes the effect of statutes, requiring them to be read and given effect in a way that is compatible with Convention rights, 'so far as it is possible'—and it leaves judges to decide what is possible **(s 3)**;

---

[39]   On the role of the EU Charter in Brexit, see 'Note on Brexit', p xxi.

- creates a new ground for quashing administrative action as unlawful if the action infringes a Convention right and is not required by statute (**s 6**);
- empowers courts to give a remedy in relation to acts that are unlawful under s 6, including an award of damages if 'necessary to afford just satisfaction' (s 8) (see 14.6);
- empowers judges to declare that a statute is incompatible with a Convention right (**s 4**) if the statute cannot be read and given effect in a way that is compatible with the right; a declaration of incompatibility triggers a fast-track amendment process (s 10);
- gives English judges new ways of imposing the rule of law on the government, because it gives effect in English law to the provisions against arbitrary detention (Art 5), the right to a fair hearing before an independent and impartial tribunal (Art 6), and the prohibition on retrospective criminal liability (Art 7);
- requires judges to decide whether interferences with some fundamental interests are proportionate to legitimate objectives; and
- leaves it to judges to find a middle way between leaving other public authorities to violate Convention rights, and imposing their own views of the public interest on other public authorities in a way that would damage the separation of powers.

- The Human Rights Act **does not**:
  - replace the common law standards of judicial review; or
  - undermine the principle of parliamentary sovereignty.

- The House of Lords has used **s 3** of the Act to give some statutes an effect that is contrary to their meaning.

- But the courts have declined some of the opportunities offered to them by claimants' barristers to use the Act to remodel English law:
  - the House of Lords' interpretation of **s 6** of the Act has protected exercises of a Convention-incompatible statutory power from being quashed on judicial review;
  - the courts have developed a **doctrine of deference** to executive and legislative authorities in making the necessary assessments of the public interest to apply the qualified Convention rights (the role of deference is dealt with in Chapter 8); and
  - the House of Lords has refrained from using **Art 6** of the Convention (the right to a fair trial) to restructure administrative decision making.

- Decisions of the **European Court of Human Rights** in Strasbourg have the same effect in international law as they had before the Human Rights Act: its decisions bind the United Kingdom. A claimant who loses on a Convention issue in the English courts under the Human Rights Act can try going to Strasbourg to seek a different decision.

- Decisions of the Strasbourg Court have a *new* effect in English law under the Human Rights Act, because English courts must take account of them (s 2).

- The Charter of Fundamental Rights of the European Union enshrines many of the same rights as the ECHR. Unlike the ECHR, it has direct effect in UK law. But it will not replace the ECHR, because its scope is restricted to actions of government in implementing EU law.

CRITICAL QUESTIONS ● ● ●

1   Is judicial review for incompatibility of administrative action with Convention rights justified by constitutional principle?

2   How does the Human Rights Act 1998 promote the rule of law? Does it pose dangers to the rule of law?

3   Should English courts be *less* deferential than the Strasbourg Court in applying the qualified Convention rights?

4   Are there proportionality tests for the application of all Convention rights?

5   Neither House of Parliament is a 'public authority' for the purposes of the Human Rights Act (s 6(3)). Why not?

6   Why does the Human Rights Act define 'primary legislation' to include an 'Order in Council made in exercise of Her Majesty's Royal Prerogative' (s 21(1))? How does that provision affect judicial review of the prerogative?

7   The Human Rights Act s 19 provides that: 'A Minister of the Crown in charge of a Bill in either House of Parliament must . . . (a) make a statement to the effect that in his view the provisions of the Bill are compatible with the Convention rights; or (b) make a statement to the effect that although he is unable to make a statement of compatibility the government nevertheless wishes the House to proceed with the Bill.' Suppose that a minister makes a statement that, in his or her view, a Bill is compatible with Convention rights, but in fact the Bill is incompatible with Convention rights. Does a person aggrieved by the minister's conduct have any legal remedy?

8   Could you get judicial review of a governmental decision not to ask Parliament to amend legislation that a court has declared to be incompatible with a Convention right?

9   Can a remedial order under the Human Rights Act s 10 be quashed by a court as *ultra vires*?

10 Why do the privacy and political freedom Articles (Arts 8, 9, 10, 11) allow only those limits on freedom and privacy that are *'necessary* in a democratic society'? Why not allow those limits that are just or reasonable?

READING • • •

Handyside v United Kingdom (1976) 1 EHRR 737

R v Home Secretary, ex p Venables and Thompson [1998] AC 407

V v United Kingdom (2000) 30 EHRR 121

R (Alconbury) v Environment Secretary [2001] UKHL 23

R (Daly) v Home Secretary [2001] UKHL 26

R (Anderson) v Home Secretary [2002] UKHL 46

Ghaidan v Godin-Mendoza [2004] UKHL 30

Bank Mellat v Her Majesty's Treasury (No 2) [2013] UKSC 39

R (Nicklinson) v Ministry of Justice [2014] UKSC 38

On protection of fundamental rights before the Human Rights Act 1998:

Stephen Sedley, 'Human Rights: A Twenty-First Century Agenda' [1995] PL 386

On the impact of the Human Rights Act in general:

Lord Irvine, 'The Impact of the Human Rights Act: Parliament, Courts and the Executive' [2003] PL 308

Alison Young, *Parliamentary Sovereignty and the Human Rights Act* (Hart 2009)

Aileen Kavanagh, *Constitutional Review under the UK Human Rights Act* (CUP 2009)

On the Human Rights Act s 3:

Philip Sales and Richard Ekins, 'Rights-consistent Interpretation and the Human Rights Act 1998' (2011) 127 LQR 217

On the relation between the Strasbourg Court and British courts:

Philip Sales, 'Strasbourg Jurisprudence and the Human Rights Act: A Response to Lord Irvine' [2012] PL 253

On proportionality in human rights law:

Paul Craig, 'The Nature of Reasonableness Review' [2013] CLP 1

Grant Huscroft, Bradley W. Miller, and Gregoire Webber, *Proportionality and the Rule of Law* (CUP 2014)

Aileen Kavanagh, 'Reasoning about Proportionality under the Human Rights Act 1998' (2014) 130 LQR 235

Philip Sales, 'Rationality, Proportionality and the Development of the Law' (2013) 129 LQR 223

On the Charter of Fundamental Rights of the European Union:

Paul Craig and Grainne de Burcá, *EU Law: Text, Cases and Materials* (5th edn, OUP 2011), p 395

On the law and politics of human rights:

Jonathan Sumption, 'Book Review of Conor Gearty, *On Fantasy Island: Britain, Europe and Human Rights*' (2017) 133 LQR 338–40

 The following online resources accompany this chapter: **summaries** of key cases and legislation; **updates** on the law; **guidance** for answering the pop quizzes and questions; and **links** to legislation, cases, and useful websites.

Part II
Process

4 Due process

Due process requires a variety of procedures for different decisions in different contexts. Good procedures are essential for responsible government. But they also increase the cost of administration. They may improve decision making; but unnecessary procedural requirements may actually stand in the way of good administration. We don't simply need more process; we need *due* process—that is, process that is suited to the type of decision, to the nature of the authority that is making it, and to the ways in which the decision affects a complainant. The attempt to achieve due process is essential to good administration and to the administration of justice. The law of due process is the judges' best contribution to administrative law.

LOOK FOR • • •

- **Proportionality** in procedural duties of public authorities.

- The three **process values**: procedural requirements can improve decisions, treat people with respect, and subject the administration to the rule of law.

- **Process cost** and **process dangers**.

- **The question of procedural justice**: what procedures should an administrative authority take?

- **The question of comity**: to what extent should judges impose their answer to the question of procedural justice on other authorities?

- The **irony of process**: in order to secure due process, the law must sometimes require procedures that impose *disproportionate* burdens on administrative authorities.

- The cases on executive decisions concerning **detention** (in parole, mental health, asylum, and terrorism), which raise questions at the frontiers of due process.

> ' . . . the Board of Education will have to ascertain the law and also to ascertain the facts. I need not add that in doing either they must act in good faith and fairly listen to both sides, for that is a duty lying upon every one who decides anything. But I do not think they are bound to treat such a question as though it were a trial. '
>
> **Board of Education v Rice [1911] AC 179 (HL), 182 (Lord Loreburn LC)**

4.1 The justice of the common law

Mr Cooper started building a house. He got as far as the second floor when the Wandsworth Board of Works 'sent their surveyor and a number of workmen, at a late hour in the evening, and razed it to the ground' (*Cooper v Wandsworth Board of Works* (1863) 14 CB (NS) 180, 182).

Cooper sued the Board for the tort of trespass to property (see 14.1). The Board's defence was that the demolition was no trespass, because it was authorized by statute. The statute required seven days' notice to the Board before any new building could be started. If a building was started without the seven days' notice, the statute said, 'it shall be lawful for the . . . board to cause such house or building to be demolished' (Metropolis Local Management Act 1855 s 76). The Board had received no notice; Cooper said he had sent one in, but admitted that he had started work five days after giving notice.

The Board of Works lost. The Court held that the demolition was unlawful. How is that possible, if Cooper had not given seven days' notice, and a statute of Parliament said that demolition 'shall be lawful' if seven days' notice was not given? The answer is that 'although there are no positive words in a statute requiring that the party shall be heard, yet the justice of the common law will supply the omission of the legislature' (Byles J, 194). The demolition was unlawful *because the Board had not given Cooper a hearing*—that is, the common law required the officials to give Cooper notice of what they had in mind, and consider what he had to say, before they could lawfully exercise the power that Parliament had given them.

Why did the justice of the common law require a hearing? Byles J took something for granted in his famous statement, which the other judges spelled out: 'no man is to be deprived of his property without his having an opportunity of being heard' (Erle CJ, 187); 'A tribunal which is by law invested with power to affect the property of one of Her Majesty's subjects, is bound to give such subject an opportunity of being heard before it proceeds' (Willes J, 190).[1] Willes J called it a rule 'of universal application, and founded upon the plainest principles of justice' (190).

To reach that decision, the judges needed to deal with two problems raised by counsel for the Board of Works in *Cooper*. The first is whether the Board of Works was right to think that its public role demanded that it get on with the job of demolishing Cooper's house without giving a hearing. The second is whether it is appropriate for judges to

---

[1]   Is due process restricted to British subjects? No. For example, today, as in the 1860s, the availability of *habeas corpus* does not depend on nationality.

impose the processes *they* consider appropriate on an executive agency. So we need to address a question of **procedural justice** and also a question of **comity**, as follows.

- What are the 'plainest principles of justice' (Willes J, 190) on which the rule of due process is founded? (See 4.2.)

- Granted that justice *sometimes* requires a hearing, why shouldn't the judges leave it to the administration to decide when? (See 4.3.)

> **Hearing** is used metaphorically for any procedure in which a decision maker considers what a person affected has to say, before making a decision. In an oral hearing (see 4.8), the decision maker listens to the person face to face.
>
> A **procedure** is something that a decision maker does for the purpose of making (or justifying, or communicating, or explaining, or reconsidering) a decision.
>
> A **process** is the set of procedures taken in the making of a decision.
>
> A **proceeding** is a set of procedures for the determination of a particular case before a tribunal or court.

4.2 Natural justice

For centuries before *Cooper*, English lawyers had been using '**natural justice**' as a technical term for the procedural duties owed by a court, or by an administrative body that makes decisions that are somewhat similar to those of a court ('quasi-judicial' decisions).[2] When you are deciding to pull down someone's house, it is unjust to act as if he or she had nothing to say on the matter.

Since Cooper was putting up the building, and the Board's decision was based on Cooper's failure to give notice, Cooper might have had new information relevant to the decision. He might have been able to show that it was only by accident (or due to the fault of a third party) that his notice hadn't reached the Board. Or, if he really had not given notice, he might be able to tell the Board something that would be relevant to the discretionary power that it had to exercise (e.g., that the construction met its standards, so that his default was a technicality that did not justify wrecking the house). It would be *substantively* unjust for the Board to pull down his house if there were good reason not to, so it is *procedurally unjust* to do so without knowing all of the information or argument that might show a good reason not to. Doing that would go against the public purpose for which the Board had been set up. The Board was not doing its job of protecting people from dangerous buildings (and not demolishing buildings that are not dangerous) if it pulled down houses on partial or faulty information.

---

[2] But the phrase 'natural justice' had earlier been used more generally for what is inherently just, in substance or in process: in *Moses v Macferlan* (1760) 2 Burr 1005, 1012, Lord Mansfield CJ said of what is now called a claim in restitution that 'the defendant, upon the circumstances of the case, is obliged by the ties of natural justice and equity to refund the money'.

But there is also another reason why it was unjust to pull down Cooper's house without talking to him about it. Even if he had *no* information to give, tearing down someone's house without telling him ahead of time shows disrespect. Counsel for the Board in *Cooper* asked (at 186): 'What necessity can there be for giving the party notice, when he well knows that he is doing an illegal act, and that the board have power to prostrate his house?' The Court's answer was that the Board owed Cooper the respect that it would have shown him if it had given notice of the plan—even if that procedural step could make no difference to the outcome. The men from the Board of Works came at night. Erle CJ said that there was evidence that they were not on 'amicable' terms with Cooper. The lack of notice and lack of a hearing were in themselves ways of abusing Cooper, by treating him as if he didn't matter.

FROM THE MISTS OF TIME

Byles J cited the 1748 case of *R v Chancellor of Cambridge, ex p Bentley* (1748) 2 Ld Raym 1334. Dr Bentley had been expelled from the University of Cambridge: Fortescue J held that, before being deprived of rights as a punishment for misconduct, 'The laws of God and man both give the party a right to make his defence, if he has any.' And he observed that 'even God himself did not pass sentence upon Adam before he was called upon to make his defence' (cited in *Cooper*, 195). The point of the story is that God already knew the facts of the case. So even if nothing can possibly be learned from the people affected by a decision, the decision maker can, and sometimes must, treat them decently by letting them have their say. Byles J said that Fortescue J's judgment 'is somewhat quaint, but it . . . has been the law from that time to the present' (*Cooper*, 195). It is still the law in the twenty-first century.

Finally, apart from showing respect for Cooper, and even if the person affected has nothing to say, the requirement of a hearing subjects the power of the Board of Works to the **rule of law** and promotes the allied value of **accountability**. Uncontrolled public decision making doesn't just lead to poor outcomes and show disrespect for the people affected; it also lacks the regularity and transparency that could distinguish it from the mere say-so of the people on the Board of Works. Procedural participation by people affected by a decision promotes the rule of law by making it more difficult for a public authority to act arbitrarily. And it is an accountability technique in itself, because it puts the public authority in the predicament of having to face up to the people affected by a decision.

These benefits are *related* to the outcome goal of getting only the unsafe houses pulled down, and to the value of showing respect for Cooper. Protecting him from an uncontrolled process is a way of showing him respect, and so is a rule making someone from the Board of Works look him in the eye before pulling down his house. But the rule-of-law value of procedures is distinct from their value in improving outcomes and showing respect. Think of an armed robber who is caught red-handed by police, and who admits the offence and does not want a trial. The police cannot just take him off to prison—English law still insists on a criminal trial, with the cumbersome procedures that a trial involves even when the accused pleads guilty. The reason is to impose the rule of law on the community's response to crimes, and to provide accountability *to the community*—not just to the person affected—for action taken on behalf of the community.

Process value: the advantages of procedural participation

- **The value of promoting good outcomes**: to improve the capacity of the decision maker to act on all of the relevant considerations. That promotes good administration, which is in the public interest.
- **The value of respect**: to treat a person who is involved in certain ways in the *outcome* of a decision as someone who should be involved in the *process*.
- **The value of imposing the rule of law on the administration**: to promote integrity in public decision making by controlling the process.

These three process values are stated very clearly in Lord Reed's explanation of 'the purpose of procedural fairness' in *Osborn v Parole Board* [2013] UKSC 61—a landmark case in the law of due process. Lord Reed held that 'one of the virtues of procedurally fair decision-making is that it is liable to result in better decisions' [67]. But there are two others: 'justice is intuitively understood to require a procedure which pays due respect to persons whose rights are significantly affected by decisions' [68], and the rule of law is the final value: procedural requirements can 'promote congruence between the actions of decision-makers and the law which should govern their actions' [71]. As is obvious from his remarks, the rule-of-law value is connected to the value of achieving better decisions.

So there is value in making the Board of Works give a hearing to people like Cooper. But we should face up to the drawbacks. First, it *costs public money*. It is cheaper to decide whether to pull down a house without paying someone to spend time giving notice to Cooper (and finding him in the first place) and listening to what he may have to say. Second, *it may actually be dangerous to the public interest*. Requiring hearings will make the officials' work less convenient, and that carries a risk of damaging the public interest. Remember that the point of the Board's powers was partly to protect the public against dangerous building practices, and a dangerous building can fall down in the time it takes to give notice and to give a defaulter the opportunity to explain. As counsel for the Board in *Cooper* pointed out, 'in many cases the object to be attained would be utterly frustrated unless done promptly' (187). No doubt, the Court would not have held the action in *Cooper* to be a tort if the Board of Works had acted in an emergency to prevent the house from falling on passers-by. But the decision in *Cooper* inevitably puts pressure on officials to be concerned with the risk of liability that they may face in pulling down a house without lawful procedures—and not just about the risk that the house will fall down.

Process cost and process danger: the disadvantages of procedural rights

- **Process cost**: the expense of procedural steps, in time and money.
- **Process danger**: the risk that, by requiring a particular procedure, the law will damage the capacity of the public authority to carry out its functions justly and effectively.

Natural justice demanded a hearing in the *Cooper* situation, in spite of the drawbacks. The danger was inconsequential, and the value of a hearing in that situation was worth the cost.

Process and substance

In *Cooper*, the Board of Works decided to pull down the house, and it decided that Cooper's failure to give notice justified it in doing so. The **substance** of the Board's decision is what it decided: *both* the action it decided to take, and the reasons for which it decided to take it. The defect in the **process** by which the Board made the decision was the failure to listen to Cooper. Substance and process are distinct, but are connected to each other. Because of the connections, the distinction can seem either mind-bending or non-existent. So hold on to the simple idea that the substance of a decision is *what was decided*. If you can write down 'the public authority decided *that* . . .', then the three dots stand for the substance of the decision (in *Cooper*, the Board decided *that* his house was to be demolished because of his lack of notice); the process is the sum of the steps by which that decision was reached. But 'steps by which a decision was reached' is ambiguous! It could refer to steps in the public authority's *reasoning*, or to things that the public authority *did* to enable it to do that reasoning (see 6.9).

Due process requires a decision maker to take the steps (in particular, to listen to people who have something to say on the issues) that are suited to making a good decision. It *also* requires actions that promote responsible decision making, such as communicating the decision, giving reasons for it (Chapter 6), and being prepared to reconsider it or to provide an appeal from it. *And* it requires those things to be done by people who can be seen by a reasonable observer to be unbiased (Chapter 5).

Of course, people like Cooper are only concerned with process when the substance of the decision is adverse to their interest; if, without giving him a hearing, the Board had made a decision not to pull down Cooper's house, he would have no complaint.

4.3 Comity between the judges and the Board of Works

The Board ought to have listened to Cooper. But what gives the judges jurisdiction to right the wrong? More recent cases take the judges' jurisdiction for granted. But it was at issue in *Cooper*. The Board of Works made an argument of comity (see 1.5.3): that even if natural justice required a hearing, it was the *Court's* job to impose it only when an official was acting 'judicially' (that is, when the official's role was to hear a dispute as to someone's legal rights). And the Board argued that it had acted 'ministerially' (that is, its function was to administer a public programme, rather than to resolve a dispute as to Cooper's legal rights). The Board had a job to do in the public interest, and while it is possible for administrators to abuse their power, 'the great safe-guard against abuses in the administration . . . is that the members of which these boards are composed are elected by the rate- payers of the district' (*Cooper*, 186). The lawyer for the Board of Works might have said something similar for *any* public authority: that the appropriate form of control is through management by an executive that is democratically accountable. In support of the argument that the Board was acting ministerially and not judicially, counsel for the Board said something that no English lawyer would say today (at 186): 'An arbitrary power is conferred upon the board, which is necessarily to be exercised without any control.'

The failure of that argument is the most important development in modern administrative law. It is the founding principle of the modern law of due process: even when the functions of a public authority are administrative or 'ministerial' rather than judicial, they must be exercised with due process, and the judges have a general jurisdiction to require due process. In the rest of this chapter, we will see that the principle is justified by the **core rationale** (see 2.8) for judicial interference with other public authorities: the judges can improve public decision making by taking on themselves the power to control the procedures by which some governmental decisions are made. It is required, as Byles J put it (at 194), by the justice of the common law.

4.3.1 Due process in judicial *and* administrative decisions

In *Cooper*, the argument that natural justice is restricted to judicial or quasi-judicial functions failed. But the judges' response to that argument in *Cooper* was muddled. It would take *Ridge v Baldwin* [1964] AC 40, a century later, to clear up the muddle. Erle CJ could not quite decide whether the decision in *Cooper* was judicial (*Cooper*, 189). Byles J said, 'I conceive that they acted judicially', but also: 'It seems to me that the board are wrong whether they acted judicially or ministerially' (194). If the Board acted ministerially, he thought that it owed Cooper no hearing, but still was bound to give notice of the demolition before carrying it out (195). Willes J said, 'it is clear that these boards do exercise judicial powers' (191), but did not say how a ministerial power would differ. After *Cooper*, it was unclear whether hearings were required in the exercise of administrative functions, and what the difference was between administrative functions and quasi-judicial functions.

One solution would be for the judges to decide (as Byles J did) that the decision was 'judicial' or 'quasi-judicial', because of the way in which it affected Cooper. The Court of Appeal took that approach in *Hopkins v Smethwick Local Board of Health* (1890) 24 QBD 712 (CA). But that approach led to confusion over how a decision had to affect a person in order to be judicial or quasi-judicial. It also led to procedural injustice: in *Nakkuda Ali v Jayaratne* [1951] AC 66, the Privy Council made room for such an injustice. The Ceylon Controller of Textiles had power to revoke a dealer's licence to deal in textiles if there were reasonable grounds to believe that the dealer was unfit. Lord Radcliffe held that the writ of *certiorari*—the courts' process for quashing decisions made without natural justice[3]— was not available because the Controller did not have a duty to act judicially (at 78):

---
[3] Today, it would be a quashing order (see 10.4.1, p 389).

> ' In truth, when he cancels a licence he is not determining a question: he is taking executive action to withdraw a privilege because he believes, and has reasonable grounds to believe, that the holder is unfit to retain it. ' [4]

That was a **process failure**. It may seem that the problem is that there is no distinction between judicial/quasi-judicial and administrative functions. But the distinction is actually quite clear: an administrative decision is designed to give effect to the policy of the government, while a judicial or quasi-judicial decision is designed to decide a dispute as to the legal position of the parties. The problem is that *these types of decision overlap*: a decision to give effect to a policy of the government often determines someone's legal position—as it did in *Nakkuda Ali*. The decision in *Nakkuda Ali* was a process failure because the judges wrongly thought that no decision giving effect to government policy requires procedural participation by the people it affects. But the administrative ('executive', as Lord Radcliffe called it) task of preventing textile trading by unfit dealers cannot be done fairly without listening to what the dealer in question has to say.

The right solution is for the common law to require due process in the exercise of administrative functions, *as well as* judicial and quasi-judicial functions. Lord Denning stated this solution in the Court of Appeal in *Padfield v Minister of Agriculture, Fisheries and Food* [1968] AC 997, 1006: 'It is said that the decision of the Minister is administrative and not judicial. But that does not mean that he can do as he likes, regardless of right or wrong. Nor does it mean that the courts are powerless to correct him.' In making administrative decisions, due process may require a hearing, because of (1) the process value of a hearing; and (2) the possibility of requiring a hearing without damaging the public authority's performance of its administrative functions. Judicial decisions may call for special procedures. But the difference between administration and adjudication does not mean that it is acceptable to make administrative decisions with no procedural participation for people affected.

If judges can impose due process on administrative authorities without hindering them from doing their job, then it is not a breach of comity for the judges to do so. Erle CJ commented in *Cooper* (at 188): 'I cannot conceive any harm that could happen to the district board from hearing the party before they subjected him to a loss so serious as the demolition of his house; but I can conceive a great many advantages which might arise in the way of public order, in the way of doing substantial justice, and in the way of fulfilling the purpose of the statute, by the restriction which we put upon them.' He exaggerated just a little, because harm *would* result from a requirement of a hearing: the Board would face the process cost of paying officials to deal fairly with people before pulling down their houses. And it would create a process danger—the danger being that the Board of Works' agents might be distracted from protecting people from dangerous buildings, by the process of communicating with the property owner. So there *is* an issue of comity,

----

[4]   But note that Lord Radcliffe also held that the Controller *had* acted with natural justice: he had given the dealer a fair hearing (*Nakkuda Ali*, 81). We don't know what the Privy Council would have decided if it had been faced with a case in which the Controller had made his decision unfairly.

because the decision interferes with the administration. And the judges in *Cooper* took it upon themselves to judge the value or detriment of interference. Judges who take that attitude might end up imposing fussy, expensive, and damaging procedures on a body that could and would act justly without them. But in cases like *Cooper* and *Nakkuda Ali*, the readiness to impose due process on the executive is essential for the rule of law.

English administrative law since the twelfth century has been prepared to take these risks and to impose these costs in *some* cases. The process danger in *Cooper* was negligible; it was only the cost of responsible government. So the judges were justified in imposing the procedural requirement in the interest of the rule of law. Even though the Chief Justice was a judge and not a works expert, he could see that the Board would be 'fulfilling [its] purpose' better, not worse, if it were to give a hearing. There is a tension in the law of due process, because it requires the judges to decide the purpose of another public authority's power. But where they can do so responsibly and without disrespecting that role, it is not a breach of comity for the judges to impose procedures on the Board of Works.

The principle of legality at work

The requirement of due process is based on the principle that the requirements of the law are to be understood in light of certain legally protected values and are limited by those values (see 1.5.5). Courts subject the general statutory power to demolish a house to a qualification that the legislature did not impose. So Lord Mustill said, in *R v Home Secretary, ex p Doody* [1994] 1 AC 531, 560, 'where an Act of Parliament confers an administrative power there is a presumption that it will be exercised in a manner which is fair in all the circumstances'. The presumption is a rule of the common law that gives effect to the principle of legality.

But because public authorities need only give *due* process, the courts will not use the principle of legality, for example, to add a common law requirement of a hearing to a statutory process by which central government can limit spending by local councils (*R v Environment Secretary, ex p Hammersmith LBC* [1991] 1 AC 521, 598–9 (Lord Bridge); on this important decision, see 7.3.2, p 262).

● *Pop quiz* ●

If the decision in *Hammersmith* was right, is that because the law does not require central government to act fairly in limiting council spending? Or because it is fair for the central government to limit council spending without giving the council a hearing?

The judges who decided cases like *Nakkuda Ali* did not think that it was okay for the administration to act unfairly: in *B Johnson & Co v Minister of Health* [1947] 2 All ER 395, 400, Lord Greene said that 'every Minister of the Crown is under a duty, constitutionally, to the King to perform his functions honestly and fairly'. Then he added, 'but his failure to do so, speaking generally, is not a matter with which the courts are concerned'. In his decision in *Associated Provincial Picture Houses v Wednesbury* [1948] 1 KB 223 (see 2.3, p 48) later the same year, Lord Greene said that the courts will quash an exercise of discretion only for certain *restricted* forms of *unreasonableness*, and in *B Johnson & Co*, he insisted that only certain *restricted* forms of *unfairness* are the courts' concern. A minister's decision in planning matters 'cannot be challenged and criticised in the courts unless he has acted unfairly in another sense, *viz.*, in the sense of having, while performing quasi-judicial functions, acted in a way which no person performing such functions, in the opinion of the court, ought to act' (*B Johnson & Co*, 400).

Today, you need to remove the words 'while performing quasi-judicial functions' from that statement of the law. Since the 1940s, it has become a basic principle that administrative functions, as well as judicial functions, must be carried out with due process. But today, the differences among decisions mean that the process that is due will differ significantly between, for example, a ministerial decision over town planning, and a decision to dismiss a public employee. Even in the landmark case of *Ridge v Baldwin*, this principle was not very clearly stated. But it was firmly established as a result of Lord Reid's approach to the case.

4.3.2 *Ridge v Baldwin*: a general requirement of due process

Charles Ridge was Chief Constable of police in Brighton, and had served twenty-three years on the police force, when he was prosecuted on corruption charges. He was acquitted, but at the end of the trial the judge said, first, that Ridge was a bad example because of his association with men suspected of bribing police, and second, that his evidence would not be trusted in future prosecutions. The day after this damaging scene, the police authority told Ridge that he was sacked. His lawyer immediately complained to the Home Secretary that the decision was contrary to natural justice, because the authority had given Ridge no hearing. The Home Secretary upheld the decision, and Ridge brought an action for a declaration that the decision was unlawful.

The police authority's defence was that: 'For those who are responsible for a police force such a dismissal is a matter of the policy of the borough and therefore in acting they need not apply the principles of natural justice' (*Ridge*, 58). It is the argument that the Board of Works had made against Cooper, and it combines the arguments of necessity and comity. The argument is that, because of the public need for effective policing, it is not unfair to proceed without a hearing, and it would be a breach of comity for the courts to require one. Counsel for Ridge had an answer to the argument (at 61):

> ' It is accepted that when administrative actions are to be considered, policy is always a factor. But the rules of natural justice are concerned with a fair form of procedure, not with controlling policy. '

That argument succeeded, and transformed administrative law. In a landmark opinion, Lord Reid harked back a century to *Cooper* and said that if Ridge's case had come a few decades earlier, it would have been plain that he had to be given a hearing. Lord

Reid thought that the courts had lost track of the scope of natural justice because 'insufficient attention has been paid to the great difference between various kinds of cases' (*Ridge*, 65). In cases of dismissal, he held, a hearing was required if, as in *Ridge*, the decision had to be made on grounds of neglect of duty.

Lord Reid's approach reconciled comity with due process, by applying the **principle of relativity** (see 1.3). The crucial point in his opinion is his response to the police authority's claim that *because it was implementing policy on behalf of Brighton*, the principles of natural justice did not apply. Lord Reid made no use of the old distinction between ministerial and judicial powers, but just pointed out the varied roles that policy might play in different decisions and the ways in which an administrative decision might still resemble the work of a judge, even when a public authority is implementing policy. He said that the police authority 'was not deciding, like a judge in a lawsuit, what were the rights of the person before it. But it was deciding how he should be treated—something analogous to a judge's duty in imposing a penalty. No doubt policy would play some part in the decision—but so it might when a judge is imposing a sentence' (*Ridge*, 72). So the police authority's responsibility for effective policing was perfectly consistent with a duty to listen to Ridge. In fact, Lord Reid might have pointed out, good policy *required* that it proceed in a manner that would put all of the relevant considerations on the table. The importance of doing so is worth the **process cost** of giving the police chief a hearing.

It may have seemed to the police authority that there was a **process danger**: a risk that policing would be damaged if it were to listen to the Chief Constable. The members of the committee that made the decision may well have thought that maintaining public confidence in the police demanded a summary dismissal as a statement. And if it really were necessary for the good of the community, it would not be unfair to dismiss Ridge without a hearing. Compare the position of Cabinet ministers, who can be sacked without a hearing at the mere say-so of the Prime Minister. And the minister cannot get judicial review! The law does not impose a duty on the Prime Minister to consider representations from the Cabinet minister before making the decision. The reason is that imposing a legal duty would not improve decision making, because of (1) the nature of the job of a Cabinet minister; and (2) the democratic value of making the Prime Minister accountable for the decision to the House of Commons and to the electorate *only*, and not to judges. So a court will not ask whether the Prime Minister has proceeded unfairly in dismissing a minister.

The decision in *Ridge* was a good one, because the judges could interfere without doing the sort of damage they would do if they were to try to supervise the dismissal of ministers. There is no need for the police authority to be able to proceed without a hearing, or to be free from judicial interference. And there is a genuine danger, in that context, that officials free from judicial interference will fail to give due process because of the pressures they may be under and because the process cost of a hearing will come out of the budget that they manage.

The effect of Lord Reid's decision was something that *Cooper* and the other cases had not said: it imposed due process generally on administrative authorities. Administrative decisions, like judicial decisions, should be made with due process (although the form of process that is *due* will be affected by the administrative nature of the decision).

The problem of comity has been solved for tearing down houses, and for sacking police chiefs. The solution is that the process values of better outcomes, showing respect to the people in question, and subjecting the administration to the rule of law are worth pursuing, in spite of the process danger and the process cost. But the Board of Works in *Cooper* was a nineteenth-century precursor of a regulatory state that has grown massive, making decisions that affect people in very diverse ways, requiring very different forms of procedural involvement for people who want a say in the process.

Like most bad arguments, the arguments of the public authorities in *Cooper* and *Ridge* (and the successful argument of the public authority in *Nakkuda Ali*) were based on a kernel of good sense: that administrative decisions do not require the same procedures as judicial processes. The mistake was the idea that justice does not demand *any* procedural protections when a decision is administrative. Even after *Ridge*, the judges had not quite finished putting the mistake to rest. Three years later, Lord Parker CJ sorted it out again, from first principles, without even mentioning *Ridge*:

> ' . . . even if an immigration officer is not in a judicial or quasi-judicial capacity, he must at any rate give the immigrant an opportunity of satisfying him of the matters in the subsection, and for that purpose let the immigrant know what his immediate impression is so that the immigrant can disabuse him. That is not, as I see it, a question of acting or being required to act judicially, but of being required to act fairly. '[5]

Lord Parker pointed out with some embarrassment that it was difficult to reconcile this view with Lord Radcliffe's opinion for the Privy Council in *Nakkuda Ali*: 'I very much doubt, however, whether it was intended to say any more than that there is no duty to invoke judicial process unless there is a duty to act judicially' (*In re HK*, 631). That generous approach to *Nakkuda Ali* retains the kernel of good sense behind a mistaken decision: that fairness demands procedures that are proportionate to the issues at stake in the administrative process.

In the rest of this chapter, and in Chapter 5, we will see how the law determines that proportion.

Latin lesson

- *Audi alteram partem*: 'listen to each side of the story'.
- *Nemo judex in causa sua*: 'no one is to decide his own case'.

Those two maxims encompass much of procedural justice, including the common law rule against bias and the right to a fair hearing. Requiring **reasons** is *partly* an instrument for requiring the decision maker to hear both sides and to decide without bias. A right to an administrative or judicial **appeal** (or to judicial review) bolsters the *audi alteram partem* rule, by guarding the integrity and soundness of the initial determination.

---

[5]   *In re HK (an infant)* [1967] 2 QB 617, 630.

4.4 Due process is proportionate process

After *Ridge*, is there a general duty to give hearings before making administrative decisions? No. Remember *R v Ministry of Defence, ex p Walker* [2000] 1 WLR 806 (see 2.1). One of the challenges to the Army's criminal injuries compensation scheme was that it lacked due process—specifically, that it was unfair for the Ministry to restrict the criminal injuries compensation scheme without announcing the change directly to soldiers or to their commanders. But the argument was unsuccessful. Walker did not even claim that he ought to have had a hearing, but only notice—and the House of Lords held that he had no right even to that. The decision to restrict the scheme is an example of the sort of administrative action that yields *no legal right to any procedural participation* by the people affected.[6]

Due process does not mean *giving a hearing*. It means *giving a person affected by a decision a way of participating in the making of the decision that is proportionate in light of the nature of the decision*. It would be a mistake to think that *Ridge v Baldwin* simplified the law of due process. It can be very difficult to decide both the question of procedural justice (what form of participation a person ought to have) and the question of comity (whether the courts should impose their own answer to that question).

There is no better example of the depth of controversy over these questions than *Bank Mellat v HM Treasury (No 2)* [2013] UKSC 39. The majority of the Supreme Court saw it as a simple application of *Cooper* and *Ridge* (see, e.g., Lord Sumption, [29] and [44]). The Treasury had imposed financial restrictions (orders under the Counter-Terrorism Act 2008 preventing UK financial institutions from dealing with Bank Mellat). The orders had a devastating impact on the Bank's business, and the Treasury imposed them without even notifying the Bank. It was somewhat like tearing down the claimant's house without giving notice and inviting representations first. Yet the Supreme Court was deeply divided, 5–4, on whether the common law required the Treasury to consult the Bank before imposing the measures.

Lord Hope said that 'the duty to give advance notice before a statutory power that may affect the subject adversely is exercised . . . is deeply rooted in the common law' (*Bank Mellat* [146]), but he pointed out that the duty depends on the circumstances. If the Treasury needs to consult a bank before issuing restrictions, a risk arises that the bank may take steps to evade the effect of the restrictions. Giving notice to the bank and inviting it to make representations would in any case lead to delay in achieving the purpose of the restrictions. And it would be a pointless exercise if the Treasury were relying on secret information (which is bound to be the case), unless the bank has recourse to judicial review at that point (which it might well seek), which would create a really serious delay [149].

Under the Counter-Terrorism Act 2008 s 63, a bank subject to restrictions can apply to the High Court to have the restrictions set aside after they are made, and the

---

6   But even where there is no right to procedural *participation*, the fairness doctrine provides procedural *protection*: the decision must be made without bias (see 5.1.2, p 166).

dissenters thought that this form of recourse was all that fairness to the Bank required. Lord Hope concluded: 'For the court to insist on a prior duty to consult at common law would be inconsistent with the purpose of the legislation, which is to protect the national interests of the United Kingdom in circumstances where there is a significant risk to those interests, and it would contradict what I would understand to have been the will of Parliament' [153].

The points that divided the justices in *Bank Mellat* concerned both the requirements of fairness to the Bank and also the nature of their own duty of comity towards the Treasury. The consultation required by the majority creates an obvious process danger. The majority decision reflects both a view that the danger was not grave and also a judgment that the judges should assess the risk, rather than defer to the government's assessment of the risk. The minority decision reflects a greater scepticism as to that judicial role. The problem with the majority decision in *Bank Mellat* is that there is no good reason to think that the judges could assess the process danger.

Ridge v Baldwin has not made the law of due process easy; it has only established that it is up to the judges to resolve these difficult questions that determine the scope of their own authority. As Lord Reid emphasized from the beginning in *Ridge*, the answers depend on the circumstances. In Lord Denning MR's words: 'The rules of Natural Justice—or of fairness—are not cut and dried. They vary infinitely' (*R v Home Secretary, ex p Santillo* [1981] QB 778, 795). There is no general answer to the question 'What procedures does the common law require for an administrative decision?'— except that it requires *due* or *proportionate* procedures.

A question of proportionality is a question of *how much*—in this case, a question of how much procedural involvement is enough to give the necessary protection to the interests of a person affected by a decision. Proportionality does not require a jury trial on a parking ticket, because that would be superfluous for the purpose. Proportionality is a relation between two things (see 3.6, p 93)—in this case, between the procedural involvement of a person affected by a decision and the issues at stake in the decision. Suppose a court considering a charge of murder invited the defendant to make written submissions, but did not hold a trial. That would fail to give the defendant the procedural protection that is proportionate to the nature of the charge.

So what determines the variation in procedures? To what should they be proportionate? Lord Denning MR, in *Santillo*, held that the Home Secretary did *not* have to give a man a hearing when he decided to deport him at the end of his imprisonment for rape after the trial judge had recommended deportation. It did not even matter if the Home Secretary had received new information that reinforced his judgment that the man should be deported. *This* part of Lord Denning's decision puts a limit on the **duty of respect**: you do not have a right to a hearing merely because you might be able to set the record straight when a public authority has heard something derogatory about you. However, Lord Denning did not hold that a convict *generally* has no right to a hearing before deportation. He said that if a 'new adverse factor may turn the scale against the man', the Home Secretary 'should invite him to deal with it' (374). In that sort of case, the Home Secretary *would* have a duty to give notice of the adverse factor and a duty to give a hearing.

Whether a particular procedure is *due* depends on the three process values: promoting good outcomes, showing appropriate respect for a person affected, and imposing the rule of law on the process. A procedure is due if it is the right way in which to pursue those purposes, given the process cost and any process danger that may be involved.

Variation across time

Through legislation and through the development of the common law, the law's answer to the question of what procedure is due has evolved. For a glimpse into the much changed law on the procedure by which the Home Office decides whether to deport a foreign national prisoner after completion of a prison sentence, compare *Santillo* in 1981 with *R (Lumba) v Home Secretary* [2011] UKSC 12, in which the duty of the Home Office to consider representations from the prisoner was taken for granted, and the Supreme Court imposed a duty to publish the details of the Home Office's policy that a prisoner 'needs to know in order to make informed and meaningful representations to the decision-maker before a decision is made' [38]. (See 8.5.) And Chapter 12 on Tribunals chronicles the implications for administrative hearings of the establishment of a systematic scheme of tribunal hearings into complaints about administrative action that was unknown in the 1980s.

The common law of due process has largely addressed these considerations in terms of the second process value, *fairness to the claimant*, because showing respect for the person affected is the courts' special concern. Promoting the public interest in good outcomes (the first process value) and imposing the rule of law on the administrative decision making (the third value) are typically the result of requiring procedures that are fair to the claimant. So we can say that, in English law, a hearing (or some other form of procedural participation) is due:

- when **legislation** (including the Human Rights Act 1998) or a public authority's own rules require it; and

- when **fairness** (in Lord Greene MR's restricted sense in *B Johnson & Co v Minister of Health* [1947] 2 All ER 395) requires it.

But there is one proviso, which Lord Greene had in mind in *B Johnson & Co* and which is often forgotten: the requirements of procedural fairness are subject to the principle of comity. A procedure is not required unless it is possible for judges to require it without damaging the decision maker's ability to do its job. There are many ways in which public authorities could act unfairly without being subject to any judicial control. The Prime Minister might dismiss a Cabinet minister unfairly and the minister would have no legal recourse.

Subject to that proviso, fairness to the claimant is the chief focus of the law of due process. In fact, fairness is sometimes spoken of as if it were the entire reason for procedural duties. But remember that the public interests in the rule of law and

in good administration also require that public authorities be subjected to procedural duties.

4.4.1 Legislation

The decision-making processes in *Cooper, B Johnson & Co, Ridge*, and *Bank Mellat* were
all governed by legislation. It may seem that a court faces no problem of comity in giving effect to legislative procedural requirements: it is simply enforcing the rules made
by Parliament (or by a minister in delegated legislation, or through the use of the prerogative). But there is still a problem for the courts: do legislative processes exclude the
common law of due process?

The judges lean in favour of saying 'no' to that question. In *Cooper, B Johnson & Co,
Ridge*, and *Bank Mellat*, the defendants argued each time that the courts should not
impose additional procedures that the legislation had not required. In *Ridge*, for example, the police authority argued unsuccessfully that it did not need to give a hearing
because, by statute, the Home Secretary had power to overturn its decision. That argument virtually always fails, as it did in *Bank Mellat*. Citing *Cooper* and *Lloyd v McMahon*
[1987] 1 AC 625, Lord Sumption said, 'the fact that the statute makes some provision
for the procedure to be followed before or after the exercise of a statutory power does
not of itself impliedly exclude either the duty of fairness in general or the duty of prior
consultation in particular, where they would otherwise arise' (*Bank Mellat* [35]). Here,
again, the principle of legality is in action, ensuring that statutory schemes are not
treated as implicitly displacing the constitutional principle of due process.

4.4.2 Fairness

A decision is **unfair** if it wrongly neglects the interest of a person it affects: it is **procedurally** unfair if it wrongly neglects a person's interest in participating in the process;
it is **substantively** unfair if its outcome wrongly injures a person's interest (see 6.9,
p 222, on the difference between substance and process).

Since *Ridge v Baldwin*, the judges have used 'procedural fairness' as a general
term for the procedural requirements that the common law imposes.[7] Even after
Ridge, judges have sometimes suggested that natural justice involves a more demanding set of procedures, which is only required if a decision is quasi-judicial. But Lord
Denning's approach has largely taken over—he used 'natural justice' and 'fairness'
interchangeably (e.g. in *Santillo*, in 4.4, p 134; Lord Slynn did the same in *R (Alconbury)
v Environment Secretary* [2001] UKHL 23 [50]).[8] Lord Bridge said that the phrase 'the
requirements of fairness' better expresses the 'underlying concept' than 'natural justice' (*Lloyd v McMahon* [1987] 1 AC 625, 702).

---

[7]   But the roots of the doctrine go back long before the 1960s: see Lord Loreburn's remark in *Board
of Education v Rice* [1911] AC 179 (HL), 182, at the beginning of this chapter.

[8]   And see Megarry V-C's discussion of the two terms in *McInnes v Onslow-Fane* [1978] 1 WLR
1520, 1530.

┌─ **FROM THE MISTS OF TIME** ─────────────────────────────────

'Fairness' may seem like a more modern label for procedural requirements than 'natural justice'. But fairness has been a legal requirement for decision making for centuries, at least for courts of specific jurisdiction. In *R v Cowle* (1759) 2 Burr 834, 861, Lord Mansfield held that any doubt 'whether a fair, impartial, or satisfactory trial or judgment can be had there' was a reason for the Court of King's Bench to quash a decision.

└──

The link between fairness and natural justice is that procedural unfairness is an injustice: the common law of due process can be summed up by saying that 'a procedure that involves significant injustice' is unlawful, unless it is expressly authorized by statute (*R (Roberts) v Parole Board* [2005] UKHL 45 [83] (Lord Woolf)). If such an injustice is authorized by statute, the statute may be incompatible with Arts 5 or 6 of the European Convention on Human Rights.

Fairness to whom?

Note that the courts will require a public authority to act fairly not just towards the parties to a dispute, and those affected by the outcome of a decision, but also towards those affected *by the process*: for example, to witnesses at a public inquiry, or in parole board hearings, or a coroner's inquest, who might be endangered by disclosure of their identity and/or testimony (*R (A) v Lord Saville of Newdigate* [2002] 1 WLR 1249).

4.5 What's at stake in the outcome, and what's at stake in the process?

To summarize, due process (often referred to as 'procedural fairness') requires a hearing when the person affected by a decision ought to have a way of participating in the making of the decision, and that will depend on proportionality between the process values that a procedure would serve (good outcomes, respect, the rule of law) and any process costs and process danger.

It may seem that what's fair depends on the impact of the decision on the person affected. After all, the prospect of the destruction of his property is what entitled Cooper to a hearing. And Ridge stood to lose his position as Chief Constable. But it is *not* just the impact on the person affected. Remember the difference between the dismissal of a Cabinet minister by the Prime Minister, and the dismissal of Ridge by the police authority (see 4.3.2). The impact of dismissal on the Cabinet minister may be just as severe as the impact on Ridge. But because of the nature of the decision (the nature of the job of a Cabinet minister, the role of the decision maker, and the context in which the decision maker acts), the Cabinet minister has no legal right to a hearing.

Many decisions that have an enormous impact on someone's life can be made fairly without involving that person in the decision-making process. If the government sends an aircraft carrier to the other side of the globe, the decision will affect the liberty of the sailors, and the business of merchants in Portsmouth, and the family life of the sailors' children, and the life of people on the other side of the globe. None of them has any legal right to advance notice of the plan, or the reasons for it, or an opportunity to put a case to the government as to why the aircraft carrier should not be sent to sea.

Rights to involvement in a decision-making process do not depend merely on the impact of the decision on a person, but on *whether the person has something to say on the issues that are relevant to the decision*. Lord Mustill summed up the law of fair procedures accurately in *R v Home Secretary, ex p Doody* [1994] 1 AC 531, 560, by saying: 'Fairness will very often require that a person who may be adversely affected by the decision will have an opportunity to make representations.' If a person is adversely affected, fairness requires such an opportunity *very often*, but not *generally*. It is unfair to make a decision that adversely affects someone without a hearing only *if* there is a **process value** that justifies a particular procedure.

A classic statement of what it is that procedural fairness depends on

'. . . what the requirements of fairness demand . . . depends on the character of the decision-making body, the kind of decision it has to make and the statutory or other framework in which it operates.'[9]

To see why procedural fairness does not depend merely on the impact of a decision on a person adversely affected, consider the difference between parking tickets and parole decisions. If a public authority is deciding whether to fine you £70 for parking on a double yellow line, you have a right to an oral hearing before an adjudicator.[10] If the Parole Board is deciding whether you should go free, or stay in prison for many months, the impact of the decision is much greater. But you may have no right to an oral hearing (see 4.8).

But we can generalize in one way: a public authority must give some form of hearing before deciding to deprive a person of property (*Cooper*). And although Ridge had no right to continue as Chief Constable if his conduct was damaging the police force, he had a right to be heard on the question of whether that was the case. There is a general duty to give a hearing to a person whom the decision will *deprive of a legal right or a legally protected interest*, as in *Ridge*. It becomes unfair to decide without giving a person a hearing when the way in which the decision affects the person makes the person's participation relevant to the process.

---

9   *Lloyd v McMahon* [1987] AC 625, 702 (Lord Bridge).

10   See http://www.londontribunals.gov.uk/about and http://www.trafficpenaltytribunal.gov.uk.

Lord Denning's answer to the question of what determines the variation in the requirements of fairness

'. . . an administrative body may, in a proper case, be bound to give a person who is affected by their decision an opportunity of making representations. It all depends on whether he has some right or interest, or, I would add, some legitimate expectation, of which it would not be fair to deprive him without hearing what he has to say. '[11]

Personal liberty, of course, is one interest that the law is especially concerned to protect. So Lord Denning also said, 'where a public officer has power to deprive a person of his liberty or his property, the general principle is that it is not to be done without his being given an opportunity of being heard and of making representations on his own behalf' (*Schmidt*, 170). We can say something stronger about a decision to deprive a person of liberty: it is not generally a matter for **administrative authorities**; it has required *judicial* process ever since *habeas corpus* developed into a general remedy against arbitrary government in the seventeenth century (see 1.1.1).

No one can lawfully be imprisoned without a judicial hearing, unless an Act of Parliament specifically authorizes it. Special procedural protection against arbitrary detention is not just part of our history; it is also guaranteed by the European Convention. Article 5 requires a prompt explanation of the reason for an arrest, and a prompt hearing by a court that can decide whether the detention is lawful. So legislation authorizing administrative detention would have to be accompanied by a derogation from the Convention, or it would be incompatible with Art 5. And the legislation would still be incompatible if the derogation were not lawful (see 1.1.2, p 8, on *A and X v Home Secretary* [2004] UKHL 56).

Sentencing of prisoners is a task for judges, and not for the administration. Yet the Parole Board, an administrative body, can decide whether a person will be released long before the end of his or her sentence, or kept in prison for more months and years. There is no automatic right to an oral hearing, because (1) the person is subject to a sentence of imprisonment and so has no legal right to be at liberty; and (2) the issues relevant to the decision concern the protection of the public and not the guilt of the prisoner. A Parole Board decision can mean the difference between immediate release and years behind bars. So its impact can be greater than the impact of a criminal trial. But the parole process offers procedural protections for the prisoner that are much less than the protections of a criminal trial.

All three reasons for process rights depend on the value of a person's participation in the determination of an issue, as follows.

- **The interest in good outcomes**: a hearing can only improve the capacity of the decision maker to act on all of the relevant considerations if a person has something to say on the issues at stake.

---

[11] *Schmidt v Home Secretary* [1969] 2 Ch 149, 170. On legitimate expectations, see 8.4.

- **The duty of respect**: it usually shows no disrespect if the public authority makes a decision without involving you in the process if there is no value in your participation.
- **The rule of law**: process rights can protect the integrity of public decision making by standing in the way of arbitrary decisions and forcing decision makers to listen to those who have something to say on the issues relevant to the decision.

4.6 The elements of process

If you do have a right to participation in a decision-making process, what does that right give you? That varies, of course. But we can find the basic elements of fair procedure in *Ridge*. Lord Reid held that the power of dismissal cannot be exercised until the police authority 'have informed the constable of the grounds on which they propose to proceed and have given him a proper opportunity to present his case in defence' (79). Lord Hodson said that 'three features of natural justice stand out—(1) the right to be heard by an unbiased tribunal; (2) the right to have notice of charges of misconduct; (3) the right to be heard in answer to those charges' (132).

We can take these elements out of the dismissal situation and generalize: a person with a legally protected interest in the outcome of a decision is presumed to have something to say on the issues that are relevant to the decision, so that procedural fairness demands (1) no bias; (2) notice; and (3) an opportunity to make representations. You might say that the first and second follow from the entitlement to make representations: a hearing is a sham if the tribunal is biased, and a person will not be able to make representations effectively without notice of the process and of the issues.

To support these basic elements, a person affected by a decision may want some or all of the following procedural benefits.

The Menu

Publication of the process to be followed

...

Disclosure of information held by the public authority or others

An oral hearing

Openness, or confidentiality, depending on the situation

The right to be represented (by a lawyer or other advocate)

Funding for representation

...

An opportunity to present evidence and argument

An opportunity to challenge contrary evidence and argument
(possibly by cross-examining witnesses)

Reasons for the decision

. . .

Time enough to prepare representations

No unreasonable delay at any stage

All steps in the proceedings to be held in a convenient location

The option of waiving procedures

Reconsideration of an adverse decision, and/or an appeal, and/or judicial review

---

The role of judicial review

Remember that, from the complainant's point of view, judicial review forms part of the whole process. *Alconbury* (see 3.5, p 90) shows the role of judicial review in fair administrative procedures: that role is *not* to do what the administrative processes were meant to do, but only to provide sufficient judicial control to ensure an independent and impartial determination of the lawfulness of the administrative decision and procedures [49].

Procedural schemes adopted by legislation or by internal guidelines in government departments can be non-specific and leave the details of the process to the persons responsible for giving a hearing (a judicial decision like *Ridge* or *Cooper* leaves details to those persons too). But some such schemes regulate all of the details on the menu.[12] In 4.7–4.10, we will see how the courts have addressed the problem of procedural justice and the problem of comity in dealing with selected items from the menu: notice and disclosure (4.7); oral hearings (including the availability of cross-examination, and the openness of hearings) (4.8); waiver (4.9); and reconsideration and appeals (4.10).

4.7 Notice and disclosure

> ' Since the person affected usually cannot make worthwhile representations without knowing what factors may weigh against his interests fairness will very often require that he is informed of the gist of the case which he has to answer. ' [13]

---

[12] For an example of an elaborate scheme, see the Parole Board Rules 2016, SI 2016/1041.

[13] *R v Home Secretary, ex p Doody* [1994] 1 AC 531, 560 (Lord Mustill).

The requirement of informing the person affected of the 'gist of the case' is designed to serve the three purposes of a hearing:

- **the interest in good outcomes**: the person with an interest can only make a useful contribution to the process if he or she knows the issues *and* the information on which the public authority may proceed to act;

- **the duty of respect**: it is not enough for this purpose to tell the person affected that there will be a hearing—he or she needs to know what is at stake; and

- **the rule of law**: notice of issues and disclosure of information to the person affected opens up the operations of the public authority to public scrutiny.

In *B Johnson & Co v Minister of Health* [1947] 2 All ER 395 (CA) (see 4.3.1, p 129), a minister had a statutory duty to consider objections to a compulsory purchase proposed by a local authority before deciding whether to confirm the plan. Lord Greene MR held that statements made to the minister by the local authority *while he was considering the objections* had to be disclosed to the claimants (the owners of the property), saying, 'it has always been naturally said that information of that kind must be disclosed to the other party to give that other party an opportunity of controverting it, or making comments upon it' (401). It is a long-established rule that a public authority (here the Secretary of State) resolving a dispute between two parties (the claimants and the local authority) must disclose to each the information provided by the other.

But *before he received the objections,* the local authority had told the minister that the claimants were 'speculative builders', implying that the claimants would make ill-founded objections to the plan. Lord Greene MR held that the law did not require the minister to disclose information 'which he has obtained as a purely administrative person' (401). *Doody,* a landmark of due process, shows how the law on disclosure has changed since Lord Greene's day. Lord Mustill said: 'I find in the more recent cases on judicial review a perceptible trend towards an insistence on greater openness, or if one prefers the contemporary jargon "transparency", in the making of administrative decisions' (*Doody,* 561).[14] Doody was a life prisoner for whom the Home Secretary was setting a tariff—the period of time that must be spent in prison for punitive purposes before the prisoner can be considered for parole. The Home Secretary had not disclosed to Doody the judge's recommendation as to sentence. The House of Lords quashed the Home Secretary's decision and required him to decide the matter afresh, after disclosing the judge's opinion and considering what Doody might have to say about it.

The Home Secretary was still clinging to a lack of transparency in 1994, when *Doody* was decided, and here we can see a hangover of the distinction between administrative and judicial decisions. Transparency had long been the rule in decisions that

---

[14]   See 1.6.1 on the Freedom of Information Act 2000, and on other aspects of the trend towards open government.

the courts considered to be judicial; disclosure is tightly connected to the commitment to judgment in open court, which goes back to the common law's roots in the twelfth century.

As Upjohn LJ put it in *Re K (Infants)* [1963] Ch 381, 405–6:

> ' It seems to be fundamental to any judicial inquiry that a person . . . must have the right to see all the information put before the judge, to comment on it, to challenge it and if needs be to combat it, and to try to establish by contrary evidence that it is wrong. It cannot be withheld from him in whole or in part. '

Since the decision in *Doody*, that principle of judicial inquiry has been extended in administrative law to any decision in which a person has a right to a hearing, with a proviso and an exception.

General rule: if a party has a right to a hearing, the decision must be based on information that has been disclosed to that party.

Proviso: a person cannot expect disclosure that is not necessary for the purposes of his or her participation in the process.

Exception: the law may forbid disclosure of information that *does* affect the complainant's participation in the process, and may authorize consideration of the secret information by an administrative decision maker, where disclosure would involve a serious process danger. (See 4.12 on secret hearings.)

Since participation is the point of disclosure, a claimant may only have a right to learn 'the gist of the case', as Lord Mustill said in *Doody*. But the disclosure has to come in time for the party to be able to use it in the administrative process (*R v Criminal Injuries Compensation Authority, ex p Leatherland, Bramall and Kay* [2001] ACD 13 (Turner J)). Note, however, that the decision maker does not have to disclose *what he or she is thinking* before making a decision. Lord Diplock pointed out that:

> ' once a fair hearing has been given to the rival cases presented by the parties the rules of natural justice do not require the decision maker to disclose what he is minded to decide so that the parties may have a further opportunity of criticizing his mental processes before he reaches a final decision. If this were a rule of natural justice only the most talkative of judges would satisfy it and trial by jury would have to be abolished. '[15]

---

[15] *Hoffmann-La Roche v Trade and Industry Secretary* [1975] AC 295, 369.

> **Open government: an aspect of due process?**
> Bear in mind the far-reaching developments in open government in the twenty-first century: see 1.6.1. Disclosure of government information has been revolutionized by the Freedom of Information Act 2000, and by common law developments of a 'common law presumption of openness' in *Kennedy v Charity Commission* [2014] UKSC 20, the duty to publish some policies established in *R (Lumba) v Home Secretary* [2011] UKSC 12, and the expansion of duties of consultation in policy formation, in *R (Moseley) v Haringey LBC* [2014] UKSC 56. All of these developments represent developments in the law of administrative process, as they change the information available to people seeking to challenge administrative action. In *Moseley*, the majority of the Supreme Court accepted Lord Wilson's view that the content of a statutory duty to consult was determined by the 'common law duty of procedural fairness' (*Moseley* [23]).

4.8 Oral hearings

4.8.1 Oral hearings are exceptional

Even when a hearing is due, there is no general requirement that the decision maker meet the complainant face to face. That is, an *oral* hearing is not generally required: 'Natural justice does not generally demand orality' (*R (Morgan Grenfell & Co Ltd) v Special Commissioner of Income Tax* [2001] EWCA Civ 329 [47] (Blackburne J)). In that case, a tax inspector asked a Special Commissioner (that is, a tax tribunal) for permission to require disclosure of documents from a taxpayer; the taxpayer sought judicial review of the Special Commissioner's refusal to give him an oral hearing on the question of whether to order disclosure. The Court of Appeal held that an oral hearing would be 'worth little without knowledge of the case that has to be met' (at [50]). And the taxpayer had no right to know the reasons why the tax inspector was asking for permission. So giving an oral hearing would be useless. And it might be worse than useless: it would be 'destructive of the whole purpose of the procedure' if it were to lead to disclosure of the reasons for the inspector's request. So **because of the process danger** that an oral hearing would involve, the Court of Appeal held that the Special Commissioner must not give an oral hearing.

But an oral hearing is not guaranteed, even when there is no such process danger and the consequences of the decision are serious. It depends on whether an oral hearing would make a difference on the issues at stake. In the classic case of *Lloyd v McMahon* [1987] AC 625, the House of Lords held that an oral hearing was unnecessary for a decision by an auditor that forty-nine councillors should reimburse Liverpool Council for a loss of more than £100,000 caused by their misconduct in delaying setting a rate (they were trying to put pressure on central government to increase the Council's funding). The case is a reminder that procedural rights do not simply depend on the impact of a decision on the claimant; they depend, instead, on the nature of the public authority making the decision, on the issues that need to be decided, and on the statutory framework in which the decision was made. And, as a result, procedural rights depend on whether the claimant has something to say on the issues. The auditor found misconduct and bad faith, and those findings will generally call for an oral hearing if they are relevant to the decision. Yet no oral hearing was called for in *Lloyd*, because it would have made no difference to the facts on which the auditor properly based his decision, after considering the councillors' written response.

Even when a Parole Board decides to revoke parole and return a prisoner to jail, the common law duty of fairness may not require an oral hearing. But it often will do so, as in *R (West) v Parole Board* [2005] UKHL 1. West had got into trouble while on parole; the facts were messy and obscure. He had been breaking his parole rules by visiting his former partner and not staying at the required address, and he wanted to do a lot of explaining. The House of Lords held that he should have been given an oral hearing, and that the duty to do so was wider than the Parole Board had thought, even though it depended on the circumstances. At [35], Lord Bingham said:

> ' Even if important facts are not in dispute, they may be open to explanation or mitigation, or may lose some of their significance in the light of other new facts. While the board's task certainly is to assess risk, it may well be greatly assisted in discharging it (one way or the other) by exposure to the prisoner or the questioning of those who have dealt with him. . . . The prisoner should have the benefit of a procedure which fairly reflects, on the facts of his particular case, the importance of what is at stake for him, as for society. '

Like the common law duty of fairness, Art 6 of the Convention does not generally demand an oral hearing for administrative decisions, either. Its title is 'Right to a fair trial', but that is misleading. It gives a right to a trial only for certain sorts of determinations of civil rights and obligations: those that call for a trial. And although it gives a right to a trial on a criminal charge, it allows some decisions determining length of custody to be made without an oral hearing. One example is *R v Home Secretary, ex p Dudson* [2005] UKHL 52, decided after the European Court of Human Rights had held that the tariff for young offenders convicted of murder had to be determined by an independent decision maker (*V v United Kingdom* (2000) 30 EHRR 121—see 3.1, p 75). In order to comply with that decision, the Home Secretary asked the Lord Chief Justice to review Dudson's tariff. Under the Home Secretary's scheme, the Lord Chief Justice decided the matter on written representations, and recommended a reduction from eighteen years to sixteen. Dudson claimed that the Lord Chief Justice's decision had been unlawful because Art 6(1) of the Convention gave him a right to an oral hearing. The House of Lords held that his original trial satisfied the right to a fair and public hearing on a criminal charge; after that, he had to be dealt with fairly, but (said Lord Hope, at [34]):

> ' ... the application of [Art 6(1)] to proceedings other than at first instance depends on the special features of the proceedings in question. Account must be taken ... of the role of the person or persons conducting the proceedings that are in question, the nature of the system within which they are being conducted and the scope of the powers that are being exercised. The overriding question ... is whether the issues that had to be dealt with at the stage could properly, as a matter of fair trial, be determined without hearing the applicant orally. '

That requirement of fairness depended on whether any information the applicant could have provided at an oral hearing would have added anything. The decision was a firm endorsement of the **principle of relativity**, even in the application of a Convention right. In fact, the requirements of Art 6 even depend, in one respect, on **process cost**: the House of Lords held that, because the Lord Chief Justice had an obligation under Art 6(1) to carry out the exercise within a reasonable time, he did not have to give hearings that would be bound to delay the review of tariffs unreasonably for no good purpose.

Oral hearings

Oral hearings are generally required for:

- deprivations of legal rights or legally protected interests, and in particular:
  - any serious disciplinary or other penalty;[16] and
  - dismissal from a public office 'where there must be something against a man to warrant his dismissal' (*Ridge v Baldwin* [1964] AC 40, 65 (Lord Reid)), and therefore a hearing is not required in dismissing a minister from office.

They are required *if* fairness demands it for:

- refusals of release on parole (*Osborn v Parole Board* [2013] UKSC 61);
- objections to a grant of planning permission (*R (Adlard) v Environment Secretary* [2002] EWCA Civ 735);
- review of tariff for young offenders (*R (Dudson) v Home Secretary* [2005] UKHL 52); and
- applications for licences (*R v Gaming Board, ex p Benaim and Khaida* [1970] 2 QB 417, 430).

They are routine for:

- parole revocation for life-sentence prisoners (*R (West) v Parole Board* [2005] UKHL 1 [27]; *Osborn v Parole Board* [2013] UKSC 61).

---

16   But *Lloyd v McMahon* [1987] 1 AC 625 is an exception.

> **Note** that although the *Osborn* decision did not require an oral hearing for all
> Parole Board decisions, it led to a massive overhaul of the process. The Parole
> Board announced that the Supreme Court decision 'fundamentally changes the
> way the Parole Board must view the concept of an oral hearing and significantly
> broadens the circumstances in which the law requires it to hold one'.[17]

The judges have a fondness for oral argument, and they are aware of the difference it
can make to the decision maker.[18] But the common view is that oral hearings are not
'the very pith of the administration of natural justice' (*R v Local Government Board, ex
p Arlidge* [1914] 1 KB 160, 192–3, endorsed by Woolf LJ in *Lloyd v McMahon* [1987]
1 AC 625, 670). They are required when the issues can only be dealt with justly and
effectively if the decision maker sees the parties face to face.

Public authorities generally have discretion to give an oral hearing in the operation of statutory schemes; this is one instance of the principle of legality (see 1.5.5). A
public authority will be treated as having a discretion to give an oral hearing even if the
statute does not confer the power to do so, and the public authority will have a duty to
do so where it would be unfair to proceed without one. We can see the principle tested
almost to its limit in *R (Hammond) v Home Secretary* [2005] UKHL 69. The Criminal
Justice Act 2003 provided that a life prisoner's tariff 'is to be determined by a single
judge of the High Court without an oral hearing' (*Hammond* [5]). The House of Lords
held that this rule was subject to the judge's discretionary power to give an oral hearing if fairness required it. This remarkable decision was only possible because of the
Human Rights Act 1988 s 3, and the issue was not argued because the Home Secretary
accepted the idea. But the fact is that the House of Lords accepted that it was 'possible'
to interpret a statute *prohibiting oral hearings* as *allowing an oral hearing* where fairness
requires it (see 3.3.1, pp 80).

4.8.2 Opportunity to cross-examine

Complainants who are dissatisfied with a decision of a public authority will often
claim (sometimes rightly) that the process was unfair because the information before
the decision maker ought to have been tested through the same sort of demanding,
adversarial procedures as in the courts. Cross-examination is the best example of such
a procedure, and it is not easy to get a court to order it.

There is no general right to cross-examine witnesses who give evidence before a
public authority (*Bushell v Environment Secretary* [1981] AC 75 (HL)). The government's duty to investigate deaths under the Convention has not changed that principle: in *R (D) v Home Secretary* [2006] EWCA Civ 143, the Court of Appeal overturned
a High Court decision that there was a right to cross-examine in a public inquiry

---

[17] http://www.gov.uk/government/collections/parole-review-changes-in-reponse-to-the-osborn-
judgment.

[18] Compare the importance that oral hearings have in tribunal proceedings: see 12.4.5.

concerning an attempted suicide in prison. There is no general right to cross-examination in the relevant legislation (Inquiries Act 2005), and the Court of Appeal held that it should be up to the chair of an inquiry. That principle concerning inquiries has a more general application: cross-examination is not a general requirement of a fair hearing, but a public authority conducting an oral hearing will generally have discretion to allow cross-examination, and must do so *if* it is necessary for the purposes that require the hearing.

4.8.3 Open hearings

Among the fundamental rules of judicial decision making, Lord Devlin included the rule 'that all justice shall be done openly' (*Re K (Infants)* [1965] AC 201, 237). It is one respect in which open government is a very old principle (see 1.6.1). There are many exceptions, even in the High Court (e.g., in family law proceedings involving children). But we can take it as a general rule that any oral hearing by an administrative authority is to be held in public unless there is reason to do otherwise. This means that 'closed material procedures' and the use of secret hearings, discussed in 4.12, ought to be very exceptional.

The same imperative was written into the requirement of a 'fair and *public* hearing' in Art 6 of the Convention. That requirement seems to be presented as a necessity for any determination of civil rights. But as with the rest of the seemingly categorical requirements of Art 6, the Strasbourg Court and the English courts have found a way to recognize the principle of relativity, and to dilute this apparent essential into a default requirement that can be overridden. For example, public inquiries are *on behalf* of the public, but they need not be *held* in public, even after the Human Rights Act 1998 (*R (Persey) v Environment Secretary* [2002] EWHC 371).

4.9 Waiver

If you have a right to a hearing, and the public authority offers to hear you and you decline, then you cannot get judicial review on the ground that you were not given a hearing. A process is not due to the claimant if the claimant waives it. So in claims for judicial review on the ground that the claimant was not given a hearing, public authorities often argue that the claimant waived a hearing; they seldom succeed.

In *R (West) v Parole Board* [2005] UKHL 1 [50], Lord Slynn said: 'On any view the applicant should be told that an oral hearing may be possible though it is not automatic; if having been told this the applicant clearly says he does not want an oral hearing then there need not be such a hearing unless the board itself feels exceptionally that fairness requires one.' So it is possible to waive an oral hearing when the Parole Board is deciding whether to revoke parole (a context in which the decision maker ought to be 'predisposed in favour of an oral hearing'). An informed and express waiver will evidently be effective unless there are exceptional reasons. The principles are tolerably clear—you can waive a hearing in an administrative process, but:

- you will not ordinarily be taken to have waived a hearing just because you did not insist on having one;

- an ill-informed waiver will not count as a genuine waiver; and

- there may be circumstances in which a process is improper because a procedure ought to have been taken even though it *was* waived.

If you think of the three reasons for process rights, these principles make sense. The **duty of respect** for the claimant means taking his or her word at face value in deciding what procedures to take. In fact, to give no effect to a well-informed waiver is to treat the claimant as incapable of making a responsible decision. Where the **interest in good outcomes** would ordinarily require some procedure, we can ordinarily be confident that a public authority can reach a good outcome without it, if the person whose interests are at stake is well informed and has waived the procedure. And it may be compatible with the **rule of law** for a person to waive a procedure, as long as the waiver is open and informed.

But for rule-of-law reasons, waiver is impossible if it would put the integrity of the process in doubt. When we come to the law of bias, we will see that, in some circumstances, the law will not allow a party to waive the right to complain that a decision was biased (see 5.2.2, p 175).

Compare the criminal process

You cannot waive a trial on a serious criminal charge, but you can plead guilty, and if you plead not guilty, you need offer no evidence. You cannot appeal from a conviction merely on the ground that you did not have a fair hearing because you pleaded guilty. These features of the process give the defendant a measure of control over his situation that is compatible with the administration of justice.

4.10 Reconsideration and appeals

Here is one fundamental difference between administrative process and judicial process: administrative decision makers have **no general doctrine of** *res judicata* (the rule that a judicial decision cannot be challenged or reopened, except in an appeal or a lawful challenge to the court's jurisdiction). The High Court ordinarily has no jurisdiction to reconsider its own decisions. But administrative decision makers do have that power:

> ❛ Fairness will very often require that a person who may be adversely affected by the decision will have an opportunity to make representations on his own behalf either before the decision is taken with a view to producing a favourable result; or after it is taken, with a view to procuring its modification; or both. ❜ [19]

---

[19]   *R v Home Secretary, ex p Doody* [1994] 1 AC 531, 560 (Lord Mustill).

A decision in your favour may give you a legitimate expectation (see 8.4, p 297) that the public authority's stance will *not* be modified. But if the decision is adverse, you may be able to ask for reconsideration (if no one else has a legitimate expectation and there is no public interest that makes it fair to refuse the request). And very commonly legislation will also give you a right to appeal a decision to another decision maker (typically to a tribunal—see Chapter 12).

Reconsideration and administrative appeals must be conducted with due process, and the complainant will ordinarily need to make use of any such process before seeking judicial review. It may seem that an administrative appeal would make judicial review on due process grounds unnecessary—and it *ought* to do so, because judicial review is not available if it is superfluous. But, in fact, the availability of an administrative appeal often does not block judicial review on due process grounds, because (1) any irregularity in the appeal will itself be ground for judicial review; and (2) a process failure in the initial decision will not necessarily be cured by an appeal.

Remember that, in *Ridge*, the police chief had actually benefited from *both* reconsideration by the police authority *and* an appeal to the Home Secretary. When Ridge brought his action for a declaration of illegality, the police authority argued that each of these procedures cured the defect in the initial decision to sack Ridge without a hearing. Lord Reid held that a proper reconsideration would have solved the defect:

> ' I do not doubt that if an officer or body realises that it has acted hastily and reconsiders the whole matter afresh, after affording to the person affected a proper opportunity to present his case, then its later decision will be valid. ' [20]

But the police authority's reconsideration was 'very inadequate' (*Ridge*, 79), because there was no disclosure of the case against Ridge. As for the appeal to the Home Secretary, the Law Lords' explanation of its role is complicated by their conclusion that the initial decision was a nullity (see 10.4.8, p 401, on the effect of nullity). That approach obscures the real problem with the appeal to the Home Secretary, which is suggested in Lord Reid's speech: the Home Secretary merely decided that there was 'sufficient material on which the watch committee could properly exercise their power of dismissal' (81). Because the appeal did not give Ridge the opportunity to contest that material, it did not correct the process failure in the initial decision. Ridge would have had no case if he had been given either a genuine rehearing with proper disclosure from the police, or a decision from the Home Secretary remitting the matter to a differently constituted committee of the authority for a proper hearing. Ordinarily, an administrative appeal can only cure a procedural defect in the original hearing if the appeal itself amounts to a whole new hearing with fair procedure, or results in the matter being sent back to the initial decision maker to be dealt with fairly.

[20]   *Ridge v Baldwin* [1964] AC 40, 79.

> ### Curing procedural defects
>
> It is possible for a defect in process to be remedied by an appeal or rehearing, but only if the new process gets to the substance of the problem. In *R (Cart) v Upper Tribunal* [2010] EWCA Civ 859, an administrative decision was made to increase the child support that the claimant had to pay, without notice to him. He appealed to the First-tier Tribunal (see 12.4.10, p 468) and lost his appeal. The Upper Tribunal held that he had no right to appeal further on the ground of the unfair procedure, because the First-tier Tribunal gave 'full and fresh consideration' to the issues that ought to have been addressed in the initial decision [44]. The question is one of proportionate process: a procedural injustice ought to be remedied by giving the person in question *enough* of a rehearing to solve the problem.

4.11 Discretion in process

Do administrative authorities have discretion in deciding what procedures to follow (see 7.2, p 247, on what discretion is)? The courts require them to give the *right* procedures, and not just to reach reasonable conclusions as to what procedures to follow. In *Osborn v Parole Board* [2013] UKSC 61, the Supreme Court emphatically rejected the idea that the role of the court is to decide whether the defendant made reasonable decisions as to what would be fair: 'That is not correct. The court must determine for itself whether a fair procedure was followed. . . . Its function is not merely to review the reasonableness of the decision-maker's judgment of what fairness required' (Lord Reed, [65]). It may seem that there is no room for discretion.

But in fact, depending on the circumstances, public authorities can have a considerable latitude of discretion in deciding on procedures. There may be different types of proceeding that are fair and are compatible with legislation. As Lord Mustill said in *Doody* (at 560–1):

> ‘ [I]t is not enough . . . to persuade the court that some procedure other than the one adopted by the decision-maker would be better or more fair. Rather, they must show that the procedure is actually unfair. The court must constantly bear in mind that it is to the decision maker, not the court, that Parliament has entrusted not only the making of the decision but also the choice as to how the decision is made. ’

In addition, the House of Lords identified an 'implied power of an administrative body to *enhance the fairness* available to a person who otherwise would be adversely affected by the lack of that power' (*R (Roberts) v Parole Board* [2005] UKHL 45 [65] (Lord Woolf)). That power implicitly gives public authorities in general a discretionary power to invent procedures that are required neither by legislation nor by the common law. But as the *Roberts* case itself shows, those inventions may be extremely controversial, and will be subject to judicial supervision, and will be ruled unlawful if the judges decide that they are unfair. So, as Lord Woolf had put it in an earlier decision, even if a public authority 'is master of its own procedure and has considerable discretion as to what procedure it wishes to adopt, it must still be fair. Whether a decision reached in the exercise of its discretion is fair or not is ultimately one which will be determined by the courts' (*R v Lord Saville of Newdigate, ex p A* [2000] 1 WLR 1855 [38]).

In summary, since proportionality is the organizing principle of due process, the judges' role in controlling procedural decisions is the same as their role in controlling those decisions of substance for which proportionality is the standard of judicial control (see 8.3). Even though it can be a very intrusive form of review, it still leaves considerable free choice to the public authority.

● *Pop quiz* ●

Inquiries, such as the 'Bloody Sunday' inquiry into deaths in Northern Ireland in the *Lord Saville* case, have 'wide discretion as to the procedure' they take.[21] Why is that?

4.12 Secret hearings and process danger

In the borderlands between administrative justice and criminal justice lie the problems of the detention of people with a mental illness who have committed acts of violence, the detention of asylum seekers, a variety of government actions in dealing with terrorism suspects, and the detention of prisoners who have completed their tariff, or who have been recalled to prison for violating conditions of parole. There is often relevant information that the decision maker, or other parties, do not want disclosed to the public, or to the person affected by the decision.

Harry Roberts was involved in the bloody murder of three policemen in London in 1966—a year after Parliament suspended the death penalty. He shot two of the officers. He was given an especially long tariff of thirty years; in periodic reviews after the tariff expired in 1996, the Parole Board had to decide whether his detention was 'no longer necessary for the protection of the public',[22] in which case he must be released. In a deeply divided decision in *Roberts*, the House of Lords approved a **special advocate** scheme that the Parole Board had invented for itself. The Home Secretary gave the Board information that the Board withheld from Roberts, in order to protect the sources [3]. But the Board appointed a lawyer to make representations on Roberts's behalf and disclosed the information to the lawyer. Roberts sought judicial review of the decision to appoint a lawyer for him, whom he was not allowed to meet.

----

21 *Bushell v Environment Secretary* [1981] AC 75 (HL) at 96 (concerning a local inquiry under the Highways Act 1959 with no statutory rules of procedure); cf. *R (Persey) v Environment Secretary* [2002] EWHC 371 (discretion whether to receive evidence in private in a public inquiry into the outbreak of foot and mouth disease).

22 By the combined effect of the Crime (Sentences) Act 1997 s 28(6) and the decision of the House of Lords in *R v Lichniak* [2002] UKHL 47 [8] and [29].

The House of Lords held by a majority that the invention of the scheme was within the powers of the Board to take steps incidental to its decisions. The decision depended on a crucial condition: the ability of the Board to withhold relevant information from prisoners. Rules made by the Home Secretary under the Criminal Justice Act 1991 s 32(5) provided that the Board could do so on the ground of 'national security, prevention of disorder or crime or the health and welfare of the prisoner or others' (*Roberts* [22]). The majority reckoned that if the Board could lawfully withhold evidence, then giving the prisoner a special advocate is better than nothing. So Lord Woolf said that the scheme 'can only enhance the rights of a life sentence prisoner' [67]. He saw the power to arrange special advocates as an instance of a public authority's implied discretion to 'enhance the fairness' of its process [65].

So why was there a vehement dissent by Lord Bingham and Lord Steyn? Lord Bingham appealed to the **principle of legality**: access to an adversarial hearing had a process value that the law protects. So, in their general power to make and to apply procedural rules, the Home Secretary and the Board should not be able to detract from that value, unless the statute expressly authorized it (and, by contrast, Parliament *has* authorized special advocate schemes in other fields—see pp 154–156).

Lord Steyn called the Parole Board's proceedings a 'phantom hearing' (*Roberts* [88]), and an 'evisceration of the right to a fair hearing' [89]. He too relied on the principle of legality [93], and said that the majority decision was 'contrary to the rule of law' [97]. He even called Roberts's situation 'Kafkaesque'.

The Kafka test for due process: what Josef K didn't know

Franz Kafka's 1925 novel *The Trial* portrays the terror and helplessness of a defendant who is arrested and not told the case against him. In fact, Josef K doesn't know:

- what the charges are;
- who is pressing the charges;
- which court is hearing the charges;
- where the court is;
- when he is supposed to appear; or
- what decisions, if any, are made during the proceeding.

Josef has a lawyer, but the lawyer talks nonsense. When Josef actually finds the court after wandering through a confusing block of flats, there are many officials doing nothing in particular, and every session ends inconclusively. *The Trial* is a nightmare in the form of a novel. Look away from the footnote if you don't want to know the ending.[23]

In *Roberts*, Lord Rodger said that references to Kafka were 'inapposite' [110].

---

23 The officials stab him to death without telling him why. It could have been worse: among Kafka's other protagonists, one commits suicide on the say-so of his father, one is transformed into a hideous insect and dies slowly, and one is mutilated by his own torture machine.

The emotional argument reflects alarm about the very idea of special advocates. The word 'special' should make the hairs stand up on the back of a lawyer's neck: it means a departure from the basic responsibility to the client, which gives a certain integrity to the lawyer's job. And the link isn't only important to the advocate: without it, the person 'represented' does not have the slightest reason to have confidence in his or her advocate. Any appointment of a special advocate represents a disruption in the ethical basis of the legal profession, and a departure from its history.

Roberts was controversial because it concerned an administrative decision about detention. Like the Parole Board, the criminal process tries to protect witnesses. That is difficult. And a secret hearing in a criminal prosecution is not an option: in English law, no one can be convicted of a crime or sentenced on the basis of secret evidence. But Harry Roberts had been convicted in an open trial, and sentenced to life in prison. Roberts's situation was *different* from the situation of Josef K in Kafka's novel, because Roberts knew exactly why he was sent to prison, *and* that he was sent to prison for life, subject to a non-judicial process for considering early release, *and* that the protection of the public is the only issue in the parole decision. So if there is a justification for the majority decision, it is that, in the administration of that life sentence, it is fair to act on secret information in the interest of protecting informants.

Lord Steyn and Lord Bingham suggested that a special advocate arrangement is *in itself* contrary to a fundamental legal value, so that it ought to require express authorization by Parliament. There has been no shortage of such statutes; they have mushroomed in the twenty-first century, and culminated in the Justice and Security Act 2013. In *Al Rawi* v *Security Service* [2011] UKSC 34, the Supreme Court had refused to approve a secret hearing in a High Court action for damages, holding that the common law did not allow such a proceeding, and that only Parliament could authorize it. Lord Brown said that the reason was 'the damage [that would be] done by a closed procedure to the integrity of the judicial process and the reputation of English justice' [83]. Yet Parliament proceeded to give the courts discretion in any civil case to follow a 'closed material procedure' (ss 6, 8). That term is only a lawyer's euphemism for a secret hearing: a closed material procedure does not just mean showing secret material to the court. Since no one but the government and the judges is allowed to see the material, it also means using a special advocate and, of course, a closed hearing in which the material is considered, and argument can be heard in secret. A closed material proceeding turns an administrative tribunal into a secret tribunal, and a court into a secret court.

Our twenty-first-century legacy: secret hearings

There were no special advocates until 1997.[24] Now, just look at the variety of schemes in which they may be used; these are just examples.

---

[24]   See *Roberts* [28], where Lord Bingham catalogues the schemes listed here.

- **Special Immigration Appeals Commission (SIAC)**: for decisions to remove foreigners from Britain on national security grounds when some of the evidence is top secret (Special Immigration Appeals Commission Act 1997 s 6). A special advocate 'shall not be responsible to the person whose interests he is appointed to represent' (s 6(4)). The advocate can see evidence that is withheld from the appellant and can cross-examine secret witnesses, but cannot communicate with the appellant without permission from the SIAC after seeing secret material.
- **Proscribed Organisations Appeal Commission**: set up to hear appeals from bodies outlawed as terrorist organizations (Proscribed Organisations Appeal Commission (Procedure) Rules 2001, SI 2001/443, r 9).
- **Pathogens Access Appeal Commission**: the Attorney General may appoint 'a person to represent the interests of any person who will be prevented from hearing or inspecting any evidence' on grounds of national security (Pathogens Access Appeal Commission (Procedure) Rules 2002, SI 2002/1845, r 8).
- **Employment Tribunals**: a minister may, 'if he considers it expedient in the interests of national security', direct an Employment Tribunal to hold a secret hearing (Employment Tribunals (Constitution and Rules of Procedure) Regulations 2004 Sch 1, r 54). See *Tariq v Home Office* [2011] UKSC 35.
- **Local planning inquiries**: if the Secretary of State decides that a local planning inquiry is to be held in secret on national security grounds, the Attorney General may appoint a special advocate to represent the Interests of any person prevented from being there (Planning and Compulsory Purchase Act 2004 s 80).
- **Terrorism prevention and investigation measures (TPIMs)**: special advocates to be appointed in the proceedings in which the Home Secretary asks for permission to impose a TPIM (that is, an order restricting the movement and providing for monitoring of persons suspected of involvement in terrorism), or a person subject to a TPIM appeals against it (Terrorism Prevention and Investigation Measures Act 2011, Sch 4).
- **Parole Board hearings**: where the Board can lawfully withhold evidence from the prisoner, it may appoint a special advocate to make representations on behalf of the prisoner (*Roberts*).
- **Financial restriction proceedings**: the Counter-Terrorism Act 2008 s 66 provides for closed material procedures in cases on measures taken by the Treasury against persons believed to have been involved in the finance of terrorism or of nuclear proliferation (see *Bank Mellat*).
- **Any civil proceeding**: where a court makes a declaration under the Justice and Security Act 2013 'that the proceedings are proceedings in which a closed material application may be made to the court' (ss 6, 9).

> ## When the courts have appointed special advocates
>
> - In an appeal against a decision of the SIAC, where necessary on national security grounds, in *Home Secretary v Rehman* [2003] 1 AC 153 [31]–[32]. It is only to be done 'in the most extreme circumstances' (Lord Woolf [31]).
> - On an application for judicial review by a member or former member of a security service, if the security service asked for consideration of material 'too sensitive to be disclosed' to the party's legal advisers: *R v Shayler* [2003] 1 AC 247 (HL) [34].
> - For deciding whether the public interest requires information to be withheld from the defence in a criminal prosecution, if 'no other course will adequately meet the overriding requirement of fairness to the defendant' (*R v H* [2004] UKHL 3 [22]).[25]

There is a **process danger**—not mentioned in the speeches in *Roberts*—that may lie behind the dissent in that case: a special advocate scheme risks making non-disclosure normal. It will be easier for the Parole Board to persuade itself to withhold information from a prisoner if there is a scheme that does something to help out the prisoner when it does so. But it should always be a crisis when a decision maker acts on secret information that is adverse to a party who has a right to a hearing.

In all of these secret hearings schemes, there is:

(1) a process danger that **motivates** the scheme—if an open hearing is the only option, the public interest (or interests of individuals) might be harmed either by the publication of sensitive information, or by the court's inability to consider relevant information; and

(2) a process danger that **results from** the scheme—secret hearings and special advocates risk sacrificing the benefits of due process (that is, good decisions, respect, and the rule of law).

The courts have, to some extent, tried to stem the tide; the *Roberts* case is exceptional, and the courts will not ordinarily approve of the invention of secret hearings without statutory authority: in *R (B) v Westminster Magistrates' Court* [2015] AC 1195, the Supreme Court refused to allow a Magistrates' Court to invent a secret hearing to consider secret evidence in extradition proceedings. And in the operation of secret hearings, the courts will err on the side of disclosure, and will require that the gist of the closed material be disclosed where possible (*Home Secretary v AF* (No 3) [2009] UKHL 28). As Mr Justice Irwin put it in *Kamoka v Security Service* [2015] EWHC 3307 [12] and [20]:

---

25   Note that secret evidence cannot be presented by the prosecution; *Re H* concerned evidence that the Crown would ordinarily need to disclose to the defendant in a criminal proceeding. The Crown asked the court to hold that the evidence was subject to 'public interest immunity'; the court will not make such an order if it would result in an unfair prosecution, and then the Crown would need to withdraw the prosecution in order to avoid disclosing the information.

> ' the closed material procedure instigated by the [Justice and Security Act 2013] is in conflict with the ordinary principles of fairness of common law . . . common law must introduce fairness so far as possible and so far as is consistent with the provisions of the Act. '

His conclusion was that as much should be disclosed as possible, and material that could not be disclosed should be 'gisted' as fully as possible. 'Beyond that, common law cannot go' [20].

Secret hearings have become a systematically entrenched aspect of administrative justice. And just once, the UK Supreme Court has held a secret hearing. It may not happen again for a long time. In *Bank Mellat v HM Treasury* (No 2) [2013] UKSC 39 (see 4.4), Lord Neuberger started off by saying: 'The idea of a court hearing evidence or argument in private is contrary to the principle of open justice, which is fundamental to the dispensation of justice in a modern, democratic society' [2]. But he was in the majority—six Justices to three—that agreed to the first ever secret hearing in the Supreme Court or the House of Lords. The Treasury lawyers said that there was information that they could only disclose under a closed material procedure, that might make a difference to the decision. The justices held a secret hearing and saw the material; after the secret hearing they all said that they needn't have seen it. That relieved them of having to give a secret judgment (that is, a set of reasons explaining their view of the 'closed material', which would amount to a secret report to the government). Lord Hope considered that prospect to be 'obnoxious' [98], and castigated the Treasury for misusing the procedure in its request for a closed material procedure in the Supreme Court [100].

The other justices shared Lord Hope's view that it will be best if the Supreme Court never has to issue a secret judgment. That attitude is bound to shape the courts' approach to the discretion they have been given under the Justice and Security Act 2013, to agree to secret hearings in any civil case. And in future, the government's lawyers are going to think long and hard before they ask the Supreme Court to hold a secret hearing.

● *Pop quiz* ●
What would happen if secret hearings were not permitted in any court or tribunal?

4.13 Conclusion: the irony of process

The justice of the common law has often misfired; when it works, it imposes due process on the administration even where Parliament (and the administration itself) failed to do so. Imposing due process is the best thing that judges can do to improve administration. The **dangers** of process are not serious dangers if process is kept in proportion. The **costs** of administrative processes are massive, but these are the costs of the rule of law, and they are, generally, a bargain for the public. As Lord Reed has pointed out, 'procedures which involve an immediate cost but contribute to better decision-making are in reality less costly than they may appear' (*Osborn v Parole Board* [2013] UKSC 61 [72]). And in any case, justice often demands that the public pay the cost: **process failure** is an invitation to arbitrary government. So process cost has a very strictly limited relevance to the question of what procedures a court should impose: 'The most that can be said is that the more burdensome and far-reaching the consequences, the more carefully must be scrutinised the rule that is said to produce them. . . . The concepts of natural justice and the duty to be fair must not be allowed to discredit themselves by making unreasonable requirements and imposing undue burdens' (*McInnes v Onslow-Fane* [1978] 1 WLR 1520, 1533–5).

But the courts have never been prepared to allow an unfair administrative procedure on the ground that a fair procedure would be costly. It is *not* usually the role of the courts to tell the government what costs it should incur (see 7.3.2). But in *R (Howard League for Penal Reform) v Lord Chancellor* [2017] EWCA Civ 244, the Court of Appeal broke new ground, holding that the Lord Chancellor had acted unlawfully in withdrawing funding for legal aid for some decisions before the Parole Board on whether prisoners could be moved to open conditions, and in Prisons Service decisions as to whether a prisoner should be assigned to a special centre for disruptive prisoners. The reasoning was carefully limited to situations in which the prisoner could not be assisted in other ways to participate effectively in the process [51], and depended on a finding of 'systemic unfairness' [6] for which the threshold is high. Yet the decision was simply based on the common law of procedural fairness, and the Court of Appeal relied on *Doody* and *Osborn* [33]–[40]. Along with the Supreme Court decision in *R (UNISON) v Lord Chancellor* [2017] UKSC 51 (quashing the Lord Chancellor's imposition of fees for bringing claims in the Employment Tribunals; see 1.5.5), the *Howard League* case shows a new willingness by the courts to outlaw governmental austerity policies, if they result in unfair processes.

The **core rationale** (see 2.8) for judicial review supports the wide-ranging common law techniques of due process. So it is not necessarily a breach of comity for courts to invent their own ways of interfering with other public authorities. Even the *Howard League* case—making it unlawful for an administrative authority *not* to spend its funds on legal aid—is not a breach of comity, unless it damages the public authority's capacity to do its job.[26] The courts do not generally damage that capacity when, for example, they require a public authority to listen to both sides, or to decide impartially, or to give *its own* reasons for decision.

But even these basics are not required of every executive decision: when the Prime Minister is thinking of dismissing a minister, she ought to listen to people who have something to say on the issues, and it may be important for her to talk to the minister first (depending on the issues), and in any case she shouldn't be biased and she should have good reasons. But *the law* does not require her to listen to anyone, or to tell anyone

---

[26]   And note that the government has the option, after *Howard League*, of asking Parliament to legislate to limit legal aid funding.

her reasons, or even to decide impartially. If procedural requirements are pointless, or if imposing them would damage the public authority's function, then comity requires the court to stay out of it.

The law has to respond to the **principle of relativity** (see 1.3). But look at the consequences: if process rights depend on the type of decision and the context in which it is made, there is considerable room for litigation over the particular requirements of the case. In *R (Thompson) v Law Society* [2004] EWCA Civ 167 [45], the Court of Appeal held that fairness may require an oral hearing for a complaint of inadequate service against a solicitor: 'What is fair depends upon the circumstances of the particular case. I can imagine circumstances in which an adjudicator or appeal panel might think it appropriate to hold an oral hearing and there may even be cases in which the court would intervene to quash a decision refusing to do so.' The result is a litigation trap: for any solicitor who loses without an oral hearing, judicial review is a potential recourse, and a potential technique for fighting the decision. The extent of the litigation trap depends, first of all, on how clearly potential claimants and potential defendants can see from a case like *Thompson* whether judicial review is pointless or promising, and second, on how stringent the judges are in granting permission for a claim for judicial review. Certainty would be gained by a blanket rule requiring oral hearings, or a blanket rule that they are not required. But either approach would fail to offer proportionate process. So the cost of *proportionate* process is the *excess* of process that is generated by the litigation trap.

> **Any obstacle to arbitrary use of power will also pose a potential obstacle to the sensible use of the power.** And it will give the losing party a technique for fighting an administrative decision that was perfectly fair and reasonable. In order to guarantee *due process*, it may be necessary to provide processes that will be *excessive* in some cases. And the availability of judicial review compounds the irony.

Here is an illustration of the irony of process, from the government's strategy for asylum and immigration:

> Some types of application raise fundamental issues. In these cases it is right that it should be possible to appeal against a decision to refuse the application. This applies to asylum applications, where the person concerned claims that they face persecution or death in their own country, and to marriage and family cases. However, applicants should not be able to abuse that right by making unmeritorious appeals to frustrate our efforts to remove them. [27]

---

[27] Home Office, *Controlling Our Borders: Five-year Strategy for Asylum and Immigration*, February 2005, Cm 6472 [32].

The irony is that there is no fair way to decide which appeals are unmeritorious, without some form of hearing. Sometimes, the entire appeal needs to be heard before it can be seen to be unmeritorious.

Because of this problem, process is extremely important. No one ever brought a procedural challenge to a decision in his or her favour. And no one needs the court to hold that procedures were unfair if he or she can get the court to interfere with the substance of a decision. And the result of a procedural challenge may be merely that the decision maker does the same thing again with a different process.

Yet the control of process is the most important and most successful part of administrative law: the judges and the legislature do not suffer the same disabilities that they face in dealing with questions of substance, and they can do justice by imposing due process on the administration.

And if it is too late for a new process to set things right, a procedural challenge may give the claimant a substantive outcome. So, in *Cooper*, the house had been pulled down, and Cooper got damages in tort because it was too late for the Court to order the public authority to make the decision again using the right process.

Also, a claimant may bring a procedural challenge in order to get the decision made by a different person or body: if a decision is quashed because the process was flawed, the new decision will often need to be made by a differently constituted decision maker.

What is more, it is a wrong in itself (a breach of the **duty of respect**) for a public authority to tear down a house or to sack an employee without hearing the other side of the story first. Even if you have had a hearing, if a decision goes against you, it is very easy to get the feeling (and it is sometimes true) that you have not *really* been listened to at all. And so a holding that a decision was made unfairly can give a claimant a sense of vindication. Allied to that potential for vindication is the simple, direct opportunity for accountability that motivates many judicial review challenges: the judicial process gives people who feel they have not been listened to the remarkable opportunity to drag the public authority in front of an independent body.

Although some of its principles are as old as (and in fact much older than) the *Bentley* decision in 1748, the law on process has seen major advances since *Ridge*. It is still in flux. As Lord Mustill said in *Doody*: 'The standards of fairness are not immutable. They may change with the passage of time, both in the general and in their application to decisions of a particular type' (560).[28] Amid all of this change, it is worth remembering that people may have *no* right to a hearing, even though an executive decision affects them very significantly. In the following cases, the affected person will ordinarily have no right to procedural participation in an administrative decision:

- a Cabinet minister who is dismissed;

- a sailor whose ship is sent to sea;

- a farmer from Ghana who is opposed to British agricultural policy;

----

[28] 'Standards and perceptions of fairness may change, not only from one century to another but also, sometimes, from one decade to another', according to Lord Bingham in *R v H* [2004] 2 AC 134 [11].

- a soldier, when the Army's compensation scheme is changed; and

- a celebrity who is not nominated for an honour.

So you do not automatically have a right to any particular form of participation in a decision-making process just because you are affected by the decision. It depends on the nature of the decision.

And still the most important development in modern administrative law is the principle that administrative decisions must be made with due process.

TAKE-HOME MESSAGE • • •

- **The three main values of procedural participation are:**
  - the value of promoting good outcomes;
  - the value of respect for persons affected by a decision; and
  - the value of imposing the rule of law on public decision making.

- **Due process is proportionate process**: whether a process is due depends on whether it promotes the three **process values**, in a way that is justifiable in light of the **process cost** and any **process danger**.

- The focal concern of the common law of due process is **fairness** to persons affected by a decision, who have something to say on the issues. Fairness requires that the public authority abide by its **duty of respect** for people affected by its decisions, and that it act on all of the **relevant considerations**. But fairness is not the only concern:
  - due process also promotes the public interest in responsible decision making, in which the outcome is based on all of the relevant considerations; and
  - due process includes procedures laid down by valid legislation, and may require conformity to procedures that a public authority has announced or has a practice of using.

- **The irony of process**: to guarantee due process, it may be necessary to afford more process than is due.

- There is no general reason to involve someone affected in the making of a decision. British farm policies affect farmers in Ghana, and if British and EU policies oppress those farmers, they have suffered an injustice. But farmers in Ghana have no legal right to participation in the policy-making process.

CRITICAL QUESTIONS • • •

1   Why shouldn't it be up to an administrative authority to decide what process is appropriate? Why should judges decide?

2   The law of due process is in flux. Considering (1) the 'continuing momentum in administrative law towards openness of decision-making' (Lord Mustill in *R v Home Secretary, ex p Doody* [1994] 1 AC 531, 566) and (2) the effect of the Human Rights Act 1998, do you think the procedures that were refused in the following decisions would be ordered by the courts today?

- *B Johnson & Co v Minister of Health* [1947] 2 All ER 395
- *Nakkuda Ali v Jayaratne* [1951] AC 66 (PC)
- *McInnes v Onslow Fane* [1978] 1 WLR 1520.

3   Can you reconcile the following two views?
- Lord Greene's view in *B Johnson & Co v Minister of Health* [1947] 2 All ER 395, 400, that a minister's duty to perform his functions honestly and fairly, 'speaking generally, is not a matter with which the courts are concerned'.
- Lord Loreburn's view in *Board of Education v Rice* [1911] AC 179 (HL), 182, that listening to both sides fairly 'is a duty lying upon every one who decides anything'.

4   No one complains about lack of due process when he or she gets the outcome that he or she wants. Sergeant Walker (see 2.1) would not have been bothered if the military had adopted a more generous compensation scheme without consulting soldiers; Charles Ridge would not have minded if the police authority had decided not to dismiss him after considering the matter without listening to him; Cooper would have had no complaint if the Board of Works had decided not to tear down his house after considering it without talking to him. Does that mean that judicial review over procedures is merely a sham for complaints that are actually about the substance of the decision?

READING • • •

Cooper v Wandsworth Board of Works (1863) 14 CB (NS) 180
Ridge v Baldwin [1964] AC 40
R v Home Secretary, ex p Doody [1994] 1 AC 531
R (West) v Parole Board [2005] UKHL 1
R (Roberts) v Parole Board [2005] UKHL 45
Osborn v Parole Board [2013] UKSC 61

On due process in general:
Paul Craig, 'Perspectives on Process: Common Law, Statutory and Political' [2010] PL 275
On special advocates:
Aileen Kavanagh, 'Special Advocates, Control Orders and the Right to a Fair Trial' (2010) 73 MLR 824
John Ip, '*Al Rawi, Tariq*, and the Future of Closed Material Procedures and Special Advocates' (2012) 75 MLR 606–23

The following online resources accompany this chapter: **summaries** of key cases and legislation; **updates** on the law; **guidance** for answering the pop quizzes and questions; and **links** to legislation, cases, and useful websites.

5 Impartiality and independence

There is an ancient common law rule against bias in judicial and administrative decision making, and its requirements are surprisingly close to those of the European Convention guarantee of impartiality in the determination of civil rights. But the Convention adds a requirement of independence. Legal requirements of impartiality and independence have an important, but limited, role in administration: they ought to be developed in ways that do not stop a public authority from the fair pursuit of its policies.

LOOK FOR • • •

- The difference between **bias** (which is unlawful), and a **lack of impartiality** (which may be lawful). Bias is unfair partiality.

- When bias will be presumed.

- The relation between **independence** and impartiality.

- The difference—and the connection—between **substance** and **process**.

- Bias as a lack of due process, **and also** as a flaw in the substance of a decision maker's reasoning.

> ' Every body in the town has already pre-engaged his opinion. The burgesses have all taken sides: the justices have already declared him so heinously guilty, that he ought to be immediately disfranchised, without waiting for a trial of the indictment. I dare say they were of that opinion, without prejudice to the man, but from indignation at his guilt: and perhaps very justly; for a man may judge impartially even in his own cause. However, we must go upon general principles. '
>
> *R v Cowle* (1759) 2 Burr 834, 862–3 (Lord Mansfield)

5.1 Impartiality and bias

In *R v Cowle*, a Berwick town council meeting had degenerated into a riot, and the defendant had been charged with assault. He complained that the trial would be unfair because the justices of the peace, who were to decide the case if the prosecution went ahead in Berwick, had brought a motion to ban him from voting in Berwick for taking part in the riot. Lord Mansfield decided that it would be unlawful for the Berwick justices to try the defendant, and the Court of King's Bench issued a *certiorari* (a quashing order—see 10.4.1, p 389) to quash the indictment, and ordered the criminal charges to be heard by a jury in Northumberland.

A decision maker is impartial if he or she is not inclined to decide one way or the other before hearing from the people who ought to be heard. Bias is partiality on the part of a decision maker who ought to be impartial, and it makes a decision unlawful. Lord Mansfield explained the law of bias as follows:

> ' If a witness in a cause has an **interest**, though it be small, he must be rejected: or if a juryman has declared his opinion by a former verdict, he may have done it very justly, but yet is liable to be challenged for this cause, on a subsequent trial. In the present case, it is impossible but that all the persons who would be concerned in trying this matter at Berwick, must be **biassed** by their **preconceived opinions**. I do not speak this, with the least imputation upon the magistrates of Berwick: but it is not fit that they should be judges in their own cause, and after having already gone so far as they have done. ' [1]

We long ago abandoned the notion that a *witness* must be impartial, but for jurors and judges we have the same rule today as in 1759.

Yet impartiality is *not* a general requirement of lawful decision making. Administrative officials ought to be partial to their policies. A **biased** decision, on the other hand, is unlawful at common law, whether it is made by a judge or an administrative official.

---

[1] *R v Cowle* (1759) 2 Burr 834, 862–3 (emphasis added).

A bias is a bad attitude. It is a disposition to make a decision against a party's interest, regardless of how the case ought to be decided.[2] As Lord Goff put it, a biased decision maker 'unfairly regard(s) . . . with favour, or disfavour, the case of a party to the issue under consideration by him' (*R v Gough* [1993] AC 646, 670).

If the decision maker has that sort of unfair attitude, no hearing can be fair. In fact, a hearing is not really a hearing at all if the decision maker is going to decide against you regardless of what he or she hears. The 'hearing' becomes a sham. So the rule against bias is part of the law of due process (see Chapter 4).

An administrative or judicial decision will be quashed for lack of due process if a decision maker had:

(1) an **improper interest** in the outcome; or

(2) a **relation** to one party to a dispute that made it **unfair** for the decision maker to decide between the parties; or

(3) an **improper preference** for one outcome (or, as Lord Mansfield called it, 'a preconceived opinion').

It is not impossible for a person to make a fair decision in spite of his or her interests and relations. A mother, for example, *can* resolve a dispute between her own child and someone else's child without leaning in favour of her own child. But the law does not trust judges or jurors to do it. As Lord Mansfield said: '[A] man may judge impartially even in his own cause. However, we must go upon general principles.' So it would be unlawful for a mother to sit as a judge in a claim in tort brought by her child against someone else.

If a decision maker has the wrong sort of interest in the outcome, or the wrong sort of relation to a party, or the wrong sort of opinion about the facts, the law **presumes** that the decision maker was influenced by it. That is, without any proof that a decision resulted from the unfair interest or relation or opinion, the law deals with the situation as if that were proved. An improper preference for or against one side is an **actual** bias; it is a ground for the decision maker to recuse himself or herself (that is, to withdraw from the proceeding and leave it to someone else to make the decision), and it is ground for an administrative decision to be quashed in judicial review if the decision maker does not do so. A decision maker should recuse himself or herself (and the decision should be quashed for failure to do so) if the decision maker has **relations** or **interests** or **preconceived opinions** that create a real possibility of a bias (that is, a real possibility of an improper preference for or against one side); in those cases, the law presumes that there was an improper preference.[3]

---

[2] What about dispositions to decide against the *public* interest? There is no legal remedy for that, *unless* a claimant in judicial review has standing to challenge the relevance of considerations on which the public authority acts. See the discussion of *R v Foreign Secretary, ex p World Development Movement* [1995] 1 WLR 386, 274, at 8.2.2.

[3] Note, however, that Lord Bingham used 'actual bias' differently, to mean 'a disqualifying interest of any kind', in *Davidson v Scottish Ministers* [2004] UKHL 34 [19]. He ought to have said that the law presumes bias when the decision maker has a disqualifying interest. On disqualifying interests, see 5.1.3, p 168.

A presumption of bias cannot be rebutted—that is, if a decision is challenged on the ground of a real possibility of bias, the decision cannot be rescued by proof that the decision maker was actually being perfectly fair-minded. We must go upon general principles, as Lord Mansfield said. And if there is one biased member of a decision-making body, *all* of the members will be disqualified, at least if the proceeding reached a point at which the members discussed the issues.[4] So Lord Mansfield was not prepared to hear that some particular justice from Berwick had no preconceived opinion about the defendant.

5.1.1 Judicial bias

The judges have not hesitated to strike down decisions by their fellow judges, to protect both the integrity of their own process and the *appearance* of integrity. The House of Lords and the Supreme Court have been extraordinarily willing to uphold complaints of bias or of the possibility of bias by lower court judges. And both the House of Lords[5] and the Court of Appeal[6] have invented judicial review of their own processes when a party wants to complain of bias or the appearance of a possibility of bias in one of their decisions. In an extraordinary process to hear a complaint that a House of Lords' decision was tainted by the appearance of a possibility of bias,[7] the Law Lords overturned the decision (*R v Bow Street Metropolitan Stipendiary Magistrate, ex p Pinochet Ugarte (No 2)* [2000] 1 AC 119). Lord Hoffmann had been the unpaid chairman of Amnesty International's fundraising organization. Amnesty International was given leave to intervene in a case over whether General Pinochet had immunity from extradition as former head of state of Chile. Amnesty, a human rights advocacy group, intervened because of its agenda to prevent (and to improve recourse against) state torture of the kind that Pinochet was accused of perpetrating. Amnesty had no material interest in the outcome of the litigation, but the Law Lords decided that it might not look right to the public for a judge to have an institutional connection with an organization that had hired lawyers to make representations to the judges. As we will see, the courts since *Pinochet* have found the appearance of a possibility of bias in very remote connections to the matter of a dispute.

5.1.2 Administrative bias

Cowle was a criminal prosecution; *Pinochet* was an extradition appeal in the House of Lords. So what do these cases have to do with administrative law? The rule against bias

---

[4]   *Re Medicaments (No 2)* [2001] EWCA Civ 1217 [99].

[5]   *R v Bow Street Metropolitan Stipendiary Magistrate, ex p Pinochet Ugarte (No 2)* [2000] 1 AC 119 (HL).

[6]   *Taylor v Lawrence* [2002] EWCA Civ 90.

[7]   Note that judges often use the phrase 'apparent bias' as a shorthand for 'the appearance of a possibility of bias': see, e.g., *Davidson v Scottish Ministers* [2004] UKHL 34 [1], [25], [44].

governs *both* judicial and administrative decision making. And the courts have long considered the application of the doctrine to judges as an example for administrative decision makers:

> ' . . . it will have a most salutary influence on these tribunals when it is known that this high court of last resort, in a case in which the Lord Chancellor of England had an interest, considered that his decree was on that account a decree not according to law, and was set aside. This will be a lesson to all inferior tribunals to take care not only that in their decrees they are not influenced by their personal interest, but to avoid the appearance of labouring under such an influence. '[8]

Why is the law on bias in *administrative* decision making linked to the cases on bias in *judicial* decision making? Partly, it is because the problems of bias in **administrative justice** (that is, in the resolution of disputes by an independent body that is not part of the court system, such as a tribunal or an ombudsman or an auditor), are much the same as the problems in courts.

Tribunals and courts differ in one way: tribunals often have members who are there because of a technical expertise, or as representatives of the community (see 12.4.3). Contrast judges, who are meant to apply the law on the basis of the evidence before the court, without acting on any technical expertise in deciding the facts and without representing any interest except the public interest in the administration of justice. When a tribunal judge decides a case on the basis of special knowledge that arises not from the hearing before the tribunal, but from his or her experience or expertise, is he or she giving a biased decision? Not according to the House of Lords: Lord Hope held that the integrity of the tribunal system 'is not compromised by the use of specialist knowledge or experience when the judge or tribunal member is examining the evidence' (*Gillies v Work and Pensions Secretary (Scotland)* [2006] UKHL 2 [23]). The rules on bias for tribunal judges are the same as the rules for jurors and for judges (*R v Gough* [1993] AC 646, 670). This section, and 5.2 and 5.3, address the decisions of bodies that are governed by the same test as judges.

And, in fact, you might say that *all* administrative decision making is governed by the same rule: that decisions must be *unbiased* (where bias is a bad attitude against one side). But it is critically important that not all administrative decision makers have to be *impartial*; some public authorities not only may, but must, have some sort of 'preconceived opinion' at the point when they hear from parties who have a right to a hearing. The application of the rule against bias raises *much* more interesting problems in some fields of administrative decision making, such as in the planning process, than it does in courts. There are two interrelated reasons, as follows.

---

[8]   *Dimes v Proprietors of Grand Junction Canal* (1852) 3 HL Cas 759, 793–4.

The two-body problem

(1) Many public authorities, *unlike* courts and tribunals, do not hear a dispute between parties, but hear responses to their own (tentative or even concluded) decisions or policies or plans. So they are already involved in the issues, rather than serving as a neutral third party resolving a dispute between two sides.

That lack of independence does not in itself create a presumption of bias. But it generates difficult problems in deciding what sort of involvement with the issues creates a real possibility of a bad attitude against a claimant. Even for administrators who do not resolve a dispute between two parties, but simply have to consider the view of a person affected by their decision before acting (such as the Board of Works in *Cooper v Wandsworth Board of Works* (1863) 14 CB (NS) 180—see 4.1, p 122), *some* interests, relations, and preconceived opinions will be improper. But the question of which are improper will be different from the question of whether a judge in a tribunal or in the High Court is biased.

The policy problem

(2) In the two-body cases, administrators, unlike judges, *ought* to bring their policy agendas to their work.

It is all right for a person who has a policy that goes against your interests to make a decision after hearing you. But *some* dispositions are improper. Essentially, those will be dispositions to make a decision that is not based on the relevant considerations. In 5.4 and 5.5, we will see how the law must do something to control the preconceived opinions of administrators in the two-body cases, and we will see how difficult it is for the court to do so without a breach of comity. And in 5.6 we will see the deep, important connection between the law on bias (for all decision makers) and the doctrine that discretionary decisions must be made on the basis of the relevant considerations. Like the law on the giving of reasons (see Chapter 6), the law on bias is a point of connection between legal control of decision-making processes and legal control of the substance of decisions.

The law of bias on the part of tribunal judges really is simply part of the law on judicial bias, and we will start with that in this chapter. Then we will come to grips with the ways in which the two-body problem and the policy problem create special difficulties for administrative decision makers who do not resolve a dispute between two parties, but simply have to give a hearing in their decision-making process.

5.1.3 The basic rule for courts and tribunals

When a court or a tribunal decides a dispute between two parties, it is unfair, and therefore unlawful, for a particular judge to participate in the decision if he or she has a hostile attitude towards one side. Of course, judges do not generally recuse themselves on the ground that they are against one of the parties. They do not generally announce in court or in their reasons that they were against one party, and decisions are not generally struck down on that basis. In an appeal or in a complaint of bias brought to a different judge of the same court, incidentally, there is simply no way to get the allegedly biased judge into a witness stand to face questioning as to what his or her views actually were. No English court has ever heard testimony from one of its judges as to what attitude he or she had towards the complainant.[9] Bias is a bad attitude, remember, and there simply are no reported cases of actual bias.

Behave yourself

Even a judge who behaves badly may decide impartially, as Lord Mansfield pointed out. Judges never quite express an opinion that a particular party ought to get it in the neck. But they have to be extremely careful about expressing attitudes of other kinds that may be prejudicial, or the Court of Appeal will throw out a decision. In *El-Farargy v El Farargy* [2007] EWCA Civ 1149 [28], the judge in a civil dispute involving an Arab sheikh had come up with a variety of digs at the sheikh, such as, 'if he chose to depart on his flying carpet never to be seen again', '. . . to see that every grain of sand is sifted', '. . . at this I think relatively fast-free time of the year', and a joke that the sheikh's case was 'a bit like Turkish Delight'. The Court of Appeal quashed the judge's decision because the remarks could be seen 'to be mocking and disparaging . . . for his status as a Sheikh' [30]. The Court of Appeal will not even ask whether a party actually got a fair hearing from a judge who said regrettable stuff about him.

What are the grounds on which there is some practical chance of challenging a judge's role in a dispute? A judge is **automatically disqualified** if he or she has a substantial financial interest in the outcome of a case (*Locabail v Bayfield* [2000] QB 451 [50]). There is no official list of the grounds for automatic disqualification, but aside from financial interests they certainly extend to any **relationship** that, on general principles, is incompatible with the neutrality of a judge (such as being the mother of a defendant or claimant, or having decided the dispute that is being appealed). The Court of Appeal has extended automatic disqualification, roughly, to *any* personal connection between the judge and a party, holding that a judge was automatically disqualified when he realized that he knew an expert witness for one party. The Court of Appeal held that he could not proceed to hear the case by proposing that the party call a different witness (*AWG Group Ltd v Morrison* [2006] EWCA Civ 6 [29]). Automatic disqualification is appropriate where the judge's involvement in a decision would reflect badly on the

---

9 Although a judge may say something about the matter in a court transcript, which would be available to an appeal court, and the judge may give reasons for a decision when a party complains of bias directly to the judge. And a court considering a complaint of bias may accept a statement from a judge or juror (*Locabail v Bayfield Properties* [2000] QB 451 [17]). In all of these cases, the complainant has no way of challenging what the judge says.

integrity of the system, regardless of what the parties to the dispute might think about it. *AWG* shows that the courts will be quick to decide that there is a problem if a judge has anything to do with one of the parties.

If a judge is not automatically disqualified, it is still unlawful for him or her to decide the matter if an interest, relation, or opinion makes it unfair to do so. And as there is no viable way for a court in appeal or judicial review to consider the judge's actual attitudes, the law needs general principles for deciding whether a process was fair. When a party complains about an interest or relation or opinion of a judge, the basic question is the *Porter v Magill* test:

When bias will be presumed

' The question is whether the fair-minded and informed observer, having considered the facts, would conclude that there was a real possibility that the tribunal was biased. '[10]

In this standard formulation, 'biased' has the meaning explained earlier—that is, a judge is biased if he or she is disposed to decide against a party regardless of the relevant considerations.[11] And bias will be presumed if the fair-minded, informed observer would think that there is a possibility of it.

The *Porter* formulation was a change from a different test that Lord Goff had set out in *R v Gough* [1993] AC 646, 670. He held that the question was whether 'there was a real danger of bias on the part of the relevant member of the tribunal in question'. *Porter* drew on Lord Phillips' decision in the Court of Appeal in *Re Medicaments (No 2)* [2001] 1 WLR 700. The Human Rights Act 1998 requires the English courts to take into account decisions of the European Court of Human Rights, and Lord Phillips held that the Strasbourg jurisprudence required the courts to pay more attention to what an observer would think, and not just to whether there really was a danger of bias. The Strasbourg Court had held that:

' It must be ascertained whether sufficient guarantees exist to exclude any legitimate doubt . . . . Even appearances may be important; what is at stake is the confidence which the court must inspire in the accused in criminal proceedings and what is decisive is whether the applicant's fear as to a lack of impartiality can be regarded as objectively justifiable. '[12]

---

[10] *Porter v Magill* [2001] UKHL 67 [103].

[11] The House of Lords in *Porter* was presupposing this, on the basis of Lord Goff's speech in *Gough*, 670, discussing the possibility that a tribunal member might be biased 'in the sense that he might unfairly regard (or have unfairly regarded) with favour, or disfavour, the case of a party to the issue under consideration by him'.

[12] *Gregory v United Kingdom* (1998) 25 EHRR 577 [42]. See also *Findlay v United Kingdom* (1997) 24 EHRR 221.

So there are three tests for the presumption that a decision was biased:

- the *Gough* test—whether there is a real danger of bias;

- the **Strasbourg test**—whether the applicant's fear as to a lack of impartiality can be regarded as objectively justifiable; and

- the *Porter* test—whether a fair-minded and informed observer, having considered the facts, would conclude that there was a real possibility that the tribunal was biased.

You might say that all three are the same: if there is no real danger of bias, an applicant's fear as to a lack of impartiality is not objectively justifiable, and a fair-minded and informed observer, having considered the facts, would conclude that there was no real possibility that the tribunal was biased. But the courts see the change from *Gough* to *Porter* as shifting the emphasis from how things are to how things look.

5.2 Appearance and reality

Why quash a decision for mere appearances? In *Cowle*, Lord Mansfield held that 'a doubt whether a fair, impartial, or satisfactory trial can be had there' was a reason to remove a case from the Berwick justices (861). It did not have to be proved that a trial there would not be fair. It was enough if it was doubtful. But whose doubt counts? The judge's, or the defendant's, or that of the people of Berwick? Or of the country? Is a misguided doubt enough?

It is very commonly said that justice must not only be done, but also be seen to be done.[13] A rule that a decision will be quashed if there is an appearance of bias (or even the appearance of a *possibility* of bias) has advantages:

- it is a guard against actual bias, which is more or less impossible to prove;

- where a decision maker was acting in good faith, but had an unfair relation or interest, it enables judges to quash an unfair decision without having to condemn the decision maker;[14] and

- it can help to enhance public respect for the courts.

In fact, being prepared to quash decisions for the appearance of a possibility of bias is absolutely crucial, because of Lord Mansfield's simple point that 'we must go upon general principles'. A connection with the case of a kind that might influence someone to decide it unfairly is embarrassing for the judge as well as alarming for the parties,

---

[13] e.g., *Davidson v Scottish Ministers* [2004] UKHL 34 [7] (Lord Bingham).

[14] As the Court of Appeal put it in *Re Medicaments (No 2)* [67]: 'It is invidious for the reviewing Court to question the word of the Judge . . . but less so to say that the objective onlooker might have difficulty in accepting it.'

and there is no way of working out whether the judge actually decided with an open mind.

The drawback, of course, is that quashing decisions for the mere appearance of bias gives a party an opportunity to try to get rid of a decision maker who may quite fairly decide against them. Or it gives the loser an opportunity to try to overturn a process after the outcome has gone the wrong way, on the ground that something didn't look right. Either way, a rule designed to protect a party from the mere appearance of bias potentially gives that party a way of tearing up the process if he or she does not like the way things are going, or the way things have gone.

The irony of process

Good process can demand that the decision maker give a party a technique for attacking a process that was not actually unfair, if he or she does not like the result.[15]

The *Porter* test and the Strasbourg cases it is based on seem to be concerned with raw public opinion. According to the unanimous House of Lords in *Lawal v Northern Spirit Ltd* [2003] UKHL 35 [14]: 'Public perception of the possibility of unconscious bias is the key.' Can a decision be quashed because the public has a *mistaken* perception that it was biased? In *Porter*, the hypothetical observer, who could presumably be either a party or the general public, must be fair-minded and informed, and must have considered the facts—and the fair-minded and informed observer will not think that there is a real possibility of bias, when there is no real possibility of bias. In *Helow v Home Secretary* [2008] UKHL 62 [3], Lord Hope said this of the 'fair-minded and informed observer':

> She is the sort of person who takes the trouble to read the text of an article as well as the headlines. She is able to put whatever she has read or seen into its overall social, political or geographical context. She is fair-minded, so she will appreciate that the context forms an important part of the material which she must consider before passing judgment.

She sounds very similar to a good judge. So there ought to be little difference in effect between the *Porter* test and the *Gough* test.

In *Lawal*, the Law Lords did not say that public *misconceptions* mattered. Should a court quash a decision on the ground that the public falsely thinks that it was biased? It may seem that it should, since respect for the courts can be affected by a totally misguided public opinion that a decision was biased. Like any public authority, courts must be accountable to the public. But the accountability they owe is to be transparent,

---

15   On the irony of process, see 4.13, p 157. On the possibility that a doctrine of waiver can prevent some abuses of the law on bias, see 5.2.2.

to guard the integrity of their processes, to promote access to justice, and to give clear and candid reasons for their decisions. They should overturn a decision where there is good reason for the public to doubt the fairness of their process. But they owe nothing to public misconceptions. The court should not quash decisions made through a process that it can see was fair, because somebody might have the misconception that it might have been unfair. The remedy ought to be for the court to explain the situation in its reasons, rather than to quash a fair decision.

In *Porter* itself, an auditor was investigating politically charged complaints that Conservative councillors had been selling off council housing at a loss, in an attempt to move Conservative voters into key wards before an election. The auditor held a televised press conference after the preliminary phase of his investigation, and posed for the cameras beside high stacks of documents in ring binders, with a security guard watching over them. The Law Lords called it an error of judgment: 'The main impression which this would have conveyed to the fair-minded observer was that the purpose of this exercise was to attract publicity to himself, and perhaps also to his firm. It was an exercise in self-promotion in which he should not have indulged. But it is quite another matter to conclude from this that there was a real possibility that he was biased' [105]. So, according to *Porter*, it is not enough that a process looks bad, or that someone might suffer from a misconception. If a decision is to be quashed, it must have looked bad in such a way that a complainant has a *justifiable* fear that the decision maker was biased.

5.2.1 The judge's opinion on the law

In the rash of bias decisions over recent years, have the judges been *too* ready to quash decisions for an appearance of bias? It depends on what they have been expecting from the 'fair-minded and informed observer' in the *Porter* test, and whether they have been too concerned with public perceptions and not enough with justifiable public perceptions. In one respect, though, they have gone beyond the true rationale for a rule against bias, which is to secure due process.

The fact that a decision maker—judge *or* administrator—has previously expressed a view that has adverse implications for a party to a dispute does not necessarily indicate bias. Otherwise, a judge would not be able to sit in a case in which one party wanted to rely on a precedent decided by that judge. Even though the fair-minded observer might think that a judge would be inclined to take the same view of the law that he or she took in a previous case, that would not be enough to make the fair-minded observer think that the judge was biased. It would be fruitless to complain that a judge should be recused when you need to ask the court to depart from a precedent that he or she decided. You might think that the court is predisposed to decide against you—and it might be true—but the judge is not disqualified on that ground. Lord Bingham has said that 'adherence to an opinion expressed judicially in an earlier case does not of itself denote a lack of open-mindedness' (*Davidson v Scottish Ministers* [10]).

Moreover, the judges may quite appropriately form a view of a case, based on the papers submitted by the parties and their own reading, before an oral hearing. That really does give the judges a predisposition before the barristers stand up to make their arguments, but there is nothing unfair about it. As Ward LJ has said: 'The business of this court would not be done if we were to recuse ourselves for entering the court having formed a preliminary view of the prospects of success of the appeal before us' (*El-Farargy v El Farargy* [2007] EWCA Civ 1149 [26]). Likewise, the Court of Appeal has held that there was no appearance of a possibility of bias where a High Court judge conducted the trial of a commercial dispute after having found the defendant guilty of lying and forgery during preliminary steps in the litigation. The Court concluded that in this situation, the judge 'is not "pre-judging" by reference to extraneous matters or predilections or preferences . . . .He is judging the matter before him, as he is required by his office to do' (*JSC BTA Bank v Ablyazov* [2012] EWCA Civ 1551 [70]).

The reason why these forms of potential or actual predisposition are fair is not simply that judges are expected to be open-minded enough to listen to arguments as to why they should change their view (although we need judges who can do that). The really important reason is that a judge *ought* to have views on what the law is (and, e.g., on whether a precedent ought to be overruled).

It would, however, be improper for a judge elevated from the High Court to the Court of Appeal to decide an appeal from his or her own decision.[16] There ought to be a simple rule that the expression of a *general* view as to the law by a judge is never good ground for a claim that there is the appearance of bias (whether it was in a law journal, or a previous decision, or an after-dinner speech). It would be different if a judge had committed himself or herself to a *particular application* of the law to the complainant's case (e.g., by writing in a law journal or saying on television that a particular party ought to lose a particular claim). But even if a general point of law is crucial to a party's case, it should be simply no objection at all that a judge has expressed a view on it.

But, in *Davidson*, the House of Lords unanimously quashed a decision for no more reason than that. Davidson wanted an injunction ordering a Scottish minister to move him to a different prison, and a three-judge court held that no injunction was available under the Scotland Act 1998 against a Scottish minister. Lord Hardie, one of the three judges, had been a government minister three years earlier, and during the passage of the Scotland Bill he had expressed the opinion in Parliament that the Bill, along with the Crown Proceedings Act 1947, would prevent injunctions against Scottish ministers. Lord Bingham held that: 'The fair-minded and informed observer, having considered the facts, would conclude that there was a real possibility that Lord Hardie, sitting judicially, would subconsciously strive to avoid reaching a conclusion which would undermine the very clear assurances he had given to Parliament' [17]. The House of Lords' decision can be explained partly by the connection with party politics: it may be thought to look bad that the judge had been speaking on behalf of the government when he expressed his opinion in Parliament. The House of Lords' decision can also be explained as a zealous attempt to follow two decisions in which

---

[16] Judges are also automatically disqualified from sitting in disputes that they were involved with in legal practice before becoming a judge.

the European Court of Human Rights had suggested that involvement in the passage of legislation disqualified a judge from later interpreting it, and held that a 'doubt in itself, however slight its justification, is sufficient to vitiate the impartiality' of the tribunal in question.[17]

No ground is offered in the *Davidson* case for thinking that the fair-minded observer (as the *Porter* test puts it) would believe that there was a possibility that Lord Hardie was biased. In light of the Law Lords' references to the Strasbourg cases, the conclusion must be that the possibility of an *unreasonable* perception of bias may be treated as a ground for quashing a decision. Given the process havoc that results, that approach is a serious mistake. A decision should only be overturned if the integrity of the judicial process is at stake; its integrity is not endangered by unreasonable misperceptions of bias.

As Lord Hope said, while concurring with the rest of the Law Lords (*Davidson* [46]):

> It would be easy, were we permitted to take a more robust view, to deplore a system which permits an unsuccessful litigant to challenge a judge's decision that has gone against him by searching after the event for previously undiscovered material, like a needle in a haystack, that might be thought to undermine his objectivity. One might think that the cost and delay of rehearing the case would only be justified if there was a real possibility that the wrong decision had been reached because of the alleged bias.

That shows the price we pay for a rule that decisions can be quashed for the appearance of a possibility of bias. There is no genuine sense in which Davidson had not got a fair hearing of his claim for an injunction against a Scottish minister. And the guarantee of impartiality in Art 6 ought to be interpreted in light of its purpose of securing due process. Although it is the judges' obligation under the Human Rights Act 1998 to take account of Strasbourg decisions, *Davidson* would have been a good case in which to depart from *obiter dicta* from the Strasbourg Court suggesting that a decision can be quashed because of the possibility of a misconception that there was a possibility of bias. The European Court of Human Rights' view that 'doubt in itself, however slight its justification, is sufficient to vitiate the impartiality' of a tribunal is, potentially, damaging to the administration of justice. Table 5.1 summarizes the facts of a number of cases that considered whether there was the appearance of a possibility of bias.

5.2.2 Waiver

Can a person waive the right to an unbiased tribunal? It would be wrong to allow it if bias is a blot on the integrity of the decision maker. And we have seen that *some* interests, relations, and opinions are inherently objectionable. The relations and interests

---

[17] *Procola v Luxembourg* (1995) 22 EHRR 193 [45]; *McGonnell v United Kingdom* (2000) 30 EHRR 289 [57].

Table 5.1 House of horrors: is it bias?

Decision maker	Relations to a party	Possibility of bias?
A juror in a burglary trial	—realized after the conviction that the defendant was the brother of her former next-door neighbour.	No[18]
A lay member on a tribunal	—during the hearing, applied for a job with a company, forgetting that one party's main witness was a director of the company.	Yes[19]
A lay member on a tribunal	—had sat on other tribunals with a lawyer for one party.	Yes[20]
A medical member of a three-person tribunal, hearing a claim against the Benefits Agency	—provided expert reports on behalf of the Benefits Agency in other cases.	No[21]
A judge	—conducted a summary trial for contempt, on grounds of the defendant's outrageous behaviour in her court.	No[22]
Conduct		
A judge in a theft trial	—accused defence counsel of 'silliness', 'nonsense', and 'being ridiculous'.	Yes[23]
A judge in a civil claim	—joked about whether an Arab sheikh would disappear on his flying carpet (etc.).	Yes[24]
A coroner	—called relatives of the deceased 'unhinged' and 'mentally unwell'.	Yes[25]

(Continued)

---

[18] *R v Gough* [1993] AC 646. But note that Lord Goff suggested in his reasons that the court should only quash the conviction if there were a real possibility of bias; in his view, an appearance of a possibility was not enough. *Porter* departed from that approach.

[19] *Re Medicaments (No 2)* [98]: '[A] fair-minded observer would apprehend that there was a real danger that Dr Rowlatt would be unable to make an objective and impartial appraisal of the expert evidence.'

[20] *Lawal v Northern Spirit* [2003] UKHL 35.

[21] *Gillies v Work and Pensions Secretary* [2006] UKHL 2.

[22] *Wilkinson v Lord Chancellor's Department* [2003] EWCA Civ 95.

[23] *R v Lashley* [2005] EWCA Crim 2016 [48]: ' . . . repeated and unnecessary demonstrations of inappropriate personal animosity towards counsel' interfered with 'the normal due process required at every trial'.

[24] *El-Farargy v El Farargy* [2007] EWCA Civ 1149.

[25] *R v HM Coroner for Inner London West District, ex p Dallaglio* [1994] 4 All ER 139.

Table 5.1 (*Continued*)

Decision maker	Conduct	Possibility of bias?
An auditor	—held a press conference to show off how thorough his investigation was, with a security guard posing beside the stacks of documents.	No[26]
A deputy prison governor	—had been present when the governor approved an order for prisoners to undergo a squat search; in disciplinary proceedings, he ruled that the governor's order was lawful.	Yes[27]
A judge	—decided in the Scottish Court of Session that injunctions could not be granted against the Scottish ministers (after giving advice to the House of Lords, as Lord Advocate, that injunctions could not be granted against the Scottish ministers).	Yes[28]
A judge in a commercial trial	—realized that an expert witness for one party was a friend of his and proposed that the party call another witness.	Yes[29]

that lead to automatic disqualification are unwaivable: it would just be improper for a judge to preside in a claim in tort against her son, even if the claimant did not object. The grounds for automatic disqualification should simply result in a judge recusing himself or herself, rather than asking the party who might suffer detriment if they mind.

But since decisions can be quashed merely because of an appearance of the possibility of bias, we really need a good doctrine of waiver. Some relations with a party that would lead to disqualification of a judge can certainly be waived. For example, if the judge is a solicitor whose firm has acted for a party, he or she has a relation that is improper unless it is disclosed; if it is disclosed, and the other party has no objection, then the judge is not disqualified, if he or she has not acted for one of the parties (*Locabail (UK) Ltd v Bayfield Properties* [2000] QB 451 [52]–[55]). The rule is that in such a case, 'a right to object to a judge on the ground of the appearance of bias can be waived, if done with full knowledge of the relevant facts and the right to object, and if done clearly and unequivocally' (*JSC BTA Bank v Ablyazov* [2012] EWCA Civ 1551 [23]).

A good doctrine of waiver must start with a duty on the judge to give full and early *notice* of any relation with a party that might give rise to an appearance of a possibility

26 *Porter v Magill* [2002] 2 AC 357.

27 *R (Al-Hasan) v Home Secretary* [2005] UKHL 13.

28 *Davidson v Scottish Ministers (No 2)* [2004] UKHL 34.

29 *AWG Group Ltd v Morrison* [2006] EWCA Civ 6.

of bias (although it needs to be flexible enough to deal with the situation in which a judge learns during a hearing that he or she has a relation to a party). And the next requirement is that, as with any waiver of procedural protections (see 4.9), a waiver of the right to insist on having the matter decided by another decision maker 'must be clear and unequivocal, and made with full knowledge of all the facts relevant to the decision whether to waive or not' (*Locabail* [15]).

Even though a waiver must be clear and unequivocal, the *Locabail* case shows that it is possible to waive a right to complain of an appearance of a possibility of bias by doing nothing. The mere fact that a party *could* have complained earlier will not be enough to count as a waiver (see *Millar v Dickson* [2001] UKPC D4). But the reviewing court will find a waiver if there is reason to think that the complainant waited to see what decision would be made before complaining. In *Locabail*, the Court of Appeal concluded that the party who complained of apparent bias, after a decision in a complex commercial dispute, had wanted 'to wait and see how her claims in the Locabail litigation turned out before pursuing her complaint of bias. [She] wanted to have the best of both worlds. The law will not allow her to do so' [69]. That appearance of opportunism was the basis for the conclusion that she had waived her right.

5.3 Independence

In order for a community to achieve responsible government, powers need to be separated not only among the executive, judiciary, and legislature, but also *within* each branch of government (see 1.5.1, p 16). The independence of judges is a crucial part of the separation of powers between the judiciary and the executive. The independence of some administrative decision makers (such as prosecutors: see 7.3.6) is a separation of powers within the executive branch of government.

Independence is a structural feature of decision makers that tends to improve their capacity to act with impartiality. It means 'not only a lack of hierarchical or institutional connection but also a practical independence' (*Ramsahai v Netherlands* (2008) 46 EHRR 43 [325]). In *Findlay v United Kingdom* (1997) 24 EHRR 221 [73], the European Court of Human Rights said: '[I]n order to establish whether a tribunal can be considered as "independent", regard must be had inter alia to the manner of appointment of its members and their term of office, the existence of guarantees against outside pressures and the question whether the body presents an appearance of independence.'

In England, administrative tribunals have been designed for more than a century to achieve more or less independent review of many forms of administrative decision; the **reconstruction of tribunals** was designed to enhance their independence (see Chapter 12). A lack of independence can be ground for judicial review of an administrative decision if it amounts to 'the effective surrender of the body's independent judgment' (*R v Environment Secretary, ex p Kirkstall Valley Campaign Ltd* [1996] 3 All ER 304 (QBD), 321 (Sedley J)). An administrative body that has been given responsibility for a decision must genuinely exercise that responsibility (see 8.1.2), and cannot surrender its judgment or be overridden by any other government agency that is not specifically authorized to do so. But at common law there has never been a general legal requirement of institutional independence in administrative decision making, and no administrative decision could be challenged as biased merely on the ground that the decision maker was not independent of government. One reason for this is that if Parliament gives a decision-making power to a public authority that is not independent of government, the courts cannot hold it to be unlawful for that authority to exercise the power.[30] The other reason is that many administrative decisions do *not* require an independent tribunal. The Board of Works in *Cooper* is a good example of the sort of administrative decision maker that decides people's rights, without being independent of government. And the police authority in *Ridge v Baldwin* [1964] AC 40 is a reminder of the varieties of independence: police authorities have an independence *from elected government* at both national and local levels. It is a form of separation of powers within the executive that is essential for the rule of law. But the police authority that sacked Ridge was not independent of the administration of the police; on the contrary, it was responsible for the administration of the police. So Ridge had not yet had an independent hearing when he was sacked. But the fact that the police authority was not independent was not a flaw in the process; the flaw was just that it had not heard his side of the story.

In the European Convention on Human Rights, independence is a distinct, additional protection for impartial decision making. So the right to an *independent* tribunal under the Convention brought something new to English law. Article 6(1) provides that:

> ' In the determination of his civil rights and obligations or of any criminal charge against him, everyone is entitled to a fair and public hearing within a reasonable time by an independent and impartial tribunal established by law. '

So, for example, investigation of government wrongdoing must be independent from government (*Edwards v United Kingdom* (2002) 35 EHRR 487 [70]).

You might think that Art 6 would revolutionize English administrative law, requiring all decisions determining rights to be made by someone (such as a judge) who is independent of government. The decision makers in *Cooper* and *Ridge* lacked independence, since the Board of Works in *Cooper* and the police authority in *Ridge* were administrative bodies that were *part of* the government. If their decision-making role were to be incompatible with Art 6, it would revolutionize administrative law.

But there has been no revolution. The change has been very significant, but limited. In *R (Anderson) v Home Secretary* [2002] UKHL 46, the House of Lords declared under the Human Rights Act 1998 that the Home Secretary's statutory power to determine tariffs for adult prisoners was incompatible with Art 6 (see 3.5). Sentencing decisions and decisions over parole must be made by persons who are independent of government. The result is that the Act shifted tariff setting into the courts. That change

----

[30] See the discussion of *R v Home Secretary, ex p Venables and Thompson* [1998] AC 407, at 3.1, p 74.

in the law is important because the inadequacy of judicial review to preserve a proper separation of powers in tariff setting was exposed in *R v Home Secretary, ex p Venables and Thompson* [1998] AC 407 (see 3.1). Before the Human Rights Act, the judges could only tell the Home Secretary what considerations he could lawfully take into account; in *V v United Kingdom* (2000) 30 EHRR 121, the European Court of Human Rights simply held that it was a breach of the Convention for a tariff to be decided by a government minister, because he is not independent.

Now, the English judges can do what the Strasbourg judges can do and declare that a statute is incompatible with the Convention. But the Act has not brought any *general* requirement of independence to administrative law. Unlike in *Anderson* or in *Venables and Thompson*, most administrative decision making does not determine how long someone stays in prison. Article 6 does not even apply to all administrative decisions, but only to those that determine 'civil rights and obligations or ... any criminal charge'. That vague phrase was used with a technical meaning that restricts the effect of Art 6. And where Art 6 *does* apply, if an initial decision maker is not independent, compound decision making (that is, the combination of the initial decision plus appeal or review) can provide the independent control over the decision that is necessary for due process (see 5.3.2).

FROM THE MISTS OF TIME

The independence of **judges** has been protected for more than 300 years in England. In 1628, King Charles I dismissed Sir Ranulf Crew for 'shewing no zeal' for the King's scheme to force nobles to give him loans,[31] and his successor, Sir Nicholas Hyde, promptly decided *Darnel's Case* (1627) 3 Howell's St Tr 1 (KB), 1 (see 1.1.1, p 5) in favour of the King and against the knights who refused to make the loan. No judge has been dismissed since then for lacking zeal for the administration's projects. The Act of Settlement 1700 provided that 'judges commissions be made *quamdiu se bene gesserint* [while they behave themselves well], and their salaries ascertained and established; but upon the address of both Houses of Parliament it may be lawful to remove them' (Art III). Before that, they had held their commissions so long as the King saw fit. Today, there is a 'guarantee of continued judicial independence' in s 3 of the Constitutional Reform Act 2005.

Temporary judges with no job security who rely on the government for promotion are not independent for the purpose of Art 6 (*Ruxton v Starrs* [2000] HRLR 191).

5.3.1 Determining civil rights

The drafters of the Convention actually *missed* an opportunity to impose due process on administration. They wrote that a person's Art 6 right to an independent and

---

[31] Sir Edward Coke, too, had been removed from office in 1616 by the Privy Council, partly for disrespect towards the King.

impartial tribunal arises 'in the determination of his civil rights and obligations'. They meant to give procedural protections in the sort of decision making that is done in the private law courts, and the criminal law courts, in European countries that have separate courts for disputes over administrative decisions.[32] That is why Art 6 is titled 'Right to a fair trial' (and the rest of Art 6(1) regulates the publicity of 'the trial'). The Article was drafted for the sort of disputes that are typically resolved in a trial.

FROM THE MISTS OF TIME

Article 6 was copied from the International Covenant on Civil and Political Rights of the United Nations.[33] In UN negotiations in 1949 over the drafting of the International Covenant, the French and Egyptians proposed a guarantee of process rights for the determination of 'rights and obligations' in general. The Danes responded that such a guarantee would be too broad:

'[I]t would tend to submit to judicial decision any action taken by administrative organs exercising discretionary power conferred on them by law . . . . the individual should be ensured protection against any abuse of power by administrative organs but the question was extremely delicate and it was doubtful whether the Commission could settle it there and then. The study of the division of power between administrative and judicial organs could be undertaken later . . .'[34]

As a result, the UN resolved to guarantee 'rights and obligations in a suit of law'. But the drafters of the European Convention could not agree that the Art 6 protections should apply *only* to law suits, so they changed the wording to 'civil rights and obligations', even though they kept 'trial' in the title of Art 6. As a result, because claimants with complaints against administrative decisions have regularly sought to argue that those decisions affect civil rights and obligations, the Strasbourg Court has been carrying out 'The study of the division of power between administrative and judicial organs' in applying Art 6, which was drafted in a way that completely fails to deal with the differences between the demands of procedural justice in a criminal trial, and in an administrative decision.

---

[32] See *Feldbrugge v Netherlands* (1986) 8 EHRR 425, cited by Lord Hoffmann in *Runa Begum v Tower Hamlets LBC* [2003] UKHL 5 [28].

[33] Article 14 of the International Covenant now provides: 'In the determination of any criminal charge against him, or of his rights and obligations in a suit at law, everyone shall be entitled to a fair and public hearing by a competent, independent and impartial tribunal established by law.' The International Covenant lacks the adjudication and enforcement facilities of the European Convention.

[34] *Feldbrugge*, 444–5.

In the cases on the applicability of Art 6, the European Court of Human Rights has extended it well beyond the sort of issues that are decided in trials. The Court has explained a 'civil' right as a right in private law (see *Albert and Le Compte v Belgium* (1983) 5 EHRR 533 [28]), without having a very definite idea of what that means. Article 6(1) applies to some indisputably administrative matters such as planning disputes (*Bryan v United Kingdom* (1995) 21 EHRR 342; *R (Alconbury) v Environment Secretary* [2001] UKHL 23). But it does not apply to discretionary criminal injuries compensation schemes (*Masson v Netherlands* (1996) 22 EHRR 491), or to decisions in tax disputes (*Ferrazzini v Italy* (2001) 34 EHRR 1068).

The really tricky cases concern social security benefits. It is clear that some benefit decisions are covered: Art 6 applies to a decision as to whether a person qualifies for a benefit under an unemployment insurance scheme (*Schuler-Zgraggen v Switzerland* (1993) 16 EHRR 405), and to decisions on entitlement to welfare benefits too, at least if you have an 'individual, economic right flowing from specific rules laid down in a statute' (*Salesi v Italy* (1998) 26 EHRR 187 [19]). So if legislation entitles you to a specific benefit in a precisely defined situation, your claim to it will be a claim to a 'civil right' (with the resultant Art 6 requirement of independence).

But what if your eligibility for a benefit depends on the judgment of the administrative authority responsible for providing the benefit? In *Ali v Birmingham City Council* [2010] UKSC 8, the Supreme Court decided that such an exercise of judgment is not a determination of civil rights in the relevant sense, so that Art 6 does not apply. The Housing Act 1996 s 193 gave the local authority a duty to make housing available to homeless people; the duty ceased if the applicant refused an offer of housing. The local authority's reviewing officer decided that its offer had been refused, so that the duty to provide accommodation had ceased. The claimants argued that Art 6 required that the decision had to be made by an independent tribunal. Lord Hope, writing the majority opinion, held that 'civil rights' under Art 6 were not being determined in ' . . . cases where the award of services or benefits in kind is not an individual right of which the applicant can consider himself the holder, but is dependent upon a series of evaluative judgments by the provider as to whether the statutory criteria are satisfied and how the need for it ought to be met' [49].

In *R (A) v Croydon LBC* [2009] 1 WLR 2557 [44] Baroness Hale said that she would be 'most reluctant' to allow Art 6 to lead to the 'judicialisation of claims to welfare services of this kind'. She pointed out that 'every decision about the provision of welfare services has resource implications for the public authority providing the service'. If independent tribunals are set up to make decisions that are currently made by the local authorities that are responsible for the expenditure, 'resources which might be spent on the services themselves will be diverted to the decision-making process'.

The approach of Lord Hope and Baroness Hale reflects the fact that the administrative decisions in these cases are paradigm examples of the decisions for which Art 6—providing a right to 'fair trial'—was not well designed. The decisions ought to be made fairly by the administrative agency (and the common law of procedural fairness requires that). And the person seeking the benefit ought to be able to complain to an independent tribunal that they have been made unlawfully (and they have that right; see 5.3.2). But there is no justification for requiring the decision on such benefits to be made by a tribunal that is independent from the authority that has to provide them.

Yet, when the claimants in the *Ali* case went to Strasbourg, a Chamber of seven judges decided unanimously that the UK Supreme Court had been wrong, and that Art 6 governs the provision of housing to the homeless (*Ali v United Kingdom* (2015) 63 EHRR 20). In *Poshteh v Kensington and Chelsea Royal LBC* [2017] UKSC 36, the UK Supreme Court resolutely stood by its decision in *Ali*, refused to go along with the Strasbourg decision, and held that the Strasbourg Court had failed to address its 'concerns over "judicialisation" of the welfare services, and the implications for local authority resources' [33].[35]

The problem is that Art 6 has a simple, serious design flaw. If it was meant to secure justice in administrative decisions, the Convention should have required fair hearings and prohibited unreasonable delay and bias, and other forms of unfairness, in administrative decisions (including decisions as to whether to provide housing or other welfare benefits). But not all such decisions require an independent decision maker, in order to be decided justly. The Convention should have required an independent tribunal only in a more narrowly restricted range of decisions (those decisions, such as sentencing, in which independence in the initial decision is necessary for due process). Requiring a hearing by an independent tribunal for the award of social welfare benefits would be a failure of proportionality in process (see 4.4).

In 5.3.2, we will see the judges' primary technique for dealing with this flaw in Art 6: the creative idea that the requirement of an independent decision maker can sometimes be met by an appeal or judicial review, when the initial decision maker is not independent.

5.3.2 Compound decision making

If Art 6 does apply to a decision and the initial decision maker does not meet the requirement of independence, then an appeal to another body, or judicial review, may prevent a breach of Art 6. The Convention, like the common law, should only protect *due* process, which means proportionate process (see 4.4). The courts have occasionally (as in *Davidson*) given claimants disproportionate protection against bias. But, otherwise, their elaboration of Art 6 has given effect to the principle of proportionate process. So, in *Porter v Magill* [2002] UKHL 67, a local government auditor acted as investigator, prosecutor, and judge. That would infringe the separation of powers within administration if it were uncontrolled. And ordinary judicial review would not be enough to vindicate Art 6. But Lord Hope held that the councillors' rights under Art 6 were protected by the availability of an appeal to the Divisional Court, which

....

[35] See 3.8 on the implications of *Poshteh* for the UK courts' relationship with the Strasbourg Court. Note that the Strasbourg Court found no violation of Art 6, on the ground that the claimants' right of appeal to a county court provided the procedure guaranteed by Art 6 (*Ali v United Kingdom* (2015) 63 EHRR 20 [82]–[85]). See 5.3.2 on compound decision making.

could confirm, vary, or quash a decision.[36] The court 'can exercise afresh all the powers of decision which were given to the auditor' [92].

Compound decision making can protect the interests at stake, while allowing a non-independent initial decision maker to pursue the public interest. For some decisions, it may be best to get a body with a policy agenda to make the initial decision, because appeal or review by an independent body may be enough to protect those interests of a complainant that ought to be protected by law. And the jurisdiction of the court in review or appeal need not be as intrusive as the court's jurisdiction was in *Porter v Magill*.

Think of the police authority in *Ridge v Baldwin* [1964] AC 40. A police authority is responsible for preserving the reputation of the police. A threat to that reputation might lead it to a conclusion that Ridge had to be sacked for the good of the police force, without due regard for Ridge's own interests. However, if the decision were left to an independent body that could pass judgment on the situation without trying to push through a policy agenda, the decision as to whether Ridge should be Chief Constable would be deeply detached from management of the police. Since the role of the Chief Constable is critical to the management of a police service, an independent body set up to decide whether a police chief should be dismissed either would become the real police service management (and then it would not be independent any more), or would make uninformed decisions. Ridge has no right to a system that detaches decisions as to his position as police chief from the management of the police force. He does have a right to judicial review to impose fair procedures on the police authority and to prevent abuse of power. Judicial review on those grounds does not detach the decision from the management of the force.

Because the managers of a police service ought to have a say in the discipline and dismissal of police officers, there is no injustice to Ridge in a general scheme that gives the police authority a power to dismiss, as long as there is independent and effective review on grounds of due process and abuse of power.

But compound decision making undoubtedly creates risks:

(1) a risk of **particular injustices** if the independent reviewer fails to identify or to remedy an injustice in the decision of the initial decision maker; and, conversely,

(2) a risk that the independent reviewer will **interfere with sound decisions**, in the mistaken view that it knows what decision the initial decision maker ought to have made.

Today, the requirements of Art 6 of the Convention are met if a public servant who is dismissed has access to an independent tribunal that can reverse the decision. Neither common law fairness nor the Convention forbids administrative bodies to determine people's rights, as long as an independent tribunal has power to determine the lawfulness of the decision.

---

[36] He also held that this view was consistent with the interpretation of Art 6 by the Strasbourg Court in *Bryan v United Kingdom* (1995) 21 EHRR 342, 360.

In *Runa Begum v Tower Hamlets LBC* [2003] UKHL 5, the Tower Hamlets Council had a legal duty to house Ms Begum, who was homeless. She complained that the home that it offered her was in a drug- and crime-infested area, that she had been robbed when she went to visit it, and that her estranged husband frequented the neighbourhood. The Council's decision was reviewed by one of the Council's own housing officers, who rejected her complaint; the housing officer decided that Ms Begum had not been robbed, that the other complaints were not serious, and that the alternatives available in the borough were no better. Ms Begum claimed that the process infringed her Art 6 right to an independent tribunal.

The housing officer certainly was not independent. But Ms Begum had a statutory appeal to the county court. Her right to determination of her civil rights by an independent tribunal was not infringed if it was the county court that determined them. But she claimed that her rights were already determined before she could get to the court, because she could only appeal on a question of law (see Chapter 9), and her complaint was against the housing officer's determination of the *facts* of her situation. So her case raised two questions: (1) did the decision as to whether she had been offered reasonable housing determine her civil rights; and, if so, (2) had her civil rights been determined by an independent tribunal?

There would be two drawbacks in a scheme providing Ms Begum with a fully independent tribunal on the question of whether the housing offered to her was reasonable.

- Process cost (see 4.2, p 123): the Council (or some other public authority) would need to pay for an independent agency to hear evidence and determine the facts of the situation.

- Process danger (see 4.2, p 123): a truly independent decision maker would not be in a position to appreciate some of the considerations relevant to the decision, which include the needs of other homeless people, and the alternatives available to the Council in housing Ms Begum.

Given those drawbacks, the Law Lords thought it appropriate that the Council's housing officer should decide whether the housing was reasonable, subject to Ms Begum's right of appeal. But how can that be squared with Art 6?[37]

The Strasbourg Court had held that if a decision determines civil rights and obligations, then the initial decision maker must either comply with the requirements of Art 6(1), or be 'subject to subsequent control by a judicial body that has full jurisdiction and does provide the guarantees of Article 6(1)' (*Albert and Le Compte v Belgium* (1983) 5 EHRR 533 [29]). That suggests, of course, that 'full jurisdiction' is compatible with a scheme in which a reviewing court does not replace the initial decision maker's view on all points with its own. The House of Lords took up this suggestion. Lord Hoffmann held in *Alconbury*, at [87], that 'full jurisdiction' does not mean full

---

[37] The majority assumed, without deciding, that Art 6 applied. After *R (A) v Croydon* (see 5.3.1, p 182), it would be possible to argue that Art 6 does not apply to a case such as *Runa Begum*.

decision-making power. It means full jurisdiction to deal with the case as 'the nature of the decision requires'; this was unanimously approved by the Law Lords in *Runa Begum*. 'Full jurisdiction' means jurisdiction that is sufficient for the purpose of vindicating the due process rights in Art 6.

As Lord Bingham put it, 'the more elastic the interpretation given to "civil rights", the more flexible must be the approach to the requirement of independent and impartial review if the emasculation (by over-judicialization) of administrative welfare schemes is to be avoided' (*Runa Begum* [5]).

This means that the **principle of relativity** (see 1.3) is a principle of the interpretation of an international human rights instrument like the Convention. Even under Art 6, the need for independent decision making depends on the context. For example, the right to an independent decision maker is violated if the Home Secretary decides a tariff (*R (Anderson) v Home Secretary* [2002] UKHL 46), but not if the Home Secretary *reviews* a tariff during the prisoner's term of imprisonment (*R (Smith) v Home Secretary* [2005] UKHL 51).

> ### Common law procedural protections extend more broadly than the protections in Art 6
>
> The common law of due process is not restricted to decisions that determine 'civil rights'. Determination of civil rights is only one consideration that goes into the due process calculation at common law (it is a ground for the right to a hearing). English courts have sometimes imposed on themselves a similar classification problem, by holding that natural justice must be given in judicial and quasi-judicial decisions, but not in administrative decisions (see 4.3.1). But the House of Lords in *Ridge v Baldwin* re-established a more flexible approach to due process at common law, which makes it unnecessary for English courts to define a boundary between decisions that do and do not require due process. So Sedley LJ has said, in *R (Wooder) v Feggetter* [2002] EWCA Civ 554, [46]:
>
> > ' One relevant divergence [between the Convention and the common law] is that the common law sets high standards of due process in non-judicial settings to which the European Court of Human Rights at Strasbourg declines to apply Art 6 of the Convention for the Protection of Human Rights and Fundamental Freedoms. Here a claimant can derive better protection from the common law than from the Convention, and the Human Rights Act 1998 s 11(a) expressly preserves his right to do so. '

In these compound decision-making cases, shouldn't the complainant still get a fair hearing before the first body? Yes, of course they should, and that is why a biased decision before an initial decision maker is always a breach of Art 6. But the guarantee of *independent* decision making in Art 6 has to be interpreted in a way that promotes due process, and independence is simply not a general requirement of fair governmental decision making, even where the decision affects people's rights and obligations.

5.3.3 The value of independence

We can conclude with three basic points about the value of independence. First, **independence is not necessarily a good thing**. It tends to improve the capacity to act with impartiality, so it may not be valuable if a decision maker need not or should not act impartially. That follows from the *Alconbury* and *Runa Begum* cases. As Lord Hoffmann has said: 'Independence makes the courts more suited to deciding some kinds of questions and being elected makes the legislature or executive more suited to deciding others' (*R (ProLife Alliance) v British Broadcasting Corporation* [2003] UKHL 23 [76]).

Second, independent decision making can sometimes be a good idea *not* because decisions as to rights need to be insulated from policy making, but because **independence may improve policy making**. One of the first initiatives of the new Labour government in 1997 was to give away the role of setting interest rates to the Monetary Policy Committee (MPC) of the Bank of England. Under the Bank of England Act 1998, the Committee is to support the government's economic policy—but that duty is subject to a *primary* duty to maintain price stability (that is, to keep inflation under control (s 11)). And questions as to what those duties require are questions for the MPC. The government cannot ordinarily give directions to the Bank as to monetary policy, although it can take over in 'extreme economic circumstances' (s 19). The idea was that independence would enhance policy making by insulating interest-rate decisions from political pressures that might influence the government to take bad risks with decisions that might boost inflation. More generally, over the next ten years, Labour governments expanded a trend that the Conservatives started in the 1980s, toward policy implementation by 'non-departmental public bodies' that operate with substantial independence from government (see 15.1.1). The Prisons Service, the Child Support Agency, the Benefits Agency, NHS trusts, and many other bodies are designed to achieve good delivery of public services in partial autonomy from government departments.

Finally, we should note that the **independence of *judges*** is part of the **core rationale** (see 2.8) for judicial review. Judicial review can be a good way of securing responsible government partly because of the protection that independent judges are able to provide *for* due process and *against* abuse of power. And by the same token the independence of tribunal judges is part of the rationale that successive Parliaments have had over a century, for committing the resolution of complaints over a wide variety of government acts to specialist tribunals (see Chapter 12).

5.4 Policy and prejudice

There is a puzzle about impartiality and independence in administrative decision making: why even bother requiring the Board of Works to give Cooper a hearing, before it tears down his house? The Board of Works is obviously predisposed against the complainant if it even reaches the point of listening to him. It only gets to that step if it thinks there is a reason to tear down his house. Or why require the police authority to give Ridge a hearing, when it is predisposed to sack him?

The answer to the puzzle is partly that officials are not incapable of responding to objections to a plan of action that they have in mind. And it is partly that compound decision making can do something to protect Cooper[38] or Ridge from unfairness. But the more important part of the answer lies in the fact that neither independence nor impartiality is necessarily a good thing. A predisposition in favour of a course of action is *not necessarily improper*. There is a rule against bias in all administrative decision making, but *not* a rule requiring impartiality in all administrative decision making. It depends on what kind of decision is being made, and on what kind of predisposition the decision maker has. Partiality is a predisposition (that is, a disposition that a decision maker has before hearing from people affected). Bias is an *unfair* predisposition, and not all predispositions are unfair.

In a criminal trial, a predisposition to convict *or* to acquit would be improper. A court should also begin the hearing of a civil claim with no predisposition in favour of either party. But an administrative decision maker can formulate a very particular, provisional policy objective (e.g., to tear down Cooper's house for non-compliance with safety legislation) and then *ask what someone involved* (e.g., the homeowner) has to say about it. That explains why it is not unfair for the police authority to have power to dismiss Ridge. This is not to say that there can be no bias on the part of a police authority. Bias would be presumed, and members of the authority automatically disqualified, if it had any financial interest in Ridge's dismissal, or if it was prejudiced against him on racial grounds, or if Ridge was in the course of a messy divorce from a member's sister. But it would not be bias, for example, for it to go into a disciplinary hearing thinking that the damage from his alleged conduct, if he actually did it, is so damaging to the reputation of the police that he should be sacked if he has no good explanation.

In a criminal trial, the prosecution puts the case to decision makers (jurors) who must start out with no suspicions. A disciplinary decision is different, and it is not impossible for a decision maker who suspects someone of misconduct to give him or her a fair hearing. Some kinds of decision are different again and are in fact the implementation of a policy as to how to pursue the public interest. In *Ridge v Baldwin*, Lord Reid pointed out 'the great difference between various kinds of cases' in which the courts have had to decide what due process requires: 'What a minister ought to do in considering objections to a scheme may be very different from what a watch committee ought to do in considering whether to dismiss a chief constable' (*Ridge v Baldwin* [1964] AC 40, 65).

The most striking challenges for the law of bias arise where a public authority has a scheme and needs to consider objections to it. If an official has a policy that counts

---

[38] *Cooper* was a claim in tort. A claim in tort against a public authority represents a form of compound decision making, because the public authority has a defence if its action was lawful. So tort claims against public authorities involve a review of the lawfulness of administrative action. See 14.2.

against your argument, can that *ever* count as bias? We will address that question by looking at decisions whether to approve plans for development of land. They are decisions that generate masses of litigation because there is a lot of money at stake, and also because people have such strong feelings in favour of projects that they reckon will improve their neighbourhoods and bitter feelings against projects that threaten them.

5.5 Bias in the planning process

Figure 5.1 is a much simplified account of the elaborate system of compound decision making in England for approval of proposals to build housing, shopping malls, leisure centres, and other developments. 'Planning permission is required for the carrying out of any development of land' (Town and Country Planning Act 1990 s 57(1)). The standard way in which to get planning permission is to apply to the local planning authority: a committee of local councillors, who hold public consultations before deciding whether (and on what conditions) to give permission. In England, the Secretary of State for Communities and Local Government can call in an application (s 77), which means deciding (in place of the local planning authority) whether the project should go ahead. The Planning Inspectorate[39]—an executive agency (see 15.1.3, p 584) of the Ministry of Housing, Communities and Local Government— hears appeals from local planning authority decisions.

An applicant can appeal to the Secretary of State (Town and Country Planning Act 1990 s 78) against a refusal of permission by the local planning authority, or against conditions imposed on a permission. The Secretary of State decides the appeal after getting a report from a planning inspector. The Secretary of State may 'deal with the application as if it had been made to him in the first instance' (s 79(1)). Only the applicant for planning permission has this appeal right (s 78), but third parties who want to complain that the local planning authority gave permission unlawfully can seek judicial review (*R v Hammersmith and Fulham LBC, ex p Burkett* [2002] UKHL 23). The Secretary of State's decision on an appeal (or the decision on an application that he or she has called in) can be challenged through a statutory judicial review process with a special (very short!) six-week time limit (Town and Country Planning Act 1990 s 288). A decision by the Secretary of State not to call in an application is subject to judicial review.

Where does the law of bias fit into that scheme of compound decision making? Here is a starting point. At *every single step* in that very complex diagram, a decision maker should be automatically disqualified if he or she has a personal financial stake in the development proposal under consideration (or if his or her child owns the property . . .). With a financial stake in the project, a local councillor on the

---

[39] https://www.gov.uk/government/organisations/planning-inspectorate.

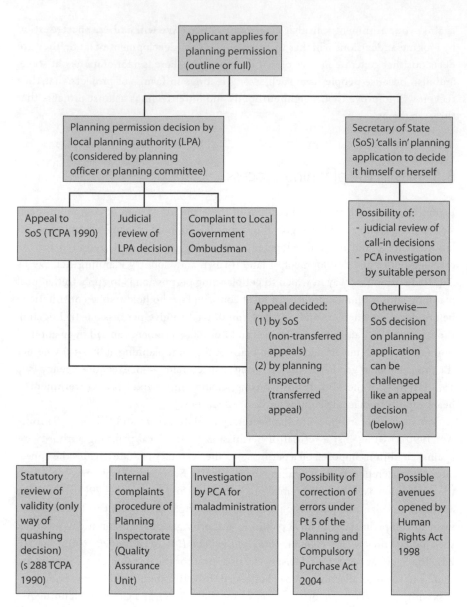

Figure 5.1 Overview of the process of applying for planning permission

planning committee should step aside and should not even play any role in discussions. A local or parliamentary ombudsman with a financial interest should leave it to someone else to investigate. The Secretary of State should declare his or her interest and the Prime Minister should ask someone else to take the decision. A judge should recuse himself or herself. And so on. The integrity of the process would be damaged at *any* point if a decision were made by a person with a private interest in the development.

What about a decision maker with another sort of interest—a person whose policy or whose aims for the area in question are in favour of the development, or against it, or are in favour of imposing particular conditions? Or a person whose political party has such policies or aims?

R v Hillingdon LBC, ex p Royco Homes [1974] QB 720 was the first decision in which the courts quashed a local authority's decision under the modern planning system.[40] The Council granted the builder permission to build houses on the condition that ten years' accommodation in the homes would be given to homeless people whom the Council had a legal duty to house. The Divisional Court quashed the permission, in a decision that the judges regarded as 'a strong step' (Bridge J, 732). Their decision was only justified because the conditions were 'the equivalent of requiring the applicants to take on at their own expense a significant part of the duty of the council as housing authority' (Lord Widgery CJ, 731). The conditions were *Wednesbury* unreasonable (that is, so unreasonable that no reasonable public authority would pursue it; see 2.3, p 48), and therefore unlawful.

But the applicant did not argue that the Council had been biased in its consideration of the application for planning permission. Why not? The Council had obviously not been impartial in imposing the conditions; it had been pursuing its policy agenda of getting the homeless housed at minimum cost. But there is a simple reason why bias was not alleged: pursuing a policy agenda is a form of partiality, but the judges can only call that pursuit an *unfair* form of partiality (and therefore it only counts as bias) if they can hold (1) that it is an unlawful policy; or (2) that the decision maker refused to consider relevant considerations that count against the policy. And if the policy is unlawful or the decision maker refuses to consider relevant considerations, then the decision is unlawful anyway, and the claimant does not need the law of bias.

Yet, increasingly in this century, people challenging planning decisions (disappointed applicants for permission, or competitors who want to stop a successful applicant from building new shops or homes, or local residents who opposed a project unsuccessfully in the planning process) have been trying to use the law of bias to argue that a councillor who has expressed views about the project is biased, or that a committee is biased if a political party endorses or opposes the project, or if the council itself, as opposed to a councillor in his or her personal capacity, has an interest. Opponents of a council's agenda have used the doctrine of bias to take their battle to the courts, after losing in the planning committee.

R v Amber Valley District Council, ex p Jackson [1985] 1 WLR 298 is a classic of administrative law: the first attempt to argue that a planning decision was biased because of the policy of the controlling political party. Woolf J held that the Labour group controlling the Council was indeed 'politically pre-disposed' in favour of the development that it proceeded to approve, but that there was nothing unlawful about it even though the objectors might well think that the planning committee would act on that political agenda (307–8):

---

[40] In the Town and Country Planning Act 1947; now the Town and Country Planning Act 1990.

> ' The rules of fairness or natural justice cannot be regarded as being rigid. They must alter in accordance with the context. Thus in the case of highways, the department can be both the promoting authority and the determining authority. When this happens, of course any reasonable man would regard the department as being pre-disposed towards the outcome of the inquiry. The department is under an obligation to be fair and carefully to consider the evidence given before the inquiry but the fact that it has a policy in the matter does not entitle a court to intervene. '

The caveats to this statement are that (1) Woolf J made it clear that the rules of fairness *are* rigidly against involvement of a councillor with a private interest in the decision (307); and (2) he insisted that the planning committee had a duty to consider the objections to the planning application on their merits (308). But if the committee members took the view that the objections were not good objections *to their own policy,* there was nothing unlawful in that.

In *R v Environment Secretary, ex p Kirkstall Valley Campaign Ltd* [1996] 3 All ER 304 (QBD), 325, Sedley J held that 'a person is disqualified from participation in a decision if there is a real danger that he or she will be influenced by a pecuniary or personal interest'. But he also held that 'the law recognises that members will take up office with publicly stated views on a variety of policy issues' (325), and that (as Woolf J had held in *Amber Valley*) those views do not count as bias unless the councillor refuses to consider objections.

Those classic cases have not stopped angry opponents of developments from alleging political bias. In *R (Lewis) v Redcar and Cleveland* [2008] EWCA Civ 746, the Court of Appeal took a step to keep the law on bias in proportion. In a challenge to a local planning authority's approval of an application to build a leisure centre on land owned by the Council, the Administrative Court judge had held that the fair-minded and informed observer in the *Porter* test for apparent bias would conclude that there is a real possibility of bias if there are 'unusual circumstances which suggest that councillors may have closed their minds before embarking upon a decision' (*Lewis* [11]), and that there were such circumstances, because the councillors who voted for the project pushed it through in the run-up to an election, and the governing coalition on the Council voted unanimously for it [12]. But the Court of Appeal overturned the judge's decision that there had been an appearance of bias. Following *Amber Valley*, the Court held that it is 'not objectionable' for members of a local planning authority to be predisposed to approve a project (*Lewis* [106]). Pill LJ said that: 'The notion that a planning decision is suspect because all members of a single political group have voted for it is an unwarranted interference with the democratic process' [38].

There is no doubt that the *Porter* test is the right way in which to decide whether there is the appearance of a possibility of bias *arising from a personal interest* on the part of a council member. But is it the right way in which to decide whether the party politics behind a council decision reflect bias? Pill LJ actually suggested that the *Porter* test does not apply to *that* question (*Lewis,* [70]–[71]):

> ⁶ The danger of the "notional observer" test [that is, the *Porter* test] is that the role of elected Councillors may not fully be taken into account. That could lead to any Councillor, elected on a pro-scheme manifesto, creating a serious risk of a Council's grant of permission being quashed if he participated in the decision to grant. That would not be in the public interest or accord with the law. It is for the court to assess whether Committee members did make the decision with closed minds or that the circumstances give rise to such a real risk of closed minds that the decision ought not in the public interest be upheld. The importance of appearances is, in my judgment, generally more limited in this context than in a judicial context. ⁹

But Longmore LJ and Rix LJ held that appearances matter, and that the *Porter* test does apply—although it must be applied in a way that is sensitive to the circumstances. They both considered that it is a very hard test to satisfy when the claimant alleges that the party politics showed a predisposition in favour of a project (*Lewis* [96] and [109]– [110]). Rix LJ said that:

> ⁶ Evidence of political affiliation or of the adoption of policies towards a planning proposal will not for these purposes by itself amount to an appearance of the real possibility of predetermination, or what counts as bias for these purposes. ⁹ [41]

Start from a point on which all of the judges agreed (a point established by *Amber Valley* and *Kirkstall Valley Campaign*): that the local council was 'an elected body entitled to make and carry out planning policies' (*Lewis* [15]). Then there can be no bias in a predisposition that arises from the councillors' policies. A refusal to pay attention to the relevant considerations—'predetermination', as Sedley J had called it in *Kirkstall Valley Campaign*, at 325—is ground for judicial review. But for predetermination it is not enough that a councillor stuck to his or her preconceived policy; there would also have to be evidence of a refusal even to consider objections.

So it seems that the Lord Justice Pill's approach must be right: there should be no *Porter*-style appearance test for predetermination, any more than there is an appearance test for *Wednesbury* unreasonableness. Imagine that Councillor Smith thinks that a development will be a great improvement to a town, and is a member of a political party that supported the idea at the last local election. Imagine that Councillor Jones owns the company that wants to develop the land. Because of the appearance of a possibility that Jones will be affected by a financial interest, the law should and does

---

[41] The Localism Act 2011, section 25 provides that '[a] decision-maker is not to be taken to have had, or to have appeared to have had, a closed mind when making the decision just because . . . the decision-maker had previously done anything that directly or indirectly indicated what view the decision-maker took, or would or might take' in relation to a relevant matter. As regards planning decisions, that provision simply restates the common law as set out by Rix LJ in *Lewis*.

presume that Councillor Jones is biased. But bias is irrelevant in the case of Councillor Smith. Councillor Smith must still listen to objections. Councillor Smith would only have a closed mind *if he or she were to refuse to consider the merits*. An opinion that the merits are in favour of a planning proposal is anything but a refusal to consider the merits. And it is not a bias, because the decision whether to approve a development is a political decision.

The Court of Appeal could have done more in *Lewis* to stop litigation in which an opponent to a scheme alleges that the pattern of voting by party members in a local planning committee might appear to an observer to involve a possibility of bias. And the Court of Appeal left the door ajar, in *Lewis*, for claimants to bring proceedings claiming that a political decision was biased because it was *too political*.

5.5.1 Due process comes to the House of Commons tea room

What about planning decisions at the central government level, by a minister? In *Broadview Energy v Secretary of State for Communities and Local Government* [2015] EWHC 1743, the Court of Appeal held that a minister deciding on a planning application has to act like a judge, so that it may be unlawful for him or her to talk to the local MP about the issues in the House of Commons tea room. The Secretary of State had called in an application for permission to build a wind farm, and a minister refused permission. The developer claimed in the High Court that because the local MP had lobbied the minister to try to persuade him to refuse permission (including stopping him in the House of Commons tea room to talk about it), there was an appearance of bias that made the decision unlawful. In the High Court, Mr Justice Cranston's straightforward response was that the planning process was designed to be a political process. Political lobbying by MPs, including in the House of Commons tea room, 'is part of our Parliamentary democracy and generally there can be no lawful objection to it' [49].

When the developer appealed, the Court of Appeal rejected Mr Justice Cranston's approach. The Court found no appearance of bias, but held that it was unlawful for the minister to talk to the MP in the tea room—a breach of the 'ordinary principles of fairness in our law' [42]; the minister had committed a 'breach of natural justice in failing to cut off the conversation and letting the conversation continue' [30] (although the Court did not quash the decision, because it was 'a technical breach which cannot have made any difference to the ultimate decision' [30]). The Court of Appeal rejected the idea that the lobbying was not unlawful because the decision was meant to be political: 'Constituency matters are one thing, but quasi-judicial decisions to be made by Ministers are another' (Lord Justice McCombe [43]).

In calling the decision 'quasi-judicial' ([29], [42]) the Court of Appeal was no doubt influenced by the fact that the Department's own guidelines stated that 'Planning ministers are under a duty to behave fairly ("quasi-judicially") in the decision-making procedure' (*Broadview Energy v Secretary of State for Communities and Local Government* [2016] EWCA Civ 562 [16]). But the 'quasi-judicial' part of that guideline is a basic mistake. The minister certainly is under a duty to act fairly, so that he had to consider what the developer had to say in favour of the development. But the House of Lords established very clearly in *Franklin v Minister of Town and Country Planning* [1948] AC 87 that ministers exercising such statutory powers of decision on planning applications do not have to do so like a judge. They have 'no judicial, or quasi-judicial, duty' (102).[42]

In *Broadview Energy*, the Court of Appeal treated the minister's planning decision precisely as they would have treated a decision to dismiss a police officer for misconduct (see [31]); that is, as if the decision maker had to act rather like a judge, who must not receive representations that the claimant did not get to respond to, in a form of hearing that the claimant did not receive. The last thing a judge in a civil or criminal trial ought to do is to talk an MP in the House of Commons tea room about what outcome the MP would like to see.

The crucial point in favour of Mr Justice Cranston's approach is an instance of the **principle of relativity** (1.3): in order to act justly, a community needs a judicial process for civil and criminal trials, and a quasi-judicial process for deciding on the dismissal of a police officer for misconduct, in order to act justly, a community needs a political process for deciding how land is to be developed.

Political processes are, of course, imperfect. The controls on bad political decisions over planning are (1) local democracy (which sometimes works very well in recognizing and promoting genuine local interests, and sometimes does not); (2) the Secretary of State's power to call in an application (and to hear appeals from a disappointed applicant); and (3) the political constraints under which the Secretary of State works. Where those political processes do not work well, the judges cannot fix them. Litigation is not an effective way to resolve the very difficult questions that a community may face about whether to build houses or a shopping mall on the edge of a town, or whether to build a wind farm in the countryside.

5.6 Conclusion

When is it bias (that is, a bad attitude) for a public authority to act on its policy? Only when it results in a closed mind (so that the authority is not paying attention to the relevant considerations at all), or when pursuit of the policy is *Wednesbury* unreasonable. So, for example, if a police authority were to have a policy of eliminating officers of a particular race, its decision to sack a police officer of that race would be biased. Notice that the problem is one of due process (because the police authority would not be giving the officer a fair hearing) *and* substance (because the authority would be acting on an irrelevant consideration). Chapter 6 looks more closely at the difference between, and the relation between, process and substance. Here, they come together. A public

---

[42] The Court of Appeal referred to this holding in *R (Lewis) v Redcar and Cleveland* [2008] EWCA Civ 746 [43].

authority that sacks a police officer on racist grounds is *both* deciding on substantively improper grounds *and* failing to treat the officer with due process. The decision is biased, but the doctrine of bias has nothing to add to the doctrines of control of discretion that addressed in Chapters 7 and 8.

This fact about bias shows, incidentally, how the entire law of due process is connected with the substance of decision making: the main point of requiring procedures, like the point of outlawing bias, is to get decisions made on the relevant considerations. As Sedley J said in *Kirkstall Valley Campaign Ltd*, at 324, the *audi alteram partem* ('listen to each side'—see 4.3.2, p 130) principle is 'one application of the wider principle that all relevant matters must be taken into account'.

Any obligation to give a hearing of any kind implies some sort of rule against bias, because a biased decision maker is not listening. Alertness to the considerations that a party may offer is an essential part of a hearing. In *Stansbury v Datapulse Plc* [2003] EWCA Civ 1951 [28], when an employment tribunal member had been drinking alcohol and fell asleep, the Court of Appeal found 'an analogy with cases of bias'. Relying on the *Porter* test, the Court quashed the decision because 'the hearing should be by a tribunal each member of which is concentrating on the case before him or her'.

Note, though, that the rule against bias applies without regard to any entitlement to a hearing, or to any procedural participation in a decision. In *McInnes v Onslow-Fane* [1978] 1 WLR 1520, 1530, it was held that even where there was no right to a hearing or to reasons for a decision not to award a boxing manager's licence, 'the board were under a duty to reach an honest conclusion, without bias, and not in pursuance of any capricious policy' (Megarry V-C).

TAKE-HOME MESSAGE • • •

- A **bias** is an unfair attitude. It is a disposition to decide against a party for some improper reason, regardless of the merits of the question being decided.

- A decision maker must be **impartial** when fairness requires it. Unfair partiality is bias, but not all decisions must be made impartially.

- The rule against bias applies to all administrative decisions by public authorities, but impartiality is only required in decision making that is relevantly similar to the role of judge or juror in a court:
  - judges and jurors need to start their hearings with no predisposition to decide one way rather than another (except that a judge may quite properly hear a case even if he or she starts out with a strongly held view on a general question of law that goes against the argument that one of the parties wants to make); and
  - it is not unfair, for example, for a public authority that suspects an employee of misconduct to make a disciplinary decision, after hearing the employee's side of the story, or for planning authorities to pursue their planning policies in a responsible way.

- The **principle of relativity** determines when impartiality is required: the fairness or unfairness of a particular sort of predisposition depends on the nature of the decision.

- **Relations** or **interests** that might lead to an improper disposition are enough to disqualify a decision maker automatically.

- The **appearance** of the possibility of an unfair disposition is enough to disqualify a decision maker.

CRITICAL QUESTIONS • • •

1   What is the point of quashing decisions for the mere appearance of a possibility of bias? Is it to avoid damage that would be done to the good repute of the legal system if bystanders were to be shocked at an unfairness? Or is it to protect the affected party from abuse?

2   Can it ever count as bias for an administrative authority to base a decision on its policy?

3   The common law of due process applies broadly, but flexibly, to administrative decisions, and that is 'one relevant divergence' between the common law and the European Convention (*R (Wooder) v Feggetter* [2002] EWCA Civ 554 [46]). What other divergences are there?

4   What difference is there, if any, between making an unreasonable decision and being biased?

5   It would have taken a 'study of the division of power between administrative and judicial organs' in order for the framers of the European Convention to deal explicitly with the role that independence ought to play in administrative decision making (see 5.3.1). What would that study have to accomplish? How could Art 6 be redrafted to address the problem explicitly?

6   The emphasis in Chapter 4 was on due process, which means proportionate process. Can the law on impartiality and bias be explained as a set of requirements of proportionate process? Or is impartiality (where it is required) an all-or-nothing matter that does not involve proportionality?

READING • • •

R v Amber Valley District Council, ex p Jackson [1985] 1 WLR 298
R (Alconbury) v Environment Secretary [2001] UKHL 23
Porter v Magill [2001] UKHL 67
Runa Begum v Tower Hamlets LBC [2003] UKHL 5

Davidson v Scottish Ministers [2004] UKHL 34
R (Al-Hasan) v Home Secretary [2005] UKHL 13
R (Lewis) v Redcar and Cleveland [2008] EWCA Civ 746
Broadview Energy v Secretary of State for Communities and Local Government [2015] EWHC 1743

On bias:
Sir Louis Blom-Cooper, 'Bias: Malfunction in Judicial Decision-making' [2009] PL 199
On bias and predetermination in the law on planning decisions:
Thomas Cross, 'Predispositions, Predeterminations and the Test for Apparent Bias' [2007] J of Planning Law 1260

 The following online resources accompany this chapter: **summaries** of key cases and legislation; **updates** on the law; **guidance** for answering the pop quizzes and questions; and **links** to legislation, cases, and useful websites.

6 Reasons: process and substance

This chapter illustrates the principle of relativity (see 1.3), by explaining why public authorities may or may not be required to give reasons for their decisions, depending on the type of decision and its context.

The chapter will conclude with an explanation of the difference, and the connection, between the substance of a decision and the process by which it is made. That will prepare the way for the discussion of how judges review the substance of decisions in the following chapters.

LOOK FOR • • •

- The reasons why public authorities should *sometimes* explain their reasons for a decision:

  - requiring reasons may improve decisions;

  - it may be unfair (to a person affected by the decision) for the decision to be unexplained; and

  - reasons may support the rule of law by facilitating judicial review, and may improve transparency and accountability in government in other ways.

- The link between duties to give reasons for a decision and duties to give disclosure before making a decision.

- The *Padfield* practicality principle: even where no one has a right to reasons, a public authority may need to give reasons, in order to avoid a conclusion on judicial review that it acted unlawfully.

- Reasons why public authorities do not always need to give reasons.

- The difference, and the relationship, between process and substance.

> ' [T]he duty to give reasons . . . is a function of due process, and therefore of justice. Its rationale has two principal aspects. The first is that fairness surely requires that the parties especially the losing party should be left in no doubt why they have won or lost. . . . The second is that a requirement to give reasons concentrates the mind; if it is fulfilled, the resulting decision is much more likely to be soundly based on the evidence than if it is not. . . . Transparency should be the watchword. '
>
> *Flannery v Halifax Estate Agencies* [2000] 1 WLR 377 (CA), 381 (Henry LJ)

6.1 Giving reasons for decisions

The giving of reasons is a procedural step that informs people affected by a decision (and, potentially, the public) of the substance of a decision. It seems to be a very attractive general notion that public authorities ought to explain their decisions. It is an advance in accountability in itself. It is a step towards open government, and it can show respect for the persons affected by a decision. And it seems that a court can require a public authority to give reasons with no breach of comity (see 4.3.1, p 128), because a requirement of reasons does not tell the public authority how to decide, but only requires it to be candid about *its own* reasons.

Even here, though, the requirements of the law ought to depend on the context. Sometimes, there is just no reason for the law to require administrative authorities to explain themselves.

Public authorities have no general legal duty to give reasons for their decisions.[1] It has often been suggested that this is an outdated idea and that the remarkable advances in procedural protections since the 1950s have reversed it, so that reasons must be given for administrative decisions unless there is some exceptional excuse.[2] The most prominent suggestion is Lord Justice Elias's remark in *Oakley v South Cambridgeshire DC* [2017] EWCA Civ 71 [30], that 'it may be more accurate to say that the common law is moving to the position [that] whilst there is no universal obligation to give reasons in all circumstances, in general they should be given unless there is a proper justification for not doing so'. He did not say that the common law had arrived at that position: 'It is firmly established that there is no general obligation to give reasons at common law, as confirmed by Lord Mustill in the *ex parte Doody* case' [29]. But you may wonder if it is the right destination point for the common law.

---

1   *McInnes v Onslow-Fane* [1978] 1 WLR 1520, 1531 (Megarry V-C); *R v Home Secretary, ex p Doody* [1994] 1 AC 531, 564 (Lord Mustill). As Sedley J said in *R v Higher Education Funding Council, ex p Institute of Dental Surgery* [1994] 1 WLR 242 (DC), 258, 'there being no general obligation to give reasons, there will be decisions for which fairness does not demand reasons'.

2   See, e.g., *R (Wooder) v Feggetter* [2002] EWCA Civ 554. In *R v Lambeth LBC, ex p Walters* (1994) 26 HLR 170, 177, Sir Louis Blom-Cooper wrote 'the absence of a general duty to give reasons is widely regarded as the greatest single defect of—indeed a blot on—administrative law'. And see *Stefan v GMC* [1999] 1 WLR 1293 at 1300.

As we will see in this chapter, this suggestion can only make sense if it is interpreted as referring to *certain sorts of decisions*, and to requests for reasons by *persons affected in certain ways* by those decisions. And then there is and should be no general duty to give reasons. This is in fact a very important and durable principle, for two reasons.

- **Standing before the public authority:** a public authority has no duty to explain a decision to people who are not affected by it. So, for example, Lord Bridge's classic statement of the doctrine of fairness in *Lloyd v McMahon* [1987] AC 625 concerns 'decisions affecting individuals' and does not give rights to one individual to be told the reasons for a decision as to another individual's position.

Standing to insist on reasons is an implicit, seldom-discussed restriction on legal duties of public authorities to explain themselves. A duty to give reasons—in the cases where there is such a duty—will only be owed to persons whose legally protected interests are affected by the decision. Thus, in *Oakley v South Cambridgeshire DC* [2017] EWCA Civ 71, which extended duties to give reasons for planning approvals (see 6.4), Elias LJ said that the extension 'would not mean that any busybody could seek reasons where permission is granted. The rules of standing ensure that only those who have a proper interest in doing so can challenge a decision' [55]. By this he meant that the duty to give reasons was imposed for the benefit of persons who could challenge the planning decision in judicial review.[3] Standing to insist on reasons is flexible: in the case of planning decisions, it includes not only persons whose property rights are affected (such as those seeking permission to put up a building on land they own),

> ## Open standing under the Freedom of Information Act 2000
> The Act gives a *general* right of access to information to '[a]ny person making a request for information to a public authority' (s 1(1)). That right gives general access to reasons for a decision *if* the public authority has a record of them, and *if* the information is not exempt from disclosure under Part II of the Act (see 1.6.1, p 30). But It does not impose a duty on the public authority to give reasons.

but also persons who have a 'strong and continuing interest they have in the character of the environment in which they live' [59]. But no one can insist on reasons for a decision, if they have no interest in it that the common law will protect.

- **The principle of relativity** (see 1.3): even individuals directly affected by a public authority's decision may have no right to know the reasons for it. For example:
  - general policy announcements by government departments will often be accompanied by reasons, but the government has no legal duty to give reasons just because it has decided on a policy; and

---

[3]   On standing before courts, see Chapter 11.

- even decisions that directly affect particular people do not necessarily carry a duty to give reasons. If 100 people apply for a job in the civil service, the ninety-nine unsuccessful applicants have no legal right to be told the reasons why the department decided to hire someone else.

To see the continued importance—in the twenty-first century—of the rule that there is no general duty to give reasons, consider *R (Hasan) v Trade and Industry Secretary* [2008] EWCA Civ 1312. The claimant argued that the common law required the government to publish reasons for decisions to grant licences for the export of military equipment to Israel, as an instance of a general duty to give reasons for decisions. The Court of Appeal held that any such general duty would be unprincipled. If there were a general duty, 'the court would be invited to require the publication of reasons whenever an individual judge was persuaded that it was a good idea' [6], and the grounds of the resulting duty would be 'simply a cocktail of the particular facts relied on' in arguments in particular cases.[4]

The absence of a general duty to give reasons does not simply mean that public authorities do not always have to explain themselves. It also means that before a court imposes any requirement of reasons on any public authority, there has to be a specific, legal reason for reasons. Reasons must have some legally recognized process value (see 4.2, p 123), or the law does not require them.

It is important to remember these points from the start, because they can easily be forgotten when you see the remarkable judicial extension of duties to give reasons since *Ridge v Baldwin* [1964] AC 40. The rationale for this extension is the same as the rationale for the extension of disclosure (see 4.7). In fact, a duty to give reasons at one stage in the administrative process *is* a duty to disclose useful information for the next stage, when a complainant seeks recourse in a complaint within a government department, or in a tribunal, or in judicial review. Reasons for the initial decision are *especially* important for those seeking judicial review, because the grounds of judicial review are restricted. If the judges were simply to give a new hearing and re-decide the issue that an administrative decision maker had addressed, the court would not need to know the decision maker's reasons.

So *R v Home Secretary, ex p Doody* [1994] 1 AC 531 is both the leading case on reasons for administrative decisions and the leading case on disclosure: the House of Lords required the Home Secretary both to *disclose* the judges' recommendation regarding the tariff to be served by a life-sentence prisoner and to *give reasons* for his own decision. Then the prisoner would be able to use those reasons as the basis for an application for judicial review. The extension of duties to give reasons is part of a trend that Lord Mustill described in that case towards greater transparency in administration.

The same things that make a hearing desirable can make the giving of reasons desirable. Sedley LJ has given a pithy statement of some of the benefits and drawbacks of reasons, and it could equally be a statement of benefits and drawbacks of hearings:

----

4   See 11.2.1, p 427, for an argument that the claimant in *Hasan* should not even have been given permission to seek judicial review.

> ' The giving of reasons may among other things concentrate the decision-maker's mind on the right questions; demonstrate to the recipient that this is so; show that the issues have been conscientiously addressed and how the result has been reached; or alternatively alert the recipient to a justiciable flaw in the process. On the other side of the argument, it may place an undue burden on decision-makers; demand an appearance of unanimity where there is diversity; call for the articulation of sometimes inexpressible value judgments; and offer an invitation to the captious to comb the reasons for previously unsuspected grounds of challenge. '[5]

So, like hearings, reasons can have:

- **process value** (the values of promoting good outcomes, showing respect for persons affected, and subjecting the administration to the rule of law);

- **process cost** (they are an expensive chore to produce, and they may generate pointless litigation over the wrong choice of words); and even

- **process danger** (the danger of distorting good decision making).

It may seem that the value of reasons is only superficial, because the public authority can simply say what it knows will sound proper, since there is no way of getting at its *real* reasons. But a right to be given reasons can be really valuable. Even a losing party who deeply disagrees with the explanation for a decision is in a better position than a losing party who is given no explanation. Reasons give the losing party something to criticize in public. The mere fact that the public authority had to give reasons confers a gesture of respect on the losing party. The value of respect is equally important in both judicial and administrative decision making: reasons treat a person affected by a decision as someone to whom an account must be given.

Reasons may promote good outcomes by focusing the mind of a decision maker who knows that the decision must not only be made, but also *explained*. What is more, giving reasons can promote good outcomes by controlling future decisions. Consider the giving of reasons *by judges* in the common law: it shows the outcome value of reasons, because it allows the courts to use a sophisticated doctrine of precedent to control the law. If judges did not give reasons, they could not make law. Publicizing their reasons gives the courts a way of developing and improving the standards that they use to decide disputes, and achieving more uniform adherence to those standards. In administrative decision making, the importance of that value is generally more limited than it is in the common law courts. But in the work of certain appeal tribunals, such as the Employment Appeals Tribunal, it has the same value as in the courts. And the Upper Tribunal has the opportunity to use its reasons to control the work of tribunals (see 12.4.6).

---

[5]   *R v Higher Education Funding Council, ex p Institute of Dental Surgery* [1994] 1 WLR 242, 257–8.

More important in administrative decision making is the rule-of-law value of giving an open account—not only to persons affected, but also to the public—of administrative conduct. A duty to give reasons creates a direct and significant way of holding a public authority to account for its adherence to the law. And reasons therefore facilitate judicial review, which in turn is designed to uphold the rule of law. So *Doody* was a major step in the process by which the judges attempted to impose the rule of law on the Home Secretary's power to set tariffs for life-sentence prisoners, before the power was taken away under the Human Rights Act 1998 (see 2.5.1).

In *judges'* decisions, reasons can promote the rule of law because the public explanation of a decision is the most important technique of judicial accountability. Courts give reasons not only for the benefit of the parties, and not only to facilitate the development of the law, but also to show the community that the judges are themselves ruled by law. Responsible judicial conduct depends on the judges' integrity, and therefore on the various institutional and cultural factors that sustain their integrity (such as a good appointments process, good legal education, and an independent-minded bar). Accountability supports responsible judging in the same way that it supports other aspects of responsible government. But in the courts the giving of reasons is the judges' *only* form of accountability, since their independence forbids any other way of calling them to account for the soundness of their decision making. In administrative decision making, by contrast, reasons play a part in a complex system of accountability involving appeals to tribunals, judicial review, investigations by ombudsmen, and inspection and regulation by auditors and other authorities.

Finally, it is worth noting the reflexive value of requiring reasons: they promote due process. Reasons vindicate a person's participation in the process by requiring the public authority to *respond* to the representations that a person made in a hearing. And reasons may expose a process failure by showing that the decision was based on considerations that a party had no opportunity to address.[6]

When does a public authority need to give reasons? As with hearings, the only general statement we can make about reasons is that they are required *if*:

- legislation (including the Human Rights Act 1998) requires reasons (see 6.1.1–6.1.3), or

- it would be unfair not to explain the decision to the person seeking reasons (see 6.1.4).

6.1.1 Legislation: The Tribunals and Inquiries Act 1958

Even before *Ridge v Baldwin*, the Tribunals and Inquiries Act 1958 required tribunals to give reasons for decisions, and in this century reasons are a deep-rooted feature of the system that is emerging from the reconstruction of tribunals (see Chapter 12).

---

[6] The plaintiff made this claim, unsuccessfully, in *Lloyd v McMahon* [1987] 1 AC 625, 697.

The effect of the 1958 Act was dramatic: in *R v IRC, ex p Federation of Self-Employed and Small Businesses* [1982] AC 617, 640, Lord Diplock pointed out that the Act had made a statement of reasons mandatory for 'many administrative decisions that had previously been cloaked in silence; and the years that followed . . . witnessed a dramatic liberalisation of access to the courts'. The giving of reasons had made it easier to challenge decisions in judicial review, and in Lord Diplock's view, that development was part of 'that progress towards a comprehensive system of administrative law that I regard as having been the greatest achievement of the English courts in my judicial lifetime' (641).

After the 1958 Act, scrutinizing a tribunal's reasons became the stock in trade of lawyers acting for people with a complaint against a public authority, both because the reasons might disclose that the decision was based on an error of law or an irrelevant consideration *and also* because an inadequacy in the reasons became a ground of judicial review in itself. And this development encouraged the development, in *Doody*, of common law duties to give reasons in decisions not governed by the 1958 Act.

6.1.2 The Human Rights Act 1998

Article 5(2) of the European Convention requires reasons to be given for an arrest. Article 6 only states that, in the determination of civil rights and obligations, 'Judgment shall be pronounced publicly.' But the European Court of Human Rights has held that pronouncing judgment generally requires reasons (*Helle v Finland* (1998) 26 EHRR 159). So, where Art 6 applies to an administrative decision (see 5.3, p 178), there *is* a general right to reasons. 'Judgment' must normally be 'a reasoned judgment' (*English v Emery Reimbold & Strick Ltd* [2002] EWCA Civ 605 [7]).

The European Court of Human Rights has linked the requirement of reasons to 'the proper administration of justice' (*Garcia Ruiz v Spain* (2001) 31 EHRR 22 [26]). It has also been linked to fairness (*English* [7]), and to the need to make appeal rights meaningful (*Hadjianastassiou v Greece* (1992) 16 EHRR 219 [33]). So the right to reasons under Art 6 has the same complex basis as rights to reasons at common law. And as with duties to give reasons in the common law: 'The extent to which this duty to give reasons applies may vary according to the nature of the decision' (*Ruiz Torija v Spain* (1995) 19 EHRR 553 [29]).

Aside from the impact of Art 6, reasons may be required for interferences with the interests protected by other Convention rights. Sedley LJ has held that Art 8 (the right to respect for private and family life) 'recognises a standard of protection of personal autonomy' (*R (Wooder) v Feggetter* [2002] EWCA Civ 554 [47]), which requires reasons for decisions that interfere with that autonomy. But he also held that the common law development since *Doody* provides the very same basis for requiring reasons. It shows that reasons requirements, like much of the law of administrative procedures, are essentially the same in the common law and under the Human Rights Act 1998.

As a result, the Human Rights Act only makes a difference to the law of reasons in two ways:

- decisions of the Strasbourg Court as to when the principles apply must be taken into account by English judges (Human Rights Act 1998 s 2); and

- by the Human Rights Act 1998 s 4, a statutory provision that reasons need not be given for such interferences with personal autonomy could be declared incompatible with the Convention.

6.1.3 European Union law

Article 296 of the Treaty on the Functioning of the European Union (TFEU) provides that:

> Legal acts shall state the reasons on which they are based and shall refer to any proposals, initiatives, recommendations, requests or opinions required by the Treaties.

Like reasons under the European Convention on Human Rights, the reasons for this EU reasons requirement lie in the same combination of fairness, the rule of law, and transparency, as in English law: '[Art 296] . . . seeks to give an opportunity to the parties of defending their rights, to the court of exercising its supervisory functions and to Member States and to all interested nationals of ascertaining the circumstances in which the Commission has applied the Treaty' (Case 24/62 *Germany v Commission* [1963] ECR 63, 69). And here, too, the principle of relativity is recognized: '[T]he statement of reasons required by Article [296] of the Treaty must be appropriate to the nature of the measure in question' (Cases C-71/95, C-155/95, C-271/95 *Belgium v Commission* [1997] ECR I-687 [53]).

The question whether a statement of reasons meets the requirements of Art 296 'must be assessed with regard not only to its wording but also to its context and to all the legal rules governing the matter in question. Moreover, the degree of precision of the statement of the reasons for a decision must be weighed against practical realities and the time and technical facilities available for making the decision' (Case C-180/96 *United Kingdom v Commission of the European Communities* [1998] ECR I-2265 [70]).

6.1.4 Fairness

As for the common law of fairness, it is in flux. We can best understand the flux as a developing attempt to give effect to the process values of showing respect for persons, promoting good outcomes, and supporting the rule of law. There is a common law duty to give reasons when it would be unfair not to do so. By focusing on fairness to the claimant, the common law incidentally promotes the rule of law and good decision making.

But the value of reasons is limited, and fairness does not require reasons that would be pointless or worse. Suppose that a police authority has to appoint a chief of police. Suppose that a good result will be the appointment (other things being equal) of the candidate with the best combination of integrity, leadership ability, expertise in police work, and organizational skills. Reaching such a result depends on the sensitivity of the committee members and the sense of the candidates' qualities that they are able to develop in the appointment process. The crucial issue in the decision is the comparison of the qualities of the candidates, and it might be difficult or impossible for the committee members to explain their assessment of the successful candidate to an unsuccessful candidate. An unsuccessful candidate has no right to an explanation of the talents of the successful candidate. Reasons would not help with an appeal, and they might not help the unsuccessful candidate to understand what had happened. They would not necessarily make the decision more transparent, and if they did, that might mean disclosing something that the public authority shouldn't be disclosing to the unsuccessful candidate (that is, the authority's assessment of other candidates).

The requirements of fairness are very different if a police authority is deciding to *dismiss* a chief of police. In *Ridge v Baldwin*, one of the Chief Constable's complaints was that, when the police authority dismissed him, it only stated a general finding of 'negligence', with no particulars. Lord Reid said: 'I fully accept that where an office is simply held at pleasure the person having power of dismissal cannot be bound to disclose his reasons' (66). The House of Lords held that there *was* a duty to give reasons in Ridge's case, because the police authority only had lawful authority to dismiss on grounds of negligence or unfitness. A dismissal on those grounds must be explained. The requirement of reasons in *Ridge* reflects all three of the process values: the value of respect, the interest in good outcomes, and the rule of law. The difference between a hiring decision and a dismissal decision is that the issues are different: the question in hiring is whether someone is the best candidate; in dismissal, the question is whether someone's misconduct or incapacity has made it impossible for the employment relationship to be sustained.

Not all public servants have a right to reasons for being dismissed. Like duties to give a hearing, duties to give reasons do not simply depend on the impact of a decision on a person. We can see this from Lord Reid's statement about offices held 'at pleasure': a dismissal from such an office has just as great an impact as the dismissal in *Ridge* (and is just as capable of being unfair), but that does not mean that the law requires reasons. It is an open question, to be resolved on the general principles of fairness. Lord Reid said that a person holding an office at pleasure 'has no right to be heard before he is dismissed' (*Ridge*, 65), but we cannot expect that courts would treat that as a general rule today. Lord Reid said that there was a clear reason for the rule (65–6): 'As the person having the power of dismissal need not have anything against the officer, he need not give any reason.' But if that person purports to dismiss for misconduct, why shouldn't he or she have to hear the officer and give reasons? Doing so might contribute to the fairness, outcome, *and* rule-of-law reasons for reasons. In Canada, the Supreme Court has held that the requirements of procedural fairness, including duties to give reasons, apply in the same context-dependent fashion to dismissal from offices held 'at pleasure' as in the rest of administrative law (*Knight v Indian Head School Division* [1990] 1 SCR 653). But that means that, *depending on the context*, there may be no duty to give reasons for a dismissal. The clearest example is the dismissal of a Cabinet minister; even though Lord Reid's general rule is in doubt, it is very clear that a minister has no legal right to be told the reasons for a dismissal.[7] The judges would be failing in the duty of comity they owe the Prime Minister if they were to order him or her to give reasons for recommending that the Crown dismiss a minister. The reason is the nature of the Cabinet minister's job: the community needs him or her to be accountable to the Prime Minister in a way that is controlled by no other institution, except Parliament. Even by imposing a legal duty to give reasons, the judges would be interfering with the Prime Minister's political responsibility.

What fairness depends on

Lord Bridge insisted in *Save Britain's Heritage v Number 1 Poultry Ltd* [1991] 1 WLR 153, 166–7, that the duty to give reasons does not 'depend on the degree of importance which attaches to the matter falling to be decided', but 'entirely on the nature of the issues falling to be decided'.[8]

The lack of a general duty to give reasons is not a special concession that the law gives to the executive. Reasons are not required for some of the most crucial decisions made *in courts*, either. In a criminal trial, juries give no reasons for a conviction. Contrast this with the decisions a trial judge makes on legal issues. Here, reasons are required to improve the decision by requiring the judge to explain it, to help the defendant with an appeal, and to improve the transparency of the decision. Yet although a murder trial is the paradigm of procedural protection for a person affected by the decision, reasons are not required for a jury conviction. Reasons would have no reliable process value. The instrument of a jury trial makes a conviction depend on whether ten out of twelve impartial citizens are convinced that the defendant committed murder; their judgment typically depends on their assessment of the credibility of witnesses, and always depends on judgments that can be very hard to explain. The jurors may have different reasons, and there is no reason to think that their explanation would tell the defendant anything he or she needs in order to understand what was happening to him or her, or give him or her any legitimate basis to appeal from a conviction.

---

[7]   'Apart from judges and others whose tenure of office is governed by statute, all servants and officers of the Crown hold office at pleasure' (*Ridge*, 65 (Lord Reid)). Most Crown servants today have a tenure of office governed by statute and statutory access to tribunals for resolution of disputes. But Cabinet ministers do not.

[8]   Approved in *South Buckinghamshire District Council v Porter (No 2)* [2004] UKHL 33 [42].

A reminder of the limited value of reasons

Fairness does not require reasons for the crucial findings in a murder trial. In *Taxquet v Belgium* (2012) 54 EHRR 26, a Chamber of the European Court of Human Rights held that a jury trial on a charge of murder was contrary to Art 6 of the Convention, because reasons were not given. The judges held that it was 'important, for the purpose of explaining the verdict both to the accused and to the public at large—the "people" in whose name the decision is given—to highlight the considerations that have persuaded the jury of the accused's guilt or innocence and to indicate the precise reasons why each of the questions has been answered in the affirmative or the negative' [48]. That decision would have destroyed the jury system as we know it—but the Grand Chamber saw reason and overturned it. The safeguards against arbitrariness in a jury include the openness of the proceeding, the judge's instructions to the jury in open court, and the simple fact that there are twelve members on the jury and that the accused will be not be convicted unless at least ten of them vote for conviction (in England and Wales). Reasons are not necessary for a fair trial.

Judges do generally give reasons for their conclusions on the main issues in a claim or appeal, but not for all decisions (*Flannery v Halifax Estate Agencies Ltd* [2000] 1 WLR 377). Reasons are not generally given for a refusal of leave to appeal, or for some procedural decisions (*McInnes v Onslow-Fane* [1978] 1 WLR 1520, 1533). Those decisions can be crucial to the parties; yet no reasons are required unless reasons would have a distinct process value. Likewise, judges do not generally need to explain why they believe one eyewitness over another. But reasons *are* to be given for preferring one expert witness over another if the decision between them depends on argument that the judge could articulate (*Flannery*, 377).

And the judge's duty to give reasons develops with the law: reasons were generally not given for an award of costs before the Civil Procedure Rules 1998, since costs went to the winner of the litigation except in exceptional circumstances. But the new Rules gave the courts wider grounds on which to use costs to encourage parties not to waste time and money in litigation, with the result that judges may have more explaining to do. If a costs award needs explanation, the Court of Appeal may send it back for the judge to give reasons (*English v Emery Reimbold & Strick* [2002] EWCA Civ 605).

The conclusion is that the question of whether fairness requires reasons does not depend on the *impact of the decision*, but on *the process value of giving the reasons*.

6.2 The deprivation principle

The process value of reasons generally does lead to a duty to explain administrative decisions that deprive a person of a right, or of a legitimate expectation. So there is a general duty to give reasons for disciplinary or punitive decisions. *Ridge v Baldwin* is an example, but the rule extends more broadly today than it did in 1964. This requirement matches the requirement of disclosure before a decision in such cases (see 4.7). The prospect of a deprivation of a right or a legitimate expectation means that the persons affected are entitled to know the case against them:

- through disclosure before a decision is made, so that the person affected can know what the public authority is thinking of doing to him or her and can participate in the decision-making process; and

- through reasons, in order to understand what has been done to them and also to pursue any available recourse (in an administrative appeal or through the courts).

Disclosure and reasons vindicate the right to a hearing in such cases.

In *McInnes v Onslow-Fane*, the plaintiff wanted to know why he was refused a licence to work as a boxing manager; Megarry V-C pointed out that: 'There may be no "case against him" at all, in the sense of something warranting forfeiture or expulsion' (1532). But how could McInnes know whether there *was* a case against him without reasons? The result of *McInnes* is that if a decision *needn't* be based on a case against the applicant, he has no right to the reasons that would let him know whether the decision *was* based on a case against him. Is that unfair? The solution to this puzzle is that because the public authority was deciding *whether to give* a licence, rather than *whether to revoke one*, it did not matter whether the decision was based on a case against McInnes. His case was not a deprivation case: he was only applying for a licence and did not even have a legitimate expectation of being given one. Megarry V-C pointed out that: 'A man free from any moral blemish may nevertheless be wholly unsuitable for a particular type of work.' He concluded that McInnes had no right to reasons 'in the absence of anything to suggest that the board have been affected by dishonesty or bias or caprice, or that there is any other impropriety' (1535).

The courts have made it clear that reasons will very often be required in order to facilitate judicial review. The point was made explicitly in the landmark decision of *R v Home Secretary, ex p Doody* [1994] 1 AC 531, 565:

> ' . . . the decision of the Home Secretary on the penal element is susceptible to judicial review. To mount an effective attack on the decision, given no more material than the facts of the offence and the length of the penal element, the prisoner has virtually no means of ascertaining whether this is an instance where the decision-making process has gone astray. I think it important that there should be an effective means of detecting the kind of error which would entitle the court to intervene, and in practice I regard it as necessary for this purpose that the reasoning of the Home Secretary should be disclosed. '

This important holding does *not* mean that reasons must be given for every decision that could be judicially reviewed (if that were the case, there *would* be a general duty to give reasons for an administrative decision). Lord Mustill's remark depended on the facts in *Doody*.[9] Reasons are required *when a claimant for judicial review needs the public authority's reasons in order for the process of judicial review to be fair*. Even that restricted requirement places a very significant onus on public authorities to give reasons for decisions that penalize, or discipline, or deprive a person of a legitimate expectation.

6.3 The duty of respect

Sometimes, what's more, a person has a right to reasons for a decision just because of the way in which it affects him or her, even when the reasons could not help in seeking recourse against the decision. 'One of the classes of case where the common law implies a duty to give reasons is where the subject matter is an interest so highly regarded by the law (e.g., personal liberty) that fairness requires that reasons, at least for particular decisions, be given as of right' (*R (Wooder) v Feggetter* [2002] EWCA Civ 554 [24] (Brooke LJ)). In *Wooder*, a psychiatrist decided that an anti-psychotic drug ought to be administered to a patient who had been detained in a mental health institution since he had killed a man in 1985. The patient did not consent; the psychiatrist prescribed the drug, and then asked for the second opinion that the law requires before drugs can be forced on a patient without consent. The second doctor agreed that the drug treatment was needed, but the patient was not given the second doctor's reasons for agreeing. The Court of Appeal held that reasons had to be given.[10]

Notice two ways in which *Wooder* goes beyond the approach that had been suggested in *Ridge*, and affirmed in *Doody*. First, there was no allegation of misconduct, for which Wooder ought to be heard in his own defence. In *Ridge*, there were suggestions (although not in Lord Reid's speech) that Ridge might not have been entitled to reasons if the police authority had dismissed him for unfitness, rather than for neglect of duty. Second, the relevant considerations in *Wooder* were a matter for professional expertise. It might seem that there is no process value in giving reasons for a decision, when a layperson would have no relevant contribution to offer to the process. Note also that because the decision was based on the doctor's professional judgement, the value of reasons to the patient in judicial review would be very limited: the court is not in a position to second-guess the second opinion. Requiring a second opinion is itself the chief legal protection against arbitrary use of the power to force drug treatment on an unwilling patient.

The duty of respect (see 4.2, p 123) calls for reasons in such a case: some decisions cannot fairly be made without the best attempt at an explanation, even if the person subject to the decision has nothing to contribute to the making of the decision. The

---

[9] As Sedley LJ pointed out in *R v Higher Education Funding Council, ex p Institute of Dental Surgery* [1994] 1 WLR 242, 257.

[10] The Court of Appeal made the duty to give reasons subject to an *exception*, where the giving of reasons itself would be 'likely to cause serious harm to the physical or mental health of the patient or any other person' (*Wooder* [30]).

only process value in disclosure is the important value of treating the person as someone to whom an explanation is due. Brooke LJ based his decision on 'the social justice benefit' of explaining the decision (*Wooder* [28]). And Sedley LJ held that the decision was 'so invasive of physical integrity and moral dignity that it calls without more for disclosure of the reasons for it' [37]. We can still say that the duty of respect does not require reasons to be given when they would be pointless—but they are not pointless when refusing to explain would itself be abusive.

● *Pop quiz* ●

In *Wooder*, should the doctors have been required to give the patient their reasons *before administering* the drug? Or is it good enough to explain afterwards?

6.4 Trigger factors for reasons

The *Wooder* approach is an important further step in the trend towards open decision making (see 4.7, p 141). It raises a question as to how far the courts will go in requiring reasons for professional assessments. Eight years before *Wooder*, a limit had been drawn in *R v Higher Education Funding Council, ex p Institute of Dental Surgery* [1994] 1 WLR 242. The Funding Council's grants to educational institutions were based on its assessment of their research quality, for which it gave no reasons. In the Divisional Court, Sedley J held that, in cases like *Doody*, 'the nature and impact of the decision itself call for reasons as a routine aspect of procedural fairness' (*Institute of Dental Surgery*, 262); where that is *not* the case, 'some trigger factor is required to show that, in the circumstances of the particular decision, fairness calls for reasons to be given'.

Compare requirements to give a *hearing*. A similar divide can be made between cases in which there is a right to a hearing because of the nature and impact of the decision (such as *Ridge* or *Cooper v Wandsworth Board of Works* (1863) 14 CB (NS) 180), and cases in which there is a right to a hearing *only if* some particular feature of the claimant's case makes it unfair for the public authority to proceed without hearing from the claimant.

Let's call the latter kind of cases 'trigger-factor cases'; *McInnes v Onslow-Fane* is an example of a trigger-factor case in which no such feature could be made out, so that it was *not* unfair to refuse to give reasons. In cases like *Ridge* (which discipline, penalize, deprive of a legal right or legitimate expectation, etc.), the common law requirement of reasons is like a statutory requirement of reasons: it makes reason giving part of the administrative routine. In trigger-factor cases, the public authority has to be ready to explain itself only if some special consideration makes it necessary.

Sedley J's example of a trigger-factor case was *R v Civil Service Appeal Board, ex p Cunningham* [1992] ICR 816 (CA). The Appeal Board in that case had power to order compensation for unfair dismissal, and without giving reasons it awarded Cunningham less than half of what he would have received from an employment tribunal; that major discrepancy provided the trigger factor that called for an explanation.

In *Institute of Dental Surgery*, 259, Sedley J held that 'purely academic judgments' are in the *Cunningham* category rather than the *Doody* category: the Funding Council had no legal duty to give reasons *unless* a trigger factor made it unfair to proceed without an explanation.

If a trigger factor is required, the court itself must be able to identify it, without passing judgments that it cannot legitimately pass. In *Institute of Dental Surgery*, the claimant argued that its widely acknowledged excellence in research was a trigger factor. But Sedley J held that the court could not conclude that the Funding Council's decision was 'so aberrant as in itself to call for an explanation. We lack precisely the expertise which would permit us to judge whether it is extraordinary or not' (261).

If the trigger factor is an apparently inexplicable feature of a decision, it must be something that the court can itself properly identify as so peculiar that it is only fair for the person affected to have an explanation. In the case of administrative assessments of dental surgery research, the trigger would have to be something 'aberrant'. But that is not a general standard. In *Oakley v South Cambridgeshire District Council* [2017] EWCA Civ 71, the Court of Appeal imposed a common law duty to give reasons for a planning approval, where the local council approved the building of a football ground in the greenbelt, against the advice of the council's planning officer. Elias LJ held that the departure from the recommendation of the planning officer on an important matter 'suggests that some explanation is required' [61], and Sales LJ held that 'a particular onus of justification arises' when a council departs from its development plan, or from the protection of the Green Belt [78]. A 'particular onus of justification' is a good phrase for the trigger, and the nature of the decision will determine what it takes for that onus to arise.

Can you get reasons for academic judgments?

Universities and colleges can grade undergraduate exam papers without giving reasons for the grade. But in examining graduate research degrees, the universities have a general and consistent practice of asking for reports from the examiners explaining the reasons for the examiners' recommendations, and those reports are regularly given to the student. If a university were to fail a doctoral candidate without providing reasons, a court in judicial review would presumably require reasons, even if the university's own rules did not require it—either because of the student's legitimate expectation based on the practice, or because of the unfairness of giving no explanation for the rejection of a thesis that represents years of work. So reasons can be expected for one of the most difficult forms of academic judgement. This is the case even though the court would defer (more or less completely) to the examiners' judgment as to whether the thesis met the standard for the degree. The reasons for reasons in such a case are analogous to the reasons in *Wooder*: to show respect for the person on whom judgment is being passed, and to bring openness and a form of accountability to a decision that would otherwise be dangerously secret.

The contrasting unavailability of reasons for undergraduate grades can be explained partly by the massive process cost that it would take to give a similar report on the strengths and weaknesses of each examination script.[11] There is no feasible method for controlling arbitrariness in undergraduate grading, except for careful use of double marking, and review by an internal committee and by external examiners. Students and universities (and, for that matter, employers reading a transcript) have to rely on the skill, commitment, and integrity of markers. Administrative law has hardly anything to contribute.

In the *Institute of Dental Surgery* case, Sedley J pointed out that undergraduate marking decisions are not insulated from judicial review, even though the court will have to defer to the academic judgement of the examiners (262):

'. . . where what is sought to be impugned is on the evidence *no more* than an informed exercise of academic judgment, fairness alone will not require reasons to be given. This is not to say for a moment that academic decisions are beyond challenge. A mark, for example, awarded at an examiners' meeting where irrelevant and damaging personal factors have been allowed to enter into the evaluation of a candidate's written paper is something more than an informed exercise of academic judgment.'

That approach does not mean that reasons will be required for an unexpectedly low grade on an examination.[12]

Awarding of grades in university is a reminder of the basic principle that public authorities have no general duty to give reasons for decisions—even decisions that affect a person profoundly.

After *Doody, Institute of Dental Surgery*, and *Wooder*, there is still a wide variety of decisions—even decisions that shape a particular person's future—for which no reasons need be given. There is no general duty to give reasons, but the cases in which reasons must be given are not exceptional, either, because there is no general power to make a decision *without* giving reasons. It all depends on the purpose of the decision and on the context. And reasons can be required in contexts where they had previously been considered unnecessary. In *Wooder*, Brooke LJ suggested that 'it should not be taken for granted that the HEFC [*Institute of Dental Surgery*] case would be decided in the

---

11 Compare the grading of GCSE and A level examinations, for which no reasons are given. There is a clerical checking service, a re-marking process, you can get your script back, and there is an appeal following a re-mark—but you do not get reasons for the mark.

12 The ombudsman service for higher education does not interfere on grounds of academic judgement, but is prepared to scrutinize a university's operation of its examination system very closely: see 13.9.1.

same way today. Indeed, it might well have been decided a different way [that is, if it had gone to the Court of Appeal] in 1993' [23].

Who or what deserves respect?

Do Cooper[13] or McInnes[14] or Ridge,[15] who are human beings, deserve a form of respect that the Institute of Dental Surgery does not deserve? The courts have not differentiated between personal claimants and businesses, and they do not generally need to. Giving process rights to business organizations shows respect for the human beings they serve, and promotes good outcomes, and serves the rule of law (compare the standing of public interest organizations to seek judicial review—see 11.2.1, p 419). *But* there are some special duties owed only to human beings, because the duty of respect puts special burdens on public authorities that do certain things that can only be done to human beings—such as detention, and dismissal from employment.

6.5 The *Padfield* practicality principle

Since *Padfield v Minister of Agriculture* [1968] AC 997 (see 2.3, p 50), it has been well established that where a public authority has no duty to give reasons, it cannot use its own silence to insulate a decision from judicial review. The Law Lords all agreed. Lord Hodson put it most strongly: if the circumstances suggest that one of the grounds of review is made out, a minister 'would not escape from the possibility of control by mandamus through adopting a negative attitude without explanation' (1049). The result is that public authorities with no *duty* to give reasons may *need* to give the aggrieved person reasons, in order to explain why their conduct is not unlawful.

Before *Padfield* reached the House of Lords, Lord Denning had paved the way in his judgment in the Court of Appeal, which is a classic of administrative law. The Minister of Agriculture had decided not to refer a complaint from farmers to a committee for investigation. Lord Denning said (at 1006–7):

> ' If the Minister is to deny the complainant a hearing—and a remedy—he should at least have good reasons for his refusal: and, if asked, he should give them. If he does not do so, the court may infer that he has no good reason. '

---

[13] *Cooper v Wandsworth Board of Works* (1863) 14 CB (NS) 180.

[14] *McInnes v Onslow-Fane* [1978] 1 WLR 1520.

[15] *Ridge v Baldwin* [1964] AC 40.

This practicality principle is expressed most neatly by Lord Keith in *R v Trade and Industry Secretary, ex p Lonrho plc* [1989] 1 WLR 525, 540: even where there is no duty to give reasons, 'if all other known facts and circumstances appear to point overwhelmingly in favour of a different decision, the decision-maker, who has given no reasons, cannot complain if the court draws the inference that he had no rational reason for his decision'. But that was not the case in *Lonrho*, and 'the absence of reasons for a decision where there is no duty to give them cannot of itself provide any support for the suggested irrationality of the decision' (539–40).

In a trigger-factor case, the question is whether it was procedurally unfair for the public authority to proceed without giving reasons (because the duty of respect called for explanation of a decision that would otherwise seem inexplicable to the complainant). The practicality principle applies even where the public authority has not acted unfairly: if the decision appears to be extremely unreasonable until it is explained, then the public authority had better explain, or the complainant may succeed in challenging the substance (see 6.9.1) of the decision. In such a case, the public authority 'will effectively be compelled to provide reasons in order to defend the case because if no reasons are given, the court may infer that the decision is bad' (*Oakley v South Cambridgeshire DC* [2017] EWCA Civ 71 (Elias LJ at [33], citing *Padfield*).

Since the possibility that a decision will appear to be unreasonable can be unpredictable to the initial decision maker (as in *Padfield*), the practicality principle means that it is good policy to explain a decision wherever it is feasible to do so, if there is someone who may seek judicial review. For this reason, *Padfield* itself has indirectly led to an increase in open government: those developments have given public authorities more cause to explain what they do.

6.6 The content of reasons

When there is a duty to give reasons, it is a duty to give *sufficient explanation, for the purpose* for which reasons are required. It was not enough for the police authority to tell Ridge that he was sacked for negligence; the authority had to explain why it had held that he had been negligent.

Proportionality alert

The content of reasons provides another instance of proportionate process (see 4.4). Reasons must be explicit and detailed *enough* for the purpose. Notice how proportionality acts as a *limit* on what the law requires of a public authority: the public authority need not say more than the purpose requires.

The content of reasons ought to depend on the purposes for requiring reasons, and those purposes are multiple. If the purpose is simply transparency, then reasons must be sufficient to demonstrate that the decision maker is acting responsibly. If the purpose is to show respect to a person affected, then the reasons will need to address the arguments (if any) that a claimant made. Reasons may also be given in the interest of good outcomes or to provide fair disclosure to a claimant who may wish to seek recourse against a decision. In those cases, grounds of appeal or of judicial review partly determine the extent of the reasons that a decision maker must give. The *Doody* principle means that the decision maker needs to give sufficient explanation of a decision to enable the court to decide whether there has been a process failure, or an error of law, or an unlawful use of a discretionary power. So reasons may need to:

- facilitate judicial review (*R v Home Secretary, ex p Doody* [1994] 1 AC 531);[16]

- explain the decision maker's response to representations made by a party;

- bring transparency to a decision to which the court will defer (*R (Wooder) v Feggetter* [2002] EWCA Civ 554, and doctoral examinations by universities).

Reasons required under the Tribunals and Inquiries Act 1958 not only must be intelligible, but also must 'deal with the substantial points that have been raised' (*Re Poyser and Mills' Arbitration* [1964] 2 QB 467, 477–8, approved by the House of Lords in *Westminster City Council v Great Portland Estates* [1985] AC 661). *Poyser and Mills* can in fact be treated as stating the general requirement for any decision given after a hearing (including in tribunals—see Chapter 12): the reasons need not address 'every particular point that has been raised at the hearing', and it takes 'something substantially wrong or inadequate in the reasons' to justify interference on judicial review (478). But the decision will be unlawful if the reasons given do not address the substance of the parties' arguments. So, in *Poyser and Mills*, the decision maker's statement of reasons was held to be inadequate when he identified the relevant issues and simply stated that the facts were sufficient to justify his resolution of the issues.

When reasons are required, their purpose is not to show the reviewing court that the decision was correct. Demanding reasons that show the decision to be the correct decision would presuppose a judicial power to replace another public authority's decision with the judge's own decision. Correctness is not a general ground of judicial review.

And the courts have not generally demanded perfect, or even complete reasons. As *Ridge v Baldwin* and *Poyser and Mills* show, it is a big mistake for a public authority merely to refer to a legislative standard that must be applied and to state that the reason for the decision is that the standard is or is not met. On the other hand, no reasons will be required that are unnecessary in the circumstances. If someone who knows the evidence given and the submissions made at a hearing can understand why the decision was made, that is enough. So, in *S v Special Educational Needs Tribunal* [1995] 1

---

[16] Note that, in *R v Home Secretary, ex p Venables and Thompson* [1998] AC 407 (see 3.1, p 74), it was the Home Secretary's reasons (the reasons that the *Doody* case required) that led to the decision being quashed on the ground of irrelevant considerations.

WLR 1627 (QBD), the High Court held that reasons have to enable a party to establish whether there had been an error of law. A legal duty to give reasons may be satisfied even if the reasons given would not adequately explain the decision to someone
who was not familiar with the making of the decision. The duty to give reasons only
requires an explanation that will serve the purpose for which the law requires it.

6.6.1 Reasons for planning decisions

When planning inspectors report on the merits of a proposed building or development, or when a local authority or a minister decides whether to approve a project,
their reports and decisions often generate anger and resentment. If the project is not
approved, a developer may have a huge financial stake in challenging the decision; if
it is approved, the neighbours and others may be determined to take any measure to
stop it. But it is very hard to challenge the substance of a report or a decision. So claimants often challenge the decision on the ground of bias (see 5.5) or on the ground that
inadequate reasons were given. It is an example of the fact that claimants resort to procedural challenges when it is hard to challenge the substance of a decision they oppose.

The House of Lords established a rule against 'excessive legalism' in reasons
requirements for controversial planning decisions (*Save Britain's Heritage v Number 1
Poultry Ltd* [1991] 1 WLR 153; for an explanation of the planning process, see 5.5).
Avoiding excessive legalism ought to be a general principle of the law of reasons for
administrative decisions.

In *Bolton v Environment Secretary* (1996) 71 P&CR 309, the House of Lords unanimously overturned a Court of Appeal decision that the Environment Secretary had to
address every material consideration, when giving reasons for granting planning permission for a shopping centre. Lord Lloyd said (at 314):

> ' What the Secretary of State must do is to state his reasons in sufficient detail to
> enable the reader to know what conclusion he has reached on the "principal impor-
> tant controversial issues". To require him to refer to every material consideration,
> however insignificant, and to deal with every argument, however peripheral, would
> be to impose an unjustifiable burden. '

The Law Lords held that reasons for planning inspectors' conclusions may be
brief, and need only explain what needs to be explained to people who are aware
of the issues and the arguments made in the inquiry. Hoffmann LJ said that: 'The
inspector is not writing an examination paper' (*South Somerset District Council v
Environment Secretary* [1993] 1 PLR 80, 83, approved in *South Buckinghamshire
District Council v Porter (No 2)* [2004] UKHL 33 [29] (Lord Brown)). Lord Bridge
held, in *Save Britain's Heritage*, that even a *deficiency* in reasons will not be enough
to justify quashing a planning report, unless 'the lacuna in the stated reasons is
such as to raise a substantial doubt as to whether the decision was based on relevant grounds and was otherwise free from any flaw in the decision-making process

which would afford a ground for quashing the decision' (168). That means—as Lord Mustill suggested in *Doody*—that reasons must be tailored to the grounds of judicial review. So in *R (Campaign to Protect Rural England) v Dover DC* [2016] EWCA Civ 936, Lord Justice Laws quashed a local council's decision to approve a development that would cause significant harm to an 'Area of Outstanding Natural Beauty'. The Council's minutes recorded only that the Council thought the impact on the Area could be minimized, and the Court of Appeal held that that was not a sufficient explanation, because of the importance of the issue. Laws LJ added that the decision 'should not be read as imposing in general an onerous duty on local planning authorities to give reasons for the grant of permissions' [32], and cited Lord Brown's remark in the *South Buckhinghamshire* case that the content of the duty to give reasons depends on the nature of the issues being decided.

Public reasons

There are many situations in which public authorities need to explain their actions to other public authorities; the examples that have special constitutional importance are the responsibility of ministers to answer questions in Parliament about the conduct of their department, and the ministers' managerial capacity to ask questions of civil servants in their departments, and of agencies that carry out public functions on behalf of the government. But departments and other public authorities may also have to explain the reasons for their decisions to independent investigators such as ombudsmen (see Chapter 13) and auditors (see 15.4.2).

Compare Art 15(3) of the European Convention on Human Rights, which imposes a control on derogations from Convention rights in time of war or other public emergency. The government must 'keep the Secretary General of the Council of Europe fully informed of the measures which it has taken and the reasons therefor'.

6.7 How to remedy a failure to give reasons

If no reasons were given where they ought to have been given, or inadequate reasons were given, it may seem that the court ought to quash the decision. But it does not follow automatically. The court need not quash the decision if it can invite the decision maker to give reasons for the decision being challenged (*Flannery v Halifax Estate Agencies* [2000] 1 WLR 377 (CA), 383). But that may no longer be possible by the time of judicial review; it was impossible in *Flannery*, a case concerning a county court decision, because the decision was more than a year old by the time it reached the Court of Appeal.

In *R (O) v West London Mental Health NHS Trust* [2005] EWHC 604, the defendant had a common law duty to give reasons for refusing to discharge a paranoid schizophrenic patient. When the patient pointed out that the stated reasons did not address the crucial question of whether he would be a danger to himself or others, the Trust gave further reasons addressing that point. On judicial review, the court held that, in a case involving personal liberty, 'the adequacy of the reasons is itself made a condition of the legality of the decision' [18], and declared that the decision was a nullity [24].

We should not conclude that the court must automatically quash a decision affecting personal liberty where the decision maker adds further explanation after giving inadequate reasons. Even if adequate reasons are a condition of the legality of a decision, the court has discretion not to give any remedy (see 10.4.6). How should that discretion be exercised? There are two points in favour of the decision in the case, which are addressed in the decision. First is the risk that the giving of new reasons after a patient complains may amount to mere rationalization (that is, phoney reasons) for a decision that was not made on the relevant considerations (but then mere rationalization is a risk whenever anyone gives reasons for anything). Second, for decisions of the kind involved in the case, it is important for the claimant to have complete reasons not at the point when he or she seeks judicial review, but when the decision is made (and invalidating the decision for lack of reasons is a way of recognizing that need for timely reasons).

But if a defect in reasons can be cured by the giving of a proper explanation in response to a query or an objection to the reasons given, then there is no good reason to invalidate a decision, even if a decision is only lawful if reasons are given. It is worth considering that the *courts* are very flexible about the remedying of their own reasons: if a party applies to a trial judge for permission to appeal on the ground of lack of reasons, the judge can give additional reasons. If a party applies to an appellate court for permission to appeal on the ground of lack of reasons, the appellate court can adjourn the application and invite the trial judge to give additional reasons (see *English v Emery Reimbold & Strick Ltd* [2002] EWCA Civ 605 [25]).

6.8 Reasons and process danger

It is a very attractive idea that, as Henry LJ put it, 'transparency should be the watchword' (*Flannery*, 381). But it is dangerous. In *Flannery*, the Court of Appeal ordered a retrial after a High Court judge said that he preferred the evidence of the defendant's expert witness, but did not explain why the other party's expert was wrong. Within a few months, the decision in *Flannery* led to a 'rash of applications for permission to appeal', which the Court of Appeal described as 'an industry which is an unwelcome feature of English justice' (*English*, [3] and [2]). In *English*, the Court dismissed three appeals in spite of 'shortcomings' in two of the sets of reasons, and held, at [118], that:

> ' . . . an unsuccessful party should not seek to upset a judgment on the ground of inadequacy of reasons unless, despite the advantage of considering the judgment with knowledge of the evidence given and submissions made at the trial, that party is unable to understand why it is that the judge has reached an adverse decision. '

It is meant to be a high hurdle: claimants have to convince the appellate court that they cannot understand why they lost. Shortcomings in the reasons are not enough.

Since the common law requirement of reasons is based on fairness, it should only require a fair explanation, not a complete or perfect explanation. The danger is that the requirement of reasons itself, if turned into a requirement of *good* reasons, will distort the administrative process—and the legal process—by generating pointless litigation by disappointed appellants who know why they lost, but want to challenge the result. This danger can be kept under some sort of control through the approach in *English*, and the same approach should be taken to judicial review of administrative decisions for inadequacy of reasons. And the same approach has been taken in the European Court of Human Rights concerning the right to reasons under Art 6. That requirement has been interpreted not to require a detailed answer to every argument of a party (*Ruiz Torija v Spain* (1995) EHRR 553, 562). And in EU law, the requirement of reasons in Art 296 TFEU does *not* mean that the Commission must 'discuss all the issues of fact and law raised by every party during the administrative proceedings' (Joined Cases 240–242/82 *Stichting Sigarettenindustrie v Commission* [1985] ECR 3831 [88]).

The law needs to avoid the danger of demanding too much in the giving of reasons for a decision. Can it ever be dangerous to require reasons *at all*? Yes. In *R (Abbasi) v Foreign Secretary* [2002] EWCA Civ 1598, Abbasi's mother claimed that it was unlawful for the Foreign Secretary to refuse to complain to the Americans about the detention of a British national in Guantánamo Bay. The Court of Appeal rejected the claim, on the ground that there were potential disadvantages in complaining to the Americans that the Foreign Secretary had to take into account, but which the judges could not assess. If that is the right decision, one question remains about *Abbasi*: why did the Court of Appeal also refuse to require the Foreign Secretary to give reasons? Here, there is no problem of justiciability: the Court would not have to answer any question it is ill-suited to answer about the disadvantages of complaining to the Americans. It need only impose on the Foreign Secretary a duty to explain *his own* reasons for not doing so. The rationale for the Court's refusal to require reasons is that *communicating reasons* would itself affect relations with the United States and other countries. Then, the mere fact of telling a public official to explain a decision might interfere inappropriately with his or her role. And then a judicial requirement of reasons would be a breach of comity between the courts and the government.

There can be process danger in ordering reasons to be given for a decision. Of course, process dangers should not be exaggerated. In *Ridge v Baldwin*, the police authority doubtless thought that the requirement of reasons was damaging to its function in serving the public interest. The House of Lords' decision in the case is a rejection of any *general* notion that it is damaging to require a public authority to explain itself.

The act of giving reasons is a *procedural* step. It tells the person affected the *substance* of the decision. Reaching a decision for the right reasons is a matter of the substance of the decision. The rest of this chapter explains the difference between process and substance.

Summary of reasons for reasons

- To vindicate other forms of procedural participation, by requiring the public authority to respond to representations of parties.
- To show respect for a person by explaining what the public authority is doing to him or her.
- To provide disclosure that may be needed for a challenge to a decision in an administrative process, or on judicial review.
- To increase openness of decision making in the public interest.
- To provide a direct form of accountability by requiring a public explanation of a decision.

These reasons may or may not arise, depending on the type of decision and the circumstances. When they do arise, they reflect the three general process values (promoting good outcomes, showing respect, and imposing the rule of law on the administration: see 4.2). Unless legislation requires reasons to be given for a particular decision, the legal duty to give reasons arises only when it would be unfair to refuse to give reasons, in spite of the process costs involved—and in spite of any process dangers.

6.9 The difference between process and substance, and why it matters

6.9.1 The ambiguity of 'process'

Calvin's mom finds a lamp broken in the living room. She asks Calvin if he knocked it over. He says that Hobbes did it. She thinks that Hobbes can't have done it, and there is no one else on the scene. So she decides that Calvin did it, and she sends him to his room for breaking the lamp.

The *substance* of her decision is *what* she decided. It can be stated like this: 'Calvin's mom decided *that . . .*'. So the conclusion that Calvin broke the lamp is part of the substance of the mom's decision (Calvin's mom decided *that he did it*).[17] The punishment is also part of the substance of her decision: she decided *to send him to his room*, and since (like public authorities) she is responsible for her decisions, that entails a decision *that sending him to his room was an appropriate response*.

----

17   Calvin's mom decided *to ask Calvin* (and to listen to what he had to say); that was the substance of a decision as to what procedure to use.

The *process* by which she decided is the way in which she decided, so it can be stated like this: 'Calvin's mom decided *by* . . .'. There is an ambiguity in this idea of the *way* in which a decision is made; it is an ambiguity in the idea of process. A decision is made:

(1) *by* taking steps to obtain information relevant to the decision (typically, steps that involve others in the making of the decision, such as the step of asking Calvin whether he did it); and

(2) *by* reasoning, for example by concluding that Hobbes can't have done it, and by reasoning that Calvin must therefore have done it.

In a 'process' in the first sense, the steps taken are procedures (see 4.6). Other, allied, actions by which a decision maker carries out its responsibility for a decision are also procedures (they include giving reasons for the decision, reconsidering it, or providing an appeal, and so on).[18] A 'process' in the second sense is a process of reasoning.

What about Calvin's mom's decision *that* Hobbes can't have broken the lamp? It is a step in reasoning to the conclusion that Calvin did it. It is part of 'process' in the sense of a process of reasoning. But it is very different from 'process' in the first sense, because *it is also part of the substance* of the decision. It is (part of) what she decided. The reasons for which she reached her conclusion, and not merely the conclusion, are the substance of the decision. They are (part of) what she decided: she decided *that* Hobbes can't have done it, and *that* therefore Calvin must have done it.

The reasoning process is part of the substance of the decision. Process in the first sense is not. Calvin's mom ought to give fair procedures, *and* the substance of her decision ought to be fair. She shouldn't base her conclusions as to what Calvin did on assumptions that she ought to know are false. She shouldn't punish him if he doesn't deserve it. And if he does deserve it, she shouldn't punish him disproportionately.

The decisions of administrative authorities, too, ought to be fair in process and fair in substance. But the difference between substance and process is very important in a system of law, in which we need one institution to control the decisions of another. The reasons for a court to defer to another public authority on matters of substance (which *include* issues of the way in which the authority reasoned) are generally different from—and more extensive than—the reasons for a court to defer on matters of process in the first sense.

We saw in Chapter 4 that courts can generally impose due process on administrative authorities without any breach of comity. They could not generally impose *due substance* without a massive breach of comity. But throughout Chapter 4 the discussion was of 'process' in the first, procedural sense, in which a decision maker's *reasoning* is not part of the process at all. Difficulty has often arisen, in English administrative law, from a confusion between the two senses of 'process'. Although it is possible for a decision to be unlawful because of the reasoning process by which it was reached,

---

18   And procedural flaws may include not only the fact that a decision maker proceeded in the wrong way, but also that it was improper for the decision to be made by the person or body that made it. See Chapter 5.

it is actually a fundamental principle of administrative law (seldom stated and often disregarded) that the law does *not* require public authorities to engage in the correct *reasoning process.*

6.9.2 *Begum*

Shabina Begum was sent home from school for wearing the jilbab, a long dress designed to hide the shape of a girl's arms and legs. Her family said that her Muslim faith demanded it. The school's uniform policy allowed the headscarf and shalwar kameeze (a smock over a long-sleeved shirt, along with tapered trousers), but not the jilbab. The school reasoned that her freedom of religion was not at stake, because mainstream Muslim opinion allowed the shalwar kameeze. She claimed that the school had infringed her right to manifest her religion under Art 9 of the Convention.

The Court of Appeal held that her freedom of religion was affected (*R (Begum) v Denbigh High School* [2005] EWCA Civ 199). And the appeal judges concluded that the school had unlawfully excluded her, even though forbidding the jilbab might be a proportionate restriction on the freedom of religion. The school had not used the appropriate process, because it ought to have *reasoned* that her freedom of religion was at stake and asked itself whether there were interests that justified a restriction on her freedom. *Begum* is the most striking example of the potential confusion between the two senses of 'process'.

The House of Lords rejected what Lord Bingham called 'the Court of Appeal's procedural approach', because 'what matters in any case is the practical outcome, not the quality of the decision-making process that led to it' (*Begum* [31]). He pointed out that the Strasbourg Court takes a 'pragmatic approach' and does not find a violation of the Convention 'on the strength of failure by a national authority to follow the sort of reasoning process laid down by the Court of Appeal' [29]. And Lord Hoffmann concluded, at [68]:

> ❛ In domestic judicial review, the court is usually concerned with whether the decision-maker reached his decision in the right way rather than whether he got what the court might think to be the right answer. But article 9 is concerned with substance, not procedure. It confers no right to have a decision made in any particular way. What matters is the result: was the right to manifest a religious belief restricted in a way which is not justified under article 9.2? . . . Head teachers and governors cannot be expected to make such decisions with textbooks on human rights law at their elbows. ❜

The Law Lords' conclusion about the Convention must be right, because Art 9 does not confer a right to a reasoning process: its purpose is to protect freedom of religion. If the school's uniform policy had the good purpose of protecting the rights and freedoms of others (by fostering an inclusive and non-competitive culture in the school), and the school pursued it without interfering disproportionately with Shabina

Begum's manifestation of her religion, then the school did not infringe her right under the Convention, even if the school authorities did not follow the correct reasoning process. It is now a well-established principle under the Human Rights Act 1998 that a decision maker does not need to refer to the Convention rights in order to act compatibly with the Convention.[19]

But head teachers and governors cannot be expected to make their decisions with textbooks on judicial review at their elbows, either. The strange thing about the decision in *Begum* is the suggestion that 'conventional judicial review' (Lord Bingham [28]) or 'domestic judicial review' (Lord Hoffmann [68]) is 'procedural', in a way that requires that decisions be based on the right reasoning. The idea sounds like a way of expressing the role of courts in imposing due process—which, as we have seen, they can do without any breach of comity. But if 'process' and 'procedural' are taken to include the way in which a decision maker *reasons*, and if the court is considered to have responsibility for due 'process' in *that* sense, then the right to have a decision made in the right way becomes a right to the right reasoning. The Law Lords in *Begum* cannot have meant that any incorrectly reasoned decision can be set aside on judicial review. Lord Hoffmann expressly denied it by saying that judicial review is not concerned with 'whether he got what the court might think to be the right answer' [68]. A duty to *follow the correct reasoning process* would yield a right to the right answer.

Conventional judicial review does not require that decisions be based on the correct reasoning process. It is true that a decision can be unlawful if it is based on an irrelevant consideration, or if a public official does not 'direct himself properly in law' (*Associated Provincial Picture Houses v Wednesbury Corporation* [1948] 1 KB 223, 229). It is these powerful techniques of judicial review, combined with the ambiguity of 'process', that lead judges to suggest that a claimant in judicial review has a right to a decision that is made by the correct reasoning process. But it should be obvious that a flawed reasoning process is not a ground for judicial review. Suppose that a local council has the misconception that its by-laws are not controlled by the rule in the *Wednesbury* case, so that it can decide on any ground it chooses. The flaw in its reasoning would do nothing, in itself, to invalidate the council's by-laws. And similarly in *Begum*: if the school were to think that its uniform policy was not subject to judicial review, it would be making an error of law, but *that* error would not give a ground for judicial review.

But now suppose that a high school prohibited the jilbab for racist reasons. Then, both on the conventional rules of judicial review and under the Human Rights Act,[20] the policy would be unlawful. And that would be the case even if reasonable school authorities might have prohibited the jilbab in the same circumstances, in order to protect the rights and freedoms of others. So a public authority's reasoning *can* make

---

[19] e.g., the Court of Appeal has held that care orders for children must not be set aside 'merely for want of a full quotation of Article 8 even if the respect mandated by the Article is otherwise demonstrable' (*Re S-H (Children)* [2010] EWCA Civ 1184 [30]).

[20] And also under the Race Relations Act 1976 ss 1(1)(a), 17, 18, and 71.

a decision unlawful all by itself. But that can happen only when the mere fact that the public authority reasoned that way is an abuse of power (e.g., because it expresses contempt for the people affected by it). There is ground for judicial review only when leaving the decision to stand would damage values that the law protects—and, ordinarily, a flaw in reasoning (whether in a Human Rights Act case *or* under conventional judicial review) only makes a decision unlawful when the decision injures values that the law protects. That is because it is part of the judicial review of the substance of decision.

6.9.3 *Venables and Thompson*: substance *and* process

The ambiguity of 'process' is not the only obstacle to understanding the distinction between substance and process. Another obstacle is the fact that some judicial review decisions control *both at once*, so that it can seem that there is no distinction between substance and process. In *R v Home Secretary, ex p Venables and Thompson* [1998] AC 407 (see 3.1, p 74), the fact that public opinion was in favour of a long tariff of imprisonment for the child murderers was an irrelevant consideration, and the House of Lords struck down the Home Secretary's decisions in its control over the *substance* of his decision. But the boys' lawyers also put *the same* complaint in terms of procedural impropriety, on the ground that the Home Secretary should not have taken account of 'expressions of opinion' from newspapers (538). So was it unfair for the Home Secretary to listen to the clamour in the media (which is a procedural defect)? Or was the media clamour an irrelevant consideration (which is a substantive defect)? The answer is that it was both—but that does not mean that there is no distinction between process and substance.

The House of Lords quashed the Home Secretary's decisions for lack of natural justice, *as well as* for irrelevant considerations. After holding that the doctrine of irrelevant considerations applied, Lord Steyn held that 'the decisions of the Home Secretary were also procedurally flawed by the credence and weight which he gave to public clamour for an increase in the level of the tariff' (519). Lord Hope held that '[n]atural justice requires' that petitions and newspaper campaigns 'be dismissed as irrelevant to the judicial exercise, as it would be unfair for the judge to allow himself to be influenced by them' and that the decisions were 'procedurally unreasonable on this ground' (538–9).

Part of the procedural problem, as Lord Hope pointed out, is that the expressions of opinion in the media 'cannot be tested by cross-examination or by any other form of inquiry in which the prisoner for his interest can participate' (538). But it was procedurally unfair for the Home Secretary to rely on what the newspapers said for a more basic reason: the clamour was irrelevant. As Lord Steyn put it, the problem of procedural unfairness 'overlaps' with the problem of irrelevant considerations. Paying attention to the newspapers (a procedural step) had nothing to contribute to the making of the decision except a potentially prejudicial consideration (that the public opinion was in favour of a long tariff), which the law forbids the decision maker to take into account.

The overlap between process and substance is not an accident. The standard reason for a procedural step is *that it will contribute to putting the relevant considerations before the decision maker.* As we have seen, that is not the only reason for procedures. Giving a hearing, and giving reasons for a decision, also serve the value of treating a person subject to the decision with respect and the value of imposing the rule of law on the decision by making it more transparent. The variety of reasons for procedures does not detract from the basic, standard connection between good administrative procedures and the substance of good decisions: the procedures should be designed to promote decisions that are good in substance. A claimant who wants procedures that put irrelevant considerations before the decision maker has no right to them, and procedures that put adverse irrelevant considerations before the decision maker are unfair. The reason is that irrelevant considerations cannot contribute anything worthwhile to the substance of the decision.

6.10 Conclusion

Procedural requirements ought to contribute to good substance. The point of procedures is to provide accurate fact finding, faithful application of the law, and responsible exercise of discretionary powers, by the best-placed decision maker, on the basis of all the relevant considerations. This is true even when a procedure is required because of the value of respect: the procedure would be a pretence, rather than a step that shows respect for the person, if it had no potential to contribute to the making of a good decision.

This deep connection between process and substance can make the distinction seem obscure. But it is actually fairly simple. A fair procedure is, typically, an action designed to achieve a good outcome. It would be a mistake to think that the law's concern is only with procedures: its concern for procedures ought to be based on a concern for substantive justice. Remember the paradigm case of a legal requirement of due process: *Cooper v Wandsworth Board of Works* (1863) 14 CB (NS) 180 (see 4.1). Erle CJ thought that a hearing should be given before the use of the power to tear down houses, *because* that power 'seems to me to be a power which may be exercised most perniciously' (188). He suggested that if the Board had listened to Cooper, he might have been able to show that, although he hadn't given notice, the building work conformed to the standards that the Board applied to new buildings. And then, Erle CJ said (188–9):

> ' I cannot conceive any harm that could happen to the district board from hearing the party before they subjected him to a loss so serious as the demolition of his house; but I can conceive a great many advantages which might arise in the way of public order, in the way of doing substantial justice, and in the way of fulfilling the purposes of the statute, by the restriction which we put upon them, that they should hear the party before they inflict upon him such a heavy loss. '

Suppose the Board had given Cooper a hearing, and he had admitted he had contravened the statute by not giving notice, but proved that the work had been done strictly in accordance with the statute. Then, it might seem that the Board could lawfully exercise the statutory power to demolish the house. But as Keating J asked, 'can any one suppose for a moment that the board would have proceeded to inflict upon the man the grievous injury of demolishing his house? I cannot conceive it for a moment' (196). And Erle CJ said, 'if he explained how it stood, the proceeding to demolish, merely because they had ill-will against the party, is a power that the legislature never intended to confer' (188).

There, in 1863, is the ancestry of the control of discretionary powers outlined in *Wednesbury*, which we saw at work in *R v Ministry of Defence, ex p Walker* [2000] 1 WLR 806 (see 2.1), and which is explained further in Chapter 7. It is a form of control over the substance of an administrative decision. And it *also* provides the standard rationale for the law of due process.

TAKE-HOME MESSAGE • • •

- You cannot get reasons for every administrative decision.

- But you have a right to reasons if it would be unfair for a public authority not to give them, or if legislation requires them.

- As with other procedural protections for persons affected by a decision, reasons are required if they have a process value that is worth pursuing in spite of the process cost, and in spite of any process danger.

- But they can only be required by someone with standing to ask for reasons.

- The substance of a decision is what was decided. The process is the set of steps by which the decision was reached.

- Judicial review is available to quash decisions made without *due process*, but the fact that a decision was made by the wrong *reasoning process* is not in itself a ground of judicial review.

CRITICAL QUESTIONS • • •

1   Can the court demand reasons without demanding correct reasoning?

2   Can you give an example of a situation in which a person would have no standing to require a public authority to give reasons for a decision?

3   What difference has the Human Rights Act 1998 made to the law on administrative authorities' duties to give reasons?

4   Should judges be more deferential in reviewing matters of substance than in reviewing matters of procedure?

5   In *Padfield v Minister of Agriculture* [1968] AC 997, the House of Lords did not impose a legal duty on the Minister to give reasons for decision. Would the courts do so today in the same situation?

6   Should the law require universities to give reasons for undergraduate examination marks?

READING • • •

Ridge v Baldwin [1964] AC 40

Save Britain's Heritage v Number 1 Poultry Ltd [1991] 1 WLR 153

R v Home Secretary, ex p Doody [1994] 1 AC 531

R (Wooder) v Feggetter [2002] EWCA Civ 554

English v Emery Reimbold & Strick Ltd [2002] EWCA Civ 605

R (Abbasi) v Foreign Secretary [2002] EWCA Civ 1598

R (Begum) v Denbigh High School [2005] EWCA Civ 199

Michael Fordham, 'Reasons: The Third Dimension' [1998] Judicial Review 158

Mark Elliott, 'Has the Common Law Duty to Give Reasons Come of Age Yet?' [2011] Public Law 56–74

 The following online resources accompany this chapter: **summaries** of key cases and legislation; **updates** on the law; **guidance** for answering the pop quizzes and questions; and **links** to legislation, cases, and useful websites.

Part III
Substance

7 Discretion and deference

The common law controls the substance of administrative decisions through the doctrine of abuse of power. The point of the doctrine is to promote responsible government. The court is to control other public authorities, but it has to do so with comity—that is, with respect for an administrative body's own decision-making role. It is not generally the judges' job to decide whether another public authority made the right decision. The challenge of comity is to work out the difference between an arbitrary decision (which the judges should remedy) and a bad decision (which may be none of the judges' business).

LOOK FOR ● ● ●

- **Deference**—a requirement of comity that depends on the reasons for allocating power to an administrative body, and on the value of review of its decisions by an independent decision maker.

- The **reasons for allocating power to an administrative body**:

  - expertise;

  - political responsibility; and

  - effective processes.

- The resulting **four reasons for a court to defer**: expertise, political responsibility, and effective processes, along with the mere fact that the law has allocated decision-making power to an administrative body.

- The **variation** in the amount of leeway that the courts leave to other public authorities in various situations, and the corresponding flexibility in the standard of review of the substance of decisions.

> ' ... the task of the court is not to decide what it thinks is reasonable, but to decide whether what is prima facie within the power of the local authority is a condition which no reasonable authority, acting within the four corners of their jurisdiction, could have decided to impose. '
>
> *Associated Provincial Picture Houses v Wednesbury Corporation*
> [1948] 1 KB 223, 233 (Lord Greene MR)

> ' It is not the constitutional role of the court to regulate the conditions of service in the armed forces of the Crown, nor has it the expertise to do so. But it has the constitutional role and duty of ensuring that the rights of citizens are not abused by the unlawful exercise of executive power. While the court must properly defer to the expertise of responsible decision-makers, it must not shrink from its fundamental duty to "do right to all manner of people". '
>
> *R v Ministry of Defence, ex p Smith*
> [1996] QB 517, 556 (Sir Thomas Bingham MR)

7.1 Abuse of power: the how-to guide

It may seem that administrative law has always been moving towards greater judicial control of executive power. But we can find very creative judicial interference with executive agencies at the beginning of the administrative state, nearly five hundred years ago. Parliament first established a permanent framework for Commissioners of Sewers in the Statute of Sewers, 1531. The Commissioners were an administrative agency authorized to build ditches and banks and flood defences. The statute said that they could survey existing defences as they 'thinke expedient', and they could build or repair or remove ditches and banks according to their 'wisdomes and discrecions'. And to fund the works, they could charge landowners for the cost, as 'shall seme moste convenient' (23 Henry VIII c 5).

The Commissioners of Sewers repaired a bank along the side of the Thames estuary. Mr Rooke owned seven acres of meadow along the riverside where they made the repairs. The Commissioners charged him for the cost, and took his goods to cover the charge. But the work didn't only protect Rooke's land; there were other landowners with 800 acres of land that was also 'subject to the like danger of drowning' if the bank was not repaired. Rooke went to the Court of Common Pleas—the common law court for disputes between private persons over property—and won his claim for the return of his property.

Sir Edward Coke reported on the decision in his law reports, and commented that:

> ' notwithstanding the words ... give authority to the Commissioners to do according to their discretions, yet their proceedings ought to be limited and bound with the rule of reason and Law. '[1]

---

[1]   *Roke v Withers* (1597) 5 Co Rep 99, 100a.

Today, judges simply refer to the rule of law, rather than 'the rule of reason and Law'. *Rooke* offers an early articulation of what English judges now call the **'principle of legality'** (see 1.5.5, p 22). The Statute of Sewers said nothing about any legal limits on the Commissioners' discretionary power. Yet it was right for the judges to subject the power to limits, to protect Rooke from being deprived of his property by an extraordinarily unfair administrative decision.

The judges' role was not to do the job of the Commissioners of Sewers, but to prevent the Commissioners from using their power arbitrarily. A decision is **arbitrary** in the relevant sense if other institutions can identify it as failing to respond to reason. And then they can rightly interfere, even though the Commissioners were given discretion. Coke wrote:

> ' For discretion is a science or understanding to discern between falsity and truth, between wrong and right, between shadows and substance, between equity and colourable glosses and pretences, and not to do according to their men's will and private affections. '[2]

Those glowing words might be taken to suggest that a judge ought to quash an exercise of discretion if the Commissioners did not get it right. Coke did not fully meet the challenge of explaining the crucial difference between a judicial decision that stands against arbitrary government and a judicial decision that takes over the job of the Commissioners of Sewers. And yet, he did pinpoint one crucial and durable idea that we can use, when he said that the discretion was not to be used according to the Commissioners' 'will and private affections'. In order for an administrative official to make a lawful decision, it has to be possible to understand it not merely as the officials' whim, but as a decision on behalf of the community, taken in good faith for the public good. If there is nothing to distinguish the administrative decision from the arbitrary say-so of the officials, then the court can interfere without failing in the duty of comity that it owes to administrative officials.

Coke found two reasons for concluding that the Commissioners had failed to abide by the rule of reason and law: first, because it was *so radically unfair* to charge Rooke for the full cost of the works, when he occupied less than 1 per cent of the land that would be protected by the works. Second, Coke said that the Commissioners' approach was not a reliable way of funding essential works, since the value of land along a river might be insufficient to pay for the works. By making it more affordable for the payers, spreading the cost among all those affected would mean that the financing, and the works themselves, could be carried out more efficiently.

Why was it up to the judges to come to these conclusions about how the Commissioners should do their job? One crucial element in the decision is the fact that the Commissioners' decision was a decision to take Rooke's property. The common law's long-standing concern for property rights undoubtedly influenced the judges to

---

[2] *Rooke v Withers* (1597) CO REP 99b, 210 (Sir Edward Coke).

take a less deferential approach to the charging decision than they would have taken, for example, if Rooke complained that the Commissioners were repairing a bank that did not need repairing. And still, Parliament had allocated the charging decision itself to the Commissioners. The judges' rationale for interfering could not simply be that another decision would have been a better way of doing the Commissioners' job. The decision had to be identifiable, from the perspective of the court, as a departure from that job.

There were reasons, after all, to appoint Commissioners of Sewers and to give them the job of building flood defences, instead of giving that job to judges. The following are three.

Three potential reasons for allocating a power to an administrative decision maker

- Expertise.
- Political accountability to the government.
- Swift and effective decision-making processes.

Given the reasons for allocating power to the Commissioners, how could it be right for the Court to step in and *contradict* the Commissioners' opinion as to how to carry out a role that Parliament had entrusted to them, and not to judges? The answer is that, even though they were not Commissioners, the judges had the opportunity to prevent injustices in the exercise of administrative power that they could identify without taking over the Commissioners' job, or preventing them from doing their job.

In deciding which injustices those are, judges need to **defer** to the person to whom the law allocates the power, in a way and to an extent that reflects the purpose of that allocation of power. And it is possible to defer more or less, and on some issues but not on others. So it is possible to defer in the way that an allocation of power demands, without leaving the power uncontrolled. None of the three reasons for allocating a power to an administrative official is a reason for allocating *uncontrolled* power to the official.

A court that is prepared to defer to the holder of discretionary power can still intervene to remedy fraud and corruption; those are instances of abuse of power, so that you might say that the Commissioners were not doing their job at all. The idea of abuse is a crucial starting point in understanding the judicial control of discretionary power: the Court in *Rooke's* case did not need to claim (and it could not claim) to be able to do the Commissioners' job better than the Commissioners could do it. The court had to claim that the Commissioners were not really doing their job at all when they imposed the whole of the cost on Rooke. Yet, since it was the Commissioners' job to decide whom to charge, the judges *did* disagree with them about the merits of their decision (that is, about how to do their job). They had to be prepared to do so, or they would not have been able to protect Rooke or anyone else from an abuse of power.

Remember this if you ever find someone saying that judicial review does not control the merits of an administrative decision. The classic example is what Lord

Brightman said in *Chief Constable of the North Wales Police v Evans* [1982] 1 WLR 1155, 1173:

> ' Judicial review is concerned, not with the decision, but with the decision-making process. ' [3]

The implication is that there is no review of the substance, or the merits of a discretionary decision. But in virtually every case discussed in this chapter, and Chapters 8 and 9, the judges display a willingness to concern themselves with the decision—its substance, and not merely the process.

> ### Substance and merits
> The *substance* of a decision is *what was decided* (see 6.9.1). A question as to the *merits* of a decision is a question as to *how good or bad its substance was*.

Judicial review must be concerned with the decision—with its substance and its merits—or it would leave the executive free to abuse its discretionary powers. If a court is to prevent abuse of power without taking over the use of the power, it has to assess the substance of exercises of discretionary power. But it has to do so in a way that gives the initial decision maker a leeway that corresponds to the reasons why the power was allocated to that person or institution.

In England in the twenty-first century, the judges still refer repeatedly to Lord Greene's attempt to find that sort of approach to the substance of administrative decisions in *Associated Provincial Picture Houses v Wednesbury Corporation* [1948] 1 KB 223 (see 2.3, p 49). That attempt was not new in 1948: it is implicit in *Rooke's* case, since the Court of Common Pleas did not claim to have authority to determine all questions as to what the Commissioners should do. And in a series of cases in the nineteenth century, the hands-off approach was articulated better than it was in *Wednesbury*. Lord Russell had sketched the approach fifty years before *Wednesbury*, in *Kruse v Johnson* [1898] 2 QB 91. And *Kruse* was not new; it was based on *Slattery v Naylor* (1888) 13 App Cas 446—which wasn't novel either. The decision in *Slattery* upheld a local by-law prohibiting the burial of bodies in cemeteries within 100 yards of a dwelling. *Kruse* was also a challenge to a local by-law (providing that 'No person shall sound or play upon any musical or noisy instrument or sing in any public place or highway within fifty yards of any dwelling-house' after being asked to desist). *Wednesbury* was a challenge to a local authority decision to allow a cinema to show movies on a Sunday, subject to a condition that children under the age of fifteen should not be admitted. So these three landmark cases concerned the exercise of statutory powers to regulate public order and conduct in the community, which local authorities had exercised for

---

[3]   Cited with approval by Lord Fraser in *Council of Civil Service Unions v Minister for the Civil Service* [1985] AC 374, 401. See 7.3.1, p 254, on the decision in that case.

purposes that they took to be in the public interest. Unlike *Rooke's* case, all three were unsuccessful challenges to the substance of a governmental decision. And the judges in each case tried to articulate a form of legal control that judges can apply with no breach of comity.

The two common strands are (1) that the judges are *not* generally to quash such decisions on the ground that they are unreasonable; but (2) that there are *certain forms* of unreasonableness that do give a ground for judges to interfere. The ground of review is not unreasonableness in general. The ground of review is that, in spite of their disadvantages in reviewing someone else's judgment, the judges can see that the decision is unreasonable in a way that calls for a judicial remedy. So the unreasonableness must be 'manifest' to a reviewing court. Table 7.1 sets out the considerations that the judges held to be grounds for quashing a decision, and the grounds that they held *not* to be grounds for quashing a decision.

Table 7.1 The classic cases: an attempt at comity

	Grounds for quashing a decision	*Not* grounds for quashing a decision
Slattery v Naylor (1888) 13 App Cas 446, 452–3 (Lord Hobhouse)	'[A] merely fantastic and capricious bye-law, such as reasonable men could not make in good faith' (452); 'capricious or oppressive' (453)	A by-law cannot be quashed 'merely because it does not contain qualifications which commend themselves to the minds of judges' (452)
Kruse v Johnson [1898] 2 QB 91, 94–5 (Lord Russell)	'[P]artial and unequal in their operation . . . manifestly unjust; . . . bad faith; . . . such oppressive or gratuitous interference with the rights of those subject to them as could find no justification in the minds of reasonable men' (99–100)	'A by-law is not unreasonable merely because particular judges may think that it goes further than is prudent or necessary or convenient' (100)
Associated Provincial Picture Houses v Wednesbury Corporation [1948] 1 KB 223, 230–1 (Lord Greene)	'[U]nreasonable in the sense that the court considers it to be a decision that no reasonable body could have come to' (230)	'It is not what the court considers unreasonable, a different thing altogether' (230)

7.1.1 The four basic reasons for deference

That hands-off approach to the initial decision is a **deferential** form of control. To defer is to leave the answer to some question, to some extent, to the initial decision maker, so that it takes some special reason for the court to interfere with that decision maker's answer to it (to defer completely is to take the attitude that there can be no reason for the court to interfere). There are **four basic reasons** for deference. In Lord Russell's reasons in *Kruse*, three are mentioned and the fourth is implicit (95):

> ' . . . the question of reasonableness or unreasonableness is one which must be decided by the **representative** body **entrusted with the power** to make by-laws, and **knowing the locality** in which they are to take effect and the needs and wishes of its inhabitants. ' [4]

(1) **Legal allocation of power**: the fact that Parliament *entrusted the power* to the local council means that the council should decide what by-laws the town should have, and the court should not interfere just because the judges would have made a different by-law.

That is important both because of the rule-of-law value of finality (that is, there shouldn't be a further proceeding to upset a decision unless there is a good reason for it), and also because the court ought to presume that the allocation of a decision-making power to a public body was done for some good reason. The three potential reasons for allocating a power to an administrative decision maker generate the second, third, and fourth reasons for deference.

(2) **Expertise**: the council's familiarity with the locality may give it a better grasp than the judges of the considerations that are relevant to the question of what by-laws their town should have.

(3) **Political responsibility**: as representatives, the councillors, unlike the court, are accountable to the people of the community and have the job of acting responsibly as their representatives.

In *Kruse*, the fourth consideration is implicit in the better grasp of the relevant considerations that Lord Russell presumed the councillors to have: it is not just that they are more skilled at assessing those considerations, but also that they have techniques for going about the task that are more effective than the limited and artificial fact-finding techniques that are available in a court.

(4) **Processes**: the councillors have ways of learning what is relevant that represent no failure of due process and which are better attuned to the decision-making task than the courts' heavily restricted processes.

The four reasons for deference are all interrelated. For example: a good power-allocation decision (by Parliament, or the Crown, or by an administrative authority with delegated power) (reason 1) is one that gives the power to a decision maker who ought to have political responsibility for it (reason 3). And it is important that responsibility for some

---

[4] Emphasis added. Compare 'the local authority are entrusted by Parliament with the decision on a matter which the knowledge and experience of that authority can best be trusted to deal with' (*Wednesbury*, 230, although Lord Greene did not mention *Kruse v Johnson*).

decisions be given to people who have the expertise (reason 2), and who have the decision-making processes and resources (reason 4), to make good decisions.

The first reason (legal allocation of power) is enough for a **presumption of non-interference by courts**. That is, if the law allocates responsibility for a decision to an administrative authority, you can never go to a court simply on the ground that the authority ought to have reached a different conclusion. Judicial review is not a second chance at the right decision; the process is a last resort (see 2.7) in which the claimant must ask the court for permission to argue that a decision was unlawful. You need a ground of *review*—a reason for a court to overturn someone else's decision. Otherwise, administrative decisions would be merely provisional, and if you did not like the result, you would be able to ask a court to do the administrative job instead.

What does it take to establish a ground of review that will overcome the presumption of non-interference by courts? It depends! The presumption of non-interference may be very weak or very strong, and its strength is determined by the widely varying ways in which the other three basic reasons for deference apply in a variety of circumstances. All we can say in general is that if Parliament has decided that responsibility for a decision ought to rest with an administrative official, then the court ought to respect that allocation of power. So, in an important restatement of the *Wednesbury* approach, in *R v Home Secretary, ex p Hindley* [1998] QB 751, 777, Lord Bingham said:

> ' . . . responsibility for making the relevant decision rests with another party and not with the court. It is not enough that we might, if the responsibility for making the relevant decision rested with us, make a decision different from that of the appointed decision maker. To justify intervention by the court, the decision under challenge must fall outside the bounds of any decision open to a reasonable decision maker. '

Administrative **expertise** (the second reason for deference) comes in a very wide variety of forms—some quite technical and some (as in *Kruse*) a matter of having a thorough familiarity with the situation in which a decision is to be made. And the **processes** by which relevant information can be found and assessed (the fourth reason for deference) vary, too. By comparison to the processes available to the initial decision maker, the judicial review process may be very effective *or* very poor at putting the relevant information in front of the judges, depending on the issues at stake.

Even the forms of **political responsibility** (the third reason for deference) are various—from the constitutional responsibility of Parliament, which makes its decisions unreviewable, to the constitutional responsibility of the Crown for international relations, to the managerial responsibility of government departments for their own operation. Political responsibility in these varying forms is supported by similarly varying forms of political **accountability**: to the voters in the case of Parliament, to Parliament in the case of the ministers of the Crown, and to superiors and ultimately to ministers in the case of civil servants. Local authorities like those in *Slattery, Kruse,* and *Wednesbury* are democratic, but they have none of the constitutional status of

Parliament, and judges have a variable record in deferring on the ground of the local voters' mandate.

The reasons for deference depend radically on the type of decision, the nature of the initial decision maker, and the context in which the decision is made. Not only do the forms of allocation of power, expertise, political responsibility, and decision-making process vary widely; their importance as reasons for deference varies too, depending on the issues at stake in a particular decision. That is why the **principle of relativity** (see 1.3) is a central principle of the control of discretionary power. What does not vary, though, is the court's constitutional responsibility for preventing administrative authorities from abusing their power, when the court can do so with no breach of comity. None of the four reasons for deference is a reason for administrative decisions to be unreviewable.

7.1.2 Abuse of power and arbitrary government

The one general feature of a decision that tends to justify review in spite of the reasons for deference is **abuse of power**, which is, as Lord Russell put it in *Kruse v Johnson*, 'such oppressive or gratuitous interference with the rights of those subject to [a decision] as could find no justification in the minds of reasonable men' (94–5). This formula, echoing *Slattery* and echoed in *Wednesbury*, makes a very important constitutional move: it preserves the principle that it is not for the judges to decide what local by-laws or licensing decisions would be reasonable, while giving the judges a role in protecting integrity in the conduct of government.

> ### Bad government, arbitrary government, abuse of power
>
> Bad government does not respond well to considerations that ought to guide it. **Arbitrary government** does not respond *at all* to considerations that ought to guide it. **Abuse of power** is the use of power for bad purposes: for example, for private gain rather than in the public interest (such as taking a bribe to release a prisoner), or with malice (such as imprisoning someone just to prevent them from criticizing the government). Abuse of power is an example of arbitrary government, because an official who abuses his or her power is not responding to the considerations that ought to guide its use at all.
>
> There are many bad government decisions that do not count as arbitrary government and are not abuses of power. If the argument against a decision is stronger than the argument for it, then the decision is a bad decision. If there is no real argument in favour of it at all, then the decision is an act of arbitrary government.
>
> Here is what makes it difficult to identify arbitrary government: it can be hard, in some cases, to distinguish between a decision that is only supported by a bad argument and a decision that is not supported by any argument at all.

Because it can be hard to distinguish between a bad argument and no argument, it may seem impossible or paradoxical to try to prevent arbitrary use of a power without deciding how a power should be used. But the judges in the three classic cases of *Slattery*, *Kruse*, and *Wednesbury* showed that it makes sense.

> **If the judges are able to say that no one in *the position of the public authority* could present the action in good faith as a genuine exercise of their discretion, then the judges can interfere with someone else's decision with no breach of comity.**

In that scenario, it becomes the judges' responsibility to interfere to prevent or to remedy arbitrary government. The judges cannot take that responsibility without assessing the merits of the decision. But the judgment they pass on the merits is restrained by the reasons for deference. The result is a restrained, flexible, vague standard of review.

There, in a nutshell, is the core of the doctrine of abuse of power in English administrative law. As a standard of judicial review for very many administrative decisions, it is justified by the **core rationale for judicial review** (see 2.8). Its vagueness gives judges a tool that they can misuse, by striking down reasonable decisions that they do not like, or by leaving abuses of power unremedied. But it also gives them the opportunity to control arbitrary use of power while acting with comity towards other public authorities.

There remains one further point to note about the scope of this doctrine in *Slattery*, *Kruse*, and *Wednesbury*. Like any precedent, the effect of those cases on the law depends on their facts. This point is crucial, because *Wednesbury* has taken on such a legendary role that sometimes it seems like a code for the control of discretionary powers. But because of the principle of relativity, there is no such code. The legal effect of the *Wednesbury* decision depends on the facts of the case.

Slattery, *Kruse*, and *Wednesbury* each concerned more or less democratic decisions of local councils—so the *ratio* in each case is limited in two ways. First, there is good reason, in reviewing some other sorts of decision, for judges to show **even more restraint** than in *Slattery*, *Kruse*, and *Wednesbury*. The ways of controlling licensing decisions that Lord Greene set out in *Wednesbury* do *not* apply to all administrative decisions; we will see, for example, that the courts are not prepared to quash certain central government spending decisions, or certain decisions as to how to conduct international relations, on the grounds on which they will quash local by-laws (see 7.3).

Second (and conversely), the doctrine of abuse of power leaves all sorts of room for courts to substitute their judgment for that of the public authorities with **less restraint**, concerning different sorts of decisions. Lord Greene refused to accept that 'the ultimate arbiter of what is and is not reasonable is the court and not the local authority' (*Wednesbury*, 230), but *that* conclusion depends on the role of the local authority in decisions of the kind it had made in that case. Sometimes, it is an extremely good idea for the courts to set themselves up as ultimate arbiter of what is reasonable, when public authorities carry out tasks that are very different from the task of making local by-laws. The classic example is *habeas corpus* (see 1.1.1): in inquiring into an administrative decision to detain a person, the court will not merely ask whether the decision to detain was 'a decision that no reasonable body could have come to'. The court actually *will* set itself up as the arbiter of what is reasonable. This is not a historical peculiarity of *habeas corpus*: in *R v Home Secretary, ex p Khawaja* [1984] AC 74, an application for a declaration and *certiorari* (a quashing order), the House of Lords decided that the court could substitute its own view for the decision of an immigration officer as to whether a person was an illegal immigrant, rather than merely ask whether any reasonable immigration officer could have reached that conclusion.

Didn't the *Wednesbury* approach apply to *Khawaja*? No. Lord Scarman agreed with the Home Secretary that if Lord Greene's approach were to apply to *Khawaja*, it would prohibit the court from substituting its own judgment for that of the immigration officer. But for that very reason the whole House of Lords refused to take that restrained approach (109–10): 'Such exclusion of the power and duty of the courts runs counter to the development of the safeguards which our law provides for the liberty of the subject.' It may sound as if *Khawaja* partly overruled *Wednesbury*, but that is not the case at all: Lord Scarman said that Lord Greene's approach 'is undoubtedly correct in cases where it is appropriate' (109).[5] *Wednesbury* does not require a restrained judicial approach to the detention of an alleged illegal immigrant, because the reasons for Lord Greene's restraint depended on the facts of the *Wednesbury* case: he was reviewing the regulation of cinemas by a local authority, not the detention of a person by an immigration officer.

More generally, we can say that the courts will take a more intrusive approach to review of an administrative decision whenever they do not have the same reasons for deference (reasons of administrative expertise, political responsibility, and effective process) as in *Slattery, Kruse,* and *Wednesbury*. So consider Lord Greene's view, in *Wednesbury*, that it 'would require something overwhelming' before a court could hold that a decision was so unreasonable that no reasonable authority could have come to it (230). Like the *ratio* of any decision of the common law, the effect of this rule is to be understood as applied to the facts of the case. There is no general rule that it 'would require something overwhelming' before a court can interfere with an administrative decision. The standard is flexible, so that it may require something overwhelming in order for judges to overturn a local council by-law, but will allow judges a more intrusive role in other sorts of decisions where the four reasons for deference apply with lesser force—such as the decision in *Rooke v Withers*, in which the discretionary power was a power to take Rooke's property.

The general rule is that in order to interfere with the exercise of a discretionary power, the court has to be able to see that the decision is unreasonable, *in spite of* the fact that the decision-making power was allocated to another authority, and in spite of any superior expertise or better process that the initial decision maker may have, and in spite of the political responsibility that the initial decision maker may have for

---

[5] But the decision *did* overrule *R v Home Secretary, ex p Zamir* [1980] AC 930 (HL), which had held that the Home Secretary's decision to remove an immigrant could only be reviewed on the ground that no reasonable person could have reached it.

the decision. What does it take to justify that conclusion? Given the flexibility of the standard, judges tend to illustrate by giving lists of instances.

The List—substantive features that make an exercise of power unlawful, *Wednesbury* version:

- **Error of law**: a person entrusted with a discretion must, so to speak, direct himself or herself properly in law.
- **Irrelevance**: he or she must call his or her own attention to the **matters that he or she is bound to consider**, and must exclude from consideration matters that are **irrelevant**.
- Something so **absurd** that no sensible person could ever dream that it lay within the powers of the authority—a decision that no reasonable body could have come to.
- **Bad faith** (225).[6]

● *Pop quiz* ●

Lord Russell's version of The List in *Kruse v Johnson* is largely the same as Lord Greene's in *Wednesbury*, except that Lord Russell *also* mentioned conduct that is manifestly unjust, capricious, inequitable, or partial in its operation, and oppression. Are those separate grounds of review that were missing from Lord Greene's version of The List in *Wednesbury*?

7.1.3 The unreasonable and the irrational

A decision is unreasonable if there is reason against it; the reasons not to do something can be stronger or weaker, so a decision can be more or less unreasonable. A decision is reasonable if it responds to reason, so that it is arguable that it is the right decision. The arguments in favour of a decision can be stronger or weaker, and so a decision can be more or less reasonable. As a result, unreasonableness is an extravagantly flexible thing: on the one hand, you might say that it is not reasonable to make the wrong decision, because there is reason to do something else; on the other hand, even if a decision is quite definitely wrong, people often say that it was reasonable, as a way of saying that there is some sort of strength in the reasoning that supports the decision.

This huge flexibility in the idea of reasonableness makes the standards of judicial review rather vague, but not as vague as you might think. For, as we saw from *Wednesbury*, there is *no general judicial review for unreasonableness*. A public authority should never use its power unreasonably, but a court will not interfere unless it finds a

---

6   Bad faith is the most powerful, but the hardest to prove, of any ground of judicial review. It is a ground of judicial review even if the substance of the decision is *not* so unreasonable that no public authority would have done it. Compare the role of bad faith in the tort of misfeasance in a public office: see 14.5.

kind of unreasonableness that it can act on, while showing respect for the fact that the power to make the decision was allocated to the initial decision maker.

The court can do that if, as Lord Greene put it, a local authority licensing decision is 'so unreasonable that no reasonable authority could ever have come to it', or, more simply, if it is 'a decision that no reasonable body could have come to' (230). The judges call that '*Wednesbury* unreasonableness'.[7] It is a form of unreasonableness that could justify the judges in interfering in a case like *Wednesbury*, even though it is not generally their job to say whether someone else's decision is reasonable.

Picking up on Lord Greene's insistence that it would take something 'overwhelming' for judges to interfere with such a decision, judges have often emphasized that judicial control of discretionary powers may be *very* restrained. The favourite way of making that point is to refer to *Wednesbury* unreasonableness as 'irrationality'.[8] Lord Diplock introduced that term in his speech in *Council of Civil Service Unions v Minister for the Civil Service* [1985] AC 374 (the '*GCHQ*' case), at 410. He tried to shoehorn the grounds of judicial review of exercises of discretionary power into the words 'illegality', 'irrationality', and 'procedural impropriety'.[9]

But 'irrationality' is a misleading term. To everyone except English public lawyers, an irrational decision is one that has no intelligible purpose. If a decision is *completely* unreasonable—so that there is no argument in favour of it at all—then it is irrational. Irrational action is inexplicable. Extremely unreasonable actions can be highly rational; irrational actions are just mad.

It should not and does not take irrationality in the ordinary sense before the judges will interfere. The decision in *Rooke v Withers* was *Wednesbury* unreasonable: no reasonable Commissioner of Sewers would inflict the cost of saving 807 acres of land on the occupier of less than 1 per cent of the land. But it was all too rational: before the Commissioners of Sewers were given their commission, the owner of that land had been maintaining the bank, so it made sense to the Commissioners to maintain the status quo. And perhaps they thought that it was more convenient to collect the whole cost from just one person. Like many abuses of public power, the Commissioners' decision was directed to an intelligible purpose. Yet the radical unfairness of the decision was a good reason for the judges to interfere.

There is probably not a single case in the law reports in which government action was irrational in the ordinary sense. When Lord Diplock wanted to explain *Wednesbury* unreasonableness, it would have been better for him to say that the

---

[7] They often call Lord Greene's version of The List of grounds of review of the substance of a decision as the '*Wednesbury* principles' or '*Wednesbury* grounds'. See, e.g., *R v Environment Secretary, ex p Nottinghamshire County Council* [1986] AC 240, 249 (Lord Scarman).

[8] *R v Ministry of Defence, ex p Walker* [2000] 1 WLR 806 is one example among hundreds (Lord Slynn, 812; Lord Hoffmann, 816). Sometimes, the judges speak of '*Wednesbury* irrationality': *Tesco Stores v Environment Secretary* [1995] 1 WLR 759, 780 (Lord Hoffmann); *R (McDonald) v Kensington and Chelsea Royal LBC* [2011] UKSC 33 [28] (Lord Walker).

[9] Lord Russell had suggested that unreasonableness is irrationality, in *Education Secretary v Tameside* [1977] AC 1014 (HL), 1074.

exercise of a discretionary power may be quashed if the courts can identify it as an abuse of power. Yet it has become standard practice for judges to say that the ground of review is 'irrationality'. When you see that word, you have to view it as code for a complex form of review, in which the courts, for a variety of reasons, conclude that a decision is *so* unreasonable that even though the administrative authority has a wide discretionary power like that in *Wednesbury*, it is no breach of comity for judges to interfere with its exercise.[10]

One danger of the word 'irrationality' is that it suggests that a court can only interfere with a public authority that has gone mad (and done something 'merely fantastic', as Lord Hobhouse called it in *Slattery*). It would indeed have taken a fairly mad by-law to justify judicial review in cases like *Slattery, Kruse,* or *Wednesbury*. Treating those cases as if they held that only irrational decisions can be quashed, judges have often suggested that the law has changed or ought to change, to go beyond 'irrationality' to allow more intrusive control of discretionary powers.[11] But there never was a rule that a court can only interfere with the substance of a decision if it is irrational. Dividing the grounds of judicial review into 'illegality, irrationality, and procedural impropriety' (see 9.4, p 356) is misconceived, even though it is very popular.

In order to understand the real complexity of judicial control of the substance of administrative decisions, we need to go beyond Lord Diplock's labels, and sort out the tools of the trade. Sections 7.2.1–7.2.3 explain what *discretion* is, what *discretionary powers* are, and how discretion is related to *powers and duties*. Section 7.2.4 explains *deference*, and its relation to discretion.

Section 7.3 explains why the courts allow massive deference to public authorities in certain areas of administration: spending decisions; decisions involving technical expertise; planning decisions; decisions approved in Parliament; investigations and prosecutions; and decisions based on impressions.

Chapter 8, conversely, explains when and why the courts afford only minimal deference to some administrative decisions—or none at all. Don't think that there are simply two categories of case; there is an indefinite variety of cases, and there is even a range of ways in which they differ. The reasons for deference are correspondingly diverse, and there is not even a single continuum of degrees of deference.

Yet, in order to understand judicial control of executive power, it is very useful to focus on some of the reasons courts can have for deferring quite radically on some issues (this chapter), and some of the reasons they can have for deferring very little— or not at all—on other issues (Chapter 8).

---

10 Brooke LJ said, 'far too often practitioners use the word "irrational" or "perverse" when these epithets are completely inappropriate' (*R (Iran) v Home Secretary* [2005] EWCA Civ 982 [12]). Compare Sedley LJ's view, in *R (Bancoult) v Foreign Secretary (No 2)* [2007] EWCA Civ 498 [59], that it is a mistake to call a decision 'irrational' if the decision maker's reasoning 'reveals no true flaw of logic but rather an inadmissible or collateral purpose'.

11 See 8.3 for the history of suggestions that *Wednesbury* ought to be replaced with a general doctrine of proportionality.

7.2 Discretion

'Discretion' is a useful word, because it is ambiguous. It refers to a freedom of choice on the part of a decision maker. On the other hand, it is also a sort of synonym for propriety and decency. The double aspect of discretion is that:

(1) the decision maker has a choice to make; and yet,

(2) since it is a *discretion*, the decision maker is to act responsibly and not arbitrarily.

So the choice is not to be made for the decision maker's own personal benefit, but for purposes that the decision maker is responsible for pursuing on behalf of the community. Having a discretion means having a choice; having no discretion means having no choice. Having a discretion does *not* mean that anything goes. Every public power must be exercised responsibly, and every public decision ought to be made reasonably. That means deciding in the public interest, and with respect for the private interests of persons affected by the decision. But for a public authority to have a discretion means that it is *up to that authority to decide* what is in the public interest, and to determine what is required by respect for private interests.

Here is one crucial point that is easy to forget: the fact that a power is to be used responsibly does not in itself mean that anyone else ought to have power to interfere with an irresponsible use of the power. A reviewing court must work out how—if at all—to control a freedom of choice that has been given to another public authority. And it is possible to limit a public authority's freedom, without taking it away.

7.2.1 Varieties of discretion

There are various ways in which a decision maker can be free to decide as he or she sees fit.

- **Express discretion**: a law maker may say that a decision maker is to have a discretion.
  - **Example**: *Rooke v Withers* (1597) 77 ER 209: the Commissioners of Sewers Act provided for Commissioners to cause ditches and banks and sewers 'to be made corrected repayred amended putt downe or refourmed as the case shall require after your wisdomes and discrecions' (23 Henry VIII c 5).

- **Implied discretion**: the same thing can be done implicitly, by saying that a decision maker *may* do something, or that it has power to do it, without saying how (or even whether) the power must be used.
  - **Example**: *Cooper v Wandsworth Board of Works* (1863) 14 CB (NS) 180—'[I]t shall be lawful for the . . . board to cause such house or building to be demolished' (Metropolis Local Management Act 1855 s 76).

The Act implied that the Board had a choice, because it did not say that the Board must demolish the building. The Act stated no limits on the discretionary power, but as *Cooper* shows, the common law may 'supply the omission of the legislature' (194) (see 4.1) and impose limits on the power. So, for instance, the Board of Works acted unlawfully by failing to give Cooper a hearing before demolishing his house.

- **Grants of power in subjective terms**: a law maker may say that a decision maker's own view is to prevail.
  - **Example**: *Associated Provincial Picture Houses v Wednesbury Corporation* [1948] 1 KB 223—the local authority could give licences 'subject to such conditions as the authority think fit to impose'.

That may seem to be the ultimate grant of discretion. The local authority in the *Wednesbury* case *did* think fit to impose the condition that the cinema challenged. So how could the cinema ask the court to pass judgment on whether the condition was reasonable? The answer is that legislation making a public authority's powers depend on what a person *thinks* is consistently read to require the person to have legitimate *grounds* for what he or she thinks. So the legal effect of that legislation ('such conditions as the authority think fit to impose') is the same as it would be if it simply read that the authority may impose conditions. A notorious case during World War II treated an objective restriction on the Home Secretary's power to detain enemy aliens (requiring him *to have reason* for suspicion of association with the enemy) as if it were satisfied if the Home Secretary *thought* he had reason (*Liversidge v Anderson* [1942] AC 206). That approach has been categorically rejected since the 1940s: see, for example, *R (Guisto) v Governor of Brixton Prison* [2003] UKHL 19 [41] (on the difference between objective and subjective tests, see 14.5.1, p 559).

- **Inherent discretion**: a power is *inherent* if a body has it simply because the power is essential if the body is to carry out its role. Inherent powers typically involve some substantial degree of discretion.
  - **Example**: *R v Ministry of Defence, ex p Walker* [2000] 1 WLR 806 (see 2.1)— the Ministry of Defence had a power to create a compensation scheme that had not been conferred on it by any statute or other law-making act; it could decide to give compensation, but it had no legal duty to do so.

All of the major authorities of the state in the British constitution have certain powers without which they could not fulfil their responsibilities. Parliament has inherent discretionary power to legislate. The High Court, too, has inherent discretionary powers to develop the law, and to control its own process (through contempt of court and through decisions concerning procedures).[12]

Administrative authorities have inherent discretionary powers, too. The **prerogative** of the Crown is an inherent discretionary power (but it *is* limited by law (see 1.5.1), and is subject to judicial review). And public authorities that do not exercise the prerogative of the Crown may have all sorts of powers of legal persons (such as the power to contract (see 15.3)) even if Parliament has not acted to give them such powers. Finally, since they need to adopt decision-making procedures if they are to

---

12   Today, the Civil Procedure Rules 1998 preserve these discretions (see 10.1).

be decision makers at all, administrative authorities have an inherent discretionary power to invent procedures. That power is recognized by the common law, but it is also limited by the duties imposed by the common law of due process.

What is and is not prerogative, and why it doesn't matter

The royal prerogative includes a variety of distinctive powers of the Crown. In *R (Heath) v Home Office Policy and Advisory Board for Forensic Pathology* [2005] EWHC 1793, a forensic pathologist challenged a decision of the Board to refer a complaint to a disciplinary tribunal on the ground that there was no statutory power to do so and that the referral to a tribunal was not an exercise of prerogative. The challenge failed because an action of a public authority does not have to be an exercise of statutory or prerogative power in order to be lawful; the court held that the referral of the complaint could be 'executive action'.

The 'executive action' label does not explain why the Board had lawful power to make the decision. *Everything* that the government does (whether lawful or unlawful, and whatever the source of the power) is executive action. The reason why the Board had lawful power to make the decision in *Heath* is a legal principle that has been acted upon, but never very clearly stated in the cases: any public authority has **inherent power** (that is, a power not conferred by any law maker) to act with legal effect where it is necessary for the proper fulfilment of its lawful functions.[13] Prerogative powers are inherent powers of the Crown.

For the purpose of deciding the standard of judicial review, it doesn't matter in a case like *Heath* whether a public authority is exercising a statutory power, or an inherent power, because the standards of review for error of law, due process, and the prevention of abuse of power do not depend on the legal source of the power.

- **Resultant discretion**: suppose I ask you to come to my party, and you ask when you should turn up. I say: 'Oh, please come early.' It may not be clear *how early is early*.[14] Then, my request is vague (because there is no sharp boundary to the actions that count as complying). I have not simply asked you to come whenever you please; I am giving you a standard for your behaviour, and if you don't come early, you won't have done what I asked. But the vagueness of my request (that is, the imprecision as to when 'early' starts and stops) gives you some degree of choice (even though there will be times that clearly are *not* early, and the discretion may be wide or narrow depending on the circumstances). The vagueness of the request

---

[13] See T Endicott, 'Lawful Power' (2017) 15 NZJPIL 1–19.

[14] Note that I also give you an implied discretion: if there is *a range of times that count as early*, my request implies that you can choose among them. An unspecific request confers an implied discretion, and a vague request confers a resultant discretion.

leaves you a choice of how to comply, even though you are acting according to a standard that regulates your conduct.

- **Example**: *R v Monopolies and Mergers Commission, ex p South Yorkshire Transport* [1993] 1 WLR 23 (see 9.3.1, p 353)—the Commission could inquire into mergers that affected a 'substantial part of the United Kingdom'.

Where the law is vague, the power to apply the law is a discretionary power, because the vagueness of the law will leave the administrative authority a choice in some cases that is not determined by law. There is a difference between enacting that a public authority shall have discretion in awarding licences and enacting that it shall give licences to persons who are suitably qualified. But both legislative techniques give discretion.

'What to justice shall appertain'

The world's greatest example of a resultant discretion was conferred on *judges* by the Habeas Corpus Act 1640, which provided that, on the issue of a *habeas corpus*, the court 'shall proceed to examine and determine whether the cause of such commitment . . . be just and legal, or not, and shall thereupon do what to Justice shall appertain, either by delivering, bailing or remanding the prisoner'.

When the law tells judges to do what to justice shall appertain, and does not say what *does* appertain to justice, a wide-ranging discretion results.

Note that all of these varieties of discretion are compatible with the principle that **they must be exercised responsibly**. And that is compatible with control by a reviewing authority on the *Wednesbury* grounds. But to the extent that a reviewing authority imposes standards that require the initial decision maker to use a discretionary power in one way rather than another, the decision maker is left with no discretion.

7.2.2 Discretion and discretionary power

A discretion is a choice that the law leaves up to a decision maker, and a discretionary power is a power that gives the decision maker such choice in *some* cases, on *some* grounds. If you have discretion, the law (while potentially ruling out all sorts of things you might wish to do) does not require a particular decision. It is quite possible that there may be only one lawful way to use a discretionary power in a particular case; *in such a case*, the holder of a discretionary power has no discretion.

Consider *Slattery v Naylor* (1888) 13 App Cas 446. Although the Privy Council decided that the Council had discretion to ban burials within 100 yards of a dwelling, it suggested that there would be no discretion to ban Roman Catholics from conducting burials. The power to make by-laws was discretionary, but it did not give the Council discretion to wage a religious war.

Note, finally, that it may be very controversial *whether* a power is discretionary, and whether the decision maker has discretion in a particular case. In *Slattery*, *Kruse*, and

Wednesbury, each dispute was as to *whether* the public authority had discretion to do what it had done.

A discretion is a freedom of choice (among options that may limited) that is to be exercised responsibly. A public authority has that freedom of choice when it has no legal duty to make one decision rather than another. When a court holds that an exercise of a discretionary power was unlawful, as in *Rooke v Withers*, it is deciding that the initial decision maker had no discretion to make the decision it made.

FROM THE MISTS OF TIME

The idea that discretionary powers are to be controlled by the High Court is very old. In *Keighley's Case* (1609) 10 Co Rep 139, 140a, Sir Edward Coke relied on *Rooke v Withers*, and said that the statutory power of the Commissioners of Sewers to act 'according to your wisdoms and discretions' (Statute of Sewers 1531, 23 Henry VIII c 5, s III) was 'to be intended and interpreted according to law and justice, for every Judge or commissioner ought to have *duos sales, viz. salem sapientiae, ne sit insipidus, & salem conscientiae ne sit diabolus* [two gifts: the gift of wisdom—not to be stupid—and the gift of conscience—not to be a devil]'.

7.2.3 Powers and duties

Giving a power to a public authority always confers discretion, unless the public authority is duty-bound to use the power in a particular way. If the law requires the authority to exercise the power in a particular way, then it imposes a legal duty and there is no discretion. The Parole Board has a discretionary power to release a prisoner after the completion of the tariff period if the prisoner poses no danger to the public. The House of Lords (following the lead of the European Court of Human Rights in *Stafford v United Kingdom* (2002) 35 EHRR 32) turned that power into a duty to release a prisoner who poses no danger. The law requires parole in that situation (*R v Lichniak* [2002] UKHL 47 [20]).

Yet a public authority may have **discretion** in the performance of a **duty**. In *Lichniak*, the House of Lords only imposed a duty to release a prisoner after the tariff *if* the prisoner posed no danger to the public, so the Parole Board had a duty to act according to a vague standard. In *deciding whether* that duty applies, the Parole Board will have a resultant discretion whenever it is unclear whether a particular prisoner poses a danger.

A public authority also has discretion whenever it has a duty to provide a service, but has a range of choices available as to how to provide the service.

....

But is it really discretion?

Can a public authority really have a *discretion* when there are principles at stake (so that it must exercise its judgment responsibly and not just act on a whim)? If not, there are no discretions, since all public powers must be used responsibly.

Sedley J suggested in *R v Tower Hamlets, ex p Tower Hamlets Combined Traders Association* [1994] COD 325 that an administrative decision-making power may be 'a matter of judgment according to the legal principles and not to discretion'.

But if those principles themselves allow the public authority the leeway to choose one way or another, then the public authority has discretion: rather than determining the outcome, the law leaves it to the public authority (to some extent) to decide what the principles require. The making of that choice does indeed require judgment, but the law does not require a particular judgment to be made. Lord Keith took this approach in *R v Devon County Council, ex p G* [1989] AC 573, 604, in deciding whether a local authority had a discretion in deciding whether free transportation was 'necessary' for school students: 'The authority's function in this respect is capable of being described as a "discretion", though it is not, of course, an unfettered discretion but rather in the nature of an exercise of judgment.'

7.2.4 Deference

Deferring to someone else means going along with their answer to a question. As Lord Slynn put it in *R v Ministry of Defence, ex p Walker* [2000] 1 WLR 806, 812 (see 2.1), as regards the deference of courts to a ministry's decisions in setting up a compensation scheme: 'It is not for the courts to consider whether the scheme with its exclusion is a good scheme or a bad scheme, unless it can be said that the exclusion is irrational or so unreasonable that no reasonable minister could have adopted it.'

You may think that deference of any kind is dangerous: it can work to insulate unjust decisions. Why *not* consider whether the administrative scheme is a good scheme or a bad scheme? If the judges were to decide that for themselves, then they would have the opportunity to improve things. If the courts defer to the executive on questions of substance, some injustices will stand uncorrected. But the danger of leaving a decision to an authority that might act unjustly is not a reason for judges to take over all public decision making; judges, too, might act unjustly. They should only interfere where the community can be confident that judicial review will improve public decision making. Their duties of comity towards other public authorities require them not to start from scratch and do the initial decision maker's job. And a court does not have to choose between refusing to review a decision and making a new decision in place of the original. It can defer more or less, and on some questions and not others.

There is a very important connection between deference and discretion. Discretion is freedom to answer a question in more than one way, and judicial deference sustains that freedom, to some extent. Every act of deference by a court towards a public authority amounts to a judicial decision not to craft legal standards that would restrict the discretion of the public authority. So deference has the opposite effect from the **principle of legality** (see 1.5.5, p 22). When the court applies the principle of legality, it is crafting a standard that restrains an authority's discretion. When the court defers, it is deciding not to do so.

But is it really deference?

In *R (ProLife Alliance) v British Broadcasting Corporation* [2003] UKHL 23 [75]–[76], Lord Hoffmann denied that the courts should defer to other public authorities:

> ' . . . although the word "deference" is now very popular in describing the relationship between the judicial and the other branches of government, I do not think that its overtones of servility, or perhaps gracious concession, are appropriate to describe what is happening. In a society based upon the rule of law and the separation of powers, it is necessary to decide which branch of government has in any particular instance the decision-making power and what the legal limits of that power are. . . . when a court decides that a decision is within the proper competence of the legislature or executive, it is not showing deference. It is deciding the law.'[15]

But deference is not necessarily servile, or a concession: an army general is a superior officer who may need to defer to a sergeant on the question of how to get a platoon across a river. The general could override the sergeant's decision (and there might even be some special reason to do so). But it may be better for the sergeant to answer the question of how to cross the river than the general (the sergeant may know the terrain and the abilities of each soldier, or it may be damaging to his relations with the soldiers if the general steps in . . .). A good general will then defer to the sergeant (to some extent), even if he or she can't see the point of what the sergeant is doing. The general is not servile, and is not making a gracious concession; the reason for deference is that, in order to do his or her own job well, the general has to respect the sergeant's role. That is, the reason for deference is comity.

Like the general, a court will often need to defer to the expertise of other decision makers in order to do its own job well. But, unlike the general, courts are not commanding officers, and they also have reasons of political responsibility to defer to other decision makers.

By contrast, think of the attitude a judge ought to take to *legal argument* made by the lawyers for a public authority: the judge should listen with respectful attention, and with an open mind, and should then decide the matter with no deference at all to either party's legal argument.

---

[15] A similar view was expressed by Lord Bingham in *Huang v Home Secretary* [2007] UKHL 11 [16], and by Lord Wilson in *R (Quila) v Home Secretary* [2011] UKSC 45 [46]. But in *R v Ministry of Defence, ex p Smith* [1996] QB 517, 556, Lord Bingham had said, 'the court must properly defer to the expertise of responsible decision-makers'.

7.3 Massive deference and non-justiciability

7.3.1 Foreign affairs and national security

In 1984, Prime Minister Thatcher decided to ban the trade union at the government's intelligence communications centre, Government Communication Headquarters (GCHQ). And she decided to do it without consulting the union first. The House of Lords held that the union had a legitimate expectation that she would consult it before banning it from the workplace (*Council of Civil Service Unions v Minister for the Civil Service* [1985] AC 374, the 'GCHQ' case; the Prime Minister is also the Minister for the Civil Service). As we will see in Chapter 8, the courts will quash a decision of a public authority that disappointed a legitimate expectation (on grounds of unfairness), if it was unfair to do so in the circumstances. Mrs Thatcher said that she had needed to ban the union without consultation because consultation would create a risk of industrial action by the union, which would endanger national security.

If consulting the union would create a serious danger to the nation, then it was not unfair for the Prime Minister to go ahead and ban the union without consulting first. If the danger that would be caused by union consultation was trivial (or even imaginary, so that the Prime Minister was really just trying to make the unions look like enemies of the nation), then it was unfair to proceed without consultation. And the Law Lords refused to decide whether consulting the union would create a serious danger to the nation. So the House of Lords would not conclude that Mrs Thatcher had acted unlawfully.

There are three key points to take from the *GCHQ* case.

GCHQ: key points

(1) The decision established clearly, for the first time, that **the courts can control the exercise of the royal prerogative**, using the same grounds of judicial review that they use when they control the use of statutory powers.[16]

(2) The judges, nevertheless, retained the idea that **some powers are non-justiciable**.

(3) The judges treated the four basic reasons for deference as considerations that *may* lead the court to consider a question to be non-justiciable.

'Justiciable' means 'suitable for a court to decide'. Lord Diplock held that the question of what would pose a danger to national security is a *non*-justiciable question, because 'the executive government bears the responsibility and alone has access to sources of information that qualify it to judge what the necessary action is' (413).

The importance of political responsibility for protecting the nation is the third of the four basic reasons for deference. Judges ought to leave the resolution of some

---

[16] There had been suggestions to the same effect in *Chandler v DPP* [1964] AC 763, and a decision under the Criminal Injuries Compensation Scheme, set up under the prerogative, was reviewed in *R v Criminal Injuries Compensation Board, ex p Lain* [1967] 2 QB 864.

questions to politicians because the fact that the politicians represent the people (and that the people can remove them) is a good control on the decision, and because the responsibility of politicians would be diluted by judicial interference. An understanding of justiciability must also involve an understanding of what judges are good at (the second reason for deference), as well as what the judicial *process* is good for (the fourth reason for deference): an issue is not justiciable if the way in which courts make decisions is the wrong way to resolve that issue.

Deference and terrorism

Expertise, process, and political responsibility can be pressing reasons for deference, and they have come to seem more urgent since the 11 September 2001 attacks on New York and Washington. In October 2001, in reviewing a Home Office decision that it was in the public interest to deport a terrorism suspect, Lord Hoffmann pointed out the government's 'access to special information and expertise in these matters', and added that decisions on how to combat terrorism 'require a legitimacy which can be conferred only by entrusting them to persons responsible to the community through the democratic process' (*Home Secretary v Rehman* [2001] UKHL 47 [62] (Lord Hoffmann)).

Similarly, the House of Lords unanimously held in *R (Corner House Research) v Director of the Serious Fraud Office* [2008] UKHL 60 that it was lawful for the defendant to halt a serious fraud investigation concerning allegations that Saudi officials had been bribed to buy British aircraft, on the ground that Saudi Arabia was threatening to withdraw its cooperation with anti-terrorism measures—a possibility allegedly creating a risk to British lives. Neither the judges nor the Director of the Serious Fraud Office could assess that risk, and the judges accepted that the Director could act on the views of government ministers (see 7.3.6).

And in *R (Bancoult) v Foreign Secretary (No 2)* [2008] UKHL 61, the House of Lords reviewed the Foreign Secretary's decision to ban the Chagos Islanders from returning to their ancestral islands in the Indian Ocean. Their families had been moved to Mauritius in the 1970s, to clear the way for the United States to build a major airbase on one of the islands. In 2008, the United States did not want any Islanders living within hundreds of miles of its airbase. The Law Lords held 3–2 that it was not an abuse of power for the Foreign Secretary to base the decision on his assessment of the value of military cooperation with the United States.

Does this approach to the 'war on terror' amount to an abandonment of the rule of law? Not necessarily, because the rule of law does not require that judges decide what would be good for national security or public safety. The role the judges play has to reflect their disadvantages in assessing dangers to the public, and it has to reflect the risk of abuse of power by a government that claims to be protecting the public from danger. There will be a failure in the rule of law if the government abuses the freedom that comes with the judges' deference. And the judges give the government a technique for abuse if their deference on issues of public safety is too great.

The most important tensions in the control of discretionary powers result from a clash between issues on which judges need to defer, and the highly justiciable values that the courts insist on protecting. These things are controversial among the judges, and there is no easy overall way of assessing their success in standing up for the rule of law. In *Bancoult*, the House of Lords was deeply divided over whether the judges needed to defer to the Foreign Secretary's assessment of the security considerations that, he said, gave reason to keep the Islanders away from the Islands. The courts could not assess the UK's need to cooperate with the United States, but Lord Bingham and Lord Mance dissented, concluding that no matter how important it is to create a secure base for the US Air Force (that was the question on which judges needed to defer), no reasonable Foreign Secretary would ban the Islanders from the Islands in order to achieve it. It seems clear that the Law Lords in the majority would have concurred in quashing the decision if the Islanders had actually been living on the Islands; the majority thought that since there was no economically viable prospect of resettlement of the Chagos Islands, the litigation really concerned the Islanders' campaign for more support from the government. If there had been a consensus among the judges that the ban on returning to the Islands was a violation of a fundamental right, there would have been a consensus that the Foreign Secretary could not violate it in order to cooperate with the United States.

And the Belmarsh Prison case (*A and X v Home Secretary* [2004] UKHL 56—see 1.1.2, p 8) shows that, in spite of their need to defer on issues of public safety, the judges will almost unanimously line up against government action in the right conditions. Those conditions arise where, as in *A and X*, persons are detained on the basis of the judgment of politicians as to what emergency steps the 'war on terror' requires.

Why justiciability?

The *GCHQ* case represented a failure to attain the rule of law if the judges, in spite of their relative inability to assess the alleged danger to national security, could still have decided whether it was unfair for the Prime Minister to ban the union without consultation (e.g., if it should have been obvious to the judges that consultation could be conducted with no detriment to the operation of GCHQ). If that was the case, we might ask, why did the Law Lords put the problem in terms of *justiciability*, instead of simply pointing out some strong reasons for deference? All of the four basic reasons for deference arose in *GCHQ*. But they all arose in *Slattery*, *Kruse*, and *Wednesbury*, too. Why didn't the judges in those cases hold that the claims were non-justiciable?

Some entire *claims* are non-justiciable, because courts have no jurisdiction to hear them.

Non-justiciable claims

- The court will not hear a defamation claim that requires it to pass judgment on the acts of another country, because 'the court would be in a judicial no-man's land' (*Buttes Gas and Oil Co v Hammer (No 3)* [1982] AC 888, 938).
- The court will refuse permission to seek judicial review where the claim would require the court to pass judgment on the lawfulness of another country's

action in international criminal law (*R (Khan) v Foreign Secretary* [2014] EWCA Civ 24—an allegation that GCHQ had violated UK and international criminal law by supplying information to the US authorities for use in drone strikes in Pakistan).

- The court will not ordinarily pass judgment on whether foreign legislation should be respected, although it *will* do so, exceptionally:
  - where the legislation is extremely abusive (*Oppenheimer v Cattermole* [1976] AC 249—a decree depriving German Jews of their German nationality); or
  - where the legislation is undeniably contrary to international law (*Kuwait Airways v Iraqi Airways (Nos 4 and 5)* [2002] UKHL 19—an Iraqi government decree purporting to dissolve Kuwait Airways and to transfer its aircraft to Iraqi Airways).
- Civil claims for damages for torture cannot be brought in the English courts against states and their representatives: state immunity is 'an absolute preliminary bar, precluding any examination of the merits' (*Jones v Saudi Arabia* [2006] UKHL 26 [33] (Lord Bingham)).[17]
- A claim for judicial review of an Act of Parliament on the ground that it was unreasonable would be non-justiciable.[18]
- A claim in defamation against an MP for what he or she says in the House of Commons is non-justiciable, because of parliamentary privilege.

In all of these cases, justiciability restricts the courts' jurisdiction: they have no power to determine the reasonableness of an Act of Parliament, or to award damages for torture against a foreign state. But in *GCHQ* the court did have jurisdiction to decide whether the Prime Minister's decision was *Wednesbury* unreasonable. Applying that standard requires the court to defer, but the question of *how much* to defer is one of degree. As Lord Bingham said in *R v Ministry of Defence, ex p Smith* [1996] QB 517, 556:

> ' The greater the policy content of a decision, and the more remote the subject matter of a decision from ordinary judicial experience, the more hesitant the court must necessarily be in holding a decision to be irrational. That is good law and, like most good law, common sense. '

---

[17] But state immunity only arises in respect of acts done in the exercise of sovereign authority, and not acts governed by private law, so that a worker in a foreign embassy can sue his or her employer in the Employment Tribunal: *Benkharbouche v Embassy of the Republic of Sudan* [2017] UKSC 62 (see 3.11).

[18] This remains the case, in spite of occasional hypothetical suggestions by judges that they 'may have to consider' whether there are some things that Parliament cannot lawfully enact (*R (Jackson) v Attorney General* [2005] UKHL 56 [102] (Lord Steyn)).

Given that explanation of the duty to defer in controlling certain discretionary powers, what does it add to say that an issue is non-justiciable (and not merely that the judges must defer)? The answer is that an issue is non-justiciable if comity requires that judges do not even address it. The puzzling part is this: if the courts won't second-guess an administrative judgment *at all*, aren't they abandoning their responsibility for the administration of justice? The key to the puzzle is to understand just which questions are non-justiciable.

Justiciability in administrative law is a feature of *issues*

In *GCHQ*, Lord Diplock concluded that 'what action is needed' to protect national security is 'a matter upon which those upon whom the responsibility rests, and not the courts of justice, must have the last word' (412). That makes it sound as if it is the question of *how to use a power* that may be non-justiciable. And Lord Roskill offered a non-exhaustive list of 'excluded categories' of prerogative power that are not susceptible to judicial review, 'because their nature and subject matter are such as not to be amenable to the judicial process': his instances were 'the making of treaties, the defence of the realm, the prerogative of mercy, the grant of honours, the dissolution of Parliament and the appointment of ministers' (418). That list was whittled down in later decisions,[19] but it took the decision in *R (Abbasi) v Foreign Secretary and Home Secretary* [2002] EWCA Civ 1598 (see 1.1, p 4) to clarify the meaning of this list. *Abbasi*, like *GCHQ* itself, was a landmark case concerning the control of the prerogative, even though the claimant lost.

Losers' landmarks

Watch for landmark cases that push the law dramatically in the direction of the *losing* party's argument! It happens quite often, not only because the judges are sympathetically trying to give the loser some consolation, but also because, in giving reasons for their decision, conscientious judges will often strive to state the argument for the losing side as favourably as it can be put, and then to explain why the case *still* needs to go the other way.

The decision in *Abbasi* pushed the imposition of the rule of law on the executive well beyond what was decided in *GCHQ*. The Court of Appeal decided that Abbasi was being arbitrarily detained in Guantánamo Bay, yet declined to reach the conclusion that the Foreign Secretary was acting unlawfully in refusing to demand Abbasi's release. The reason was that the proper exercise of the discretionary power to make representations to another country on behalf of the Crown involved considerations that were not justiciable. The Court of Appeal decided that it was inappropriate for

---

[19] e.g., in *R v Home Secretary, ex p Ruddock* [1987] 1 WLR 1482, Taylor J made it plain that a claim that national security was at stake did not (in itself) prevent the court from exercising its supervisory jurisdiction. And in *R v Home Secretary, ex p Bentley* [1994] QB 349, the court reviewed the exercise of the prerogative of mercy.

judges even to ask the questions that they would need to answer if they were to decide whether the Foreign Secretary had exercised the discretion properly. Those questions included whether and how Britain ought to cooperate with the United States in the 'war on terror'. The repercussions for relations with the United States (and for that matter with France and Pakistan) were relevant considerations and were non-justiciable.

If those questions are not for judges to answer, then whether the Foreign Secretary's decision was wise or foolish, just or unjust, the English judges have no jurisdiction to tell the Foreign Secretary how to respond to the relevant considerations. They lack the expertise, the techniques of inquiry, and the political accountability that are all essential for taking responsible decisions based on those considerations. *Abbasi* is a demonstration of the fact that judges have no general jurisdiction to do justice. Comity forbids them to impose a just foreign policy on the government.

In reaching its decision in *Abbasi*, the Court of Appeal clarified two points:

- no prerogative power is unreviewable; but

- judges cannot interfere with the exercise of a discretionary power (statutory or prerogative) if they would need to decide a non-justiciable issue in order to apply the grounds of review.

It is not a *power*, or the exercise of a power, that is justiciable or non-justiciable; what may be non-justiciable is a particular *issue* that would need to be decided, in order to give the remedy that the claimant seeks.

The Court of Appeal dismissed the claim for judicial review because, even after deciding that Abbasi was being arbitrarily detained, the judges were not in a position to find that the Foreign Secretary's refusal to complain to the Americans was itself an abuse of power. The new step in *Abbasi* was that the Court *was* prepared to apply the doctrine of **relevance** (see 8.2) to an exercise of the prerogative power to conduct relations with other states. The Court held that Abbasi's arbitrary detention in a foreign country was relevant to the Foreign Secretary's decision. It is implicit in the Court of Appeal decision that, if the Foreign Secretary:

(1) had refused to consider a request that he challenge the United States; or

(2) had denied that Abbasi was being arbitrarily detained; or

(3) had denied that the conditions of Abbasi's detention were relevant to his decision,

the Court could have declared that he had reached his decision unlawfully, and required him to make the decision again on the basis of the relevant considerations (see *Abbasi* [99]–[100]). The point is emphasized by another Court of Appeal decision following *Abbasi*: in *R (Al Rawi) v Foreign Secretary* [2006] EWCA Civ 1279, the Court rejected an argument that the Foreign Secretary had failed to attend to all of the relevant considerations when he refused to demand the release of detainees from Guantánamo Bay. Laws LJ held that: 'The court's role is to see that the government strictly complies with all formal requirements, and rationally considers the matters it has to confront. Here, because of the subject-matter, the law accords to the executive an especially broad margin of discretion' [148]. But, Laws LJ implied, judicial review is still available to require the government to *consider* 'the matters it has to confront'.

Abbasi made it clear that no administrative power is exempt from judicial review for abuse of power. But the exercise of some powers will be largely unreviewable in effect, because they will almost always involve non-justiciable considerations. It is an inescapable conclusion, implicit in *Abbasi*, that non-justiciable issues are likely to be at stake in the decision whether to make demands to another country.

A mistake in *Miller*

In *R (Miller) v Secretary of State for Exiting the European Union* [2017] UKSC 5, the Supreme Court held by an 8–3 majority that the Prime Minister could not initiate the process under the EU Treaty to take the UK out of the EU by exercise of the prerogative. The Court held that only Parliament could authorize her to do so. The judges felt that Brexit was too constitutionally important for it to be commenced by an administrative act [82]:

> ' We cannot accept that a major change to UK constitutional arrangements can be achieved by ministers alone; it must be effected in the only way that the UK constitution recognises, namely by Parliamentary legislation. '

The majority said that this conclusion followed from 'the ordinary application of basic concepts of constitutional law' [82], and 'long-standing and fundamental principle' [81]. But they did not say what the concepts or the principle were, as Lord Reed, Lord Carnwath, and Lord Hughes pointed out in their dissents.[20]

Ironically, while taking away the treaty prerogative in the case of constitutionally important matters, the majority justices remarked, *obiter*, that 'the general rule is that the power to make or unmake treaties . . . is not reviewable by the courts' [55]; see also [92]. It would certainly have been true to say that the proper exercise of the treaty power is very commonly based on considerations that are not justiciable, and that judicial review is not available where the courts would have to pass judgment on such considerations. But it was a mistake for the majority to suggest that *the power is not reviewable*. Suppose that a claimant alleged that the Prime Minister had made or terminated a treaty in exchange for a bribe. There is no reason at all why the court should not review the exercise of the power and, if the allegation were proven, hold the act to have been an abuse of the prerogative, and declare it to have been unlawful. In their dissenting judgments in *Miller*, Lord Carnwath thought that the majority was wrong on this point [267], and Lord Reed said that he expressed no view on whether the exercise of the treaty prerogative might be subject to judicial review [239].

20 See T Endicott, 'Lord Reed's Dissent in Gina Miller's Case and the Principles of our Constitution' (2018) UK Supreme Court Yearbook 259–81.

Are questions of international law justiciable?

It is primarily *issues* that are justiciable or non-justiciable. A *claim* is non-justiciable if the court would have to pass judgment on a non-justiciable issue, in order for the claim to succeed. But no administrative power or action is non-justiciable. How, then, can we understand the remarkable justiciability case of *R v Prime Minister, ex p Campaign for Nuclear Disarmament* [2002] EWHC 2712? The CND asked the court to declare that the Prime Minister would be acting contrary to international law if he were to send troops into Iraq without a resolution from the United Nations Security Council specifically authorizing it. The Court of Appeal held that the issue of whether the Prime Minister would be acting contrary to international law was non-justiciable. But why? It was *not* beyond the ability of judges to decide whether it was lawful in international law to invade Iraq. In terms of expertise (the second basic reason for deference) and processes (the fourth), the judges were in a better position than the executive to determine this question. So why was this issue (and thus the claim) non-justiciable?

The courts will decide questions of international law whenever they need to (as in *Kuwait Airways v Iraqi Airways (Nos 4 and 5)* [2002] UKHL 19). But they only do so in order to determine some question of rights and duties between two parties; they will not determine what international law requires without a dispute under English law. There was no such dispute in the *CND* case. In fact, since international law binds other nations too (but the orders of English courts do not), it would be 'an exorbitant arrogation of adjudicative power' for the English court to pass judgment (*CND* [37]). Even though the issues were quite manageable for judges, it is not their role to make a declaration of their opinion on a point of international law that does not need to be decided for any purpose of English law. The English judges cannot authoritatively determine the British government's obligations in international law. If the British government invades another country in violation of international law, the *CND* case shows that the English courts will not interfere.

Similarly, in *Corner House Research*, the House of Lords rejected an argument that the judges should require the Director to act on the judges' interpretation of the UK's obligations under the international Convention on Combating Bribery of Foreign Public Officials 1997. The House of Lords held that it would not be unlawful in English law for the Director of the Serious Fraud Office to violate international law by acting incompatibly with the Convention on Combating Bribery (Lord Bingham [47]).[21]

Non-justiciability is a special reason for complete deference, but only for complete deference *on some particular issue*. Even though non-justiciability seems like an all-or-nothing matter, it is surprisingly flexible, because it can be generated by the four basic reasons for deference. And those reasons have varying force in different circumstances.

---

[21] For confirmation from the Court of Appeal that there is no general rule of English law that a public authority may not violate a treaty obligation of the United Kingdom, see *Morgan v Hinton Organics* [2009] EWCA Civ 107.

Political questions in the United States

In 2004, a court in California dismissed the complaint in *Taxpayers of United States of America v Bush* without a trial. The plaintiffs claimed that the Bush government had conspired with the government of Saudi Arabia to conduct the 9/11 attacks on the World Trade Center and the Pentagon, in order 'to gather public support for the military invasion of Iraq and persuade Congress to enact the U.S.A. Patriot Acts' (2004 WL 3030076 (ND Cal), Illston J, 30 December 2004). The court struck out the claim on the ground that the issues were non-justiciable under the 'political questions' doctrine.

In a classic statement of that doctrine in *Baker v Carr* 369 US 186, 216 (1962), the US Supreme Court held that the court should refuse to answer a question on the ground of:

' . . . a textually demonstrable constitutional commitment of the issue to a coordinate political department; or a lack of judicially discoverable and manageable standards for resolving it; or the impossibility of deciding without an initial policy determination of a kind clearly for non-judicial discretion; or the impossibility of a court's undertaking independent resolution without expressing lack of the respect due coordinate branches of government; or an unusual need for unquestioning adherence to a political decision already made; or the potentiality of embarrassment from multifarious pronouncements by various departments on one question. '

7.3.2 Money

The best examples of massive deference in the English law of judicial review are the cases on local council funding under the Thatcher government: *R v Environment Secretary, ex p Nottinghamshire County Council* [1986] AC 240, and *R v Environment Secretary, ex p Hammersmith and Fulham LBC* [1991] 1 AC 521. Parliament had authorized the Environment Secretary to assess whether local authorities were setting excessive budgets. Central government could control local expenditure by reducing its support grant to local authorities (*Nottinghamshire*), and by capping the community charges that local authorities could impose (*Hammersmith and Fulham*). The Conservatives punished dozens of Labour councils for spending too much, and the local authorities went to court to challenge the decisions on the *Wednesbury* grounds. Lord Scarman hinted in *Nottinghamshire* that there was no justiciable issue (247); in *Hammersmith and Fulham*, Lord Bridge said that 'the merits of the policy underlying the decisions are not susceptible to review by the courts and the courts would be exceeding their proper function if they presumed to condemn the policy as unreasonable' (597). The House of Lords held in both cases that the *Wednesbury* grounds of review were unavailable. The Minister's decisions could not be challenged on the ground of *Wednesbury* unreasonableness, according to Lord Scarman in *Nottinghamshire*, but only on the ground of bad faith or improper motive, or on the ground that the decision was 'so absurd that he must have taken leave of his senses' (596). If that sounds like irrationality, it just shows why the popular use of the term 'irrationality' for *Wednesbury* unreasonableness is dangerous and confusing. 'So absurd that he must have taken leave of his senses' is a very good synonym for 'irrational', but Lord Scarman was deliberately trying to identify a way of controlling the financial control discretion that was *more restrained* than the way of controlling local by-laws that was set out in *Slattery, Kruse,* and *Wednesbury*. In *Hammersmith and Fulham,* Lord Bridge held that not just any irrationality would do as a ground of judicial review of a decision to cap the community charge (527): '[I]t is not open to challenge on the grounds of irrationality short of the extremes of bad faith, improper motive or manifest absurdity.'

These cases show that *Wednesbury* does not offer a general set of standards of review of executive action.[22] No clearer illustration could be given of the **principle of relativity** (see 1.3). The courts will not necessarily quash a decision for *Wednesbury* unreasonableness; it depends on the issues at stake. Even in *Hammersmith and Fulham,* the House of Lords did not say that the decision was unreviewable: the local authorities would have won if they could have shown bad faith (e.g., that the Environment Secretary had taken a bribe, or that he had targeted Labour councils on grounds other than their spending plans). But it is not the judges' job to decide whether the amount of a government grant to a local authority is so unreasonable that no reasonable cabinet minister could have decided to make it.

Justiciability reminder

Remember that it is a particular question or issue that is justiciable or non-justiciable (see 7.3.1, p 254). *Decisions* are reviewable; *issues* are justiciable or not justiciable. Lord Scarman suggested in *Nottinghamshire* that while the interpretation of a statute giving a wide discretion over public expenditure *is* 'justiciable', the 'matters of political judgment' that have to be decided in exercising the discretion are for the ministers and the House of Commons, and 'are not for the judges or your Lordships' House in its judicial capacity' (247). But a funding decision is not unreviewable: it could be quashed in judicial review on grounds of bad faith (as Lord Greene pointed out in *Wednesbury*), because the court would not need to pass judgment on anything non-justiciable in order to quash the decision.

When can a public authority take the cost of a decision into account?

In general, the courts are extremely unwilling *to tell public authorities how to spend money,* yet not unwilling at all *to make them spend money.* If a public authority has a discretionary power to decide how to spend money, the courts will be as restrained as

---

22 As Lord Scarman said: 'There is a risk . . . that the judgment [in *Wednesbury*] may be treated as a complete, exhaustive, definitive statement of the law' (*Nottinghamshire,* 249).

they were in *Nottinghamshire* and *Hammersmith and Fulham*. And the expense of using a discretionary power in one way rather than another may be a relevant consideration: in *R (Bancoult) v Foreign Secretary (No 2)* [2008] UKHL 61 (see 7.3.1, p 255), the House of Lords held that, in deciding whether to prohibit the Chagossians from returning to the Indian Ocean islands from which they had been removed in the 1970s, 'the advice that the cost of any permanent resettlement would be "prohibitive" was an entirely legitimate factor for the Government—which is responsible for the way that tax revenues are spent—to take into account' (Lord Rodger [113]; cf. Lord Hoffmann [55]).

But the fact that a public authority's legal duty requires it to spend money will not stop the court from enforcing the duty. First of all, the classic cases on due process such as *Cooper v Wandsworth Board of Works* (1863) 14 CB (NS) 180 make the government spend money on administrative procedures, and the process costs that the law imposes in the twenty-first century are really serious. Second, in many cases on the exercise of discretionary power, the courts are prepared to tell public authorities that the impact on their resources is an *irrelevant* consideration.

The leading decision is *R v East Sussex County Council, ex p Tandy* [1998] AC 714 (HL). Beth Tandy could not go to school for medical reasons, so the local education authority provided her with tuition at home. After three years, the authority decided to cut the teaching from five hours a week to three hours a week, to save money. The education authority had a statutory duty to provide a 'suitable education'; that duty gave it a **resultant discretion** (see 7.2.1, p 249) in deciding what was suitable for a particular student. But the House of Lords held that the decision had to be made without regard to the authority's financial resources.

Yet, in other contexts, the courts sometimes show massive deference towards public authorities on decisions about how to spend their money. In *R v Cambridge Health Authority, ex p B* [1995] 1 WLR 898 (CA), the health authority decided to deny life-saving treatment to a nine-year-old girl. Sir Thomas Bingham MR said: 'Difficult and agonising judgments have to be made as to how a limited budget is best allocated to the maximum advantage of the maximum number of patients. That is not a judgment which the court can make' (906).[23]

If we can reconcile *Tandy* with *B*, we will have a clear idea of the legally permissible role of financial considerations in administrative discretions. And, in fact, the distinction between the two classes of case is clear and important: if a decision maker has a duty to abide by a standard that does not depend on its resources (such as a duty to provide a 'suitable education'), then it cannot get out of its legal duty on financial grounds. But if it has a wide discretion that includes the responsibility to decide how to distribute resources among competing needs (as health authorities often have in deciding what treatments to provide), then financial considerations become relevant: the public authority has a discretionary power to choose among different potential allocations of its resources. The courts will give practically no protection against bad

---

[23]   Compare *R (Pfizer Ltd) v Secretary of State for Health* [2002] EWCA Civ 1566, in which a drug company unsuccessfully challenged restrictions on the circumstances in which the NHS would supply Viagra.

decisions in the allocation of a limited budget among competing needs; '[t]hat is not a judgment which a court can make', as Sir Thomas Bingham MR said in *B* (137).

This approach leaves the provision of some crucial social services up to the largely uncontrolled choice of administrative officials. If they make an overly stingy decision about whether to provide a crucial medical treatment, the courts will not put it right. That is justifiable, because of the court's limited capacity to decide how much expenditure on a service would be appropriate. Of course, administrative authorities may make bad decisions. If the difficult case of *B* had been decided the other way, the resulting turn towards more intrusive judicial review would have given judges the opportunity of righting wrongs—but this opportunity would have come at the risk of irresponsible judicial interference with public service provision. It is one of the drastic implications of comity that the judges cannot right all wrongs.

So open-ended discretionary powers and duties to provide public services can be exercised on the basis of the administrative authority's judgment as to the best use of resources, with very little control. In *R v Chief Constable of Sussex, ex p International Trader's Ferry Ltd* [1999] 2 AC 418 (HL), 430, Lord Slynn cited the *B* case and held that the police could take the impact on their resources into account in deciding how much police protection to provide for an animal exporter against animal rights demonstrators. The police had a duty to provide protection, but they also had a discretion as to how to carry it out, and the House of Lords was not prepared to tell them how much of their budget to commit to the claimant's problem.

> ### The public-sector equality duty
>
> The Equality Act 2010 s 149 controls spending decisions by requiring public authorities to have due regard to the impact of spending on equality of opportunity (see 8.3.2).

7.3.3 Planning

In reviewing decisions to give or to refuse permission for new building projects, the courts will defer massively to the views of a local planning inspector (*R (Springhall) v Richmond upon Thames* [2006] EWCA Civ 19) or the Environment Secretary (*Tesco Stores v Environment Secretary* [1995] 1 WLR 759), as to what is in the public interest.

In *First Secretary of State v Hammersmatch Properties Ltd* [2005] EWCA Civ 1360, the judge in the Administrative Court had quashed a decision of a planning inspector to preserve a building in Welwyn Garden City rather than to allow a redevelopment. The Court of Appeal reversed the Administrative Court decision on the ground that the judge 'entered the arena of planning merits and has thereby exceeded his powers.... Planning judgments are for planning authorities and not the courts' [32]–[33]. Pill LJ relied on the restatement of *Wednesbury* unreasonableness by Lord Bingham CJ in *Hindley*: 'To justify intervention by the court, the decision under challenge must fall outside the bounds of any decision open to a reasonable decision maker' (*R v Home Secretary, ex p Hindley* [1998] QB 751, 777).

Massive deference: vague, but very significant

Because the *Wednesbury* principles are so vague, you may start to think that the judges just quash whichever decisions they don't like and say that no reasonable person could have made the decision. It is not surprising if that happens sometimes, since it is easy for any of us to jump from thinking that a decision was wrong to thinking that no reasonable person could agree with it.

But the *Hammersmatch Properties* case shows that the judges actually can refrain from interfering with decisions that they do not like. Lady Justice Smith plainly disagreed with the decision, but said that her 'personal view' was 'irrelevant in the present proceedings' [36]. Staughton LJ said: 'If I were the planning authority, I would stop preserving the Vospor building as a useless object . . . I suspect that it was what the people of Welwyn Garden City wanted, or some of them. However, I am not the planning authority, and neither is the judge' [40].

Notice also that sometimes the courts expressly state that a decision on some point can lawfully be made *either way* by a public authority. *Boddington v British Transport Police* [1999] 2 AC 143 is an example: Lord Steyn stated that the railway company could permit some smoking or forbid all smoking on its trains, as it saw fit; either policy would be 'within the range of reasonable decisions open to a decision maker' (175). *R v Monopolies and Mergers Commission, ex p South Yorkshire Transport* [1993] 1 WLR 23 (see 9.3.1, p 353) is another classic example.

So the hands-off standards of control of discretionary powers make a difference: although the judges *can* use the vague grounds of judicial review to step in and impose what they think the original decision maker ought to have done, they often succeed in leaving the public authority to do its own job.

7.3.4 Decisions approved in Parliament

Statutes often require that a particular kind of administrative decision (usually, administrative regulations) must be laid before Parliament for approval before becoming valid, or is subject to annulment by Parliament after being made. If the Houses of Parliament have approved a decision, it may seem that the courts should not review its substance at all, because of the **political responsibility** reason for deference (the third of the four basic reasons for deference). In fact, the situation is more complex.

In *Hammersmith and Fulham* (see 7.3.2), the fact that the rate-capping decisions could only take effect with the approval of the House of Commons seems to have made the House of Lords all the more reluctant to interfere with decisions about national financial policy: '[I]t is in the political forum of the House of Commons that they are properly to be debated and approved or disapproved on their merits' (*R v Environment Secretary, ex p Hammersmith and Fulham LBC* [1991] 1 AC 521, 597 (Lord Bridge)).

But the effect of approval in Parliament depended on the nature of the decision in the *Hammersmith and Fulham* case. There is no rule that any decision is unreviewable just because it has been approved by both Houses of Parliament. The constitutional difference between a statute and a 'statutory instrument' approved by both Houses is fundamental. The difference has long been recognized (see *R v Electricity Commissioners, ex p London Electricity Joint Committee Co* [1924] 1 KB 171, 208), and was reasserted in *Bank Mellat v HM Treasury (No 2)* [2013] UKSC 39 [39]–[40].

With statutory instruments, the question of whether parliamentary approval makes any difference to judicial review depends on the nature of the decision. The very deferential approach in the *Hammersmith and Fulham* case depends on the national finance issues that were at stake; the House of Commons was well placed to pass judgment on those issues, and there was really no additional role for the courts to play in assessing the reasonableness of the public finance decisions.

Bank Mellat, by contrast, concerned a direction to financial institutions not to deal with the claimant bank, on the ground that it was involved in financing the Iranian nuclear weapons programme: 'The direction, although made by statutory instrument, involved the application of a discretionary legislative power to Bank Mellat. . . . It was as good an example as one could find of a measure targeted against identifiable individuals' (Lord Sumption [46]). The parliamentary process, therefore, made no difference to the claimant's argument that the Treasury should have consulted the Bank before proposing the direction. In such a case, the role of the House of Commons should be seen as an additional safeguard, with different purposes from the safeguard of judicial review on the *Wednesbury* principles. That approach reflects the different capacities of courts and of the House of Commons to secure responsible government (see 2.5.3).

Lord Sumption suggested, in *Bank Mellat*, at [43], that Parliamentary approval generally makes no difference:

> ‘ The reason why this does not intrude on the constitutional primacy of Parliament is not simply that delegated legislation, however approved, does not have the status of primary legislation. It is that a statutory instrument is the instrument of the minister (or other decision-maker) who is empowered by the enabling Act to make it. The fact that it requires the approval of Parliament does not alter that. The focus of the court is therefore on his decision to make it, and not on Parliament's decision to approve it. ’

But in cases such as *Hammersmith and Fulham*, the approval of Parliament makes a very significant difference, because of the nature of the issues at stake. And in *Bank Mellat*, Lord Sumption went on to say that 'respect for Parliament's constitutional function calls for considerable caution', and that there is special reason for a cautious approach to review of 'legislative instruments founded on considerations of general policy' [44].[24] So the majority's non-deferential approach in *Bank Mellat* is compatible

----

[24] Approved in *R (SG) v Secretary of State for Work and Pensions* [2015] UKSC 16 (Lord Reed [94]).

with the very deferential approach in the *Hammersmith and Fulham* case. The House of Commons was well placed to pass judgment on the national finance issues at stake in *Hammersmith and Fulham*, and there was really no additional role for the courts to play in assessing the reasonableness of the public finance decisions. The difference that approval in Parliament makes, if any, depends on the issues in the case.

● *Pop quiz* ●

If the focus of the court is on the minister's decision to make a statutory instrument and not on Parliament's decision to approve it, could you seek judicial review to quash a decision by a minister to present a Bill to Parliament, and argue that the court should focus on the minister's decision and not on Parliament's decision to approve the Bill?

7.3.5 Acts of the Scottish Parliament

In *AXA General Insurance v HM Advocate* [2011] UKSC 46, insurance companies sought judicial review of an Act of the Scottish Parliament on the ground that it was irrational, and therefore ought to be held unlawful under common law standards of judicial review. The Supreme Court held that the availability of judicial review depended on the nature of the power in question—but even though the Scottish Parliament has a 'plenary' power to legislate (subject to compatibility with the European Convention on Human Rights), the justices were not prepared to say that judicial review was not available on common law grounds. But they would not decide the purposes for which the Scottish Parliament's purposes are to be used (Lord Reed [147]), so that the proper purposes doctrine from *Padfield v Minister of Agriculture* [1968] AC 997 (see 2.3) does not apply. And judicial review is not available on the ground of 'irrationality' (*AXA* [52] and [154]). This is another reminder that the *Wednesbury* case does not give a general code of judicial review of public decisions.

Legislation that is incompatible with Convention rights is outside the competence of the Scottish Parliament (Scotland Act 1998 s 29), and can be struck down by the courts on that ground; common law judicial review adds little or nothing. Lord Hope suggested that the courts might quash an Act of the Scottish Parliament that sought 'to abolish judicial review or to diminish the role of the courts in protecting the interests of the individual' [151]. It seems that the judges' deference is so massive that common law judicial review of legislation of the Scottish Parliament will make no difference unless the Scottish Parliament were to find a way to restrict access to courts, without breaching any Convention right. The assertion of a judicial power to quash Acts of the Scottish Parliament, as a result, is really only a symbolic assertion of judicial responsibility for the rule of law.

● *Pop quiz* ●

Lord Hope held in *AXA* that, 'as there is no provision in the Scotland Act which excludes' judicial review, 'it must follow that in principle Acts of the Scottish Parliament are amenable to the supervisory jurisdiction of the Court of Session [which in this respect is the same as the jurisdiction of the High Court in England

and Wales] at common law' [47]. What if the Scotland Act had provided that there could be no judicial review of the lawfulness of an Act of the Scottish Parliament? Would such an exclusion of judicial review be lawful?

7.3.6 Legal processes

Public authorities may have massive leeway in making decisions about the conduct of litigation, or the conduct of investigations into criminal allegations. 'Absent dishonesty or mala fides or an exceptional circumstance', a decision of the Director of Public Prosecutions (DPP) to consent to a criminal prosecution 'is not amenable to judicial review' (*R v DPP, ex p Kebilene* [1999] 3 WLR 972, 985; cf. *Sharma v Antoine* [2006] UKPC 57 [14]). As Lord Bingham has put it, 'only in highly exceptional cases will the court disturb the decisions of an independent prosecutor and investigator' (*R (Corner House Research) v Director of the Serious Fraud Office* [2008] UKHL 60 [30]).

There has been just one notable judicial interference with the discretion of the DPP, and that was not to tell the DPP who could be prosecuted, but to require him to publish a policy on how the decision would be made. In *R (Purdy) v DPP* [2009] UKHL 45, the House of Lords held that Art 8 of the European Convention entitled the claimant, who had progressive multiple sclerosis, to know the policy that the DPP would follow, in deciding whether to prosecute her husband for the crime of assisting suicide, if he were to help her to travel to another country for the purpose of committing suicide. Requiring the DPP to publish a policy was extraordinary.[25] The Law Lords were careful not to say whether it ought to be a crime for Ms Purdy's husband to help her to commit suicide ('We do not venture into that arena, nor would it be right for us to do so'—Lord Hope [26]). But the only explanation for interfering at all rests in the Law Lords' view that the offence involved an intrusion into the claimant's private and family life. In *Pretty v UK* (2002) 35 EHRR 1 [77], the Strasbourg Court had rejected a claim that the Convention required the DPP to say in advance whether a person would be prosecuted for assisting suicide in a particular case. And the Supreme Court reaffirmed in *R (Nicklinson) v Ministry of Justice* [2014] UKSC 38 that it is not the courts' job to tell the DPP what his or her policy should be.

Judicial review of decisions to investigate and to prosecute is ordinarily very restrained. The rationale for restraint is that, for a defendant against whom an unreasonable investigation is conducted or an unreasonable prosecution is pursued, the criminal justice process itself provides a fair hearing, when the person is prosecuted. Judicial review is a last resort (see 2.7), so it is not needed where the claimant has access to another judicial process.

But consider a decision *not* to investigate or to prosecute, and how dangerous such a decision could be if it concerned allegations against a public official or the

....
[25] The DPP publishes a Code for Crown Prosecutors: https://www.cps.gov.uk/publication/code-crown-prosecutors. The House of Lords held that the Code provided 'almost no guidance at all' in the circumstances of *Purdy*, at [53]. The policy on assisted suicide, published as a result of *Purdy*, is at https://www.cps.gov.uk/publication/assisted-suicide.

investigation of wrongdoing in which the government has an interest. An independent and committed prosecution service is crucial to the rule of law. In England, this role is given to the Crown Prosecution Service (CPS), and its independence is guarded by a politician, the Attorney General. He or she is traditionally meant to act independently from the government, but is appointed on the advice of the Prime Minister and attends Cabinet meetings. The DPP (the head of the CPS) has day-to-day responsibility, subject to his or her accountability to the Attorney General, and subject to the possibility that individuals may initiate a private prosecution. Much of the decision turns on highly educated guesswork as to the likelihood that a jury will convict, and the courts will interfere only to insist that the prosecutors take into account the relevant considerations (*R v DPP, ex p Manning* [2001] QB 330).

Is there any role for judges in a decision not to investigate wrongdoing, or not to prosecute, because doing so would not be in the public interest? No such decision had been quashed before the Divisional Court's decision in *R (Corner House Research) v Director of the Serious Fraud Office* [2008] EWHC 714, striking down a decision by the Director of the Serious Fraud Office (an investigator who, like the DPP, makes independent decisions, but is accountable to the Attorney General). The Director had called off the investigation of allegations that British Aerospace, a private company, had committed an offence in UK law by giving bribes to foreign officials in negotiating the sale of fighter aircraft to Saudi Arabia. The Divisional Court held, at [60], that the Director had unlawfully surrendered to a threat from Saudi Arabia to withdraw from cooperation with the British government in fighting terrorism, if the investigation continued:

> ' The rationale for the court's intervention is its responsibility to protect the rule of law. . . . The surrender of a public authority to threat or pressure undermines the rule of law. '

The House of Lords overturned the Divisional Court's decision, and restored the deferential approach to judicial review of independent investigations. The Law Lords all held that the Director could lawfully take into account an alleged risk to British lives if the Saudis were to withdraw from cooperation in fighting terrorism (*R (Corner House Research) v Director of the Serious Fraud Office* [2008] UKHL 60). They left it to the Director to assess the risks, and they also allowed him to defer to others (such as the British Ambassador to Saudi Arabia, the Prime Minister, the Foreign Secretary, and the Defence Secretary) who might know better what Saudi Arabia was likely to do and what effect it might have in Britain. And they left it to him to weigh the supposed risk against other considerations, including the importance of upholding the rule of law.

The result of *Corner House Research* is a very hands-off form of review. The Saudis threatened not only to stop cooperating in fighting terrorism, but also to stop buying British aircraft. The government and the arms manufacturer were urging the Director to stop the prosecution. A commercial threat *would* have been an irrelevant consideration. There was no evidence that the Director had based his decision on the commercial threat. But even though the Director had clearly come under pressure to stop the investigation for patently irrelevant commercial reasons, the Law Lords were not prepared to assess the issue that did matter (whether stopping the investigation might cost British lives).

The Divisional Court thought that, as judges, they had to quash a decision that was based on a threat because: 'At the heart of the obligations of the courts and of the judges lies the duty to protect the rule of law' ([2008] EWHC 714 [63]). They quoted Lord Hope's remark in *R (Jackson) v Attorney General* [2006] 1 AC 262 [107], that 'the rule of law enforced by the courts is the ultimate controlling factor on which our constitution is based'. The House of Lords' decision in *Corner House Research* underlines a harsh reality that the courts have to face: they cannot always enforce the rule of law. Protecting the rule of law is much more a responsibility of the executive than it is the responsibility of the courts (see 1.5.1), and the courts have a limited capacity to supervise the government's fulfilment of that responsibility.

Corner House Research leaves open a genuine risk that the government will pressurize prosecutors into abandoning the rule of law on trumped-up grounds of public safety, when they have other interests in mind; the Law Lords' justification for their decision was, in effect, that the courts could not guard against that risk, because they had to leave it to an independent investigator (and indirectly to government officials who were far from independent) to assess a risk to British lives. It may, in those circumstance, be a breach of comity for the courts to enforce the duty of the executive to protect the rule of law.

7.3.7 Decisions based on impressions

A court may be 'less qualified to make the decision under challenge than the decision maker' (*Higham v University of Plymouth* [2005] EWHC 1492 [29]), simply because the initial decision maker had a process by which he or she could see the people involved face to face. The University in the *Higham* case had a power (and duty) to remove a medical student from the register if it could not certify his or her fitness to practise medicine. The really crucial reason for deference was a **process reason**: Stanley Burton J held that the University's committee 'had the advantage of seeing and hearing the witnesses and, perhaps most importantly, Mr Higham himself, and were able to form a view of him and his personality that a consideration of the documents by this Court cannot approach' [29]. The court 'must approach that decision fairly made by those qualified to make it with the respect and deference due in such circumstances' [29].

Apart from any problems arising from the passage of time, you might think that this advantage of the initial decision maker could be solved through a hearing in the Administrative Court. But it is only in special circumstances (see 9.2.5) that the court will repeat the fact-finding inquiry. The **presumption against interference** (see 7.1.1, p 240) is also a presumption against starting from scratch on an assessment of the facts. Finding the facts all over again would be a way of solving mistakes in the first decision. But it would be a way of introducing new mistakes, too, and there is no reason for it unless the claimant can show *either* a lack of due process, *or* that the substance of a finding of fact was patently unreasonable. That is why judicial review is not *generally* available against findings of fact, although a court will ask whether there is special reason to overturn a decision as to the facts (see 9.2).

7.3.8 Policy in general?

The instances of massive deference outlined here are some of the most dramatic, but they are only instances. The four basic reasons for deference play out in varying ways in diverse cases in which courts are very unwilling to interfere. *R v Ministry of Defence, ex p Walker* [2000] 1 WLR 806 (see 2.1) is an instance of massive deference: if the military uses its inherent discretionary power to provide for soldiers by setting up a compensation scheme for injuries, and the scheme is not contrary to any statute, the courts will not want to strike down the eligibility criteria unless they really are extremely bad. So the House of Lords held in *Walker* that the criteria would have to be 'irrational' (812). The massive deference in the case is explained partly by the fact that Sergeant Walker was challenging a decision as to how to spend money. But deference was also due to the military's expertise in (and responsibility for) assessing the conditions of troops, and the risks they faced in Bosnia and Northern Ireland.

Such decisions, it is often said, are policy decisions, and that explains the massive deference they attract in a variety of contexts. Apart from deference on matters of impression, can we say that all of the instances of massive deference reflect the courts' unwillingness to pass judgment on policy matters? Yes, if you like, because the word 'policy' is so flexible. It can include *any* reason for a public decision (and in that sense of 'policy', there is no general deference on policy matters). Or it can mean a reason that calls for judicial deference to another decision maker. In the *GCHQ* case, Lord Diplock said that challenges to 'the application of Government policy . . . do not normally involve questions to which . . . the judicial process is adapted to provide the right answer' (*Council of Civil Service Unions v Minister for the Civil Service* [1985] AC 374, 411). But 'policy' in Lord Diplock's sense only gives an overall label to the considerations that reflect the four basic reasons for deference. To say that an issue is a matter of 'policy', in the sense that requires courts to defer to other public authorities, is just to say that the responsibility to decide it has been allocated to another public authority, and that the authority's expertise, or political responsibility, or processes put it in a better position than the court to decide the issue.

7.4 Conclusion

Because judges have taken dramatic steps to control abuses of power, it is tempting to exaggerate the importance of judicial review in administrative law. To put it in perspective, consider the following summary of the ways in which the law controls the exercise of discretionary powers.

In summary—the law may control a discretionary power by:

(1) **allocating it to a particular person or agency;**

(2) **defining its extent:**
  - powers conferred by statutes and regulations are defined by the legislation that confers them;

(3) **imposing standards that the decision maker must apply, or identifying considerations on which a public authority must act;**

(4) **requiring a public authority to adhere to procedural requirements:**
  - openness and notice;
  - hearings;
  - lack of bias; and
  - reasons;

(5) **providing for review:**
  - internal review or appeal within an agency;
  - administrative justice processes (tribunals, ombudsmen, inquiries, etc.); and
  - judicial review and statutory appeals; and

(6) **imposing liabilities:**
  - for crimes and torts;
  - and in any other way Parliament sees fit to provide (e.g., liability of councillors to make good any losses occasioned by the failure to make a rate—*Lloyd v McMahon* [1987] 1 AC 625).

That summary is actually a summary of administrative law—this whole book is about legal conferral and legal control of discretionary powers. Judicial review plays an important, but limited, role; it is just one line in the summary. It is not even the primary technique for controlling the use of discretionary powers. Courts are only one of the institutions that review decisions. The tribunals system controls administrative decisions in much larger numbers than courts do (see Figure 12.1, p 449), and often with less deference.

It is also important not to understate the role of judicial review. While the judges have little control over the allocation of discretionary power,[26] they have played a leading role in the development of the law of due process, and they continue to take a dynamic approach to it. Appeals from the Tribunal system to the Court of Appeal and the Supreme Court give the judges an important role in controlling and developing the work of tribunals (see Chapter 12), and judges even control the work of ombudsmen (see Chapter 13). And the judges have played a central role in developing the liabilities of public authorities in tort and contract (see Chapters 14 and 15). To the overall structure of administrative law, the judges' law-making role is more important than their role in resolving particular disputes and preventing particular abuses of power.

---

[26] They can decide under the Human Rights Act 1998 that an allocation of power is incompatible with a Convention right: see 2.5.1. And they have had a very important incidental role, for example, in deciding which powers ministers can lawfully delegate to civil servants (see 15.1.2).

And the dramatic role of judges in reviewing the substance of administrative decisions is not as important as their role in imposing due process on the executive. That is because the judges' contribution to the law of due process brings a general change to the whole game; by contrast, the quashing of a decision on substantive grounds is always particular. The law of due process is capable of *guiding* the administration: officials can change their behaviour to respond to a requirement to give a hearing or to give reasons, but they cannot change their behaviour to respond to a requirement that they must not make extremely unreasonable decisions, or that they must interpret the law correctly. Public authorities do not need the courts to tell them that legislation should be interpreted correctly, or that they should not act irrationally. Regardless of judicial review, every public authority ought to use its power reasonably and on a correct interpretation of the law in every case.[27] And they more or less always think that their interpretations are correct and their actions are reasonable. The Commissioners in *Rooke v Withers* (1597) 5 Co Rep 99 doubtless thought that they were being reasonable. The effect of judicial review of the substance of decisions is to allocate power to the courts to decide what counts as a reasonable decision or a correct interpretation.

The real difficulty in judicial control of discretionary powers is that it seems, on the one hand, that the judges should not be interfering with a power that has been allocated to someone else—and, on the other hand, that the judges should not leave a claimant to suffer the injustice of a bad decision. The mere fact that a power has been allocated to another body raises the presumption that judges should not interfere. That presumption may be very strong or very weak, depending on the context. So the crucial element in resolving this apparent puzzle is the **principle of relativity** (see 1.3). The reasons for deference to the initial decision maker vary widely; they may require the courts to treat some issues as simply non-justiciable. It is the judges' responsibility not to turn a non-justiciability doctrine into something that the government can use to cloak abuses of power that the judges could identify. And remember that, although a court should not pass judgment on non-justiciable issues in reviewing an exercise of a discretionary power, such issues do not give a rationale for violating a claimant's legal rights. No government official can use non-justiciable arguments of state interest to violate the law (see 8.1).

Injustice is not a general ground of judicial review!

It would be a breach of comity if judges were to take it on themselves to right every injustice caused by administrative decisions. If this seems shocking, revisit the cases discussed in this chapter in which the courts were very deferential—such as *R v Environment Secretary, ex p Nottinghamshire County Council* [1986] AC 240—and ask yourself if the court ought to have decided those cases without deferring in any way to the initial decision maker. That is what it would require for the judges to review all decisions on the ground of injustice. No public decision should be unjust, but it is not always the judges' job to decide what is just.

---

27 The doctrine of legitimate expectations, discussed in 8.4, includes a form of substantive control of discretionary power that *does* create a new obligation that public authorities can use to guide their decisions: it requires them to abide by certain sorts of expectation unless there is special reason to depart from what was expected.

TAKE-HOME MESSAGE • • •

- The control of discretion requires courts to examine the substance of the justification of executive action, *but*:

  - that does not mean that judges need to decide all questions as to the grounds on which the executive ought to act; *and*

  - the standard on which judges ought to intervene varies—it depends on the nature of the executive action under review.

- A discretionary power (such as a power to hire employees) is a power that gives some degree of choice as to how it is to be applied. A discretion is a choice. A public authority has no **discretion** to hire on racist or other abusive grounds, even though it has a discretionary power to hire employees.

- Judges **defer** when they leave it up to an administrative authority, to a greater or lesser extent, to make a decision. They defer completely on issues that they hold to be **non-justiciable**.

- Issues (not powers, or exercises of power) can be justiciable or non-justiciable. A *claim* is non-justiciable if it could only succeed if the judges were to decide a non-justiciable issue.

CRITICAL QUESTIONS • • •

1 Administrative authorities always ought to make the best possible decision. So why isn't judicial review generally available on the ground that an authority did not make the best possible decision?

2 Does the difference between inherent discretions and discretions conferred expressly by statute make any difference to judicial review?

3 Are there any unfettered discretionary powers?

4 Are there any unreviewable administrative decisions?

5 Can you reconcile judicial control of discretionary power with the principle that judges are only to strike down an action that the public authority had no power to take?

6 What is the relationship between the law of due process (Chapter 4) and the law of control of discretionary powers?

7 When a court questions the validity of a regulation approved in both Houses of Parliament, is it acting contrary to Art 9 of the Bill of Rights ('the freedom of speech and debates or proceedings in Parliament ought not to be impeached or questioned in any court or place out of Parliament')?

READING ● ● ●

Rooke v Withers (1597) 5 Co Rep 99

Slattery v Naylor (1888) 13 App Cas 446

Kruse v Johnson [1898] 2 QB 91

Associated Provincial Picture Houses v Wednesbury Corporation [1948] 1 KB 223

R v Home Secretary, ex p Khawaja [1984] AC 74

Council of Civil Service Unions v Minister for the Civil Service [1985] AC 374 (*'GCHQ'*)

R v Environment Secretary, ex p Nottinghamshire County Council [1986] AC 240

R v Environment Secretary, ex p Hammersmith and Fulham LBC [1991] 1 AC 521

R (Abbasi) v Foreign Secretary and Home Secretary [2002] EWCA Civ 1598

R (Corner House Research) v Director of the Serious Fraud Office [2008] UKHL 60

R (Bancoult) v Foreign Secretary (No 2) [2008] UKHL 61

Bank Mellat v HM Treasury (No 2) [2013] UKSC 39

R (Nicklinson) v Ministry of Justice [2014] UKSC 38

R (Miller) v Secretary of State for Exiting the European Union [2017] UKSC 5

On the *Miller* case:

Nick Barber, Tom Hickman, and Jeff King, 'Reflections on Miller' (2016–2017) 8 UK Supreme Court Yearbook 212–237

Richard Ekins, 'Constitutional Practice and Principle in the Article 50 Litigation' (2017) 133 LQR 347–53

Timothy Endicott, 'Lord Reed's Dissent in Gina Miller's Case and the Principles of our Constitution' (2016–2017) 8 UK Supreme Court Yearbook 259–81

On which powers are prerogative powers:

Margit Cohn, 'Judicial Review of Non-statutory Executive Powers after *Bancoult*' [2009] PL 260

On judicial review of spending decisions:

Jeff King, 'The Justiciability of Resource Allocation' (2007) 70 MLR 197

Jeff King, 'The Pervasiveness of Polycentricity' [2008] PL 101

On deference:

Jeff King, 'Institutional Approaches to Judicial Restraint' (2008) 28 OJLS 409

Alison Young, 'In Defence of Due Deference' (2009) 72 MLR 554

On the *Bancoult* decision (see 7.3.1):

Mark Elliott and Amanda Perreau-Saussine, 'Pyrrhic Public Law: *Bancoult* and the Sources, Status, and Content of Common Law Limitations on Prerogative Power' [2009] PL 697

On inherent power:

Timothy Endicott, 'Lawful Power' (2017) 15 NZJPIL 1–19

 The following online resources accompany this chapter: **summaries** of key cases and legislation; **updates** on the law; **guidance** for answering the pop quizzes and questions; and **links** to legislation, cases, and useful websites.

8 Substantive fairness

When there is reason for non-deferential judicial review, deference would mean aban-doning the rule of law. The more interventionist grounds on which judges will control the substance of some decisions—**relevance**, **proportionality**, and **legitimate expec-tations**—may involve little deference, depending on the type of decision and the con-text in which it is made.

Each of the interventionist doctrines gives the judges the opportunity to do justice for a claimant and to improve public administration. For the very same reasons, each doctrine poses a danger that the judges will make themselves into surrogate adminis-trators by overextending the grounds of judicial review.

LOOK FOR • • •

- The extent to which judges should and should not defer to administrative authori-ties in giving effect to these grounds of judicial review of the substance of decisions:

  - Relevance.

  - Proportionality.

  - Legitimate expectations.

  - Abuse of power.

> ' The differences in approach between the traditional grounds of review and the proportionality approach may . . . sometimes yield different results. . . . This does not mean that there has been a shift to merits review. On the contrary, . . . the respective roles of judges and administrators are fundamentally distinct and will remain so. '
>
> *R (Daly) v Home Secretary* [2001] UKHL 26 [28] (Lord Steyn)

8.1 Minimal deference and the principle of legality

Deference is not a default setting for judicial review; it depends on the issue. The **four basic reasons for deference** (see 7.1.1) depend on the type of decision and the context in which it is made. In this chapter, we will see that the judges need to substitute their own judgment for that of an administrative authority on some issues, in order to give effect to the **principle of legality** (see 1.5.5, p 22). The most non-deferential grounds of decision in English judicial review are relevance (8.2), proportionality (8.3), and legitimate expectations (8.4).

The theme of this chapter is that none of these adventurous doctrines has led to a general rule that judges can review decisions without deferring to the judgment of the initial decision maker. Along the way we will see some hasty suggestions from the judges that these non-deferential doctrines have taken over judicial review, replacing the earlier, deferential approach of *Associated Provincial Picture Houses v Wednesbury Corporation* [1948] 1 KB 223. But they have not. There is no general rule authorizing judges to review administrative decisions without deference. But where judges can improve administrative decision making by passing judgment on the very questions of substance that the administrative authority had to decide, it is no breach of comity for them to do so. And where it is necessary to prevent arbitrary government, the rule of law demands that they do so.

We can start with *zero* deference: the courts do not defer to administrative authorities on the question of whether they should carry out a legal duty.

8.1.1 Zero deference: no discretion to act unlawfully

The court will not leave it up to an administrative authority to choose whether to violate a legal rule. This simple point is a reminder of the difference between *discretionary power* and *discretion* (see 7.2.2): even if a public authority has a very wide discretionary power, it has no discretion to use that power to do anything that is prohibited by law. As a result, the law of tort (see Chapter 14), the criminal law (see 14.5.4) and the law of contempt of court (see 10.4.5) are parts of administrative law, and in fact, parts of our constitution: no one has any exemption from tort liability or criminal liability, or from the duty to abide by a court order, on account of being a public official.

8.1.2 Zero deference: the genuine exercise rule

An administrative authority also has no discretion to abdicate its powers. Every discretionary power carries with it a legal duty to consider whether and how to exercise it. In *R (Abbasi) v Foreign Secretary* [2002] EWCA Civ 1598, comity required the Court not to interfere with the Foreign Secretary's judgment as to whether to demand the release of British prisoners in Guantánamo Bay (see 1.1, p 4). The Court of Appeal deferred radically to the Foreign Secretary's judgment on the question of whether to make diplomatic representations on behalf of a subject whose fundamental rights were being violated by another country. But the Court made it plain that it would step in if the Foreign Secretary were to refuse even to consider whether to do so. In that case, the Court would 'make a mandatory order to the Foreign Secretary to give due consideration to the applicant's case' [104]. On the issue of whether the Foreign Office should *consider* making representations, the judges will not defer to the Foreign Secretary's judgment at all.

Similarly, it is unlawful for an administrative authority to **fetter** its own discretion by, for example, adopting rules that prevent it from considering particular cases on their merits. But that does not mean that administrative authorities cannot lawfully adopt rules or act on policies. In fact, we will see in this chapter that a claimant can be entitled to some form of judicial protection for expectations that are based on authorities' policies (8.4). The rule against fettering means, instead, that a decision maker may need to be prepared to consider an argument that an exception should be made to a policy for some special reason in a particular case (*British Oxygen Co Ltd v Board of Trade* [1971] 1 AC 610). The question ought to be whether the purposes for which the authority has the power require it to be willing to consider special circumstances.

In the exercise of statutory powers, the basis of the no-fettering principle is that by giving a discretionary power, Parliament impliedly imposes a duty to consider exercising it. In *R (Sandiford) v Secretary of State for Foreign and Commonwealth Affairs* [2014] UKSC 44, the defendant's power was not a statutory power, but the prerogative power to assist British nationals overseas. Lindsay Sandiford was convicted in Indonesia of attempting to smuggle cocaine into Bali, and was sentenced to death; she asked the Foreign Office to give her legal aid to seek clemency; she was told that the government had a strict policy against funding legal representation overseas for British nationals. She argued that the Foreign Office had infringed the rule against fettering its discretion.

The Supreme Court rejected that argument, on the basis that in the case of a prerogative power, no one has imposed on the holder of the power a duty to consider different possibilities for its exercise; so the Foreign Office's general policy did not amount to an unlawful fettering of its discretion. That does not make its decision immune from review; it is still possible to challenge such a policy on grounds of 'irrationality' [65]–[66]. The Supreme Court decision in *Sandiford* suggests that the rule against fettering simply does not apply to prerogative power. But if, in the exercise of the prerogative, the decision maker adopted a rule or policy and *arbitrarily* refused to consider the situation of a person affected by the policy, then it might be justifiable for the court to require the decision maker to consider the case: and indeed, that is actually implicit in the holding in *Abbasi* (not contradicted in *Sandiford*) that the court might order the government to consider a request that the prerogative be exercised for the benefit of a claimant.

An administrative authority must not unlawfully **delegate** its decision-making power to anyone else. But that does not mean that all delegation is unlawful. For example, when the Home Secretary had statutory power to decide the tariff for life prisoners, the House of Lords held that it was lawful for him to delegate that decision to a junior minister (*R v Home Secretary, ex p Doody* [1994] 1 AC 531, 566). The common law frequently allows ministers' statutory responsibilities to be carried out by civil servants (see 15.1.2, p 582). The question is whether delegation is incompatible with the reasons for which the power was given to the authority named in the statute.

These rules—against refusing to consider using a power, and against fettering or unlawfully delegating the exercise of a power—are, potentially, compatible with comity between judges and administrative authorities. Zero deference on the question of whether to consider exercising a discretion is compatible with due deference on the question of how to exercise it. The courts are not taking over the administrative officials' job if they only make sure that the administrative officials actually make a genuine exercise of their own responsibility.

But the dangerous word in the doctrine is 'genuine'. There is a standing impulse for judges to say that a bad exercise of discretion was not an exercise of the authority's power at all. So this doctrine is only *potentially* compatible with comity between judges and administrative authorities. Depending on what they count as genuine, the judges may end up using the genuine exercise doctrine to replace other public authorities' judgment with their own. But as a technique for judicial innovation it has been overtaken by the more openly non-deferential doctrines.

8.1.3 The principle of legality and the value of liberty

The courts will not treat general powers as authorizing decisions that disregard certain fundamental values (see 1.5.5, p 22). This reading-down of powers is the most important general technique by which judges limit public authorities' leeway in the use of discretionary powers. Which interests will be protected? There is no catalogue, and it is not the judges' job to codify the principle of legality. But it is their job to identify specific instances of it, and if there were a catalogue, it would certainly include the following.

Examples of values protected by the principle of legality

- Liberty (*A and X v Home Secretary* [2004] UKHL 56—see 1.1.2, p 8)
- Property (*Rooke v Withers* (1597) 5 Co Rep 99—see 7.1; *Entick v Carrington* (1765) 19 Howell's St Tr 1029—see 14.1; *Ahmed v HM Treasury* [2010] UKSC 2)
- Access to courts (*R v Home Secretary, ex p Simms* [2000] 2 AC 115)
- Administrative due process (*Cooper v Wandsworth Board of Works* (1863) 14 CB (NS) 180)

Note the overlaps! Administrative due process and access to the courts protect property and liberty.

The judges will not allow the use of a power to detract from these values disproportionately even if a statute conferring a power says nothing about the matter, and even when there are other relevant considerations at stake.

Liberty

In English law, 'every imprisonment is *prima facie* unlawful and . . . it is for a person directing imprisonment to justify his act' (*Liversidge v Anderson* [1942] AC 206, 245 (Lord Atkin)).[1] Lord Atkin called that 'one of the pillars of liberty'. Liberty is the first and most famous of the values protected by the principle of legality.

Habeas corpus is available as a process for challenging detention if no other adequate process is available. But, today, all of the important forms of executive detention—by mental health authorities, or the police, or immigration officials—are regulated by statutory schemes. An application for *habeas corpus* will fail where a statute authorizes the detention. And *habeas corpus* is not available where a statutory scheme provides an adequate process for a court to determine whether the detention is lawful.[2] The judges will take the same creative approach to their task in controlling those statutory schemes as they took centuries ago in developing *habeas corpus* (see 1.1.1, p 5).

> #### Instances of the special judicial concern for liberty: the prisoner cases
>
> - In *R v Home Secretary, ex p Doody* [1994] 1 AC 531, *R v Home Secretary, ex p Pierson* [1997] 3 All ER 577 (HL), and *R v Home Secretary, ex p Venables and Thompson* [1997] 3 WLR 23, the judges insisted on due process in the Home Secretary's decisions setting tariffs for life prisoners, and used the relevance doctrine to control the grounds on which the Home Secretary decided a tariff.
> - Then, under the Human Rights Act 1998, the courts declared that the mere fact that the Home Secretary had power to decide the tariff was incompatible with the right to an independent tribunal in Art 6 of the Convention (*R (Anderson) v Home Secretary* [2002] UKHL 46). Parliament changed the legislation as a result, and tariff setting for life-sentence prisoners is no longer a problem of administrative law; the initial decision is made by a judge.
> - In *R v Home Secretary, ex p Simms* [1999] 3 All ER 400 and *R (Daly) v Home Secretary* [2001] UKHL 26, the courts protected a prisoner's freedom to communicate with lawyers and the media (see 8.3).

Judges have extended their scrutiny beyond the decision to detain, to impose intensive control on the treatment of a detained person. In *R (Wilkinson) v Broadmoor Special*

---

[1] Lord Atkin was dissenting; his dissent has come to be accepted as good law (*Inland Revenue Commissioners v Rossminster* [1980] AC 952).

[2] Extradition is governed by a statutory regime that retains *habeas corpus*: see the Extradition Act 1989. For an example of a grant of *habeas corpus* in the House of Lords in extradition proceedings, see *R (Guisto) v Governor of Brixton Prison* [2003] UKHL 19.

Hospital [2001] EWCA Civ 1545, the doctors at a mental hospital decided that they needed to administer medical treatment under restraint to a patient who was detained because of a mental illness. The Court of Appeal held that, in judicial review, the court's task was to make 'its own assessment of the relevant facts' [34], and to conduct 'a full merits review of the propriety of the treatment proposed' [36]. So instead of deferring to the mental health experts, the court has to decide whether it is right to impose the treatment on the patient, using evidence from the doctors, given under cross-examination. Because the treatment is forced, the courts treat the administrative decision as only provisional, and the treatment that ought to be given is an open question for the court to decide.

8.2 Relevance

It seems to be part of the genuine exercise rule: a public authority that does not act on relevant considerations is not *genuinely* doing what it was given power to do. Yet this ground of review can be dynamite. Lord Greene put it this way in *Wednesbury* (228):

> ' If, in the statute conferring the discretion, there is to be found expressly or by implication matters which the authority exercising the discretion ought to have regard to, then in exercising the discretion it must have regard to those matters. Conversely, . . . the authority must disregard . . . irrelevant collateral matters. '

Twenty years after *Wednesbury*, the House of Lords made this doctrine into the basis of a highly political interference with the Minister of Agriculture's management of a milk marketing scheme, in *Padfield v Minister of Agriculture, Fisheries and Food* [1968] AC 997. The Minister had a discretionary power to refer complaints to a committee, and he refused to refer a complaint because he did not want to generate political pressure in favour of the opponents of the scheme. Lord Reid held (at 1030):

> ' Parliament must have conferred the discretion with the intention that it should be used to promote the policy and objects of the Act, the policy and objects of the Act must be determined by construing the Act as a whole and construction is always a matter of law for the court. '

Public authorities always ought to act for proper purposes and on the basis of the relevant considerations. But in a doctrine that courts are to decide which purposes are proper and which considerations are relevant, there is potential to abolish all deference to administrative authorities.

A *consideration* is simply something that a decision maker might take into account in a way that would affect the decision; it can be a **general** consideration as to the purpose of the decision-making power (as in *Padfield*), or it can be one of the **facts** of a particular case. A *relevant* consideration is one that the decision maker *ought to* take into account.

Relevant considerations include legitimate general grounds for decision, and also those facts of the particular case on which the legitimate general grounds of decision depend.

In judicial review, should the judges decide what is relevant? The crucial point that will emerge from the following is that they must be prepared to *control* administrative judgments of relevance. Yet it is not generally the judges' job to do so by replacing the administrators' view of what is relevant with their own view of what is relevant.

The remarkable thing about the decision in *Padfield* is not that the judges interfered in politics. They have been interfering in politics at least since the *Case of Proclamations* (1611) 12 Co Rep 74 and *Prohibitions del Roy* (1607) 77 ER 1342 in the seventeenth century (see 1.5.1, p 17). But in those earlier decisions the judges only decided what actions the Crown did or did not have power to undertake. In *Proclamations*, Sir Edward Coke held that the King could not act like Parliament: he could not create new offences. In *Prohibitions*, Coke held that the King could not sit as a judge. In *Padfield*, the House of Lords told the government (some of) *the grounds on which it could and could not decide* whether to take actions that Parliament had authorized the government to take. Is that approach compatible with the deferential approach that Lord Greene was outlining in *Wednesbury*? Or did the judges abolish deference in *Padfield*, by taking it on themselves to tell the government the grounds on which it could act? The answer has to be that *Padfield* did not abolish deference. But let's consider why it may seem to do so.

8.2.1 Relevance, deference: a contradiction?

Whenever a different decision ought to have been taken, you can explain why by pointing out a consideration that the decision maker should have acted on, or should not have acted on. So it may seem that under *Wednesbury*, with its doctrine of relevant considerations, the judges must determine all questions as to what decision ought to have been taken. And then you may think that administrative law contains a massive contradiction: judges should defer to some extent, on some issues (since they are only reviewing the lawfulness of the decision, rather than making a new administrative decision), yet they should not defer (since a decision is to be quashed if it was based on an irrelevant consideration). How can we resolve the contradiction?

In a New Zealand case, *CREEDNZ Inc v Governor General* [1981] 1 NZLR 172, Cooke J started out by saying that a decision will only be quashed for failure to attend to relevant considerations 'when the statute expressly or impliedly identifies considerations required to be taken into account by the authority as a matter of legal obligation. . . . It is not enough that a consideration is one that may properly be taken into account, nor even that it is one which many people, including the court itself, would have taken into account if they had to make the decision' (183). The House of Lords adopted that reasoning in *Re Findlay* [1985] AC 318, 334. On this approach, the relevance doctrine is really a rule that the court may quash a decision if the law specifically requires consideration of something that the decision maker ignored (or requires the decision maker to ignore something that they did not ignore), *or* if the decision maker ignored something so *obviously* relevant (or acted on a ground so *obviously* irrelevant) that they can be said not to have properly exercised the power they were given. It is not, in fact, a doctrine that all questions of relevance are for the court.

To test the extent to which a court should be prepared to overrule the judgment of an administrative authority on a question of relevance, let's look at one of the most remarkable examples of the use of the relevance doctrine: the *Pergau Dam* case.

8.2.2 *Pergau Dam*

In 1993, the Foreign Secretary, Douglas Hurd, decided to spend £234 million to build a dam in Pergau, Malaysia. It was the largest single project that had been financed by the Overseas Development Administration (ODA), and it was a waste of money. The National Audit Office (see 15.4.3) and even the ODA's own economists said that it was a waste. The money was spent because Prime Minister Thatcher had promised financial assistance to Malaysia while she was negotiating an arms deal in which Malaysia was to buy more than £1 billion worth of British fighter planes. Instead of using the development budget for development, the British government was using it as a sweetener to promote British arms sales.

In *R v Foreign Secretary, ex p World Development Movement* [1995] 1 WLR 386 ('*Pergau Dam*'), the High Court held that the government had acted unlawfully in providing money for the dam from the overseas aid budget. The remarkable thing about the decision is that the judges were prepared to hold a spending decision unlawful when the purposes of the decision were highly political and involved foreign relations. The minister argued that the judges should defer to his view as to what purposes were within the statute. The court disagreed (401):

> ' Whatever the Secretary of State's intention or purpose may have been, it is, as it seems to me, a matter for the courts and not for the Secretary of State to determine whether, on the evidence before the court, the particular conduct was, or was not, within the statutory purpose. '

This does *not* mean that the court will not defer on the relevant considerations. It means that the court will not defer *on the question of what considerations the legislation rules out*. And that is so even where there is a reasonable argument in favour of the minister's view as to which considerations the legislation rules out.

But the minister does have discretion to choose among the purposes that the law does not prohibit. The Overseas Development and Co-operation Act 1980 s 1(1) gave the Secretary of State power to make grants 'for the purpose of promoting the development or maintaining the economy of a country or territory outside the United Kingdom, or the welfare of its people' (*Pergau Dam*, 390). He was certainly maintaining the economy of Malaysia by giving the government £400 million from the overseas development fund. It is not implausible to argue that the Act authorized the action. But the court quite rightly rejected a plausible interpretation, in favour of an interpretation that better fulfilled the development purpose of the legislation.

● *Pop quiz* ●

Can you distinguish *R v Foreign Secretary, ex p World Development Movement* [1995] 1 WLR 386 from *R v Environment Secretary, ex p Hammersmith and Fulham LBC* [1991] 1 AC 521 (see 7.3.2)? Both were challenges to government funding decisions under statutory powers, but in *Hammersmith and Fulham*, the House of Lords refused to interfere with a funding decision unless it was 'so absurd that he must have taken leave of his senses'. Why wasn't the same hands-off standard applied in *World Development Movement*?

Often, the courts suggest that all questions of relevance are for the court, but that it is up to the decision maker to decide their weight, as in this classic statement by Lord Keith in *Tesco Stores v Environment Secretary* [1995] 1 WLR 759, at 764:

> It is for the courts ... to decide what is a relevant consideration. ... But it is entirely for the decision maker to attribute to the relevant considerations such weight as he thinks fit, and the courts will not interfere unless he has acted unreasonably in the *Wednesbury* sense.

But the fact that some consideration is or is not very weighty is itself a highly relevant consideration: that simply demonstrates that not all questions of relevance are for the courts.

8.2.3 Questions of relevance are not necessarily for courts

Several cases have emphasized this point: a decision maker may have discretion in deciding which considerations are relevant. In *Findlay*, the House of Lords held that the law neither required the Home Secretary to consider the Parole Board's view before making a policy change, nor prohibited him from doing so. Consider the following cases in which the judges have refused to decide what was relevant.

- *R v Panel on Take-overs and Mergers, ex p Guinness Plc* [1990] 1 QB 146: Lord Donaldson MR held that the Panel was 'a body which is itself charged with the duty of making a judgment on what is and what is not relevant, although clearly a theoretical scenario could be constructed in which the panel acted on the basis of considerations which on any view must have been irrelevant' (159).

- *R (Khatun) v Newham LBC* [2004] EWCA Civ 55: a local authority was making decisions as to where to house homeless people without letting them see the property first. The claimant asked for the decision to be quashed on the ground that the potential tenant's view as to the suitability of the property was a relevant consideration that the local authority had ignored. The Court of Appeal refused; following *Findlay*, Laws LJ held that, 'where a statute conferring discretionary power provides no lexicon of the matters to be treated as relevant by the decision-maker, then it is for the decision-maker and not the court to conclude what is relevant subject only to *Wednesbury* review' (*Khatun* [35]).

- *R (Al Rawi) v Foreign Secretary and Home Secretary* [2006] EWCA Civ 1279: 'In this area of the government's responsibility to make decisions touching the conduct of foreign relations, the class of factors which are neither compulsory nor forbidden, but which it is open to the decision-maker to treat as relevant or not, must be particularly wide' (Laws LJ [131]).

- *R (Hurst) v London Northern District Coroner* [2007] UKHL 13: 'Some considerations are required to be taken into account by decision makers. Others are required not to be. But there is a third category: those considerations which the decision maker may choose for himself whether or not to take into account' (Lord Brown [57]).

- *R (Corner House Research) v Director of the Serious Fraud Office* [2008] UKHL 60: 'A discretionary decision is not in any event vitiated by a failure to take into account a consideration which the decision-maker is not obliged by the law or the facts to take into account, even if he may properly do so: *CREEDNZ Inc v Governor General* [1981] 1 NZLR 172, 183' (Lord Bingham [40]).

- *R (South Staffordshire and Shropshire Healthcare NHS Foundation Trust) v St George's Hospital* [2016] EWHC 1196 (Admin): Cranston J held that if legislation specifically requires a consideration to be taken into account, or it is 'so obviously material' that the decision maker must have regard to it, then a failure to take it into account makes a decision unlawful. But a decision is not unlawful just because it ignores considerations that the court considers relevant 'unless not to do so is *Wednesbury* unreasonable'. He added: 'Those considerations can be characterised as permissive considerations, in that it is up to the decision-maker to take them into account if she so chooses' [34].

In none of these cases did the courts refuse to control the administrative authority's decision as to what is relevant. In none of them did the courts treat judgments of relevance as judgments for the courts. That is the right approach, because *control* over judgments of relevance is essential if the courts are to prevent arbitrary government. But comity requires courts not to interfere with a reasonable judgment as to what is relevant.

Relevance and the courts

Lord Greene did not treat questions of relevance generally as questions for the court. In *B Johnson & Co v Minister of Health* [1947] 2 All ER 395, 400, decided less than four months before the *Wednesbury* hearing, he refused to substitute 'the opinion of the court as to what considerations should weigh with the Minister for the opinion of the Minister himself, which had been made by Parliament the decisive matter'.

8.3 Proportionality and deference

It is unreasonable to use a sledgehammer to crack a nut, or to make a mountain out of a molehill. It is unreasonable to act in a way that has a disproportionate impact on people affected by a decision, and no public authority should act unreasonably. But that does not mean that judges should interfere when an administrative authority does so. The point of the *Wednesbury* doctrine was that comity generally requires judges not to decide what would be a reasonable decision, but only to interfere with a decision that no reasonable person *in the position of the administrative authority* would take. The *Wednesbury* principles apply quite broadly (although even those principles do not apply to all decisions by public authorities—see 7.3.2), because they offer ways in which judges can identify administrative decisions as arbitrary. But it is not necessarily arbitrary to do too much or too little. So judicial review on the ground of proportionality calls for some rationale other than the judges' general responsibility to impose the rule of law on other public authorities. Proportionality should only be a ground of judicial review where the law recognizes an interest that ought to be protected by a judicial inquiry as to whether it has been or may be damaged in a way that is out of proportion to the attainment of a public objective (see 3.6).

It sometimes seems that proportionality is poised to take over judicial review. To his version of 'The List' of the grounds of judicial review (see 9.4, p 356), Lord Diplock said that further grounds might be added in time, and mentioned 'the possible adoption in the future of the principle of "proportionality"' (*Council of Civil Service Unions v Minister for the Civil Service* [1985] AC 374 ('*GCHQ*'), 410). And after the enactment of the Human Rights Act 1998, judges started to suggest that proportionality *has* become a general feature of English administrative law. For proportionality really did become a test of compatibility of administrative action with Convention rights (see 3.6 for an account of the structure and the role of proportionality reasoning under the Convention). And it came to seem to some, such as Lord Slynn, that proportionality cannot be restricted to European Union law and the effect of Convention rights:

> ' I consider that even without reference to the Human Rights Act 1998 the time has come to recognise that this principle is part of English administrative law. . . . Trying to keep the *Wednesbury* principle and proportionality in separate compartments seems to me to be unnecessary and confusing. ' ³

More recently, in a series of cases—*Kennedy v Charity Commission* [2014] UKSC 20 [54], *R (Sandiford) v Secretary of State for Foreign and Commonwealth Affairs* [2014] UKSC 44 [66], *Pham v Home Secretary* [2015] UKSC 19 [113], *Keyu v Foreign Secretary* [2015] UKSC 69 [132] and [304], and *Youssef v Foreign Secretary* [2016] UKSC 3 [51]–[61]—the Justices of the Supreme Court have been asking themselves whether the time has come, as Baroness Hale put it in *Keyu* [303], 'to recognise proportionality as

---

³   *R (Alconbury) v Environment Secretary* [2001] UKHL 23 [51].

a further basis for challenging administrative actions, a basis which, if adopted, would be likely to consign the *Wednesbury* principle to the dustbin of history'.

In *Keyu*, the claimants argued that the four-stage proportionality test set out in *Bank Mellat* (see 3.6) 'should now be applied in place of rationality in all domestic judicial review cases' [131]. Lord Neuberger said that 'It would not be appropriate for a five-justice panel of this court to accept, or indeed to reject, this argument, which potentially has implications which are profound in constitutional terms and very wide in applicable scope' [132]; Lord Kerr agreed but added, 'I suspect that this question will have to be frankly addressed by this court sooner rather than later' [271]. In *Youssef*, Lord Carnwath said, 'It is to be hoped that an opportunity can be found in the near future for an authoritative review in this court of the judicial and academic learning on the issue' [55].

The Supreme Court will no doubt be addressing the matter again and again. But the time will never come for a proportionality test in the judicial review of all administrative decisions. As Baroness Hale put it very succinctly in *Keyu*, 'it is one thing to apply a proportionality analysis to an interference with, or limitation of, a fundamental right and another thing to apply it to an ordinary administrative decision such as whether or not to hold some sort of inquiry' [304]. There is actually a very good rationale for what Lord Slynn called 'separate compartments': in judicial review on the ground of proportionality, the judges put some interest or interests asserted by the claimant into one side of the scales and public interests (or the interests of other individuals) into the other side, and decide which is weightier. Proportionality has no place in judicial review unless there is some special reason *for judges to decide* when government action *too great* an adverse impact on some interest or interests that the law protects.

There is such a special reason for judges to engage in proportionality reasoning in Convention rights adjudication. For the Strasbourg judges, the reason is that the United Kingdom has adopted the Convention as a way of protecting certain interests of persons. For UK judges, the reason is that the Human Rights Act requires them to protect those interests.

And proportionality reasoning is not restricted to Convention rights adjudication: where the values protected by the principle of legality (see 1.5.5) are at stake, there is special reason for the judges to use proportionality reasoning to provide that protection. The classic example is *R (Daly) v Home Secretary* [2001] UKHL 26. The Home Secretary, exercising a statutory power to make rules for management of prisons, instructed prison governors to exclude prisoners from their cells while making searches. The House of Lords held that the policy was unlawful because it created a risk that prison guards would read the prisoner's correspondence with his lawyer, which in turn would inhibit a prisoner from communicating freely with his lawyer. That interfered *too much*—that is, disproportionately—with the prisoner's freedom to communicate with his lawyer. The decision was 'an orthodox application of common law principles derived from the authorities and an orthodox domestic approach to judicial review' (Lord Bingham [23]). It was orthodox because the requirement of proportionality is a way of protecting a 'common law right' ([10] and [15]) of privileged communication with a lawyer. And the role of that right in *Daly* reflects the fact that there is not, and there should not be, any general doctrine of proportionality in judicial review of administrative action.

Think about the difference between the decision in the *Daly* case and the decision in a case like *World Development Movement*, or a case like *R v Environment Secretary, ex p Hammersmith and Fulham LBC* [1991] 1 AC 521 (see 7.3.2, p 262). If proportionality were a general standard of judicial review of administrative action, then in a case like *Hammersmith and Fulham* the court would have to decide whether the central government's decision to cap the spending of local authorities was proportionate (in its impact on their finances, presumably, and on their ability to spend public money) to the pursuit of legitimate central government objectives. The court would have to quash a decision if it did not allow local authorities to spend *enough*. But there is no reason for the country to be governed by the judges' view, instead of central government's view, as to how much local authorities should be able to spend.

In spite of the many suggestions over more than thirty years since Lord Diplock's remark in the *GCHQ* case in 1984, there is no reason for the judges to make proportionality into a general ground of judicial review.

8.3.1 Deference and the Human Rights Act 1998

In Human Rights Act adjudication, the role of proportionality is deeply entrenched and very wide ranging. In a Human Rights Act claim, the question for the court is whether a person's Convention rights have been violated, and *not* whether a public authority has used its power reasonably. So it may seem that the Human Rights Act imposes a legal limit on the exercise of discretionary powers, which involves no deference to the decisions of an administrative authority. A breach of a Convention right is simply unlawful (unless it was required by statute), whether or not it is so unreasonable that no reasonable public authority would act that way.

And yet, deference plays a crucial role in judicial decisions concerning Convention rights. Some of the most important judicial accounts of deference to administrative authorities come in decisions under the Human Rights Act, when the judges are rejecting a claimant's argument that the judges should impose the decision that they would have made if they had the job of the initial decision maker. In *R v Director of Public Prosecutions, ex p Kebilene* [2000] 2 AC 326, 381, Lord Hope said: 'In some circumstances it will be appropriate for the courts to recognise that there is an area of judgment within which the judiciary will defer, on democratic grounds, to the considered opinion of the elected body or person whose act or decision is said to be incompatible with the Convention.'

No case illustrates the role of deference in applying the Human Rights Act 1998 better than *R (Begum) v Denbigh High School* [2006] UKHL 15. Shabina Begum claimed that her school had violated her freedom of religion by enforcing a uniform policy that banned the jilbab (see 6.9.2, p 224). You might think that the House of Lords would simply decide whether the policy was 'necessary in a democratic society . . . for the protection of the rights and freedoms of others'—as it says in Art 9(2) of the

Convention. But, in fact the House of Lords firmly refused to decide for itself what was necessary in Denbigh High School. Lord Bingham said [34]:

> ‘ It would in my opinion be irresponsible of any court, lacking the experience, background and detailed knowledge of the head teacher, staff and governors, to overrule their judgment on a matter as sensitive as this. The power of decision has been given to them for the compelling reason that they are best placed to exercise it, and I see no reason to disturb their decision. ’

And Lord Hoffmann agreed that ‘an area of judgment, comparable to the margin of appreciation, must be allowed to the school’ [64].

The issue in *Begum* was whether the impact of the school’s uniform policy on Shabina Begum’s freedom of religion was disproportionate to its value in protecting other girls’ freedom. Do the **four basic reasons for deference** apply to the judges’ decision on *that* issue? The first reason—the allocation of decision-making power to the administrative agency—is put in question by the passage of the Human Rights Act 1998: Parliament may have allocated power to schools to determine uniform policies, but in the Human Rights Act, Parliament allocated power *to courts* to decide what counts as a breach of the freedom of religion under Art 9. So the **presumption of non-interference** (the principle that a court should not interfere with someone else’s decision unless there is a special reason to do so—see 7.1.1, p 240) does not apply.

Another basic reason for deference does apply, however, and it is very important: it is the familiarity of the school authorities with the needs of the pupils, which is a form of expertise. On that issue, the school authorities are better informed than judges, in a way that cannot be remedied through the litigation process. A sensitive understanding of the social pressures faced by the girls is crucial to a good decision as to whether it is legitimate to prohibit the jilbab, and people working in the school are better placed to reach the necessary understanding than people working in a court.

The House of Lords’ deference to the school in *Begum* does not mean that the court will not control the school’s decisions. The court will ask whether the school’s choice was made responsibly, with due process, and on the relevant considerations. Its deference is limited, and is left rather vague by the decision in *Begum*, but can best be summed up by saying that the judges will not interfere with reasonable decisions of a school as to whether a school needs a uniform policy that limits religious expression. The law requires the school not to ban the jilbab unless the ban is necessary for the protection of the freedom of others. But the judges will not pass judgment on that question; they will leave it to the school unless they can see—in spite of the advantages that the school authorities have—that there is no justification for the policy.

This approach is *less* deferential than the ordinary common law of control of discretionary powers, yet deference is still essential. But notice that the judges did not defer on the question of how to interpret the Convention. The Human Rights Act requires the judges to do that without deferring to the public authority whose decision is being challenged. The deference arises because *the application of the Convention rights themselves* sometimes requires assessments that can best be made by public authorities other than courts.

Lord Brown explained, in *Tweed v Parades Commission for Northern Ireland* [2006] UKHL 53 [55], that 'it is the court's recognition of what has been called variously the margin of discretion, or the discretionary area of judgment, or the deference or latitude due to administrative decision-makers, which stops the challenge from being a merits review'. And Lord Reed has said that the courts should 'give weight', in proportionality reasoning, to the initial decision maker's view on issues that 'are by their nature more suitable for determination by Government or Parliament' (*R (Nicklinson) v Ministry of Justice* [2014] UKSC 39 [296]; see also *R (SG) v Secretary of State for Work and Pensions* [2015] UKSC 16 [92]). He added that 'There is nothing new about this point. It has often been articulated in the past by referring to a discretionary area of judgment' [296]. The same point has often been articulated by referring to 'giving weight' to the government's assessment of relevant considerations, as in the landmark case of *Ali v Home Secretary* [2016] UKSC 60 [46] on deportation from the UK of foreign criminals. Lord Reed held for the Supreme Court that:

> ' where the Secretary of State has adopted a policy based on a general assessment of proportionality, as in the present case, [tribunals and judges] should attach considerable weight to that assessment. . . . '

The Court accepted the Home Secretary's judgment that imprisonment for four years or more 'represents such a serious level of offending that the public interest in the offender's deportation almost always outweighs countervailing considerations of private or family life' [46]. Lord Reed cited (at [44]) a remark by Lord Bingham that 'giving of weight to factors such as these is not . . . aptly described as deference'.[4] That remark reflects the hesitancy of some judges to see themselves as deferring (see 7.2.4). But other judges such as Lord Hope and Lord Brown (see above) have described the very same approach as deference. And it is a legitimate and in fact essential judicial approach in such cases: judges defer when they allow executive officials a discretionary area of judgment, and when they give weight to the judgment of an official. The result of cases such as *Begum* and *Ali* is a flexible, variable doctrine of deference in the application of proportionality reasoning, even in Human Rights Act claims.

One of the more spectacularly doomed proportionality challenges to government policy making was brought by protesters against the 2010 increase in university student fees in England and Wales to £9,000 per year. In *R (Hurley) v Secretary of State for Business Innovation and Skills* [2012] EWHC 201, the claimants argued that the change was a breach of the right to education under Art 2 of Protocol 1 to the Convention. The government had decided to shift a large part of the public funding of education from grants to loans; the court was—it should be needless to say—not prepared to hold that the new funding policy violated the Convention. The government is accountable to

---

4   *Huang v Home Secretary* [2007] 2 AC 167 [16].

Parliament, and not to the courts, for this aspect of policy.[5] In order to hold that the policy violated the Convention, the judges would need to be able to pass judgment on the public interest in reducing the cost to the Treasury of higher education, and on the prospect that access to education would be hindered by perceptions of the risk of taking loans, and weigh the two in the balance. There was no prospect that the judges would do that. But a doomed claim may not be futile from the campaigner's point of view: accusing the government of violating human rights puts a political issue in a new light, and forces the government to defend itself in court. The litigation frames that issue as a dispute in which the campaigners are holding the government to account before an independent authority. 'Public interest' cases can be a way of getting a message to the public, even if the claimant is bound to lose (see 10.3.2).

8.3.2 Equality

Like proportionality, equality is a relation. But it is a relation *among people*. Is there a general principle of judicial review that people should be treated as equals? Yes, according to the old line of cases leading to *Wednesbury*. In *Slattery v Naylor* (1888) 13 App Cas 446, 453 (see 7.1, p 237), Lord Hobhouse suggested that the court might set aside some by-laws as unreasonable 'such, for instance, as a bye-law providing that the Roman Catholic cemetery should be closed to the Roman Catholic community, but remain available for others'. And Lord Russell said in *Kruse v Johnson* [1898] 2 QB 91, 99, that by-laws would be unlawful '[i]f, for instance, they were found to be partial and unequal in their operation as between different classes'. So there is an unspecific anti-discrimination principle in English administrative law that is more than a century old. It is simply *part* of the doctrine of relevance.

But it would be going too far to say that a court can generally quash a decision that does not treat the claimant equally with other people. As Lord Hoffmann held in *Matadeen v Pointu* [1999] 1 AC 98 (PC), 109: 'The fact that equality of treatment is a general principle of rational behaviour does not entail that it should necessarily be a justiciable principle— that it should always be the judges who have the last word on whether the principle has been observed.' The judges' role in insisting on equality should be restricted (as *Slattery* and *Kruse* suggest) to decisions that would show an arbitrary disrespect for people (see Lord Hoffmann in *R (Carson) v Work and Pensions Secretary* [2005] UKHL 37).

But in respect of racism, sexism, and other forms of prejudice, legislation has given the judges such a role. In the 1970s, Parliament prohibited certain forms of discrimination (not only by public authorities, but also by private persons and companies) on the basis of race and sex, and the European Union has taken further measures that have effect in English law.[6] Those measures were designed to respond to traditional

---

[5] On the variability of judicial deference to policy decisions, see 7.3.8.

[6] The Race Relations Act 1976, Sex Discrimination Act 1975, and Equal Pay Act 1970. The Disability Discrimination Act was added in 1995. Article 10 of the Treaty on the Functioning of the European Union (TFEU) provides that the European Union 'shall aim to combat discrimination based on sex, racial or ethnic origin, religion or belief, disability, age or sexual orientation'.

prejudices that caused particularly unfair disadvantages to people who had suffered discrimination. It took legislation to respond effectively to those grounds of discrimination; the legislation has been consolidated and extended in the Equality Act 2010, which has created a field day for equality litigation.

The public-sector equality duty

The claimants in *R (Hurley) v Secretary of State for Business Innovation and Skills* [2012] EWHC 201 never stood a chance of persuading a court that the huge rise in university tuition fees violated the European Convention on Human Rights (see 8.3.1, p 289). But they succeeded in one aspect of their case: the court held that the decision had been made unlawfully, because the Secretary of State did not give the 'rigorous attention' that he was required to give to his public-sector equality duties ('PSEDs') [97].

The Equality Act 2010 s 149 frames the public-sector equality duty as follows:

> (1) A public authority must, in the exercise of its functions, have due regard to the need to—
>
> (a) eliminate discrimination, harassment, victimisation and any other conduct that is prohibited by or under this Act;
>
> (b) advance equality of opportunity between persons who share a relevant protected characteristic and persons who do not share it . . .

The Act replaces the earlier provisions for race, sex, and disability, and also extends the duty to include age, gender reassignment, pregnancy and maternity, religion or belief, and sexual orientation as protected characteristics (s 149(7)), and there is a separate duty on some authorities to 'have due regard to the desirability' of exercising their functions 'in a way that is designed to reduce the inequalities of outcome which result from socio-economic disadvantage' (s 1(1)).

The duty is onerous:

> . . . the 2010 Act imposes a heavy burden upon public authorities in discharging the PSED and in ensuring that there is evidence available, if necessary, to demonstrate that discharge. It seems to have been the intention of Parliament that these considerations of equality of opportunity (where they arise) are now to be placed at the centre of formulation of policy by all public authorities, side by side with all other pressing circumstances of whatever magnitude. [7]

The PSEDs apply extraordinarily broadly, to the 'functions' of a public authority. They do not require pointless steps to be taken where the needs identified in the Equality Act 2010 are irrelevant: 'There is no need to enter into time consuming and potentially

---

[7] *R (Bracking) v Secretary of State for Work and Pensions* [2013] EWCA Civ 1345 [59].

expensive consultation exercises or monitoring when discrimination issues are plainly not in point' (*R (Elias) v Defence Secretary* [2005] EWHC 1435 [96] (Elias J)). And the judges have resisted attempts 'to get the Court to "micro-manage" the information gathering aspect of the PSED' (*R (Aspinall) v Secretary of State for Work and Pensions* [2014] EWHC 4134 (Admin) [123]). Yet the PSED has opened up new possibilities for challenging policy decisions in the courts: wherever a policy involves a potential benefit to or detriment to people with the protected characteristics, the courts will find a breach of the PSED unless a decision maker can show that attention was given to each of the statutory considerations. If that cannot be done, the public authority may be held to be in breach of the duty even where 'there has on any view been very substantial compliance with these equality duties' (*Hurley* [95]).

The requirement of 'due regard' might have been taken to introduce a proportionality test, so that the court must decide whether the public authority has *done enough* to remove disadvantages and to meet the needs of people with the protected characteristics. But in *R (Baker) v Secretary of State for Communities and Local Government* [2008] EWCA Civ 141, the Court of Appeal established that a statutory duty (in that case, under the Race Relations Act 1976) to have due regard to the impact of a decision on equality is *not* 'a duty to promote equality of opportunity between the appellants and persons who were members of different racial groups' (Dyson LJ [31]). Dyson LJ held that 'due regard' is 'the regard that is appropriate in all the circumstances', including the way in which the disadvantaged racial group is affected, but also including 'such countervailing factors as are relevant to the function which the decision-maker is performing' [31]. As a result, the PSED has the effect of (1) creating an onerous obligation to take procedural steps, involving the preparation and use of equality impact assessments; and (2) requiring public authorities to take the resulting considerations into account (so that the PSED is a particularly intense, statutory form of the doctrine of relevant considerations). If the impact of a decision on equality is properly considered, then the administrative authority's evaluation of that impact 'will only be treated as unlawful where it is "unreasonable or perverse"' (*R (S) v Justice Secretary* [2012] EWHC 1810 [99] (Sales J).

It is important that, in *Hurley*, although the PSED had not been carried out, the court did not interfere with the decision to raise college fees to £9,000 per year: 'It would cause administrative chaos, and would inevitably have significant economic implications, if the regulations were now to be quashed' (*Hurley* [99]). The decision in *R (Hunt) v North Somerset Council* [2013] EWCA Civ 1320 was similar: the Court of Appeal held that the Council had not fulfilled its PSEDs, because although the right sort of equality impact assessment had been prepared before a decision to reduce spending on youth services, and had been provided to the councillors, the councillors had not actually been told that they had to read it and take it into account. But to uphold the claim the Court would have had to quash the Council's entire budget for the previous financial year, and the Court refused to do so because it would have been 'highly impractical and detrimental to good administration' [90].

The PSED has restructured policy making. And it has created a new frontier in administrative law litigation, because it gives a novel technique to challenge funding decisions in a court. But because of that great breadth, the duty lacks depth: if the right processes have been conducted, and the considerations resulting from an equality impact assessment have been considered, then the resulting decision will be lawful. And even if a decision is unlawful, the court will refuse a remedy that would be detrimental to good administration. As a result, the really important effect of the Equality Act 2010 will not be the stream of litigation that it has generated, but the structural change that it has brought to public decision making. Public expenditure decisions (and, in particular, decisions to cut funding to deal with the strain on public finance) now involve a public process of explicit consideration of the impact on people with the protected characteristics.

Non-discrimination under the ECHR

We have seen that the statutory public-sector equality duties use a heightened form of the doctrine of relevant considerations to restrain public authorities in making policy decisions that have a particular impact on disadvantaged groups. The European Convention on Human Rights provides proportionality protection against discrimination, in Art 14. That may seem a much stronger form of protection. But it is very significantly limited by judicial deference, both in Strasbourg and in the UK courts, to Parliament and to the executive.

Article 14 provides that:

> ' The enjoyment of the rights and freedoms set forth in this Convention shall be secured without discrimination on any ground such as sex, race, colour, language, religion, political or other opinion, national or social origin, association with a national minority, property, birth or other status. '

The Strasbourg Court has interpreted Art 14 as meaning that a policy needs a proportionality justification, if there is 'a difference in the treatment of persons in analogous, or relevantly similar, situations':

> ' Such a difference of treatment is discriminatory if it has no objective and reasonable justification; in other words, . . . if there is not a reasonable relationship of proportionality between the means employed and the aim sought to be realised. ' [8]

But in making this proportionality assessment, 'a wide margin is usually allowed to the state under the Convention when it comes to general measures of economic or social strategy. . . . the court will generally respect the legislature's policy choice unless it is "manifestly without reasonable foundation"' [9] (see 3.7 on the margin of appreciation).

---

[8] *Carson v United Kingdom* (2010) 51 EHRR 369 [61].

[9] *Stec v United Kingdom* (2006) 43 EHRR 1017 [52].

In *R (SG) v Secretary of State for Work and Pensions* [2015] UKSC 16, the claimants tried to use Art 14 to challenge a politically significant element in the government's austerity programme. The Department for Work and Pensions had imposed a benefit cap, to reduce housing benefit where the total welfare benefits received by a household exceeded net median earnings in working households. The claimants argued that the cap violated Art 14 and was therefore unlawful under the Human Rights Act; the argument was that the cap discriminated against women, because it particularly affected single-parent households, most of which are headed by women.

The government stated its objectives as saving public expenditure for the economic good of the country, incentivizing work to reduce long-term unemployment, and changing the benefits culture. Having accepted those aims as legitimate, the Supreme Court (with Baroness Hale and Lord Kerr dissenting) held that the benefit cap was not a disproportionate way of pursuing them. Lord Reed emphasized that although the Human Rights Act 'entails some adjustment of the respective constitutional roles of the courts, the executive and the legislature', the courts still need to give weight to the determination of some issues by Parliament and to the executive [93]:

> ' ... the question of proportionality involves controversial issues of social and economic policy, with major implications for public expenditure. The determination of those issues is pre-eminently the function of democratically elected institutions. It is therefore necessary for the court to give due weight to the considered assessment made by those institutions. Unless manifestly without reasonable foundation, their assessment should be respected. '

That 'manifestly without reasonable foundation' test, used by the Strasbourg Court and the UK Supreme Court on questions of general economic strategy, is very much like *Wednesbury* unreasonableness. It is a strong form of judicial deference. But the deference does not *prevent* the judges from interfering. In *R (MA) v Secretary of State for Work and Pensions* [2016] UKSC 58, the government had instituted a 'bedroom tax'— a similar austerity initiative to restrict welfare benefits. The regulations capped housing allowance for claimants who had more bedrooms than the Department thought they needed. The judges held that there was manifestly no reasonable foundation for counting a family as having too many bedrooms when medical reasons prevented adults from sharing a bedroom, or required a child to have an overnight carer.

The deferential approach of the majority of the Supreme Court in these cases is entirely justified. The question of how much to spend on welfare benefits is a critically important question for every developed country, and bad judgements in favour of austerity will inflict hardship on the economically disadvantaged (who are not mentioned in Art 14), and on women and children and the disabled, who are overrepresented among the economically disadvantaged. That hardship reflects a social injustice, to the extent that the UK could do better at alleviating it. Yet if the judges were to abandon the deferential approach of *SG*, they would be controlling the country's public expenditure while suffering from a major disability. The judges lack the techniques to manage the economy, or even to manage public revenue and expenditure, and a community can only make good decisions on welfare expenditure by integrating them into the overall management of public revenue and expenditure. There is no effective solution to injustice in social security through litigation.

You may think that there is no effective solution through politics either, since democratic processes do not reflect the interests of the disadvantaged. But consider this surprising fact: since the European Convention on Human Rights was established in 1950, the really significant improvements in the situation of disadvantaged people in the United Kingdom have been achieved through the politics of the welfare state— chiefly in the forms of public education, the National Health Service, public housing, and welfare benefits—rather than through the role of courts in giving effect to human rights law. There is no reason to think that the UK would have done better, if judges showed less deference to Parliament and the executive on questions of economic strategy.

8.4 Legitimate expectations

In *R (Bibi) v Newham LBC* [2001] EWCA Civ 607, a local authority promised to give permanent accommodation to Manik Bibi and his family within eighteen months. The local authority thought that the family, who were homeless, had a legal right to it. Then the House of Lords held that local authorities had no obligation to give homeless people permanent accommodation, and should not be bumping homeless people up to the front of the housing queue (*R v Brent LBC, ex p Awua* [1996] AC 55). The Council refused to provide the permanent accommodation it had promised, and the claimants sought judicial review. The Court of Appeal issued a declaration 'that the authority is under a duty to consider the applicants' applications for suitable housing on the basis that they have a legitimate expectation that they will be provided by the authority with suitable accommodation on a secure tenancy' (*Bibi* [69]).

That phrase 'legitimate expectation' is a technical term.[10] A legitimate expectation might better be called a 'legally protected expectation'. If a person has a legitimate expectation, it is not merely legitimate for him or her to expect something; the law will give the expectation some form of protection in judicial review. *Bibi* shows why this technique has been developed. On the one hand, Bibi had no legal right to permanent accommodation.[11] On the other hand, it would be unfair to Bibi, and it would put the

---

[10]   Lord Denning used it in a 1969 decision in which he held that before a foreign national's permission to stay in the UK is revoked early, they should be given an opportunity to make representations, even though they have no right to remain in the United Kingdom, because they have 'a legitimate expectation of being allowed to stay for the permitted time' (*Schmidt v Home Secretary* [1969] 2 Ch 149, 171).

[11]   The promise from the local authority gave them no rights in contract law, because it was a gratuitous promise (Bibi gave no consideration for it). On what a right is, see 3.4.

integrity of public services in doubt, if a public authority were to pay no attention to what it had said that it would do. As Lord Fraser put it in the *GCHQ* case, 'even where a person claiming some benefit or privilege has no legal right to it as a matter of private law, he may have a legitimate expectation of receiving the benefit or privilege, and, if so, the courts will protect his expectation by judicial review as a matter of public law' ([1985] AC 374, 401). Remember that word 'protect': the courts will *not* necessarily order a public authority to do what the claimant expected it to do.

The courts have been working—in a process that is still in flux—to find a way for the law to protect expectations that public authorities generate. In doing so, courts face a special and rather delicate problem of comity: how can they complete this development without taking over the judgments that a good administrator would make, in reconciling the protection of legitimate expectations with conflicting interests? In *Bibi*, at [64], Lord Justice Schiemann resolved the problem of comity in the following way:

> In an area such as the provision of housing at public expense where decisions are informed by social and political value judgments as to priorities of expenditure the court will start with a recognition that such invidious choices are essentially political rather than judicial. In our judgment the appropriate body to make that choice in the context of the present case is the authority. However, it must do so in the light of the legitimate expectations of the respondents.

So in a case like *Bibi*, the court:

- will defer very substantially on general questions as to priorities of expenditure;

- will not defer at all on the question of whether expectations induced by the public authority are relevant; and

- will defer to some extent on the question of whether the promise should be carried out, in a way that will vary substantially depending on the circumstances.

That last form of deference explains the difference between a legitimate expectation of housing and a right to housing. If a person has a right to housing (conferred by statute or contract), the court will order housing (or compensation) to be provided. Courts do not defer to administrative authorities on the question of whether to respect someone's legal rights.

But if the claimant has a legitimate expectation, the court will defer to the public authority in a way that depends both on the authority's responsibility for setting funding priorities and on the authority's capacity to identify the interests of third parties, such as people waiting in the queue for permanent housing ahead of the Bibi family. Those third parties would not be treated fairly if their interests were simply subordinated to the expectations of the claimants. But if the claimants had a legal right to housing, the authority's expenditure priorities would be irrelevant, and so would the interests of third parties.

As Schiemann LJ said, if a claimant has a legitimate expectation of a housing benefit, the court 'will not order the authority to honour its promise where to do so would be to assume the powers of the executive' (*Bibi* [41]). He held that a local authority is 'abusing its powers' if it acts without even considering the fact that it is going back on a legitimate expectation [39]. The gist of the doctrine of legitimate expectation is that the court will quash a decision if the public authority's approach to the claimant's expectation was an abuse of power. There may or may not be 'only one lawful ultimate answer to the question whether the authority should honour its promise' [43].

8.4.1 What generates a legitimate expectation?

An expectation does not deserve legal protection merely because it was reasonable for a claimant to expect a particular action. There must have been a pattern of conduct, or a representation, or a promise, that makes it unfair for the public authority to disregard the expectation. Then, it becomes the business of the courts to protect the expectation in some way.

If the alleged legitimate expectation was generated by a promise, it must have been 'clear, unambiguous and devoid of relevant qualification' (*R v Inland Revenue Commissioners, ex p MFK Underwriting Agents* [1990] 1 WLR 1545, 1569 (Bingham LJ); see also *R (Bancoult) v Foreign Secretary (No 2)* [2008] UKHL 61 [60]). Ironically, it can be very unclear whether there has been a clear promise, and very controversial. In *Bancoult* (see 7.3.1, p 255), the House of Lords was deeply divided 3–2 over whether the Foreign Secretary had clearly promised that the Chagossians would be allowed to return to the Chagos Islands.

An expectation can deserve judicial protection even if the public authority did not actually make a promise. A legitimate expectation may arise from 'the existence of a regular practice which the claimant can reasonably expect to continue', as Lord Fraser said in the *GCHQ* case ([1985] AC 374, 401). In that case, the practice of consulting unions had given the unions reason to believe that the practice would continue; the reason was that the practice created a relationship between the government as employer and the union, in which the government was committed to recognizing the union's role in decision making. Similarly, the (then) Inland Revenue's twenty-year-old practice of allowing late claims for a form of tax relief gave rise to a legitimate expectation in *R v Inland Revenue Commissioners, ex p Unilever* [1996] STC 681 (CA), so that it was an abuse of power for the Revenue to pull the rug out from under the claimants' feet by suddenly refusing late claims.

Whether it arises from government practice or from a statement, the expectation must be one that the courts can legitimately protect. In *R v Environment Secretary, ex p Hammersmith and Fulham LBC* [1991] 1 AC 521, the government had announced that the Environment Secretary would not cap the spending of local authorities that set 'sensible' budgets. The local authorities argued that they *had* set sensible budgets, and that it was therefore a breach of their legitimate expectation for the government to cap their spending. The argument failed so comprehensively that Lord Bridge only said that it was 'plainly misconceived', and did not even take the trouble to explain why. The reason was that, by promising not to interfere with 'sensible' budgets, the government was not pinning itself down to any particular view of what counted as sensible. If the court had been willing to decide what was a sensible budget, it would have been taking over the minister's job. There was nothing wrong with the local authorities expecting to be able to set a sensible budget without being capped—but they had no hope of getting a court to protect that expectation by deciding what would be a sensible local council budget.

Even more radically, in *Wheeler v Office of the Prime Minister* [2008] EWHC 1409, a claimant tried to argue that there was a legitimate expectation of a referendum before the ratification of the European Union's Treaty of Lisbon, because Prime Minister Tony Blair had promised a referendum before ratification of another treaty (the claimant said that the two treaties had the same effect). The Administrative Court held that there was no legitimate expectation. Even if the promise of a referendum applied to the new Lisbon Treaty (and the court doubted whether that was justiciable [37]), the promise did not generate an expectation that the court would protect [43]: 'In our view a promise to hold a referendum lies so deep in the macro-political field that the court should not enter the relevant area at all.'

> There is no legitimate expectation, unless *a court* is in a position to decide that it would be an abuse of power to disappoint the expectation.

8.4.2 Does reliance matter?

Yes. If a claimant acted to his or her detriment because of an expectation that a public authority induced, then that fact will count in favour of an argument that it would be an abuse of power for the public authority to ignore the expectation. But reliance is not conclusive, because the requirements of public policy and the interests of third parties may mean that it is not an abuse of power to disappoint an expectation, even after a claimant has relied on it. And reliance is not necessary, either: 'It is not essential that the applicant should have relied upon the promise to his detriment, although this is a relevant consideration in deciding whether the adoption of a policy in conflict with the promise would be an abuse of power' (*Bancoult (No 2)*, Lord Hoffmann [60]). Since it is relevant, there are bound to be cases in which the very fact that a claimant did not rely on a representation or practice means that he or she has no legitimate expectation. *R v Education Secretary, ex p Begbie* [2000] 1 WLR 1115 is an example. Peter Gibson LJ said: 'It is very much the exception, rather than the rule, that detrimental reliance will not be present when the court finds unfairness in the defeating of a legitimate expectation' [48].

> ### Estoppel and legitimate expectation: the land by the lake
> Suppose I promise to give you my piece of land by the lake, and say that you can build a cabin there and move in. But I like the new cabin so much that I decide to

keep the land, and try to have you ejected. I will be estopped (which is Norman French for 'stopped') from asserting my right in court. Does a legitimate expectation estop a public authority from asserting the lawfulness of an exercise of public power? No. I am estopped from asserting my right to the land by the lake because it would be unconscionable (that is, selfish in a way that the law should not tolerate) for me to do so after I induced you to act to your detriment.

Although there is 'an analogy between a private law estoppel and the public law concept of a legitimate expectation created by a public authority' (Lord Hoffmann in *R (Reprotech) v East Sussex County Council* [2002] UKHL 8 [34]), the analogy is dangerous, because the rationale for protecting a legitimate expectation is not that the public authority is using private legal rights unconscionably. The rationale is abuse of public power. The question is not limited to the private rights or interests of the claimant: 'remedies against public authorities also have to take into account the interests of the general public which the authority exists to promote' (*Reprotech* [34]). The court will insist that a legitimate expectation should be fulfilled only if it would be an abuse of power for the public authority not to do what the claimant expected. Both Lord Scarman and Lord Fraser made the same point in *Newbury District Council v Environment Secretary* [1981] AC 578, 616, 617.

● *Pop quiz* ●

What if a public authority does the very things that would create an estoppel if they were done by a private person? Is the public authority estopped from asserting its right to the land by the lake? Or does the other party need to ask the court for protection of its legitimate expectation?

8.4.3 What if a claimant expected that a public authority would do something unlawful?

A public authority's conduct or representation may lead a claimant to expect the authority to do something that is against the law. Even if the claimant's expectation is perfectly reasonable (e.g., if the claimant had no reason to think that the expected conduct was unlawful), it cannot count as a legitimate expectation. In order to generate an expectation that the law will protect, a public official's promise or undertaking 'must not conflict with his statutory duty or his duty, as here, in the exercise of a prerogative power' (*R v Home Secretary, ex p Ruddock* [1987] 1 WLR 1482, 1497 (Taylor J)). That does not only mean that no legitimate expectation arises from a representation that a public authority will do something that is specifically prohibited by law. It also means that, if there *is* a legitimate expectation, it does not stop the public authority from being able to change a policy, or to act on all of the relevant considerations: '[T]he Secretary of State cannot fetter his discretion. By declaring a policy he does not preclude any possible need to change it' (*Ruddock*, 1497).

If a public authority cannot fetter its discretion, it may seem that a claimant cannot have a legitimate expectation that a public authority will use a discretion one way rather than another. But no: the *Ruddock* decision simply means that the doctrine of legitimate expectation does not necessarily prevent a public authority from changing a policy that would have benefited a claimant.

The courts have tried to reconcile the protection of expectations with the need for public authorities to be able to change policies. In *Re Findlay* [1985] 1 AC 318, Lord Scarman said that a prisoner had no legitimate expectation of being treated according to the parole policy that was in effect when he went to prison (338): 'The most that a convicted prisoner can legitimately expect is that his case will be examined individually in the light of whatever policy the Secretary of State sees fit to adopt provided always that the adopted policy is a lawful exercise of the discretion conferred upon him by the statute.' The House of Lords was concerned to ensure that the law should not protect an expectation if doing so would prevent a public authority from exercising its responsibilities, which might include changing a policy.

8.4.4 Procedural and substantive protection for legitimate expectations

In the 1980s and 1990s, there was much controversy over whether the doctrine gave substantive protection for legitimate expectations, or whether a public authority merely needed to listen to what the person affected had to say, before deciding to disappoint a legitimate expectation. In *GCHQ*, Lord Diplock had suggested that 'where the decision is one which does not alter rights or obligations enforceable in private law but only deprives a person of legitimate expectations, "procedural impropriety" will normally provide the only ground on which the decision is open to judicial review' ([1985] AC 374, 411); cf. *O'Reilly v Mackman* [1983] 2 AC 237, 275 (Lord Diplock). It seemed to some that an authority with a discretionary power had to be free to act regardless of the expectations of persons affected by the decision, or the courts would be taking away the discretion (and by the same token, they would be giving public authorities a technique for taking away *their own* discretion, by promising someone that they would use a power in one way rather than another).

But as *Bibi* shows, that controversy is long over. The claimants in *Bibi* did not merely get a declaration that they were entitled to a hearing; by telling the local authority that the claimants' legitimate expectation had to be taken into account, the Court spelled out considerations on which it had to decide. And that means determining part of the *substance* of the decision that it had to make. The authority could not deny Bibi what he had been promised unless there were overriding reasons not to give it to him. Although this was not clear when the *GCHQ* case was decided in 1984, there was clear authority for substantive protection for legitimate expectations in *R v Home Secretary, ex p Khan* [1985] 1 All ER 40, and Taylor J unequivocally stated that the doctrine of legitimate expectation is 'not confined' to a right to be heard in *R v Home Secretary, ex p Ruddock* [1987] 1 WLR 1482, 1497. In fact, it should always have been obvious that the doctrine gave substantive protection. After all, it follows from the *Wednesbury* doctrine that if no reasonable public authority would disappoint an expectation, then it is unlawful to do so. And that is unquestionably a matter of substance.

Is substantive protection of expectations dangerous? Does it restrict a public authority's capacity to change its policy? And does it enable an authority to bind itself illegitimately, evading the law that requires it to make a genuine exercise of its discretion (see 8.1.2)? Not necessarily. As Taylor J pointed out, substantive protection for legitimate expectations need not fetter the discretion of a public authority (*Ruddock*, 1497). It can be a good *exercise* of discretion for a public authority to commit itself (after all, public authorities can enter binding contracts—see 15.3.2). But the substantive impact of the doctrine ought to be limited, because no one can *legitimately* expect a public authority to be unable to change its policy under any conditions. Stanley Burton LJ said for the Court of Appeal: 'A minister is entitled to review, to change and to revoke his policy whenever he considers it to be in the public interest to do so' (*Rahman v Home Secretary* [2011] EWCA Civ 814 [43]). We can make that into a complete statement of the substantive effect of legitimate expectations if we say that a minister is entitled to review, to change, and to revoke a policy where it would not be an abuse of power, in light of the claimant's expectations, to do so.

The result in *Bibi* shows that the courts can protect legitimate expectations with out taking away a public authority's discretion. In fact, in *Bibi*, the doctrine of legitimate expectation **simply acts as an instance of the relevance doctrine**, because the Court held that the law required the authority to take its promise into account in exercising its discretion. That fact itself shows, first of all, that the doctrine of legitimate expectation is not a novelty, and second, that it must provide some form of substantive protection. Like *Wednesbury* unreasonableness, the relevance doctrine unquestionably controls the substance of decisions. The strenuous debates over the legitimate expectation doctrine have really concerned the extent of substantive protection. We will look at that problem in this section; it tests the limits of the judges' role.

In the idea that courts should prevent abuse of power, there is a rationale for some form of substantive protection for expectations that administrative authorities have induced. The courts must apply it with comity towards administrative authorities. You might think that it is no breach of comity for the judges to hold an administrative authority to a policy choice to which *the authority has committed itself*. Yet the courts still need to defer to some extent, as Lord Scarman explained in *Findlay*, because a public authority may have legitimate reasons to change a policy, or to create exceptions to it, and may need to reconcile it with competing interests. The deference the courts need to show may make it impossible for them to decide whether it is appropriate for a public authority to disappoint a legitimate expectation. The judges do not always keep hold of the principle of comity as clearly as they did in *Bibi*.

The leading case is *R v North and East Devon Health Authority, ex p Coughlan* [2001] QB 213 (CA). A car accident had left Miss Coughlan in need of constant nursing care. After she had been in a hospital for more than twenty years, the health authority promised her that, if she moved into a new nursing home called Mardon House, she could stay there for life. She agreed, but after five years the authority decided to close Mardon House and to move her again. The decision was made for financial reasons and because the facility was not clinically well suited for other health service functions that were located there [53]. The Court of Appeal held that the decision had been unlawful. The authority had deliberately considered the fact that Miss Coughlan had been promised a home for life, so the decision shows how legitimate expectation can move beyond the relevance doctrine.

Lord Woolf MR, for the Court of Appeal, pointed out that different expectations may deserve different forms of legal protection (at [57]):

> ' (a) The court may decide that the public authority is only required to bear in mind its previous policy or other representation. . . . Here the court is confined to reviewing the decision on *Wednesbury* grounds. . . . (b) On the other hand the court may decide that the promise or practice induces a legitimate expectation of, for example, being consulted before a particular decision is taken. Here it is uncontentious that the court itself will require the opportunity for consultation to be given unless there is an overriding reason to resile from it. . . . (c) Where the court considers that a lawful promise or practice has induced a legitimate expectation of a benefit which is substantive, not simply procedural, authority now establishes that here too the court will in a proper case decide whether to frustrate the expectation is so unfair that to take a new and different course will amount to an abuse of power. Here, . . . the court will have the task of weighing the requirements of fairness against any overriding interest relied upon for the change of policy. '

Of Lord Woolf's three categories of protection, the first is an application of the relevance doctrine,[12] and the second is an application of the law of due process.

If legitimate expectations can be protected in different ways, what determines the form of protection? The Court held that Miss Coughlan's case came within category (c), because the promise was so important to her, the persons affected by the promise were few, and the consequences of holding the authority to its promise were 'likely to be financial only' [60].

Lord Woolf's category (c) is a form of protection against substantive unfairness. But not just any unfairness. In order for a court to interfere, the claimant has to show that frustrating the expectation was unfair in a way that the judges can identify as an abuse of power. So it seems that Miss Coughlan did not win merely because the health authority had not given the right weight to her expectation. She won because their decision was *so unfair* as to be an abuse of their discretionary power. Understood in that way, the case is an orthodox application of principles that go back to *Kruse* and earlier; it is only remarkable because, by deciding that the decision was an abuse of power, the judges took it on themselves to discount the financial consequences of keeping open an almost-redundant nursing home.[13]

---

12 See *Coughlan* [73].

13 In the Court's reasons in *Coughlan* there is simply no assessment of the interests that, the defendant argued, gave an overriding reason of public interest for going back on the promise. Those were the cost of continuing to use Mardon House (which is not stated in the judgment), and the detrimental consequences for patient care of providing different sorts of service there [87]. The decision in *Coughlan* is only warranted on an assumption as to the facts, which the judgment does not explain: that the cost, and the detriment to patient care, were both so little that it was an abuse of power not to incur them.

Yet the judges also said, that 'it is for the court to decide' whether a decision in category (c) 'strikes a proper balance between the public and the private interest' [52], and 'the Health Authority failed to weigh the conflicting interests correctly' [89]. The Court also held that: 'The propriety of such an exercise of power should be tested by asking whether the need which the Health Authority judged to exist to move Miss Coughlan to a local authority facility was such as to outweigh its promise that Mardon House would be her home for life' [83]. That would indeed have been the way for the health authority to decide whether to move Miss Coughlan—but the way *for a court to decide whether it was lawful* is (according to the Court of Appeal in *Coughlan* itself) to ask whether it was *so* unfair as to amount to an abuse of power for the health authority to reach the conclusion that it reached ([57] and [67]–[71]). So there is an ambiguity in *Coughlan*: is it the judges' job to identify an abuse of power? Or to determine whether a public authority decided proportionately (that is, to impose the court's weighting of the conflicting interests)?

In *R v Ministry of Agriculture, Fisheries and Food, ex p Hamble Fisheries Ltd* [1995] 2 All ER 714, 731, Sedley J had held that the court's duty was 'to protect the interests of those individuals whose expectation of different treatment has a legitimacy which in fairness *outtops* the policy choice which threatens to frustrate it' (emphasis added). Hamble Fisheries had refitted a boat to take advantage of the Ministry's way of counting fishing quotas; the Ministry changed its policy, and refused to make an exception to allow the company to take advantage of the old scheme. The word 'outtops' in Sedley J's reasons shows that he took it upon himself to decide whether the Ministry made the correct decision. In *R v Home Secretary, ex p Hargreaves* [1997] 1 All ER 397, Hirst LJ called Sedley J's approach 'heresy'. The heresy was that Sedley J judged whether the policy change was important enough to justify the impact on Hamble Fisheries, instead of deferring to the Ministry's view of the importance of the policy change. Hirst LJ said, in *Hargreaves*: 'On matters of substance (as contrasted with procedure) *Wednesbury* provides the correct test. . . . while Sedley J's actual decision in the *Hamble* case stands, his ratio in so far as he propounds a balancing exercise to be undertaken by the court should in my judgment be overruled' (412).

Did *Coughlan* rehabilitate *Hamble Fisheries* after it was called 'heresy' in *Hargreaves*? No, because *Coughlan*, according to the Court of Appeal, involved an abuse of power. Consider the fact that the Court of Appeal in *Coughlan* relied on *Kruse v Johnson* (*Coughlan* [72]). It would be completely foreign to Lord Russell's approach in *Kruse* to say that the court must decide whether the policy objective was important *enough* to justify the impact on the defendants. His approach was not even to ask that question, but to ask instead, in anticipation of *Wednesbury*, if decisions were 'manifestly unjust; if they disclosed bad faith; if they involved such oppressive or gratuitous interference with the rights of those subject to them as could find no justification in the minds of reasonable men' (*Kruse v Johnson* [1898] 2 QB 91, 99–100—see 7.1, p 237).

The Justices of the Court of Appeal in *Coughlan* (which included Sedley LJ) certainly wanted to reject the *Hargreaves* view that *Wednesbury* provides the correct test for substantive protection of legitimate expectations. They held that, in category (a) (where the public authority need only bear in mind its policy or representation), 'the court is confined to reviewing the decision on *Wednesbury* grounds'—implying that, in category (c), the court is *not* confined to reviewing the decision on *Wednesbury* grounds. And the Court suggested that the right approach 'is to ask not whether the decision is ultra vires in the restricted *Wednesbury* sense but whether, for example through unfairness or arbitrariness, it amounts to an abuse of power' [67]. That presents *Wednesbury* as if it were restricted to irrationality (see *Coughlan* [62]). Then the Court held that the decision of the health authority in *Coughlan* was perfectly rational, but could be quashed for unfairness amounting to abuse of power (citing *Kruse* [72]). The Court presented the resulting doctrine of substantive protection for legitimate expectations as a progression beyond *Wednesbury*.

But the result in *Coughlan*, and the reasons for it, are compatible with Lord Greene's reasons in *Wednesbury*. Precisely because the Court held the decision in *Coughlan* to be an abuse of power, there is no ground for the Court's suggestion that *Coughlan* required a ground of review other than those that Lord Greene identified. No reasonable public authority would exercise its power in a way that is so unfair as to amount to an abuse of power. It would be deeply contrary to Lord Greene's approach in *Wednesbury* to say that a decision might be so unfair as to amount to an abuse of power, and yet still lawful because it was not irrational. The Court of Appeal in *Coughlan* had a convincing argument that a decision does not have to be irrational before it can be quashed as an abuse of power. But that convincing argument only shows that it has always been a mistake for the courts to describe *Wednesbury* unreasonableness as 'irrationality' (see 7.1.3). The very fact that the Court of Appeal could rely on *Kruse* shows that *Coughlan* does not support the *Hamble Fisheries* rule that it is unlawful for a public authority to disappoint a substantive legitimate expectation whenever the courts decide that the impact on the claimant outtops the public interest in a policy change. Its conclusion that the health authority had abused its power meant that *Coughlan* was simply too strong a case to give the Court an opportunity to rehabilitate *Hamble Fisheries*.

Yet, in its conclusion on the legitimate expectation issue, the Court really did state the old heretical line from *Hamble Fisheries*—the line that the Court of Appeal had overruled in *Hargreaves*—by asking if the health authority had correctly weighed its reasons for wanting to close Mardon House against its promise not to (*Coughlan* [89]). If *Coughlan* stands for the principle that the judges have that job, then it was revolutionary. But it is better to take the case as standing for the proposition asserted repeatedly through the decision—a proposition that is compatible with *Wednesbury* and which (as the judges suggested by citing *Kruse*) goes back much further than *Wednesbury*. It is the proposition that an exercise of discretion can be quashed for 'unfairness amounting to an abuse of power' (*Coughlan* [89]).

When the judges say, as in *Coughlan*,[14] that it is their job to decide whether the value of pursuing the public authority's purpose by disappointing the expectation is proportionate to the impact on the claimant of doing so, perhaps they are counting the disappointment of a legitimate expectation as an abuse of power, and therefore

---

[14] See also *Nadarajah v Home Secretary* [2005] EWCA 1363 [68] and *UK Association of Fish Producer Organisations v Secretary of State for Environment* [2013] EWHC 1959 [92].

unlawful, where they can see that the impact on the claimant is disproportionate even after they have deferred (to whatever extent may be appropriate) to the public authority's assessment of the value of the course of action that would disappoint the expectation. They will quash a decision that disappoints a legitimate expectation if it is obviously, manifestly disproportionate, and a manifestly disproportionate use of power is an abuse of power.

8.4.5 Legitimate expectations: conclusion

What more does legitimate expectation give than the ordinary doctrines of due process and control of discretionary powers? Nothing: it is *part of* those doctrines. It can be procedurally unfair to disappoint an expectation without a hearing, and it can be substantively unfair to disappoint an expectation. And then the decision is unlawful if it is procedurally unfair, or if it is so unfair in substance that it is an abuse of power.

The key concept that explains substantive protection for legitimate expectations is abuse of power. What is an abuse of power? The cases, of course, give no precise answer. 'Abuse' is vague. But the crucial point is that abusing power is *worse* than just making the wrong decision. An abuse of power is a departure from responsible government (see 1.4.2). As Laws LJ said in *R v Education Secretary, ex p Begbie* [2000] 1 WLR 1115 [81], to call someone's conduct an abuse of power is a 'condemnation'. The reason for condemnation is that the decision maker has abandoned the standards that are meant to guide his or her conduct. So, for example, an error of law (by a judge or by an administrative authority) is not an abuse of power, as Lord Griffiths said in *R v Hull University Visitor, ex p Page* [1993] AC 682, 693:

> ' I do not regard a judge who makes what an appellate court later regards as a mistake of law as abusing his powers. . . . I used the phrase "abuse of power" to connote some form of misbehaviour that was wholly incompatible with the judicial role that the judge was expected to perform. I did not intend it to include a mere error of law. '

We can say the same about exercises of discretionary power. If the health authority in *Coughlan* moved Miss Coughlan when it did not need to do so, it made the wrong decision. If it abused its power, it did worse than that; it engaged in a form of misbehaviour that was wholly incompatible with the public role that the health authority was expected to perform.

Like the other vague terms that judges have used to explain their role (such as 'irrational', or 'perverse', or 'so unreasonable that no reasonable official could have done it'), the vagueness of the standard leads to a risk that judges will see a decision they do not like and just call it an 'abuse of power'. But that only means that it is an idea that is open to misuse—not that it is meaningless. The special feature of abuse of power is that judges ought to be able to identify it without needing to second-guess the decision maker on matters that call for deference. *Wednesbury* unreasonableness was Lord

Greene's attempt to articulate the basis of abuse of power: it is conduct that a court ought to condemn because, even from the court's detached point of view, it can be seen that no one in the decision maker's position could seriously defend the decision.

Ordinarily, a decision is an abuse of power if it is abusive towards the claimant. That is only the *ordinary* case: consider *R v Foreign Secretary, ex p World Development Movement* [1995] 1 WLR 386, in which the government took money that Parliament had allocated for overseas aid and used it to give Malaysia a financial incentive to buy British military aircraft (see 8.2.2, p 284). What made that decision an abuse of power—the thing that distinguishes it from simply making the wrong decision—is that it showed a flagrant disregard for the purposes for which a public authority has been given a power. The government did not merely make a bad overseas aid decision; it did not make an overseas aid decision at all. It decided to use the overseas aid fund for something else instead.

8.5 Consistency

In *R (Rashid) v Home Secretary* [2005] EWCA Civ 744, the claimant was a Kurd from Iraq, whose application for asylum was turned down on the basis that he could have escaped persecution within Iraq by relocating to the Kurdish zone. Neither Rashid, nor his advisers, nor the Home Office caseworker who dealt with his claim knew that the Home Secretary had a policy that asylum claims were not to be refused on that ground. The Court of Appeal held that the rejection of the claim was an instance of unfairness amounting to an abuse of power.

The Court of Appeal described its decision in *Rashid* as an application of the doctrine of legitimate expectation. But Rashid had no expectation! He did not know about the Home Secretary's policy. In *Coughlan*, and even in *Bibi*, the public authority's conduct was substantively unfair *because the defendant had led the claimant to expect a different course of conduct.*

What is the real rationale for the decision in *Rashid*? The explanation is that the courts consider it to be their responsibility to require some degree of consistency from administrative authorities in adhering to their policies. In *Nadarajah v Home Secretary* [2005] EWCA Civ 1363 [68], Lord Justice Laws said that it is:

> ' a requirement of good administration, by which public bodies ought to deal straightforwardly and consistently with the public. '

In the landmark case of *Mandalia v Home Secretary* [2015] UKSC 59, the Supreme Court adopted Lord Justice Laws' view, and we now have a new doctrine of consistency in the application of policy. Lord Wilson said for the unanimous Court that 'the applicant's right to the determination of his application in accordance with policy is now generally taken to flow from a principle, no doubt related to the doctrine of legitimate expectation but free-standing, which was best articulated by Laws LJ [in

Nadarajah]' (Mandalia [29]). Lord Wilson restated the principle (citing *Mandalia*) in *R (Lee-Hirons) v Secretary of State for Justice* [2016] UKSC 46 [17]:

> ' Where a public authority issues a statement of policy in relation to the exercise of one of its functions, a member of the public to whom it ostensibly applies, . . . has a right at common law to require the authority to apply the policy, so long as it is lawful, to himself unless there are good reasons for the authority not to do so. '

Laws LJ based the principle on good administration. It is not *generally* the job of judges to tell government departments what good administration requires. Courts should only do so if their view can be imposed on the department with no breach of comity. In *Nadarajah*, *Mandalia*, and *Lee-Hirons*, it is the fact that the public authority had itself chosen the policy that made the judges feel free to require adherence to it.

Yet a public authority ought to be able to change its policy; the doctrine of legitimate expectation does not stop them from doing so (*R (Niazi) v Home Secretary* [2008] EWCA Civ 755), and neither should the doctrine of consistency in the application of policy. Sometimes, it will be unclear whether a public authority has unlawfully neglected its policy, or has lawfully changed it. In *Nadarajah* itself, the Court held against the claimant on the ground that the Home Office had changed its policy in a way that involved no abuse of power. This crucial aspect of the doctrine of consistency will be worked out through the elaboration of an important proviso that Lord Justice Laws stated in *Nadarajah* [68], and that Lord Wilson restated in *Lee-Hirons*—that the law does not require a public authority to adhere to its policy where 'there is good reason not to do so'.

The new doctrine of consistency has to be targeted at arbitrary, irresponsible use of power (that is, use of power that does not respond to the considerations that it ought to respond to). That is how the doctrine is related to the doctrine of legitimate expectations: both grounds of review are justified by the court's role in preventing acts of government that the court can identify as arbitrary.

● *Pop quiz* ●

The doctrine adopted in *Mandalia* and *Lee-Hirons* is that a public authority may not lawfully depart from a policy that favoured the claimant, unless it has good reason. After *Mandalia*, should we conclude that there is no need for a doctrine of legitimate expectations, since unfairly disappointing a legitimate expectation will count as an instance of departing from a policy without good reason?

8.6 Substantive unfairness

The judges in *Coughlan* held that the ground for quashing the decision to move Miss Coughlan was 'an abuse of power or a failure of substantive fairness' [76]. Are they the same thing? Is substantive unfairness a ground of judicial review?

It is sometimes said, as Lord Diplock said in *R v Inland Revenue Commissioners, ex p National Federation of Self-Employed and Small Businesses* [1982] AC 617, 637, that judicial review is not available 'for acts done lawfully in the exercise of an administrative discretion which are complained of only as being unfair or unwise'. Yet Lord Scarman said in *R v Inland Revenue Commissioners, ex p Preston* [1985] AC 835, 851:

> ' I must make clear my view that the principle of fairness has an important place in the law of judicial review: and that in an appropriate case it is a ground upon which the court can intervene to quash a decision made by a public officer or authority in purported exercise of a power conferred by law. '

Who was right?

They were both right. If the claim is *only* that a decision was substantively unfair, that is not a ground of judicial review. But *certain forms* of unfairness can justify judicial review. In the ferment of judicial review in the 1980s (see 2.6), this point became clear: the House of Lords held unequivocally and unanimously, in *Preston*, that the judges in judicial review can give relief against unfairness in the exercise of an administrative discretion, but *only* if the unfairness means that the judges could conclude that the decision was an abuse of power by the commissioners (see Lord Templeman, at 864).

That sort of unfairness may, as in *Coughlan*, arise because of an expectation that the public authority has induced. But a decision can be substantively unfair without any legitimate expectation. Legitimate expectation is indeed, as the judges suggested in *Coughlan*, an instance of a general doctrine of substantive unfairness. But substantive unfairness is a general ground of judicial review only when it amounts to abuse of power.

It is not even enough that a decision is *very* unfair—after all, it did not matter how unfairly the Conservative government was acting in capping the local authorities' rates in *R v Environment Secretary, ex p Hammersmith and Fulham LBC* [1991] AC 521 and *R v Environment Secretary, ex p Nottinghamshire County Council* [1986] AC 240 (see 7.3.2, p 262); it was still not the judges' job to remedy the unfairness. The local by-laws in both *Wednesbury* and *Kruse* were substantively unfair if they were disproportionate (if the by-law in *Wednesbury* restricted access to the cinema *too much*, or if the by-law in *Kruse* did not give people *enough* freedom to sing hymns in public). But the judges in both cases insisted that it was not for them to decide those questions. Contrast the great case of *Rooke v Withers* (1597) 5 Co Rep 99 (see 7.1): when the Commissioners of Sewers charged Rooke for the whole cost of flood defence work that would not only protect his seven acres but also 800 acres owned by others, the substantive unfairness was something that the court—even without usurping the role of the Commissioners—could identify as an abuse of the charging power.

It is the principle of comity that distinguishes forms of substantive unfairness that the court can and cannot remedy. Procedural unfairness *generally* justifies judicial review, because the judges can generally require another public authority to use a fair procedure, without interfering with that authority in a damaging way. But judges cannot generally decide whether the substance of an administrative decision was fair without damaging the work of administrative authorities. If you think this is wrong—because unfair decisions shouldn't happen—go back to *Hammersmith and Fulham* and *Nottinghamshire*, and they will remind you that the courts cannot remedy all bad decisions. Substantive unfairness does *not* generally justify judicial review. The added something that is required is something that *the court is in a position to identify* as an abuse of power, something that is *manifestly* unfair—'conspicuous unfairness' (*Rashid* [19]). That is, judicial review requires unfairness that is manifest *to a reviewing court*. That is the general standard today for review of the substance of the exercise of discretionary power. It is vague, and offers courts the temptation just to quash any decision when they think that a different decision ought to have been made. If they do that, they are stepping beyond the role of judges.

As Lord Scarman put it in *Nottinghamshire*: '[T]he courts may intervene to review a power conferred by statute on the ground of unfairness but only if the unfairness in the purported exercise of the power be such as to amount to an abuse of the power' (249–50).[15]

8.7 European Union law: legitimate expectations and proportionality

For generations, the European Union has been paying farmers to produce crops and livestock for which there is no adequate market. The Common Agricultural Policy (CAP) has sustained the farmers' way of life.[16] It has also consumed vast resources and distorted international markets, hurting poorer farmers in developing countries who are trying to compete with European farmers. The EU has made fitful attempts to reform this massive administrative and financial programme. In 2003, the Council adopted Regulation 1782/2003, designed to replace payments for production with direct payments that would give cotton farmers no incentive to overproduce cotton. To avoid a sudden upheaval in the cotton market, the regulation provided for 65 per cent of the payments to be given as income support, rather than as a production subsidy. Not only that: the definition of 'production' was changed, so that farmers could collect the full payments without the cotton actually reaching harvest.

Spain's complaint was that the result would be such a reduction in production that the Spanish cotton-processing industry would go out of business (which in turn would hurt those farmers who were still trying to harvest cotton, since they would have no one to process their crop). What recourse did Spain have in EU law? The Court of Justice of the European Union (CJEU) can review the legality of certain acts of the European Parliament, the Council, and the Commission, under Art 263 TFEU. In just

---

[15] Citing Lord Templeman's speech in *Preston*, 864–5.

[16] The TFEU itself enshrines the extravagant aim of ensuring 'a fair standard of living for the agricultural community, in particular by increasing the individual earnings of persons engaged in agriculture' (Art 39).

a few words, the statement of the grounds of review provides an interesting comparison with the English grounds of judicial review:

> ' . . . lack of competence, infringement of an essential procedural requirement, infringement of the Treaties or of any rule of law relating to their application, or misuse of powers. '

You will recognize these grounds: the first three are roughly the same as lack of jurisdiction (see 9.1.1, p 319), lack of due process (see Chapters 4–6), and failure to abide by a legal duty (see 8.1.1). The fourth is something like abuse of power (see 7.1).[17] Where do legitimate expectations come in? Just as they form part of the law of due process and abuse of power in English law, they can be a basis for identifying an 'essential procedural requirement', or a 'misuse of powers', in EU law.

8.7.1 Legitimate expectations in the EU

In Spain's cotton case, Case C-310/04 *Spain v Council* [2006] ECR I-07285 [81], the Court held that 'the principle of the protection of legitimate expectations is one of the fundamental principles of the Community'. But no one has a legitimate expectation that institutions with power to change the CAP will not do so: 'if a prudent and circumspect operator could have foreseen that the adoption of a Community measure is likely to affect his interests', the principle is not violated if the measure is adopted. To rub it in, the Court added that 'economic operators are not justified in having a legitimate expectation that an existing situation which is capable of being altered by the Community institutions in the exercise of their discretionary power will be maintained, particularly in an area such as that of the common organisation of the markets, the objective of which involves constant adjustment to reflect changes in economic circumstances' [81]. As in English law, the doctrine of legitimate expectations is meant to support the capacity of public authorities to make appropriate changes to their policies.

The Court held that the Spanish had no legitimate expectation that the old production supports would be maintained, partly because fundamental reform had been under discussion for more than ten years. The only legitimate expectation they had was that no reform would be made in a way that *disproportionately* damaged their operations. So when it comes to the substance of a policy change, all that a claimant gets from the doctrine of legitimate expectation is something that could be stated as a distinct principle of EU law in any case: that the Regulation should not interfere disproportionately with the farmers' operations.

---

[17]   When the TFEU says 'misuse of powers', it must be understood to mean what English lawyers call 'abuse of power', or it would be the judges' job to quash any act that the Parliament or the Council or the Commission should not have adopted. That was patently not the intention of the parties to the Treaty.

8.7.2 Proportionality in the EU

The Court declared that the Council had infringed the principle of proportionality. But the form of review was very hands-off, and it is important to see just what the Court meant; Spain actually won on the EU law equivalent of the requirement of genuine exercise of discretion, which the Court linked to its own relevance doctrine, at [122]:

> ' ... the Community institutions which have adopted the act in question must be able to show before the Court that in adopting the act they actually exercised their discretion, which presupposes the taking into consideration of all the relevant factors and circumstances of the situation the act was intended to regulate. '

The principle of proportionality, 'one of the general principles of Community law', requires the following (at [97]):

> ' ... that acts adopted by Community institutions do not exceed the limits of what is appropriate and necessary in order to attain the legitimate objectives pursued by the legislation in question; where there is a choice between several appropriate measures, recourse must be had to the least onerous, and the disadvantages caused must not be disproportionate to the aims pursued. '

If proportionality is a general doctrine of EU law, it may seem that it is the judges' job to decide *how much* disadvantage to a claimant is *too* much. But in *Spain v Council*, the Court did *not* decide 'the limits of what is appropriate and necessary in order to attain the legitimate objectives'—any more than Lord Russell decided what sort of by-laws would be reasonable in *Kruse v Johnson* [1898] 2 QB 91. Instead, the Court decided that, 'bearing in mind the wide discretion enjoyed by the Community legislature where the common agricultural policy is concerned, the lawfulness of a measure adopted in that sphere can be affected only if the measure is manifestly inappropriate in terms of the objective which the competent institution is seeking to pursue' [98].[18]

That word 'manifestly', repeated several times in *Spain v Council*, is the same word that Lord Russell used in *Kruse v Johnson*, and that Lord Bridge used in *R v Environment Secretary, ex p Hammersmith and Fulham LBC* [1991] 1 AC 521. And they all used it for the same purpose: to emphasize the court's limited role in passing judgment on the substance of a decision, when the decision maker has a broad discretionary power.

The considerations in *Spain v Council* depended on the especially political role that the treaties gave the EU legislative institutions in operating (and reforming) the CAP. In other contexts, the CJEU will be less deferential. But remember: even though

---

[18] The 'manifestly inappropriate' standard, and much of the rest of the Court's account of the law, can be found repeated verbatim in several cases reaching back to Case 265/87 *Schräder v Hauptzollamt Gronau* [1989] ECR 2237 [22]: '[T]he legality of a measure adopted [to give effect to the Common Agricultural Policy] can be affected only if the measure is manifestly inappropriate having regard to the objective which the competent institution intends to pursue.'

'proportionality' is a general principle of EU law, there *is no* general doctrine of EU law that courts will quash measures that are disproportionate to their objectives. Where the institution responsible for the measure has a wide discretion, the Court will only interfere if the measure has a *manifestly* disproportionate impact.

In *Spain v Council*, the Court decided that the Council 'has not shown before the Court that in adopting the new cotton support scheme established by that regulation it actually exercised its discretion, involving the taking into consideration of all the relevant factors and circumstances of the case' [133]. It is an EU version of the **genuine exercise** rule (see 8.1.2), and not a general rule that judges must decide how much is too much.

The law of the European Convention has not brought a general standard of proportionality into English law, and neither has EU law. The CJEU defers to the Council, to some extent, on the implementation of the CAP. Notice that this does not mean that deference is the default position in CJEU review of the lawfulness of EU measures. As in English administrative law, whether and how a court should defer to another public authority is an open question, which depends on the type of decision, the nature of the decision maker, and the decision-making context. We cannot say that there is a general rule of deference, *or* a general rule of no deference.

> Deference (see 7.2.4) means not minding, or not asking (to some extent), whether the initial decision was right or wrong! You can see why judges sometimes have difficulty deferring to administrative authorities.

8.8 Conclusion

Does abuse of power unify the grounds of judicial review? Lord Scarman thought so:

> ❛ The ground upon which the courts will review the exercise of an administrative discretion by a public officer is abuse of power. Power can be abused in a number of ways: by a mistake of law in misconstruing the limits imposed by statute (or by common law in the case of a common law power) upon the scope of the power; by procedural irregularity; by unreasonableness in the *Wednesbury* sense; or by bad faith or an improper motive in its exercise. ❜ [19]

But that only stretches 'abuse of power', to make it into a catch-all phrase for the grounds of judicial review. It is no abuse of power for a public official to come to a different view of the law from a judge. To act in bad faith, on the other hand, really is an abuse of power. An abuse of power is an abandonment of responsible government. The important point to bear in mind is that judges should not invent for themselves the power to interfere with another public authority simply because it ought to have used its power differently.

---

[19] *R v Environment Secretary, ex p Nottinghamshire County Council* [1986] AC 240, 249.

The courts have a very wide-ranging responsibility to interfere with official action that is unlawful because it does not conform to standards that Parliament has set for public authorities (e.g., in the Race Relations Act 1976, or the Human Rights Act 1998, or the European Communities Act 1972). Judges should only impose standards of their own devising when doing so is justified by the **core rationale** for judicial review—that is, to promote responsible government by holding it unlawful for a public authority to act in a way that judges can identify as arbitrary (see 2.8). It is the judges' duty of comity that distinguishes decisions that should have been different (which may be none of the judges' business) from decisions that ought to be quashed on judicial review.

This means that substantive unfairness—like unreasonableness (see 7.1.3)—is not in itself a ground of judicial review. But *some forms* of substantive unfairness justify interference by a court. The nineteenth-century law is still good on this point, and much of the twentieth- and twenty-first-century progress has been to apply it more broadly, and with particular attention to special aspects of substantive unfairness: to the interests that may arise from expectations generated by officials, and to the potential for judges to protect certain interests of a claimant by asking (with a greater or lesser degree of deference where comity requires it) what setbacks to those interests are disproportionate to the public interests that a public authority is pursuing. The basic principles are more than a century old. Decisions 'such as reasonable men could not make in good faith' are one thing (and courts may quash them unless the issues at stake are non-justiciable) (*Slattery v Naylor* (1888) 13 App Cas 446, 453). But decisions are not to be struck down as unreasonable (or disproportionate, or a breach of legitimate expectation) merely because they do not 'commend themselves to the minds of judges' (*Slattery*, 453).

Summary

Judges may control a discretionary power by:

- applying (and developing) the law of due process;
- applying any legal prohibition on the use of power (such as the prohibition in the Human Rights Act 1998 s 6 on acting incompatibly with a Convention right, when primary legislation does not require it);
- deferential[20] review of fact finding (see 9.2);
- non-deferential review of interpretations of the law (see 9.1);
- protecting a legitimate expectation (by procedural or substantive means);
- deferential review for reasonableness (the extent of deference varies dramatically with the context).

Of course, you might say that the last point encompasses all of the others: it is not the judges' job to tell another public authority how to use its power, *or even what would be reasonable*. But if the court can determine that a power has been exercised unreasonably without breaching its duty of comity to another public authority, there is ground for judicial review.

---

[20] Depending on the type of decision: see 9.2.4.

TAKE-HOME MESSAGE • • •

• The doctrines of **relevance**, **legitimate expectations**, and **proportionality** all require judges to pass judgment on the substantive fairness of administrative decisions.

• But there is still no general doctrine that an administrative decision should be struck down just because it is substantively unfair.

• Only certain forms of substantive unfairness justify judicial review. The vague general test for those sorts of unfairness is that the courts will interfere with an *abuse of power*.

• The application of that general test depends on the type of decision and the context in which it is made. Judges really will substitute their own judgment for that of the initial decision maker on certain questions—in particular, on whether there are grounds for the use of a discretionary power to detain a person.

CRITICAL QUESTIONS • • •

1   Are there any grounds *other than abuse of power* on which judges may interfere with the substance of an exercise of a discretionary power?

2   Can a public authority lawfully act contrary to a legitimate expectation?

3   Should the courts defer to a public authority on the question of what purposes the authority's powers can properly be used to pursue?

4   Should the courts defer to a public authority on the question of what considerations are relevant to the exercise of a discretionary power?

5   Why is proportionality a general principle of the law of due process, but not a general principle of the control of discretionary powers?

6   The courts have a doctrine of precedent (requiring them to abide by [some] previous decisions), and a doctrine of *res judicata* (giving conclusive effect to a decision once it is made and is not subject to any appeal). Is there a doctrine of precedent or a doctrine of *res judicata* for public authorities in general?

7   Your local council sends you a cheque for £1,000, with a letter explaining that you paid too much council tax. You deposit the cheque (quite reasonably thinking that the council must know what it is doing). Then the council accountants realize that, because of a clerical error, they wrote the cheque and sent the letter to the wrong person. Can they demand the money back?

8   The government has a regular practice of responding to a declaration of incompatibility under the Human Rights Act 1998 by making an amending order. If a statute is declared incompatible, does a person affected by it have a legitimate expectation that the government will do so?

READING • • •

Re Findlay [1985] AC 318

R v Foreign Secretary, ex p World Development Movement [1995] 1 WLR 386

R (Daly) v Home Secretary [2001] UKHL 26

R (Bibi) v Newham LBC [2001] EWCA Civ 607

R v North and East Devon Health Authority, ex p Coughlan [2001] QB 213

R (Begum) v Denbigh High School [2006] UKHL 15

Case C-310/04 *Spain v Council* [2006] ECR I-07285

R (Corner House Research) v Director of the Serious Fraud Office [2008] UKHL 60

R (Hurley) v Secretary of State for Business Innovation and Skills [2012] EWHC 201

R (Bracking) v Secretary of State for Work and Pensions [2013] EWCA Civ 1345

On the *Corner House Research* case:

Lord Steyn, 'Civil Liberties in Modern Britain' [2009] PL 228, 233–5

On proportionality and deference:

Tom Hickman, 'The Substance and Structure of Proportionality' [2008] PL 694

Julian Rivers, 'Proportionality and Variable Intensity of Review' (2006) 65 CLJ 174

On legitimate expectations:

Philip Sales, 'Legitimate Expectations' [2006] Judicial Review 186

Rebecca Williams, 'The Multiple Doctrines of Legitimate Expectations' (2016) 132 LQR 639–63

Joanna Bell, 'The Doctrine of Legitimate Expectations: Power-constraining or Right-conferring Legal Standard?' [2016] PL 437–55

On EU law—legitimate expectations and proportionality:

Paul Craig, 'Unreasonableness and Proportionality in UK Law', ch 5 in Evelyn Ellis, *The Principle of Proportionality in the Laws of Europe* (Hart 1999)

Jürgen Schwarze, 'The Convergence of the Administrative Laws of the EU Member States' (1998) 4 EPL 191

 The following online resources accompany this chapter: **summaries** of key cases and legislation; **updates** on the law; **guidance** for answering the pop quizzes and questions; and **links** to legislation, cases, and useful websites.

9 Errors of law and control of fact finding

Administrative authorities deciding someone's legal position must determine what the law is, and find the facts, and apply the law to the facts. This chapter asks how the courts control the exercise of power involved in those three judgments.

LOOK FOR • • •

- Review for error of law, review of findings of fact, and review of the application of law to the facts.

- Deference on questions of law: is there any?

- The fundamental union (downplayed and sometimes denied by the judges) between these three forms of review, and other forms of control of discretionary power.

> ' We cannot correct an error in their proceedings, and ought to suppose what is done by a final jurisdiction, to be right. '
>
> *Moses v Macferlan* (1760) 2 Burr 1005, 97 ER 676 (KB), 679
> (Lord Mansfield CJ, on reviewing decisions of the Court of
> Conscience, a local small claims court set up by statute)

> ' . . . in general any error of law made by an administrative tribunal or inferior court in reaching its decision can be quashed for error of law. '
>
> *R v Hull University Visitor, ex p Page* [1993]
> AC 682 (HL), 702 (Lord Browne-Wilkinson)

9.1 Errors of law

9.1.1 The discretionary power to determine the law

When Sergeant Walker applied to the Ministry of Defence for criminal injuries compensation in *R v Ministry of Defence, ex p Walker* [2000] 1 WLR 806 (see 2.1), the Ministry of Defence had to answer three questions in order to decide whether he was entitled to compensation.

> **Three questions in the application of the law:**
>
> 1. What were the rules of the compensation scheme?
> 2. What had happened to Sergeant Walker?
> 3. What did the rules of the scheme require in his case?

In a nutshell, English law controls these administrative decisions through:

(1) a rule that an administrative decision is unlawful if it is based on an error of law—that is, on any error the court finds in the administrative authority's answer to question 1 (9.1);

(2) a more hands-off form of control of administrative fact finding, in which the judges only interfere when for some special reason it is obvious that the administrative authority got the facts wrong (9.2); and

(3) a rule that, unless the administrative authority got question 1 wrong, the court will only interfere with its answer to question 3 if the administrative decision as to how the rules apply is so unreasonable that no reasonable decision maker could have reached it (9.3).

By creating a scheme of criminal injuries compensation for its soldiers, the Ministry of Defence took on responsibility for deciding whether a particular soldier's claim (such as Sergeant Walker's claim) fitted the scheme's criteria for eligibility. The criteria would obviously be met in some cases, and in those cases it would be wrong for the Ministry to refuse compensation. But the operation of any such scheme will yield cases (such as Sergeant Walker's case) in which it would be reasonable to decide that the claimant is eligible, and also reasonable to decide that the claimant is ineligible. Every uncertainty in the application of its terms in particular cases leaves a **resultant discretion** (see 7.2.1, p 249) to the decision maker: a freedom to resolve the uncertainty as the decision maker sees fit, with no duty to decide one way rather than another. The scheme itself gives the choice to the body responsible for operating the scheme. The choice is to be made in light of the purposes of the scheme, but sometimes those purposes will be compatible with a decision either way. So, in Walker's case, the Ministry's power to apply the scheme was a discretionary power: it created a discretion to hold that the claimant was or was not eligible for compensation.

A legal power to decide a claim with legal effect is a **jurisdiction**. The Ministry had jurisdiction to decide Sergeant Walker's claim, and that power was subject to judicial review. You might think that this discretionary power would be controlled, like all discretionary powers, in the deferential style explained in Chapter 7, with attention to the principle of comity. But on one aspect of the exercise of an administrative jurisdiction the judges do not defer. In Walker's case, Lord Slynn said: 'It is plainly open to the court on an application for judicial review to consider whether the Ministry of Defence has correctly interpreted the scheme . . . or whether its decision involves an error of law' (810).

If the judges' role is to control the Ministry's exercise of its jurisdiction as it controls other discretionary powers, why did Lord Slynn claim that it was the judges' job to make sure that the scheme was interpreted *correctly*? The answer involves one of the most remarkable lines of cases in the history of English law. In the cases leading up to *R v Hull University Visitor, ex p Page* [1993] AC 682, the courts took upon themselves a power to review exercises of administrative jurisdiction for **error of law**. That development was grounded on mistaken arguments of precedent, and it cannot be justified on grounds of constitutional principle. The development of review for error of law made it seem confusing and irrelevant to think of administrative agencies as having any jurisdiction at all—when, in fact, jurisdiction is a crucial tool for understanding the legal powers of public authorities (see 9.1.7). And along the way, the judges disregarded an Act of Parliament. This chapter explains these remarkable developments leading up to *Page*, and also explains the substantial discretions that remain to administrative decision makers in identifying the facts and in applying the law to the facts.

Error of law, when it isn't even law

An 'error of law' does not actually have to be an error of law; as we saw in *Walker*, the courts will quash a decision if it is based on an interpretation of rules that the public authority has made for its own conduct, in operating a scheme of criminal injuries compensation that conferred no legal rights on the claimant (see 2.2). And in *Mandalia v Home Secretary* [2015] UKSC 59, the Supreme Court quashed the Home Office's instructions to the Border Agency caseworkers who were processing applications for visas. Lord Wilson held that the interpretation of the instructions 'is a matter of law which the court must therefore decide for itself', and that 'previous suggestions that the courts should adopt the Secretary of State's own interpretation of her immigration policies unless it is unreasonable . . . are therefore inaccurate' [31].

● *Pop quiz* ●

The implication of *Mandalia* is that the Home Office cannot act on its own reasonable interpretation of its own policies, if the judges' interpretation is different. Is that a breach of the duty of comity that judges owe toward administrative authorities (see 1.5.3)? Or does it protect claimants from misinterpretation of the standards that the Home Office is committed to applying?

The traditional doctrine was that a public authority acts unlawfully if it makes an error of law of a kind that leads it to act outside its jurisdiction. And that is what the House of Lords held in *Anisminic v Foreign Compensation Commission* [1969] 2 AC 147. Yet the Law Lords went on in later cases to invent a rule that it is unlawful for a public authority to make a decision based on *any* error of law. One remarkable feature of the novel doctrine is the way in which it arose from a myth about *Anisminic*.

9.1.2 *Anisminic*: the myth

The myth has taken on the aura of accepted doctrine in English administrative law. Lord Diplock said, in *Racal* [1981] AC 374 (HL), 383, that *Anisminic* was 'a legal landmark' that made the following 'break-through' in judicial control of administrative tribunals and authorities:

> ' . . . the old distinction between errors of law that went to jurisdiction and errors of law that did not, was for practical purposes abolished. Any error of law that could be shown to have been made by them in the course of reaching their decision on matters of fact or of administrative policy would result in their having asked themselves the wrong question with the result that the decision they reached would be a nullity. '

And in *O'Reilly v Mackman* [1983] 2 AC 237, 278 (see 10.2.1, p 370), Lord Diplock expanded on the 'break-through', in an account of the contributions that Lord Reid had made to judicial review:

> ' *Anisminic* . . . liberated English public law from the fetters that the courts had theretofore imposed upon themselves so far as determinations of inferior courts and statutory tribunals were concerned, by drawing esoteric distinctions between

errors of law committed by such tribunals that went to their jurisdiction, and errors of law committed by them within their jurisdiction. The break-through that the *Anisminic* case made was the recognition by the majority of this House that if a tribunal whose jurisdiction was limited by statute or subordinate legislation mistook the law applicable to the facts as it had found them, it must have asked itself the wrong question, i.e., one into which it was not empowered to inquire and so had no jurisdiction to determine. '

In *Page*, at 702, Lord Browne-Wilkinson endorsed Lord Diplock's view as to the effect of *Anisminic*, and immediately added: 'Therefore, . . . in general any error of law made by an administrative tribunal or inferior court in reaching its decision can be quashed for error of law.' Lord Browne-Wilkinson offered no authority for the rule, except Lord Diplock's account of *Anisminic*. And he offered no rationale for the rule; in fact, it seems to have appealed to him as providing *its own* rationale: an error of law is to be quashed *for error of law*. But all of the Law Lords agreed with that view, and the consensus was repeated in *Boddington v British Transport Police* [1999] 2 AC 143 (HL) (Lord Irvine, at 158). It has become a standard notion in the lore of administrative law, as expressed by Baroness Hale and Lord Dyson in *R (Cart) v Upper Tribunal* [2011] UKSC 28:

' In holding that [the ouster clause] was not effective to oust the jurisdiction of the High Court to set aside a decision which was a nullity, and that a decision made in error of law was a nullity, the House of Lords effectively removed the distinction between error of law and excess of jurisdiction. ' [1]

' . . . the importance of the *Anisminic* case is that it showed that a material error of law renders a decision a "nullity" so that the decision is in principle judicially reviewable. ' [2]

There is a double irony in these remarks. First of all, the *Cart* decision itself established that the Upper Tribunal was not necessarily acting in excess of jurisdiction, if it made an error of law. If the Upper Tribunal errs in law in refusing to allow a claimant to appeal a First-tier Tribunal decision, the claimant can only seek judicial review if the decision involves an important point of principle or practice, or there is some other compelling reason for judicial review (on this important case, see 12.4.10). A material error of law does not render a decision of the Upper Tribunal a nullity.

Second, the judges in *Anisminic* were careful *not* to remove the distinction between error of law and excess of jurisdiction. But beginning with *Racal*—long before *Cart*—the judges came to talk as if it had done so.

....

[1]   *Cart* [18].

[2]   *Cart* [110]. Compare Lord Dyson's statement in *R (Lumba) v Secretary of State for the Home Department* [2011] UKSC 12 [66], that 'The importance of *Anisminic* is that it established that there was a single category of errors of law, all of which rendered a decision ultra vires.'

9.1.3 *Anisminic*: the decision

What actually happened in the *Anisminic* case? Counsel for Anisminic did indeed ask the House of Lords to abolish the distinction between error of law and excess of jurisdiction. But although the five Law Lords were deeply divided, *each* of them refused to do that—including the three in the majority.

(1) **Lord Wilberforce** approved a remark of Lord Denning that '[a] tribunal may often decide a point of law wrongly whilst keeping well within its jurisdiction' (*R v Northumberland Compensation Appeal Tribunal, ex p Shaw* [1952] 1 KB 338, 346). He held that 'the commission has (admittedly) been given power, indeed required, to decide some questions of law', but that it did not have 'power to decide those questions which relate to the delimitation of its powers' (*Anisminic*, 209).

(2) **Lord Reid** held to the view he had expressed, in *R v Governor of Brixton Prison, ex p Armah* [1968] AC 192, 234, that if 'a magistrate or any other tribunal' acts within jurisdiction, '[n]either an error in fact nor an error in law will destroy his jurisdiction'. In *Anisminic*, he added that a court can quash the decision of a tribunal 'not because the tribunal has made an error of law, but because as a result of making an error of law they have dealt with and based their decision on a matter with which, on a true construction of their powers, they had no right to deal' (174).

(3) **Lord Pearce** implied that there is a difference between 'excess of jurisdiction' and 'error of law', and held that the decision maker will 'step outside its jurisdiction' only if it asks itself the wrong question (195).

But those three judges *did* decide that the particular error of law that they found in the decision made the public authority's decision a nullity. Why did they hold that it was a nullity, rather than that the Commission had made an error of law that was within its jurisdiction? The key to all of the confusion over *Anisminic* is the 'ouster clause'—a provision in the Act that set up the Foreign Compensation Commission:

> ' The determination by the Commission of any application made to them under this Act shall not be called in question in any court of law. ' [3]

Anisminic made an application to the Commission for compensation for the loss of a manganese mine, worth £4 million, which the Egyptian government had confiscated in the 1956 Suez crisis. Anisminic was able to put enough commercial pressure on the Egyptian government to induce it to 'buy' the mine the Egyptians had seized, for £500,000. Then, a reconciliation between Britain and Egypt led to a grant of £27.5 million from Egypt to compensate the owners of property that Egypt had confiscated in the crisis.

....
[3]   Foreign Compensation Act 1950 s 4(4). On the courts' approach to ouster clauses, see 2.7.1.

The British government's regulations on eligibility for the compensation stated that the applicant had to be the owner of the property or the 'successor in title' of the owner, and that 'any person who became successor in title' of the applicant had to be British.[4] The Commission considered Anisminic's application, and decided that the Egyptian government was Anisminic's successor in title. And since the Egyptian government was not British, Anisminic was ineligible under the compensation scheme.

Anisminic claimed that the Commission had misinterpreted the obscure, badly drafted clause concerning the 'successor in title' of the applicant. But this is where the ouster clause kicks in: if the determination of the Commission could not be called in question in any court of law, how could Anisminic challenge the Commission's interpretation? Anisminic's lawyers claimed that, because of the alleged misinterpretation, the Commission had *not* made a determination. They said that its so-called 'determination' was a 'nullity'.[5] They could not ask the judges to question a determination, so they asked them to declare that there *was no* determination.

The majority in the House of Lords accepted this argument. Yet that meant denying the undeniable: that the Commission had determined the company's application. As Lord Morris put it in his dissent: 'That which, they [the majority] say, should be disregarded as being null and void, is a determination explained in a carefully reasoned document nearly ten pages in length which is signed by the chairman of the commission. There is no question here of a sham or spurious or merely purported determination' (*Anisminic*, 181). It may seem absurd that the majority could say that the Commission's determination was not a determination. In fact, although it was wrong, it was not absurd. The majority's decision took a sound basic principle, and overextended it.

9.1.4 *Anisminic*: the kernel of good sense

Even if Parliament forbids the courts to interfere with a determination, the courts still have to decide whether a determination is genuine. After all, a legal rule that you must accept a £20 note as legal tender does not require you to accept a counterfeit £20 note. It was already 'well established' in the nineteenth century that the ouster clauses of the day—statutory provisions prohibiting *certiorari* (see 10.4.1)—simply did not apply when a claimant challenged a decision on the ground that it was made without jurisdiction (*Ex p Bradlaugh* (1878) 3 QBD 509). As Lord Reid said in *Anisminic*, the word 'determination' in the statute does not include 'everything which purports to be a determination but which is in fact no determination at all' (170). Lord Reid gave the example of a forged 'determination', which is obviously not a determination.

The kernel of good sense in the reasoning of the majority in *Anisminic* includes both this obvious point that a forged 'determination' is *not* a determination, *and* the sound insight that this reasoning can be taken further: there may be 'determinations'

....

[4] See *Anisminic*, at 172.

[5] On the role of nullity in judicial review, see 10.4.8.

made by genuine public authorities that are not genuine determinations. How far can the point be taken? What is the difference between a *bad* determination and something that is *not* a determination? Lord Reid's answer is given in a list of things a tribunal might do or fail to do that are 'of such a nature that its decision is a nullity' (171).

The List (of things that make an administrative decision a nullity): Lord Reid's version

(1) 'It may have given its decision in bad faith.'
(2) 'It may have made a decision which it had no power to make.'
(3) 'It may have failed . . . to comply with the requirements of natural justice.'
(4) 'It may in perfect good faith have misconstrued the provisions giving it power to act so that it failed to deal with the question remitted to it and decided some question which was not remitted to it.'
(5) 'It may have refused to take into account something which it was required to take into account.'
(6) 'Or it may have based its decision on some matter which, under the provisions setting it up, it had no right to take into account.'[6]

The first two grounds are straightforward: if the Commission had acted in bad faith by, for example, taking a bribe from Anisminic's enemies, it would make sense for a court to conclude that it had not made a real determination of Anisminic's application at all. And if the Commission were to issue a 'determination' in which it claimed to fine Anisminic for misconduct, the court would have jurisdiction to declare that the 'determination' has no effect: the Commission had no power to fine applicants, and Parliament only enacted that no determination *of an application for compensation* is to be questioned in a court. So bad faith and lack of the necessary power would be good grounds for holding that a so-called 'determination' is not really a determination; they illustrate the kernel of good sense in the majority's reasoning.

What about failure to proceed in accordance with natural justice? Five years earlier, in *Ridge v Baldwin* [1964] AC 40, Lord Reid and the majority of the House of Lords had held that *any* procedural unfairness in an administrative decision is ground for holding that it was made without jurisdiction, so that it is a nullity. This radical approach to due process amounts to saying that a decision maker is not deciding at all if it decides without due process. And perhaps that radical approach is justified by the courts' capacity to apply it with no breach of comity (as long as the courts remember their discretion over judicial review remedies—see 10.4.6).

---

6 Compare this later remark by Lord Reid about what counts as a genuine use of a *discretion*, in *Dorset Yacht v Home Office* [1970] AC 1004, 1031: 'Then there may, and almost certainly will, be errors of judgment in exercising such a discretion and Parliament cannot have intended that members of the public should be entitled to sue in respect of such errors. But there must come a stage when the discretion is exercised so carelessly or unreasonably that there has been no real exercise of the discretion which Parliament has conferred. The person purporting to exercise his discretion has acted in abuse or excess of his power.'

Now, what about the fourth, fifth, and sixth items on Lord Reid's list: misconstruction of 'the provisions giving it power', and failing to take into account things the Commission was required to take into account, and taking into account things it had no right to take into account? These grounds of nullity led to Lord Diplock's misinterpretation of the case. They are ambiguous, because they may be taken to mean either:

(1) that *some* misconstructions, or irrelevant considerations, or mistakes as to the basis of the decision can make a 'determination' null and void; or

(2) that a determination is null and void if it involves *any* misconstruction, or irrelevant consideration, or mistake as to the basis of its decision.

Lord Diplock assumes that Lord Reid took the second view. In fact, Lord Reid relied on the distinction between mistakes of law that *are* 'of such a nature that its decision is a nullity' (*Anisminic*, 171), and mistakes of law that *are not* of such a nature.

So Lord Reid's judgment does not support Lord Diplock's rule. But the drawbacks in Lord Reid's explanation of his decision are both general (he did not explain how to distinguish between errors of law that do and do not make a decision a nullity) and particular (he gave no justification for the conclusion that the Commission had not determined Anisminic's application for compensation). Lord Morris's vehement dissent argued that Anisminic had to satisfy the Commissioners that it met the eligibility criteria, and that, in deciding the meaning of the criteria, the Commissioners 'were at the very heart of their duty, their task and their jurisdiction. It cannot be that their necessary duty of deciding as to the meaning would be or could be followed by the result that if they took one view they would be within jurisdiction and if they took another view that they would be without' (189). The majority did not explain what it was about the Commissioners' view that took them outside their jurisdiction; that is what led to misinterpretation of the case.

9.1.5 Lord Diplock's rule

It seems that the current, orthodox doctrine of judicial review for error of law is founded on *obiter dicta* by Lord Diplock,[7] based on a misinterpretation of the judgment in a single case (*Anisminic*) that was wrongly decided by a badly divided House of Lords.

----

[7]   In fact, all of the House of Lords' and Supreme Court's assertions of the rule have been *obiter*, although there is no reason to doubt the authority of the consensus in favour of it. Lord Diplock's statements of his rule were *obiter* in *Racal* (because the House of Lords held that the rule does not apply to decisions of the High Court) and in *O'Reilly* (in which Lord Diplock was only pointing out just how powerful judicial review is—see 10.2.1). The Law Lords' endorsement of the rule was *obiter* in *Page* (because the rule does not apply to university Visitors), and in *Boddington* (there was no error of law in that case). The statements of the doctrine by Baroness Hale and Lord Dyson in *R (Cart) v Upper Tribunal* [2011] UKSC 28 were *obiter* because according to *Cart*, a decision of the Upper Tribunal is not subject to judicial review simply on the ground that it was based on an error of law: see 9.1.2.

Is it possible to say anything better than that for Lord Diplock's interpretation of *Anisminic*? How about this: the three Law Lords in the majority in *Anisminic* may have *attempted* to retain the distinction between errors of law that make a decision a nullity and errors of law that do not. But the distinction is so unstable that their decision must be construed as having the *effect* of abolishing it. When an administrative authority has to apply legal standards, as in *Anisminic*, any error of law results in asking the wrong question. Lord Reid said (174), 'The question I have to consider is not whether they made a wrong decision but whether they inquired into and decided a matter which they had no right to consider.' But if they made any mistake in interpreting the rules they were applying, then they would presumably have chosen a mistaken test for deciding that matter. Which means that they would have asked *whether their mistaken test was satisfied*, and (since the test is mistaken) that is the wrong question. So any decision based on an error of law is reached by asking the wrong question (that is, by getting the legal test wrong, and then asking whether the wrong legal test is satisfied). And then, on the authority of *Anisminic*, any decision based on an error of law is a nullity.

This construction of the decision in *Anisminic* will not wash, partly because only Lord Pearce expressed the majority conclusion by saying that a decision maker steps outside its jurisdiction if it asks itself the wrong question (195). Lord Wilberforce carefully rejected the idea (at 210):

> A tribunal may quite properly validly enter upon its task and in the course of carrying it out may make a decision which is invalid—not merely erroneous. This may be described as "asking the wrong question" or "applying the wrong test"—expressions not wholly satisfactory since they do not, in themselves, distinguish between doing something which is not in the tribunal's area and doing something wrong within that area—a crucial distinction which the court has to make.

The problem with Lord Wilberforce's speech is that it faces the same general objection and particular objection as Lord Reid's speech: he did not explain how the court was to make the crucial distinction, and he did not justify his view that the Commission's decision in the case was 'invalid—not merely erroneous'.

9.1.6 Lord Diplock's presumption: law is for the judges

You may say that it is not particularly important that Lord Diplock's rule is based on a misinterpretation of *Anisminic*. If the rule is sound, it does not matter that the House of Lords invented it in mistaken *obiter dicta* in *O'Reilly* and *Page*, rather than in *Anisminic*.

And the rule may seem to be sound, because you may think that no determination based on a misconstruction of the law is a genuine determination *of the issues that Parliament established the Commission to determine*. Parliament must have established the Commission to allocate compensation on the basis of the *correct* interpretation of the criteria, and not on a misinterpretation. And then, if the Commission interprets the criteria incorrectly, it is not doing what Parliament created it to do.

This seductive line of reasoning completely misses a basic point: the mere fact that a public authority must do the right thing does not mean that a court has jurisdiction to decide what is right. Administrative authorities should certainly act on the correct view of the law. That does not actually require that courts should quash their decisions for error of law. All public authorities ought to make the best possible decisions (and Parliament can be presumed to intend that they should do so). But that does not mean that the judges have jurisdiction to hold that a decision was *ultra vires* on the ground that it was not the best decision that could have been made.

But, of course, the discretionary power *to identify the law* seems to be the special preserve of the judges. That is what Lord Diplock thought: he held that *Anisminic* 'proceeds on the presumption that . . . Parliament intends to confine [an administrative agency's] power to answering the question as it has been so defined: and if there has been any doubt as to what that question is, this is a matter for courts of law to resolve in fulfilment of their constitutional role as interpreters of the written law and expounders of the common law and rules of equity' (*Racal*, 383). Of course, Parliament requires public authorities to answer the question that Parliament has set—but why presume that it is for courts to resolve any doubt as to what that question is? The presumption was new in English law—it only dates to the work of Lord Denning[8] and Lord Diplock.[9] This novel presumption was foreign to Lord Mansfield.[10] It is not found in *Anisminic*, in which Lord Wilberforce said: 'I think that we have reached a stage in our administrative law when we can view this question quite objectively, without any necessary predisposition . . . that questions of law, or questions of construction, are necessarily for the courts' (209). Since *Page*, the judges have adopted the very predisposition that Lord Wilberforce rejected.

A presumption is a rule that an issue (such as whether an administrative tribunal is the final arbiter of questions of law) is to be decided in a certain way, unless there is overriding reason to decide in a different way. One objection to the supposed presumption is that, applied to *Anisminic*, it would make nonsense out of Parliament's adoption of the ouster clause. The majority in *Anisminic* took the statutory provision,

> ' The determination by the Commission of any application . . . shall not be called in question in any court of law '

---

8   *Pearlman v Keepers and Governors of Harrow School* [1979] QB 56.

9   Lord Browne-Wilkinson endorsed it in *Page*, 703, saying that there was 'a presumption that the statute conferring the power did not intend the administrative body to be the final arbiter of questions of law'.

10 See the quotation from *Moses v Macferlan* (1760) 2 Burr 1005, at the beginning of this chapter.

and gave it the ambiguous effect that it would have if it said:

> The determination by the Commission of any application . . . shall not be called in question in any court of law, but the High Court may declare that a purported determination is a nullity if the Commission arrived at it by inquiring into a matter which it had no right to consider.

Lord Diplock's rule gives the statutory provision the *incoherent* effect that it would have if it said:

> The determination by the Commission of any application . . . shall not be called in question in any court of law, but the High Court may declare that a purported determination is a nullity if it is based on an error of law.

The majority disregarded the statute in *Anisminic*, because the Commission really had (as Lord Morris said) determined the company's application. Lord Diplock's rule commits the courts to disregard Parliament, whenever Parliament provides that an administrative decision is not to be questioned in a court.

Now, let's forget the ouster clause that generated the confusion in *Anisminic*, and ask whether either the *Anisminic* approach, or Lord Diplock's rule, is generally the right approach to judicial review of the determinations of law made by another public authority (if there is no ouster of the court's jurisdiction).

There is still an objection to the presumption that Parliament intended all questions of law to be decided by courts. The crucial point is that the current rule—Lord Diplock's rule—is a rule against judicial deference to the public authority whose decision is under review. Lord Reid's approach did leave room (without explaining it) for deference. Even where there is no ouster clause, the judges should be prepared to defer to an interpretation of an administrative scheme by the public authority that is responsible for giving effect to the scheme, to some extent, in ways that ought to vary with the context.

Constitutional principles justify review for lack of due process, and for abuse of power, and for use of power in a way that is unreasonable in a justiciable respect, and for purported decisions made with no jurisdiction. Do those principles also justify review for error of law?

The **rule of law**, of course, requires all public authorities to apply the law faithfully, according to its terms. That may seem to justify Lord Diplock's rule. But that seemingly attractive view would be a mistake. It really is a failure in the rule of law when any public authority acts on a misguided view of the law. But why expect that the judge's view of the law will be better than the administrative authority's view? That might be the case **if the judges are more expert** at understanding and developing the standards of the law than the public authority in question. Or it might be good for the judges to impose their view if that would achieve **consistency** among a variety of uncoordinated decision makers.[11]

---

[11] Lord Denning mentioned this justification for judicial review for error of law in *Pearlman v Keepers and Governors of Harrow School* [1979] QB 56.

The potential benefits of expertise and coordination do not justify Lord Diplock's rule. Judges are not *generally* more expert at the job of interpreting an administrative scheme than the very diverse administrative authorities are themselves. The Foreign Compensation Commission might understand the foreign compensation rules as well as or better than the judges do. And whether the judges can bring consistency to administrative practice depends on whether there are a number of uncoordinated decision makers in the particular context.

Here is another potential justification for judicial review for error of law, which is quite distinct from the benefits that justify appeals within the courts: if the public authority has an agenda or an incentive to develop and elaborate its standards in the wrong way, then the judges' **independence** means that they can do a better job of it. But the value of this important feature of judicial review also depends on the context. The independence of administrative decision makers varies widely. And the *need* for independence varies widely, too (see 5.3.3).

The general rule of review for error of law is not justified by constitutional principle, because the benefits of imposing the judges' interpretation of the law do not apply generally; they depend on the type of decision and the context in which it is made.

The new Tribunals system

Parliament reconstructed the Tribunals system in 2007 to create an Upper Tribunal that hears appeals on a point of law from the First-tier Tribunals (see 12.2). Further appeals are available from the Upper Tribunal to the Court of Appeal on a point of law, and you might think that those appeals would function just like judicial review for error of law, with no judicial deference to the Tribunals' views on the interpretation and application of the statutory schemes that they apply. But in *R (Jones) v First-tier Tribunal* [2013] UKSC 19, the Supreme Court held that 'the development of a consistent approach to the application of [the legislation in question] . . . was a task primarily for the tribunals, not the appellate courts' (Lord Dyson [47]). That view is a departure from Lord Diplock's general idea that law is for the judges in the High Court. The approach that the Court of Appeal and the Supreme Court take to their role in appeals from the Upper Tribunal has to be understood in the light of the structure and operation of the new system: see Chapter 12.

9.1.7 Is there any such thing as jurisdiction?

Is it even *possible* for someone other than a High Court Judge to have legal power to decide what the law is? Yes. English law still recognizes jurisdictions within which the courts will not interfere on the ground of an error in interpreting the law. In *Page* itself, the House of Lords would not interfere with a university Visitor on the ground of error of law.

The Arbitration Act 1996 provides a scheme of arbitration of commercial disputes; the scheme allows the parties to agree that there will be no appeal on a question of law, and then an appeal can only be brought on the ground that the tribunal exceeded its powers. And an arbitrator does *not* exceed his or her powers by making an error of law. In *Lesotho Development v Impregilo SpA* [2005] UKHL 43 [25], Lord Steyn held:

> ' The reasoning of the lower courts, categorising an error of law as an excess of jurisdiction, has overtones of the doctrine in *Anisminic* . . . which is so well known to the public law field. It is, however, important to emphasise again that the powers of the court in public law and arbitration law are quite different. '

An error of law does not *necessarily* take a decision maker outside a limited jurisdiction. And, indeed, the courts used to treat some public authorities like arbitrators, as we can see from *Board of Education v Rice* [1911] AC 179 (HL), 182 (Lord Loreburn LC):

> ' The Board is in the nature of the arbitral tribunal, and a Court of law has no jurisdiction to hear appeals from the determination either upon law or upon fact. But if the Court is satisfied either that the Board have not acted judicially . . ., or have not determined the question which they are required by the Act to determine, then there is a remedy by mandamus and certiorari. '

The county court system is another notable statutory jurisdiction, with which the High Court judges will not interfere on grounds of error of law. In *R (Sivasubramaniam) v Wandsworth County Court* [2002] EWCA Civ 1738, the claimant sought judicial review of a refusal of a circuit judge to grant permission to appeal against the decision of a district judge. The Court of Appeal held that the High Court had jurisdiction to give judicial review, because 'the judge in question has limited statutory jurisdiction and . . . it must be open to the High Court to review whether that jurisdiction has been exceeded' [54]. But because there was within the county court a 'proportionate' system for reviewing the merits of decisions made by district judges, the Court of Appeal would not review county court decisions *for error of law*. Lord Phillips added, at [56]:

> ' The possibility remains that there may be very rare cases where a litigant challenges the jurisdiction of a circuit judge giving or refusing permission to appeal on the ground of jurisdictional error in the narrow, pre-*Anisminic* sense, or procedural irregularity of such a kind as to constitute a denial of the applicant's right to a fair hearing. '

So the county court—a statutory body—can make errors of law within jurisdiction that the High Court will not treat as grounds for judicial review. The reason is not that the county court is above the law; the reason is proportionate process. If a litigant has had a fair hearing on an application for leave to appeal within the county court, it would only involve excessive litigation if he could raise the same question on judicial review in the High Court.

There is, moreover, an extremely important tribunal that is not subject to judicial review for error of law: the Upper Tribunal (see 12.2). An appeal can be brought from a decision of the Upper Tribunal to the Court of Appeal only if the appeal would raise an important point of principle or practice, or there is some other compelling reason. Judicial review is not available on the ground that there was an error of law in a decision of the Upper Tribunal, if the decision does not meet those criteria (see 12.4.9).

We can see that Lord Diplock's rule does not follow necessarily from the limited powers of public authorities, or it would have to apply to university Visitors, and arbitrators, and the county court, and the Upper Tribunal, each of which has a limited power. Lord Diplock's rule is a novel technique of the English judges for controlling administration, by imposing their own understanding of the rules that other public authorities are responsible for applying. It is not required by the logic of the law, but only by the judges' view that it is their task alone—and not the task of other public officials—to decide what the law is in the field of public administration.

While Lord Browne-Wilkinson's speech in *Page* offered no reason in favour of the general rule that administrative authorities may be reviewed for error of law, we can learn something from the reasons he offered for *not* applying the doctrine to university Visitors:

- there is a centuries-old common law doctrine that decisions of university Visitors on fact and law were not to be reviewed;[12] and

- the Visitors have a special, domestic jurisdiction—'the visitor is applying not the general law of the land but a peculiar, domestic law of which he is the sole arbiter and of which the courts have no cognisance' (*Page*, 702).

Why not say that the Foreign Compensation Commission was applying not the general law of the land, but a specific legal scheme of which (given Parliament's decision that its determinations were not to be questioned in court) it was sole arbiter? The answer given in *Page* was only that the Visitor's role is *domestic*—that is, it operates within a society (a university) that has its own rules. But that does not give any reason in itself for treating the Visitor as special, once it is admitted (as Lord Browne-Wilkinson admitted) that the university is not a private club, but a public authority that can be controlled in judicial review.

There *is* good reason for a court to defer to a university Visitor in interpreting the university's rules, but the reason is not limited to domestic rules of a university. The rules of the university have a special context with which the Visitor is familiar: that context gives a reason for anyone reviewing a decision from outside to defer, to some extent—as the House of Lords did in *Page*—to the Visitor's expertise. The rules of foreign compensation, too, had a special context, and the Commission was familiar with

---

12   'If the judgment of the visitor be ever so erroneous, we cannot interfere in order to correct it' (*R v Bishop of Ely* (1794) 5 Durn & E 475, 477 (Lord Kenyon CJ)).

it: this context gives a reason for anyone reviewing the Commission's work from outside to defer to the Commission's expertise. Consider that, in *Anisminic*, at 206, Lord Pearce said that it is 'a matter of opinion' whether it would be unfair to treat someone who had already got partial compensation from the Egyptian government in the same way as someone who had got none. That point, absolutely crucial to the interpretation of the confusing eligibility criteria in the case, is one on which the Court ought to have deferred to the much better-informed opinion of the Commission unless, from the Court's detached perspective, it was possible to identify the Commission's approach as unreasonable or abusive.

The rule of law is against *arbitrary* decision making. The rule of law is perfectly compatible with the deference that the House of Lords showed to university Visitors in *Page*, and it would be compatible with deference to other public authorities on questions of interpretation of legal standards.[13] The fact that the law requires every public authority to act in accordance with the law does not tell us who is to decide how to interpret the law. And while judges ought to *exercise control* over all such decisions, the UK constitution does not require that judges must *make* those decisions.

Reasons for deference

There are two good reasons for the judges not to replace a university Visitor's understanding of the university's rules with their own understanding. The **first** is that the Visitor can be expected to have a sensitivity to and familiarity with the needs of the university community and its members, which give the court reason to defer to his or her judgement on how to interpret and to elaborate its rules. Lord Browne-Wilkinson accepted this point in the case of university Visitors, adopting Lord Kenyon's view, expressed 200 years earlier, that 'any interference by us to control the judgment of the visitor, would be attended with the most mischievous consequences, since we must then decide on the statutes of the college, of which we are ignorant, and the construction of which has been confided to another forum' (*R v Bishop of Ely* (1794) 5 Durn & E 475, 477).

The judges may be as ignorant of the rules of a foreign compensation scheme as they are of the statutes of a university. In *both* cases, of course, they can learn the rules, and hear argument as to their interpretation. But as Lord Kenyon put it, there may still be reason for the judges to defer to another forum, to which the construction of the rules 'has been confided'. The point applies to university Visitors and, for the same reasons, it applies to any administrative decision maker whose familiarity with a scheme of regulation (and its context) is helpful in deciding how to interpret and how to elaborate the rules of the scheme.

---

[13] In *R v Charity Commissioners for England and Wales* (2001) 33 HLR 48, Jack Beatson QC held that the exception in *Page* also extends to the Charity Commissioners: in deciding whether trustees have complied with their duties, the Commissioners are similarly exercising a 'domestic' jurisdiction, and their decisions are only reviewable for lack of jurisdiction 'in the narrow sense', lack of natural justice, and abuse of power. But there has been no move to extend the same reasoning to administrative authorities in general.

The **second** reason for deference to university Visitors is a reason of process, which Lord Browne-Wilkinson pointed out in *Page* (at 704):

> ' The advantage of having an informal system which produces a speedy, cheap and final answer to internal disputes has been repeatedly emphasized in the authorities. . . . If it were to be held that judicial review for error of law lay against the visitor I fear that, as in the present case, finality would be lost. . . . Although the visitor's position is anomalous, it provides a valuable machinery for resolving internal disputes which should not be lost. '

Even though it is hard to generalize about administrative justice systems, these points about the process value of finality in decision making apply to many administrative decision-making institutions: they generally provide 'a valuable machinery', from which review for error of law may detract. The irony of *Page* is that Lord Browne-Wilkinson's good reasons for deference to university Visitors count *against* Lord Diplock's rule.

Summary of potential reasons for deference to administrative authorities on questions of law

(1) **The potentially better capacity of the administrative authority to form a good judgment as to how to interpret and elaborate the rules** (because of its experience with the scheme in question, and its understanding of the context in which the scheme operates).

(2) **Process**: if the court starts all over again in interpreting the scheme in question in judicial review, it may detract from the work of a valuable machinery for resolving disputes.

These considerations can justify a form of judicial review that gives an authority some leeway in interpreting its scheme. Their importance varies with the context, and neither consideration would justify judicial refusal to control the way in which an administrative authority interprets its scheme. In a brief remark at the end of his reasons, Lord Browne-Wilkinson asserted a jurisdiction to review *Visitors'* decisions (*Page*, 704):

> ' Judicial review does lie to the visitor in cases where he has acted outside his jurisdiction (in the narrow sense) or abused his powers or acted in breach of the rules of natural justice. '[14]

---

[14] In *R v Visitors to the Inns of Court ex p Persaud* [1994] QB 1, the Court of Appeal extended this same standard of review to decisions of High Court judges serving as visitors in deciding appeals by barristers against disciplinary decisions. The phrase 'jurisdiction (in the narrow sense)' was borrowed from *Anisminic*, in which Lord Reid suggested that, in a wide sense, a tribunal 'acts without jurisdiction' when its decision is a nullity. But he said that 'it is better not to use the term except in the narrow and original sense of the tribunal being entitled to enter on the inquiry in question' (at 171).

Just like that. He offered no authority or rationale for this assertion of judicial power over visitors. Yet it does have a sound justification, in the **core rationale** for judicial review (see 2.8): the Administrative Court's independence, its openness, its adversarial process, and its effective power give it the opportunity to prevent abuses of power and to impose good process on other university Visitors, in a way that will show no disrespect for the exercise of their jurisdiction. So Lord Browne-Wilkinson's residual standard of review for university Visitors—as casually as he stated it—provides a sound template for judicial review in general. It is a form of judicial review that might have emerged from a good interpretation of the ambiguous decision in *Anisminic*. Judges will be preventing arbitrary use of power, without a breach of the comity they owe to a university Visitor, if they quash a decision that was based on an interpretation of the university's rules that they can see to be unreasonable from their detached perspective.

● *Pop quiz* ●

What do *you* think about these three questions?

(1) Was *Anisminic* rightly decided?

(2) Does *Anisminic* support Lord Browne-Wilkinson's conclusion in *Page* that 'in general any error of law made by an administrative tribunal or inferior court in reaching its decision can be quashed for error of law'?

(3) Does *Page* set the right standard for judicial review?

9.1.8 Deference, North American style

Canada

Just before Lord Diplock took the law in a new direction, the Supreme Court of Canada had taken a decisive turn in the other direction, by clarifying the distinction (left obscure in *Anisminic*) between errors of law that do and do not make a decision a nullity. In *Canadian Union of Public Employees v New Brunswick Liquor Corporation* [1979] 2 SCR 227 ('*CUPE*'), the Liquor Corporation had been using managers to run its shops during a strike. The provincial Labour Relations Board—whose decisions were protected by an ouster clause like that in *Anisminic*—held that the policy was an unlawful interference with the strike. In judicial review, the Supreme Court of Canada rejected the idea that the Board's decision should be quashed if it was based on a misinterpretation of the law. Dickson J's reasons adopted the kernel of good sense in *Anisminic*: that if the Board misinterpreted the Act in such a way 'as to embark on an inquiry or answer a question not remitted to it', then it would have acted without jurisdiction. But he resolved the ambiguity in *Anisminic* by holding that the decision maker would only be embarking on an inquiry not remitted to it if its interpretation was 'so patently unreasonable that its construction cannot be rationally supported by the relevant legislation and demands intervention by the courts upon review' (*CUPE*, 237).

That reasoning neatly debunked the idea that *there is no* distinction between errors of law that do and do not make a decision a nullity. On the *CUPE* approach, the distinction is vague (just as any standard of review for reasonableness is vague), but perfectly coherent. If an interpretation is *patently* unreasonable, or 'cannot be rationally supported', then it makes sense to say that the decision maker has not made a decision within its jurisdiction at all. And then its so-called 'determination' is not a determination. That is not because its interpretation was wrong, but because it was so clearly unreasonable that acting on that so-called 'interpretation' does not count as exercising the jurisdiction at all.

After the *CUPE* decision in 1979, the Canadian Supreme Court developed Dickson J's approach into a 'pragmatic and functional approach' aimed directly at giving effect to 'the role of the superior Courts in maintaining the rule of law' (*Union des employés de service v Bibeault* [1988] 2 SCR 1048 [123] and [127] (Beetz J)). The courts applied three standards for review of administrative interpretations of the law (correctness, reasonableness, and the 'patently unreasonable' standard), with the choice depending on four factors:

- whether there is an ouster clause or a statutory right of appeal;

- the relative expertise of the tribunal and of the reviewing court;

- the purposes of the legislation; and

- the nature of the question.[15]

That approach adopted Lord Wilberforce's view that questions of law are not necessarily for courts, but that the courts must impose the rule of law on the exercise of an administrative jurisdiction to apply the law. It allows judges to ask just the right questions as to their role in controlling other public authorities. But as we will see, its flexibility came at a cost.

● *Pop quiz* ●

How would *Anisminic* have been decided if the House of Lords had adopted the *CUPE* standard, that an interpretation of the law by an administrative tribunal will only be set aside if it was patently unreasonable?

The United States: the 'principle of deference to administrative interpretations'

In the 1980s, the US Supreme Court, too, established a 'principle of deference' to an administration's interpretation of a statute, in *Chevron v Natural Resources Defense Counsel* 467 US 837 (1984). That decision has been cited thousands of times, and is still good law; it has been called a 'quasi-constitutional text'.[16] As in many landmark

---

15 See the cases cited in *Zenner v Prince Edward Island College of Optometrists* [2005] 3 SCR 645 [28].

16 Cass Sunstein, '*Chevron* Step Zero' (2006) 92 Virginia L Rev 187, 187; cf. Antonin Scalia, 'Judicial Deference to Administrative Interpretations of Law' [1989] Duke LJ 511.

decisions, the Court claimed to be giving effect to long-established doctrine. And indeed, the US Supreme Court had held in 1827 that: 'In the construction of a doubtful and ambiguous law, the cotemporaneous construction of those who were called upon to act under the law, and were appointed to carry its provisions into effect, is entitled to very great respect' (*Edwards' Lessee v Darby* 25 US 206, 210 (1827)).

If Congress expressly gives the agency power to *make* rules, then those rules are subject to judicial review on the same ground as in English law: the court will overturn them if they are 'arbitrary, capricious, or manifestly contrary to the statute' (*Chevron*, 844). But US law treats administrative agencies as having discretion not only when they make rules, but also when they interpret statutes, if there is an 'interpretive gap created through an ambiguity in the language of a statute's provisions' (*National Cable & Telecommunications Association v Brand X Internet Services* 125 S Ct 2688, 2712 (2005) (Breyer J)). When Congress delegates power implicitly, by authorizing an agency to give effect to legislation that does not resolve the precise question at issue in a dispute, the court will only overturn a decision if it is based on an unreasonable construction of the statute. The agency is 'the authoritative interpreter (within the limits of reason) of such statutes' (*Brand X*, 2701 (Thomas J)).

Under the *Chevron* doctrine, the court is to ask:

(1) whether Congress has 'directly spoken to the precise question at issue'.

If so, then the court must override any contrary interpretation by an agency. But if not, then 'the court does not simply impose its own construction on the statute', as if it were the initial decision maker. Instead, the court is to ask:

(2) 'whether the agency's answer is based on a permissible construction of the statute' (843–4). The court decides if the administrative agency has reasonably exercised its implicit power to resolve a question of interpretation of the rules it applies.

We can think of it all as a single, vague, flexible test of reasonableness, since it would be unreasonable to adopt an interpretation that is inconsistent with what Congress has enacted if Congress has 'directly spoken to the precise question at issue'. So, in US law, a court cannot simply substitute its own interpretation of a statute for the agency's interpretation; it must give 'considerable weight' to the agency's interpretation and uphold any 'reasonable' construction (844–5).

Like the Canadian approach, the *Chevron* doctrine does not presume that questions of law are for judges. That is not because Americans underestimate the importance of judges in establishing the law. The courts' responsibility for the law is built into the US Constitution, and the Supreme Court established more than 200 years ago that it is 'emphatically the province and duty of the judicial department to say what the law is' (*Marbury v Madison* 5 US 137, 177 (1803) (Marshall J)). The *Chevron* doctrine preserves the courts' responsibility for the rule of law; it recognizes that Congress can lawfully give discretion to an administrative agency to interpret the scheme for which it is responsible. The US judges assert control over that discretion, without eliminating it.

Like the Canadian approach, though, it creates deep controversy in the courts. The best example of controversy over *whether an administrative interpretation of the law is unreasonable* is the US Supreme Court's first case on global warming. The Environmental Protection Agency under George W Bush's administration decided that it could not regulate carbon dioxide emissions, because carbon dioxide did not count as 'air pollution'. On the question of whether the Agency's interpretation was reasonable, a narrow 5–4 liberal majority quashed the Agency's decision, with an energetic conservative dissent insisting that the Court should have deferred to the Agency's decision under the *Chevron* doctrine (*Massachusetts v Environmental Protection Agency* 127 S Ct 1438 (2007)).

In 9.1.9, we will see that although the American and Canadian approaches are better justified in constitutional principle, the difference in the effect of the English doctrine is not as great as you might think—except for the deep controversies that the more principled North American doctrines generate over the standard of review.

9.1.9 The limits of the error of law doctrine

The rule that all administrative decisions are subject to judicial review for error of law unjustifiably presumes that judges will be better than the statutory decision maker at interpreting the rules of a statutory scheme. The judges impose their own view, when they ought to be assessing the reasonableness of the initial decision maker's view.

But the effects of this excessive judicialisation of administration are not always damaging. And it might be worse for judges to abdicate their responsibility to quash arbitrary administrative decisions than it is for them to exaggerate their responsibility. Moreover, the doctrine has a restricted scope, the alternatives would create problems, and it still leaves discretion to administrative authorities in applying the law.

The restrictions on the scope of the doctrine

In addition to the fact that it does not apply to arbitrators, county courts, the Upper Tribunal, or university Visitors, Lord Diplock's rule is restricted in the following ways:

- the error must be 'relevant' (*Page*, 702), or operative—a court will not quash a decision just because the tribunal made an error of law, if the error did not affect the outcome;

- even a decision that was reached on the basis of an error of law will not be quashed, if the decision did no substantive injustice;

- the error must be on a question of law—not on a question of fact (see 9.2), or a question of the application of the law to the facts (see 9.3).

The problems with the alternatives

In Canada, the law grew extremely complex, and there was enormous flexibility—and therefore room for controversy—in the application of the four factors used to decide which of the three standards (correctness, reasonableness, or patent unreasonableness) to apply. Some judges complained that the difference between 'unreasonableness' and 'patent unreasonableness' was obscure (*Voice Construction Ltd v Construction & General Workers' Union* [2004] SCC 23 [2004] 1 SCR 609 [40]–[41] (Lebel J)). The question of the standard of review that ought to apply to a particular administrative interpretation was a matter of huge controversy, going up to the Supreme Court again and again,[17] before the judges even got to the point of applying the standard.

So in *Dunsmuir v New Brunswick* [2008] SCC 9, the Supreme Court of Canada rewrote the law, abolishing the distinction between unreasonableness and patent unreasonableness, and requiring courts to apply either a standard of correctness, or a standard of reasonableness (with the extent of the court's deference under the reasonableness test depending on the same range of factors on which the choice between unreasonableness and patent unreasonableness had depended). Reasonableness has become a general standard for judicial review of interpretations of the law, with judicial review on a standard of correctness limited to 'questions of law that are of central importance to the legal system as a whole and that are outside the [administrative authority's] expertise' (*Canadian Human Rights Commission v Canada (Attorney General)* [2011] SCC 53 [18]).

Dunsmuir simplified the law. But the Canadian approach still calls on the judges to pay attention to all of the relevant circumstances in deciding what sort of deference they owe to an administrative interpretation of a statute. And, for that very reason, it still invites appellate litigation over the approach that the court should take to its own role in particular circumstances. The very clear and well-established doctrine of judicial deference to administrative authorities does not generate a consensus as to which interpretations of the law are reasonable, and cases have frequently proceeded all the way to the Supreme Court of Canada, and have divided the justices of the Supreme Court, on the application of that deferential standard (see, e.g., *CEPUC v Irving Pulp & Paper* [2013] SCC 34).

Similarly, in the United States, the *Chevron* approach generates huge controversy at each of its two steps: disagreement as to whether Congress has directly spoken to the issue in dispute, and over whether an administrative agency has exercised its interpretative discretion reasonably. *Chevron* deference varies in accordance with the same considerations that the Canadians have tied to different 'standards of review', including the relative expertise of the agency and the court, and the nature of the question. On these questions, the US judges are deeply divided. The US Supreme Court has divided angrily along political lines—not only in *Massachusetts v Environmental Protection Agency* (see 9.1.8), but also in *Rapanos v US* 126 S Ct 2208 (2006) (over whether it was plausible to conclude that drains that dry up for part of the year count as part of the 'waters of the United States'). In another decision ten days after *Rapanos*, Justice Scalia referred to the dissenting judges in *Rapanos* as having reached the 'wildly

---

[17] See the 33 Supreme Court decisions since *CUPE* that were cited in *Dunsmuir v New Brunswick* [2008] SCC 9.

implausible conclusion that a storm drain is a tributary of the waters of the United States' (*Hamdan v Rumsfeld* 126 S Ct 2749, 2839 (2006)). The remarkable fact about the *Chevron* doctrine is that it leaves room for bitter disagreement among the judges of the US Supreme Court—not merely over how to interpret a statute, but also over whether an agency's interpretation is even plausible, and over the degree of deference the judges owe to a particular agency in a particular situation.

At present, there are no such disagreements in England over the standard of review. The standard is correctness. So disagreements work themselves out simply as disagreements over how best to interpret the legislation.

Here is the moral of the story: suppose that the English judges had moderated Lord Diplock's rule and adopted a form of deference to administrative decisions interpreting the law. That would bring the legal doctrine of English judicial review closer to the constitutional justification that it needs. The core rationale for judicial review requires judges to prevent arbitrary decision making, but does not require judges to replace other public authorities' judgment on all questions of law. But that change could generate the massive controversies that have been the focus of debate in dozens of decisions in the highest courts in Canada and the United States.

If judges really were to ask the pertinent question (the question of what sort of deference they ought to accord to an administrative interpretation of the law, given the nature of the agency and the nature of the question), judicial review would be a battleground for competing understandings of the relative expertise and responsibility of courts and other public authorities. It *is* a battleground, as we saw in Chapter 8, when the judges decide how to control discretionary powers. But on questions of the interpretation of statutes, English judicial review gains a certain eerie calm from the fact that the barristers do not argue and the judges do not reflect on the rationale for interfering with an administrative authority's interpretations of the law. You may conclude that it is better to have review for error of law (and to trust the judges to apply it with an unstated respect for the initial decision maker's interpretation) than to have a complex doctrine of deference, because we would gain too little and pay too much if the judges were to address the real issues at stake in justifying judicial review. Lord Diplock did not offer that rationale for his rule, but no other is available.

The remaining discretion

Lord Diplock's rule of review for error of law requires no deference by courts to other public authorities on questions of the law that they administer. So, in English law, administrative authorities have no discretion to act on a view of the law that is incompatible with the view that the court comes to. But since the power the judges have taken on themselves is itself a discretionary power, there is actually nothing to *stop them* from deferring to the public authority to which the decision was entrusted. That is, they can benefit from the reasons of the initial decision maker in deciding what to make of the law.

What's more, judicial review for error of law does *not* mean that administrative authorities have no discretion in applying the law, because the judges' view of the law may leave a range of lawful decisions to the administrative authority. If there is more than one correct way in which to apply the law, the court will not interfere with the administrative authority's choice.

We will see in 9.3 that this generates an important form of administrative discretion. To understand it, we first need to understand the ways in which judges control fact finding.

9.2 Control of fact finding

The result can be as unjust when an administrative body gets the facts wrong as when it gets the law wrong. Perhaps that explains the emergence of a new myth that is even more remarkable than the error of law doctrine: the myth that a mere error of fact is ground for judicial review.

A claimant in judicial review can ask the court to determine the law, and then to quash the decision if the judge's view of the law is incompatible with the view of the administrative authority. That turns judicial review into a form of appeal. If there were judicial review for error of fact, then a claimant could ask the court to determine the facts, and to quash the decision if its view of the facts is incompatible with the view of the defendant public authority. That would turn judicial review into a rehearing of the original decision.

This had better not be the state of the law, because there are two reasons why courts should often defer to the initial decision maker's judgment as to the facts.

- **Process**: in judicial review, the court does not have good techniques for finding the facts.

- **Comity**: it would show disrespect for the good functioning of other authorities if the judges were to take over the job of identifying the facts for administrative decisions in general.

9.2.1 Fact-finding processes

The courts act through a process that is not tailored to the particular situation in which a public authority finds the facts; it is tailored to the task of controlling a wide variety of decision-making processes, to restrain arbitrary decision making.

The processes for fact finding in ombudsman's reports and planning inquiries and parole board hearings and social security appeal tribunals (and so on) are extremely diverse. The processes used by those decision makers are more or less investigative, inquisitorial, or adversarial, depending on their particular purposes. Unlike judicial processes, many of them are quite appropriately designed to take advantage of information-gathering techniques that involve no rules of evidence except the rules that are necessary for due process—that the decision maker should give parties an opportunity to respond to adverse information where fairness demands it.

Unless those processes are badly designed, they will be much better for their purposes than the court's attempt to identify the facts in judicial review. For the court's process is summary (see 10.3)—that is, there is ordinarily no trial. In a claim for judicial review, the judges read the parties' sworn statements, and order cross-examination where it seems necessary. The courts do have discretion to order a trial. But there is no general reason to think that a trial will identify the facts more accurately than the initial decision maker could do through its fact-finding processes. For example, in order to review an ombudsman's conclusions as to the facts on a standard of *correctness*, the judges would need to conduct an ombudsman's investigation.

Finally, the courts will be at a comparative disadvantage in many situations simply because the initial decision maker made its inquiry into the facts *earlier*.

9.2.2 Fact finding and comity

The reasons of process and comity are connected: because judges do not have the processes needed for finding the facts, an attempt to do so would damage some of the administrative schemes whose operation is challenged in judicial review. Moreover, aside from their more effective processes, the people who make administrative decisions may have expertise or experience in their field that enables them to understand the facts of a case better than judges can (see 12.4.3 on expert membership in tribunals).

But comity can be a reason for deference even where it would be possible for judges to do a good job of finding the facts. For judicial review *controls* other decision-making processes, and does not *replace* them. Even if another decision maker made a mistake, a claimant does not automatically have a right to a judicial rehearing of the decision. Judicial interference needs a rationale in constitutional principle. The fact that administrative decision makers can get the facts wrong does not mean that the legal system should give you a right to another fact-finding inquiry by a different agency.

Remember the four basic reasons for deference (see 7.1.1, p 238).

- Legal allocation of power
- Expertise
- Political responsibility
- Processes

The first two and the fourth are reasons for deference to administrative authorities on questions of fact. The mere fact that a statute has entrusted the fact-finding power to the administrative authority means that the court should not decide the facts afresh, but only supervise the work of that authority. And if the authority has relevant expertise, or has fact-finding processes that are better for the purpose than the adversarial presentation of evidence in a courtroom, then those are reasons for greater deference to the authority's conclusions.

So judicial control of fact finding is limited by a variable, but important, requirement of judicial deference. The traditional role of the judges has been to decide whether a decision maker has 'acted without any evidence or upon a view of the facts which could not reasonably be entertained' (*Edwards v Bairstow* [1956] AC 14, 29 (Viscount Simonds)). That applies the restrained *Wednesbury* approach to the control of fact finding. As Lord Brightman put it in *R v Hillingdon LBC, ex p Puhlhofer* [1986] AC 484 (HL), 518:

> ' Where the existence or non-existence of a fact is left to the judgment and discretion of a public body and that fact involves a broad spectrum ranging from the obvious to the debatable to the just conceivable, it is the duty of the court to leave the decision of that fact to the public body to whom Parliament has entrusted the decision-making power save in a case where it is obvious that the public body, consciously or unconsciously, are acting perversely. '

This restrained form of control would only deserve a brief note, except for two huge problems: first, we need to decide what to make of some revolutionary, yet popular, judicial assertions of a general power to review administrative decisions for error of fact; then, we need to work out what sort of defect in fact finding makes a decision 'perverse' in Lord Brightman's sense.

9.2.3 An error of fact revolution?

When the Criminal Injuries Compensation Board decided against a claim without having seen a crucial police doctor's report, the claimant argued that 'there is jurisdiction to quash the board's decision because that decision was reached on a material error of fact' (*R v Criminal Injuries Compensation Board, ex p A* [1999] 2 AC 330, 344). Lord Slynn agreed. Citing Wade and Forsyth's view that '[m]ere factual mistake has become a ground of judicial review . . .' (344), he said: 'I would accept that there is jurisdiction to quash on that ground in this case, but I prefer to decide the matter on the alternative basis argued, namely that what happened in these proceedings was a breach of the rules of natural justice and constituted unfairness' (345).[18]

Lord Slynn's apparent revolution had been anticipated by Sedley J in *R v Parliamentary Commissioner for Administration, ex p Balchin* [1997] JPL 917 (see 13.8.1). In reviewing a report by the Parliamentary Ombudsman, he said that: 'If there is [a reviewable error], . . . it does not have to be classified as one of law or of fact (the latter too being reviewable if crucial to the decision . . .)' (928).[19] The views of both Lord

------

[18] Compare *R v Transport Secretary, ex p Alconbury* [2001] UKHL 23 [53] (see 3.5), in which Lord Slynn said that the court has 'jurisdiction to quash for a misunderstanding or ignorance of an established and relevant fact'. His remarks in both *A* and *Alconbury* were *obiter*.

[19] This remark, too, was *obiter*. And contrast Sedley J's remark, in *R v Education Secretary, ex p Skitt* [1995] ELR 388, 398, that striking down a decision for error of fact would be a 'novelty in English law'.

Slynn and Sedley LJ can be traced back through their reasons to *Education Secretary v Tameside Borough Council* [1977] AC 1014—a remarkably intrusive House of Lords' decision controlling the Education Secretary's statutory power to reverse unreasonable decisions of local education authorities. Lord Wilberforce said that, in controlling a minister's discretionary powers, the courts 'cannot substitute their opinion for that of the minister: they can interfere on such grounds as that the minister has acted right outside his powers or outside the purpose of the Act, or unfairly, or upon an incorrect basis of fact' (1047).

If this remark seems to give authority for a general power of judges to reverse administrative decisions that were based on an error of fact, the impression is very misleading. Lord Wilberforce *started* from the principle that the court cannot substitute its opinion for that of the minister. The court must have a power to control the minister's fact-finding role, in order to carry out its role of preventing arbitrary uses of administrative power. But controlling that role does not justify replacing the minister's opinion on the facts with that of the courts. It only justifies interfering when, from its detached vantage point and with the limited techniques available in the judicial review process, the court can see that the minister got the facts plain wrong. We have to interpret Lord Wilberforce's statement that courts can interfere if a minister has acted 'upon an incorrect basis of fact' in light of this duty of judicial deference.

Consider, similarly, a remark in a commentary on the development of judicial review in *Kennedy v Charity Commission* [2014] UKSC 20 [54], in which Lord Mance said that 'the remedy of judicial review is in appropriate cases apt to cover issues of fact as well as law'. It may suggest that we have undergone a revolution and now have review for error of fact, just as we have review for error of law. But Lord Mance was right to limit the remark to 'appropriate cases'. It would not be appropriate for judges to treat all issues of fact as a matter for determination by the court. Judges have no general power to substitute their judgment for the judgment of an administrative decision maker on questions of fact—not even on crucial questions of fact.

Consider again *Runa Begum v Tower Hamlets LBC* [2003] UKHL 5 (see 5.3.2, p 185), a case that shows the courts' limited capacity to control fact finding. The decision depended on the reviewing officer's assessment of Ms Begum's credibility, because she claimed to have been robbed in the area in which the local authority offered to give her housing. What is the appropriate form of judicial control of that assessment? The local authority's housing officer was in a much better position than judges to assess Ms Begum's credibility, partly because her familiarity with the area gave her an understanding of what Ms Begum was talking about. And the reviewing officer had the advantage of meeting Ms Begum and asking her questions in a different situation from the artificial setting of a court hearing, and of doing so earlier than the court could. These advantages have an important result: a judge in judicial review would not be able to do as good a job of deciding whether Ms Begum was credible as a housing officer who talked to her.

The House of Lords concluded that the authority had discretion in reaching its conclusions on those questions (and that the discretion was not a breach of Art 6 of the European Convention): '. . . the decision as to whether the accommodation was suitable for Runa Begum was a classic exercise of administrative discretion, even though it involved preliminary findings of fact' (Lord Hoffmann [56]). Lord Millett held that [99]:

> *'* A decision may be quashed if it is based on a finding of fact . . . which is perverse or irrational; or there was no evidence to support it. . . . The court cannot substitute its own findings of fact for those of the decision-making authority if there was evidence to support them; and questions as to the weight to be given to a particular piece of evidence and the credibility of witnesses are for the decision-making authority and not the court. *'*

Note the benefits *and* drawbacks of deferential review of fact finding . . .

It may seem that the judges should find the facts for themselves, because that is the only way to put things right if the housing officer has made an error of fact. But the standard should still be deferential because:

- the deferential standard will provide a substantial protection against bad decision making (and fact finding by judges would not provide perfect protection); and
- the fact that the standard will not guard against imperfect fact finding does not demand a second hearing on the facts by a decision maker that is not as well placed as the first decision maker to decide the facts.

Proportionate process requires the form of review that will provide a reasonable protection against bad decisions, without generating rehearings that are not equipped to yield better decisions.

Runa Begum unequivocally establishes the limited approach to review of fact finding (and establishes that it is compatible with the European Convention on Human Rights).[20] And in the context of appeals from the Tribunal system (see 12.4.9), the Court of Appeal put it even more strongly in *Criminal Injuries Compensation Authority v First-tier Tribunal* [2014] EWCA Civ 65: on a question of fact, the Court of Appeal will only overturn a conclusion of the First-tier Tribunal if 'it is one to which no rational tribunal could properly have come' (Lord Justice Moore-Bick [10]). These decisions can be reconciled with *Tameside* if we pay attention to Lord Justice Scarman's point in the Court of Appeal in *Tameside* that, in order for the court to intervene, the actual state of the facts must be 'plainly established'. That is, it must be plain to everyone (so that the court can see it in spite of its relative disadvantages as a tribunal of fact) that the initial decision maker got the facts wrong. A claimant in judicial review cannot ask the court to *establish* the facts by conducting the inquiry that it would take to do a better job than the initial decision maker. But in order to do what judges can do to guard

---

[20] Reaffirmed in *Poshteh v Kensington and Chelsea Royal LBC* [2017] UKSC 36 [42].

against arbitrary decision making by the housing officer, the court should interfere if it is patently obvious, even from the judge's relatively disadvantageous position, that the officer has made a mistake.

Article 6 and fact finding

You might think that the right to an independent tribunal in Art 6 of the European Convention would require courts to find the facts afresh in judicial review of administrative bodies that are not independent. But in another example of the judicial construction of Art 6 as only requiring procedures that are fair and reasonable (see 5.3.2, p 183), Lord Hoffmann said that he did not think that Art 6 'mandates a more intensive approach to judicial review of questions of fact' (*Runa Begum* [50]). A process for determining civil rights that is not independent of government does not infringe Art 6 if a court on judicial review has 'full jurisdiction to deal with the case as the nature of the decision requires' (*Alconbury* [87], Lord Hoffmann). Deferential review of fact finding meets that requirement.

There is a difference between review on questions of fact and review on questions of law. The English judges view questions of law as questions for the court (see 9.1.6), but they do not take the same attitude to questions of fact. Lord Slynn and Lord Justice Sedley may seem to be exceptions, but it seems hard to imagine that they would actually consider that the Administrative Court should make its own finding as to, for example, whether a drug problem in a neighbourhood in Tower Hamlets is bad enough to make it an unsuitable place to house a homeless person.

In *E v Home Secretary* [2004] EWCA Civ 49, the Court of Appeal reviewed the law on errors of fact (although without citing *Runa Begum*, which the House of Lords had decided a few months earlier), and held that, at least in some contexts, 'the time has now come to accept that a mistake of fact giving rise to unfairness is a separate head of challenge in an appeal on a point of law' (*E* [66]). In spite of the suggestion that the doctrine was new, the carefully reasoned decision actually amounts to a new articulation of the traditional, limited approach. And it is a helpful new articulation: an error of fact is not enough, but the court can quash a decision if it can see that an error of fact gives rise *to unfairness*.[21] The Court gave the following 'ordinary requirements for a finding of unfairness', at [66]:

> ' First, there must have been a mistake as to an existing fact, including a mistake as to the availability of evidence on a particular matter. Secondly, the fact or evidence must have been "established", in the sense that it was uncontentious and objectively verifiable. Thirdly, the appellant (or his advisers) must not have been responsible for the mistake. Fourthly, the mistake must have played a material (not necessarily decisive) part in the tribunal's reasoning. '

---

[21] Compare 'unfairness arising out of a mistake of fact' (*Connolly v Secretary of State for Communities and Local Government* [2009] EWCA Civ 1059 [37]).

That helpful articulation of the traditional approach confirms that, even if it is the judges' job to decide whether other public authorities have got the law right, it is not generally the judges' job to decide whether they have got the facts right.

9.2.4 What does it take for a finding of fact to be perverse?

Is *R v Hillingdon LBC, ex p Puhlhofer* [1986] AC 484—holding that the courts should leave the fact finding to the body subject to judicial review, unless it was acting perversely—still good law? Yes, *if* we understand Lord Brightman's requirement of 'perversity' to be met where, as the Court of Appeal put it in *E*, a mistake of fact has given rise to unfairness.

In order for judicial interference to be justified, an error of fact need not be outrageous or scandalous, and the decision maker need not have been at fault (as Lord Brightman made clear in *Puhlhofer*).[22] In order for a court to intervene, it must simply be obvious, from the detached vantage point that the judge has in judicial review, that an injustice has arisen from an error of fact.

Asylum seekers often challenge fact-finding decisions, and their cases give examples of errors of fact that do and do not justify review. Keene LJ held in *R (Ahmed) v Home Secretary* [2004] EWCA Civ 552, [12]:

> ' … while errors of fact often will not require a decision to be upset, these errors are so strange as to leave one wondering what was happening when the adjudicator wrote his determination. It is possible that he was confusing this appellant with another appellant or this case with another case. '

In that sort of case, judicial review is justified whether the mistake was reasonable or not. The rationale for review is that the court is in a position to identify a mistake in spite of the initial decision maker's advantages. Perhaps we could say that the role of perversity is that the court will interfere not merely with a finding of fact that was *made* perversely, but also where it would be perverse to let the decision stand. So Lord Brightman was not quite right in *Puhlhofer*: it does not have to be 'obvious that the public body, consciously or unconsciously, are acting perversely'. It only needs to be obvious that an injustice has been caused *by an error that the judges can identify with no breach of comity.*

The court may therefore quash a decision that was made with **no evidence** (such a decision is 'perverse' in Lord Brightman's sense: *R v Bedwellty Justices, ex p Williams* [1997] AC 225). But the 'no evidence' rule has to be understood in light of the context. In *B Johnson & Co v Minister of Health* [1947] 2 All ER 395 (CA), 400 (see 4.3.1, p 129), Lord Greene said that it would be 'fallacious' to think that a minister's decision about a planning inquiry 'is in some sense a quasi-judicial decision which can be challenged on the ground of lack of evidence, for instance, in the courts in the same way

---

[22] And see *E v Home Secretary* [2004] EWCA Civ 49 [63] and [65].

as a judicial decision might be challenged'. Even though the antique 'quasi-judicial' terminology is dangerous (it was used in the early twentieth century to restrict the law of due process—see 4.3), there is an important point here: lack of evidence is not a ground on which planning decisions should be reviewed *in the same way* as convictions in magistrates' courts.

Ministers' decisions concerning planning inquiries must be made with due process, but due process in planning inquiries does not demand the same sort of evidence as in criminal proceedings. So in *R v Bedwellty Justices, ex p Williams* [1997] AC 225 (HL), 233, Lord Cooke held that: 'To convict or commit for trial without any admissible evidence of guilt is to fall into an error of law.' That sort of decision requires evidence of the kind that courts expect in the criminal justice process. A minister's planning decision, by contrast, will only be set aside for error of fact if the court is able to decide that it was made without the sort of information that ministers ought to use in deciding whether a building project is in the public interest.

9.2.5 Radical fact finding

To understand the principle of relativity (see 1.3), it is essential to note that, in some areas, the courts really have quite properly jumped in and decided the facts for themselves. Yet that does not support the myth of judicial review for mere error of fact, because you need special circumstances if you are to persuade judges to find the facts for themselves.

In *Khawaja v Home Secretary* [1984] AC 74 (HL), 109–10, Lord Scarman pointed out that the form of review outlined by Lord Greene in *Wednesbury* 'excludes the court from substituting its own view of the facts for that of the authority. Such exclusion of the power and duty of the courts runs counter to the development of the safeguards which our law provides for the liberty of the subject.' That does not mean that there is anything wrong with what Lord Scarman called 'the *Wednesbury* principle'; it means that the common law does not apply the principle in the review of an executive decision to detain a person. When a man is detained as an illegal entrant, 'It is not enough that the immigration officer reasonably believes him to be an illegal entrant if the evidence does not justify his belief. Accordingly, the duty of the court must go beyond inquiring only whether he had reasonable grounds for his belief' (Lord Fraser, *Khawaja*, 97). Likewise, if a decision puts a claimant's life at risk, 'the basis of the decision must surely call for the most anxious scrutiny' (*Bugdaycay v Home Secretary* [1987] AC 514, Lord Bridge at 531).[23] The anxious scrutiny doctrine is very close to a doctrine that the court will determine the facts (the 'basis') for itself. But in *R (Kiarie) v Home Secretary* [2017] UKSC 42 [47], Lord Wilson held that it was not close enough. The claimant argued that deporting him would violate his rights under Art 8 of the ECHR, and challenged the Home Secretary's decision to certify his claim as 'clearly

---

23 Cf. *R (Brown) v Home Secretary* [2015] UKSC 8 [31].

unfounded', so that he could be deported before having a chance to appeal the decision in the UK. Lord Wilson held that the Court had to be prepared to determine the facts (concerning a claimant's family circumstances, for the purpose of Art 8 of the ECHR) for itself, rather than reviewing—even with 'anxious scrutiny'—the reasonableness of the Home Secretary's findings of fact.

The most striking instance of the principle of relativity in administrative law?

Even though it is *not* generally the job of the courts to determine the facts on which an executive decision ought to have been based, there is no deference to executive authorities' view of the facts that ground a decision to detain a person. (For the principle of relativity, see 1.3.)

This extraordinary review for error of fact in detention cases amounts to a rehearing. Why isn't it a breach of comity? Part of the reason is that the judicial process is well equipped to identify the relevant facts. The crucial facts tend to be facts concerning the individual who is being detained, of a kind that courts are used to determining (in criminal matters in particular), rather than the facts that an administrative authority identifies when it is making general policy. As a result, rehearing the facts would not usually damage the public interest that potentially required the detention. But more fundamentally the reason is a justification of necessity in the interests of justice. When the decision is an extraordinary administrative decision to detain a person, or puts the claimant's life at risk, or risks violating a Convention right, it is not a breach of comity for judges to call it into question in a way that overrides the initial decision maker's fact finding. The decisions in *Khawaja* and *Bugdaycay* do not support general review for error of fact, and the decision in *Kiarie* does not support a general replacement of administrative fact finding with judicial fact finding. Those cases show the principle of relativity at work: the judges will never take over fact finding in planning cases, in the way that they have done in cases that involve detention, or a risk of death, or a risk of the violation of Convention rights. It is important to note that, in *Runa Begum*, Lord Bingham rejected an argument that the fact finding in a housing case should be subjected to the sort of 'anxious scrutiny' or 'close and rigorous analysis' adopted in *Khawaja*, 'if by that is meant an analysis closer or more rigorous than would ordinarily and properly be conducted by a careful and competent judge determining an application for judicial review' (*Runa Begum* [7]).

9.2.6 Jurisdictional facts?

In *R (A) v Croydon LBC* [2009] UKSC 8, the local authority had a statutory duty to provide accommodation to 'any child in need within their area who appears to them to require accommodation'. The statute defined 'child' to mean 'a person under the age of

18'. Baroness Hale held, at [26]–[32], that the question (1) whether a person is a child; and (2) whether he or she is in need are 'different kinds of question':

> ' The question whether a child is "in need" requires a number of different value judgments. What would be a reasonable standard of health or development for this particular child? How likely is he to achieve it? What services might bring that standard up to a reasonable level? . . . it is entirely reasonable to assume that Parliament intended such evaluative questions to be determined by the public authority, subject to the control of the courts on the ordinary principles of judicial review. Within the limits of fair process and "*Wednesbury* reasonableness" there are no clear cut right or wrong answers.
>
> But the question whether a person is a "child" is a different kind of question. . . . it defines the outer boundaries of the jurisdiction of both courts and local authorities under the 1989 Act. This is an Act for and about children. If ever there were a jurisdictional fact, it might be thought, this is it. '

She held that questions of type (1) (such as whether a person is a child) were questions 'for the courts rather than for other kinds of decision-makers' [27].

Baroness Hale's reference to 'jurisdictional fact' may seem to take administrative law back to past centuries. In *Groenvelt v Burwell* (1700) 1 Ld Raym 454 (see 2.5.3, p 59), the College of Physicians of London fined and imprisoned Dr Groenvelt for selling poisons; Lord Chief Justice Holt in the Court of King's Bench refused to decide whether Groenvelt had done so, because 'the judges do not understand medicines sufficiently to make a judgment' (471). But he insisted that the Court *would* decide whether the College had acted within its jurisdiction, and implicit in that form of judicial review is a responsibility on the part of the Court to decide any facts that need to be decided in order to identify jurisdiction.

For more than two centuries (until the flexible approach in *Edwards v Bairstow* made it less important), the courts struggled to find a way of deciding whether a question of fact has to be decided by the court in order to determine the power of the administrative decision maker, or whether a question of fact was committed to the decision maker (so that the court could not decide it). The decision in *R (A) v Croydon* is not likely to lead to further centuries of puzzling over the nature of jurisdiction; Baroness Hale did not rely on the fact being jurisdictional [29].[24] Yet she focused on an issue that gives us a good understanding of the local authority's jurisdiction: in the scheme of social support for children that Parliament had set up, what sort of questions needed to be left to the local authority in order to achieve the purposes of the scheme? The answer is that the local authority needed to be able to make the value judgments

---

[24] Note that Lord Scarman had used the jurisdictional approach in *Khawaja*: '[W]here the exercise of executive power depends upon the precedent establishment of an objective fact, the courts will decide whether the requirement has been satisfied' (*Khawaja v Home Secretary* [1984] AC 74, 110).

involved in determining need, and on those issues the courts ought to defer to it in the way that Baroness Hale did. But the courts can decide who counts as a child without detracting from the local authority's public role in the welfare scheme.

Similarly, in *R (Al-Sweady) v Defence Secretary* [2009] EWHC 2387, the question was whether a claimant's nephew had died in custody at a British Army base (in which case, he would be able to assert rights under the European Convention on Human Rights), or on the battlefield in Iraq (in which case, the Convention would not apply). The judges held that '"*hard-edged*" questions of fact [such as the question of where the nephew died] represented an important exception to the rule precluding the court substituting its own view in judicial review cases' (Scott Baker LJ, [19]).

That approach, like Baroness Hale's approach in *R (A) v Croydon*, respects the requirement of judicial comity toward other public authorities. It leaves matters of judgment to the initial decision maker, while protecting the claimant against patent mistakes and against risks of distorted fact finding.

R (A) v Croydon and *Al-Sweady* can be described as offering different tests for different sorts of fact. But they can also be described as offering a single test (which applies differently to different sorts of fact): assuming it is a fact of a kind that the court can decide for itself, will the court interfere inappropriately with the proper function of the administrative authority if it does so? That is the question of comity.

To summarize, an administrative decision ought to be quashed in judicial review if it was based on a finding of fact that can be seen *from the court's detached and restricted vantage point* to result in an injustice. In special circumstances in which the courts are capable of passing judgment on the facts in question, and justice demands it for the protection of essential interests such as liberty and security of the person, the courts can jump in and find the facts for themselves, quashing a decision merely on the basis that, in some relevant respect, the facts were not as the public authority had thought they were. The purpose of the doctrine is to hold public authorities accountable, and it does *not* allow the courts to substitute their judgment for the judgment of other public authorities on questions of fact in general. There is still no general judicial review for error of fact.

9.3 Applying the law to the facts: a 'permissible field of judgment'

Here is a puzzle about *R v Ministry of Defence, ex p Walker* [2000] 1 WLR 806 (see 2.1). The criminal injuries compensation scheme included a provision that no compensation was available for injuries caused by 'military activity by warring factions'. The Ministry decided that the restriction applied to the facts of Walker's case, so that he was not eligible for compensation. We have seen that the courts will review an interpretation of such a scheme on a standard of correctness: Lord Slynn said that the court had to decide whether the Ministry of Defence had interpreted the compensation scheme **correctly** (810). We have seen that it would review decisions as to the facts of a particular case on a standard of reasonableness.[25] What is the standard of review for a decision as to how to apply the scheme to the facts?

Lord Hoffmann thought that the court had to decide whether the Ministry had applied its rules **reasonably** (815):

> ' The next question is whether the injury to Sergeant Walker fell within the terms of the exclusion announced by the minister. I think it plainly did. He was fired upon by a Serbian tank. I do not see how it can be said that the ministry could not reasonably take the view that this was military activity by a warring faction. '

If the court had to decide whether the Ministry interpreted the scheme *correctly*, then why was Lord Hoffmann concerned with whether it was *reasonable* to take the view that the exclusion applied to Walker?

The answer to the puzzle is that both Lord Slynn and Lord Hoffmann were right, because **interpreting** the scheme is different from **applying** it to a case. According to Lord Diplock's rule, the court will insist on its own interpretation of the scheme, and will quash a decision that is incompatible with its interpretation. But the court's interpretation may allow the administrative decision maker to apply the law for *or* against a claimant—and then the court will not interfere.

There are two reasons why the courts do not apply a standard of correctness to decisions applying the law, in spite of the doctrine of judicial review for error of law:

(1) **deference on questions of fact**—the judges are at a disadvantage in applying the law to the facts; and

(2) **the resultant discretion** (see 7.2.1, p 249) **that vague standards give the initial decision maker**—the court's interpretation of the law may or may not require a particular outcome in a given case.

The second of these points is especially important: if the correct view of the law does not require one particular decision, then a public authority is free to decide one way or another.

That may seem impossible, if you think that there is no difference between **interpreting the law** and **deciding how to apply the law**. In fact, the distinction between questions of interpretation and questions of application is simple, although vague. The distinction *seems* extremely confusing, because understanding it means working out two potentially mind-boggling questions: what interpretation is, and which questions are questions of law.

9.3.1 What is interpretation?

The interpretation and the application of the law are related, because an interpretation of the law is a rule for applying the law. If an administrative decision maker explains how, in its view, the law is to be applied, then it is giving its interpretation, and the court will decide whether it is mistaken or correct. If the court decides that the interpretation

---

25   There was no dispute as to the facts in *Walker*.

is mistaken, the court will correct the error (and will hold the administrative decision to be unlawful if it was based on the error). If the interpretation that the decision maker offers is correct, then the court will not interfere, unless the decision maker's application of the law to the facts is incompatible with that interpretation. As Cranston J has put it: '[I]f the relevant statutory agencies adopt the correct legal interpretation the court will not substitute its own judgment for how that approach fits in its precise application to particular facts. At least analytically there is a distinction between interpretation and application' (*R (UNISON) v Monitor* [2009] EWHC 3221 [60]).

In a case like *Walker*, the correct interpretation may leave a wide discretion to the decision maker to decide in favour of an application *or* against it. The court will only interfere if the Ministry's interpretation of the scheme was incorrect, or if the Ministry's decision not to compensate, given the facts of Walker's case, was incompatible with the correct interpretation of the scheme. The power to apply the scheme is a discretionary power, because the best interpretation of the scheme may leave the administrative decision maker a choice to apply it in Walker's favour or not.

The classic case on judicial review of decisions applying the law was a statutory appeal on a question of law: *Edwards v Bairstow* [1956] AC 14. The leading recent authority is a decision on judicial review: *R v Monopolies and Mergers Commission, ex p South Yorkshire Transport* [1993] 1 WLR 23. Both cases show that administrative decision makers have discretion in applying the law, even though the courts will quash their decisions (either on a statutory appeal or in judicial review) for error of law.

In *South Yorkshire Transport*, a bus company was buying up local bus services after the Thatcher government's deregulation of the industry. The Conservative Trade and Industry Secretary wanted to break up this monopoly, so he referred the matter to the Monopolies and Mergers Commission. The Commission had power to investigate acquisitions of companies that affected 'a substantial part of the United Kingdom' (and to unwind them, after investigation, if they were not in the public interest). The South Yorkshire bus companies had routes that affected an area between Leeds and Derby that covered 1.65 per cent of the land area of the United Kingdom (with 3.2 per cent of the population—see Figure 9.1). South Yorkshire said that it was not a substantial part of the United Kingdom, so that the Commission had no jurisdiction to investigate.

South Yorkshire Transport was asking the court to answer the question of whether the area between Leeds and Derby is a substantial part of the United Kingdom. It claimed that: 'If the commission has reached a different answer it is wrong, and the court can and must intervene' (32). But Lord Mustill did not altogether agree: he said that it *was* the court's job to identify 'the criterion for a judgment', even if 'opinions might legitimately differ' as to what the criterion ought to be. So he endorsed Lord Diplock's rule that the court should impose its understanding of the scheme on the authority responsible for operating the scheme, even if the authority's understanding was reasonable. But, he added at (32), if the 'criterion so established' is vague:

> ' . . . the court is entitled to substitute its own opinion for that of the person to whom the decision has been entrusted only if the decision is so aberrant that it cannot be classed as rational: *Edwards v Bairstow* [1956] AC 14. '

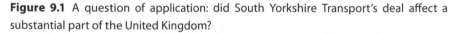

Figure 9.1 A question of application: did South Yorkshire Transport's deal affect a substantial part of the United Kingdom?

To identify the criterion for a judgment is to interpret the law. The criterion that Lord Mustill established in *South Yorkshire Transport* (his interpretation) was vague. He interpreted 'substantial part of the UK' to mean 'of such size, character and importance as to make it worth consideration for the purposes of the Act' (32), and he found that the Commission's decision was within the 'permissible field of judgment' (33) allowed by that criterion. Once the court has established its interpretation of the law, the court will interfere with decisions applying that interpretation only on the 'rationality' ground of review that is used in control of discretionary powers. Whether the rationality requirement leaves the administrative decision maker any leeway depends on how vague the 'criterion for a judgment' is. The standard that the House of Lords adopted in answering the question of law in *South Yorkshire Transport* left the Commission a very wide leeway.

That leeway is one example of the leeway that administrative authorities have in the exercise of discretionary powers. And in other cases, the judges have made it very clear that the general standard of review of decisions applying the law is *Wednesbury* unreasonableness. Lord Donaldson MR held in *O'Kelly v Trusthouse Forte plc* [1984] QB 90, 123, that if a tribunal has stated the law correctly, an appellate court can interfere with the application of the law to the facts only if 'no reasonable tribunal, properly directing itself on the relevant questions of law, could have reached the conclusion under appeal'. And in *Moyna v Work and Pensions Secretary* [2003] UKHL 44 [25], Lord Hoffmann held that the court cannot overturn a decision 'whether the facts as found or admitted fall one side or the other of some conceptual line drawn by the law . . . unless it falls outside the bounds of reasonable judgment'.

If it still seems odd that the doctrine of review for error of law can leave a wide 'permissible field of judgment' in applying the law, you should consider the decision that Lord Donaldson, Lord Mustill, and Lord Hoffmann all cited in *O'Kelly, South Yorkshire Transport*, and *Moyna*. Lord Radcliffe's classic speech in *Edwards v Bairstow*.

Harold Bairstow had bought a lot of spinning machinery for £12,000, and promptly sold it in bits at a profit of £18,000. The tax inspector claimed that the deal was an 'adventure or concern in the nature of trade', so that Bairstow had to pay income tax. Bairstow claimed that the deal did not count as trade because it was a one-off sale of an asset; the tax inspector thought it was still trade because Bairstow flipped it—that is, he bought it for the purpose of selling it at a profit. The tax commissioners (the tribunal for taxpayer complaints) decided that the deal did not count as trade. The tax inspector appealed on a question of law to the High Court. The High Court and the Court of Appeal upheld the tribunal's decision, but the House of Lords decided that the tribunal had erred in law, on the ground that the only reasonable conclusion was that the sale of the machinery counted as trade.

Note that, according to Lord Radcliffe, the court's role in deciding whether there was an error of law was *not* necessarily to decide whether a particular transaction counted as 'trade' (at 34): 'There are many combinations of circumstances in which it could not be said to be wrong to arrive at a conclusion one way or the other.' This statement takes the approach of *Slattery, Kruse*, and *Wednesbury* (see 7.1), and uses it to control the discretion that administrative tribunals have in applying the law. Lord Radcliffe's speech has become the standard reference point for judges explaining the way in which they control the application of the law—although he rightly claimed to be stating old and well-established law.

9.3.2 What is a question of law?

You can see why the courts have struggled to decide whether a question of the application of a statute is a question of law or a question of fact. In an appeal on a point of law (e.g., in *Edwards v Bairstow*), the appellant needs to persuade the court that the error that it alleges was an error on a question of law, or there is no jurisdiction to overturn the decision. And in judicial review (e.g., in *South Yorkshire Transport*), the claimant tries to persuade the court that the error it alleges was an error on a question of law to get the court to substitute its judgment for the judgment of the administrative tribunal.

Is a question of the application of a statute a question of law or a question of fact? The key to this problem is that the question of the application of the law is a question of law if the law demands a particular answer to it. A question of application is not a question of law if (as in *South Yorkshire Transport*) the law allows the tribunal to decide it either way.

When it is reasonable to decide that the facts do *or* do not fall within the relevant legal category, the issue is *not* a question of law, which means that it is not a question on which the court needs to impose its own judgment. As Lord Simon later said, in explaining *Edwards v Bairstow*, if 'certain conduct must as a matter of law fall within the statutory language (as was the actual decision in *Edwards v Bairstow*)' or if it 'must as a matter of law fall outside the statutory language', then the question of application is a question of law (*Ransom (Inspector of Taxes) v Higgs* [1974] 1 WLR 1594 (HL), 1618).

It is, of course, tempting for a court in judicial review, or in an appeal on a question of law, to conclude that there must have been an error of law if the reviewing court thinks that a tribunal or other authority misapplied the law. But the Supreme Court has held to the orthodox doctrine that a decision should not be overturned on the ground that the law was misapplied to the facts, unless it is 'quite clear' that the initial decision maker must have misunderstood the law. In reviewing the application of the law by the Asylum and Immigration Tribunal, *AH (Sudan) v Home Secretary* [2007] UKHL 49, [30], Baroness Hale said:

> ' This is an expert Tribunal charged with administering a complex area of law in challenging circumstances . . . . [T]he ordinary courts should approach appeals from them with an appropriate degree of caution; it is probable that in understanding and applying the law in their specialised field the Tribunal will have got it right . . . . Their decisions should be respected unless it is quite clear that they have misdirected themselves in law. Appellate courts should not rush to find such misdirections simply because they might have reached a different conclusion on the facts. '

9.4 Conclusion: the underlying unity of control of discretionary powers

Judicial control of administrative jurisdictions to apply the law can promote the rule of law. The judges' independence, the openness of the courts, their adversarial process, and the effectiveness of judicial orders give the courts the opportunity to prevent abuses of power and to impose good process on other decision makers. The remarkable doctrine of review for error of law gives the judges the more dramatic opportunity to improve administrative decision making, or to damage it by imposing the judges' misinterpretations on a decision maker that understands the purpose of the scheme in question better, and is responsible for applying it. *Edwards v Bairstow* and *South Yorkshire Transport* show the discretion that administrative authorities may have in applying the court's interpretation. The breadth of that discretion may be substantial: the courts will defer to a reasonable administrative decision as to how the law is to be applied.

No one has overruled Lord Diplock's rule that the courts will not defer on questions of law. But *AH (Sudan)* shows a final, notable reason why the doctrine of review for error of law need not be damaging in its effect: while it allows the judges to ignore and to set aside the judgment of the initial decision maker, it also allows them to learn from the initial decision maker. And if they take Baroness Hale's approach and treat the decision of initial decision makers with respect 'unless it is quite clear that they have misdirected themselves in law', then the standard of review will, in effect, involve a healthy form of judicial deference. And it will be compatible with the responsibility of the judges to secure the rule of law.

It is popular to divide the law of judicial review into two compartments: control of discretionary powers (with *Wednesbury* as the leading case), and control of decisions applying the law (with *Anisminic*, as reinterpreted by Lord Diplock, as the leading case). It may seem to be an attractive division, because exercising a discretion is a matter for the body given the discretion, but applying the law seems to be a matter for judges. But that would be a basic mistake. It ought to have become clear in the course of this chapter that **a power to apply the law is a discretionary power**.

Consider the following puzzle about the relation between having a discretion and applying the law: in *R v Gaming Board for Great Britain, ex p Kingsley* [1996] COD 178, the Gaming Board had to decide whether Kingsley was a 'fit and proper person' to operate casinos. Was the Board applying the law, or exercising a discretionary power? The answer is that it was doing *both*. The Board had to decide whether the legal category 'fit and proper person' applied to Kingsley. That category was so vague that the Board had a very wide resultant discretion in deciding whether to count Kingsley as being within the category. If the Board misinterpreted the term in the statute, it would *for that very reason* be acting on irrelevant considerations. So there is an underlying unity between the error of law doctrine (which concerns the interpretation of legal categories) and the control of discretionary power.

The Queen's Bench Division held in *Kingsley*, by the way, that it was for the Board to decide what considerations it would take into account in deciding whether a person is fit and proper, as long as it kept in mind the purpose of the legislation. That decision reflects both the discretion that a public authority still has in applying the law (in spite of the doctrine of review for error of law) and the rule that deciding which considerations are relevant is not generally a matter for the court (although the court has a general power to quash a decision based on an unreasonable view as to what is relevant—see 8.2.3). So here is a template for the form of judicial review power that judges can legitimately take upon themselves. It is a model for ways in which they ought to give effect to the core rationale for judicial review.

The template for the judges' supervisory jurisdiction

Judicial review ought to be generally available to ask whether an administrative authority has:

- acted without jurisdiction; or
- acted without due process; or
- acted contrary to any legal rule that the judges can identify with no breach of comity; or
- acted on a view of the facts that can be seen, even from the judges' detached point of view, to be manifestly wrong; or
- used its discretionary powers (including any discretionary power to interpret or elaborate the rules that it is responsible for applying) in a way that judges can identify as unreasonable with no breach of comity.

Appendix: The List (of grounds of judicial review)—Lord Diplock's version

'Judicial review has I think developed to a stage today when without reiterating any analysis of the steps by which the development has come about, one can conveniently classify under three heads the grounds upon which administrative action is subject to control by judicial review. The first ground I would call "illegality," the second "irrationality" and the third "procedural impropriety".'[26]

This seemingly neat list is very popular,[27] but it is incoherent. 'Procedural impropriety' makes sense—that means lack of due process. Lord Diplock meant 'irrationality' as a label for *Wednesbury* unreasonableness—but it is a misleading label (see 7.1.3). And if 'illegality' means unlawfulness, it covers all of the grounds of review.[28]

Lord Diplock tried to explain (*GCHQ*, 410): 'By "illegality" as a ground for judicial review I mean that the decision-maker must understand correctly the law that regulates his decision-making power and must give effect to it.' But all the grounds of judicial review are part of the 'law that regulates' a decision-making power. Perhaps Lord Diplock thought of 'illegality' as a label for the doctrine of review for error of law, which he had been crafting in decisions just before the *GCHQ* case (*Racal* [1981] AC 374 (HL); *O'Reilly v Mackman* [1983] 2 AC 237 (HL)). Or perhaps he meant illegality as a label for everything except procedural

---

[26] *Council of Civil Service Unions v Minister for the Civil Service* [1985] AC 374, 410.

[27] Prominent House of Lords decisions adopting Lord Diplock's list include: *R v Environment Secretary, ex p Hammersmith and Fulham LBC* [1991] 1 AC 521, 594; *Boddington v British Transport Police* [1999] 2 AC 143 (HL), 152; *R v Lord Chancellor, ex p Page* [1993] AC 682, 701.

[28] So, e.g., in *R v Environment Secretary, ex p Nottinghamshire County Council* [1986] AC 240, 249, Lord Scarman said that Lord Greene's speech in *Wednesbury* outlined 'the circumstances in which the courts will intervene to quash as being illegal the exercise of an administrative discretion'.

impropriety and irrationality, as Lord Bridge suggested in *R v Environment Secretary, ex p Hammersmith and Fulham LBC* [1991] 1 AC 521, 597. For judges who think that the *Wednesbury* principles (including the doctrine of judicial review for bad faith and, crucially, the doctrine of relevance) do not all fit into 'irrationality', it is a popular move to squeeze them into 'illegality' (along with the doctrine of legitimate expectations).

There is no particular reason to use 'illegality' as a label for bad faith and irrelevant considerations if we do not use it as a label for procedural impropriety and irrationality (whatever may be meant by that) as well. And classifying relevance as a matter of 'illegality' would be dangerously misleading.[29] It would suggest that the standard for identifying the considerations on which a decision should be based is one of correctness (like the standard for determinations of law). But that is a mistake that generates excessive judicialisation of administrative decision making: judges ought to defer to public authorities, to some extent, on the question of what considerations are relevant to the public authority's decision (see 8.2.3).

It is impossible—and unnecessary—to encapsulate the grounds of review in three big words.

TAKE-HOME MESSAGE • • •

- It should not be the judges' job to correct every **error of law**, although that is what the well-established doctrine requires. They should quash **unreasonable interpretations** of the standards that a public authority has responsibility for applying.
- It is not the judges' job to correct every **error of fact**. But they should quash decisions based on a conclusion as to the facts that they can see to be patently mistaken (from their detached perspective).
- A question of **how the law applies to a particular case** may or may not be a question of law. It is a question of law if the law requires it to be answered in a particular way, but it is not a question of law if the law allows it to be answered in different ways. As a result, administrative authorities have discretion (which may be wide or narrow depending on the law in question) in applying the law to the facts of a case.

CRITICAL QUESTIONS • • •

1   **Is there any difference between judicial review for error of law and a statutory appeal to the Upper Tribunal (see Chapter 12) on a question of law?**

---

[29] Sometimes, judges have treated irrelevant considerations as part of the 'irrationality' ground of review: Lord Donaldson spoke of '[i]rrationality, . . . in the sense of failing to take account of relevant factors or taking account of irrelevant factors . . .' (*R v Panel on Take-overs and Mergers, ex p Guinness Plc* [1990] 1 QB 146, 159).

2   What is jurisdiction? Do administrative authorities have any?

3   Can you reconcile the decision in *Anisminic* with the statutory ouster clause? Would the approach of the majority in *Anisminic* have been the right approach if there had been no ouster clause in the legislation setting up the Commission?

4   Is fact finding a discretionary power?

5   What is the relationship between 'The List' of things that make an administrative decision a nullity in Lord Reid's speech in *Anisminic* (see 9.1.4, p 325), and 'The List' of substantive features of an exercise of power that make it unlawful in Lord Greene's reasons in *Wednesbury* (see 7.1.2, p 244)?

6   Every fact that is relevant to the exercise of a power is a relevant consideration. So if there is judicial review for failure to decide on the relevant considerations, doesn't that mean that there must be judicial review for error of fact?

7   Decisions of the High Court are not susceptible to judicial review. Does that mean that the High Court has unlimited jurisdiction?

READING • • •

Edwards v Bairstow [1956] AC 14
Anisminic v Foreign Compensation Commission [1969] 2 AC 147 (HL)
Re Racal [1981] AC 374 (HL)
O'Reilly v Mackman [1983] 2 AC 237 (HL)
R v Lord Chancellor, ex p Page [1993] AC 682
R v Monopolies and Mergers Commission, ex p South Yorkshire Transport [1993] 1 WLR 23
Moyna v Work and Pensions Secretary [2003] UKHL 44
E v Home Secretary [2004] EWCA Civ 49

On errors of law:
Rebecca Williams, 'When is an Error not an Error? Reform of Jurisdictional Review of Error of Law and Fact' [2007] PL 793
Paul Daly, 'Deference on Questions of Law' (2011) 74 MLR 694
On review of fact finding:
Paul Craig, 'Judicial Review, Appeal and Factual Error' [2004] PL 788
On the distinction between questions of law and questions of fact:
Timothy Endicott, 'Questions of Law' (1998) 114 LQR 292

The following online resources accompany this chapter: **summaries** of key cases and legislation; **updates** on the law; **guidance** for answering the pop quizzes and questions; and **links** to legislation, cases, and useful websites.

Part IV
Litigation

10 How to sue the government: judicial processes and judicial remedies

This chapter addresses the process of judicial review, and the extraordinary remedies available to the court. The process and remedies are compared to the process and remedies in ordinary claims (which can also be used to challenge administrative action). In controlling these complex processes, the challenge for judges is to keep things in proportion: due process in judicial control of administrative action is essential to the administration of justice.

LOOK FOR ...

- **Proportionality** as the key principle of judicial process (just as it is the key principle of administrative process).

- The courts' discretionary control over their own process (developed at common law, and preserved in modern reforms).

- **Process danger**: can the courts control their own process in a way that does justice and respects the public interest? Or does the process need to be controlled by rules that restrict the courts' discretion?

- The **irony of process** (see 4.13, p 157) again: in order to protect the administration of justice, the courts may need to provide forms of process that are excessive and wasteful in some cases.

> '*A mandamus* . . . ought to be used upon all occasions where the law has established no specific remedy, and where in justice and good government there ought to be one. Within the last century, it has been liberally interposed for the benefit of the subject and advancement of justice.'
>
> *R v Barker* (1762) 3 Burr 1265, 1267 (Lord Mansfield)

10.1 The judicial process puzzle: why is this a problem?

In 2013, David Cameron's government set out to reform the judicial review process, aiming 'to tackle the burden that unmeritorious judicial reviews have placed on stretched public services whilst protecting access to justice and the rule of law.'[1] The consultation process generated opposition to the proposals, on the basis that the government was actually trying to insulate itself from the rule of law.[2] But the reforms went ahead, first with changes to the Civil Procedure Rules to rule out oral hearings on permission to seek judicial review where a claim is 'totally without merit' (see 10.3.2). And then Parliament enacted a variety of steps to curtail judicial review in the Criminal Justice and Courts Act 2015. The Act makes claimants face more of the costs of litigation and disclose their financial resources to the court and (ordinarily) to the defendant (see 11.3), and requires courts to refuse relief in judicial review, even where the court decides that a decision was made unlawfully, where the result would have been the same if the decision had been made lawfully (see 10.4.7). The reforms were initiated in the face of a huge increase in applications for permission to seek judicial review, which had more than tripled in ten years from 4,200 in 2004 to 15,600 in 2013 (see Figure 10.1). But the increase had come almost entirely in immigration cases (and judicial review of immigration decisions was transferred to the Upper Tribunal in 2013); the number of non-immigration judicial review claims has actually risen very little in twenty years.

Was the government right to seek to protect public authorities from judicial review? Or do the reforms represent an attack on the rule of law? To answer these questions, you will need to understand the variety of judicial processes, the special time limits and permission requirements in claims for judicial review, the remedies the judges can order, and the ways in which the judges have exercised their discretion in controlling the proceedings, and in issuing remedies. At that point—by the end of this chapter—three principles should be evident.

---

[1] From the government's consultation report, 'Judicial Review: proposals for further reform', 12 March 2014: http://www.consult.justice.gov.uk/digital-communications/judicial-review/. And see: http://www.bbc.com/news/uk-politics-20389297.

[2] See especially 'Judicial Review: Proposals for Reform (CP25/2012) JUSTICE Response'— http://www.justice.org.uk/judicial-review-consultation/.

- Strange as it may seem, **the rule of law does not automatically require that an unlawful decision should be quashed in judicial review**.
- But the rule of law does require **proportionate process** in judicial review. That is, the law must not only impose standards of lawful conduct on public authorities, but must also provide processes and remedies that are sufficient to give claimants a genuine opportunity to seek justice, and that are sufficient to make the UK a country that is ruled by law, and not by arbitrary decision making.
- There may be no way to provide proportionate process, without providing claimants with techniques that will enable them to impose costs on the public and to obstruct perfectly legitimate administrative decisions. That is **the irony of process**.

These principles are illustrated further in Chapter 11, which explains the requirement of standing for judicial review, and the opportunity that judicial review gives to advocacy groups to pursue political activism through the courts.

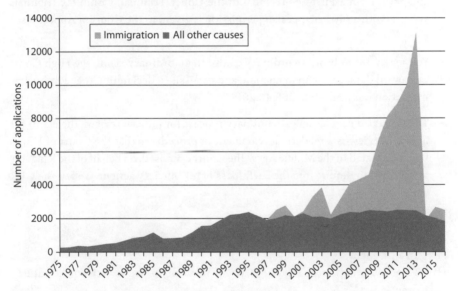

Figure 10.1 Applications for permission for judicial review in the High Court, 1975–2016 Reproduced from Christopher Hood and Ruth Dixon, *A Government that Works Better and Costs Less?* (OUP 2015), Fig. 6.3a, with additional data from Ministry of Justice, *Civil Justice Statistics Quarterly: January to March 2017*.

10.1.1 The variety of judicial processes

The history of the common law has given the judges far-reaching discretionary power over their own jurisdiction to control administrative action. And in the twenty-first century, the Civil Procedure Rules 1998 (CPR) have extended that judicial power.

Due process is the goal for courts in controlling their own proceedings. That means affording claimants a way of challenging unlawful behaviour that is proportionate to the interests at stake—the claimant's interest in getting a hearing from the court, and in getting a remedy against unlawful government action, and competing interests of other private persons and of the public in (1) finality in administrative decision making; and (2) the effective operation of a process that can impose the rule of law on administration.

If you are affected by an administrative action that you believe to be unlawful, what can you do? You might think this would be easy—that claimants would simply be able ask a court to apply the grounds of judicial review. Those grounds, introduced in Chapter 2 and unpacked in Chapters 3–9, are powerful techniques for judging administrative action to be unlawful. But there are *many* potentially useful judicial processes for pursuing a claim that administrative action is unlawful.

- You may be able to bring an **appeal** (typically on a point of law, which will include error of law, unfair process, and unlawful exercise of discretion). The process for appeal to the courts from most administrative tribunals has now been unified into an appeal from a First-tier Tribunal to the Upper Tribunal, within the tribunals system (with a further appeal, if permission is given, to the Court of Appeal—see Chapter 12).

- You may want to bring an **ordinary claim**. In an ordinary claim, the High Court can award damages or an injunction, and can issue a declaration that administrative action was unlawful (CPR 40.20).

- The CPR also provide an extraordinary process for judicial review. The **claim for judicial review** is a modern development of procedures that the Court of King's Bench invented in the Middle Ages. The Court exercised, on behalf of the King, his prerogative to inquire into the lawfulness of his officials' actions. Today, the CPR define it as:

> ' . . . a claim to review the lawfulness of—
> (i) an enactment; or
> (ii) a decision, action or failure to act in relation to the exercise of a public function. ' [3]

This process offers special remedies (still called 'prerogative' remedies) that are available only through a claim for judicial review: a 'quashing order' to nullify a decision; a 'mandatory order' to require some official action; and a 'prohibiting order' to ban some official action. They were called *'certiorari'*, *'mandamus'*, and 'prohibition' until the CPR 1998 came into effect. Declarations and the ordinary remedies of damages and injunctions are also available in a claim for judicial review.

---

[3]   CPR 54.1(1)(2)(a).

- *Habeas corpus* is available to challenge unlawful detention in a very simple process that was invented in the Middle Ages, and reformed in the Habeas Corpus Acts 1640 and 1679 (the process is now regulated by Rules of the Supreme Court (RSC) Order 54).

- **Proceedings under the Human Rights Act 1998 s 7** are available to a person who claims to be a victim of an action that is unlawful under s 6 of the Act. The proceedings may be brought either by ordinary claim or by a claim for judicial review, and the court can award 'such relief or remedy … within its powers as it considers just and appropriate' (s 8(1)). Damages can be awarded for loss caused by action that is unlawful under s 6 if 'it is necessary to afford just satisfaction' (s 8(3)(b)— see 14.6). If primary legislation necessitates the breach of a Convention right, the breach is not unlawful under s 6, but the High Court can declare that the legislation is incompatible with the Convention (see 3.3).

- Finally, as a defendant in a civil claim or a criminal prosecution that depends on an administrative decision, you may be able to argue in your **defence to proceedings** that the decision was actually unlawful (if the decision was incompatible with the Convention, you may rely on the Convention right if you were a victim of breach of the right (s 7(1)(b))).

The naming of parties

Before the changes to the CPR,[4] a person seeking judicial review was called an **applicant**; the applicant sought **leave** to bring an **application for judicial review** of the conduct of a **respondent**. Now, a **claimant** seeks **permission** to bring a **claim for judicial review** of the conduct of a **defendant**. In ordinary proceedings before 2000, a **plaintiff** brought an **action** against a **defendant**; now a **claimant** brings a **claim** against a **defendant**. These are only changes of terminology. Since the procedural reforms in 1978, '**judicial review**' has often been used as a term for the process that used to be an application for judicial review and is now a claim for judicial review. But of course, judges review the lawfulness of governmental action in all sorts of proceedings, including tort claims (see Chapter 14) and criminal prosecutions (*Boddington v British Transport Police* [1999] 2 AC 143 (HL)).

You cannot ask the judges to apply their supervisory techniques in a claim for judicial review to control a defendant's purely private decisions. Judges can only review 'the exercise of a public function' (CPR 54.1), and much litigation has concerned the twilight zone between public decisions and private decisions (see 15.5.1). You might think that the blurred boundary between public and private functions would be the only problem about judicial procedures in administrative law, and that anyone who alleges unlawful administrative action would simply be able to pick the most convenient

---

4   The CPR were overhauled in 1998 on the basis of a report by Lord Woolf, but the judicial review procedure was left untouched until 2000: see CPR 54.

judicial process from this extravagant array, in order to vindicate the rule of law by getting the public authority in front of the High Court.

But, in fact, English law does *not* allow a judicial process for every complaint of unlawful public action. You can only bring an ordinary claim if you assert a **right of action** (that is, a right to a remedy if you prove your case, also called a 'cause of action'). Chapters 14 and 15 address claims that assert a right of action in tort and contract against public authorities.

By contrast with an ordinary claim in which the claimant asserts a right of action, no claimant has a right to bring a claim for judicial review; at the beginning of the process, the claimant must ask the court for **permission** to proceed (10.3.2). The process is also restricted by **time limits** (see 10.3.1) and a requirement of **standing** (Chapter 11). And at the end of the judicial review process, the **remedies are discretionary** (10.4.6). Only damages and *habeas corpus* are available as of right (*Jenke's Case* (1676) 6 St Tr 1189, 1207–8), and damages are only available when the claimant would have a right of action in an ordinary claim.

Why aren't the judicial processes freely available to anyone who alleges unlawful administrative conduct? Because the rule of law does not actually demand that. In fact, the rule of law requires a system that presumes that administrative decisions are lawfully effective, and brings an end to disputes about their effect. As the European Court of Human Rights put it, it is 'an important element of the rule of law . . . that the verdicts of a tribunal should be final and binding unless set aside by a superior court on the basis of irregularity or unfairness' (*Pullar v United Kingdom* (1996) 22 EHRR 391, [32]).[5]

So there is no general right to pursue a complaint against a public authority by a judicial process. The jurisdiction of the courts over administrative action is 'supervisory', but the judges are not the sort of supervisors who can decide what questions to ask. They do not inspect government departments to impose the rule of law; they resolve disputes brought against a defendant by a claimant who has standing to make a claim. Courts have to wait for a claimant to bring proceedings, and they are restricted in the form of remedies they can give. And the courts will exercise their discretion not to hear a claim if there is another remedy that will do justice. Judicial review is meant to be a last resort (see 2.7).

Just as the judges have been creative in extending the grounds of judicial review, however, they have been creative in extending their processes. The judges' attitude in the twenty-first century is the same as Lord Mansfield's attitude in the eighteenth (see the quotation at the beginning of this chapter): they want to find a way of hearing serious claims of unlawful administrative action.

A very complex tension results, between the judges' urge to curb unlawful administrative conduct and the need to adhere to the adversary system that gives judges their role *as judges* (and not as superintendents of administration). In this chapter, we will see the very real ways in which the courts' processes limit the role of judges in controlling administration. We will also see the ways in which the judges have expanded their opportunities to subject governmental conduct to the scrutiny of the courts. In

---

5   The remark concerned a judicial tribunal, but the same principle applies, for the same reasons, to administrative tribunals too.

administrative law, the ways in which disputes come to court raise the fundamental problems of accountability and comity among public authorities.

> **The judicial process problem**
>
> There is no general right to litigate a complaint that a public authority has acted unlawfully. And, in particular, there is no general right to seek judicial review. It is not enough to allege that a public authority has acted unlawfully; you also need a further reason why you are entitled to initiate a *judicial process in response to the allegation.*

The judges' discretion over every stage of their process (from permission to remedies) enables the judges to achieve **proportionate process** (see 4.4) in their own proceedings— at least, if they use their discretion responsibly. The CPR have very deliberately retained and, in fact, enhanced the judges' control over their proceedings, by establishing 'the overriding objective of enabling the court to deal with cases justly' (CPR 1.1(1)). Dealing with cases justly requires judges to make judgments of proportionality, because it includes:

> ' . . . dealing with the case in ways which are proportionate—
> (i)   to the amount of money involved;
> (ii)   to the importance of the case;
> (iii) to the complexity of the issues; and
> (iv)   to the financial position of each party. '[6]

That provision extends to the judges' judicial review jurisdiction, and it gives them responsibility for their process. This chapter introduces some of the remarkable inventions of doctrine and practice by which the courts have tried to take responsibility for a process that gives effect to the purposes of judicial control of administration.

10.2 Ordinary claims

It is a basic constitutional principle that an ordinary claim (or a criminal prosecution) can be brought against a public official in the same way as against a private defendant. Both the substance of the claim and the process are the same. The various opportunities for claimants are the same (such as the opportunity to get disclosure of information relevant to the claim from the defendant). And the protections for the defendant are the same—notably, limitation periods, and the opportunity to ask the court to strike out a claim that discloses no right of action.

But one important feature of ordinary claims has special implications for public authorities. The court may issue a declaration against a public authority, as against a private defendant. A claimant may seek a declaration without seeking any other remedy. So

---

[6]   CPR 1.1(2)(c).

claimants have long used ordinary claims for a declaration to ask the court to declare that a public authority has acted unlawfully, and to declare the public authority's legal duties. Why hasn't the ordinary claim for a declaration become the universal judicial process in administrative law? The reasons are complex; they become apparent once we understand the creative things that people have tried to do with the claim for a declaration.

10.2.1 Claims for a declaration and O'Reilly's problem

The twentieth-century classics of judicial review were not claims for prerogative remedies. *Associated Provincial Picture Houses Ltd v Wednesbury Corporation* [1948] 1 KB 223 (see 2.3) was an action against the local authority, for a declaration that a restriction on the cinema's Sunday opening was *ultra vires*. *Ridge v Baldwin* [1964] AC 40 (see 4.3.2) was an action against the members of the police authority for a declaration that Ridge's dismissal was *ultra vires*. *Anisminic v Foreign Compensation Commission* [1969] 2 AC 147 (see 9.1.2) was an action against the Foreign Compensation Commission for declarations that their determination was a nullity and that Anisminic was entitled to compensation.

Cases like these were brought as actions for a declaration (rather than as applications for judicial review) because of the short time limits for applications for judicial review, and because of restrictions on the judicial review process, imposed by the judges on the ground that the process did not involve a trial. In *Anisminic*, the plaintiff needed disclosure of the Commission's reasons, and the courts at that time did not order disclosure in applications for judicial review.[7] Given the advantages of bringing an action in those cases, should a claimant simply be able to choose the proceeding that is better suited to his or her claim? The courts allowed the actions in *Wednesbury*, *Ridge*, and *Anisminic* to proceed, without really thinking about it. But the House of Lords expressly endorsed a flexible approach in *Pyx Granite Co Ltd v Ministry of Housing and Local Government* [1960] AC 260, a case in which the Ministry claimed that the plaintiff ought to have proceeded by judicial review. Lord Goddard said: 'I know of no authority for saying that if an order or decision can be attacked by certiorari the court is debarred from granting a declaration in an appropriate case. The remedies are not mutually exclusive' (290).

In the report that led to reforms in 1978, the Law Commission said that ordinary actions should remain available, and that the reformed judicial review procedure 'should not be exclusive in the sense that it would become the only way by which issues relating to the acts or omissions of public authorities should come before the courts'.[8] The new rules of the Supreme Court in 1978 said nothing about the choice of procedure.

But the Law Lords set out to resolve the question, in *O'Reilly v Mackman* [1983] 2 AC 237. Lord Diplock attempted to bring 'speedy certainty' to administrative law. Instead of certainty, the decision generated litigation: eight other claims were argued all the way to the House of Lords, on the issue of whether judicial review should have

---

[7]   See *O'Reilly v Mackman* [1983] 2 AC 237, 280. In *Ridge*, 126, Lord Morris said that 'considerations of convenience [presumably the need for disclosure] would probably have pointed against' seeking *certiorari*. The reasons for seeking a declaration are not mentioned in *Wednesbury*.

[8]   *Report on Administrative Law Remedies*, Law Com No 73, 1976, Cmnd 6407 [34].

been used to bring the act or omission of a public authority before the courts.[9] This fiasco of judicial process was largely resolved by clever back-pedalling in a succession of House of Lords' cases. But the injustice of *O'Reilly* itself has never been put right. We will see why the Supreme Court would be justified in reversing the House of Lords' decision, if faced with a case on all fours with *O'Reilly*.

Christopher O'Reilly was serving fifteen years for robbery in Hull Prison. In 1976, there was an extremely violent four-day riot in the prison. The prisoners ransacked the canteen, assaulted prison officers, and camped out on the roof, throwing slates at the police. After the dust settled, the Prison Board of Visitors held an inquiry. They sentenced O'Reilly to a heavy penalty: 196 days in solitary confinement, and the loss of 510 days' early release. O'Reilly said he had an alibi. But the Board of Visitors would not listen to O'Reilly's witnesses. He wanted the court to declare that the decision was *ultra vires*, because he had not had a fair hearing.

How was O'Reilly to get the Board of Visitors into court? He was out of time for an application for judicial review. He could not bring an action for false imprisonment, because he was under a lawful sentence of imprisonment, and was subject to an administrative imposition of solitary confinement and to a loss of discretionary early release. He had to get a decision that those administrative and discretionary measures were unlawful. So, like the plaintiffs in *Wednesbury, Ridge*, and *Anisminic*, he commenced an action for a declaration that the Board of Visitors' decision was *ultra vires*. But the House of Lords struck out his pleading, using the High Court's common law power to prevent an abuse of its process. O'Reilly was left to spend more than six months in solitary confinement, and an extra year-and-a-half in prison, without his claim of procedural injustice being heard.

Why did the Law Lords think that it would be an abuse of process for O'Reilly to commence an action against the Board of Visitors? Once the 1978 reform had improved the application process, it seemed unnecessary to allow the kind of ordinary action for a declaration that had proceeded in *Wednesbury, Ridge*, and *Anisminic*. There had been a short, six-month limit on judicial review applications; the new improved judicial review procedure had an *even shorter* three-month deadline for applications for judicial review. If people like O'Reilly could choose between an ordinary action and an application for judicial review, then the three-month deadline would be a bit pointless: it would only mean that, after three months, he would have to bring an action for a declaration rather than an application for judicial review. Lord Diplock decided that the short time limit and the **summary** process of an application for judicial review had a purpose of bringing 'speedy certainty' to the administration, which O'Reilly's action would thwart. A summary process is a judicial process designed to resolve a dispute without a trial.

That was the gist of the House of Lords' reasoning in *O'Reilly*. Lord Diplock paid tribute to the ways in which Lord Reid had advanced judicial review in *Padfield*,[10]

9   *Cocks v Thanet DC* [1983] 2 AC 286; *Davy v Spelthorne* [1984] 1 AC 262; *Wandsworth LBC v Winder* [1985] AC 461; *Roy v Kensington & Chelsea FPC* [1992] 1 AC 624; *Mercury Communications v Director General of Telecommunications* [1996] 1 WLR 48; *Boddington v British Transport Police* [1998] 2 All ER 203; *Steed v Home Secretary* [2000] 1 WLR 1169; *Kay v Lambeth LBC* [2006] UKHL 10 [30].

10 *Padfield v Minister of Agriculture, Fisheries and Food* [1968] AC 997.

Ridge, and *Anisminic*. And he decided that now that Lord Reid had made judicial review into a *powerful* technique for control of public authorities, the judges needed to *protect* public authorities from it. He reckoned that it was fair to insist on that protection, now that the rules committee of the Supreme Court had improved the process on an application for judicial review. So he viewed it as an abuse of process, after the 1978 reforms, for the court to allow the sort of action that had proceeded in *Wednesbury*, *Ridge*, and *Anisminic*.

Table 10.1 lists the main differences between the process in an ordinary claim and a claim for judicial review.

Table 10.1 Procedures in an ordinary claim and in a claim for judicial review

	Time limit	Permission	Discovery[11]	Cross-examination	Remedies
Ordinary claim	None fixed[12]	Not required	By right	By right	Ordinary remedies (damages, declaration, injunction)
Judicial review proceedings pre-1978	Six months	Required	None in practice (the judges could have allowed it)	None in practice (the judges could have allowed it)	Prerogative orders only: *certiorari* (quashing order), prohibition (prohibiting orders), and *mandamus* (mandatory order)
Judicial review proceedings post-1978 (Order 53)[13]	Three months	Required	Available by order	Available by order	Prerogative order and ordinary remedies

[11] Discovery is disclosure of the other side's information and documents. Each side in a judicial dispute must disclose information that is relevant to the dispute, unless it is privileged.

[12] There are limitation periods on rights of action, but no time limit on the process. A court could, in principle, strike out a claim as an abuse of process on ground of delay if the delay were unfair to the defendant.

[13] The 1978 reforms were made by the Rules Committee of the Supreme Court, in Order 53; the reforms were then given statutory force in the Senior Courts Act 1981 s 31. The Supreme Court Act 1981 was renamed the Senior Courts Act 1981 by the Constitutional Reform Act 2005.

Of these changes, Lord Diplock treated the changes to discovery, cross-examination, and remedies as the removal of *disadvantages* of the old process. He treated the leave (permission) requirement and the time limit as *protections for public authorities*. His conclusion was that, given the removal of disadvantages, it had become unacceptable for a complainant to evade the protections for public authorities (*O'Reilly*, 285):

> ' . . . it would in my view as a general rule be contrary to public policy, and as such an abuse of the process of the court, to permit a person seeking to establish that a decision of a public authority infringed rights to which he was entitled to protection under public law to proceed by way of an ordinary action and by this means to evade the provisions of Order 53 for the protection of such authorities. '

The 'protection' of the time limit is the key to the *O'Reilly* problem, because it is the short three-month time limit that makes Lord Diplock's general rule *harsh*, and yet it is the time limit that seems to make the general rule *necessary*. There would be nothing wrong with a rule that a claimant cannot bring an ordinary claim if permission to seek judicial review was refused (or would have been refused).[14] But what about someone like O'Reilly, who simply wants to go to court long after the three-month limit on judicial review (in fact, four years later in O'Reilly's case)? If it is allowed, it seems to make the time limit pointless, and the judges hate to treat a provision of the rules of court— let alone the Senior Courts Act 1981—as pointless.

Speedy certainty and proportionate process

If an action has no time limit, is it an abuse of process for a claimant to proceed with an action after the time limit has run out for a *different* process? Here's how to decide: ask whether the time limit is necessary for good public administration, so that it is fair to tell a claimant that he or she can no longer drag a public authority into court three months after the claim arose. The crucial failing in Lord Diplock's reasoning is his overly general assumption that the time limit has that kind of importance to administration in all decision-making contexts. Counsel for O'Reilly argued that the action should go ahead, because the court could use its discretion to refuse a remedy if the delay amounted to 'tardy harassment' of the public authority (284). Lord Diplock's response was, in effect, that there would be a **process danger** even in letting the litigation proceed that far: it 'would defeat the public policy that underlies the grant of those protections: *viz.*, the need, in the interests of good administration and of third parties who may be indirectly affected by the decision, for speedy certainty as to whether it has the effect of a decision that is valid in public law' (284).

Sometimes, it is crucially important to the public interest (and to the private interests of third parties) to know with speedy certainty whether a public decision will stand up. The best examples come from the law of planning and compulsory purchase:

---

14   Lord Denning made this point in the Court of Appeal in *O'Reilly* [1982] 3 WLR 604, 622.

speedy certainty as to the lawfulness of a decision as to how land may be used is often essential, either in the public interest (in order for a public authority to proceed with a public building project), or for the good of private parties given planning permission, or third parties (so that they can know that the permission will not be overturned after they have invested in the project). Where an applicant for planning permission appeals to the Secretary of State against the decision of a local planning authority, the Town and Country Planning Act 1990 provides that the validity of the Secretary of State's decision must be challenged within six weeks (s 288(3)), and the Acquisition of Land Act 1981 imposes the same very short time limit for challenging compulsory purchase decisions (s 23(4)). But the shortest time limits are in the law of asylum: there is a ten-day limit on appeals from the Immigration and Asylum Tribunal to the First-tier Tribunal for persons in the UK, and a five-day limit for those in immigration detention in the UK.[15] Those short limits are imposed because of the ways in which planning, compulsory purchase, and asylum decisions affect the community and the persons subject to them. Public decisions are incredibly diverse, and they do not *generally* affect public or private interests in the same ways. So there is no *general* need for speedy certainty. In cases in which speedy certainty is unnecessary, Lord Diplock's rule represents a failure of proportionate process.

O'Reilly itself, ironically, is *a model example of a case in which speedy certainty has no value*. Imagine that the House of Lords had allowed O'Reilly to proceed with his action. The result would have been that, four years after the Prison Board of Visitors' decision, the Board would face litigation over whether it had given O'Reilly a fair hearing. If he won, he might walk out of prison earlier, on the ground that he had been unfairly deprived of time off his sentence. If a man walks out of prison early because an unfair punishment has been nullified, there is no detriment to the public interest or to the private interests of third parties. Compare a criminal conviction in the High Court: the Court of Appeal will overturn it decades later if the prisoner comes up with new evidence that exposes the conviction as a miscarriage of justice. The fact that the conviction happened years ago does not generate any public interest in keeping the prisoner in prison. In this context, speedy certainty is just not an issue. The administrative justice process by which O'Reilly was disciplined is similar to a criminal trial in this way: the public interest will not be damaged if either process is challenged years after the events in question. There is simply no general need for the speedy certainty of a three-month time limit on challenging administrative decisions.

Even though speedy certainty is not needed in O'Reilly's particular situation, it *would be* necessary to apply the rule generally, if it were impossible for courts to distinguish justly between cases in which speedy certainty is and is not needed. In fact, the Senior Courts Act 1981 presupposes it: the court may refuse to grant permission to proceed with a claim on the ground of delay *within* the three months' time limit 'if it considers that the granting of the relief sought would be likely to cause substantial hardship to, or substantially prejudice the rights of, any person or would be detrimental to good administration' (s 31(6)).

---

15 Asylum and Immigration Tribunal (Procedure) Rules 2005, SI 2005/230, r 7.

The final possible argument for refusing O'Reilly's action is that the court should not turn the time limit into a dead letter even if it is overly general (especially since the Senior Courts Act 1981 gave it statutory force). But note that, before 1978, the courts had allowed plaintiffs to evade the more generous six-month time limit on applications for prerogative orders by bringing a claim for a declaration. And Parliament's purpose in the Senior Courts Act was only to give effect to a scheme that had been worked out as a reform of the court's own rules.

Exceptions and 'exceptions'

General rules may allow exceptions; rules that are *overly* general cry out for exceptions. Lord Diplock said that: 'There may be exceptions, particularly where the invalidity of the decision arises as a collateral issue in a claim for infringement of a right of the plaintiff arising under private law' (*O'Reilly*, 285). And the courts immediately started crafting new exceptions, because the three-month time limit makes Lord Diplock's general rule harsh.

One important exception is that if legal proceedings are taken against you, you can argue in those proceedings that a public authority's decision was unlawful. The defence is a '**collateral**' (that is, indirect) **challenge** to the public authority's decision. Arguments that the defendant ought to have brought a direct challenge to the decision by judicial review have consistently failed. So it is not an abuse of process for a tenant to argue that a public authority's rent increase was unlawful, in defence to an action for the rent, even if he could have challenged it by an application for judicial review (*Wandsworth LBC v Winder* [1985] AC 461). And the validity of a public authority's decision can be challenged in a defence to a criminal prosecution (*Boddington v British Transport Police* [1999] 2 AC 143 (HL)). And European Convention arguments, which could be made in a claim for judicial review, can be used as a defence to a landlord's proceedings for possession of property (*Kay v Lambeth LBC* [2006] UKHL 10 [30]). It is unfair to expect potential defendants to take on the burden of litigating the validity of a decision. That is why the rule about defences is an exception to Lord Diplock's rule.

What is an exception?

If a rule does not apply in a class of cases, that class represents an exception to the rule if the rule *would* apply except for a special reason for not applying it in those particular circumstances; if the special reason is not compatible with the rationale for the rule itself, then the rule is, to some extent, undermined. The old saying that 'the exception proves the rule' is a confusing way of saying that you can tell that people are following a rule if they depart from its general requirements only when there are special considerations, which are compatible with the rationale for the rule.

But in the ensuing line of decisions, the House of Lords crafted so-called 'exceptions' that put the rule itself in question. It has come to be established that **any claim with a private law element** can be litigated in an ordinary claim, even where the validity of the public authority's decision was not *collateral* to a claim of right in private law, but actually *determined the extent* of the claimant's private law rights.

In *Roy v Kensington & Chelsea FPC* [1992] 1 AC 624, a health authority had reduced a doctor's pay because, they said, he had been away from his NHS practice too much (631). Dr Roy wanted to argue that health authority had misapplied the NHS regulations. He could undoubtedly have challenged the decision in an application for judicial review; instead, he brought an action (long after the three-month limit for applications for judicial review). The House of Lords allowed his action to proceed. Lord Bridge said that it didn't matter if the claim 'may incidentally involve the examination of a public law issue' (628). But the public law issue in *Roy* was not incidental (or collateral). The public law issue determined his private law entitlement to salary. In order to make his private law argument, Roy had to assert that the decision of the committee was unlawful. Roy was doing just what Lord Diplock said was an abuse of process: in an ordinary action, he was 'seeking to establish that a decision of a public authority infringed rights to which he was entitled to protection under public law' (285).

Roy left it unclear whether the rule was being confined to cases like O'Reilly's, in which the claimant has no relation with the public authority in private law. In *Mercury Communications v Director General of Telecommunications* [1996] 1 WLR 48, Lord Slynn said that flexibility was essential because 'the precise limits of what is called "public law" and what is called "private law" are by no means worked out' (57). That statement is true, but it is irrelevant to the application of Lord Diplock's rule. There was no problem of the limits between public law and private law in *Mercury*: the public law issue (whether the public authority defendant had set Mercury's charges lawfully) determined Mercury's rights in private law against BT. The important effect of the decision in *Mercury* lay in Lord Slynn's conclusion that: 'It has to be borne in mind that the overriding question is whether the proceedings constitute an abuse of the process of the court' (57). *O'Reilly* held that ordinary actions seeking 'protection under public law' for the plaintiff's rights *were* an abuse of process unless there was some exceptional reason for allowing it. After *Mercury*, it seems, there is no such general rule.

Lord Slynn's flexible approach in *Mercury* suggests that Lord Diplock's rule is no longer in effect. The rule has been distinguished away.

How to distinguish a precedent

Cases on relevantly similar facts are to be decided in the same way as previous cases, and a court that is bound by precedent (such as the High Court) is bound to treat the *ratio* of a decision as a reason for reaching the same decision on the same facts in a future case. The *ratio* is the reasoning that the court gives for its conclusion. If the facts of a new case are relevantly different from an earlier case, and if the *ratio* in the earlier case does not apply, then the earlier decision does not apply. In that situation, the earlier case *doesn't need* to be distinguished; it is not a precedent for a decision in the later case (although lawyers and judges often talk of 'distinguishing' an earlier case as if 'distinguishing' meant 'explaining why the earlier case is irrelevant').

If the facts of the new case are the same, then the earlier case cannot be distinguished.[16] If the facts of the new case are relevantly different, but the *ratio* (that is, the court's reasoning) in the earlier case applies to the new case, then the later court **can distinguish** the earlier decision. The later court does this by deciding that the difference in the facts justifies restricting the *ratio* of the earlier case so that it still applies to the earlier case, but is inapplicable to the new case.

Roy and *Mercury* are textbook cases of distinguishing. Lord Diplock's general rule applied to those cases, but the House of Lords restricted the rule, by excluding cases in which the claimant argues that a private law right was defeated by an unlawful decision of a public authority. That **does not overrule** *O'Reilly*, since the results in *Roy* and *Mercury* are consistent with the result in *O'Reilly* (*O'Reilly*, remember, had no private law right).[17] But by distinguishing *O'Reilly*, *Roy* and *Mercury* departed from Lord Diplock's general rule against seeking the protection of public law in an ordinary action.

The decision in *O'Reilly* will only be overruled if the Supreme Court expressly overrules it, or implicitly overrules it by deciding a case with the same facts differently from *O'Reilly*.

What is the effect of the twenty-first-century CPR on these developments? In *Dennis Rye Pension Fund Trustees v Sheffield City Council* [1998] 1 WLR 840, 849 Lord Woolf, who led the reforms, diverged from the general rule in *O'Reilly*: 'If the choice [of proceeding] has no significant disadvantage for the parties, the public or the court, then it should not normally be regarded as constituting an abuse.' On this approach, abuse of process is the exception that only arises in special circumstances.

And then Lord Woolf followed up with a more radical departure from the rule in *O'Reilly*, in *Clark v University of Lincolnshire & Humberside* [2000] 1 WLR 1988. A student brought an action for breach of contract against her university on grounds that could have been pursued in an application for judicial review. She claimed that the university breached its own regulations in punishing her for plagiarism [9]. The Court of Appeal rejected the university's application to strike out her claim. Following *Roy*

---

[16] It can be overruled by a higher court.

[17] O'Reilly had no private right to liberty, because he was in the middle of serving a prison sentence.

would have been enough to decide the case;[18] like Dr Roy, Joanne Clark had a contract with the public authority. But Sedley LJ and Lord Woolf changed the law in a way that took Lord Slynn's flexible approach substantially further. They focused squarely on the crucial issue of the time limit, acknowledging that the ability to bring an action rather than an application for judicial review would enable a claimant to evade the judicial review time limit. But they held that the new CPR allowed the Court to prevent exploitation of the procedures 'without resorting to a rigid exclusionary rule capable of doing equal and opposite injustice' (Sedley LJ [17]). The new Part 24 of the CPR enables the court to take delay into account in giving summary judgment in an ordinary claim, so that if a claimant brought an ordinary action after an 'unjustified delay' [35], the court could strike it out. The effect is that there *is no* general rule that an action after the three-month time limit for an application for judicial review is an abuse of process if the claimant is seeking the protection of public law [38]. More clearly than Lord Slynn had done, the Court held that no general rule governs the issue.

As a result of the CPR, Woolf LJ said: 'The emphasis can therefore be said to have changed since *O'Reilly v Mackman*.' The basic principle is 'the overriding objective of enabling the court to deal with cases justly' (CPR 1.1(1)) and, crucially, at the centre of Part 1 is the principle of proportionate process. That is just the principle that was missing in *O'Reilly*.

But the courts were already equipped to take delay into account in applications to strike out claims before the new CPR, as Woolf LJ pointed out at [33]. So the courts in the 1980s had every opportunity to give effect to proportionality. *O'Reilly* was implicitly based on a judgment that proportionality did not demand a hearing in that type of case. If Lord Diplock's general 'speedy certainty' argument were sound in 1983, it would be sound in the twenty-first century, even after the CPR.

The Court of Appeal will still have to follow *O'Reilly* today, in a case with the same facts. And, in fact, the precedent of *O'Reilly v Mackman* is still treated as prohibiting ordinary claims for a declaration if there is no private law element in the action. In *Trim v North Dorset DC* [2010] EWCA Civ 1446, [23], Carnwath LJ adhered to the principles from *O'Reilly*, 'that purely public acts should be challenged by judicial review, and that it is in the public interest that the legality of the formal acts of a public authority should be established without delay'. In *Trim*, a landowner tried to challenge a notice of breach of planning controls by an ordinary claim for a declaration, after the time limit for judicial review had run out. It was a case—unlike *O'Reilly*—in which there actually was a 'strong public interest' in speedy certainty [26].

By retreating from *O'Reilly* without overruling it, the courts have left the law in a topsy-turvy state. In a case like *Roy*, delay really does create administrative problems: the availability of an ordinary claim leaves the public authority uncertain as to its budget for years, because it cannot know whether its administrative decision will be challenged.[19] An ordinary claim is available even though speedy certainty would

---

[18] As Sedley LJ shows at [16].

[19] This problem does *not* mean that the claimant should not be able to proceed by an ordinary claim in a case like *Roy*; that depends on whether the damage to the public interest is so great that it would be fair to refuse to listen to Dr Roy after three months.

be valuable. Yet, in a case like *O'Reilly*, in which there is no need for speedy certainty (either in the public interest, or for the good of third parties), the law still forbids an ordinary claim (because no private law right was affected by the decision in that case).

The Supreme Court ought to overrule the decision if a case arises that is on all fours with *O'Reilly*. It would be unjust to send the claimant away without hearing his or her complaint of breach of procedural unfairness, because (1) hearing his or her complaint in a claim for a declaration would not damage the administration of the prison; and (2) the courts are able to distinguish between ordinary claims after the expiry of the time limit that would be damaging to the public interest and claims that would not. In a case like *Trim*, the courts could refuse to allow an action for a declaration to proceed because there actually is detriment to administration, and not because of a general rule that purely public acts cannot be challenged in an action for a declaration.

> **Why we need different forms of proceeding**
>
> (1) Summary process is reasonable for some disputes, while a trial is needed for others.
>
> (2) Some decisions should be subject to judicial review and some should not (see 15.5.1).

10.3 Claims for judicial review

A claim for judicial review is something out of the ordinary: the court decides the dispute without a trial. The point of a trial in an ordinary claim is to resolve the issues of fact on which a claim is based. The summary process in a claim for judicial review is designed on the assumption that resolving issues of fact is not the point of the litigation. The point is for the court to review the lawfulness of a public authority's conduct, and there is often no dispute as to what the public authority has done or proposes to do.

But the exceptions are numerous—perhaps increasingly numerous. Facts are often disputed in judicial review. There is a particular need for the courts to have effective fact-finding techniques in Human Rights Act 1998 cases that depend strongly on facts that are disputed (see, e.g., *R (Al-Sweady) v Defence Secretary* [2009] EWHC 2387). In *R (A) v Croydon* [2009] UKSC 8 (see 9.2.6, p 349), the defendant argued that the Court should avoid making findings of fact in a claim for judicial review because the process was 'not well suited to the determination of disputed questions of fact'. Baroness Hale responded: 'This is true but it can be so adapted if the need arises' [33].

There is ordinarily an oral hearing in a claim for judicial review (although the rules allow for it to be decided without one, if the parties agree). But the hearing is not a trial. The hearing is an opportunity for each side (and, often, intervenors) to make legal argument, on the basis of facts that have been presented on paper (and shown to the other side) in sworn witness statements. The court may allow a party to cross-examine the witnesses who made sworn statements for the other party, but cross-examination will be conducted outside the courtroom, and the judges hearing a claim for judicial review will have a written record of the cross-examination. Cross-examination ought to be ordered if there is contentious evidence on which the court needs to pass judgment in order to decide the claim.[20]

In *R (Wilkinson) v Broadmoor Special Hospital Authority* [2001] EWCA Civ 1545, a patient detained in a secure hospital challenged his doctors' decision to give him antipsychotic medication against his will (see 8.1.3, p 281). The Court of Appeal made an order that the doctors should be cross-examined. Since their evidence was contested, and the judges decided that they needed to pass judgment on the issues that the affidavits addressed, it became obvious that cross-examination should be ordered. This follows from the often-unstated principle of our adversarial system of litigation: that the court should act only on evidence presented by a party, and only after giving the other party an opportunity to contest it.

If a claim against a public authority involves a substantial dispute as to the facts, and cross-examination based on written statements is not enough to resolve it, the court can permit oral evidence at the judicial review hearing (CPR 8.6). But another possibility is for the court to transfer a claim for judicial review to the ordinary claim process, so that the facts can be determined in a trial (CPR 54.20).

10.3.1 Time

The **bad news** for claimants is that the general time limit of three months for a claim for judicial review (CPR 54.5(1)(b)) is short. The **further bad news** is that, even within the three months, the claim must be brought 'promptly' (CPR 54.5(1)(a)), which means that the court can refuse permission to bring a claim for judicial review on the ground of delay *within* the time limit. And even if permission is given, the court can later refuse the claim because of undue delay (Senior Courts Act 1981 s 31(6)).[21] But the claim can only be refused on that ground if it would damage the interests of third parties (*R v North West Leicestershire District Council, ex p Moses* [2000] Env LR 443), or 'would be detrimental to good administration' (s 31(6)).

The **good news** for claimants is that the CPR give the court an undefined discretion to extend the three-month time limit ('the court may extend or shorten the time for compliance with any rule': CPR 3.1(2)(a)).[22] But the courts will not extend the time limit just because it is hard on the claimant. In *R (M) v Oxford County Council* [2001] EWHC 245 (Admin), a group of families asked for permission to seek judicial review, three months and one day after the Council decided to close Oxford's middle schools. Jackson J refused permission, following a line of cases taking 'the firm approach' [20],

---

20 See, e.g., *R (Bancoult) v Foreign Secretary* [2012] EWHC 2115.

21 An example is *R (Corbett) v Restormel Borough Council* [2001] EWCA Civ 330 (relief denied at the judicial review hearing, partly because of the claimant's delay of three years). When this happens, it makes you wonder why the court ever gave permission in the first place. But this way of proceeding can be appropriate if the court cannot tell, at the permission stage, whether there is some good reason to listen to the claim in spite of the delay.

22 Note, though, that the time limit 'may not be extended by agreement between the parties'— an innovation in the 2000 reform to the CPR (CPR 54.5(2)). But the consent of the defendant would, no doubt, be relevant to the court's discretion to extend the time limit (CPR 3.1(2)).

especially in challenges to school reorganization. The firm approach is justified if the claim for judicial review would interfere with a public project that needs to proceed quickly. As Lord Justice Schiemann put it: 'Applicants in these school cases must realise that it is important to give early warning as to what is going on so that people can endeavour to conclude matters soon, so that the whole education system in the city is not kept in suspense while legal proceedings drag on' (*R v Leeds City Council, ex p N* [1999] ELR 324 (CA), 334). And where a claimant is out of time in challenging a decision to give planning permission for a development, the courts tend to refuse to extend the limit. In *Gerber v Wiltshire Council* (2016) EWCA Civ 84, the claimant sought judicial review to challenge the grant of planning permission for a neighbour to build a solar farm, more than a year after the permission was given; the Court of Appeal refused to extend the three-month time limit. The claimant's interest in challenging the lawfulness of the decision has to be taken into account, but it is hard to persuade the court that it outweighs the developer's interest in being able to proceed, along with the public interest in the project going ahead (Sales LJ [46]).

Yet, conversely, the courts have sometimes been generous in deciding when the clock starts running, even in cases in which there *was* a public interest in speed. In *R (Burkett) v Hammersmith and Fulham LBC* [2002] UKHL 23, Lord Steyn said, 'operation of a time limit may deprive a citizen of the right to challenge an undoubted abuse of power. And such a challenge may involve not only individual rights but also community interests, as in environmental cases' [45].

How can we square these varying tendencies to be firm and to be generous? They result from the judges' attempt to achieve proportionality in the exercise of their discretion over time limits. The really essential issue is how to reconcile the need for speedy certainty—where there is one—with the reasons in favour of hearing the claim. Those reasons may include protecting private interests from an injustice, as well as protecting the public interest in the rule of law. So Laws J had a point, in *R v Trade and Industry Secretary, ex p Greenpeace Ltd* [1998] Env LR 415, 424, when he said that 'the rule of law is not threatened, but strengthened' by 'a strict discipline' in controlling judicial proceedings in a way that brings finality to administrative decision making. The rule of law can demand finality *or* judicial review, depending on the circumstances. It requires a reasonable opportunity for people affected by an unlawful decision to get the problem before an independent reviewing court. That is compatible with time limits, even though time limits inevitably mean that some challenges to unlawful decisions cannot proceed. But the rule of law is not compatible with an arbitrary requirement of speed. The requirement is arbitrary if speed would not protect the interests of others than the claimant, and if there is no public interest in speed.

A floodgates argument that works!

Public authorities often argue that a claim should be rejected to prevent a flood of similar claims. A floodgates argument may be (1) that the courts cannot cope with the flood; or (2) that the potential defendants (or third parties) ought to be protected from the flood. Sometimes, a floodgates argument is a bad argument

because there will be no flood: the new liability may lead the potential defendants to change the behaviour that generates the claims. Even if there really will
be a flood, a floodgates argument is ordinarily a bad argument. If the claims are
just, the flood ought to flow.

So floodgates arguments are typically bad arguments.[23] But here is a good
one, which Lord Goff used in interpreting the phrase 'detrimental to good
administration' in the Senior Courts Act 1981 s 31(6). In *R v Dairy Produce Quota
Tribunal for England and Wales, ex p Caswell* [1990] 2 AC 738 (HL), a group of
farmers wanted to challenge the milk production quota that the tribunal had
assigned them. The tribunal had to share out 'a finite amount of quota' among
farmers, and the judge found on the leave application that allowing a claim
'would lead to re-opening the allocation of quota over a number of years'.
So Lord Goff held that allowing the delayed claim would have a retrospective effect on a quota scheme that needed to operate prospectively, which
would be detrimental to good administration (750). Floodgates arguments
are bad arguments, unless there is a serious process danger (see 4.2, p 125),
as in *Caswell*.

In working out the requirements of proportionate process, the courts now have to
consider whether the CPR and their own practice are compatible with the requirements of the European Convention on Human Rights. In *Burkett*, Lord Steyn not
only took a generous approach to counting the three months, but also questioned
whether CPR 54.5(1)(a), requiring the claim to be brought 'promptly' even within
the three months, is compatible with Art 6 of the Convention: '[T]here is at the
very least doubt whether the obligation to apply "promptly" is sufficiently certain to
comply with . . . the Convention' [53]. The courts have dealt with that uncertainty
by developing a doctrine that, within the three-month time limit, a claimant will
be held to have proceeded promptly unless there is an urgent public or third-party
interest in speed that ought to have been evident to the claimant. The Administrative
Court found such a public interest in *R (Liverpool City Council) v Secretary of State
for Health* [2017] EWHC 986. The claimants were local authorities who wanted to
argue that central government was unlawfully failing to provide them with enough
funding to carry out their legal obligations. They applied for permission for judicial
review two days before the end of the three months, but the Court refused permission on the ground that beginning a claim for judicial review nearly three months
after the year's allocation was made would cause such difficulties for the government's budgeting process that it was not 'prompt'.

---

[23] As, e.g., in *R v Home Secretary, ex p Doody* [1994] 1 AC 531 (HL) and *R (Javed) v Home Secretary*
[2001] EWCA Civ 789, in which the courts brushed off the Home Secretary's argument that
thousands of life prisoners (*Doody*) and asylum seekers (*Javed*) might bring claims if the courts
imposed due process.

Table 10.2 summarizes the time limits for claims in the High Court, complaints to an ombudsman, and appeals within the tribunals system.

Table 10.2 Time limits

For	Time limit
A claim for judicial review	Three months (*and* even within that time you must act promptly, *but* there is a discretion to extend the time for special reasons)
Ordinary claims for damages	Six years for most claims in tort and contract; three years for personal injury claims (Limitation Act 1980 ss 2, 5, 11)
A claim that a public authority has acted unlawfully under the Human Rights Act 1998 s 6	One year, subject to an equitable jurisdiction to extend the time (Human Rights Act 1998 s 7(5))
Complaints to an ombudsman	Twelve months (*but* the ombudsmen can decide to accept a late claim)[24]
Appeals from a First-tier Tribunal to the Upper Tribunal	Depends on the nature of the case: e.g. 3 days in asylum support cases, 56 days in tax cases, 90 days in criminal injuries compensation cases[25]

● *Pop quiz* ●

Is the three-month time limit on claims for judicial review compatible with the right to a fair hearing in Art 6 of the Convention?

10.3.2 Permission to proceed

The application for permission to proceed with a claim for judicial review is ordinarily made without a hearing. The claimant submits written evidence along with the claim form. But, in a small revolution in the CPR in 2000, the permission procedure became *inter partes* rather than *ex parte*. That is, the defendant public authority is given notice of the application for permission, and may briefly notify the court of its grounds for resisting the claim in its acknowledgement of service. A judge of the Administrative Court then decides whether to give permission on the basis of the papers (CPR Practice Direction 54.8.4). The judge has a discretion to direct an oral hearing (CPR 54.12), and a claimant who is refused permission on the papers can ask

---

[24] Parliamentary Commissioner for Administration Act 1967 s 6(3); Local Government Act 1974 s 26(4).

[25] Tribunal Procedure (First-tier Tribunal) (Social Entitlement Chamber) Rules 2008, SI 2008/2685 (L 13), r 22; Tribunal Procedure (First-tier Tribunal) (Tax Chamber) Rules 2009, SI 2009/273, r 39.

for reconsideration in an oral hearing (CPR 54.12(3)). Oral advocacy might serve to answer the judge's doubts about the claim, so the court ought to allow an oral hearing unless it is clear from the papers that oral representations would not make a difference. The 'paper hearing' has survived a claim that it was *ultra vires* and incompatible with Arts 6 and 8 of the Convention in *R (Ewing) v Department for Constitutional Affairs* [2006] EWHC 504. If there is an oral hearing, the defendant may (but need not) take part (CPR 54.9(1)(a)). The oral hearing on permission can be combined with a hearing of the claim itself in a 'rolled up' hearing (see, e.g., *R (HS2 Action Alliance) v Secretary of State for Transport* [2014] EWHC 2759).

The decision on the papers was one of two twenty-first-century innovations designed to deal with a massive volume of applications for permission. The second innovation was the **Pre-Action Protocol for Judicial Review,**[26] which encourages the parties to use ombudsmen, mediation, and early neutral evaluation (see 12.5), and states: 'The Courts take the view that litigation should be a last resort, and that claims should not be issued prematurely when a settlement is still actively being explored.' It is not a mere gesture: in *R (S) v Hampshire County Council* [2009] EWHC 2537, one of the reasons for refusing permission for judicial review was that the claimant had not followed the Pre-Action Protocol.

'Push me, pull you'

The courts are trying to encourage alternative dispute resolution (ADR), but the time limit damages the prospects! It forces claimants to start legal proceedings right away, rather than negotiate another way forward with the prospective defendant. The **Pre-Action Protocol** warns that the action it requires for trying to resolve the dispute before seeking judicial review 'does not affect the time limit' for bringing a claim.

In *R v Hammersmith and Fulham LBC, ex p Burkett* [2002] UKHL 23 [53], Lord Steyn agreed with Paul Craig's view that: 'The short time limits may, in a paradoxical sense, increase the amount of litigation against the administration.'

The requirement of permission reflects the extraordinary process: no one needs permission to bring an ordinary claim, because an ordinary claim asserts a right to a remedy. Since no one has a right to a prerogative remedy,[27] the centuries-old practice of the courts was to allow judicial review proceedings to commence only after a judge had decided to give permission. The reforms of the judicial review procedure in 1978 and 2000 have sustained that ancient practice by giving the court discretion to decide the test for permission. But the discretion is constrained—the court should deny permission if it is evident from the papers that:

---

[26] http://www.justice.gov.uk/civil/procrules_fin/contents/protocols/prot_jrv.htm.

[27] With the exception of *habeas corpus* (see 1.1.1).

- undue delay in the application will cause undue detriment to administration;

- the claimant does not have a sufficient interest in the matter of the claim (Senior Courts Act 1981 s 31(3)); or

- an alternative remedy should have been pursued, instead of judicial review.

As for any further test for permission, there is not a peep in the CPR, which only say that: 'The court's permission to proceed is required in a claim for judicial review' (CPR 54.4). Lord Diplock said that the purpose of the requirement of permission 'is to prevent the time of the court being wasted by busybodies with misguided or trivial complaints of administrative error', and to remove uncertainty (*R v IRC, ex p Federation of Self-Employed and Small Businesses Ltd* [1982] AC 617, 643). But people who are not busybodies may still be wasting the court's time. The crucial question seems to be whether the court can see, at the permission stage, that the proceedings are doomed to failure. So the most common way of describing the test for permission is to say that the claimant must have an 'arguable case' (*R v Home Secretary, ex p Swati* [1986] 1 WLR 477: '[A]n applicant must show more than that it is not impossible that grounds for judicial review exist. . . . he must at least show that it is a real, as opposed to a theoretical, possibility. In other words, he must have an arguable case' (Sir John Donaldson MR, 485)). In *R (English Bridge Union) v Sport England* [2015] EWHC 1347, Mostyn J gave permission to the claimant to challenge Sport England's refusal to recognize bridge as a sport, saying that the requirement of an arguable case was met 'by a very slender margin' [8].[28]

It seems that permission should not be denied merely on the ground that the judge thinks that the claim will probably fail, since the judge has not heard the matter. Even if there is an oral hearing on the issue of permission, it may remain unclear whether there is any prospect of success if permission is granted. Then the only appropriate course is to give permission. Permission should only be denied if the judge can see from the papers, or can conclude from oral argument about permission, that the case is unarguable.

It is hard to draw conclusions from statistics, without knowing the strength of each case. But the proportions given permission certainly suggest that the judges tend to be demanding. In 2000, 29 per cent of applications for permission were successful; that rate has noticeably declined, and in the first half of 2017, 17.5 per cent of the 1,300 applications for permission for judicial review were successful. A further 3 per cent of claimants were given permission after asking for reconsideration in an oral hearing.[29]

'Totally without merit'—a barrier to justice?

Reasonable people often seek permission for claims that have no prospect of success, because (1) the three-month time limit forces some people to seek permission

---

[28] In the end, the Administrative Court dismissed the claim: *R (English Bridge Union) v Sport England* [2015] EWHC 2875.

[29] Ministry of Justice, Civil Justice Statistics Quarterly, July to September 2016, p 16 and April to June 2017, p 7: https://www.gov.uk/government/collections/civil-justice-statistics-quarterly.

in a hurry, before they know how strong their case is; (2) the very existence of the permission process encourages people to seek permission for judicial review as part of negotiations with a public authority; and (3) even doomed litigation can generate very gratifying publicity in a campaign against the government. For an opponent of government policy, the process of applying for permission is itself a way of challenging the government. If permission is refused on the papers, the CPR allow claimants to ask for a renewed oral hearing on the question of permission, in which they can pursue that challenge further.

In 2013, the CPR were amended to rule out oral hearing on permission, where a claim is 'totally without merit' (CPR 54.12(7)). The claimant gets a fresh hearing on the papers from a Court of Appeal judge on the question of whether the case is totally without merit, but if the appeal judge then holds that the claim is totally without merit, the claimant will be refused permission without ever having had an oral hearing. In *R (Grace) v Home Secretary* [2014] EWCA Civ 1091, the Court of Appeal rejected an argument that 'totally without merit' should be restricted to claims that are vexatious (that is, claims in which the claimant is abusing the process). The Court held that, because the provision was intended to relieve public authorities from some of the pressure of responding to doomed claims for judicial review, the phrase 'totally without merit' should be interpreted to mean 'bound to fail'. Kay LJ concluded that 'CPR 54.12.7 so applied does not detract from the vital constitutional importance of the judicial review jurisdiction' [15]. It is a reminder that the law does not give unlimited opportunities to challenge the lawfulness of official action: if two judges independently decide that a claim is bound to fail, the claimant does not get a day in court.

As with the other steps taken by David Cameron's government to protect public authorities from judicial review (see 10.1), the actual effect of the new rule will depend on how the judges use their discretion. In *R (Wasif) v Home Secretary* [2016] EWCA Civ 82, Lord Dyson said that 'judges should feel no inhibition about certification when they believe the criteria are met' [18]; but he pointed out that an oral hearing gives 'an opportunity for the claimant to address the perceived weaknesses in the claim which have led the judge to refuse permission on the papers' [17]. 'Totally without merit' means something more extreme than not having an arguable case, since an oral hearing is allowed on the question of whether there is an arguable case; and 'the claimant should get the benefit of any real doubt' [17].

If the court refuses permission when it is not possible to determine justly that the claim for judicial review is bound to fail, it abdicates its responsibility for the rule of law. If the court gives permission when the claim for judicial review is bound to fail, it authorizes a costly and pointless litigation process that may prevent the defendant—and other private persons who are affected by the decision—from relying on a decision for no good reason.

And, believe it or not, the courts sometimes grant permission where they consider the claim to be of great public interest, *even where the claimant has no arguable case*. In *CND v Prime Minister* [2002] EWHC 2777, the Administrative Court gave permission for the Campaign for Nuclear Disarmament to make a claim that the Court simultaneously held to be non-justiciable, and therefore categorically unarguable: that the Prime

Minister would be violating international law if he were to order the invasion of Iraq without waiting for a specific UN resolution authorizing it (see [47] and [49]). And in *R (Gentle) v Prime Minister* [2006] EWCA Civ 1078, the Court of Appeal gave permission to seek judicial review of the government's refusal to hold an independent public inquiry into the circumstances leading up to the Iraq war. Permission was given 'not on the basis that we have concluded that the application for judicial review has a real prospect of success . . . but on the basis that because of the importance of the issues and the uncertainty of the present position there is a compelling reason' [22] to hold a full hearing of the claim for judicial review. Other important examples of doomed claims that were permitted to proceed are the *Abbasi* case (see 1.1, p 4), and *R v Foreign Secretary, ex p Rees-Mogg* [1994] QB 552 (see 11.2.1, p 421).

In such cases, the grant of permission sometimes amounts to a symbolic gesture of openness, because the court is able to dismiss the substantive claim for judicial review at the same time that it grants permission, without further procedural steps. But sometimes, as in *Gentle*, it leads to a fuller hearing in which opponents of government policy, who have no plausible argument that the policy is unlawful, suffer a legal defeat and score a media victory.

Permission to appeal

The Administrative Court can give permission to appeal to the Court of Appeal; if it is refused, the claimant can ask the Court of Appeal for permission (both decisions are discretionary). If there is no prospect of success in an appeal, the general importance of the issues may not in itself justify an appeal, even if permission for judicial review was granted. Simon Brown LJ refused permission to appeal in the *CND* case, saying, 'there comes a point in litigation when however momentous the issues raised, it cannot sensibly be permitted to continue' [64]. But in *Gentle*, the Court of Appeal reached the opposite conclusion, and granted leave to appeal on the same basis on which permission for judicial review had been given: that there was a public interest in a full hearing.

Even where permission is refused, the decision is often made after long argument and deliberation by the judges. That is what happened in *Al-Haq v Foreign Secretary* [2009] EWHC 1910. A Palestinian human rights organization claimed that the British government was violating international law and English law through its support for Israel. Permission to seek judicial review was refused, but the hearing on the application for permission gave the claimant a public forum in which to pursue its argument against the government, and it forced the government to respond. It is a classic case of the **irony of process** (see 4.13, p 157) at work: *just on the issue of permission*, the court may have to give a hearing that is out of proportion to the legal merit of the complaint. That may need to be done in order to sustain a system capable of giving litigants a fair hearing.

Costs warning!

One damper on speculative applications for permission is that a successful defendant can ask the court to order the would-be claimant to pay part of its legal costs—not only after judicial review, but also **after a failed application for permission** (*R (Mount Cook Land Ltd) v Westminster City Council* [2004] 2 P&CR 405). On the role of costs in judicial review, and the impact of the changes to costs in the 2015 reforms to judicial review, see 11.3, p 429.

Permission after the Criminal Justice and Courts Act 2015

The Cameron government's reforms to judicial review include a rule that the court cannot ordinarily give relief in a claim for judicial review where it is highly likely that the outcome would have been the same if the decision under review had been made lawfully (see 10.4.7). The legislation also provides for the court to consider that question *in the application for permission*, and to refuse permission if it is highly likely that the outcome 'would not have been substantially different if the conduct complained of had not occurred' (s 84(2)). The courts will not be quick to refuse permission on that ground, because of their general resistance to the idea that it may make no difference that a decision was made unlawfully (see 10.4.7), and also because they may find it difficult to come to a conclusion on that issue without hearing the full claim for judicial review. In *R (Logan) v Havering London Borough Council* [2015] EWHC 3193 [59], Blake J said:

> 'I do not rejoice in the prospect of having to make such assessments in cases like the present at the permission stage. It seems to me to have the potential for increasing the length, cost and complexity of the proceedings and bringing an unwelcome constraint on the court's flexible assessment of the interests of justice.'

10.4 Judicial remedies

The court's powers in judicial review proceedings are extremely flexible. From the twelfth century to the twentieth, claimants went to court seeking a particular remedy, and there were different forms of proceeding for different remedies. For all of its foibles, the 1978 reform nicely harmonized the procedures for different remedies. Declarations and injunctions and (most importantly) damages were added to the judicial review toolkit, and it no longer matters which remedy the claimant seeks. It used to be possible for a claimant to lose as a result of seeking the wrong remedy.[30] Now,

---

[30] e.g., *Re HK (an infant)* [1967] 2 WLR 962, in which the administrative decision was fairly made, so it couldn't be unwound by *certiorari* or *habeas corpus*; *mandamus* might have worked to make the officer consider new information, but it was not given, because the applicant had not applied for it.

instead of bringing proceedings for a particular remedy, a claimant simply brings judicial review proceedings, and the remedies for unlawful administrative action can be worked out as the court sees fit. And, as a result, there is a good deal of redundancy: the judges' toolkit is full of devices that can be used together or interchangeably. Some of them are very, very old, and very useful.

10.4.1 Prerogative remedies

The naming of prerogative remedies

Until 2004, a **quashing order** was called an **order of** *certiorari*, a **mandatory order** was called an **order of** *mandamus*, and a **prohibiting order** was called an **order of prohibition**.[31] Until 1938, they were all called '**prerogative writs**'.[32] But *habeas corpus* is still a writ.[33]

The double importance of the prerogative origins of the ancient common law writs is (1) that the **process** for seeking them has always been by summary application rather than the ordinary trial process; and (2) that they are issued at the **discretion** of the Crown (a discretion that the judges exercise for the Crown), as an instance of the Queen's prerogative to hold her officials to account. The orders have a statutory basis now under the Senior Courts Act 1981, but the same discretion remains under the Act and the CPR.

FROM THE MISTS OF TIME

Although the prerogative features of the writs were ancient, it seems that the first time they were grouped together and called 'prerogative' was in *R v Cowle* (1759) 2 Burr 834, 855–6; Lord Mansfield called *mandamus*, prohibition, *habeas corpus*, and *certiorari* 'Writs not ministerially directed', because they were not automatically issued by the court office at the request of a claimant to commence proceedings. He said that they were 'sometimes called prerogative writs, because they are supposed to issue on the part of the King'. Lord Mansfield was a royalist judge who wanted to emphasize that it was the King's prerogative to do justice according to law by bringing complaints of unlawful administration before his Court of King's Bench.

---

[31] Civil Procedure (Modification of Supreme Court Act 1981) Order 2004, SI 2004/1033, Art 3.

[32] The Administration of Justice Act 1938 s 7 abolished the prerogative writs of *mandamus*, prohibition, and *certiorari* (which the courts had developed at common law), and replaced them with 'orders' of the same names. The point was to signal a simplification in procedure, and *habeas corpus* was left untouched for symbolic reasons.

[33] See Rules of the Supreme Court Order 54, which is in CPR Sch 1 (not to be confused with CPR Part 54, which governs all claims for judicial review other than a claim for a writ of *habeas corpus*).

At common law,[34] the prerogative remedies largely developed as techniques by which the judges could control the jurisdiction of **inferior courts** (courts of specific jurisdiction). **Prohibition** was a way of stopping proceedings in progress before lower courts that were acting outside their limited jurisdiction.[35]

Certiorari also started as a way of controlling courts of specific jurisdiction after they had made a decision. It was actually a direction to a public authority to bring the record of its decision to the court (that is, to certify its record); the judges would then decide whether to quash the decision (see, e.g., *Ex p Stott* [1916] 1 KB 7). But it was natural to translate the name as 'quashing order' in the CPR, because '*certiorari*' had come to be used as a term for the whole business of ordering a decision to be brought up to the court and then quashing it. A *mandamus* required a public authority to use a legal power in a particular way; it was generally harder to get than *certiorari* (and the procedure was more difficult for the claimant), because the court had to decide that the law gave the public authority no choice but to act in the required fashion. *Certiorari* only quashed a decision; by *mandamus*, the court actually told the public authority what to do (although it was often simply an order to a lower court to carry out its legal duty to hear a matter). In *R v Barker* (1762) 3 Burr 1265, 1267 (see the quotation at the start of this chapter), Lord Mansfield said that *mandamus* 'was introduced, to prevent disorder from a failure of justice, and defect of police'. By 'police', he meant, roughly, public policy. Lord Mansfield viewed it as a potentially wide-ranging remedy that ought to be issued where justice and good government required it, 'from analogy and the reason of the thing' (1267).

10.4.2 Declarations

A declaration states the law on the issues in dispute. A claimant with no entitlement to any other remedy can ask the court simply to say that an action of a public authority was (or would be) unlawful. It is unlike a mere statement of the law given in reasons for judgment, because it *is* a judgment. So a declaration puts an end to the proceedings; conversely, if the claimant is unsuccessful, the court will dismiss the claim and issue no declaration.

A declaration is not exactly a remedy (it is often described as 'relief' rather than a remedy). It does not order the public authority to do this or that. Yet it changes the legal position, by making it impossible for the defendant to dispute the claimant's legal position. And it has an extremely useful remedial effect, because of the governmental practice of adhering to the law as stated in a declaration (backed, in many contexts, by the remedies that a claimant would have if the public authority were to act in a way that, according to the declaration, is unlawful). This extremely flexible judicial technique is the youngest, dating from as late as the nineteenth century. The judges had not

---

[34] But the prerogative writs were also available under the equitable jurisdiction of the Court of Chancery.

[35] e.g., *R v Horseferry Road Justices, ex p Independent Broadcasting Authority* [1987] QB 54.

been willing to issue declarations (except incidentally when making another order); they wanted to keep a tight rein on their process by ordering what was to be done, rather than merely saying what the law was.

The Court of Chancery Procedure Act 1852 s 50 authorized courts to issue declarations without any court order being sought or made. But the judges still wouldn't do it—until, in *Dyson v Attorney-General* [1911] 1 KB 410, the Court of Appeal suddenly saw its potential, and decided that a declaration was a good way to impose the rule of law on the Inland Revenue Commissioners. Dyson asked for a declaration that a demand for tax returns was unlawful, so that he wouldn't face the choice between complying, or waiting to be prosecuted. The Attorney General made a floodgates argument (see 10.3.1, p 381): listening to Dyson's claim would be inconvenient, because there would be 'innumerable other actions for declarations as to the meaning of numerous other Acts of Parliament which impose a penalty, thus adding greatly to the labours of the law officers' (413). The Court of Appeal had no sympathy for that argument. Farwell LJ pointed out that the courts had a discretion to refuse to listen to unnecessary claims (and to 'punish with costs'). But, he added, 'if inconvenience is a legitimate consideration at all, the convenience in the public interest is all in favour of providing a speedy and easy access to the Courts for any of His Majesty's subjects who have any real cause of complaint against the exercise of statutory powers by Government departments and Government officials' (423).

After *Dyson*, why didn't the declaration become the all-purpose judicial technique for dealing with unlawful conduct of public bodies? It nearly did: think of *Ridge v Baldwin*, *Anisminic*, and *Wednesbury*. A declaration was available in an ordinary action, and Anisminic and Charles Ridge got everything that they could have got through *certiorari* in judicial review. In *Anisminic*, counsel for the Foreign Compensation Commission claimed that the Court had no jurisdiction to issue a declaration, partly because of the ouster clause (see 2.7.1), and partly because, 'If a declaration can be granted here, it is hard to see why certiorari and mandamus should even be used at all' (167). The Law Lords brushed this argument aside (Lord Reid, 169, Lord Pearce, 196), and allowed declarations to coexist with the prerogative remedies.

Then, the 1978 reform made declarations available in judicial review proceedings. Since then, a declaration can accomplish anything that the prerogative remedies can. So, for example, if O'Reilly (10.2.1) had been allowed to proceed with an action for a declaration, he would have got the same result that he could have achieved in an application for *certiorari*. The prison authority could have been expected to comply with a declaration that the decision to discipline him was a nullity.

A claimant can even ask for a declaration that will determine the legal position of the Crown (Crown Proceedings Act 1947 s 21). That has to be done in an ordinary claim (against the relevant department or the Attorney General), because although the Senior Courts Act 1981 s 31(2) gives the court power to issue a declaration in a claim for judicial review, it does not give the court power to give judicial review of the Crown.

No prerogative remedies against the Crown

It is in theory the Queen who brings claims for judicial review, and she does not bring them against herself. There are no claims for judicial review called *R v R, ex p Bloggs*. In *R v Powell* (1841) 1 QB 352, 361, Lord Denman CJ said that the court could not issue the prerogative writs if there was no one against whom they could be enforced, and also that 'there would be an incongruity in the Queen commanding herself to do an act'.

But don't worry: you can seek judicial review of the conduct of the minister or other person or agency that decided on the action that was taken in the name of the Crown. It seems never to have been done until the nineteenth century, and even then only concerning exercise of statutory powers. Today, 'a distinction probably no longer has to be drawn between duties which have a statutory and those which have a prerogative source' (*M v Home Office* [1994] 1 AC 377, 417 (Lord Woolf)), and all conduct of ministers is amenable to judicial review if the issues at stake are justiciable. Examples of judicial review of ministers' actions on behalf of the Crown include *GCHQ* [1985] AC 374 and *Padfield v Minister of Agriculture, Fisheries and Food* [1968] AC 997.

CPR 54.6(1) and 25.1(1)(b) even provide for interim declarations. These seemed impossible at common law, because a declaration was meant to lay down the law, and the court did not want to do that before a hearing. But there is actually no problem: before the hearing, the court can declare the legal duties that the public authority has at that time, in light of the fact that the court has yet to resolve the issue (e.g., it can declare that the law requires the public authority to maintain the status quo until the hearing is complete).

There are, however, at least four reasons why the declaration has not become the universal remedy, as follows.

(1) **A declaration is partly redundant, since the procedure for seeking prerogative remedies has improved since *Ridge v Baldwin* and *Anisminic* were decided.** Most often a claimant challenging the act of a public authority asks for 'a declaration that the act was unlawful and/or a quashing order' (*ID v Home Office* [2005] EWCA Civ 38 [59]).[36]

(2) **A declaration binds a public authority only in the way in which any legal duty binds it, and not in the way in which a compulsory order of a court binds.** So contempt of court is only available to back up the mandatory and prohibiting orders and injunctions.

(3) **When the claimant is challenging an administrative determination of his or her legal status, a quashing order will sometimes be a complete solution in itself.** This is especially the case in judicial review of the sort of decision that the CPR call a 'judgment, order or conviction' (CPR Practice Direction 54.5). In such a case (let's call it a 'determination case'), declaratory relief (typically requested

---

36 Examples are very common: see *R v DPP, ex p Kebilene* [1999] 3 WLR 175.

along with a quashing order) will be refused as unnecessary. *R v Home Secretary, ex p Venables and Thompson* [1998] AC 407 is an example.

(4) **The court can use a quashing order to nullify an unlawful determination of the claimant's position, even if a declaration would establish that such a determination is a nullity.**

Yet the declaration is still very common, and very important. Often, in determination cases, a declaration will be added to the quashing order, to settle the basis on which any new determination would have to proceed. Several of the great Home Secretary cases have been resolved in this way (*R v Home Secretary, ex p Khawaja* [1984] AC 74 (HL); *R v Home Secretary, ex p Doody* [1994] 1 AC 531 (HL); *R (Javed) v Home Secretary* [2001] EWCA Civ 789).

And the declaration really has taken over in cases in which the court decides that the public authority has acted unlawfully, otherwise than in making a legal determination of the claimant's position. A pattern has emerged in several of these important cases: the claimant asks for a quashing order and a declaration, and the court upholds the claim, but issues a declaration alone as sufficient to accomplish the court's purpose (e.g., *R v Foreign Secretary, ex p World Development Movement* [1995] 1 WLR 386; see 8.2.2). Even in a determination case, if it is too late for a quashing order or a mandatory order to do any good, a declaration is standard. So in *R (Begum) v Denbigh High School* [2005] EWCA Civ 199, the claimant abandoned the claim for a mandatory order, and the Court of Appeal issued declarations (which were overturned when the House of Lords held that the school's conduct had been lawful—see 6.9.2).

10.4.3 Injunctions

Injunctions require someone to do or to refrain from doing something that the court describes—just like mandatory and prohibiting orders. But their history is entirely separate from the prerogative writs. Injunctions developed in equity as a judicial order in private law, to restrain a tort or other unlawful action. It offers claimants the prospect of asking the court to force a public authority not to do something the law forbids, or to do something the law requires.

But injunctions should be unnecessary in administrative law, given the jurisdiction to issue mandatory orders and prohibiting orders. The use of injunctions in public law reflects the haphazard history of procedural drawbacks in the judicial review procedure. Before the 1978 reforms, actions for an injunction were used where the plaintiff wanted to obtain disclosure and cross-examination. But they had their own drawbacks; a special requirement of standing prevented them from playing a major role in the development of public law. Since 1978, they have been available in claims for judicial review, with the same relaxed standing requirement as all judicial review remedies. They can be useful because the court can grant an interim mandatory injunction (in exceptional circumstances) but, it seems, not an interim mandatory order.[37] And, since *R v Transport*

---

[37] *R v Kensington and Chelsea Royal LBC, ex p Hammell* [1989] QB 518 (to get an interlocutory mandatory injunction, the claimant must have permission to proceed with judicial review, and a very strong *prima facie* case).

Secretary, ex p Factortame (No 2) [1991] 1 AC 603 and *M v Home Office* [1994] 1 AC 377, it has been possible to get an interim injunction against a minister of the Crown (that is, an injunction issued before the dispute is resolved, to prevent the irreparable damage to the parties' interests that might otherwise be caused in the meanwhile).

10.4.4 Damages

The 1978 procedural reform provided for the award of damages in judicial review. In 2004, the legislation was amended to allow 'restitution or the recovery of a sum due' as well,[38] so that debts of public authorities can be pursued by an ordinary claim.[39] But, crucially, the court must be satisfied 'that such an award would have been made if the claim had been made in an [ordinary] action begun by the applicant at the time of making the application' (Senior Courts Act 1981 s 31(4)(b)). So the change did not impose any new liabilities on public authorities. There is no general right to compensation for loss caused by unlawful action (see 14.2). To obtain damages in judicial review, the claimant must show 'a cause of action sounding in damages' (*R v Deputy Governor of Parkhurst Prison, ex p Hague* [1992] 1 AC 58, 155), just as if the proceeding were an ordinary claim. And damages can only be sought in a claim for judicial review if the claimant is also seeking one of the prerogative remedies, or a declaration, or injunction (CPR 54.3(2)).[40] So simple claims in tort or contract, in which the claimant does not allege any wrong on the part of the public authority other than the tort or breach of contract, must still be conducted through an ordinary claim. Note that many tort claims—especially in misfeasance in public office, and breach of statutory duty— depend on an argument that a decision of a public authority was unlawful in ways that would give grounds for judicial review. In such a case, the claimant can proceed with an ordinary claim in tort without asking the court for a quashing order or declaration.

For the grounds on which damages will be awarded against public authorities, see Chapter 14.

Substitutionary remedies

In 2000, a far-reaching provision for a 'substitutionary remedy' was added to the CPR (CPR 54.19(3)), authorizing the Administrative Court to step in and make the decision that the public authority should have made if 'there is no purpose to be served in remitting the matter to the decision-maker'. The court does not have to require a new and wasteful administrative justice process if it is unnecessary, but can resolve the dispute straight away at the point at which it decides that the initial administrative decision cannot stand.

---

[38] Civil Procedure (Modification of Supreme Court Act 1981) Order 2004, SI 2004/1033, Art 4(4).

[39] See *Dennis Rye Pension Fund Trustees v Sheffield City Council* [1998] 1 WLR 840, 849–51 for the problem that was solved by this reform.

[40] See discussion in *ID & others v Home Office* [2005] EWCA Civ 38 [58].

10.4.5 Contempt of court

Contempt of court is either an interference with court process, or a refusal to abide by the requirements of a court order. When it is done by a public authority, it shows what you might call a criminal lack of comity toward the court.

In 1922, the High Court imprisoned thirty Labour councillors from Poplar (a very poor borough in what is now part of Tower Hamlets in east London) for contempt (*R v Poplar Borough Council, ex p London County Council (No 2)* [1922] 1 KB 95). They had refused to obey a *mandamus* issued by the High Court to force the borough to pay contributions to London County Council expenses (*R v Poplar Borough Council, ex p London County Council (No 1)* [1922] 1 KB 72). Poplar Council had withheld the contributions on the ground that structural injustices in the rates system left them unable to help the poor in their borough, while requiring them to make disproportionate contributions to the costs of services for London, in a scheme that favoured rich boroughs. The Poplar councillors wanted to spend the money fighting tuberculosis, distributing free milk, and paying the Council's own employees (both men and women) a minimum wage of £4 per week.

The Poplar councillors would not cooperate even after being held in contempt, and they spent six weeks in prison before the government backed down and reformed the contribution system. The fiasco shows (1) that court orders in public law can be backed by coercion; (2) that the prerogative remedies can get extremely personal (it was a public authority—the Council—that failed to levy the necessary rates and pay the contributions, but the *mandamus* was addressed personally to the human beings on the Council); and (3) that even a conviction for contempt and imprisonment itself may be used as tools in a political campaign.

Action that is incompatible with the legal position as stated in a declaration is not contempt of court; it is only unlawful conduct. But failure to comply with a mandatory order, a prohibiting order, or an injunction is a contempt of court. The court can punish contempt with a fine or imprisonment.

And public authorities are also constrained by the rule that impeding the process of the courts is contempt. In *Raymond v Honey* [1983] 1 AC 1 (HL), a prison governor intercepted a prisoner's letter to his solicitor. As a result, the prisoner wrote up an application to have the governor committed to prison for contempt of court; he asked for it to be delivered to the court, but the governor stopped that package from being delivered as well. The House of Lords held that it was not proven that intercepting the first package was a contempt. But 'any act done which is calculated to obstruct or interfere with the due course of justice, or the lawful process of the courts, is a contempt of court' (Lord Wilberforce, at 10), so it was a contempt of court for the prison governor to stop the prisoner from writing to the court to commence a proceeding. The fact that he was acting in a public office did not help the prison governor at all.

The courts exercise the judicial power of the Crown, and it has always been accepted that the Crown cannot hold itself in contempt of court. That doctrine would represent a failure of the rule of law, if it could be used as a shelter for government to ignore court orders. But a minister exercising a power on behalf of the Crown can be held in contempt in his or her capacity as a minister. After many centuries of English legal history, it was done for the first time in *M v Home Office* [1994] 1 AC 377. A High Court judge had issued an injunction against the Home Office to prevent the deportation of an asylum seeker until his case had been heard; the Home Office proceeded with the deportation, and the Court declared that the Home Secretary was in contempt of court. The House of Lords upheld that decision, and rejected 'the proposition that the executive obey the law as a matter of grace and not as a matter of necessity, a proposition which would reverse the result of the Civil War' (Lord Templeman, 395). But a minister still cannot be imprisoned for contempt. Lord Woolf said (at 425) that:

> the Crown's relationship with the courts does not depend on coercion and in the exceptional situation when a government department's conduct justifies this, a finding of contempt should suffice. In that exceptional situation, the ability of the court to make a finding of contempt is of great importance. It would demonstrate that a government department has interfered with the administration of justice. It will then be for Parliament to determine what should be the consequences of that finding.

Costs as a sanction against government

In *R (YA) v Home Secretary*, 23 August 2017 (Administrative Court, unreported), the Court had ordered the Home Office to release an asylum seeker from detention within fourteen days of the order and to provide him with housing; it took more than four weeks, and the Home Office did not give the written reasons for the failure that the judge had ordered it to give. Nicola Davies J responded by ordering 'indemnity costs' (that is, a special order of costs to pay legal expenses that are not usually covered in court-ordered costs). That amounted to a symbolic penalty for non-compliance with the court's decision.

● *Pop quiz* ●

Would it have been justifiable for the Court to hold the Home Secretary in contempt in the *YA* case, on the basis of *M v Home Office*?

10.4.6 Judicial discretion over remedies

In an ordinary claim, a claimant who establishes a cause of action has a right to a remedy (whether the defendant is a public authority or a private person). But the remedies available in judicial review are discretionary.[41] In *R (Hurley) v Secretary of State for Business Innovation & Skills* [2012] EWHC 201, sixth-form students challenged the government's decision to allow universities to raise undergraduate fees to £9,000 per year. The

---

[41] It is a discretion *of the court*, and not of the Administrative Court judges. So the Court of Appeal and the Supreme Court will not defer to the decision of the Administrative Court, but will 'exercise the discretion which ought to have been exercised in the first instance' by the Administrative Court (*R v IRC, ex p Federation of Self-Employed and Small Businesses Ltd* [1982] AC 617, 664 (Lord Roskill)).

Administrative Court held that the government had failed in its legal duty under anti-discrimination legislation to consider the impact on disadvantaged groups (see 8.3.2). But the court refused to quash the decision to allow the fee rise, Elias LJ saying, at [99]:

> ' . . . all the parties affected by these decisions—Government, universities and students—have been making plans on the assumption that the fees would be charged. It would cause administrative chaos, and would inevitably have significant economic implications, if the regulations were now to be quashed. '

As a result, although the court issued a declaration that the Secretary of State failed to carry out the equality duties, it decided that quashing the decision would not be a 'proportionate remedy' [99]. Elias LJ emphasized that the Secretary of State had engaged in an 'appropriate analysis' in setting the higher fee cap, and also that the decision might have gone the other way if the breach of the equality duties had been more significant.

Likewise, the court has discretion whether to grant a declaration in an ordinary claim, as Lord Diplock pointed out in *O'Reilly*: '. . . the remedy by way of declaration of nullity of the decisions of the board was discretionary—as are all the remedies available upon judicial review' (*O'Reilly v Mackman* [1983] 2 AC 237, 284).

Discretion is the same thing when judges have it as when other public authorities have it: a power to choose one way or another with legal effect, with no legal duty to make one choice rather than another. A power may be discretionary even though the law controls its exercise, as long as the law does not require a particular result. The court's discretion may be taken away by any rule of law that requires a particular result. To understand the discretionary nature of the remedies, you need to consider the reasons for it, and the constraints the law imposes on it.

Reasons for discretion in remedies

(1) An ordinary claim vindicates claims of right; the remedies in judicial review vindicate claims that a public authority has acted unlawfully. And what, if anything, the public authority should do to put things right partly depends on the public interest.

(2) Judicial review is (and has been since the Middle Ages) a proceeding through which the state controls itself; the form of control ought to depend on the implications of unwinding an administrative course of action.[42]

(3) The court's discretion over remedies is justified by the same considerations that justify its discretion over whether to give permission for judicial review.

---

[42] But note that one way in which the state must control itself is by assuring that its agencies respect the legal rights of persons affected by its decisions. So *some* claims for judicial review vindicate the legal rights of the claimant. In *Ridge v Baldwin* [1964] AC 40 (see 4.3.2), Charles Ridge had a right to a fair hearing before being dismissed, and it could be pursued either in an application for a prerogative remedy against unlawful conduct, or in an action for a declaration of his legal right.

Constraints on discretion in remedies

The judges' discretion over remedies, like administrative discretions, is:

- **limited** (there are many cases in which it would be improper not to give a remedy);

- **supervised** (by the availability of appeals to the Court of Appeal and Supreme Court); and

- **regulated** (by the law on the particular point in issue).

It may seem that a decision such as *Hurley* involves a failure in the rule of law, since unlawful conduct by officials may not result in any judicial remedy. But on the contrary, the rule of law does not demand that the legal system's response to a breach of the law should ignore the consequences of quashing a decision (see 10.4.8). The rule of law is compatible with what Elias LJ in *Hurley* called 'proportionate remedies'. Likewise in *R (Moseley) v Haringey LBC* [2014] UKSC 56 (see 1.6.1), the Supreme Court issued a declaration that the Haringey Council had acted unlawfully in conducting a legally required consultation over its scheme to deal with council tax reductions. But the Court refused to order a new consultation: Lord Wilson held that 'it would not be proportionate to order Haringey to undertake a fresh consultation exercise in relation to a [scheme] which will have been in operation for two years and which it is not minded to revise' [33].

And in that judgment of proportionality, the remedy requested may even be weighed against the claimant's own conduct. In *R (Youssef) v Secretary of State for Foreign and Commonwealth Affairs* [2016] UKSC 3, the claimant challenged the lawfulness of the Foreign Secretary's participation in a process by which the United Nations added him to a list of persons associated with Al Qaeda (and therefore subject to sanctions). But it was established in the litigation that the claimant was 'at least a strong vocal supporter of Al-Qaida and its objectives' [61]. Lord Carnwath said that 'Judicial review is a discretionary remedy',[43] and held that 'Even if the appellant were otherwise entitled to some relief, I would be very hesitant about granting it so long as these allegations stand unrefuted' [61].

But is it really discretion?

Concerning the decision whether to quash a planning permission, Sedley LJ has said: 'I am hesitant to treat a decision so fraught with basic principles as one simply of discretion. It seems to me . . . to be better described and regarded as a matter of judgment' (*R (Corbett) v Restormel Borough Council* [2001] EWCA Civ 330 [29]).

---

43   It is not unusual to find judges calling judicial review a 'remedy': see Lord Woolf in *M v Home Office* [1994] 1 AC 377, 417. See also *R v Inland Revenue Commissioners, ex p National Federation of Self-employed and Small Businesses* [1982] AC 617, 639: 'judicial review is a remedy that lies exclusively in public law'. That is shorthand for saying that judicial review is a proceeding in which the court decides whether to give a remedy.

The important truths are that legal principle will, in all cases, forbid *some* conceivable remedial decisions (and the court has no discretion to make those decisions) and may, in some circumstances, demand a particular remedial decision (and then the court has no discretion in that particular situation). The *power* is discretionary because in some cases, the legal principles at stake allow the judge to decide either way without acting unlawfully. And the fact that it is a matter of judgment does not mean that it is not a matter of discretion; it is *both*, if the law leaves to the judge a choice that must be exercised with judgment. All discretionary powers are like this—including administrative discretions (see 7.2.2), and other judicial discretions (e.g., as to sentence after a criminal conviction, or as to costs). They must be used responsibly, and in some cases there may be only one way to exercise them, so that there is no discretion in the particular case.

Discretion and remedies under the Human Rights Act 1998

Declarations of incompatibility under the Human Rights Act 1998 are discretionary (*Lancashire County Council v Taylor* [2005] EWCA Civ 284 [42] (Lord Woolf)). Section 4(2) provides that if a statute is incompatible with the Convention rights, the court 'may' make a declaration of incompatibility. Lord Neuberger emphasized the court's discretion as to whether to grant a declaration under s 4(2) in *R (Nicklinson) v Ministry of Justice* [2014] UKSC 39, [114], adding, 'the power to grant declaratory relief is anyway inherently discretionary'.

By contrast, s 6 is not written in discretionary terms: 'It is unlawful for a public authority to act in a way which is incompatible with a Convention right', unless primary legislation requires it (see 3.3). Yet here, too, if a claimant establishes that a decision was unlawful under s 6, the remedies for the unlawfulness remain in the discretion of the court (s 8—the court 'may grant such relief or remedy, or make such order, within its powers as it considers just and appropriate').

Section 3 says that legislation 'must' be given effect in a way that is compatible with Convention rights, so far as possible. That provision gives no express discretion, but by leaving the court to decide what is possible, it gives a far-reaching resultant discretion (see 7.2.1). Section 4(4) gives an implied discretion concerning declarations of incompatibility: it states that '[i]f the court is satisfied . . . it may make a declaration of that incompatibility'.

How can remedies under the Human Rights Act 1998 be discretionary if their whole point is to vindicate rights? The Convention itself delegates the remedial responsibility to contracting states, and allows a discretion in carrying it out. The Strasbourg Court affords a margin of appreciation (see 3.7) in applying Art 13 of the Convention, which requires 'an effective remedy before a national authority' for victims of a violation of Convention rights: *Vilvarajah v United Kingdom* (1992) 14 EHRR 248 [122].

Collateral effects of unlawful administrative actions

Although the power to give a remedy at common law or under the Human Rights Act 1998 s 8 is discretionary power, the court does not have discretion over the effects of unlawfulness. If, for example, a by-law were contrary to a Convention right, or unlawful according to the rule in *Kruse v Johnson* [1898] 2 QB 91 (see 7.1), the court would have no discretion to uphold a conviction under it. And remember *Cooper v Wandsworth Board of Works* (see 4.1): once it was decided that the decision to tear down Cooper's house was unlawful, the Court had no discretion to decide that the Board of Works had a defence to the tort of trespass.

10.4.7   What if a legal flaw in a decision made no difference to the outcome?

In the Cameron government's initiatives to protect government agencies from judicial review, there is one that goes to the heart of the role of the courts. The Criminal Justice and Courts Act 2015 requires courts to refuse relief in a claim for judicial review, 'if it appears to the court to be highly likely that the outcome for the applicant would not have been substantially different if the conduct complained of had not occurred' (s 84).[44]

The courts' discretion over remedies always implied that they could refuse to quash a decision if it would be pointless to do so. The fact that a decision maker did something unlawful in the course of making a decision has never meant that the decision must automatically be quashed. For example, when a tribunal gives various reasons for rejecting a claimant's evidence, and some of those reasons are unlawful, the question will 'normally' be 'whether one can be tolerably confident that the tribunal's decision would have been the same on the basis of the reasons which have survived its scrutiny' (*HK v Home Secretary* (2006) EWCA Civ 1037 [45] (Lord Neuberger)). It would be a massive excess of legalism, rather than success in achieving the rule of law, if the courts thought that unlawfulness in the making of a decision should automatically lead to quashing the decision.

Yet, before the 2015 Act, it was a matter for the courts' exercise of discretion. And they had generally been inclined to quash a decision that had been made unlawfully, in spite of arguments by defendants that the unlawfulness made no difference. In *R (Mavalon Care Ltd) v Pembrokeshire County Council* [2011] EWHC 3371 [61], Beatson J said:

> ' The court does not ask whether the decision-maker would, or probably would, have come to a different conclusion. It only has to exclude the contrary contention, that the decision-maker necessarily would still have made the same decision. '

----

44   The Act provides that relief can be given for 'reasons of exceptional public interest' (s 84(1)), in spite of this duty.

In the Criminal Justice and Courts Act, Parliament took away this element in the judges' discretion, and imposed a duty on them: where it is 'highly likely' that the result would have been the same if the decision had been made lawfully, the court 'must refuse to grant relief' (s 84(1)).

In the case of some legal flaws in a decision-making process—such as failure to give a hearing, or failure to give reasons, or failure to comply with a Public Sector Equality Duty (see 8.3.2)—the new legislation means that lawyers for public authority defendants should always consider asking the court to hold that it is highly likely that the decision would have been the same without the legal flaw. The judges will no doubt seek to comply with their duty: for example, in *R (Hawke) v Secretary of State for Justice* [2015] EWHC 4093, in refusing to transfer a prisoner to a prison closer to the home of his disabled wife, the Court held that the Secretary of State had failed to carry out his Public Sector Equality Duty. When counsel informed him of the new rule in the Criminal Justice and Courts Act, Holman J concluded, 'I am . . . forbidden by statute from granting the declaration which in paragraph 47 above I had previously contemplated granting' [327]. But he said that the Secretary of State had acted unlawfully, and he added that just saying so was a 'declaratory judgment', even though he was prohibited from issuing a formal declaration.

It is evident that the judges will approach their new statutory duty with a tendency to think that unlawfulness makes a difference. In *R (Logan) v Havering London Borough Council* [2015] EWHC 3193 [55], Blake J expressed this attitude, saying that 'it would undermine the efficacy of judicial review as an instrument to ensure that the rule of law applies to decision making by public authorities' if a defendant could say that the unlawfulness made no difference. He added, 'It may well be that the new provision was only intended to apply to somewhat trivial procedural failings that could be said to be incapable of making a material difference to the decision made' [55]. Taken at face value, that would mean that the 2015 Act has made no change to the common law as stated by Beatson J in the *Mavalon Care* case. Parliament's evident purpose of restricting judicial review means that the Act ought to be understood to have changed the common law. But it is justifiable for the judges to conclude that they are only barred from granting relief where it is very clear that the decision maker would have reached the same conclusion if it had acted lawfully.

10.4.8 The nullity paradox

Since *Ridge v Baldwin* in 1964, the judges have viewed an unlawful decision as a nullity. When a court issues a quashing order, or a declaration that a decision was unlawful, the court is not overturning a decision that was valid when it was made. It is deciding that there never was any valid decision.

And then, you might say, if some action of a public authority is held to have been unlawful (like the decision to sack Ridge), the judges cannot possibly have any discretion over remedies. It seems contrary to the rule of law for anyone to have a discretion to let an unlawful decision stand. Lord Hobhouse said that this puzzle about nullity is a paradox, because it presents the possibility of 'the illegal act which the court nevertheless does not restrain, the ultra vires act which is nevertheless effective' (*Attorney-General's Reference (No 2 of 2001)* [2003] UKHL 68 [122], and see his speech in *Crédit Suisse v Allerdale Borough Council* [1997] QB 306, 350).

A **paradox** is a chain of reasoning that seems to be sound, but seems to lead to a contradiction. Here, the premise that a decision was unlawful, plus the premise that a court has discretion over remedies, seems to lead to contradiction: that a court of law can give legal effect to an unlawful decision. As in all paradoxes, the contradiction in this one is only apparent.

If there is ground for judicial review of a decision, then the decision is unlawful—that is, the process by which it is made, or its substance, does not meet the standards that the law imposes. But that does not determine what is to be done about it. The paradox seems to arise only because it seems that if a decision was unlawful, the court *just must* hold that it has no legal effect.

The appearance of paradox is heightened by the fallout from *Anisminic v Foreign Compensation Commission* [1969] 2 AC 147. Lord Reid held that the Commission's decision was a nullity, because the error that he found in the Commission's interpretation of the compensation regulations meant that it had reached its decision without jurisdiction. And Lord Diplock[45] transformed that holding into a doctrine that any administrative decision is a nullity if it is based on an error of law. And in *R v Lord President of the Privy Council, ex p Page* [1993] AC 682, 701, Lord Browne-Wilkinson extended this doctrine into a uniform view that administrative action in general is *ultra vires* if it is based on an error of law, or made 'in a manner which is procedurally irregular or is *Wednesbury* unreasonable'. Then, it seems, wherever there is ground for judicial review of an administrative decision, the decision is a nullity (and not a decision at all).[46] It is like a counterfeit £20 note: a counterfeit £20 note is *not* a £20 note.

The artificial reasoning generated by the ouster clause in *Anisminic* has become the general orthodoxy of administrative law today: the orthodoxy is that any ground of judicial review makes an administrative decision a nullity. But the decision does not count as a nullity in law unless a court determines that it was a nullity. And judges have discretion not to issue a declaration or a quashing order even if a decision *was* a nullity. *Except* as regards ouster clauses, the orthodoxy is no different in effect from a doctrine that decisions are valid unless a court decides to invalidate them. The orthodoxy supports Lord Reid's technique for evading ouster clauses (see 2.7.1).

The orthodoxy seems to suggest that there is nothing to be done about an unlawful decision but to declare it a nullity. But in fact, the judges have held on to the principle that, in the interests of the rule of law itself, they need to control their process by retaining discretion in remedies. The solution to Lord Hobhouse's paradox is that, strange as it may seem, the rule of law may actually require that the law courts should give legal effect to a decision that was not legally valid.

---

[45]   In *Re Racal* [1981] AC 374 and *O'Reilly v Mackman* [1983] 2 AC 237 (see 9.1.2, p 321).

[46]   Lord Browne-Wilkinson, cited in *In re Daws* (1838) 8 Ad & E 936. In fact, the idea may be as old as the seventeenth century: Sir Edward Coke said, in the *Case of Proclamations* (1611) 12 Co Rep 74, 'we do find divers precedents of proclamations which are utterly against law and reason, and for that void'.

In *R (Corbett) v Restormel Borough Council* [2001] EWCA Civ 330, a council was held to have given planning permission unlawfully. The Environment Secretary modified the permission—which stopped the development, but potentially entitled the landowner to compensation. A councillor asked the Court to decide that 'the permission which had been unlawfully granted should be treated as though it had never had any legal existence' [15]—so that the council would not be on the hook for compensation. Schiemann LJ saw 'a certain elegance' [15] in the argument, but pointed out that it had to be qualified to account for the Court's remedial discretion, and for the potential that justice might demand protection of reliance induced by unlawful decisions. He said that the **principle of legal certainty** and the **principle of legality** may clash with each other [16]; the elegance of the principle of legality led him to conclude that an unlawful decision is to be quashed on judicial review 'unless the person resisting the quashing can show at least that he would be harmed by the quashing or some other reason is shown for not striking down' [17]. Sedley LJ, likewise, held that quashing is 'the usual consequence of illegality in public law' [34], but that it should not be done in *Corbett* (chiefly because of the landowner's reliance on the unlawful planning permission).

Corbett shows the complex orthodoxy at work:

(1) if any of the grounds of judicial review apply to a public authority's decision, the decision is a nullity;[47] but

(2) there is a presumption of validity;[48] that is, no public authority's decision is to count as a nullity unless a court decides (in a proceeding that is brought properly) to treat it as a nullity; and

(3) there is a further presumption that the court will treat such a decision as a nullity (if a proceeding is properly brought to challenge its lawfulness); although

(4) the court has discretion not to do so where there is special reason.

Sometimes, by contrast with *Corbett*, the judges seem to conclude that the paradox of nullity is unavoidable, so that a decision that was *ultra vires* just cannot conceivably be given legal effect. This happened in the Supreme Court in *Ahmed v Her Majesty's Treasury* [2010] UKSC 5. The Treasury had used a statutory power to issue orders freezing assets of suspected terrorists; the Supreme Court struck down the orders on the ground that they were not authorized by the statute. The Treasury asked for the Court's judgment to be suspended for six weeks, to make it possible to propose legislation to Parliament that would lawfully freeze the assets. Lord Philips for the majority

----

47 Compare the view of Sedley LJ in *R v Higher Education Funding Council, ex p Institute of Dental Surgery* [1994] 1 WLR 242, 259, that violation of a public authority's legal obligation, such as an obligation to give reasons, is 'a ground of nullity'.

48 It is called 'the presumption *omnia praesumuntur rite esse acta* [everything is presumed to have been done properly]' (*Inland Revenue Commissioners v Rossminster* [1980] AC 952, 1013 (Lord Diplock)). The presumption is that the public authority subject to judicial review acted *intra vires*. It can be displaced by showing any ground of judicial review, but that can only be shown if the claimant has standing and proceeds in time, etc.

held that because the orders were 'ultra vires and of no effect in law' the 'object of quashing them is to make it quite plain that this is the case'. As a result, since the Court had decided that the orders were invalid, the Court would only be 'obfuscating' its judgment if it were to suspend its order (*Ahmed*, judgment as to remedy [4]–[5]). There was no mention in the majority reasons of the cases in which unlawful decisions have been given legal effect (such as *Corbett*—see 10.4.6—or *Hurley*—see 8.3.2).

Ahmed can be read as impliedly holding that no unlawful decision can be given lawful effect. That would destroy a significant element of the courts' discretion as to remedies, and it may be better to interpret *Ahmed* (as Lord Hope did, in his dissent on the issue of the suspension of the judgment, at [18]) as an *exercise* of that discretion, based on the Court's conclusion in the particular case that it would not be appropriate to suspend the effect of its judgment.

The orthodox set of doctrines is capable of achieving the right approach to remedies, *in spite* of the confusing language of nullity generated in *Ridge* and *Anisminic*, and the ruling in *Ahmed*. But the confusing language of nullity does not help. The same results could be achieved more straightforwardly without using the idea of nullity at all as a part of the courts' technical equipment,[49] on the following basis.

(1) If any of the grounds of judicial review apply to a public authority's decision, then it was unlawful for the public authority to make the decision that it made.

(2) The court has discretion to deal with the unlawfulness in a way that is just and in the public interest, taking into account the legitimate interests of the claimant, and any effect on parties who reasonably relied on the decision, and considerations of good administration.

That approach would enable the courts to do the right thing in extraordinary cases like *Corbett*.

A holding of invalidity is the law's response to unlawful conduct

The core question that the courts need to ask is **whether the decision under review was unlawful**. The only other question they need to ask is **what response the rule of law requires** to unlawful conduct, in the circumstances. The courts do not need to ask whether the decision was void, and the idea that an unlawful decision is a nullity *is not useful for their purpose*. Where it is justifiable to treat a decision as invalid, that conclusion follows from the first two steps: that the decision under review was unlawful, and that, in the circumstances, the rule of law requires that the court respond to the unlawfulness by treating the decision as ineffective. If the courts call an unlawful decision a 'nullity', then they need to have a doctrine that a court still has discretion to treat a nullity as having legal effect.

---

[49] *Except* that Lord Reid's treatment of ouster clauses in *Anisminic* really does require the nullity technique: in order to get around a statute that protected a decision from judicial interference, he had to say that there was no decision.

As Lord Radcliffe said, in *Smith v East Elloe Rural District Council* [1956] AC 739, 769:

> An order, even if not made in good faith, is still an act capable of legal consequences. It bears no brand of invalidity upon its forehead. Unless the necessary proceedings are taken at law to establish the cause of invalidity and to get it quashed or otherwise upset, it will remain as effective for its ostensible purpose as the most impeccable of orders.

10.5 Conclusion

Why do the names of judicial review cases begin with 'R' for *Regina*? It leads judges to make quite divergent remarks about what is going on in judicial review:

> In judicial review proceedings there is no true *lis inter partes* or suit by one person against another. [50]

> In reality, such proceedings represent a contest between the applicant, who both initiates and pursues the proceedings, and the authority against which the proceedings are brought. Judicial review proceedings are brought neither by nor at the instigation of the Crown. [51]

These statements reflect important aspects of judicial review, but both are wrong, in a sense: there really *is* a dispute between parties in a claim for judicial review. The proceeding is brought by the Crown against the defendant, on behalf of the claimant. And it isn't merely old-fashioned to say that the Crown brings the proceedings; it reflects the nature of judicial review in the twenty-first century. It is an extraordinary process which, in the public interest, is made available (if the court exercises its discretion to give permission) to a claimant who does not need to have a right of action. And the remedies—even where a public authority is shown to have acted unlawfully—are in the discretion of the court. The principle is still as Lord Mansfield put it: that the courts ought to use their remedial powers 'upon reasons of justice . . . and upon reasons of public policy, to preserve peace, order, and good government' (*R v Barker* (1762) 3 Burr 1265, 1267). When the courts have an overly general concern not to interfere with the administration (as in *O'Reilly v Mackman* [1983] 2 AC 237), the result is injustice. When they forget that not every unlawful action demands a judicial process, the result is a lack of comity toward other public authorities.

---

50 *R v Stratford-on-Avon District Council, ex p Jackson* [1985] 1 WLR 1319, 1323 (May LJ). So issue estoppel (the rule that a party may not raise an issue in litigation that has been decided in previous litigation between the same two parties) does not operate in judicial review (*R v Environment Secretary, ex p Hackney LBC* [1984] 1 WLR 592 (CA)).

51 *R (Ben-Abdelaziz) v Haringey LBC* [2001] 1 WLR 1485 [29] (Brooke LJ).

The extraordinary discretionary power of the judges over the process has a principled basis: the rule of law does not generally demand *or* forbid the provision of a judicial process for remedying unlawful official conduct. The rule of law *does* demand a judicial process, where that is what it takes to prevent arbitrary government, or to give a remedy to a claimant where one is due. The rule of law demands the processes that are best for those purposes. And so the judges must be prepared to use their various discretions for the purpose of preventing arbitrary government. That means, for example, never refusing permission for judicial review, and never refusing a remedy, merely because it would be better that way for the state. The legitimacy of the processes depends on the judges' independence from government interference, and also on the independent attitude of the judges, and their willingness to take responsibility for the administration of justice, and to act with comity toward other public authorities.

TAKE-HOME MESSAGE ● ● ●

- The **rule of law** does not require unlimited opportunities to challenge the lawfulness of official action. It requires (1) proportionate processes for the vindication of the legal rights of claimants; and (2) proportionate processes for the review of official action where a review is in the public interest.

- The CPR give the judges a flexible, discretionary power to hear claims for judicial review with proportionate process.

- The **discretionary power** of judges to control their own process extends to the remedies they give.

- A claimant has a right to a remedy against an infringement of his or her **legal rights** by administrative action. But a claimant has no right to a remedy against **unlawful government action** in general.

- **Comity** among public authorities requires judges not to impose processes on administrative agencies that are disproportionate to the nature of a claim. And it requires other public authorities to comply with orders of the court, and to act in accord with declarations as to their legal position.

CRITICAL QUESTIONS ● ● ●

1   'How, one wonders, is good administration ever assisted by upholding an unlawful decision?' (*R (Corbett) v Restormel Borough Council* [2001] EWCA Civ 330, [32] (Sedley LJ)). Can you answer Lord Justice Sedley's question?

2   '. . . the judicial review court, being primarily concerned with the maintenance of the rule of law by the imposition of objective legal standards upon the conduct of public bodies, has to adopt a flexible but principled approach to its own jurisdiction' (*R v Trade and Industry Secretary, ex p Greenpeace Ltd* [1998] Env LR 415, 424

(Laws J)). Is it possible for the law on access to judicial review to be both flexible and principled?

3 Do the judicial processes measure up to the requirements of due process (see Chapters 4, 5, and 6) that judges impose on *other* public authorities?

4 What is the purpose of the requirement of permission to apply for judicial review? Is it to control the workload of the Administrative Court? Is it to protect defendants from litigation?

READING • • •

Ridge v Baldwin [1964] AC 40
O'Reilly v Mackman [1983] 2 AC 237
M v Home Office [1994] AC 377
Clark v University of Lincolnshire & Humberside [2000] 1 WLR 1988
R (Corbett) v Restormel Borough Council [2001] EWCA Civ 330
Trim v North Dorset District Council [2010] EWCA Civ 1446
R (Moseley) v Haringey LBC [2014] UKSC 56
R (Wasif) v Home Secretary [2016] EWCA Civ 82

On discretion in public law remedies:
Sir Thomas Bingham, 'Should Public Law Remedies be Discretionary?' [1991] PL 64
On the reforms to judicial review process in the Criminal Justice and Courts Act 2015:
Judicial Review and the Rule of Law: An Introduction to the Criminal Justice and Courts Act 2015, Part 4, Bingham Centre for the Rule of Law, JUSTICE and the Public Law Project, London, October 2015

 The following online resources accompany this chapter: **summaries** of key cases and legislation; **updates** on the law; **guidance** for answering the pop quizzes and questions; and **links** to legislation, cases, and useful websites.

11 Standing: litigation and the public interest

The law determines who can seek judicial review, on which issues, and who can bring an ordinary claim against whom. The law is very generous to claimants, because the judges want to find a way to hear genuine complaints of unlawful administrative conduct. But the courts' doors are not open to everyone who wants to complain that a public authority has acted unlawfully: the requirement of standing reflects the basic principle that judicial process requires a dispute between interested parties, and requires that it should be in the public interest for the court to determine the matter.

LOOK FOR • • •

- The purpose of judicial review: is it to police the lawfulness of administrative action? To right injustices to claimants?

- The relation between standing (the entitlement to be heard by a court) and the purposes of judicial review.

- The increasing potential for political campaigners to use judicial review as a platform to hold the government to account.

- The role of intervenors in litigation against public authorities (and the very relaxed approach to intervention in the English courts).

> ' I regard it as a matter of high constitutional principle that if there is good ground for supposing that a government department or a public authority is transgressing the law, or is about to transgress it, in a way which offends or injures thousands of Her Majesty's subjects, then any one of those offended or injured can draw it to the attention of the courts of law and seek to have the law enforced, and the courts in their discretion can grant whatever remedy is appropriate. '
>
> *R v Greater London Council, ex p Blackburn*
> **[1976] 1 WLR 550, 559 (Lord Denning MR)**

> ' ...not every applicant is entitled to judicial review as of right... '
> *R v Inland Revenue Commissioners, ex p Federation of Self-Employed*
> *and Small Businesses Ltd* **[1982] AC 617, 645 (Lord Fraser)**

11.1 The butcher, the baker, and the grave lacuna

In *R v Home Secretary, ex p Ruddock* [1987] 1 WLR 1482, Taylor J advanced the judicial review of the prerogative, and the doctrine of legitimate expectations. Only there was no such case as *R v Home Secretary, ex p Ruddock*. Joan Ruddock was the chair of the Campaign for Nuclear Disarmament. Ruddock and the vice-president, John Cox, sought judicial review, claiming that MI5 had breached the government's guidelines by tapping Cox's phone. Taylor J held that Ruddock did not have 'a sufficient interest to apply for any relief' (1485). Ruddock's complaint was that the Home Office had tapped Cox's phone, and judicial review was not available to everyone Cox spoke to. 'Otherwise,' Taylor J said, the Home Secretary 'would be open to judicial review at the instance of his butcher, his baker and whichever other innocents were intercepted on his line.' So the case is really *R v Home Secretary, ex p Cox*; it is in the law reports as '*ex p Ruddock*' only because it had commenced with Joan Ruddock's name on the application for permission. Joan Ruddock had no standing to seek judicial review.

11.1.1 What is standing?

Standing is the entitlement to be heard. No judicial process of any kind may proceed without it. In an ordinary claim, the claimant's standing is based on his or her assertion of grounds for a claim to a remedy (the old-fashioned name for those grounds is 'a cause of action'). You needn't establish that there are *good* grounds for a claim in order to have standing—that is the question to be decided at trial. So, for example, in an action for damages for breach of contract, the claimant has standing because he or she asserts that he or she has a contract with the defendant and that the defendant is in breach of it. But if a statement of case 'discloses no reasonable grounds for bringing ... the claim' (Civil Procedure Rules (CPR) 3.4(2)), the claimant has no standing to proceed to a trial. The court may strike out the claim, on its own initiative or on the application of the defendant (CPR Practice Direction 3.4).[1] No one has standing to proceed with an ordinary claim if his or her statement of case does not state grounds on which a right to a remedy can be claimed.

In a claim for judicial review, the claimant does not need to assert a right to a remedy. An allegation of a tort or a breach of contract gives the victim standing, but an allegation of unlawful administrative conduct does not by itself give anyone standing. So how can a claimant have standing for judicial review? The answer lies in the medieval constitutional roots of the remedies given in judicial review—a heritage that suited the twentieth-century judicial adventure (see 2.6) very well. In the origins of the common law, the judges were not only commissioned to give effect to legal rights in an ordinary action, but also to hear pleas that the King should exercise his prerogative to do justice. The judges had discretion to do so, when a claimant alleged an unlawful action, but could assert no legal right to a remedy. Lord Mansfield took the jurisdiction to new frontiers in *R v Barker* (1762) 3 Burr 1265. Yet he claimed to be following ancient doctrine when he said the following of *mandamus* (the prerogative remedy that evolved into what the CPR now call a 'mandatory order'), at 1267:

> ‘ A mandamus is a prerogative writ; to the aid of which the subject is intitled, upon a proper case previously shewn, to the satisfaction of the Court. The original nature of the writ, and the end for which it was framed, direct upon what occasions it should be used. Therefore it ought to be used upon all occasions where the law has established no specific remedy, and where in justice and good government there ought to be one. ’

Pentecost Barker was one of the trustees of a Presbyterian meeting house in Plymouth; after a disputed election for a new pastor, the dissidents sought *mandamus* to compel the trustees to acknowledge the election of their candidate. Lord Mansfield decided that the dispute was 'of a nature to inflame men's passions' (1269), and could lead to a breach of the peace, and that was enough to persuade him to hear the case. Whether the case should be heard was a matter for the satisfaction of the court, and the court would be satisfied if 'justice and good government' required the dispute to be heard.

Discretion and jurisdiction

Standing determines the court's *jurisdiction* (that is, whether the court can lawfully decide the claim),[2] and yet standing is subject to the *discretion* of the court (that is, to some extent the court gets to choose whether to grant standing). This may seem bizarre, but it simply reflects the High Court's remarkable

---

[1] On standing to bring an ordinary claim for a declaration, without asserting a right to a remedy, see 11.4.

[2] See *R v Social Security Secretary, ex p Child Poverty Action Group* [1990] 2 QB 540, 556; *R v Foreign Secretary, ex p World Development Movement* [1995] 1 WLR 386, 395.

discretionary control over its own process: the court's jurisdiction is, to some extent, up to the court. This discretion was a feature of the court's inherent jurisdiction over the administration of justice at common law, and is preserved by the Senior Courts Act 1981 and the CPR.

By the twentieth century, standing requirements were more complex and varied for different prerogative writs, and it was less clear that the judges had such a wide discretion—but it was a fair generalization when Lord Wilberforce said, in *Gouriet v Union of Post Office Workers* [1978] AC 435, 482, that 'the courts have allowed . . . liberal access [to judicial review] under a generous conception of *locus standi*' (*locus standi* meaning standing—'a place to stand').

When the judges and Parliament reformed the judicial review process in the 1978 Rules of the Supreme Court and the Senior Courts Act 1981, they provided that an applicant for judicial review needed to have a 'sufficient interest in the matter' in order to proceed.[3]

11.1.2 Standing to seek judicial review: 'sufficient interest'

There are three crucial points to note about the statutory requirement of a 'sufficient interest'.

(1) **Although it is often described as a vague test of standing, it is actually not a test at all. It is a shorthand way of saying that the court is to decide the test.**

Imagine that your mother asks you to bring home eggs from the market. You ask how many, and she says 'sufficient'. She has left it to your judgement. Likewise, the Senior Courts Act 1981 does not say what kind or degree of interest is sufficient; it leaves that question to the court. The evident purpose of the provision was to preserve the court's control over (and responsibility for) its own process.

The phrase was borrowed from judicial decisions, in which the judges had said that they would exercise their discretion to allow an application for *certiorari* (today, a quashing order) only if the applicant had a 'sufficient interest' (*Ex p Stott* [1916] 1 KB 7, 9). The point of that wording in the judgments was to emphasize that although an applicant could not seek judicial review without any interest in the matter, there was no need to allege an infringement of a legal right (such as a taking of property). Not just any interest would do, but the courts were prepared to work out what was sufficient case by case.

Rights and interests

Your **interest** is what's in it for you. Your interest is legally protected if the law requires someone deciding the matter to take into account what would be good

---

[3] Rules of the Supreme Court Order 53 r 3(5); Senior Courts Act 1981 s 31(3). The Rules have been superseded by the Civil Procedure Rules; the Senior Courts Act is still in force.

for you. You have a **right** if your interest ought to be protected or promoted regardless of (some) contrary considerations. You have a **legal right** if the law requires someone to protect or promote your interest regardless of (some) contrary considerations.

Example: I have an interest in whether planning permission will be granted for a development on my land, but I have no right to be given permission. But I have a right not to have my land trespassed upon by strangers.

But 'a sufficient interest' was not an agreed, general formulation of what the judges were looking for; in some cases, it had been held that an applicant for *certiorari* must be a person 'aggrieved', and an applicant for *mandamus* must have 'a specific legal right' at stake (*R v Russell, ex p Beaverbrook Newspapers Ltd* [1969] 1 QB 342, 348).[4] So although the new rules borrowed language from the judges, the 1978 Rules of the Supreme Court and the Senior Courts Act 1981 did change the law, simplifying it and evidently making standing more widely available. The Senior Courts Act preserved the discretion the judges had (in their inherent jurisdiction over prerogative proceedings) to decide what was required for standing, at the same time *limiting* it by preventing them from hearing a case in which the claimant has no interest at all. Although the remaining discretion is very wide, that does not mean that the judges can treat just any interest they like as sufficient. As Lord Wilberforce said in *R v Inland Revenue Commissioners, ex p National Federation of Self-Employed and Small Businesses Ltd ('Fleet Street Casuals')* [1982] AC 617, 631, 'the court must decide on legal principles'. What are those principles? That depends on the second crucial thing to note about 'sufficient interest'.

(2) 'Sufficient . . .' implies '. . . for some purpose'.

The relevant purpose is the purpose of bringing a claim for judicial review. So the Senior Courts Act 1981 s 31(3) should be read as requiring enough of an interest in the matter *to justify allowing this claimant to pursue this claim against this defendant*. The question is not, 'Is the claimant seriously affected by the decision?', but, 'Does the claimant have an interest that gives the court a reason to hear his or her claim (and, incidentally, to make the defendant respond to it)?'

For which reasons should the court allow a claimant to pursue a claim? In order to redress an injustice to the claimant? Or to stamp out unlawful conduct in general? If the former were the only reason, then no one should have standing unless they claim to be the victim of an injustice. If the latter is enough, then anyone who alleges unlawful behaviour should be allowed to proceed. The judges' vision of the purpose of the judicial review procedure is not entirely clear, although it has some perfectly clear aspects. They will not give standing just because the claimant alleges unlawful conduct by a public authority. But they will listen to claimants who have suffered no injustice.

---

[4]   And in *Ex p Stott*, 9, the court suggested that an applicant for *certiorari* had to be aggrieved by the decision in order to have a sufficient interest.

(3) **Sufficiency is a question of proportionality.**

The court faces the question of what kind of interest is needed, and also how much of an interest is enough. So the test of standing is a proportionality test. As a requirement of proportionate *process*, it is part of the general law of due process, which applies generally across the vast variety of administrative and judicial decision making (see Chapter 4). Proportionality in this case is a relation between the value of hearing a claim for judicial review and the process cost, and any process danger that may result.

The result of these three points is that the court has wide-ranging discretion to give proportionate process in a way that supports the purposes of judicial review (which the judges have not stated very clearly). There is nothing more definite than that in the *'Fleet Street Casuals'* case—the only House of Lords' or Supreme Court decision on what counts as a sufficient interest. Thousands of casual newspaper workers had been cheating on their income tax, by giving the newspapers false names. The Inland Revenue worked out a deal to end the frauds and to create a new reporting system, while seeking repayment of only part of the back taxes. A federation of angry businessmen wanted to challenge the deal as a breach of the Inland Revenue's statutory duty to assess and collect tax; the federation claimed that it should be given standing because its members, like all taxpayers, were adversely affected by the frauds.

The Law Lords decided that the federation did not have a sufficient interest, but in the course of doing so they established a liberal approach to standing. The crucial point in the decision was the Law Lords' conclusion that although the Revenue owed a duty of fairness to taxpayers in general, that duty allowed for the sound management of taxes, which gave it a discretion to decide whether it was better tax policy to go after all of the tax that the casuals owed, or to cut a deal with them that would improve tax collection. The House of Lords concluded that federation did not have standing to challenge the lawfulness of the Revenue's approach, although it *would* have had standing if it had alleged something outrageous: 'some exceptionally grave or widespread illegality' (Lord Fraser, 647), 'a case of sufficient gravity' (Lord Wilberforce, 633), or a breach of statutory duty due to 'some grossly improper pressure or motive' (Lord Roskill, 662). Although Lord Diplock similarly said the federation would have standing if it had alleged 'flagrant and serious breaches of the law' (641), he also suggested (unlike the other Law Lords) that the federation would have standing to seek judicial review of any *ultra vires* conduct (644).[5]

It may seem that the House of Lords decided that the federation's allegation of unlawful conduct had no merit, and *then* decided that the federation had no standing. That would put the cart before the horse, because the question of whether the claimant has standing 'has to be answered affirmatively before any question on the merits

---

[5]   Note that all of the important cases on standing, including the *Fleet Street Casuals* case, were decided when the permission decision was made *ex parte* (i.e., without hearing from the defendant at all). The Civil Procedure Rules now allow the defendant to respond to the application for permission on paper, which enables the defendant to argue that the claimant has no sufficient interest.

arises' (Lord Fraser, 645). Yet the Law Lords decided that the conduct was not unlawful, and *on that basis*, it seems, they decided that the federation had no sufficient interest. Does that mean that the court needs to decide the merits (that is, how good the claimant's case is), in order to decide standing? Yes and no, unfortunately. It is wrong to say that no question of the merits arises until standing is decided. But it is also a serious (but popular) mistake to think that 'in reality the issue of standing collapses into the wider question of substantive merit'.[6] Questions of merits are not *generally* relevant to standing; instead, they are relevant in two particular ways, as follows.

- **No one has standing to proceed with a claim that patently has no merit.**

This isn't something special about judicial review; at any point in any proceeding, if the court can determine through a fair process that the claim has no merit, the right thing to do is to dismiss it. So, in any proceedings, including judicial review, the court may give summary judgment (that is, decide the dispute without a trial) if the claimant 'has no real prospect of succeeding on the claim' (CPR 24.2(a)(i)). And in an ordinary claim the court may strike out a statement of case if it 'discloses no reasonable grounds' for a claim (CPR 3.4), or if it is 'totally without merit' (CPR 3.3(7)). In judicial review, the claimant has to ask for permission before proceeding. The requirement of an arguable case at the permission stage *is a standing requirement*. If the court can see that the claim cannot possibly succeed, the claimant has no standing to proceed to a judicial review hearing.

- **In order to decide whether the claimant's 'interest in the matter' is sufficient to justify a hearing, the court needs to decide *what the 'matter' is*.**

In the *'Fleet Street Casuals'* case, the federation would have had standing if 'the matter' it was alleging were something outrageous (*unless* the court could tell at the permission stage that the claim was not arguable). The court could only decide whether the application made an allegation of outrageous conduct after considering the Inland Revenue's explanation of the role of the impugned decision in tax management. That explanation persuaded the House of Lords that a taxpayer had no sufficient interest to challenge the decision on the grounds the federation offered, given the discretion of the Inland Revenue in deciding what was required for the sound management of taxes. The more serious the alleged conduct (so long as the allegation is arguable), the less individual involvement the applicant needs in order to have a sufficient interest in it.

Very often, as in the *'Fleet Street Casuals'* case, the court will only be able to decide that the claimant has no right to a hearing after having given a hearing. It is another example of the **irony of process** (see 4.13, p 157). The reason for it is not that the court needs to decide *the merits* of the claim in order to decide standing, but that the court needs to decide how serious *the matter* (that is, the claim) is, in order to decide whether the claimant has a sufficient interest in it to justify a hearing.

---

6   As was said by counsel for the applicant seeking standing in *R v Employment Secretary, ex p Equal Opportunities Commission* [1995] 1 AC 1, 19.

> **The irony of process**
> The fact that standing plays a role in the substantive hearing of a claim for judicial review is an instance of the irony that parties often need to be given *more* process than is actually due to them. A claimant without a sufficient interest in a matter is not entitled to be heard, but it is often necessary to hear the whole story from the claimant *and* the defendant in order to decide whether the claimant has a sufficient interest. So the court must sometimes give a process that turns out to be more than what is due to the claimant—and that is what happened in the *'Fleet Street Casuals'* case.

Once a court decides the merits of a claim, of course, the claimant's standing is exhausted (although an unsuccessful claimant may then have standing to bring an appeal).

So merits are relevant to standing in those two ways, and yet Lord Fraser in the *'Fleet Street Casuals'* case was right in a sense when he said that the standing question was prior to that of the merits: a claim may have no merit whatsoever, and yet the claimant may have standing to proceed to a hearing if the court cannot yet see that the claim has no merit.

It is a popular idea, drawn from the *'Fleet Street Casuals'* case, that 'standing should not be treated as a preliminary issue' (*R v Foreign Secretary, ex p World Development Movement* [1995] 1 WLR 386, 395). But it is a mistake. Standing *is* a preliminary matter, because the Administrative Court is not allowed to give permission to proceed if it is apparent at that point that the claimant does not have a sufficient interest (Senior Courts Act 1981 s 31). But the court often has to allow a claim to proceed past the permission stage without having been able to determine *whether* the claimant should be given standing or not.

11.1.3 Standing and the purpose of judicial review

Does *'Fleet Street Casuals'* give us any picture of the purpose of judicial review? There are suggestions that the purpose is ordinarily to right an injustice to the claimant. All of the Law Lords (except Lord Diplock) indicated that a taxpayer might only have standing to pursue an allegation of illegality in the treatment of another taxpayer where it is exceptionally grave.[7] And since the decision, it has been held that a claimant has standing to challenge the Inland Revenue's treatment of another taxpayer *if* that

---

[7] A taxpayer can even challenge the legality of a governmental expenditure decision (at least, if the issue is of general importance) (*R v HM Treasury, ex p Smedley* [1985] 1 QB 657, 670 (Slade LJ)). But it will ordinarily be difficult to show the arguable case that is required for permission to seek judicial review, because of judicial deference to government on spending decisions: see 7.3.2.

treatment unfairly makes it cheaper for that other taxpayer to produce the same product that the claimant is producing (*R v The Attorney-General, ex p Imperial Chemical Industries* [1987] 1 CMLR 72 (CA), 107). Why does standing normally require some impact on the claimant? Why isn't it enough that the claimant is alleging that the public authority acted unlawfully? Lord Diplock, alone, suggested in the *'Fleet Street Casuals'* case that a mere allegation of unlawful conduct is enough for standing (at 644, emphasis added):

> ' It would, in my view, be a **grave lacuna** in our system of public law if a pressure group, like the federation, or even a single public-spirited taxpayer, were prevented by outdated technical rules of locus standi from bringing the matter to the attention of the court to vindicate the rule of law and get the unlawful conduct stopped. '

This grave lacuna is a bit of a mystery. Lord Diplock's talk of 'bringing the matter to the attention of the court' suggests that the courts have a general responsibility to listen to anyone in order to vindicate the rule of law whenever a public authority has acted unlawfully. Was he saying that anyone can bring any allegation of unlawful conduct in front of a court? Let's call that an 'open doors' policy on standing. The rest of this section aims to explain why it would be a mistake to think that the law has or ought to have an open doors policy.

If all unlawful official conduct just must come before a court to get quashed, then we really do need an open doors policy. But what is the point in making something unlawful? Doing so has all sorts of particular purposes; generally, the point is simply to guide and to constrain public authorities to act justly and for the public good. The point is *not* to turn the judges into a general government complaints department. If it seems pointless to make something unlawful without automatically providing a process to 'get the unlawful conduct stopped', remember that processes need a justification of their own. They can be absolutely crucial (so that the law can become pointless if the process fails). But they need some justification other than the mere fact that a public authority has allegedly done something unlawful.

The rule of law may not require a legal response to unlawful conduct!

It may sound surprising, but there is no general public interest in having a court hear a complaint that a public authority has acted unlawfully. The rule of law *does* require that officials (and people in general) abide by the law. But when they don't, the rule of law requires the operation of a process for interfering only when that process itself will enhance conformity to the law—which it might do if it changes official conduct for the future, or remedies the unlawful consequences of a particular action. As Lord Reed said in *Axa General Insurance v HM Advocate* [2011] UKSC 46 [170], 'the protection of the rule of law does not require that every allegation of unlawful conduct by a public authority must be examined by a court, any more than it requires that every allegation of criminal conduct must be prosecuted'. Similarly, although the rule of law requires a process enabling one private person to seek a remedy against a tort by another person, it does not require that every tort should result in a claim in the High Court. There is no lapse in the role of law if the victim of a tort decides not to sue.

So there is no grave lacuna just because some unlawful conduct does not come before a court, any more than there is a grave lacuna if a tort is not brought 'to the attention of the court to vindicate the rule of law and get the unlawful conduct stopped'.

Remember the butcher and the baker from *Ruddock*. If they phone someone whose phone is being unlawfully tapped by MI5, they have no standing to seek judicial review. What if the person whose phone was tapped does not want to seek judicial review (or has left the country, or has died)? Then, it seems, the rules of standing mean that no one[8] can bring the matter to the attention of the court—even a person with an arguable claim that a public authority has acted (or is acting) unlawfully. And that is not because the standing requirements are 'outdated technical rules' (*'Fleet Street Casuals'*, 644); they reflect a judgment (first of the courts, and then of Parliament: Senior Courts Act 1981 s 31(3)), that it is not the role of the courts to vindicate the rule of law by listening to all plausible allegations of unlawful official conduct. Judicial review is to be a procedure in which the claimant must have an interest in the matter that gives the court some reason to listen to them. The opportunity to stamp out unlawful administrative conduct in general does not justify a judicial review proceeding. It is not enough for the claimant to assert a general interest in getting unlawful conduct stopped. And yet, as we will see, if the claimant can persuade the court that a hearing would be in the public interest, *that* may be enough.

Representative standing

Notice that even if the Inland Revenue's decision had been unfair to the angry businessmen, it wouldn't have been unfair *to the federation itself* as an organization. So the federation had no stake in the litigation! But in fact, associations of all kinds are regularly given standing for judicial review in a very relaxed fashion (the question of whether the federation had standing to represent its members in court was not even argued in the *'Fleet Street Casuals'* case; the only issue there was whether the members had a sufficient interest). Standing of associations actually *is* a problem in ordinary claims, because the association can only be a claimant if it can assert a cause of action. But there is no such problem in judicial

---

[8] Except the Attorney General, who has standing on behalf of the public, and has a general responsibility for safeguarding the rule of law: see 11.7. And the Attorney General has no general duty to bring proceedings whenever something unlawful has occurred; he or she has a discretionary power.

review. For the purpose of litigating matters in which the people they represent have a sufficient interest, the courts have given standing to trade unions, the Association of British Civilian Internees—Far East Region, the British Parachute Association, and the president of a Jewish Burial Society.[9]

The courts have consistently been willing to assume that pressure groups work in the interest of the people they claim to represent. No doubt, a failure to do so would be a ground to refuse standing, but the defendant would need to press the matter. The courts prefer to presume that a well-known advocacy organization like Greenpeace is acting responsibly, instead of scrutinizing its structures and behaviour.

11.2 Campaign litigation: a special standing problem

In 2012, archeologists found the remains of King Richard III (1452–85) under a car park owned by the University of Leicester. The University, the City of Leicester, and Leicester Cathedral agreed to arrange for reburial in the Cathedral; the exhumation and reburial needed government approval under the Burial Act 1857, which the Justice Secretary gave. A group of individuals claiming to be sixteenth-generation relatives of Richard III wanted the remains to be reburied in York. They sought judicial review of the decision under the name of a company they created, 'Plantagenet Alliance Ltd'.

How could the Plantagenet Alliance have a sufficient interest to justify judicial review? The Alliance claimed that some of its members had an interest as relatives of King Richard III; that was rather frivolous (he had no children, and his nieces and nephews may have millions of descendants), and the judge said that their relationship after sixteen generations or more was 'attenuated in terms of time and lineage'. But he held that the Alliance had standing to proceed, because 'the points raised have a broader public interest sufficient for the Claimant to have standing in this case as a public interest litigant' [82].

Advocacy groups often use litigation as an instrument in a political campaign for purposes that they argue are in the public interest. If (as in the *Plantagenet Alliance* case) democratic politics are against a group's purposes, it may be possible to persuade a court to impose the group's purposes on the government. And litigation can be useful even if there is no good legal argument in favour of the group's claim: win or lose, judicial review gives the group a voice in a prestigious and high-profile forum, and gets attention from the BBC,[10] and puts the government in the position of having to defend

---

[9] *R v Trade and Industry Secretary, ex p UNISON* [1996] ICR 1003; *R (British Civilian Internees— Far Eastern Region) v Defence Secretary* [2003] EWCA Civ 473; *R v Shrewsbury Coroners Court, ex p British Parachute Association* (1988) 152 JP 123; *R v Greater Manchester North District Coroner, ex p Worch and Brunner* [1987] 2 WLR 1141.

[10] http://www.bbc.co.uk/news/uk-england-leicestershire-23929989.

itself before an impartial authority. The courts have to decide whether the claimant's interest gives a reason for access to that forum.

The federation in the *'Fleet Street Casuals'* case[11] asked for standing on the ground of its members' own private interest. Its grievance was that the Inland Revenue was being unfair *to the federation's members* in making a special deal for the casual workers. It claimed that it had therefore been adversely affected by the deal as an association (see Lord Roskill's speech, at 660). But counsel for the Inland Revenue said that the federation 'are seeking to represent the public interest and this they cannot do. A fortiori, . . . they can have no "sufficient interest" to bring these proceedings' (621). This argument was not addressed explicitly in the speeches in the case. Imagine if the federation were alleging some grossly improper conduct (in which case it would have standing to proceed). It is not clear whether the Law Lords decided that, in such a case, the federation would have a *private* interest sufficient to justify its proceeding, or whether it would be treated as having a sufficient interest on the ground that the proceeding would be in the *public* interest. But Lord Diplock's grave lacuna is certainly a matter of the public interest, and he proposed that the lacuna might be filled by giving standing to 'a single public-spirited taxpayer'. But why a taxpayer? If the Inland Revenue is behaving grossly improperly, why not let just anybody fill the grave lacuna? Can public spirit give a claimant standing if the law requires that the claimant must have an interest in the matter?

In *World Development Movement*, the High Court held that the government had used the foreign aid budget unlawfully to support an uneconomical dam project in Malaysia. It was a remarkable instance of judicial control of discretionary power (on the substance of the decision, see 8.2.2); it was also remarkable that the court listened to the application at all. The Movement was a 'non-partisan pressure group' (393). The whole point of the Movement was to promote *other people's* interests. So how could the Movement have a sufficient interest in the matter?

The idea of an interest is ambiguous: in one sense, you have an interest in a matter if it affects you for good or ill; in another sense, you have an interest in a matter if you find it interesting. By requiring a 'sufficient interest' in the matter, the Senior Courts Act 1981 cannot have meant that the claimant must find the matter sufficiently interesting. But the courts have treated persons who are *involved with a matter* as having a potentially sufficient interest, even if the resolution of a dispute does not affect them for good or ill. What more does it take, then, than just finding the matter interesting?

11.2.1 Factors in the standing of a campaign litigant

Rose LJ set out the following factors in the *World Development Movement* case, at 395:

- 'the importance of vindicating the rule of law' (citing Lord Diplock's comment on the grave lacuna in the *'Fleet Street Casuals'* case, at 644);

- 'the importance of the issue';

---

[11]   *R v Inland Revenue Commissioners, ex p National Federation of Self-Employed and Small Businesses Ltd* [1982] AC 617.

- 'the likely absence of any other responsible challenger';

- 'the nature of the breach of duty' (but of course this is part of 'the importance of the issue');

- 'the prominent role of these applicants' in the field of foreign aid.

The first factor does not actually help: even though the rule of law requires official conformity to the law, it does not *generally* demand judicial process for interfering with unlawful conduct. It is important to vindicate the rule of law *by judicial process* only if the proceeding is in the public interest. So we can generally say that a litigant seeking to promote the public interest will be given standing for judicial review if the following criteria are met.

The three requirements in *World Development Movement*

A campaign litigant has standing if:

(1) the issue is important to the public;
(2) no one else could make a responsible challenge; and
(3) the claimant has a 'prominent role' in the field.

Only the last of these factors has anything at all to do with the claimant's interest in the matter. The importance of the case and the 'no one else' factor are considerations that can make it a good idea to allow campaign litigation; the role of those considerations is to lead the court to treat a claimant such as the World Development Movement as *having an interest* in the matter that is sufficient to justify judicial review, even though *the group's interests are not at stake* in the decision.

Representation by campaign groups

Campaign litigation involves an element of representation when it is conducted by a pressure group that has members or supporters. The representative role of the group played no important role in *World Development Movement*. It had standing *not* because its members were affected by the decision, but because its membership and organization made it an effective body to make a case that the government had acted unlawfully.

In *R v Inspectorate of Pollution, ex p Greenpeace (No 2)* [1994] 2 CMLR 548 [81], Otton J suggested that the most important reason for giving standing to Greenpeace was that it had 2,500 members in Cumbria, who 'are inevitably concerned about . . . a danger to their health and safety from any additional discharge of radioactive waste even from testing'. But the Cumbrian members seem to be a red herring, given the nature of Greenpeace: it is a global environmental campaign organization, and not a Cumbrian residents' health and safety association. That is, the representative role of the pressure group should have been no more relevant in that case than it was in *World Development Movement*.

Campaign litigation creates a real danger that argument in court will become a phoney substitute for the political debates that ought to be conducted in Parliament, or in local councils, or in the media. And that is often precisely what a claimant is seeking to achieve by bringing a claim for judicial review, when the political process has not yielded the result that he or she wanted. The examples include challenges to the signing of treaties, such as *Blackburn v Attorney-General* [1971] 1 WLR 1037 (seeking a declaration that it would be unlawful for the government to sign the Treaty of Rome to bring Britain into the European Community) and *R v Foreign Secretary, ex p Rees-Mogg* [1994] QB 552, in which a member of the House of Lords sought to litigate issues (concerning the signing of the Maastricht Treaty) on which he had lost the debate in Parliament. In cases like these, the claimant's lawyers will be explaining to them from the start that there is no chance of success; the claimant goes ahead anyway for publicity purposes, and for the symbolic value of forcing the government to justify its actions before a judge. Even where there is no chance of success, getting a court to *question* the lawfulness of government action can be a campaign success.

It would be entirely reasonable to deny standing in cases like *Blackburn* and *Rees-Mogg*.[12] But the courts prefer to deal with them by means of (1) the requirement of an arguable case; and (2) the grounds of judicial review, with the limits that they impose on the judicial role. If the judges are self-disciplined and do not extend their reach beyond the lawful grounds of judicial review, then generous standing for campaign litigants does not raise a danger of illegitimate judicial interference with government—just a risk of wasted court time and significant cost in proceedings that will generate publicity for the campaign group, but cannot succeed. In *Blackburn* and *Rees-Mogg*, the courts gave no serious consideration to the question of standing. Blackburn's claim for a declaration was struck out on the ground that he had no arguable case. The *Rees-Mogg* litigation involved four days of hearings at substantial public expense on an application that was, all along, plainly unarguable.

Even in a case like *Rees-Mogg*, there may be a certain sort of value in a careful judicial explanation of why there are no grounds for judicial review. The proceeding becomes the court's way of reminding the community of how limited the court's responsibility is for good government. If that function can be carried out at the permission hearing, as in *Blackburn*, then the courts have no business humouring a politician (as in *Rees-Mogg*) by allowing a pointless judicial proceeding to go on to a full hearing.

Generous standing *is* justified—because it actually will promote the rule of law—where (1) there is a significant public interest at stake; and (2) the claimant alleges that the public authority's behaviour was a flagrant abuse of a legal power; and (3) the case is arguable. Then (as in the *World Development Movement* case), the litigation will be justified. But in the *Plantagenet Alliance* case, the second of those requirements was entirely missing, and it was clear to the judges in the substantive hearing of the

----

12 Compare *R (Wheeler) v Prime Minister* [2008] EWHC 1409, in which the Divisional Court heard and dismissed a claim for a declaration that it had been unlawful for the Prime Minister not to hold a referendum concerning the Treaty of Lisbon. The patently untenable claim had been allowed to proceed to judicial review; the decision does not discuss standing.

claim that the third requirement was not met. It is hard to disagree with the view of the Mayor of Leicester that the judicial review proceedings were 'plainly daft'.[13] At the substantive hearing, even as they decided that there was no basis whatsoever for the claimant's arguments that the court should order the defendants to conduct a public consultation about the reburial of Richard III's mortal remains, the Divisional Court endorsed the claimant's standing. Its reason was that 'the points raised have a broader public interest sufficient for the Claimant to have standing in this case as a public interest litigant' (*R (Plantagenet Alliance Ltd) v Justice Secretary* [2014] EWHC 1662 [82]). But the purpose of the process is not to give campaign groups a forum to advocate their views on issues that have broad public interest; the purpose is to bring claims before the court that call for judicial review. For that purpose, the claimants must have some genuine prospect of persuading the court in the substantive hearing to give a remedy against seriously unlawful conduct.

FROM THE MISTS OF TIME

Public interest standing is nothing new. At common law, the courts in principle actually did have an open doors policy, because of their responsibility for 'public order in administration of law' (*Worthington v Jeffries* (1875) LR 10 CP 379, 383). So the judges might listen to a claim, 'by whomsoever brought before them, that an inferior Court is acting without jurisdiction, or is exceeding its jurisdiction' (*Worthington*, 383, and see *Wadsworth v Queen of Spain* (1851–2) LR 17 QB 215). In *The King v Speyer* [1916] 1 KB 595, a mere 'stranger' challenged the validity of the appointment of two Privy Councillors, and the Chief Justice said that the applicant 'appears to have brought this matter before the Court on purely public grounds without any private interest to serve, and it is to the public advantage that the law should be declared by judicial authority' (613). The judges in the late twentieth century saw themselves as developing a new, more liberal approach to standing, but it is not nearly as liberal as the older common law. In those earlier cases, though, the courts did not have to deal with pressure groups like Greenpeace or World Development Movement.

In more recent times, Lord Denning advocated an open doors policy: he held that 'the discretion of the court extends to permitting an application to be made by any member of the public' (*R v Greater London Council, ex p Blackburn* [1976] 1 WLR 550, 559). But Lord Denning's open doors policy was restricted to claimants who allege that a public authority is breaking the law 'in a way which offends or injures thousands of Her Majesty's subjects' (*Attorney-General, ex rel McWhirter v Independent Broadcasting Authority* [1973] QB 629, 649). It was *not* a doctrine that anyone can bring a claim for judicial review if they allege that a decision of a public authority was unlawful, and in particular, it did not apply to 'busybodies'.

---

[13] http://www.bbc.co.uk/news/uk-england-leicestershire-23929989.

No one likes a busybody: in *'Fleet Street Casuals'*, Lord Fraser said 'a mere busybody does not have a sufficient interest. The difficulty is . . . to distinguish between the desire of the busybody to interfere in other people's affairs and the interest of the person affected by or having a reasonable concern with the matter to which the application relates' (646). Perhaps there is no better definition of a 'busybody' for standing purposes than that he or she does not have a reasonable concern with the issues: Lord Reed has held that 'A busybody is someone who interferes in something with which he has no legitimate concern' (*Walton v The Scottish Ministers* [2012] UKSC 44 [92]).

To be a busybody, it is not enough to be a member of the House of Lords who wants to continue a debate in court after losing in Parliament—or standing would have been denied in *R v Foreign Secretary, ex p Rees-Mogg* [1994] QB 552. In fact, the *Rees-Mogg* case makes it hard to imagine who does count as a busybody. The court in *Rees-Mogg* said, 'we accept without question that Lord Rees-Mogg brings the proceedings because of his sincere concern for constitutional issues' (562). So perhaps a busybody is a person with an *insincere* interest in the issues. If the claim raises any serious issue of abuse of power, and no one else is in a better position to bring the claim, then it seems that no one is a busybody unless he or she is acting in bad faith.

● *Pop quiz* ●

Remember the landmark case of *Ridge v Baldwin* [1964] AC 40 (see 4.3.2), in which the House of Lords upheld Charles Ridge's claim that the police authority acted unlawfully by dismissing him without giving him a hearing on allegations of misconduct. In a case like that today, suppose that the person dismissed chooses not to challenge the decision in court, but a concerned citizen, or an advocacy group for fairness in government, seeks permission to bring a claim for judicial review, on the grounds that succeeded in *Ridge v Baldwin*. Should the Administrative Court give them standing?

Table 11.1 summarizes the leading cases on standing in campaign litigation since the 1980s.

Has the law reached an open doors policy for campaign litigants? Schiemann J denied it in *R v Environment Secretary, ex p Rose Theatre Trust* [1990] 1 QB 504. A trust company was formed to campaign for the preservation of the remains of a Shakespearian theatre, and it sought judicial review of a minister's refusal to list the remains as a monument. Schiemann J pointed out that 'the law does not see it as the function of the courts to be there for every individual who is interested in having the legality of an administrative action litigated' (522). That is quite true: the law requires something extra. But he went on to say that the extra is that an individual claimant, or the individuals represented by a pressure group, must have 'a greater right or expectation than any other citizen of this country to have that decision taken lawfully' (522).

Table 11.1 Standing in campaign litigation

Decision	Standing given	The claimant	The matter
R v IRC, ex p National Federation of Self-Employed [1982] AC 617	✗	Businessmen's pressure group	Whether the Inland Revenue could lawfully overlook some of the tax owed by other taxpayers
R v Social Security Secretary, ex p Child Poverty Action Group [1990] 2 QB 540	✓*	Two national associations that 'play a prominent role in giving advice, guidance and assistance' to claimants for social security benefits (Woolf LJ, 546)	Whether the minister had misinterpreted his statutory duties in deciding claims for supplementary benefit
R v Foreign Secretary, ex p Rees-Mogg [1994] QB 552	✓*	A member of the House of Lords with 'sincere concern for constitutional issues' (Lloyd LJ, 562)	The lawfulness of signing the Maastricht Treaty
R v Inspectorate of Pollution, ex p Greenpeace (No 2) [1994] 2 CMLR 548	✓	'. . . a well-known campaigning organisation which has as its prime object the protection of the natural environment' (Otton J, 551)	Whether new operations at a nuclear power plant could lawfully be carried out by a variation of old licences
R v Foreign Secretary, ex p World Development Movement [1996] 1 WLR 386	✓	Non-partisan pressure group promoting interests of the poor in the developing world	Whether it was unlawful for the Foreign Secretary to use the overseas development fund for non-development purposes
R v Somerset County Council, ex p Dixon [1998] Env LR 111	✓	Local resident, parish councillor, environmentalist, election candidate in the area affected	Whether a grant of planning permission was lawful
R (Hasan) v Trade and Industry Secretary [2007] EWHC 2630	✓	A Palestinian living in territory occupied by Israel	Transparency in the award of arms export licences
Al-Haq v Foreign Secretary [2009] EWHC 1910	✗	A pro-Palestinian non-governmental organization based in Ramallah	Whether the British government was acting unlawfully by supporting the state of Israel

(Continued)

Table 11.1 *(Continued)*

R (Chandler) v Secretary of State for Children, Schools and Families [2009] EWCA Civ 1011	✗	A mother of school children who was opposed to the government's policy of encouraging the creation of academy schools	Whether the defendant had complied with the Public Contracts Regulations 2006
R (Plantagenet Alliance Ltd) v Justice Secretary [2014] EWHC 1662	✗	A group of people who wanted Richard III to be reburied in York	Whether the government should have conducted a public consultation

Notes: All of these decisions, except *Dixon* and *Al-Haq*, were made after the permission stage, at the judicial review hearing.
✓ The claimant was given standing.
✗ The claimant was not given standing.
* Standing was not disputed.

The other cases on campaign litigation have made no such requirement—almost the reverse. Instead of requiring any special private interest, they have welcomed pressure group litigation where, as in *R v Foreign Secretary, ex p World Development Movement* [1995] 1 WLR 386, it is unlikely that someone else could make a responsible challenge.

So that remark of Schiemann J no longer represents the law.[14] But that does not mean that the outcome in *Rose Theatre Trust* was wrong. In fact, it is remarkably similar to the *'Fleet Street Casuals'* case, and can be reconciled with most other decisions as a case in which the claimants would only have had a sufficient interest in seeking judicial review if they had been alleging a serious abuse of power by the minister. The one case that is irreconcilable with *Rose Theatre Trust* is *Plantagenet Alliance* (a decision in which *Rose Theatre Trust* was not mentioned). There was no allegation of abuse of power in *Plantagenet Alliance*, but only a claim that there should have been a public consultation, before a decision that had involved extensive public discussion, and local and central government deliberation, and discussion in Parliament. If the Court of Appeal has the opportunity to sort out this inconsistency, it should do so by fitting judicial review to its purpose of preventing abuse of power, and not by extending judicial review—as it was extended in *Plantagenet Alliance*—into a forum for discussion of matters of public interest that involve no abuse of power.

In *R v Somerset County Council, ex p Dixon* [1998] Env LR 111, 117, Sedley J made this connection between public interest litigation and abuse of power: '[T]here will be, in public life, a certain number of cases of apparent abuse of power in which any individual, simply as a citizen, has a sufficient interest to bring the matter before the court.' That decision is consistent (as Sedley J pointed out) with *Rose Theatre Trust*; Sedley J

---

[14] In *R v Somerset County Council, ex p Dixon* [1998] Env LR 111, 117, Sedley J said that he 'would decline to follow the decision' in *Rose Theatre Trust* (a case in which he had successfully opposed standing, as counsel for the intervening landlord).

agreed with Schiemann J's view that 'not every member of the public can complain of every breach of statutory duty' (*Rose Theatre*, 520). The cases in which 'any individual, simply as a citizen, has a sufficient interest' will include claims of grossly improper conduct, and may include *any* claim of 'general public importance' (as it was put in *World Development Movement*) in which the claim has enough merit to meet the test of an arguable case.

The *Dixon* decision was a return to the view of the old common law, and of Lord Denning, that a good citizen ought to be able to bring *some* complaints of abuse of power to the court, as long as they have no 'ill motive' (*Dixon*, 121).

Notice that it is not enough that the claimant alleges that the defendant has acted unlawfully. In *R (UNISON) v NHS Wiltshire Primary Care Trust* [2012] EWHC 624, a union was denied standing to challenge NHS outsourcing decisions on the ground that NHS trusts were violating the Public Contracts Regulations 2006 (see 15.4.4). The court held that the claim did not involve a grave enough departure from public law obligations to justify standing for the union as a public interest litigant. Likewise, in *R (Chandler) v Secretary of State for Children, Schools and Families* [2009] EWCA Civ 1011, the Court of Appeal held that the claimant had no standing to challenge the defendant's compliance with the Public Contracts Regulations. The claimant opposed the government's policy of favouring the establishment of 'academy' schools, and thought that schools ought to be run by local education authorities. Lady Justice Arden said, 'She is thus attempting, or seeking, to use the public procurement regime for a purpose for which it was not created. . . . it would, in our judgment, be outside the proper function of public law remedies to give Ms Chandler standing to pursue her claim.' The problem was not simply that the alleged unlawfulness was not grave enough, but that the regulations on public contracting were not designed to enable opponents of the government's education policy to challenge the implementation of its policy.

So the doors are *almost* open in campaign litigation cases, with the following important provisos:

(1) if there is some **particular potential claimant** who is specially affected, the court will not be prepared to hear a claim from anyone else (so if Cox's phone has been tapped, the court will not hear a claim for judicial review from people who phoned him);[15]

(2) and claimants must do more than allege unlawful conduct; they will need to allege **abuse of power**, or some form of unlawfulness that makes judicial review appropriate, and

(3) **busybodies** do not have a sufficient interest (117).

Because of these essential provisos, it is clear that we have not quite arrived at an open doors policy.

We have, though, reached a point at which standing will be given to anyone who, in good faith, looks set to make a responsible claim based on abuse of power, on a matter

---

[15] As in *R v Home Secretary, ex p Ruddock* [1987] 1 WLR 1482 (see 11.1).

of general public importance (unless perhaps some other litigant is in a better position to do it). And in *R (Hasan) v Trade and Industry Secretary* [2007] EWHC 2630, Collins J extended to a *non-citizen* the standing that Sedley J gave to 'any citizen' to challenge abuses of power, holding that a Palestinian living in territories occupied by Israel had standing to seek judicial review of decisions granting licences for arms manufacturers to export arms to Israel. The claimant asked the court to order the Secretary of State to give an explanation of the decisions that would go beyond the requirements of a statutory scheme of disclosure in Parliament, and beyond the additional voluntary disclosure that the government had given. The government did not oppose standing at the hearing, and Collins J granted it on the ground that the claimant was 'indirectly affected by any trade in military equipment to Israel' [8]. It is true that people living in Israeli-occupied territory (and, in fact, anywhere that Israel can exert military force) are indirectly affected by trade in military equipment to Israel. But the case offers no explanation as to why being indirectly affected by trade to a foreign country gives standing to ask the English courts to review the lawfulness of a decision on the regulation of trade. Perhaps this is one aspect of the liberal approach to standing: the courts do not address hard questions as to why they should listen to a claimant.

Hasan's case was decided in a 'rolled up' hearing [7] (see 10.3.2), in which permission and the merits of the claim were decided at once. That enabled a foreign citizen to challenge British arms exports in court, in a case that had no prospect of success at all. The decision offers access to judicial review for the billions of people around the world who may be indirectly affected by British arms exports (or other forms of trade?). That result would actually follow from the ruling in *World Development Movement*, *if* the litigation alleges a serious abuse of power and is conducted by a campaign group that can be expected to make an effective argument. But the court ought to have denied standing in *Hasan*, on the ground that the claimant was not alleging any abuse of power, but was only seeking transparency from the government. A refusal of standing would have been entirely compatible with the liberal approach of *World Development Movement* and *Dixon*.[16] Perhaps the decision in *Hasan* reflects a judicial instinct to be even more liberal in granting standing than *World Development Movement* demands. But standing is not open: in *Al-Haq v Foreign Secretary* [2009] EWHC 1910, without referring to *Hasan*, the Administrative Court held that the claimant (a non-governmental human rights organization based in Ramallah in the Israeli-occupied territory) had no standing to pursue its claim in judicial review. The group sought a declaration that the British government's support for the state of Israel was unlawful (see 10.3.2, p 387). Permission was refused, because the claim was doomed on the merits. But Pill LJ and Cranston J also refused to grant standing. That decision was justified, because although there is a critical public interest in a just national policy on relations with Israel and with

---

[16] The case went to the Court of Appeal in *R (Hasan) v Trade and Industry Secretary* [2008] EWCA Civ 1312. Sir Anthony May stated that neither party had questioned the judge's decision on standing, but commented that the claimant 'may be seen as a nominal representative of the public interest . . . not as an individual whose personal human rights are likely to be affected by a decision . . .' [8].

the Palestinians, there is no public interest in making the Administrative Court into a forum in which advocacy groups are entitled to ask judges to make, or even to influence that policy.

Perhaps the best summary of the interest that is required for judicial review is in the words of Lord Hope in *Axa General Insurance v HM Advocate* [2011] UKSC 46, [63]. That interest is:

> ' . . . the interest of the person affected by or having a reasonable concern in the matter to which the application related. . . . A personal interest need not be shown if the individual is acting in the public interest. '

But the court does not actually need to decide that the individual is acting in the public interest. A judge can give permission to Greenpeace or World Development Movement to seek judicial review without passing judgment on whether they are acting in the public interest; it just has to be in the public interest to hear from them. And we should not forget that the requirement of an arguable case is part of the test for standing for public interest litigation: a campaign group has no standing to get an airing in court of complaints that do not involve an arguable claim on justiciable matters.

Note, finally, that it is not only pressure groups and campaigning individuals that can be given standing in the public interest. Journalists also have standing to challenge decisions of public authorities prohibiting publication of information, apparently in the public interest rather than for the journalists' own sake.[17] But the family of a murder victim does not have standing to challenge the tariff of imprisonment set for a person convicted of the murder. Because the Crown is a party to the criminal proceedings, including the tariff-setting decision, 'there is no need for a third party to seek to intervene to uphold the rule of law'—that is the role of the Crown (*R (Bulger) v Home Secretary* [2001] EWHC 119 (Admin) [21] (Rose LJ)).

Environmental law: standing for ospreys

In *Walton v The Scottish Ministers* [2012] UKSC 44, Lord Hope pointed out that any individual with a genuine interest[18] may have standing to challenge a public decision on environmental grounds, even if the decision does not affect the person's property or other rights. He imagined a hypothetical case in which there is risk 'that a route used by an osprey as it moves to and from a favourite fishing loch will be impeded by the proposed erection across it of a cluster of wind turbines' [152]. He said that it would be wrong to refuse to give standing to an

---

17 *R v Felixstowe Justices, ex p Leigh* [1987] QB 582; *R v Home Secretary, ex p Brind* [1991] 2 WLR 588.

18 According to Lord Hope, 'this must not be seen as an invitation to the busybody to question the validity of a scheme or order under the statute just because he objects to the scheme of the development' [153].

individual seeking to challenge the decision in such a case, just because the decision did not affect their property or interests [152]:

> 'That would seem to be contrary to the purpose of environmental law, which proceeds on the basis that the quality of the natural environment is of legitimate concern to everyone. The osprey has no means of taking that step on its own behalf, any more than any other wild creature. If its interests are to be protected someone has to be allowed to speak up on its behalf.'

Judicial review offers special opportunities to environmental campaigners because of this approach to standing, and also because of special rules on awards of costs against unsuccessful claimants. EU law requires member states to give members of the public an enhanced role in decision making on environmental issues by ensuring that it is not 'prohibitively expensive' for them to pursue claims in court.[19] This rule not only affects legal aid, but is also a reason for a favourable approach to costs capping orders (see 11.3), and for reduced awards of costs, which amount to public funding for environmental claims; see *R (Edwards) v Environment Agency* [2013] UKSC 78.

11.3 Costs in campaign litigation: the bad news and the good news

Campaign litigation doesn't just a raise a problem of standing; there are also special implications for costs.

The bad news is that the ordinary rule is the starting point: the court will order an unsuccessful litigant to pay a substantial part of the winner's costs, unless there is some special reason not to. The courts have long been prepared in principle to 'punish with costs persons who might bring unnecessary actions' (*Dyson v Attorney-General* [1911] 1 KB 410, 423 (Farwell LJ)). And you cannot create a company to serve as claimant just to avoid the effect of an order of costs.[20]

And although a public interest case may just succeed (as in the *World Development Movement* case), it is a risky business. Public interest claims tend to be more speculative than other claims (the *Greenpeace* and *Rees-Mogg* and *Plantagenet Alliance* cases are examples). Claimants bring such chancy claims partly because of one of the really salient features of campaign litigation: it offers **good publicity**, and a form of **accountability**, even if the prospects for a favourable outcome are slim or non-existent. Whatever

---

[19] Directive 2011/92/EU, Art 11.

[20] If you try it, the company may be refused standing or the court may order the company to give security for costs before proceeding. See *R v Environment Secretary, ex p Kirkstall Valley Campaign Ltd* [1996] 3 All ER 304, 309 (the company was allowed to proceed because it was not formed as a way of avoiding costs).

the outcome, the process itself is a way of bringing public authorities to account by forcing them to explain themselves to a court. And **even losing** may have benefits to the pressure group, because the litigation itself still shows the group's supporters how serious the group is.

But a public interest litigant, like any litigant, needs to think about the financial implications of losing: '[A]n unprotected claimant . . . if unsuccessful in a public interest challenge, may have to pay very heavy legal costs to the successful defendant, and . . . this may be a potent factor in deterring litigation directed towards protecting the environment from harm' (*R (Burkett) v Hammersmith and Fulham LBC (Costs)* [2004] EWCA Civ 1342 [80] (Brooke LJ)). And the court can even order that the claimant give security for costs (that is, deposit with the court an amount to cover the costs of the public authority) if the prospect of success is not high and there is doubt as to whether the claimant will pay an award of costs, at the end of the proceedings.

The good news is that courts will not require you to give security for costs if that would prevent a public interest case from proceeding. And what's more, you can apply for an order providing that you will not need to pay the defendant's costs if you lose, or capping the amount that you will be liable to pay. In *R (Plantagenet Alliance) v Secretary of State for Justice* [2013] EWHC 3164, for example, the court refused to order security for costs, and gave a protective costs order (that is, a costs capping order) to let the claimant proceed with a claim that was held in the end to be groundless, in confidence that it would not have to face the ordinary costs consequences. That amounts to requiring the government to carry an additional part of the cost of litigation, where the judge thinks a case ought to proceed.

The courts have always had a discretion to do this, but until the twenty-first century they were extremely wary, and treated it as something to be done 'only in the most exceptional circumstances' (*R v Lord Chancellor, ex p Child Poverty Action Group* [1999] 1 WLR 347, 355 (Dyson J)). Things have changed. The first reported case of such an order was in *R v The Prime Minister, ex p Campaign for Nuclear Disarmament* [2002] EWHC 2712. The Campaign for Nuclear Disarmament (CND) asked the court to declare that United Nations resolutions did not authorize the use of force against Iraq. The Administrative Court capped CND's costs exposure at £25,000.

If it really is in the public interest that the litigation should proceed, then it may be better for the public to bear the costs than for the private claimant to be deterred by the risk. But it is remarkable that judges should take it on themselves to decide that public authorities are to fund litigation against themselves. When the argument to be made in the *CND* claim was so speculative and, in fact, obviously bound to fail, this decision amounted to ordering public funding of the group's pursuit of its political campaign. Judges are generally wary of deciding how public authorities should spend their money (see 7.3.2); they felt able to do so in this context because of their very wide discretion over litigation costs under the CPR, and because of their concern (evident in *CND* and *Plantagenet Alliance*) to hear speculative claims that might not come before them without financial support.

The Court of Appeal set out a list of criteria in *R (Corner House Research) v Trade and Industry Secretary* [2005] EWCA Civ 192 [74], providing that costs would be capped if:

> (i) the issues raised are of general public importance;
> (ii) the public interest requires that those issues should be resolved;
> (iii) the applicant has no private interest in the outcome of the case;
> (iv) having regard to the financial resources of the applicant and the respondent(s) and to the amount of costs that are likely to be involved, it is fair and just to make the order; and
> (v) if the order is not made the applicant will probably discontinue the proceedings and will be acting reasonably in so doing.

The orders were meant to be exceptional, but *Corner House Research* removed an earlier requirement that the court must be able to see that the case has sufficient merit (*R v Lord Chancellor, ex p Child Poverty Action Group* [1999] 1 WLR 347, 358).

In the reforms to judicial review procedure in the Criminal Justice and Courts Act 2015, Parliament put costs capping orders on a statutory footing (ss 88–89). The legislation requires courts to consider the same list of considerations that the Court of Appeal developed in *Corner House Research*, but seeks to restrain the orders in three important ways:

- by providing that they are only available after the claimant has been granted permission for judicial review (CJCA 2015 s 88(3));

- by requiring a claimant seeking a costs capping order to disclose its financial resources (the defendant will be able to see the financial information, unless the court orders otherwise) (CJCA 2015 s 88(5));[21] and

- by providing that if a court caps the costs that the claimant will have to pay to the public authority defendant if it loses, the court must also cap the costs that the defendant will have to pay to the claimant, if the claimant wins (CJCA 2015 s 89(2)).

That final requirement had also been developed in the Court of Appeal. In *R (Buglife) v Thurrock Thames Gateway* [2008] EWCA Civ 1209, the Court of Appeal insisted that public authorities need to be protected from litigation costs where there is a substantial likelihood that the claimant will lose. When the Court capped the claimant's liability to pay the public authority's costs if the claimant lost, it also capped the public authority's liability to pay the claimant's costs if the claimant won [41].

Under the 2015 legislation, as long as the issues are of general public importance, the claimant can apply for a costs capping order without showing that their case is any

---

[21] The details are set out in CPR 46.17, added by the Civil Procedure (Amendment No. 2) Rules 2016.

stronger than it needs to be to get past the permission stage. But would-be claimants still face a financial risk, because the orders are unavailable before permission is given to seek judicial review. According to the Court of Appeal, the rule that costs can be awarded against a claimant who is not given permission 'must not be applied in a way which seriously impedes the right of citizens to access to justice' (*R (Ewing) v Office of the Deputy Prime Minister* [2005] EWCA Civ 1583 [41]). So costs awards on failed applications for permission are modest. As Collins J said in *R (Gentle) v Prime Minister* [2005] EWHC 3119 [108]: 'This may seem thoroughly unfair to the public body which is on the receiving end of a claim', but it is 'a price that must be paid to ensure that there is no unreasonable fetter on the right to come to court and seek redress for a supposed breach of rights, or an unlawful decision made, or an unlawful administrative action taken, against an individual'.

The costs capping provisions in the Criminal Justice and Courts Act 2015 went along with two other reforms on costs, designed by David Cameron's government to deter judicial review claims:

- Claimants must provide courts and, ordinarily, the defendant, with information about their financial resources, and information about the resources of third parties who may be supporting the litigation (CJCA 2015 ss 85–86).

- Intervenors (advocacy groups or individuals who apply to make argument in a judicial review case, without being either a claimant or defendant) can only receive their own costs in exceptional circumstances, and they face the risk of being made to pay the defendant's costs in some circumstances (CJCA 2015 s 87).

Both of these provisions are aimed against techniques of campaign litigation that the government saw as abuses, in which an advocacy organization brings a claim in the name of a claimant who has no resources, so that if the litigation is unsuccessful, the advocacy organization will not have to pay the costs of the defendant. Both provisions risk deterring the bringing of claims, and the making of arguments, that the courts ought to hear. Just as in the case of costs capping orders, though, the legislation gives the courts discretion over the operation of the disclosure requirement and the liability of interveners to costs orders, and the *Gentle* decision shows the attitude of the judges: they will avoid putting an 'unreasonable fetter on the right to come to court'.

That attitude to the cost of public interest litigation is further demonstrated by *R (Evans) v Secretary of State for Justice* [2011] EWHC 1146, in which the court quashed amendments to the Legal Services Commission Funding Code, which would have ruled out legal aid funding for public interest litigation (except in environmental cases) by restricting legal aid to cases in which the claimant or the claimant's family stood to benefit from the outcome. Laws LJ quashed this initiative to reduce the government's exposure to public interest litigation, on the ground that the Ministry of Defence was concerned about the risk that public interest claims brought with legal aid could have consequences that are 'extremely serious for our defence, security, and foreign policy interests' [24]. Laws LJ held, at [25], that the law prohibited the government from acting on that consideration:

> ' For the state to inhibit litigation by the denial of legal aid because the court's judgment might be unwelcome or apparently damaging would constitute an attempt to influence the incidence of judicial decisions in the interests of government. It would therefore be frankly inimical to the rule of law. '

We should face the fact that there is a real risk—since judges are human, and their processes are imperfect, and they can only decide on the basis of what is submitted to them—that a court's judgment might not just be apparently damaging, but actually damaging, not only to the interests of government, but also to the interests of the community and to the interests of justice. But the courts are not prepared to allow the government to make litigation funding decisions on the basis of that risk.

11.4 Standing in an ordinary claim for a declaration

You can ask for a declaration in an ordinary claim, and unlawful administrative action is a ground for a declaration. So if you do not have an interest in the matter that is sufficient for the court to allow you to seek judicial review, can you seek a declaration instead? No: an action for a declaration has its own special standing requirement.[22] *Because* you can seek a declaration without having a cause of action (*Dyson v Attorney-General* [1911] 1 KB 410), the courts developed a standing requirement to decide whether to hear claims for a declaration, and this common law requirement is in fact much stricter than the standing requirement for judicial review.

A claimant must allege 'either an interference with some private right of his or an interference with a public right from which he has suffered damage peculiar to himself' (*Barrs v Bethell* [1982] Ch 294, 306 (Warner J)). Warner J held that 'local authorities and their members [such as the defendants in that case] are particularly vulnerable to actions by busybodies and cranks' (313). But the rule is consistent with other cases on declarations, and can be regarded as a general rule of standing for an ordinary claim for a declaration.

It may seem strange to impose one standing requirement on a claimant seeking a declaration in a claim for judicial review and a different requirement on a claimant seeking a declaration in an ordinary claim. But it makes sense for a reason emphasized in the *Barrs* case: the permission requirement gives a reason for the liberal standing doctrine in a claim for judicial review. If a claimant who would not be given permission to seek judicial review could seek a declaration in an ordinary claim instead as a matter of right, it would allow vexatious litigants to circumvent the permission requirement. This really *would* be an instance of the abuse of process that Lord Diplock had in mind in *O'Reilly v Mackman* [1982] 2 AC 237, 285 (see 10.2.1).

---

22 The same is true of an ordinary claim for an injunction.

Note that the 1978 judicial review reforms[23] liberalized proceedings for a declaration by providing that a declaration could be sought in an application for judicial review, and by *hinting* that it could be done when the applicant did not have the standing to bring an action for a declaration (because the 'sufficient interest' provision applied to all applications for judicial review, without regard to the remedy). It was only a hint, because the courts might have decided that a person seeking a declaration does not have a sufficient interest unless the matter adversely affected his or her private interests. But in the *'Fleet Street Casuals'* case, the majority held that the issue of standing was the same regardless of the remedy.

> ### Standing is not more restricted in judicial review
> The standing requirements for judicial review are not special obstructions restricting judicial review: standing in judicial review is actually *more generous* to litigants than the requirement in an ordinary claim, for which the claimant must either have a right of action (see *Ewing v Office of the Deputy Prime Minister* [2005] EWCA Civ 1583 [35]), or else fulfil the strict test of standing to bring an ordinary action for a declaration.

11.5 Standing in Human Rights Act proceedings

By the Human Rights Act 1998 s 6, an action of a public authority that is incompatible with a Convention right is for that reason unlawful (unless the public authority could not have acted differently because of primary legislation). So you might think that any campaign litigant would be able to bring the unlawful conduct before a court. But no: s 7(1) provides that a claimant can *only* bring proceedings based on s 6 'if he is (or would be) a victim of the unlawful act'. If the proceeding is a claim for judicial review, the claimant only has a sufficient interest to raise a Convention right issue if he or she is or would be a victim (s 7(3)). That reflects the Convention itself, which provides that claims may be brought in the Strasbourg Court by 'any person, non-governmental organisation or group of individuals claiming to be the victim of a violation by one of the High Contracting Parties of the rights . . .' (Art 34). The Strasbourg Court has held that the 'victim' requirement 'does not permit individuals to complain against a law *in abstract* simply because they feel that it contravenes the convention'; the claimant must be 'directly affected' (*Klass v Germany* (1978) 2 EHRR 214 [33]).

> ### A very important exception!
> The Equality Act 2006 creates an express exception to Human Rights Act 1998 s 7(1) and (3), giving the Equality and Human Rights Commission (see 13.12)

---

23 Rules of the Supreme Court Order 53, given statutory force in the Senior Courts Act 1981 s 31.

> standing to bring Human Rights Act proceedings. It only needs to show that
> there is or would be some actual victim (Equality Act 2006 s 30(3)). This provision
> creates a technique for litigation in the English courts by an independent advo-
> cacy commission.

Subject to the special statutory role of the Equality and Human Rights Commission, it is 'doubtful in the extreme' that a court would use its discretion to declare that a statute is incompatible with a Convention right if the person seeking the declaration were not a victim of the incompatibility (*Lancashire County Council v Taylor* [2005] EWCA Civ 284 [42] (Lord Woolf)).

The distinction between standing in general judicial review and standing under the Human Rights Act 1998 reflects the different responsibilities of the court in applying the Convention rights, on the one hand, and engaging in judicial review on the common law grounds, on the other. In applying the Convention rights, the court is given no general responsibility for overseeing government; its job is only to hear a claim of right. In judicial review, the courts have a more general responsibility for reviewing allegations of unlawful administrative action, so that the focus of the court's attention is not simply on protecting someone whose rights have been violated.

So the restriction on standing under the Human Rights Act does not leave a grave lacuna in our public law. It goes to show that the rule of law does not require an open doors policy; judicial processes for giving effect to the law are absolutely crucial, but they do not need to be engaged in every case of unlawful conduct. In the case of the Human Rights Act, the purpose of s 6 is to give legal effect to the Convention rights. Limiting standing strictly to victims is compatible with that concern for those rights; the purpose of making official conduct unlawful (giving effect to the Convention rights) can be met if standing is restricted to the victims of unlawful conduct.

So is there no room for campaign litigation over Human Rights Act issues? There is plenty of room, actually, but the proceedings need to be fronted by a representative claimant who is a victim of the alleged violation of a Convention right. An advocacy group can support the litigant (in fact, it can persuade the litigant to start proceedings in the first place), or can apply to intervene, to make legal argument in the proceedings (see 11.8). Moreover, an intervenor need not be a victim, and the courts are generous in allowing intervention in Human Rights Act proceedings (*R (MH) v Health Secretary (Application for Permission to Intervene)* [2004] EWCA Civ 1321).

The possibility of public interest Human Rights Act litigation does not mean that the 'victim' requirement is meaningless. It not only means that the pressure group needs to persuade such a person to put their name to the proceedings; but also means that the argument and the reasoning of the judges are focused on the effect of an incompatibility on that party. As Lord Woolf has put it for the Court of Appeal: 'The primary objective of the Convention is to secure for individuals the rights and freedoms set out in the Convention', and Human Rights Act proceedings are designed to focus on that objective (*Lancashire County Council v Taylor* [2005] EWCA Civ 284 [37]). Table 11.2 summarizes the requirements for standing in a variety of administrative law proceedings.

Table 11.2 Summary of standing requirements

In order to:	You must:
Bring a claim for judicial review	Have a sufficient interest in the matter
Seek a declaration or injunction in an ordinary claim	Assert a private right, or be subject to special damage
Bring a claim in contract or tort	Assert a right of action (see Chapter 14)
Bring proceedings under the Human Rights Act 1998	Be the victim of an alleged breach of a Convention right (s 7(1))
Bring proceedings in the CJEU	Be the addressee of the measure that is being attacked, or be directly and individually concerned by the measure[24]
Bring a complaint to an ombudsman	Complain that you have suffered injustice as a result of maladministration[25] *and*, in the case of the Parliamentary Ombudsman, find an MP willing to refer the complaint.
Seek information under the Freedom of Information Act 2000	**Standing is open:** 'Any person' can request information—s 1(1)

11.6 Standing before the Court of Justice of the European Union

Article 263 of the Treaty on the Functioning of the European Union (TFEU) allows any person to bring proceedings in the Court of Justice of the European Union (CJEU) to challenge a decision of the EU institutions if it was 'addressed to that person' *or* 'is of direct and individual concern' to them. So, as with the Human Rights Act 1998, standing cannot be given in the public interest in the way that standing can be given for judicial review in English law. But the claimant does not need to be the victim of an adverse decision. The provision concerning 'direct and individual concern' suggests a halfway house, but the CJEU has treated it restrictively. 'Individual concern' is treated as requiring that the act in question concerns the claimant just as specifically as it concerns a person to whom it is addressed. As the Court has put it, the act must concern the claimant 'by reason of certain attributes peculiar to them, or by reason of a factual situation which differentiates them from all other persons and distinguishes them individually in the same way as the addressee' (Case C-50/00 P *Unión de Pequeños*

---

[24] Article 263 TFEU. The European Parliament, Council, Commission, and member states are 'privileged' applicants with special standing; the Court of Auditors and the European Central Bank are 'quasi-privileged' applicants.

[25] Parliamentary Commissioner Act 1967 s 5(1). A complainant before the European Ombudsman need not have suffered injustice as a result of maladministration (and the European Ombudsman can initiate his or her own investigations): see 13.10.

Agricultores v Council of the European Union [2002] ECR II-6677 [36]).[26] It must be the case that the law maker actually took the applicant into account (or ought to have) in making the decision.

The Court insisted, at [37]–[38], that its strict approach to standing did not abandon the rule of law:

> ' The European Community is . . . a community based on the rule of law in which its institutions are subject to judicial review of the compatibility of their acts with the Treaty and with the general principles of law which include fundamental rights. Individuals are therefore entitled to effective judicial protection of the rights they derive from the Community legal order . . . '

Notice the emphasis on rights, which is the common thread in the doctrine of standing before British courts under the Human Rights Act 1998, and before the CJEU under EU law. Effective judicial protection of rights does not require campaign litigation; it requires a process adapted to the purpose of the law. So this strict doctrine does not create a grave lacuna in EU law, either; the purpose of judicial proceedings need not be to open the doors to all complaints of illegality.

Finally, note that the system of EU law relies on the national courts of member states. Those courts do not have jurisdiction to declare EU measures invalid (Case 314/85 *Foto Frost* [1987] ECR 4199). But any person who wishes to rely on the invalidity of an EU measure can ask the national courts to make a reference to the CJEU for a ruling on validity. And it is up to the national courts to operate procedural rules for people who want the courts to give effect to EU law. A campaign litigant in judicial review proceedings could ask the English courts to make a reference to the CJEU for a preliminary ruling on the validity of an EU measure, under Art 267 TFEU.

And if a claimant wants to argue that the action of a public authority in England is contrary to a directly effective provision of EU law, the national court must provide a process for the claim. The process may be subject to the same procedural restrictions (such as a requirement of standing) as in domestic law, *except* that if the restrictions make it practically impossible to enforce the right claimed under EU law, the national court must remove them. So a claimant must be given standing in judicial review, even if standing would ordinarily be refused, if denying standing would make 'the enforcement of a directly effective provision of the Treaty practically impossible' (*R v The Attorney-General, ex p ICI* [1987] 1 CMLR 72 (CA) [92]).

. . . .

Greenpeace in the CJEU

Greenpeace has pushed unsuccessfully for campaign litigation before the CJEU. It had no hope, as a campaign litigant, of establishing (1) that it was representing its members; and (2) that the European Union's decision to give millions of euros to

. . . .
[26] It is an ancient case law doctrine, dating back to *Case 25/62 Plaumann v Commission* [1963] ECR 95.

Spain for a nuclear power plant (a project that allegedly violated an EU environmental directive) was of individual concern to its members. For while representative standing is allowed, the case was doomed by the strictness of the 'individual concern' doctrine. The Court held that the financing was only indirectly of concern to Greenpeace's members, so that Greenpeace did not have standing (Case 321/95 P *Stichting Greenpeace Council (Greenpeace International) v Commission* [1998] ECR I-1651). In any case, as the Court pointed out, Greenpeace's members had redress for any breach of the directive in administrative proceedings in the national courts.

11.7 Standing for public authorities

The **Attorney General**, the Cabinet minister responsible for government legal services, has standing on behalf of the Crown to seek prerogative writs, and can also bring ordinary claims for an injunction or declaration. These special privileges in litigation reflect the fact that the government has a general responsibility for the rule of law. Not that the Attorney General must use these powers whenever he or she hears of unlawful conduct; it is up to him or her to decide when the public interest requires it. He or she can commence litigation at the request of (or 'at the relation of') any person; his or her discretion whether to conduct such 'relator' proceedings is (more or less) unreviewable (*Gouriet v Union of Post Office Workers* [1978] AC 435). A relator claim (brought as an ordinary claim for an injunction or declaration, or by the judicial review procedure) may be brought against a public authority on the same grounds as in a claim for judicial review. It may also be brought against any private person committing a public nuisance or otherwise violating what used to be called 'public rights'. Lord Wilberforce in *Gouriet* called the distinction between private rights and public rights one of the 'pillars' of the law (482); if it seems quaint today, that is because increasingly sophisticated regulatory regimes since the 1970s have generally accomplished the protection of certain public interests (particularly in pollution control) without the need for the Attorney General to initiate judicial proceedings. It seems that a public right arises where the law imposes a duty on a person for the public good, without giving anyone else a corresponding right to a remedy for breach of the duty.

FROM THE MISTS OF TIME

In *R v Inhabitants of Clace* (1769) 4 Burr 2456, 2458, Lord Mansfield said:

> 'I remember a case from Bristol, where the Attorney General, on behalf of the Crown, moved for a certiorari to remove some orders of two justices made for the relief of glassmakers from an over-charge upon them by the officers of Excise: and it was holden "that the King had a right in every case where the Crown is concerned, to demand a certiorari; and that the Court are bound to grant it, unless the King's right to it is restrained by some Act of Parliament".'

Lord Mansfield remembered the case from Bristol because he was the Attorney General who made the argument (see *R v Amendt* [1915] 2 KB 276).

Largely because of the courts' generous approach to standing in judicial review, relator proceedings are now obsolete, for practical purposes. They are still available, and it would be possible to imagine circumstances in which they would be useful, but there have been no relator claims in England in the twenty-first century. Yet, in principle, in *any* public interest claim, the Attorney General could have brought proceedings to uphold the rule of law. But although officials of the Crown ought to be good at upholding the rule of law in criminal prosecutions (where the problem is how the criminal justice system should respond to crimes by private persons), they are systematically ineffective at bringing each other to account for unlawful conduct. So, for example, in the *World Development Movement* case, the Attorney General could have brought proceedings for a declaration that the Foreign Secretary had unlawfully plundered the overseas development budget. But in spite of a constitutional convention that the Attorney General is meant to give advice to the government on the law as he or she sees it, without political bias, he or she does not have the independence that it would take to make him or her a watchdog over unlawful administrative action.

● *Pop quiz* ●

Why hasn't the Senior Courts Act 1981 s 31(3) removed the prerogative to bring relator proceedings? It says 'no application for judicial review shall be made unless the leave of the High Court has been obtained in accordance with the rules of court; and the court shall not grant leave to make such an application unless it considers that the applicant has a sufficient interest in the matter'.

Only the Attorney General has this special, open standing at common law. But standing can be conferred by statute; a very important example concerns **local authorities**. Judicial review has long been used by and against local authorities,[27] but it took an Act of Parliament to establish their general access to the courts. They can 'appear in any legal proceedings and, in the case of civil proceedings, may institute them in their own name', if they 'consider it expedient for the promotion or protection of the interests of the inhabitants of their area' (Local Government Act 1972 s 222).[28] They would not be given standing if they unreasonably considered the proceedings expedient (*Stoke-on-Trent City Council v B&Q* [1984] AC 754). But their standing is ordinarily taken for granted.

Public authorities very commonly seek judicial review, and standing is seldom argued. But without the sort of legislative authorization provided by s 222, a public

....

[27] e.g., the London County Council used *mandamus* to enforce a borough's legal obligations in *R v Poplar Borough Council, ex p London County Council (No 1)* [1922] 1 KB 72 (see 10.4.5).

[28] A classic instance is *R v Environment Secretary, ex p Hammersmith and Fulham LBC* [1991] 1 AC 521 (see 7.3.2), in which twenty local authorities unsuccessfully challenged the government's funding policies (their standing is not discussed in the case). And, on a more local scale, the ability to seek injunctions has proven useful in enforcing such local decisions as tree preservation orders: *Kent County Council v Batchelor (No 2)* [1979] 1 WLR 213. Note that s 222 even allows local authorities to seek injunctions to enforce the criminal law: *Kirklees Metropolitan Borough Council v Wickes Building Supplies* [1993] AC 227.

authority, like any other claimant, needs to have a sufficient interest under the Senior Courts Act 1981 s 31(3).

In *R v Environment Secretary, ex p Hammersmith and Fulham LBC* [1991] 1 AC 521, Lord Bridge suggested that public authorities may have standing for the same reason as private persons. He held that due process protects private parties who may be affected by decisions of public authorities 'in their person, their property or their reputation', and he concluded that: 'The principle equally applies to public bodies or public authorities affected by an administrative decision [of another public body] which is based upon . . . [the other public body] . . . having acted, or which necessarily implies that they have acted, unlawfully or discreditably' (598). But protecting the person, property, or reputation of public officials cannot be the main reason for giving one public authority standing to seek judicial review of the conduct of another. The central justification, implicit in most claims brought by public authorities, is a form of public interest standing: the public purposes for which the public authority exists may sometimes be legitimately pursued through judicial review of the lawfulness of another public body's conduct. That implicit rationale for local authority standing is essentially the same as the rationale spelt out in the Local Government Act 1972 (that is, standing 'for the promotion or protection of the interests of the inhabitants of their area').

Strange standing

Occasionally, local councillors have been given standing on behalf of a local council to challenge the council's own planning decisions. The Court of Appeal has endorsed this arrangement as 'convenient and appropriate' if it 'is not abused' (*R v Bassetlaw District Council, ex p Oxby* [1998] PLCR 283, 293).[29] It gives the council a way of referring its own decision to the court to be quashed. The only way in which it can be done while maintaining an adversarial proceeding is if (as in *Oxby*) there is a party adverse in interest to the councillor and the council who can intervene.

This public interest rationale for litigation by public authorities has been recognized in *R v Employment Secretary, ex p Equal Opportunities Commission* [1995] 1 AC 1. The Employment Secretary argued that the Equal Opportunities Commission (EOC) had no standing to seek judicial review of compliance with EU law on equal pay for men and women. The EOC was an independent commission established by Parliament (see 13.12). The Employment Secretary's argument was that the EOC had no right, interest, or legitimate expectation at stake, and had suffered no damage. That was all irrelevant in the view of the majority: the question of whether the EOC had a sufficient interest in the matter depended on its public role. Lord Keith pointed out that the Sex Discrimination Act 1975 gave the EOC responsibility 'to work towards the

---

[29] See also *R (Corbett) v Restormel Borough Council and Land and Property Ltd* [2001] EWCA Civ 330.

elimination of discrimination' (s 53(1)). That was enough to support the conclusion that 'the statutory duties and public law role of the EOC' gave it a sufficient interest in the matter (Lord Keith, 26). This result may seem comparable to the standing of local authorities—that is, it is a standing conferred by statute. But the better view is that the capacity to have standing without having anything to gain or lose from the decision follows from the Commission's role in promoting the public interest. It has standing because of the purpose for which Parliament set it up, and not because Parliament decided to give it standing.

There is one aspect of litigation by public authorities that creates a special problem of comity for the courts: some public authorities have tried to use judicial review to escape the consequences (or merely the disappointment) of being criticized by government agencies such as Local Government Ombudsmen (e.g., *R v LCA, ex p Croydon LBC* [1989] 1 All ER 1033) and the Audit Commission (*R (Ealing LBC) v Audit Commission* [2005] EWCA Civ 556). In those cases, the courts have to be especially careful to avoid pointless and expensive interference with another independent decision maker (see 13.8.3).

● *Pop quiz* ●

The Parliamentary Commissioner Act 1967 prohibits the Parliamentary Ombudsman from investigating complaints by local authorities, and by public authorities whose members are appointed by the Crown or whose funds are mainly granted by Parliament (s 6(1)). Why might that be?

11.8 Standing to intervene

A claimant in judicial review proceedings must 'state the name and address of any person he considers to be an interested party' (CPR 54.6(1)). The court will ordinarily allow those parties to 'take part' in the proceedings. So there is very easy access for private parties who are adverse in interest to a claimant.[30] What's more, anyone who wishes can apply to intervene, and the court has an undefined discretion to allow him or her to file evidence or make representations at the hearing (CPR 54.17(1)).

The courts also allow public interest intervention, and the test is really quite relaxed. The matters the intervenor raises must be of 'of some general importance', and there must be 'a real possibility that the court would be assisted by its intervention' (*R (MH) v Health Secretary (Application for Permission to Intervene)* [2004] EWCA Civ 1321 [8], allowing Mind, a national mental health advocacy organization, to intervene in a claim that the Mental Health Act 1983 was incompatible with the Convention). Public authorities do not generally have an incentive to oppose

---

[30] *R (Corbett) v Restormel Borough Council and Land and Property Ltd* [2001] EWCA Civ 330 is an example. And British Nuclear Fuels Plc intervened in *R v Inspectorate of Pollution, ex p Greenpeace (No 2)* [1994] 2 CMLR 548.

intervention; although intervention will slightly increase the public authority's costs, it may be politically unattractive to stand in the way of advocacy groups having an input in the litigation.

Perhaps the most extravagant example of public interest intervention yet was *R v Bow Street Metropolitan Stipendiary Magistrate, ex p Pinochet Ugarte (No 3)* [1999] 2 WLR 827, in which Amnesty International, the Medical Foundation for the Care of Victims of Torture, the Redress Trust, the Association of the Relatives of the Disappeared Detainees, and three individuals were given leave to intervene, and Human Rights Watch was permitted to present written submissions.

Life and death

The Court of Appeal accepted written submissions from the Archbishop of Westminster in *A (Children) (Conjoined Twins: Medical Treatment) (No 1)* [2000] 4 All ER 961. The Court did not explain why the submissions were accepted, although Ward LJ stated that doing so was exceptional (966). And the House of Lords accepted written submissions from the Archbishop of Cardiff (again, without giving reasons) in *R (Pretty) v DPP (Home Secretary intervening)* [2001] UKHL 61, in which Mrs Pretty unsuccessfully challenged the DPP's refusal to grant immunity to her husband should he help her to commit suicide. The courts' acceptance of the submissions reflects an openness to contributions from campaigners on the basis of the same sort of grounds as in *R v Foreign Secretary, ex p World Development Movement* [1995] 1 WLR 386: the intervenor's serious concern with the issues, experience in advocacy work, and resources for providing information or making an argument. The question of whether a person has wisdom to offer on ending human life because he is an archbishop is not justiciable. But this is true of the question of the wisdom of any public interest intervenor.

In the European Court of Human Rights, Convention contracting states other than the defendant, and other persons, can ask for leave to submit written comments or take part in a hearing,[31] and it will be granted if it is 'in the interest of the proper administration of justice' (Art 36).

But the CJEU takes a tougher stance, which matches its approach to standing: intervention will only be allowed if the party's legal position would be directly changed by the ruling in the case; it is not enough that the intervenor might have something to say that would assist the court (see Case T-201/04 R 5 *Microsoft Corporation v Commission* [2006] 4 CMLR 9, denying leave to 'think tanks' advocating policies that related to the issues in the case).

---

[31] A contracting state has a right to intervene if one of its nationals is seeking a remedy against another contracting state.

11.8.1 Intervention by public authorities

The courts are very liberal in allowing public authorities to intervene in proceedings started by private claimants: see *R (Pretty) v DPP (Home Secretary intervening)* [2001] UKHL 61, and note the important case of *R v North and East Devon Health Authority, ex p Coughlan* [2001] QB 213, in which the Secretary of State for Health was given leave to intervene and was treated as a party (the Royal College of Nursing also made written submissions [5]). As is common in intervenor decisions, no reasons were given—but it is evidently enough that the intervenors have an interest in the matter that makes it potentially useful for the court to hear them in order to decide the issues raised by the claimant and defendant.

11.9 Conclusion: the limits of administrative law

The point of administrative law is to facilitate and to control decision making in the public interest. The rule of law requires that official action should accord with the law. But if an official has engaged in unlawful conduct, there may or may not be a public interest in making any response to it. The rule of law only demands judicial processes that are needed for the purpose of preventing arbitrary government. So **proportionate process** is a principle that ought to govern judicial processes as well as administrative processes.

The public interest in imposing the rule of law on the administration does not demand unrestricted access to judicial process. Requirements of standing that restrict access to judicial review are justifiable. For the purposes that justify administrative law, access to justice is crucial. But the doors of the courts do not need to be open, and are not open, to everyone who complains that the government has acted unlawfully. The courts, in their enthusiasm for access to justice, are more prone to give too much access to judicial review, than too little. In the *Plantagenet Alliance* case, the three key obstacles to judicial review were all very low hurdles. If you agree with the court's decision on the claim for judicial review, you may conclude that the claimant had no arguable case (see 11.2.1, p 419), had no interest in the proceedings that was sufficient to justify the judicial review process, and had no justification for being protected from bearing the ordinary costs consequences of a losing claim. Yet all those matters were decided in the activists' favour in the initial application for permission to proceed to judicial review, in a High Court decision that reflects the judges' special zeal for judicial supervision of government action.

There is not a grave lacuna in our system of public law just because some unlawful conduct cannot be brought before the court. But there *will* be a grave lacuna if there is no process for a person with sufficient interest to seek a remedy, when a remedy is owed to the claimant, or is called for in the public interest.

TAKE-HOME MESSAGE ● ● ●

- The requirement of '**sufficient interest**' for standing to seek judicial review gives the court a discretionary power to decide who should be given standing—that is, to whom the courts should listen.

- The courts' doors are not open to everyone who alleges that a public authority has acted unlawfully. For example, judges will not ordinarily give standing to an individual to argue in judicial review that another individual has been treated unlawfully.

- Standing will be given to **campaign groups** to seek judicial review if they have an arguable case on an issue of public importance, and there is no particular claimant who would be better placed to seek judicial review, and the group has a prominent role in the field in question.

- Standing to seek remedies under the Convention in the Strasbourg Court, and under the Human Rights Act 1998 in the English courts, is more limited: the claimant must be a victim of an alleged violation of a Convention right.

- Standing for private parties to seek invalidation of EU measures in the CJEU, too, is limited to persons who are themselves directly affected.

CRITICAL QUESTIONS • • •

1   In enforcing the criminal law, it is the task of the police to investigate any serious allegation of criminal conduct from anyone who has information to offer. Is the task of the courts in administrative law similar—that is, to investigate any allegation of unlawful conduct from anyone who has information to offer?

2   How would an open doors policy on standing to seek judicial review (giving standing to anyone with an arguable case that a public authority has acted unlawfully) differ from the standing rules we have?

3   Was the *'Fleet Street Casuals'* case an example of public interest litigation?

4   Should leave to apply for judicial review be refused in a case in which the applicant could have gone to an ombudsman?

READING • • •

R v Inland Revenue Commissioners, ex p National Federation of Self-Employed and Small Businesses Ltd [1982] AC 617 *('Fleet Street Casuals')*
R v Home Secretary, ex p Ruddock [1987] 1 WLR 1482
R v Inspectorate of Pollution, ex p Greenpeace (No 2) [1994] 2 CMLR 548
R v Foreign Secretary, ex p World Development Movement Ltd [1995] 1 WLR 386
R v Somerset County Council, ex p Dixon [1998] Env LR 111

Carol Harlow, 'Public Law and Popular Justice' (2002) 65 MLR 1

On standing to intervene:
Michael Fordham, 'Public Interest' Intervention' [2007] PL 410

 The following online resources accompany this chapter: **summaries** of key cases and legislation; **updates** on the law; **guidance** for answering the pop quizzes and questions; and **links** to legislation, cases, and useful websites.

Part V
Administrative justice

12 Tribunals

Panels, committees, tribunals, referees, adjudicators, commissioners, and other public authorities decide many thousands of disputes each year over (for example) entitlement to benefits, or tax liability, or refugee status, or the detention of a patient in a secure hospital. The massive array of agencies reflects the great variety of benefits and burdens that twenty-first-century government assigns to people. The array had no overall organization until 2007, when Parliament transformed it into a complex system. Integrating these decision-making agencies brings advantages, but the law needs to tailor their structure, processes, and decision-making techniques to the variety of purposes they serve. And the law needs to achieve proportionate process, by reconciling competing interests in legalism and informality in tribunal processes.

LOOK FOR • • •

- The new administrative justice system established by the **Tribunals, Courts and Enforcement Act 2007** (TCEA).

- The balance between legalism and informality in the tribunals system.

- Proportionate dispute resolution.

- The irony of process: in order to do justice, tribunals need to give processes that may be *more than* proportionate in some cases.

' The edifice of administrative and adjudicative tribunals created by the Tribunals, Courts and Enforcement Act 2007 (TCEA) is a landmark in the development of the United Kingdom's organic constitution. For the first time, a single structure has been created within which a huge variety of existing tribunals is gathered. '

R (Cart) v Upper Tribunal [2010]
EWCA Civ 859 [1] (Sedley LJ)

12.1 Introduction: proportionate process in administrative justice

Every programme of government generates grievances. Those that especially affect particular individuals generate disputes that need a legally binding resolution. **'Administrative justice'** is a term for processes that are designed to resolve disputes over the implementation and operation of those projects. It is not an ancient term. Until well into the twentieth century, it was generally presumed that there was only one way of securing justice: the common law courts ought to resolve disputes between government and subject.

Government schemes are incredibly diverse. They give social security benefits, and impose taxes, and award compensation for criminal injuries, and give refugee status or immigration status, and regulate food production and workplace safety, and keep people locked in hospitals on the ground that they are dangerous to others. They have been launched (most of them over the past 100 years) with ad hoc legislation, resulting in an extravagant variety of techniques for redress of grievances caused by the schemes' operation. The variety reflects the diversity of the projects. The disputes that they generate are similarly diverse. And the number of claims in tribunals is far greater than the number of claims for judicial review in the courts. Figure 12.1 illustrates the volume of cases in major tribunals in the ten years after they were reorganized by the Tribunals, Courts and Enforcement Act 2007.

Among the most important bodies dealing with grievances about government services are the Social Security and Child Support Appeals Tribunal, the First-tier Tribunal (Tax), the Immigration and Asylum Tribunal (IAT), the Mental Health Tribunal, the Criminal Injuries Compensation Tribunal, and the school admissions and exclusion appeal panels. There are dozens more, such as the Traffic Penalty Tribunal, the National Lottery Commission, and some that have never sat, such as the Sea Fish Licence Tribunal and the Antarctic Act Tribunal.

And those are only the 'person-and-state'[1] tribunals: they hear appeals against decisions made by or on behalf of the government. Others are 'party-and-party' tribunals, government agencies designed to resolve disputes between private persons. These include the employment tribunals, the Copyright Tribunal (which controls collective

---

[1] They are often called 'citizen-and-state' tribunals, but one of the largest—the Immigration and Asylum Tribunal—does not involve citizens.

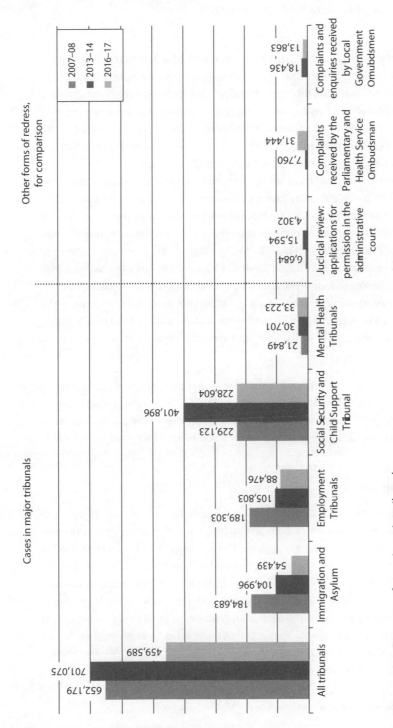

Figure 12.1 Ten years of cases in major tribunals

Sources: Ministry of Justice Tribunal Statistics Quarterly and Civil Justice Statistics Quarterly (both available at https://www.gov.uk/government/collections/); Parliamentary Ombudsman Annual Reports (available at https://www.ombudsman.org.uk); Local Government Complaint Reviews (available at http://lgo.org.uk/information-centre/reports/annual-review-reports/local-government-complaint-reviews). The reduction in tribunal cases after 2013 resulted from (1) the imposition of high fees in the Employment Tribunals (the fees were held to be unlawful in R (UNISON) v Lord Chancellor [2017] UKSC 51; see 1.5.5); (2) a new process of reconsideration of Social Security decisions; and (3) new restrictions on eligibility to bring claims in the Immigration and Asylum Tribunal.

licensing of copyright material), and the Residential Property Tribunal Service (which decides disputes between landlords and tenants).

Are party-and-party tribunals a concern of administrative law?

The employment tribunals hear complaints against private employers by private individuals. So what does this type of tribunal have to do with administrative law, when it decides relations between two private parties? The tribunals are governed by administrative law, because they are public authorities (including for the purposes of the Human Rights Act 1998). The power that such public authorities wield over private parties needs to be controlled by law.

But person-and-state tribunals raise one crucial public law problem that does not arise with party-and-party tribunals. It is a problem of separating powers. In a hearing before a person-and-state tribunal, the tribunal is part of the apparatus of the state, and it decides a dispute between the person and the state. The tribunals system has dealt with this problem by taking tribunals out of the departments of government, creating a Tribunals Service in 2006, which was then merged with the Courts Service to form Her Majesty's Courts and Tribunals Service in 2011.

A party-and-party tribunal (such as an employment tribunal, where the employer is a private company) is independent of the parties. Most of the discussion in this chapter deals with person-and-state tribunals.

The diversity of tribunals is reflected in their names, but only imperfectly: the names have been thought up (and often changed) in a series of historical accidents reflecting decisions about how best to present new decision-making authorities to the public. The terms are used in various ways, and only some very general pointers as to their use are possible.

What's in a name?

- **'Commissioner'** and 'Commission' are ancient terms,[2] and imply appointment by the Crown with a commission that is more-or-less akin to the commission of a judge. From the introduction of the income tax in 1799, the Tax Commissioners were appointed to serve both as tax collectors and as an appeal body; their work became purely adjudicative in 1946, and they became the Tax Chamber of the First-tier Tribunal under the new tribunals system. In the twenty-first century, the term 'commissioner' is used for some important bodies that have oversight responsibilities for particular areas of government (e.g., the Care Quality Commission for health care and the Equality and Human Rights Commission for combating discrimination).[3]

---

[2] The Commissioners of Sewers date back to the Middle Ages: see 7.1.

[3] It is also used for one important tribunal, the Special Immigration and Appeals Commission: see 12.6, p 473.

- The more common term **'tribunal'** can simply mean 'decision-making body' (that is its meaning in the European Convention on Human Rights Art 6). But since the aftermath of World War I, when the first major tribunals were created to deal with complaints about war pension decisions, the term 'tribunal' has been used in English administrative law to refer to a body outside the ordinary courts that has legal power to decide disputes between parties.[4]
- **'Adjudicator'** is sometimes used for a person who resolves a dispute ('referee' is sometimes used that way, too). But 'adjudicator' is sometimes used for an ombudsman.
- **'Ombudsman'** means an officer who receives and investigates a complaint and reports on the result of the investigation (see Chapter 13).
- **'Service'** means the same as 'agency', but is meant to sound more consumer-friendly.
- **'Authority'**, **'board'**, **'agency'**, and **'panel'** are neutral terms for public authorities, some of which are tribunals, which may have a variety of functions and powers.

The principle of **proportionate process** (see 4.4) means that these various bodies need different decision-making techniques for their various purposes. Some tribunals reconsider the denial of a benefit, such as Disability Living Allowance or compensation for criminal injuries. Others, such as the Immigration and Asylum Tribunal and the Mental Health Tribunal, determine personal freedom. These differences have crucial implications for the personnel of tribunals (that is, whether the members should be lawyers, or experts in some relevant profession, or laypeople, or some combination). Special technical issues (such as mental health) may affect not only the membership of the tribunal itself, but also the use of assessors to advise the tribunal, or the taking of expert evidence. The same particularities determine whether an oral hearing is essential, whether complainants need legal representation or special advice, what form of appeal is necessary, if any, and what form of independence is needed.

Yet there are common features among all tribunals:

- they hear a dispute between parties (in a person-and-state tribunal, one of the parties is a government agency);

- they determine a resolution to the dispute with binding effect;

- they determine the case according to the law;

- their jurisdiction is restricted to a specified subject matter; and

- they are not courts.

---

[4]   The term 'tribunal' has sometimes been used for an inquiry, ever since the Tribunals of Inquiry (Evidence) Act 1921. 'Tribunals of inquiry', or just 'inquiries' are public investigations. They are often chaired by a judge and involve testimony under oath. Since they are investigations rather than a process for resolving a dispute between parties, they are dealt with in Chapter 13.

Or, more precisely, they are not courts like the High Court. They are established by statute, and they have no inherent jurisdiction (that is, they only have the jurisdiction conferred on them by the legislation). Until the new tribunals system was established in 2007, they were ordinarily subject to the supervisory jurisdiction of the High Court in judicial review.[5]

Superior courts, inferior courts, and tribunals

An inferior court is subject to the supervision of the High Court by judicial review. Magistrates' courts and coroners' courts are examples of inferior courts. The Crown Court, the High Court, the Court of Appeal, and the Supreme Court are not subject to that supervision (there are statutory rights of appeal from one level to a higher level, but they are not subject to judicial review). Those are superior courts (see *Re Racal Communications* [1981] AC 374 (HL)). The Special Immigration and Appeals Commission was made a 'superior court of record' so that its decisions would not be subject to judicial review, but only subject to appeal to the Court of Appeal (like judgments of the High Court) (Anti-terrorism, Crime and Security Act 2001 s 35—see 12.6, p 474).

But there is no general legal distinction between courts and tribunals. As Lord Edmund-Davies said: '[I]t has unfortunately to be said that there emerges no sure guide, no unmistakable hallmark by which a "court" or "inferior court" may unerringly be identified' (*Attorney-General v BBC* [1981] AC 303, 351). The word 'court' has no fixed legal meaning, although it is very commonly used (including in this book) as a shorthand for 'superior court'. Any tribunal that applies the law is a 'court' in a sense. The distinction between courts and tribunals is not as important as the distinction between bodies that are and bodies that are not covered by contempt of court, or bound by rules of evidence, or required to give an oral hearing, and so on.

12.2 The reconstruction of tribunals

The TCEA has brought some unity to tribunals.[6] From November 2008, they have operated in a system of First-tier Tribunals with a unified system of appeals to the Upper Tribunal.

Given the diversity of the bodies, is it valuable to unify tribunals? The unification creates new tensions between legalism and informality, and between uniformity and

---

[5]   See 12.4.8 and 12.4.9 on ways in which tribunals continue to be subject to supervision by the ordinary courts.

[6]   Part 1 of the Act (the part dealing with the reconstruction of tribunals) is based on a White Paper (i.e., a government policy proposal) of 2004: Secretary of State for Constitutional Affairs, *Transforming Public Services: Complaints, Redress and Tribunals*, July 2004, Cm 6243; hereafter 'the White Paper'.

flexibility. But we will see that the new tribunals system has distinct and important advantages.

The diversity of the tribunals themselves remains. Tribunals do not merely apply different statutory schemes within their different jurisdictions; they also have different processes. But the diversity now operates within a system.

> ### Not included
>
> Local government tribunals are excluded from the tribunals system. And two of the largest tribunal schemes (immigration and employment) have not had their jurisdictions transferred to the new system under the TCEA: the Immigration and Asylum Tribunal, and the employment tribunals and the Employment Appeal Tribunal. They will be served by the Courts and Tribunals Service, and overseen by the Senior President of Tribunals, but will continue to exercise their old jurisdictions. The Immigration and Asylum Tribunal has been kept separate to maintain its single-tier structure, introduced in 2004 in an attempt to reduce appeals in asylum cases (Asylum and Immigration (Treatment of Claimants, etc.) Act 2004). The employment tribunals and the Employment Appeal Tribunal are party-and-party tribunals with an existing appellate structure, and the government decided to leave it alone.

The Courts and Tribunals Service is an agency of the Ministry of Justice. It has responsibility for the management of cases and the allocation of tribunal resources. Sharing building space with the courts allows more economical use of resources, contributing at the same time to the integration of tribunals with courts. The Courts and Tribunals Service also looks after the crucial business of communicating with complainants.

The judicial branch of the administrative justice system has a Senior President, appointed by the Queen on the recommendation of the Lord Chancellor (TCEA s 2), who has standing and experience equivalent to a Court of Appeal judge, and has overall responsibility for running and developing the tribunal judiciary. Below the Senior President are the presidents for seven 'chambers': the General Regulatory, Health Education and Social Care, Immigration and Asylum, Property, Social Entitlement, Tax, and War Pensions and Armed Forces Compensation Chambers.[7] The chambers bring together jurisdictions of the old tribunals. For example, the new Social Entitlement Chamber deals with asylum support, social security and child support, and criminal injuries compensation. The chambers allow for more flexible judicial appointments (because the Senior President can assign the same judge to more than one chamber). Chamber presidents are judges who are responsible for running the judicial work for their particular tribunal jurisdictions (including the issuing of guidance on changes in law and practice as they relate to their chambers).

---

[7] http://www.justice.gov.uk/tribunals.

The unified judicial office has two tiers, with the titles of 'judge of the First-tier Tribunal'[8] and 'judge of the Upper Tribunal' (TCEA s 4). There is a core of salaried judicial officers and part-time ('fee paid') judges. Both will tend to specialize; they can work in more than one chamber, but they need to be assigned by the Senior President (TCEA Sch 4 para 9) to each chamber in which they work. There are sometimes lay members (called 'member' rather than 'judge') on a First-tier Tribunal (see 12.4.3).

The most significant aspect of the unification of tribunals is the new appeals system. Appeals in the old days were specific to each tribunal. From some, there was a right of appeal to another tribunal; from others, there was a right of appeal on a point of law to the High Court, or no appeal at all. Under the unified system, the first general rule is that the First-tier Tribunal can review its own decisions, either on its own initiative or on an application from a complainant (TCEA s 9). And then there is an appeal on a point of law from a First-tier Tribunal to a unified appellate tier (the Upper Tribunal—TCEA s 11), if the First-tier Tribunal or the Upper Tribunal gives permission to appeal.[9] The Upper Tribunal is made up of the Senior President, chamber presidents, judges of the ordinary courts, and the current appellate members of the tribunal system (TCEA s 5). The Upper Tribunal, too, can review its own decisions (s 10), and there is an appeal from the Upper Tribunal on a point of law to the Court of Appeal (TCEA s 13) if the Upper Tribunal or the Court of Appeal gives permission to appeal; permission is only to be given if 'the proposed appeal would raise some important point of principle or practice; or ... there is some other compelling reason for the relevant appellate court to hear the appeal'.[10]

The power of both levels of tribunal to review their own decisions is designed to avoid unnecessary appeals: it provides for a form of alternative dispute resolution (ADR) within the tribunal system, and it distinguishes them from courts.[11] It is quite likely that the tribunals will only set aside their own decisions where there has been an obvious mistake: particularly in a challenge to a first-tier decision, a really controversial challenge will deserve to be heard as an appeal in the Upper Tribunal.

One final aspect of the integration of tribunals with the courts is very important: **the Upper Tribunal has a judicial review jurisdiction** (TCEA ss 15–21). It serves the same role as the Administrative Court in judicial review cases delegated to it by the High Court under rules made by the Lord Chief Justice and approved by the Lord Chancellor. From its inauguration, the Lord Chief Justice gave the Upper Tribunal responsibility for judicial review of the Criminal Injuries Compensation Scheme, and of First-tier Tribunal decisions where there is no right of appeal to the Upper Tribunal. Section 19 of the TCEA amends the Senior Courts Act 1981 to require the High Court

---

[8] A tribunal member who is not legally qualified is simply called 'member of the First-tier Tribunal'.

[9] See 12.4.9 for what happens next if both tribunals refuse permission.

[10] TCEA s 13(6); Appeals from the Upper Tribunal to the Court of Appeal Order 2008, SI 2008/2834.

[11] The High Court cannot review its own decisions. But the Supreme Court has inherited the power that the House of Lords had 'to correct any injustice caused by an earlier order of this House' (*R v Bow Street Metropolitan Stipendiary Magistrate, ex p Pinochet Ugarte (No 2)* [2000] 1 AC 119, 132 (Lord Browne-Wilkinson)).

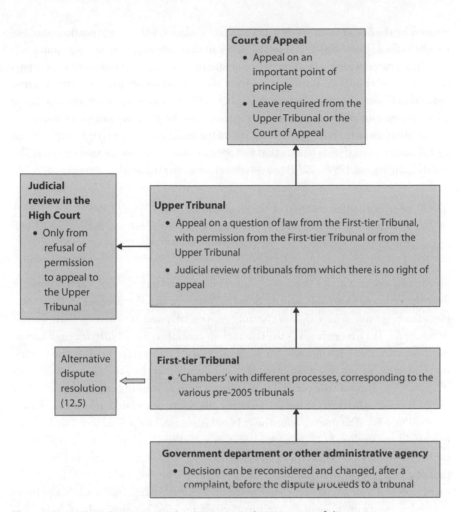

Figure 12.2 The administrative justice system: the progress of disputes

to transfer claims for judicial review covered by those rules to the Upper Tribunal, and empowers the High Court to transfer other claims where the High Court judge decides that it would be just and convenient to do so. The Crime and Courts Act 2013 s 22 provides for claims for judicial review in immigration and asylum cases to be transferred to the Upper Tribunal.

Figure 12.2 charts the progress of disputes in the administrative justice system.

12.3 The judicialization of tribunals

These were major changes to the organization of tribunals. They created a new system of administrative justice alongside, similar to, and connected with, the system of ordinary courts. Many of the changes are similar to changes made earlier for social security appeals by the Social Security Act 1998. That legislation led to a unification of tribunals in its field (particularly in appeals), and it judicialized social security disputes.

The features of judicialization in social security included the unification of appeal tribunals under a judicial President, division of the social security tribunal service into judicial and administrative branches (with a full-time social security judiciary), the effective abolition of lay membership on panels, and the gradual removal of inquisitorial decision-making techniques.[12] The last of these changes was partly brought about by a change in the considerations that an appeal tribunal was to take into account. The Social Security Act 1998 s 12(8) provided that an appeal tribunal:

> (a) need not consider any issue that is not raised by the appeal; and
> (b) shall not take into account any circumstances not obtaining at the time when the decision appealed against was made.

Think for a moment about these two features of the new way of resolving a complaint over the refusal of a social security benefit. They regulate the process in a way that gives the government new, tighter control over a massive and expensive welfare benefit programme. The **first rule** gives the tribunal no general responsibility for *good administration*, but only a responsibility to hear issues raised by a party. It makes the process more adversarial, and less of an investigation into whether the scheme is achieving its purposes. The **second rule** prevents the tribunal from assuming general responsibility for *good social security provision*, by reducing the range of considerations on which a tribunal may act. The question for the tribunal is not *whether a good social security system would give the benefit to the complainant*, but *whether the decision of the department conformed to the rules when it was made*. By making the job of the tribunal more like that of a court, these changes constrain the tribunal's power, and tighten the government's control over social security. The tribunal judges' independence actually *serves* the government's purpose of controlling decision making, because judicial independence goes along with the application of rules in a way that is not directed to the judge's own view of good social policy.

Ombudsmen, tribunals, courts

Judicialization of tribunals strengthens the basic distinction between tribunals and ombudsmen: a tribunal hears a dispute between parties; an ombudsman investigates a complaint. Making tribunals more like courts makes them less like ombudsmen, by focusing the tribunals' work on resolving a dispute as to the application of rules, and turning it away from any general inquiry into good administration (see Chapter 13 on ombudsmen).

---

[12] For a discussion, see Nick Wikeley, 'Burying Bell: Managing the Judicialisation of Social Security Tribunals' (2000) 63 MLR 475.

Judicialization brings with it the promise of impartiality, and the trained scrutiny of decisions that can be expected from lawyers, and good process. Those features may seem to reduce the government's control over decisions. Yet the judicialization of the tribunal process also brought with it features that *enhance* the government's control over social security. By restricting tribunals to the sort of considerations that judges typically handle, the reforms reduce the discretionary element in dispute resolution.

At the same time, the system is firmly committed to *avoiding* or reducing certain forms of judicialization, especially legal representation before tribunals. The new system will, as a result, need to resolve inbuilt tensions between legalism and informality. In the following discussion of the reconstruction of tribunals in general, we will need to keep in mind the ways in which judicialization will promote good administration and due process, and the ways in which it can potentially—ironically—detract from both.

12.4 Testing the system: ten elements of administrative justice

The administrative justice system needs to get each of the following elements right, in order for the system to be just overall:

12.4.1 Appointments	12.4.7 Representation and advice
12.4.2 Judicial offices	12.4.8 Appeals to the Upper Tribunal
12.4.3 Role of non-lawyer members	12.4.9 Appeals from the Upper Tribunal to the Court of Appeal
12.4.4 Evidence	12.4.10 Judicial review of tribunal decisions
12.4.5 Hearings	12.4.11 Administration and independence
12.4.6 Reasons for decisions	

12.4.1 Appointments

Appointment of tribunal judges is done on the recommendation of the same Judicial Appointments Commission that appoints High Court judges (TCEA s 48(1)). Appointment of non-legal members is also on the recommendation of the Judicial Appointments Commission, with the difference that the Commission takes advice from professional bodies on qualifications of professional experts. This change is a dramatic feature of the reconstruction. Under the Tribunals and Inquiries Act 1992, the Council on Tribunals could give advice on appointments, but the tribunal chairman was usually appointed by a departmental minister from a panel selected by the Lord Chancellor (s 6). The Lord Chancellor appointed most tribunal members, but others were simply appointed by the minister responsible for the department that made the original decision. And the departmental minister paid them (and could remove them—Tribunals and Inquiries Act 1992 s 7), and ran the tribunal.

The change to court-style appointments reflects the legalization tension: it makes tribunal members more independent, and it makes them more like judges of the High Court, complementing the titles (judge of the First-tier Tribunal, judge of the Upper Tribunal). But it downplays the differences between their work and the work of the courts.

The assignment of judges to a particular chamber is done by the managing judges (the Senior President, with the concurrence of the chamber presidents and the judge who is to be assigned—TCEA s 7(8)).

12.4.2 Judicial offices

One of the biggest symbolic changes in the reconstruction is the creation of a 'single judicial office': legal members on a First-tier Tribunal are called 'judges of the First-tier Tribunal', and on Upper Tribunals they are called 'judges of the Upper Tribunal'. A Senior President is the head of the entire 'tribunal judiciary', which potentially gives tribunal judges a collective voice that they have never had before. The status of the Senior President as a Lord Justice of Appeal will add both to the prestige and to the sense of judicial hierarchy in the tribunals; the presidents of particular chambers are High Court judges or Court of Appeal judges. Tribunal judges now have a similar title and similar forms of career progression and self-government to those of judges in the courts.

12.4.3 Role of non-lawyer members

As for the non-lawyers serving on tribunals (including the doctors, accountants, surveyors, and others who bring expertise to the making of decisions), the TCEA did not change their position. They are part of a unified 'judiciary', yet their role is put in question. The White Paper asked what the function of non-lawyer members should be: '[I]s it to add balance to the panel? Or to ensure particular interests are represented?' (White Paper, 6.67).[13] Moreover, the White Paper cast doubt on the fairness of tribunals with expert members (White Paper, 6.67):

> ' [F]or expert members a further area that needs to be developed is whether in fact it is desirable for a tribunal to have a particular expert on the panel as opposed to being available as a witness for the tribunal. Where an expert member carries out his or her own examination or investigations the parties are unable to question that member or rebut his or her conclusions. Indeed it may even give the impression that the tribunal will favour the views of that expert over the case findings of witnesses who are equally expert. '

This attitude to tribunals applies the model of courts. Judges in the law courts must decide a dispute on the basis of the evidence put before the court by the parties, and not on the basis of the judge's own views, or on information the judge receives from

---

13   See 12.2, p 452, n 6, on the White Paper.

any other source. But the point of expert membership on tribunals is that tribunals are different from courts: the purpose of a member's expertise is not to enable him or her to compete with the witnesses, but to help the tribunal to understand the witnesses and the complainant. The point is to bring perspective to the deliberations of the lawyers and lay members on a panel. And it is not necessarily unfair, because of the ways in which the issues before tribunals differ in various ways from the issues in trials in the ordinary courts.

It has long been recognized that the members of some tribunals may properly rely on their own knowledge and experience, while still abiding by the rules of natural justice.[14] Yet the White Paper suggested that there is something improper about a tribunal member bringing any perspective to a dispute other than the perspective of a High Court judge.

The role of non-lawyers varies, even on a single tribunal. Panels of the Mental Health Tribunal consist of a lawyer (who chairs the panel), a consultant psychiatrist, and a lay member who is neither a doctor nor a lawyer. If the psychiatrist member disagrees with an expert witness, he or she must say so at the oral hearing, to give the parties a chance to respond. The three members of a panel decide cases by majority vote. Risk of injustice arises from the possibility that the panel will mistakenly trust the psychiatrist member's opinion over that of other medical experts, or that the role of the lay member will introduce a biased agenda into the deliberations. Those risks could be met by the legalistic model that the White Paper hinted at. But the legalistic model has risks too: it would leave resolution of an adversarial battle between the parties' expert witnesses to a non-expert, and it would choose the lawyer's perspective on the situation over the common-sense perspective that the lay member potentially offers.

Experts on tribunals

Unlike the White Paper, the judges have no doubts about the fairness—or the value—of having non-lawyer expert membership on tribunals. In *Gillies v Work and Pensions Secretary (Scotland)* [2006] UKHL 2, [22], Lord Hope said:

> 'One of the strengths of the tribunal system as it has been developed in this country is the breadth of relevant experience that can be built into it by the use of lay members to sit with members who are legally qualified … its integrity is not compromised by the use of specialist knowledge or experience when the judge or tribunal member is examining the evidence.'

12.4.4 Evidence

Closely allied to the role of lay members is the use of evidence. Tribunals are not generally bound by the law of evidence that restricts the information that the High Court can consider (e.g., the prohibition on hearsay, and the prohibition on a judge using his

---

[14]   See, e.g., *Attorney-General v BBC* [1981] AC 303, 351 (Lord Edmund Davies).

or her knowledge of facts that cannot be 'judicially noticed').[15] The point of an expert tribunal is that it should be able to rely on its own expert knowledge. As Edmund Davies LJ said in *Metropolitan Properties Ltd v Lannon* [1969] 1 QB 577, 603: '[M]embers [of tribunals] are not restricted to the evidence adduced before them; they are free to draw upon their cumulative knowledge and experience of the matter in hand.'

This difference in evidence rules between tribunals and courts cannot be justified on the ground that courts decide more important disputes. A tribunal decision can win you back your job, or lead to your deportation, or uphold your detention in a secure hospital. The justification has to be that there are different risks of prejudice from unrestricted information in courts, and that tribunals can do a fair job of handling a less restricted range of information on the specific range of issues that they decide.

The law of evidence in the High Court is deeply tied to the common law adversarial system of dispute resolution. The information before the court in criminal proceedings is restricted because those proceedings subject one party to charges of wrongdoing against the community. The common law has always held that, in those proceedings, the court should not consider any information that the defendant cannot effectively challenge during the hearing. And even in civil proceedings in the common law courts, information is put before the court only by the parties, and each party has an opportunity to challenge the other party's evidence. Tribunals do not need to hold as strictly to that adversarial model as the High Court does. Since the question in a person-and-state tribunal is always a question as to the lawfulness and justice of administration, the tribunal can take a more inquisitorial role than a High Court judge takes in a claim for breach of contract.

12.4.5 Hearings

The new system borrows case management from the law courts. Some tribunals already had it, but there was no uniformity. Case management is designed to avoid a costly hearing, if it is unnecessary. It means that the tribunal controls the progress of the dispute; the tribunal can require the parties to meet to discuss settlement, and can expedite the process when one party is delaying.[16]

But case management will only happen once the dispute reaches the tribunal. And tribunals are different from courts: in social security and tax in particular, appeals against the government department's decision have always been filed with the department in question. That allows the department to reconsider and to defuse some disputes by changing its mind before a tribunal hearing. The new system is committed to ADR, so complainants will still file appeals with departments in most cases.

---

[15] Judges in the High Court will take notice of facts without proof if they are so obviously true that it is not unfair to the disadvantaged party for the court to accept it without making the other party prove it. The court, e.g., will accept without proof that there are many men in southeast London who fit the description 'a tall black man wearing a black hood' (*R v Irvin* [2007] EWCA Crim 2701 [11]).

[16] The Tribunal Procedure Committee can make case management rules: see TCEA Sch 5.

The earlier reform of social security tribunal processes had involved a reduction in oral hearings—from a presumption that a hearing was to be given to a requirement of permission for an oral hearing. The White Paper took the same approach, aiming in general to avoid unnecessary oral hearings (although promising that 'No appellant will lose their right to a hearing': White Paper, 6.31). The reasoning was that oral hearings are not only expensive, but also stressful and painful for complainants. The TCEA empowers the Tribunal Procedure Committee to make rules for dealing with a matter without a hearing (s 22(3), Sch 5 para 7).

Even if oral hearings are stressful, there is no doubt that they tend to benefit complainants. In a major study of Disability Living Allowance in 2003, the Auditor General found as follows:

> ' Of 34,000 [social security benefit] appeals cleared at oral hearing between April and June 2002, 52 per cent were decided in favour of the customer, compared with 23 per cent of the 11,000 paper hearings. For Disability Living Allowance, 61 per cent of oral hearings were decided in favour of the customer, compared with 34 per cent of paper hearings, and the President of Appeal Tribunals has indicated that the presence of the appellant has a significant impact on the outcome. ' [17]

Perhaps it would be best to have no presumption for or against oral hearings. Their value and importance depend on whether they are necessary in order for the claimant to have an effective way of participating in the process, and that depends on the context in which a decision is made.

12.4.6 Reasons for decisions

The TCEA says nothing about whether tribunals will give reasons; perhaps that reflects the degree to which reason giving has come to be taken for granted as a requirement of due process for any body that determines a claim to legal rights (see 6.2). Not that tribunals in the new system will always give reasons. The social security tribunals do not give reasons as a matter of course, because it would cause too much expense and delay. But a complainant who wants to appeal can request a statement of reasons.

The Tribunals and Inquiries Act 1958 had made a huge step forward by imposing a general duty on the tribunals it covered to give reasons for decision (s 12).[18] As Lord Diplock put it, the Act filled a 'lacuna' in the law, because tribunals had been able to avoid effective judicial review before that by declining to give reasons (*O'Reilly v Mackman* [1983] 2 AC 237, 277).

Reasons are all the more important under the new system of tribunals, because decisions of the Upper Tribunal are binding precedents. Reasons are needed for

---

[17] *Getting it Right, Putting it Right*, Report to the House of Commons, HC 1142, 7 November 2003 [4.17]–[4.18].

[18] The provision was retained in the Tribunals and Inquiries Act 1992 (s 10(6)).

the development of precedent, as well as for fair communication with the parties to the decision. So tribunals must generally give reasons, or be prepared to do so on request.

What must the reasons include? The requirement of reasons in the Tribunals and Inquiries Act 1958 was given teeth in *Re Poyser and Mills' Arbitration* [1964] 2 QB 467, 478, when Megaw J held that Parliament's requirement of reasons 'must be read as meaning that proper, adequate reasons must be given. The reasons that are set out must be reasons which will not only be intelligible, but which deal with the substantial points that have been raised'. Yet reasons that would fail to explain a decision to an outsider do not necessarily make a tribunal's decision unlawful, as long as they are sufficiently clear to enable an aggrieved party to establish whether there was an error of law (*S v Special Educational Needs Tribunal* [1996] 1 All ER 171): 'A reasons challenge will only succeed if the party aggrieved can satisfy the court that he has genuinely been substantially prejudiced by the failure to provide an adequately reasoned decision' (*South Buckinghamshire District Council v Porter (No 2)* [2004] UKHL 33 [36] (Lord Brown)). Like other duties to give reasons (see Chapter 6), the reasons requirement for tribunals needs to be tailored to its purpose. So proportionate process is the principle. On an appeal to the Court of Appeal, the judges will not expect the tribunals to have given perfect reasons, but reasons that are sufficient for the purpose. And the judges will not jump to the conclusion that a tribunal has gone wrong just because of a deficiency in the reasons given. As Lord Hope said in *Jones v First Tier Tribunal* [2013] UKSC 19, [25]:

> ' It is well established, as an aspect of tribunal law and practice, that judicial restraint should be exercised when the reasons that a tribunal gives for its decision are being examined. The appellate court should not assume too readily that the tribunal misdirected itself just because not every step in its reasoning is fully set out in it. '

12.4.7 Representation and advice

The government favours a policy of reducing legal representation in tribunal hearings. The White Paper pointed out that there is no absolute right to publicly funded legal advice in the tribunal process, and that 'full-scale legal representation at the taxpayer's expense in every administrative dispute or tribunal case would be disproportionate and unreasonable' (White Paper, 10.3). But that sensible principle is turned into a general purpose of avoiding legal representation, which itself risks a failure of proportionality in process (White Paper, 10.1):

> ' [W]e aim to create a situation where individuals in dispute with the State or who might be taking a case to a tribunal, or defending one, will be able to have their case resolved with little or no support or assistance. '

That aim is at odds with the judicialization of tribunals under the reconstruction. And, for years, free legal representation has been available before many tribunals, including asylum tribunals, the Mental Health Tribunal, and the Employment Appeal Tribunal (although not in the employment tribunals).

The TCEA adds nothing to the law on legal representation, and takes nothing away. Legal representation is hard to avoid in many tribunal hearings, for various reasons:

- the complexity of the legal issues and of the presentation of relevant facts;

- the need for skilled advocacy in a court-like tribunal;

- disabilities or lack of relevant skills on the part of complainants; and

- the use of expert witnesses, which will make it more valuable to have a lawyer as advocate.

It is highly unlikely that the law of tax, or asylum, or even disability benefits can ever be made simple enough that complainants will be able to challenge all official decisions effectively without representation by a lawyer or a specialist advocate. Representation not only gives help with complex legal problems, but also helps complainants who (apart from any disability) simply don't have the self-confidence or the skills to challenge an official decision. Representation also helps complainants by making their complaint look more serious from the point of view of the tribunal. Although it is certainly not necessary to have a lawyer speaking for you at every tribunal hearing, the increased judicialization of tribunals in the new system has made it harder for complainants to put their case without representation.

Unlike in the law courts, the need for representation can be met without a barrister or a solicitor, and a variety of voluntary or private independent advisers and representatives can potentially help with tribunal proceedings. Lay representation is important in practice (especially representation by welfare rights workers). Nevertheless, it will be very useful to have a lawyer at certain stages, since appeals to the Upper Tribunal are to be on a point of law. And the judicial nature of the hearing and the mystique of the legal profession make it look even more useful than it is.

In 1989, Hazel and Yvonne Genn wrote a report for the (then) Lord Chancellor's Department on *The Effectiveness of Representation at Tribunals*, which reached the unambiguous conclusion that complainants with representation were more successful in the four tribunals they studied: '[I]n all four tribunals, the presence of a skilled representative significantly and independently increased the probability that a case would succeed.'[19]

Advocacy helps even in an informal tribunal. Representation is not needed merely because of legal technicalities. In a disability benefits case, even if the issue is simply whether you can cook for yourself, it will be useful for you to have an advocate stand up and put the case, and to rebut arguments from the department's representatives.

---

[19] Hazel Genn, 'Tribunals and Informal Justice' (1993) 56 MLR 393, 400.

Nothing in the White Paper addresses these points. The White Paper makes the same generalizations that policy makers used to make in the 1980s, without any empirical support (10.11):

> ' Tribunals bear many similarities to courts but the hearings are intended to be less formal and adversarial in nature which ought in time to reduce the need for representation. The relevant law may also be simpler than in many court cases and even where it is not in many tribunals there will rarely be a need for a party to concern themselves with technical evidential issues or to deploy the traditional lawyer skill of cross-examination of witnesses. '

That may be true in some cases, such as a hearing before a parking adjudicator in which the complainant wants to argue that the traffic warden made a mistake. But advocacy will be useful in most tribunal hearings, including social security benefit appeals. Legal representation is not always in the interest of the claimants themselves, but we need a system that will make it available when it *is* needed. Unfortunately, as with so many procedural steps, there is no fair way of allowing representation when it is needed, and *only* when it is needed. Perhaps the solution to this dilemma is partly that many complainants do not need a *lawyer*, although they do need an advocate: someone with experience of the tribunal in question, knowledge of the regime it applies, and the skills needed to represent the complainant.

12.4.8 Appeals to the Upper Tribunal

In the old days, some tribunal schemes had appeals tribunals and some did not. The dramatic unifying feature of the reconstruction of tribunals is the appellate system. Any party can appeal on a point of law to the Upper Tribunal if permission is given by the First-tier Tribunal or by the Upper Tribunal. The Upper Tribunal functions much as the High Court used to function in hearing an appeal on a question of law from a tribunal. And the membership of the Upper Tribunal includes Court of Appeal and High Court judges seconded to tribunals (TCEA s 6); all the judges in the ordinary courts are judges of the First-tier and Upper Tribunals.

Statutory appeals could be brought to the High Court from twelve types of tribunal under the Tribunals and Inquiries Act 1992 by a party 'dissatisfied in point of law' (s 11 and Sch 1), and there were dozens of other statutes providing for an appeal on a question of law.[20] That work is now done by the Upper Tribunal, rather than by the High Court. It represents a large volume of litigation. By taking it over, the Upper Tribunal is also taking over the role of developing the law for tribunals. It is this step that creates a new kind of judicial institution in our legal system: the Upper Tribunal is an administrative appeals court.

---

[20] One important example was the Social Security Administration Act 1992 s 24 (appeal from Commissioners to the Court of Appeal on a question of law).

In appeals on a point of law, what attitude should the Upper Tribunal take towards the judgment of the First-tier Tribunal on the point of law? In the old statutory appeals on a point of law, Lord Denning stated that the correct meaning of a statutory term was a question of law for the court, *and* also that a tribunal erred in law if it drew the wrong conclusion from the primary facts: *Woodhouse v Peter Ltd* [1972] QB 520.[21] The more orthodox approach was that of Lord Radcliffe, who said in *Edwards v Bairstow* [1956] AC 14 (HL), 36, that an appeal would not be granted on a question of law unless 'the true and only reasonable conclusion contradicts the determination'.[22] That landmark decision introduced a reasonableness test for the way in which a tribunal applies the law to the facts: if a decision either way is reasonable, the court will not interfere, but if only one decision is reasonable, the court will hold the tribunal to it (see 9.3.1, p 353).

Moyna v Work and Pensions Secretary [2003] UKHL 44 confirmed the *Edwards v Bairstow* approach to a statutory appeal from a tribunal. Mrs Moyna suffered angina attacks, which meant that, for one to three days in a week, she could not cook for herself. She applied for the lowest form of Disability Living Allowance, which is available to a person who 'cannot prepare a cooked main meal for himself if he has the ingredients' (Social Security Contributions and Benefits Act 1992 s 72(1)(a)(ii)). She was turned down; she appealed to the tribunal and lost on the ground that she could 'on most days, prepare a cooked main meal for herself, and that it is not unreasonable to expect her to do so' [13]; she appealed to the Commissioner (an appeal tribunal) on a question of law, and lost again; then she appealed to the Court of Appeal, and won on the ground that the Commissioner and the tribunal had erred in law. The Secretary of State appealed to the House of Lords, and Mrs Moyna finally lost.

In a matter worth £15 pounds per week (for a year-and-a-half until her condition worsened), on the issue of whether she could cook for herself, these five tiers of decision making cannot be called proportionate dispute resolution. The expense of the first tribunal hearing must have been greater than the amounts that were at stake in the claim. Lord Hoffmann, though, made a general holding that ought to reduce the number of cases that go through a series of decisions up to the highest court in the land: he overturned the Court of Appeal decision on the ground that the initial tribunal's decision was 'within the bounds of reasonable judgment' [28].

Under the new tribunals system, Mrs Moyna would be refused permission to appeal from the Upper Tribunal to the Court of Appeal unless she could persuade one or the other that her case raised a matter of principle of general importance. And Lord Hoffmann's decision binds the Upper Tribunal. So an appeal to the Upper Tribunal should not be a rehearing of the matter, but an appeal on the *Edwards v Bairstow* standard, which recognizes that it may be lawful for the First-tier Tribunal to decide either way (within the bounds of reasonable judgment) in the application of imprecise standards.

....

[21] Compare *Pearlman v Keepers and Governors of Harrow School* [1979] QB 56 (Lord Denning).

[22] Lord Radcliffe borrowed the phrase 'true and only reasonable conclusion' from Lord Cooper's speech in *IRC v Toll Property Co Ltd* [1952] SC 387 (HL), 393.

12.4.9 Appeals from the Upper Tribunal to the Court of Appeal

The role of the Upper Tribunal takes the place of judicial review and appeals to the Administrative Court from tribunal decisions. But an attempt to insulate the tribunal system from any control by the ordinary law courts would have been politically costly, or ineffective, or both. So the TCEA allows the losing party in the Upper Tribunal to bring an appeal to the Court of Appeal on a question of law of general importance if permission is given either by the Upper Tribunal itself or by the Court of Appeal (s 13). That mechanism elevates the status of the Upper Tribunal, by treating its decisions as important enough that they should be reviewed by the Court of Appeal, rather than by the Administrative Court. And it was the obvious strategy for the government to take in drafting the legislation, because losing parties in the Upper Tribunal would certainly have applied to the Administrative Court for judicial review if the TCEA had provided no appeal from the Upper Tribunal. The appeal provision neatly leaves out the Administrative Court, while accepting that the Court of Appeal and the Supreme Court must have control over the Upper Tribunal.

Will the increased judicialization of tribunals and the innovative role of the Upper Tribunal affect the standard applied in those new appeals? There is no general doctrine of restraint in appeals from the High Court to the Court of Appeal: the Court of Appeal simply grants an appeal if the decision of the High Court was based on an error of law. But the Upper Tribunal itself forms an appeal court within the administrative justice system, and it has become clear that the Court of Appeal and the Supreme Court will defer to some extent to the Upper Tribunal's judgment on the law that the tribunals apply. The rationale lies in the specialization of the tribunals, and the kinds of cases that they decide, and the Upper Tribunal's capacity to exercise a supervisory role. As Baroness Hale said in *Hinchy v Work and Pensions Secretary* [2005] UKHL 16 [49]: '[I]f the specialist judiciary who do understand the system and the people it serves have established consistent principles, the generalist courts should respect those principles unless they can clearly be shown to be wrong in law.' Very many appeals in the tribunal system concern complaints that a social security decision imposes a burden on a claimant that is unreasonable or disproportionate in light of a public authority's purposes; on those issues, the Court of Appeal will defer to 'evaluation and judgment by a specialist appellate tribunal with a particular expertise in the field of social security law' (*Obrey v Work and Pensions Secretary* [2013] EWCA Civ 1584 [18]).

Parties who lose in the Upper Tribunal will often want the Court of Appeal to hold that the law was misapplied to the facts. In *R (Jones) v First-tier Tribunal* [2013] UKSC 19 [16], the Supreme Court made it clear that on these questions the appellate courts will defer very significantly to the Upper Tribunal. Lord Hope said that, 'An appeal court should not venture too readily into this area by classifying issues as issues of law which are really best left for determination by the specialist appellate tribunals.' When the question is how to apply the relevant legislation to the facts of the case, the approach established in *Jones* is that the Court of Appeal and the Supreme Court should not uphold an appeal on a point of law unless, in spite of the deference they accord to the tribunals, they can see that the law has clearly been misapplied.

The nature of an 'issue of law' (see 9.3.2) may seem to be very mysterious, if it is to be explained by asking which issues are best left to the decision maker that is subject to review, and which issues are best decided by the reviewing court or tribunal. But it is not really mysterious; the approach in *Jones* can best be seen as a way of working out the implications of Lord Radcliffe's decision in *Edwards v Bairstow* [1956] AC 14 (see 12.4.8), on the general approach the courts ought to take to complaints that a public authority has misapplied the law to the facts. 'There are many combinations of circumstances in which it could not be said to be wrong to arrive at a conclusion one way or the other' (*Edwards v Bairstow*, 34). There is no error on a point of law, if the appellate court cannot say that it would be wrong to decide the question of application in the way that the First-tier or Upper Tribunal decided it; and the appellate court cannot say that, if the right answer is best determined by the tribunal.

And on questions of fact, the Court of Appeal will only overturn a conclusion of the First-tier Tribunal if 'it is one to which no rational tribunal could properly have come' (*Criminal Injuries Compensation Authority v First-tier Tribunal* [2014] EWCA Civ 65).

12.4.10 Judicial review of tribunal decisions

Since there is an appeal on a question of law, decided by judges in the Upper Tribunal, it may seem that judicial review of tribunal decisions in the Administrative Court is a thing of the past. One of Lord Denning's rationales for aggressive judicial review of tribunals in the twentieth century was the fact that the High Court could impose consistency on a variety of tribunals (*Pearlman v Keepers and Governors of Harrow School* [1979] QB 56). The new Upper Tribunal can apply a doctrine of precedent, and will be able to impose uniformity *within* the tribunal system. And the provision for appeals to the Court of Appeal on points of law of general importance gives the Court of Appeal and the Supreme Court the opportunity to supervise the Upper Tribunal's role in developing the law. So it may seem that there is no longer any role for judicial review of tribunal decisions.

● **Pop quiz** ●

Isn't a decision based on an error of law a nullity? Imagine that the Upper Tribunal decides against you, and both the Upper Tribunal and the Court of Appeal refuse to give you permission to appeal to the Court of Appeal, because the case does not raise any important point of principle or practice. Remember the doctrine developed by Lord Denning and Lord Diplock, that an error of law by an administrative tribunal makes its decision a nullity (see 9.1.2). Can you ask the Administrative Court in judicial review for a declaration that the decision is a nullity?

But the reconstruction of tribunals in the TCEA did not completely *eliminate* judicial review of tribunal decisions. If both the First-tier Tribunal and the Upper Tribunal refuse to give permission for an appeal from the First-tier Tribunal to the Upper Tribunal, TCEA s 13 provides that the disappointed party *cannot* appeal that refusal to the Court of Appeal. In that situation, the statutory right to pursue the complaint is at an end, and the complainant's lawyer will start thinking about seeking judicial review in the Administrative Court, to challenge *the Upper Tribunal's decision to refuse permission to appeal.*

That happened for the first time in *R (Cart) v Upper Tribunal* [2011] UKSC 28, a landmark case that led to original assessments of the legal nature of the tribunal system by Laws LJ in the Administrative Court, and by Sedley LJ in the Court of Appeal, and by Baroness Hale in the Supreme Court. Laws LJ held that the Upper Tribunal is an 'alter ego' of the High Court ([2009] EWHC 3052, [94]): '... an authoritative, impartial and independent judicial source for the interpretation and application of the relevant statutory texts'. So judicial review in the High Court is not ordinarily called for, because of the stature of the Upper Tribunal. Even so, he said, if the Upper Tribunal 'were to embark upon a case that was frankly beyond the four corners of its statutory remit ... I see no reason why the High Court should not correct it' [99]. And, he thought, the Administrative Court should be prepared to give judicial review on the ground of 'a wholly exceptional collapse of fair procedure: something as gross as actual bias on the part of the tribunal' [99]. But he held that a decision of the Upper Tribunal is not review-able for error of law [98]. The Court of Appeal did not agree that the Upper Tribunal is an alter ego or 'avatar' of the High Court ([2010] EWCA Civ 859 [19]), but upheld the conclusion that a refusal of permission to appeal by the Upper Tribunal should be subject to judicial review only on restricted grounds. Sedley LJ said that the Court should interfere 'only on grounds of pre-*Anisminic*[23] jurisdictional error (which we will call out-right excess of jurisdiction) or a denial of the right to a fair hearing' [4].

In the Supreme Court ([2011] UKSC 28 [37]), Baroness Hale asserted the principle of proportionate process (see 4.4):

> ' [T]he scope of judicial review is an artefact of the common law whose object is to maintain the rule of law... . Both tribunals and the courts are there to do Parliament's bidding. But we all make mistakes. No-one is infallible. The question is, what machinery is necessary and proportionate to keep such mistakes to a minimum? In particular, should there be any jurisdiction in which mistakes of law are, either in theory or in practice, immune from scrutiny in the higher courts? '

The Supreme Court's unanimous answer to the first question was that it is necessary and proportionate to give judicial review to quash a refusal of permission to appeal to the Upper Tribunal, where it is arguable that the Upper Tribunal erred in law in refusing permission, and the appeal would raise some important point of principle or practice, or there is some other compelling reason for the relevant appellate court to hear the appeal. That is, the Supreme Court adopted the test for appeals from the Upper Tribunal to the Court of Appeal, and decided that the High Court in judicial review should apply the same test, when deciding whether to quash a refusal of permission to appeal to the Upper Tribunal [57].

....
[23] *Anisminic v Foreign Compensation Commission* [1969] 2 AC 147.

The answer to Baroness Hale's second question, although she does not spell this out, is that the Upper Tribunal does have a jurisdiction in which mistakes of law are immune from scrutiny in the higher courts: a mistake of law by the Upper Tribunal in refusing permission to appeal from the First-tier Tribunal will be immune from scrutiny in the higher courts, unless the case raises an important point of principle or practice, or there is some other compelling reason for the High Court to interfere with it (and a mistake of law by the Upper Tribunal in deciding an appeal is immune to the same extent from scrutiny in the Court of Appeal, under the criteria for appeal from the decision of an appeal by the Upper Tribunal).[24]

It was right for the courts to reject the position, argued for by the appellants, that 'judicial review should be permitted whenever there is an arguable case that the Upper Tribunal has made any error of law' (Lord Phillips [73]). Every claimant has a right to succeed in a good claim, but no claimant has a right to unlimited opportunities to challenge a determination of his or her claim. The result of the appellants' argument in *Cart* would be a lavish excess of process rather than proportionate process.

Did the Supreme Court make the right assessment of proportionality? Lord Brown said: 'The rule of law is weakened, not strengthened, if a disproportionate part of the courts' resources is devoted to finding a very occasional grain of wheat on a threshing floor full of chaff' [100]. Yet he shared in the unanimous consensus of the judges in the Divisional Court, the Court of Appeal, and the Supreme Court that the High Court should have some sort of role in supervising the Upper Tribunal's decisions on permission to appeal. That reflects the judges' deep allegiance to judicial oversight of determinations of the law by other bodies.

Remember that a party seeking judicial review of the Upper Tribunal decision has already had an independent hearing of his or her complaint against a government decision, in the First-tier Tribunal. And then there have been two independent decisions (by the First-tier Tribunal and the Upper Tribunal) that there is no case that justifies hearing an appeal. Judicial review of the Upper Tribunal then gives the party, in principle, another hearing in the High Court, and appeal from its decision to the Court of Appeal. It is hard to see how these four levels of process (after the claimant has already had a hearing from an independent tribunal) can be proportionate, unless there is something wrong with the Upper Tribunal's role in deciding permission to appeal. The judges rightly addressed the matter as a question of proportionate process, but they could not help approaching the proportionality question with the preconception—shared with Lord Denning and Lord Diplock—that law is for the judges of the High Court. Said Baroness Hale, at [43]:

> ' There is therefore a real risk of the Upper Tribunal becoming in reality the final arbiter of the law, which is not what Parliament has provided. Serious questions of law might never be "channelled into the legal system" (as Sedley LJ put it [2011] QB 120, 169, para 30) because there would be no independent means of spotting them. '

---

24 For other instances of decision makers whose mistakes of law are immune from scrutiny in the higher courts, see 9.1.7.

'Channelled into the legal system' is a telling turn of phrase: the tribunals are, needless to say, part of the legal system. Yet the judges of the Court of Appeal and the Supreme Court do not think that proceedings have come into the legal system, until they reach the High Court or the Court of Appeal.

Parliament, for its part, did not provide that the Upper Tribunal was the final arbiter of the law, and it created a right of appeal on some matters to the Court of Appeal. The effect of the Supreme Court's decision in *Cart* is the same as if the TCEA had allowed an appeal on a point of law of general importance to the High Court from a refusal of permission to appeal by the Upper Tribunal. There is no ground for attributing to Parliament the notion that such an avenue should be available.

It is possible to imagine Upper Tribunal judges erring in law in refusing permission to appeal (just as it is possible to imagine High Court judges erring in law in refusing permission to appeal). But bearing in mind that the claimant will already have had two hearings (before the First-tier and Upper Tribunals), this danger is not of a kind that justifies the dynamic, open-ended judicial review role for the High Court that the Supreme Court has established in *Cart*. The result of the decision is to invite every litigant who is disappointed after losing twice in seeking permission to appeal in the tribunal system, to try his or her luck in the High Court. Given the Supreme Court's decision, he or she will often lose (as did the appellant in *Cart* itself), on the ground that the complaint about the First-tier Tribunal's decision does not involve a point of general importance. But very few litigants will take the view that their case has no general importance, when they consider the invitation from the Supreme Court to seek judicial review. It is a recipe for pointless litigation, to guard against a risk that judges of the Upper Tribunal will wrongly refuse permission to appeal in cases involving important points of principle.

The jurisdiction of the High Court ought to be fashioned in a way that provides proportionate process. It would have been perfectly consistent with the constitutional importance of that jurisdiction if the Supreme Court had held that the Administrative Court should not give permission to any claimant to seek judicial review of a refusal of permission to appeal from the First-tier Tribunal to the Upper Tribunal. But it would have been unthinkable to the judiciary of the ordinary courts.

Keeping the process under control

Responding to a suggestion from Lord Phillips ([2011] UKSC 28 [93]), the Civil Procedure Rules Committee created a new rule (CPR 54.7A) abbreviating the judicial review process, specifically to keep *Cart*-style judicial review under control. Applications for permission must be made within sixteen days of the Upper Tribunal decision. Permission is to be decided on the criteria set out in *Cart*, without the usual right to ask for an oral hearing on permission for judicial review. If permission for judicial review is given, the High Court will automatically quash the Upper Tribunal's decision not to give permission to appeal after fourteen days, unless the Upper Tribunal or an interested party requests a hearing.

12.4.11 Administration and independence

In the old days, tribunals were operated by the government department that had made the decision being challenged. The minister in charge of the department appointed the members, the department paid them and administered their work, and the department provided information about the tribunal to complainants. The tribunal members might still have an independent attitude, but they looked as if they were dependent on the department. By the 1990s, some tribunals had already changed in this respect (social security is an example). But one important feature of the reconstruction is the general end of sponsorship of tribunals by the department whose decision was being questioned. They have now been taken out of those departments, and have merged for administrative purposes with the courts, in the Courts and Tribunals Service. That is a radical change in the administration of tribunals.

It is also of symbolic importance that s 1 of the TCEA amends the Constitutional Reform Act 2005 s 3, to extend the guarantee of continued judicial independence to tribunal members. So, like other judges, they are covered by the duty of the Lord Chancellor and ministers to uphold their independence. The other increase in the independence of tribunals lies in appointments: the Judicial Appointments Commission that advises the Lord Chancellor on appointment of judges will also advise him on appointment of tribunal members (TCEA Sch 8 para 66).

The guarantee of independence and the use of the Judicial Appointments Commission will not only make tribunal membership more independent; they will also make tribunals more like courts. Along with the administration of the unified tribunal system in the Ministry of Justice, the new appointments technique will change the appearance (if not the ethos) of tribunals into an independent system.

12.5 Alternatives to tribunal hearings: proportionate dispute resolution

The TCEA requires the Senior President to attend to 'the need to develop innovative methods of resolving disputes that are of a type that may be brought before tribunals' (s 2(3)(d)). Alternative dispute resolution involves a tension between the value of providing quicker, cheaper, less confrontational resolutions, on the one hand, and, on the other hand, the danger of railroading disadvantaged complainants into shortcut processes that do not give them a real hearing and outcomes that violate their rights or disregard their interests. There is a risk of process failure, because the very reasons for having an independent and impartial tribunal may be reasons not to leave the parties to the outcome of a process that avoids a hearing before a tribunal. But it is still a good idea for the administrative justice system to work at alternatives to tribunal hearings, because sometimes the complainant really does not need a hearing.

And the system can already provide useful alternatives. Section 24 of the TCEA provides for a tribunal member to serve as a **mediator**—that is, as someone who discusses the complaint with the two parties, to help them to reach an outcome that both agree to. Section 24(1) restricts mediation—the restrictions are meant to prevent mediation from interfering with the complainant's right to a hearing:

> (a) mediation of matters in dispute between parties to proceedings is to take place only by agreement between those parties;
> (b) where parties to proceedings fail to mediate, or where mediation between parties to proceedings fails to resolve disputed matters, the failure is not to affect the outcome of the proceedings.

The tribunals' case management powers under the Act would enable the Tribunal Rules Committee to encourage the use of ADR before a tribunal hearing, but s 24 makes it clear that the rules cannot impose compulsory mediation. The rules could, however, empower a tribunal to postpone formal proceedings during a case to carry out ADR through the s 24 mediation process, or to allow the parties to pursue other options. The options all depend on some sort of agreement between the parties. **Negotiation** is simply a discussion between the parties aimed at settlement; **mediation** is negotiation with an intermediary as a facilitator; **arbitration** is dispute resolution that is binding because the parties agree in advance to accept whatever the arbitrator decides. But there are other possibilities, too, such as **early neutral evaluation**, which gives the parties an independent opinion on their case, in order to help them to decide whether to reach an agreement without a hearing.

In the ordinary courts, pre-action protocols encourage the use of ADR before proceeding to a trial (see 10.3.2, p 384). Similar protocols could be used before tribunal hearings. But in the courts this aspect of case management works because the court can award very substantial legal costs against a party that does not cooperate. There have generally been no costs awards in tribunals. The TCEA s 29 provides that the tribunal has discretion over costs, subject to Tribunal Procedure Rules (Sch 5 Pt 1 para 12 includes a power to make rules concerning costs). Control over costs may allow greater scope for tribunals to press complainants to try ADR. The Tribunal Rules Committee, composed of the senior tribunal judges and other tribunal members, will need to work out whether that would conflict with the evident commitment in the TCEA to voluntary ADR processes. The rule against compulsory mediation suggests that ADR ought to be voluntary, which calls into question the use of cost penalties to back up case management powers.

How can the new system deal with these challenges? Proportionate dispute resolution is meant to be the harmonizing principle, but that is only a way of posing the difficult question: how much pressure to settle a dispute is compatible with fair process and good decision making? That question of proportionality depends on the reconciliation of various potential advantages and disadvantages of ADR, as shown in Table 12.1.

A good resolution to an administrative dispute should follow a process that is no more expensive, time-consuming, legalistic, and formal than it needs to be for its purposes. Those purposes are:

- to give the complainant a decent voice in the proceedings;

- to reach an outcome that gives effect to the complainant's legal rights, while showing respect for the complainant's private interests and responding to them in a way that is in the public interest;

Table 12.1 Pros and cons of ADR

Pros	Cons
Compared with a tribunal hearing, the alternative may: • be **quicker**; • be **less expensive** to the parties and to the administrative justice system; • give the complainant a form of **involvement** in a consensual resolution that enhances his or her control over the process and the outcome; • cause **less stress**; and • **reconcile parties** who may need to be able to cooperate in future. Further, ADR may lead to a resolution that the court could not have ordered, since the parties can be **more flexible** in reaching an agreement than the court could be in applying the law to the issues raised in a complaint.	If the parties have **unequal bargaining power**, then a mediated agreement may not be fair (unless the mediator abandons his or her neutrality). **The impartiality of the tribunal itself may come into question**, since it is common practice for a mediator to have discussions with each party separately. Any steps that a tribunal takes to encourage mediation may put pressure on the parties, and it will be difficult to guard against **undue pressure**. A good outcome **cannot influence other cases in the way that a precedent influences other cases after a tribunal decision**.

- to hold a public authority accountable for its conduct; and

- to shape the law in a way that (so far as the law is able to do it) promotes good administration.

Doing all that may require a process that is expensive, time-consuming, legalistic, and formal. And the irony of process means that the system may have to overdo the process in order to make sure that the rights and interests at stake do not get trampled in the rush to a resolution.

12.6 Tribunal engineering: flux in the immigration and asylum tribunals

The reconstructed tribunal system needs to meet the challenge of the diversity of tribunals. And it will need to respond to the variation over time that has arisen and will continue to arise from political pressures to respond to real or perceived problems by tampering with tribunal processes. The immigration and asylum system provides the best example of flux.

Since signing the Geneva Convention on the Status of Refugees in 1951, the UK has been committed to giving asylum to refugees (persons seeking safety in a foreign country for fear of persecution at home). And, under a varying set of entry criteria, the UK has also been prepared to accept immigrants who are not refugees. Since 1969, there has been a tribunal system for deciding appeals over whether would-be entrants fit the immigration criteria, or qualify for refugee status. The initial appeal was considered by an adjudicator (appointed by the Home Secretary), who heard an appeal on the merits of the decisions of the immigration officers or the Home Secretary. From the adjudicator's decision, there was an appeal to the Immigration Appeal Tribunal (whose members were appointed by the Lord Chancellor) (Immigration Appeals Act 1969).

The Immigration and Asylum Act 1999 allowed any dissatisfied party to bring a further appeal to the Immigration Appeal Tribunal (IAT), after an adjudicator's decision on the first appeal (Sch 4 para 22). The Court of Appeal held that the IAT had to identify an error of fact or law, and could not overturn merely on the ground that the IAT would have reached a different decision (*Subesh v Home Secretary* [2004] EWCA Civ 56).

The radical changes to this system began after 11 September 2001 ('9/11'), when fear of terrorism coincided with a media frenzy about large numbers of asylum seekers who were supposedly abusing the IAT process to stay in the UK. The Nationality, Immigration and Asylum Act 2002 changed the appeals provisions to provide an appeal to the adjudicator on facts or law, but no appeal to the IAT on the facts or the merits.[25] Appeals to the IAT required the permission of the IAT.

Under that system, the government became badly vexed by large volumes of judicial review decisions overturning refusals of permission to appeal. So, in 2004, Parliament replaced the two tiers with one Immigration and Asylum Tribunal (Asylum and Immigration (Treatment of Claimants, etc.) Act 2004); the Immigration and Asylum Tribunal was replaced in 2010 by immigration and asylum chambers of the First-tier Tribunal and the Upper Tribunal. The adjudicators and the members of the IAT all became members of the new tribunal. Most initial First-tier Tribunal decisions are made by a single immigration judge. There is an appeal from the First-tier Tribunal to the Upper Tribunal on a point of law, if either the First-tier Tribunal or the Upper Tribunal gives leave (see 12.4.8 and 12.4.9).

Meanwhile, if the Home Secretary proposes to remove a person from the country for reasons of national security or international relations, or the appeal requires disclosure of sensitive information, there is no appeal from the Home Secretary's decision (Nationality, Immigration and Asylum Act 2002 s 97). The only recourse is to the Special Immigration Appeals Commission (SIAC), under the Special Immigration Appeals Commission Act 1997. The word 'special' reflects its unusual secrecy, and 'commission' marks the government's purpose of keeping it out of the ordinary appeal processes of tribunals. The SIAC makes decisions by a panel of three members, one of whom has held high judicial office and another of whom has been an immigration judge. There is an appeal from the SIAC to the Court of Appeal on a question of law (Anti-terrorism, Crime and Security Act 2001 s 35).

Does all of this legislation amount to a progression toward proportionate dispute resolution? Proportionality is, of course, always under pressure from claimants determined to pursue any available avenue of recourse. And it is under constant political

---

[25] 'A party to an appeal to an adjudicator … may … appeal to the Tribunal against the adjudicator's determination on a point of law': Nationality, Immigration and Asylum Act 2002 s 101. See *CA v Home Secretary* [2004] EWCA Civ 1165 [10] and [30] (Laws LJ).

pressure from public anxiety both about immigration and about terrorism, and from government anxiety to be seen to be doing something. The steps in the progression have been dictated by crises such as the 9/11 attacks on the United States. Panic measures are dangerous ways of dealing with problems of due process. A community committed to the rule of law has to face the cost involved: the irony of process (see 4.13, p 157) is that we have to allow procedures that will be disproportionate in particular cases (procedures that allow some people to go on challenging a decision farther than is warranted), in order to ensure proportional process for people who need it.

12.7 Conclusion: the irony of process

The most striking feature of the tribunals system is the Upper Tribunal, which has the role of a new administrative appeals court. The new appeal process unifies tribunal appeals, and the Upper Tribunal plays a major role in administrative law.

Its focal challenges are to promote the two purposes of tribunals: administrative justice and proportionate dispute resolution. A cynic might say that 'administrative justice' means 'you don't get your day in court', and 'proportionate dispute resolution' means 'you get as little process as possible'. An optimist might say that the reconstruction promises the administration of justice in a way that is tailored to the needs of the people who are seeking justice, without imposing alienating (and, incidentally, expensive) formal procedures. The cynic and the optimist would both be overemphasizing aspects of a complex situation; the same governmental impulses have led to a really impressive reconstruction of tribunals, and *have also* created new risks of process failure. In the *Cart* case, the Supreme Court created a profusion of process, to guard against a risk of process failure where two tribunals have already held that there is no ground for an appeal to proceed.

The reconstruction of tribunals in TCEA 2007 has created an administrative justice system for the first time. Its main features reflect an evolution of the welfare state. In the earliest schemes for national insurance and soldiers' pensions before and after World War I, decision making was non-judicial, relatively informal, geared to reflect expertise and the purpose of the benefit in question. The massive development of the welfare state after World War II created a chaotic and expensive system. Since the 1980s, the trend has been to increase control of the costs both of benefits, and of the decision-making process. But it is a complex trend, involving substantial judicialization of processes, but also countervailing moves toward ADR and decision making without oral hearings and without representation.

Are tribunals the exception to a rule that disputes ought to be resolved by courts?

The Franks Committee in 1957 held on to a general principle that 'a decision should be entrusted to a court rather than to a tribunal in the absence of special considerations which make a tribunal more suitable'.[26] Yet Franks saw benefits that can often make tribunals more suitable: '... openness, fairness and impartiality'.[27] And the Franks Committee's recommendations, including the first Tribunals and Inquiries Act and the Council on Tribunals, contributed to making tribunal decision making a standard feature of the legal system, rather than a special exception to judicial decision making.

Our legal system has now abandoned the principle that courts are the standard way of deciding entitlements under government schemes, and the idea that tribunals are an exception needing special considerations. Instead, proportionate decision making is the general principle (White Paper, 3.23). The presumption that disputes as to legal rights are to be determined by the courts has been abandoned; meanwhile, the tribunals are becoming more like courts. The reconstruction has undoubtedly enhanced the impartiality of tribunals; its impact on their openness and fairness is much more complex.

The principle of proportionate process has to be applied with a healthy awareness of the irony of process: all process is imperfect, so that it is necessary to create processes that will be *disproportionate* in some cases, in order to guarantee the protections that will be necessary in other cases. Processes must be sufficient to do justice. If they do not allow scope for waste and even abuse (e.g., by asylum seekers who have no good claim to be given asylum, or people making fraudulent benefit claims), they will not be sufficient to do justice (e.g., for refugees and for people who need welfare benefits).

There is no good way of deciding which hearings are pointless without a hearing. Consider what proportionality requires in the most politically contentious tribunal scheme, immigration and asylum:

- *enough* procedural protection to asylum seekers and would-be immigrants to secure just decisions with fair participation by the people affected;

- *without* furnishing illegal immigrants and people falsely claiming to be refugees with ways of staying in the country or delaying their removal.

The irony of process is that it is impossible to accomplish both. Without serious reconsideration on an appeal to an independent decision maker, there is no good way of sorting the refugees from the non-refugees. There is no way of setting up such a process without giving people who have no right to asylum a technique to delay, or even to deceive, a tribunal or court that cannot assess the situation perfectly. So a commitment to justice in immigration and asylum matters requires a commitment to provide processes that can be abused. That is actually true of *all* tribunals, and of courts, too.

[26]   *Report of the Committee on Administrative Tribunals and Enquiries*, 1957, Cmnd 218 [38].

[27]   *Report of the Committee on Administrative Tribunals and Enquiries*, 1957, Cmnd 218 [41].

Governmental instincts (to cut the costs of waste in the tribunals, and to streamline decision making) risk misjudgments of proportionality. But the increased independence and the unification in the reconstruction of tribunals are impressive. As Sedley LJ said in *R (Cart) v Upper Tribunal* [2010] EWCA Civ 859 [42], the new system 'is something greater than the sum of its parts':

> It represents a newly coherent and comprehensive edifice designed, among other things, to complete the long process of divorcing administrative justice from departmental policy, to ensure the application across the board of proper standards of adjudication, and to provide for the correction of legal error within rather than outside the system, with recourse on second-appeal criteria to the higher appellate courts.

The crucial features of the reconstruction of tribunals are the removal of tribunal sponsorship from departments, the appointment of tribunal judges on the recommendation of the Judicial Appointments Commission, and the creation of a unified appeals tribunal in the Upper Tribunal, with appeals to the Court of Appeal. Those major reforms bring their own costs, through the increased judicialization of tribunals. The costs will be well worth paying if the system helps people to get fair hearing in, for example, a claim for disability benefits.

FROM THE MISTS OF TIME

Albert Venn Dicey is famous for arguing that, in England, the rule of law is secured by making the lawfulness of administrative action a matter for the ordinary courts (*Introduction to the Study of the Law of the Constitution* (Macmillan 1885)). The reconstruction of tribunals creates, in the Upper Tribunal, an administrative appeals court that is not part of the ordinary courts. Today, if a tribunal has decided your complaint unlawfully, you cannot go to the High Court. So is the reconstruction anathema to the traditions of the British constitution?

In his Preface to the 8th edition in 1914, Dicey wrote:

> 'France has with undoubted wisdom more or less judicialised her highest administrative tribunal, and made it to a great extent independent of the Government of the day. It is at least conceivable that modern England would be benefited by the extension of official law. Nor is it quite certain that the ordinary law Courts are in all cases the best body for adjudicating upon the offences or the errors of civil servants. It may require consideration whether some body of men who combined official experience with legal knowledge and who were entirely independent of the Government of the day, might not enforce official law with more effectiveness than any Division of the High Court.'

Today, in England, the reconstruction of tribunals has judicialized administrative tribunals, and they have the independence that Dicey considered essential to the rule of law. Even on Dicey's view, the reconstruction represents a new way of imposing the rule of law on administration, and not a departure from the rule of law.

TAKE-HOME MESSAGE ● ● ●

- The most important features of the reconstruction of tribunals in the **Tribunals, Courts and Enforcement Act 2007** are:
  - the new **appeal process in the Upper Tribunal** (along with its judicial review jurisdiction over some tribunal matters), with a further appeal to the Court of Appeal;
  - **the Upper Tribunal's opportunity to develop case law** that will govern the work of tribunals;
  - **appointment of tribunal judges** through the same independent process as appointment of judges in the ordinary courts;
  - support and oversight for the administrative justice system from:
    - — a unified Courts and Tribunals Service;
    - — a Tribunal Procedure Committee; and
    - — a move toward encouraging **ADR** in matters brought before tribunals.

- The Upper Tribunal is an innovation of constitutional significance: it is the closest thing that the UK has ever had to an **administrative court** distinct from the High Court.

- The reconstruction creates new tensions in the system between **informality** and legality:
  - it makes tribunals more like courts in some ways (in the method of appointment of tribunal judges, and their independence, and the government's aims to move away from expert and lay membership on tribunals); and yet
  - it aims to keep proceedings informal, and to restrict legal representation before tribunals.

CRITICAL QUESTIONS ● ● ●

1   What can courts do that tribunals cannot do?

2   What can tribunals do that courts cannot do?

3   What is the purpose of tribunals, and why is it best served by a tribunal as opposed to a court or some other dispute resolution system?

4   If a tribunal fails to give a fair hearing, is the possibility of an appeal on a question of law enough to remedy the unfairness?

5   Is there any good reason for the Immigration and Asylum Tribunal to have a different structure and process from other tribunals?

6   Is there any general difference between a person-and-state tribunal decision and the decision of a court in a tort action against a public authority? Why couldn't tribunals take over the complaints that are currently pursued in the tort actions discussed in Chapter 14?

7   What is the difference between the principle of proportionate decision making
and the principle (from the 1957 Franks Committee) that a dispute should be
resolved by a court unless special considerations make a tribunal preferable?

READING ● ● ●

Edwards v Bairstow [1956] AC 14 (HL)
Moyna v Work and *Pensions Secretary* [2003] UKHL 44
R (Cart) v Upper Tribunal [2011] UKSC 28
Jones v First Tier Tribunal [2013] UKSC 19

Secretary of State for Constitutional Affairs, *Transforming Public Services: Complaints,
Redress and Tribunals*, July 2004 , Cm 6243 ('the White Paper')
Tribunals, Courts and Enforcement Act 2007, Part 1
Peter Cane, Administrative Tribunals and Adjudication (Hart 2009)—a comparison
of tribunal systems in the United Kingdom, United States, and Australia, putting them in their historical context and offering an explanation of the nature of
administrative adjudication

On the reconstruction of tribunals:
Peter Cane, 'Judicial Review in the Age of Tribunals' [2009] PL 479
Hazel Genn, 'Tribunals and Informal Justice' (1993) 56 MLR 393
Genevra Richardson and Hazel Genn, 'Tribunals in Transition: Resolution or
Adjudication?' [2007] PL 116
On the *Cart* case:
Janina Boughey and Lisa Burton Crawford, 'Reconsidering *R (on the application of
Cart) v Upper Tribunal* and the Rationale for Jurisdictional Error' [2017] Public Law
592–608
**For comment on the new system ('a radical restructuring of the existing tribunal
jurisdictions into a coherent two-tier model'), from the first Senior President
of Tribunals:**
Sir Robert Carnwath, 'Tribunal Justice: A New Start' [2009] PL 48

   The following online resources accompany this chapter: **summaries** of key
cases and legislation; **updates** on the law; **guidance** for answering the pop
quizzes and questions; and **links** to legislation, cases, and useful websites.

13 Ombudsmen

Instead of adversarial litigation in a court or tribunal, an independent investigation of a complaint may be the best process for securing administrative justice. Here, we look at ombudsmen and other forms of investigation of the working of government, and the ways in which they can resolve disputes and improve administration.

LOOK FOR ● ● ●

- The ombudsmen's four keys:
  (1) they are independent;
  (2) they investigate a complaint;
  (3) they look for injustice caused by maladministration; and
  (4) they make a report.
  That's all they do!

- The way(s) in which the government ought to respond to reports by ombudsmen.

- The use of inquiries by government as a way of dealing with crises and scandals, and the ways in which the law controls their use.

- The role of courts in controlling investigation processes.

> ' Access to justice is achievable as often through institutions other than the courts of law. '
>
> *R v Lambeth LBC, ex p Crookes* (1997) **29 HLR 28** (QBD), 39 (Sir Louis Blom-Cooper)

13.1 Introduction: the 'Debt of Honour' investigation

In 2000, years of lobbying paid off for people who had been interned by the Japanese in World War II. After half a decade of campaigns, political pressure in the House of Commons pushed the government into a sudden announcement of a scheme of payments. Administrators from various departments were quickly assembled for a working party, which met on a Friday, and had to make proposals to ministers the following Monday. Just eight days later, on 7 November, a minister announced in the House of Commons that the government would make payments of £10,000 each to former detainees, not as compensation, but to recognize the country's 'debt of honour' to those who endured captivity in the Far East during World War II. He said that the payments would go to 'British civilians who were interned'.

Thousands of payments were made, starting in January 2001.[1] But the government never adopted any view on what 'British civilians' meant until March 2001, when an interdepartmental working group decided that payments would be made only to civilian internees who were born in the United Kingdom, or who had a parent or grandparent born in the United Kingdom. This 'blood link' test was not announced until July 2001. The blood-link test ruled out hundreds who had been British subjects during World War II. It not only denied those British subjects the £10,000, but it also antagonized them, because it suggested that the country did not owe them a debt of honour. The Japanese had interned them because they were British, and they were 'British civilians' in the sense that they were British subjects at the time of their internment, but under the blood-link test they did not count.

Jack Hayward complained to the Parliamentary Commissioner for Administration (the 'Parliamentary Ombudsman'). His father was a British subject born in India, and his mother was born in Iraq; after the war, he came to the UK to live with an aunt, went to school and university and did National Service in England, and eventually became a professor of politics. He had been interned as a Briton with his family, and he thought he would qualify when the government announced payments to 'British civilians'. But his application was rejected in June 2001, because he did not satisfy the blood-link test. The Parliamentary Ombudsman investigated Hayward's complaint as a representative

---

[1] By 2004, more than 23,000 payments of £10,000 had been made.

of many other complaints, and reported that maladministration in the development of the scheme had caused him an injustice. It was a 'significant departure from standards of good administration' to announce the scheme in a way that raised the hopes of all British detainees, without clearly saying who would be eligible.[2]

In July 2005, the Ombudsman's report recommended that the Ministry of Defence review the operation of the scheme, and reconsider the position of Hayward and those in a similar position. She also recommended an apology, and that the Ministry should consider expressing regret 'tangibly'.[3]

The Ministry of Defence accepted the finding of maladministration, and the last two recommendations. But it refused to review the operation of the scheme, or to reconsider Hayward's eligibility for the payment. So the Parliamentary Ombudsman used her power under the Parliamentary Commissioner Act 1967 s 10(3) to issue a special report to Parliament, indicating that she had found injustice caused by maladministration, which the government did not propose to remedy. After that report, and the intervention of the Public Administration Select Committee, the government finally revised the eligibility criteria in March 2006, to include people like Jack Hayward.

> ### Four findings of maladministration: the Parliamentary Ombudsman's summary
>
> * The scheme was devised too quickly and in a way that made eligibility unclear.
> * The ministerial statement was confusing.
> * The government should have reviewed the blood-link test to ensure that it did not lead to unequal treatment.
> * The government failed to inform complainants that the criteria had been clarified when they were sent a questionnaire to establish their eligibility.[4]

The 'Debt of Honour' case demonstrates the strengths and the limitations of ombudsmen. An investigation of a complaint provides a form of scrutiny of administration that neither MPs nor judges can offer. What the complainant does not get from an ombudsman is a legal remedy. But, on the other hand, the ability to place a special report before Parliament when injustice is not remedied provides a form of response to a complaint that no court can give. As a technique for controlling administration, ombudsmen are distinctly different from courts, and they can be more valuable to people with a complaint.

13.2 The ombudsman process: four keys

Ombudsmen share the following traits.

---

2   Parliamentary Ombudsman, 'A Debt of Honour': The Ex Gratia Scheme for British Groups Interned by the Japanese during the Second World War, HC 324 (2005–06) [155]–[159].

3   Parliamentary Ombudsman, 'A Debt of Honour' [212]–[218].

4   Parliamentary Ombudsman, 'A Debt of Honour' [199].

The keys of the ombudsman process

- Their independence: they are free of control by the bodies they scrutinize.
- Their investigative process: their scrutiny takes the form of investigation of a complaint.
- Their task: they look for injustice caused by bad administration.
- Their reporting function: the result of the process is simply a report on the investigation; it may make recommendations as to redress, if the ombudsman concludes that injustice has been caused by bad administration.

You can see how different their role is from the role of a public authority in considering a complaint about its own conduct. And, on the other hand, it is different from the role of a tribunal, or of a court in judicial review. To unpack these key features of ombudsmen, we will start with the central government ombudsman, who is a *Parliamentary* Ombudsman because of a uniquely British effort to squeeze the Scandinavian ombudsman model into our constitution.

Thank you, Sweden

When Sweden lost Finland to Russia in 1809, the Swedish nobles deposed the King and appointed a new one. They retained the constitutional allocation of executive power to the King, and legislative power to Parliament. But they took the opportunity to invent a 'iustitie-ombudsman': a representative appointed by Parliament for people with a complaint, whose job was to protect individual rights against the executive. There was no legal technique for the ombudsman to invalidate executive action; he simply investigated and made a report. It worked.

Modern ombudsmen are impartial investigators, not representatives. Otherwise, though, the first ombudsman's office nearly 200 years ago has been the model for the modern public-sector ombudsman: an independent public official appointed to investigate complaints against administrative acts of government. Since the 1960s, the model has spread throughout the common law world.

The Parliamentary Ombudsman was the first ombudsman in the UK. The Local Government Ombudsmen were set up by statute in 1974. Their powers and their role are different, in ways that reflect differences between central and local government.

The role of ombudsmen's investigations in both local government and central government *overlaps* with the role of judicial review. Moreover, courts have taken upon themselves the task of reviewing the work of the local and parliamentary ombudsmen. Judicial review of the work of ombudsmen raises a difficult question about the purpose of judicial review itself: why should courts interfere at all in the work of another independent institution set up to do justice for complainants? The judges have given judicial review of ombudsmen's reports, but they have not answered this question.

13.3 The Parliamentary Ombudsman

The idea of the Parliamentary Commissioner Act 1967 was to take advantage of the Scandinavian model to create an informal investigator. But we ended up with a special British version of the institution, because of a British problem. The office of ombudsman seemed to be at odds with the tradition that complaints against the administration of government are to be resolved by writing to one's MP. An MP can pursue a complaint by contacting the department in question. By convention, the department must respond to inquiries from MPs, and an MP who is not satisfied with the response can raise the matter in the House of Commons. The role of an ombudsman as an informal investigator of central government administration seemed to clash with that role of MPs as the people's representatives. And it may have seemed to the politicians that it was not quite right for the British government to face investigation by any authority outside Parliament.

The solution to the clash was to make the ombudsman *parliamentary* in three respects: the Ombudsman (1) investigates a complaint only on referral from an MP; (2) makes reports to the House of Commons (an annual report—s 10(4)—and a special report on any failure by a public authority to comply with a report on an investigation); and (3) is supported by a select committee of the House of Commons (it is not mentioned in the Act, but the Public Administration Select Committee considers the Parliamentary Ombudsmen's reports on behalf of the House of Commons). The reporting role, together with the connection to the Committee, provides a resolution to the tricky question of the effect of ombudsmen's reports.

Before drawing general conclusions about the value of the office in the control of administration, we will need to look in detail at the scheme of the 1967 Act, and at the ways in which the Parliamentary Ombudsmen have developed their role.

13.3.1 The Parliamentary Commissioner Act 1967

(1) **Who** is the Parliamentary Commissioner for Administration (the 'Parliamentary Ombudsman')?

She is appointed by the Crown (Parliamentary Commissioner Act 1967 s 1(2))—that is, by the government. But after appointment, she is independent of the government. Like a judge, she holds office 'during good behaviour' (s 1(2)), which means that she can only be removed by addresses from both Houses of Parliament (s 1(3)).[5] And her salary is fixed by a resolution of the House of Commons, not by the government.

---

5   But she can be removed by the Crown on grounds of medical incapacity: Parliamentary and Health Service Commissioners Act 1987 s 2.

(2) **Whom** can the Ombudsman investigate?

The major government departments[6] and more than 200 agencies are open to investigation. The 1967 Act gave a list (Sch 2); the government can extend it, but only to governmental bodies exercising functions on behalf of the Crown, or set up by the government and receiving at least half their revenue from Parliament (s 4). Educational institutions, bodies that regulate the professions, complaints investigators, and commercial bodies are excluded.[7]

(3) **How** does a complaint get to the Ombudsman?

The Ombudsman does not act on her own initiative. She can only investigate matters raised by a complaint. And the 'MP filter' in the 1967 Act provides that she can only act on a complaint after an MP refers it to her (s 5(1)—see 13.3.2).

(4) What can the Ombudsman **not** investigate?

The legislation rules out:

- complaints by a public body (e.g., a local authority, s 6);

- complaints about 'any action in respect of which the person aggrieved has or had' a remedy before a tribunal or a court. But the Ombudsman may investigate even if there is such an alternative, if 'it is not reasonable to expect him to resort or have resorted to it' (s 5(2)—see 13.5.3);

- complaints about excluded subject matters listed in Sch 3 to the 1967 Act, including international relations, crime, and security investigation, contracts, or other commercial transactions (but the compulsory acquisition of land is fair game), and personnel (pay, appointments, etc.).

(5) **When** must a complaint be brought?

Complaints must have reached an MP within twelve months after the complainant had notice of the problem—although the Ombudsman has a discretion to take complaints out of time, if there are special circumstances (s 6(3)). (Remember, this is more generous than the three-month *prima facie* time limit on judicial review—see 10.3.1.)

(6) How does the Ombudsman proceed?

- First, she decides whether a complaint is duly made (s 5(9)).

- Then, the Ombudsman decides whether to investigate, over which she has discretion (s 5(5)).[8]

---

[6] But not the Law Officers' Department, the Offices of the Leader of the House of Commons, or the Privy Council. The Parliamentary Commissioner Act 1994 extended the Ombudsman's role to investigating the administration of tribunals.

[7] Parliamentary and Health Service Commissioners Act 1987 s 1, amending s 4 of the 1967 Act. On higher education, see 13.9.1 on the Office of the Independent Adjudicator.

[8] On the discretion whether to investigate, see *R (Goldsmith IBS Ltd) v Parliamentary and Health Service Ombudsman* [2016] EWHC 1905.

- She gives the public authority an opportunity to comment on the complaint (s 7(1)).

- She conducts her investigation in private, in the manner she considers appropriate (s 7(2)).

- She can require a department or a public body to furnish information and documents relevant to the investigation, and can summon witnesses. For these purposes, the Ombudsman has the same powers as the courts (s 8).

- Public interest immunity (see 1.6.1, p 30) does not apply to Ombudsman investigations (s 8(3)), but Cabinet proceedings cannot be disclosed to her (s 8(4)).

- Obstruction of an investigation will be treated like a contempt of court (s 9).

(7) **What** does the Ombudsman look for?

The Ombudsman reports on whether 'injustice has been caused to the person aggrieved in consequence of maladministration' (s 10(3)). 'Mal–' just means 'bad'. That is an extremely broad, undefined remit.

(8) **What outcome** does the Ombudsman give?

- If she decides not to conduct an investigation, she must send a statement of her reasons to the referring MP (s 10(1)).

- A report of the results of an investigation must be sent to the complainant, to the MP, and to the investigated department/body (s 10(2)).

- After conducting an investigation, if it appears to the Ombudsman that the government is not going to remedy an injustice caused by maladministration, she may lay a special report before each House of Parliament (s 10(3)), as she did in the 'Debt of Honour' case.

So the Ombudsman is different from courts in her process, and in the substance of her inquiry, and instead of giving a remedy she makes a report. Her process is investigative rather than adjudicative. And she looks for bad administration, not unlawful administration. Those essentials apply to all ombudsmen. But before delving further into those essentials, we need to see why the Parliamentary Ombudsman is *parliamentary*, and how the Local Government Ombudsmen are different.

13.3.2 The Parliamentary Ombudsman and Parliament

The most important feature of the Ombudsman's relationship with Parliament is her ability to lay reports before each House, and her link with the Public Administration Select Committee. These features defuse the potential for crisis when a public body wants to reject a recommendation of the Ombudsman, making the issue a matter for Parliament, and giving the Ombudsman a special technique for bringing it to the attention of Parliament (see 13.7.1).

The more controversial feature of the Ombudsman's parliamentary role has been the MP filter. Its rationale was to preserve the role of MPs (and in fact to enhance it by giving them an investigative facility to invoke when they receive a complaint). But it has faced widespread criticism outside Parliament, and it is not even popular with MPs. After a review in 2000, the government actually accepted the view that the filter should be removed. But this reform is unlikely to find its way to the top of the political agenda.

And in practice the MP filter is a minor issue. Since the 1970s, the Ombudsman has been forwarding direct complaints to the constituency MP of the person complaining, rather than rejecting them.[9] Today, you can find your MP and email him or her directly from the Ombudsman's website. If your MP does not want to ask the Ombudsman to investigate, you can find another MP. Upheld by the courts,[10] and not likely to be removed soon by legislation, the MP filter has become a technicality with some symbolic value in asserting the responsibility of MPs for involvement in complaints against government. It is potentially a nuisance, but not a serious obstruction to justice.

Timing

The Parliamentary Ombudsman's process was designed to provide informal and easy redress for grievances, but the investigations can take a long time. The 'Debt of Honour' investigation took two years; the investigation did not even start for eighteen months after the complaint was made, as the Ombudsman waited for the related *ABCIFER*[11] litigation to end. That was extraordinary; the Ombudsman apologized for the delay, but of course much of it was not caused by her office. The information that the Ombudsman requests from government departments is likely to take months to emerge, especially when the issues are complex, several departments or agencies are involved, the files are massive, and the civil servants are busy with other crises.

13.4 Local Government Ombudsmen

The Local Government Act 1974 provided for Commissioners for Local Administration ('Local Government Ombudsmen') to investigate complaints of maladministration by local government. The difference between local and central government makes for some important differences from the role of the Parliamentary Ombudsman.

- People can **complain directly** to the Local Government Ombudsmen. There was initially a filter through councillors, like the Parliamentary Ombudsman's MP filter, but it was removed in 1988,[12] and investigations jumped by 44 per cent in one year.

---

[9]   See Carol Harlow, 'Ombudsmen in Search of a Role' (1978) 41 MLR 446, 451.

[10]   The court will not make any order inviting or requiring an MP to submit a complaint, or inviting or requiring the Ombudsman to investigate (*R (Murray) v PCA* [2002] EWCA Civ 1472).

[11]   *R (Association of British Civilian Internees—Far Eastern Region) v Defence Secretary* [2003] EWCA Civ 473.

[12]   Direct access was provided in the Local Government Act 1988 s 29.

- Unlike central government departments and agencies, the local authority **must be given an opportunity to consider the complaint** before the Ombudsman can investigate (s 26(5)).

- The local authority investigated **must respond** to an adverse report. Failing to do so can result in a further Local Government Ombudsman report, and continued inaction can result in the local authority being required to publish the Ombudsman's recommendations in local newspapers (with their reasons for non-compliance, if they wish).[13]

- The Local Government Act 1974 s 31(3) gave local authorities an **express power to pay compensation** to a person suffering injustice in consequence of maladministration.

These differences are explained by the difference between the role of Parliament and the more limited role of local democracy. First of all, local councillors do not have the special constitutional role that MPs have in holding the government to account. Second, whereas the Parliamentary Ombudsman reports to Parliament, it was felt necessary to give some independent clout to Local Government Ombudsman reports by requiring the local authority to reply. The Local Government Ombudsmen actually conform more closely to the Scandinavian model of ombudsmen, because their role is not complicated by the special place of Parliament in the British constitution. But, by the same token, the Local Government Ombudsmen lack the support that the Parliamentary Ombudsman gets from the Public Administration Select Committee. And the Local Government Ombudsmen are subject to a special limitation that the Parliamentary Ombudsman does not face: they cannot investigate matters that concern most or all of the inhabitants of an area.[14] That prevents them from investigating any general complaint about local council spending.

But the range of subject matter for Local Government Ombudsmen is vast; it includes education (including the contentious business of school choice and provision for special educational needs), social services, housing, Council Tax, and planning. They handle more than five times as many complaints in a year as the Parliamentary Ombudsman.

Like the Parliamentary Ombudsman, they can ordinarily take on an investigation only if the complaint is made within twelve months of the matter coming to the attention of the complainant. But they can give themselves a wide latitude where there are special considerations: in the *Balchin* investigation (see 13.8.1), the Local Government Ombudsman considered a complaint made twelve years after the events that were investigated.

---

[13] Local Government Act 1974 s 31, as amended by Local Government and Housing Act 1989 s 26.

[14] Local Government Act 1974 s 26(7).

> **Investigation of local governance**
> The Local Government Act 2000 set up a 'Standards Board' to oversee local
> authorities' codes of conduct for council members, and to investigate complaints
> of breaches of those codes. In the Localism Act 2011, Parliament abolished the
> Standards Board as part of a range of measures designed to give more power
> and responsibility to local authorities. They must now have their own codes of
> conduct and investigation arrangements (ss 27, 28), and it is a criminal offence
> for councillors to withhold or misrepresent a financial interest (s 34).

13.5 Bad administration and unlawfulness, ombudsmen and courts

13.5.1 What is maladministration?

Maladministration is just bad administration. It has an unlimited variety of forms. The
legislation does not lay down the grounds on which an ombudsman may conclude that
there has been maladministration. As Lord Denning said in *R v LCA, ex p Bradford
Metropolitan City Council* [1979] QB 287 (CA) 311, 'Parliament did not define "maladministration." It deliberately left it to the ombudsman himself to interpret the word
as best he could.' In *R (Rapp) v Parliamentary and Health Service Ombudsman* [2015]
EWHC 1344 [38], Mrs Justice Andrews held that:

> ' The question whether any given set of facts amounts to maladministration or
> causes injustice to a complainant is a matter for the Ombudsman alone. Whatever
> it may think about the conclusion reached, and even if it fundamentally disa-
> grees with that conclusion, the Court may not usurp the statutory function of the
> Ombudsman. It can only interfere if the decision reached was irrational. '

We should immediately note that this approach is at odds with *R v PCA, ex p Balchin*
[1997] JPL 917, which held that questions of what considerations might be relevant to
an ombudsman's finding that there was or was not maladministration are questions for
the Court: see 13.8.1. But the judges have generally avoided laying down rules for what
an ombudsman should treat as maladministration. Perhaps the most important judicial decision on maladministration established that it is not to be approached using
standards of lawfulness developed in judicial review. When Liverpool City Council
gave planning permission for Liverpool Football Club to build a new stand at Anfield,
the Local Government Ombudsman made an adverse report after investigating complaints that Council members should have revealed that they were season ticket hold-
ers or regularly attended matches. The Council sought judicial review of that report,
partly on the ground that instead of applying the standard of disclosure of interests
in the Councillors' Code of Conduct, the Ombudsman ought to have used the less

stringent test for bias developed in judicial review. The Court of Appeal held that although there is a substantial overlap between maladministration and unlawfulness, there is no reason why the considerations determining maladministration should be the same as those determining unlawfulness. In investigating complaints of maladministration, the Ombudsman need not be 'constrained by the legal principles which would be applicable if he were carrying out the different task (for which he has no mandate) of determining whether conduct has been unlawful' (*R v LCA, ex p Liverpool City Council* [2001] 1 All ER 462 (CA) [47] (Chadwick LJ)).

13.5.2 Maladministration, merits, and unlawfulness

There is no closed set of criteria of maladministration. Yet there are still three important, but rather vague, constraints on both the subject matter of investigations, and the content of reports:

(1) the problem has to be bad *administration*;

(2) ombudsmen may not investigate maladministration that could have been remedied in judicial review, unless it is unreasonable to expect the complainant to go to court (s 5(2) of the 1967 Act; s 26(6) of the 1974 Act—see 13.5.3);

(3) ombudsmen are not authorized to 'question the merits of a decision taken without maladministration' (s 12(3) of the 1967 Act; s 34(3) of the 1974 Act).

The legislation does not say that ombudsmen cannot question the merits of a decision taken *with* maladministration. This statutory conundrum leaves it to the ombudsman to resolve the tension between telling the administration what policies to pursue (which is not meant to be the ombudsman's job), and telling the administration how to administer them (which is the ombudsman's job).

In the 'Debt of Honour' investigation (see 13.1), the Parliamentary Ombudsman complimented the government on a scheme that 'was, after all, a highly commendable attempt to recognise "a debt of honour"', but she could not resist saying what she thought of the merits of the blood link test for payments:

> In the circumstances, it is not for me to address the aspect of the complaints I have received which relates to the fairness of the specific criterion. I will go no further than to say that it is perhaps surprising that this particular criterion was chosen as being the means to repay "a debt of honour" to those interned as British civilians by the Japanese. [15]

In straying into the merits, the Ombudsman still showed restraint: she did not recommend a change in the criterion (even though she recommended a review of the 'operation of the scheme'). The decision to adopt the criterion was taken *with*

---

[15]   Parliamentary Ombudsman, '*A Debt of Honour*' [229] and [163].

maladministration, but the Ombudsman resisted the temptation to base any recommendation on the merits of the blood-link test.

● *Pop quiz* ●

Since it is impossible to investigate maladministration without criticizing government policy, does the work of the Parliamentary Ombudsman clash with the political responsibility of the House of Commons?

What is the relation between maladministration and unlawful administration? Consider the litigation in the 'Debt of Honour' case. Before they complained to the Ombudsman, the internees had sought judicial review of the blood-link test, in the *ABCIFER* case.[16] In a complex decision, the Administrative Court rejected the argument that British civilians in general who had been interned by the Japanese had a legitimate expectation (see 8.4) of a payment. The minister's initial announcement of the scheme had been too woolly to count as the 'clear and unequivocal representation' that would give rise to a legitimate expectation. The Ombudsman picked up where the Court left off, referring to that decision and saying, 'in my view, it is precisely that lack of clarity which represents such a significant departure from standards of good administration to the extent that it constitutes maladministration'.[17]

Finally, *after* the Ombudsman's report, in *R (Elias) v Defence Secretary* [2006] EWCA Civ 1293, the Court of Appeal held that the blood-link test was a form of indirect race discrimination, and therefore unlawful under s 1(1)(b) of the Race Relations Act 1976. If a statute makes it unlawful to adopt a policy that indirectly discriminates, then you need a court rather than the Ombudsman: the Ombudsman cannot say that indirect racial discrimination is maladministration. But the pattern of litigation and investigation in the 'Debt of Honour' case shows one way in which the ombudsmen's remit is much more far-reaching than judicial review: bad administration is *not necessarily unlawful*. Since the early days of the ombudsmen, it has been clear that maladministration and unlawfulness are different, as the Court of Appeal pointed out in *Congreve v Home Office* [1976] QB 629, 654–5 (Roskill LJ):

> ' No criticism of a government department could be more devastating than that contained in the Parliamentary Commissioner's Report. It is no part of our duty in this court to condemn the conduct of the Home Office. If their various actions vis-à-vis the plaintiff after March 26 were lawful, they do not become unlawful because the Home Office conducted the whole matter both before and after that date with lamentable incompetence. If their actions were at any time unlawful, they cannot be made lawful merely because the Home Office had acted, if they had, with extreme administrative efficiency and the most laudable of motives in serving what they believed to be the true public interest. '

---

[16] *R (Association of British Civilian Internees—Far Eastern Region) v Secretary of State for Defence* [2003] EWCA Civ 473.

[17] Parliamentary Ombudsman, 'A Debt of Honour' [155].

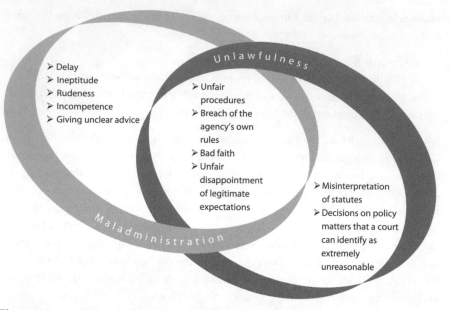

Figure 13.1 Maladministration and unlawfulness: the overlap

Note, however, that much bad administration *is* unlawful! (See Figure 13.1 for areas of overlap.) Consider the open-ended list of forms of maladministration given to the House of Commons by Richard Crossman, the minister proposing the Parliamentary Commissioner Bill in 1967: '... bias, neglect, inattention, delay, incompetence, ineptitude, perversity, turpitude and so on'.[18] Bias affecting a decision is unlawful (see Chapter 5). Turpitude implies bad faith, and that is unlawful (see 7.1). Those things are unlawful, and are also maladministration. Moreover, as has been pointed out by the High Court: 'Every procedural irregularity is likely to exhibit maladministration' (*R v Lambeth LBC, ex p Crookes* (1997) 29 HLR 28 (QBD), 36 (Sir Louis Blom-Cooper)).

But then, much maladministration is *not* in itself unlawful—such as delay and ineptitude. Note also that much unlawful conduct is not maladministration: a *Wednesbury*-unreasonable policy decision may be unlawful,[19] but does not count as maladministration for the ombudsmen's purposes. So the ombudsmen can address both more and less than judicial review addresses.

---

[18] Note the 'and so on', which reflects the open-ended nature of the Ombudsman's remit. Crossman's list of forms of maladministration was cited in *R v LCA, ex p Bradford Metropolitan City Council* [1979] QB 287 (CA), 311 (Lord Denning MR), and *R v Parliamentary Commissioner for Administration, ex p Balchin* [1997] JPL 917, 925.

[19] Remember that the courts will not apply the *Wednesbury* unreasonableness standard to all decisions, so that an extremely unreasonable policy decision may not be unlawful (see 7.3.2).

13.5.3 The ombudsmen or judicial review?

The ombudsmen legislation excludes investigation if the complainant 'has or had a remedy' in a court, unless 'in the particular circumstances it is not reasonable to expect him to resort or have resorted to it' (s 5(2)(b) of the 1967 Act; s 26 (6) of the 1974 Act). Because much maladministration is also unlawful, this exclusion of matters that could be remedied in court means that an ombudsman cannot investigate *all* complaints of maladministration. A complainant must take a complaint of unlawful administration to a court, unless he or she cannot reasonably be expected to do so. Does the reasonableness proviso mean that the ombudsman cannot investigate unless for some reason it would be especially difficult for the complainant to go to court? Or can the ombudsman investigate whenever an investigation would be a better way for the complainant to get his or her problem solved (so that it would be unreasonable to expect the complainant to engage in litigation that would be more expensive or slower or more complex)?

Given the mandate to report on injustice caused by maladministration, there is every reason for an ombudsman to take a generous approach to these questions of access. The nature of the ombudsman's office is at stake. Narrowly interpreted, s 5(2) of the 1967 Act can scarcely ever bar a complaint, because it is generally unreasonable to expect a person to engage in stressful and expensive litigation rather than take advantage of the free ombudsman process, with its investigative access to government information. Widely interpreted, s 5(2) forbids an ombudsman investigation whenever the same conduct could have been brought into question on judicial review.

In the 'Debt of Honour' investigation, the Parliamentary Ombudsman postponed the decision whether to investigate until the *ABCIFER* litigation was completed, and then asked herself whether Jack Hayward (the complainant) had exercised a judicial remedy or could reasonably be expected to do so. She concluded that Hayward *had not* exercised an alternative remedy because he had not been party to the *ABCIFER* litigation [23]. But even if he had already sought judicial review, he would not have had an alternative remedy if he was complaining of maladministration that was not unlawful. And the Ombudsman made this crucial point in deciding that it would not be reasonable to expect Hayward to seek another remedy: if the complaint is that lawful actions amounted to maladministration, then the complainant *has no* remedy in judicial review. After the *ABCIFER* litigation, it was clear to the Ombudsman that the very conduct that she considered to be maladministration (the unclear announcement, and the lack of certainty that the blood-link test was consistently applied) was not unlawful.

Note that the Ombudsman also held that the emotional and financial costs of the potentially distressing adversarial process of judicial review were relevant [26]–[27]: 'Court proceedings are adversarial in nature and ... I did not consider it reasonable to expect [Professor Hayward] to have to resort to such a process when that could have been distressing.'

The Ombudsman also pointed out that her fact-finding powers made an investigation very attractive to Hayward, who did not have the Ombudsman's access to the files and to the civil servants of the various departments involved in the payment scheme. In judicial review, the court can order disclosure, but the claimant needs to know what to ask for; in an Ombudsman's investigation, the Ombudsman can go looking for information that might turn out to be important.

The Ombudsman concluded that an investigation was 'more appropriate than expecting Professor Hayward to initiate legal proceedings' [28]. That approach is lenient toward complainants; it is more than Hayward needed (since it was evident after the *ABCIFER* case that he *had no* alternative remedy), and it turns the proviso in s 5(2)(b) of the 1967 Act into a way of allowing any complaint to go to the Ombudsman when investigation would be more appropriate than litigation. That generous interpretation of the proviso is a good interpretation: it helps the complainant in a way that cannot be detrimental to the administration (unless the Ombudsman wastes a public body's time by investigating a bad complaint on behalf of a vexatious complainant who could never have afforded litigation). The generous approach to access to the Ombudsman improves access to justice.

Meanwhile, the *courts* have also had to consider when a complaint ought to be brought to an ombudsman, and when it ought to go to judicial review. Remember that courts have a discretion whether to give permission to a claimant to seek judicial review (see 10.3.2): they can refuse permission on the ground that another remedy was available. The trend has been towards encouraging or even requiring complainants to use ombudsmen rather than courts where possible. In *R v Lambeth LBC, ex p Crookes* (1997) 29 HLR 28, 39, Sir Louis Blom-Cooper held that complaints of delays and procedural failings in paying housing benefit were 'incomparably better conducted through the informal procedure of the local government ombudsman than in the restrictively forensic forum of the courts', and concluded that 'any complaint of injustice resulting from maladministration, dressed up in the language of procedural irregularity for the purposes of judicial review, ought initially to be directed to the local government ombudsman'.

The law on this point is in flux, and we certainly cannot say in general that the High Court will exercise the discretion over relief in judicial review to send away anyone who could have taken a complaint of poor procedures to an ombudsman. But at least we can say that the ombudsmen should feel encouraged to take a positive approach to their capacity to start an investigation even when the complainant might have been entitled to some form of relief in judicial review.

And the positive approach of the Parliamentary Ombudsman in the 'Debt of Honour' case was endorsed in the leading judicial decision on the point, *R v LCA, ex p Liverpool City Council* [2001] 1 All ER 462 (CA) (see 13.5.1, pp 489–90). Liverpool City Council argued that the Ombudsman should not have started an investigation, because the complainants could have sought judicial review. The Court of Appeal held that it was a clear case in which the proviso in s 26(6) of the 1974 Act applied: even though the complainants could seek judicial review, it was not reasonable to expect them to, because they were unlikely to have the means to fund judicial review, and because the investigative role of the Ombudsman could uncover what really went on (whereas they would not have been able to get the evidence they needed for judicial review). Henry LJ said, 'the commissioner's investigation and report can provide the just remedy when judicial review might fail to do so' (472). This result supports the Parliamentary Ombudsman's approach in the 'Debt of Honour' investigation. It means that an investigation can be started whenever it would provide a better way for the complainant to seek justice.

There is every reason for a relaxed approach to the scope of ombudsmen's investigations. In one respect, though, the courts and ombudsmen have taken a strict approach: an applicant who succeeds in judicial review cannot go on to an ombudsman afterwards, and seek a recommendation of compensation for loss caused before the judicial review decision put an end to unlawful conduct.[20] That rule means that a person with a complaint should consider going to an ombudsman *first*. An ombudsman can recommend compensation for the effects of past maladministration, as well as a change for the future.

13.6 Injustice

An ombudsman cannot investigate just any maladministration. For an investigation to begin, the complainant must claim 'to have sustained injustice in consequence of maladministration' (s 5(1)(a)).

This restriction has the effect of a requirement of standing (see Table 11.2, p 436) for complaints to the ombudsman, because the ombudsman will not investigate maladministration that could not have caused you injustice. This is a *more restrictive* requirement than the requirement of standing to seek judicial review (see 11.2). Yet it can be met as long as you were affected by the maladministration in some way. In the 'Debt of Honour' case (see 13.1), Hayward had suffered no material loss from the maladministration that the Parliamentary Ombudsman found; he had no right to a payment, and he would not necessarily have received a payment if the scheme had been administered well. But the Ombudsman decided that he and the others in his position 'suffered outrage at the way in which the scheme has been operated and distress at being told that they were not "British enough" to qualify for payment under the scheme. That outrage and distress constitutes an injustice' [207].

This broad understanding of 'injustice' will eliminate the statutory requirement, if ombudsmen find that the complainant has suffered injustice whenever he or she is angry about the maladministration. But it is an approach that the courts have been willing to accept in judicial review of the ombudsmen. And as in the case of maladministration, the judges have used Richard Crossman's remarks in the House of Commons as a starting point. Proposing the Parliamentary Commissioner Bill, he said that injustice was meant to include 'the sense of outrage aroused by unfair or incompetent administration, even where the complainant has suffered no actual loss'.

---

[20] *R v Commissioner for Local Administration, ex p H* [1999] ELR 314 (CA).

So in the *Balchin* litigation (discussed in detail in 13.8.1), Sedley J said that 'injustice' can include a sense of outrage at maladministration (*R v Parliamentary Commissioner for Administration, ex p Balchin* [1997] JPL 917, 926 ('*Balchin (No 1)*')). If some stranger were genuinely outraged at the treatment that Hayward or Balchin received, his or her sense of outrage would count as injustice on Crossman's formulation or Sedley J's formulation.

Outrage is not injustice: outrage is a person's *response* to injustice. Injustice is a wrongful feature or effect of a decision that may give someone reason to be outraged. The ombudsman should be willing to investigate even when the victim of maladministration has suffered no material loss, but the requirement of injustice in the act should be construed as requiring that the complainant was a victim of unjust treatment by the administration. So it has been held in one judicial review of a Local Government Ombudsman that 'some prejudice' to the complainant had to be shown for a finding of injustice to be justified (*R v Commissioner for Local Administration, ex p S* (1999) 1 LGLR 633). The outrage felt by someone like Hayward is his or her response to an injustice or perceived injustice; if there is an injustice, it is that officials have treated him or her contemptuously (even if it did not cause loss).

Of course, the injustice requirement is not only a restriction on standing; it has an effect on the outcome of the investigation too, because the ombudsman's report will not recommend any action in the complainant's favour if the maladministration did not cause the complainant injustice.

13.7 What is an ombudsman's report actually worth to the complainant?

The outcome of an investigation for the complainant depends on what the ombudsman recommends, and on whether the government goes along with it. The 'Debt of Honour' investigation got Hayward an apology and, eventually, payment of £500 as a tangible gesture indicating the government's regret at the maladministration that the Parliamentary Ombudsman had identified. He did *not* immediately get the payment of £10,000 that the government gave to some British internees. But then he had no legal entitlement to the £10,000 (as the *ABCIFER*[21] litigation shows). And the government refused to reconsider his case. In the end, though, intervention by the Public Administration Select Committee put pressure on the government, and the criteria were changed to include Hayward. Sometimes, the Ombudsman gets a really valuable result for a complainant.

---

[21] *R (Association of British Civilian Internees—Far Eastern Region) v Secretary of State for Defence* [2003] EWCA Civ 473. The decision in *R (Elias) v Secretary of State for Defence* [2006] EWCA Civ 1293 that the blood-link test was unlawful under the Race Relations Act 1976 did not give the persons affected a right to the £10,000 either, as the decision left it open for the government to impose new, non-discriminatory criteria.

13.7.1 Compliance: a crisis?

Public authorities *almost* always carry out ombudsmen's recommendations. Over ten years from 1996 to 2006, the Local Government Ombudsmen found maladministration causing injustice 1,531 times, and the authority's response was found to be unsatisfactory only twelve times.[22] The Parliamentary Ombudsman has only rarely had to use the s 10(3) power to report the government to Parliament for non-compliance.

So the government's rejection of part of the 'Debt of Honour' report was exceptional. But it was not unique: in March 2006, the Parliamentary Ombudsman found maladministration in the role played by the Department for Work and Pensions in explaining private occupational pension schemes to the public. After massive shortfalls left some pensioners without the benefits they expected, the Ombudsman reported that the Department had not adequately explained the risks, and had published leaflets that were 'sometimes inaccurate, often incomplete, largely inconsistent and therefore potentially misleading'.[23] She recommended that the Department consider restoring part of the pension funding to provide the benefits that had been expected in some cases (and that the Department consider consolation payments to members). The costs would have been in the billions—perhaps £15 billion over sixty years.

For the first time ever, the Department both decided not to take the steps the Ombudsman had recommended, and comprehensively rejected her findings of maladministration. The Department's view was that the leaflets had not been misleading, and that the scheme members would not have saved themselves billions by making different investments if the information provided by government had been more complete. So the Department thought it had good reason to reject the report's conclusions. How should such a clash be resolved?

The 1967 Act makes Parliament the appropriate forum. The Act says nothing about any duties of government agencies that are subject to an adverse report by the Ombudsman; it authorizes the Ombudsman to lay before each House of Parliament an adverse report if it appears to her that 'the injustice has not been, or will not be, remedied' (s 10(3)). The Ombudsman must lay before each House of Parliament an annual general report, and may lay other reports before Parliament as she sees fit (s 10(4)). Since 1967, the Public Administration Select Committee has become the House of Commons' way of scrutinizing her reports, and the government's responses.

The Ombudsman laid her adverse report on the pensions investigation before Parliament under s 10(3); in testimony to the Committee, she said that she was 'disappointed to see the Government picking over and reinterpreting my findings of maladministration and injustice, re-arranging the evidence, re-doing the analysis and acting as judge on its own behalf'.[24] The Committee felt the same: 'We are disappointed that the Government has chosen to act as judge on its own behalf by rejecting and

---

[22]   See Local Government Ombudsman, *Annual Report 2006–07*, Appendix 3.

[23]   Parliamentary Ombudsman, *Trusting in the Pensions Promise: Government Bodies and the Security of Final Salary Occupational Pensions*, 6th Report of Session 2005–06 (HC 984).

[24]   http://www.publications.parliament.uk/pa/cm200809/cmselect/cmpubadm/219/219.pdf, Ev l.

qualifying a number of the Ombudsman's findings.'[25] So the pensions report created a crisis in relations between the government and the Ombudsman.

The power to report to both Houses of Parliament (and then to attend the Public Administration Select Committee for discussion) is all that the Ombudsman has. According to Cecil Clothier, Parliamentary Ombudsman from 1979 to 1984, it is 'as good an enforcing power as any reasonable Ombudsman could wish for'.[26] Clothier thought that the power to make a mandatory order would be a 'despotic power', which could only be controlled by an appeals system that would rob the ombudsmen of their speed and finality.

Meanwhile, the dispute was not just between the Ombudsman and the government. There were also the people who had complained to the Ombudsman in the first place. In *Bradley v Work and Pensions Secretary* [2007] EWHC 242, dissatisfied pensioners brought the first judicial review challenge to a governmental decision to reject a Parliamentary Ombudsman's report. The Administrative Court judge held that the minister was not legally bound to do what the Ombudsman recommended, but *was* legally bound to accept the Ombudsman's findings of maladministration, unless they were 'objectively shown to be flawed or irrational, or peripheral, or there is genuine fresh evidence to be considered' [58].

In the Court of Appeal, counsel appeared for the Parliamentary Ombudsman, and argued that 'the Secretary of State must proceed on the basis that the ombudsman's findings of injustice caused by maladministration are correct unless they are quashed in judicial review proceedings' (*Bradley v Work and Pensions Secretary* [2008] EWCA Civ 36 [135]). That was in accord with the Administrative Court's decision, and it would have meant a damaging judicialization of the Ombudsman's office. But the Court of Appeal unanimously overruled that approach, holding that it is not necessarily unlawful for a public authority to reject the Ombudsman's conclusions. The judges held that it would be 'wholly foreign to the purpose' [41] of the 1967 Act to require a minister to seek judicial review to quash an Ombudsman's report, instead of defending his or her rejection of its conclusions in Parliament. Said Sir John Chadwick, [41]:

> ' The minister whose department had, on investigation, been found by the commissioner to have been guilty of maladministration must expect to have to justify, in the parliamentary arena, why his department has not put in hand arrangements to provide a remedy in respect of the citizen's complaint. But there is, as it seems to me, no reason to think that it was any part of the Government's intentions, in introducing the legislation, to preclude a minister who was called to account before Parliament from explaining, as part of his justification for the decision to provide no remedy in respect of the complaint, his reasons for rejecting the commissioner's finding of maladministration. '

---

[25] http://www.publications.parliament.uk/pa/cm200809/cmselect/cmpubadm/219/219.pdf, 3.

[26] Cecil Clothier, 'The Value of an Ombudsman' [1986] PL 204, 209.

Yet the Court of Appeal upheld the conclusion that the minister had acted unlawfully: '[T]he focus of the court must be on [the minister's] decision to reject' [71], and the minister's decision to reject an Ombudsman's report must be 'based on cogent reasons' [72]. According to *Bradley*, the Court should quash the minister's response as unlawful 'if no reasonable Secretary of State could rationally disagree' with the Ombudsman's findings [73], and no reasonable Secretary of State would disagree with the findings unless there were cogent reasons for doing so [72] and [97]. That approach means that a decision to reject an Ombudsman's findings is unlawful unless there are cogent reasons for rejecting them. The Court of Appeal dismissed the Secretary of State's appeal against the quashing of his decision. That did not require the minister to do as the Ombudsman recommended, but it required him to make a fresh decision on the basis that she was right that the leaflets were misleading.

Granted that a department ought to consider an Ombudsman's report, and ought to have cogent reasons for rejecting a finding of maladministration (and granted that the Secretary of State should accept the Ombudsman's findings if no reasonable Secretary of State could rationally disagree), why are the courts involved? Is there any reason for judicial review to give effect to the proper departmental response to a report? *Bradley* gives no explanation. It appears to have seemed obvious to the judges: the minister had a discretionary power to act on the Ombudsman's report, and the court was only applying the ordinary *Wednesbury* principles to control that discretionary power.

The result of *Bradley* is that, as far as the law is concerned, a department can reject a Parliamentary Ombudsman's report and face the music in Parliament. A department need not seek judicial review, if it disagrees either with a finding of maladministration or with a recommendation in a report. The Court of Appeal made the crucial point that the House of Commons is the right arena for consideration of a department's response to recommendations.

Yet, according to *Bradley*, the complainants can drag the matter out of the parliamentary arena into the judicial arena—and get a new inquiry, by judges, into the facts of the case. That inquiry itself may interfere with the parliamentary process, as the Public Administration Select Committee and the House of Commons will need to suspend consideration of a department's response while legal proceedings are under way to determine whether the government's response was unlawful.

In *R (Equitable Members Action Group) v Her Majesty's Treasury & PCA* [2009] EWHC 2495, the Administrative Court applied the law as the Court of Appeal had stated it in *Bradley*. The claimants challenged the government's adverse response to a very complex report on the regulation of a large pension fund that had run into serious financial trouble. Applying the *Bradley* test of 'cogent reasons', in *Equitable Members* the Administrative Court held that the government did not have cogent reasons for rejecting some of the Ombudsman's findings. The case shows the impact of *Bradley*: although the courts say that a minister must justify a response to an Ombudsman's report 'in the parliamentary arena', a disappointed complainant can get what amounts to legally binding enforcement of the Ombudsman's findings—to the extent that the government does not persuade a court that there were good reasons for rejecting them.

The missing element in the Court's reasoning in *Bradley* is an explanation of the rationale for judicial review. When the Home Secretary makes a *Wednesbury*-unreasonable decision to deport an asylum seeker (see 7.1.3), the **core rationale** for judicial review (see 2.8) applies. The rationale for judicial review goes without saying: it is necessary in the interests of justice for the court to impose the rule of law, to stop the deportation. No other suitable remedy is available against the abuse of power. But if a minister makes a *Wednesbury*-unreasonable decision that the Ombudsman was wrong to find maladministration, there is an alternative process, established by statute: she can report to Parliament. That process is proportionate because her findings are designed to identify bad administrative practice, rather than unlawful action. And by the practice of the House of Commons, the Public Administration Select Committee provides an arena in which the Ombudsman's findings of fact and the department's response can be scrutinized. The judicial interference with the process in *Bradley* would only be justified if the parliamentary process (so carefully explained by the Court of Appeal in *Bradley*) were inadequate for remedying an unreasonable refusal by a department to accept the findings of the Ombudsman. And although it is easy to imagine the Public Administration Select Committee or the House of Commons going along with an unreasonable conclusion of a department after such a dispute, the judges are in no position to reach the conclusion that the parliamentary process is inadequate. In *Bradley*, the courts took on responsibility for reviewing matters that can be reviewed in Parliament. Judicial review is supposed to be a last resort (see 2.7), and it should not have been made available when there is another resort.

Meanwhile, in December 2007, before the *Bradley* case reached the Court of Appeal, the government announced enhanced compensation for pensioners, which amounted to compliance with the Ombudsman's main recommendation. The litigation may well have served as an instrument in the pensioners' political campaign for a spending decision in their favour. But if judicial review is a last resort, there was no reason for the litigation. In *In the matter of an application by JR55 for Judicial Review (Northern Ireland)* [2016] UKSC 22, Lord Sumption remarked *obiter* that 'The decision in *Bradley* raises delicate questions about the relationship between judicial and Parliamentary scrutiny of a minister's rejection of the recommendations of the Parliamentary Commissioner for Administration.'[27] But the Court did not reassess *Bradley*, as it did not need to do so in that case. If the issue does reach the Supreme Court, there is a good argument that the 'cogent reasons' standard in *Bradley* should be overruled, and that the Administrative Court ought to refuse permission to seek judicial review on the ground that a government department has disagreed with findings of the Parliamentary Ombudsman.

---

[27] In *R (Evans) v Attorney General* [2015] UKSC 21 (see 1.6.1), on whether the Attorney General must go along with a decision of the Upper Tribunal on a Freedom of Information Act request, the various judgments discuss a possible analogy with the question in *Bradley*, as to whether the Department of Work and Pensions must go along with the findings of the Ombudsman (see, e.g., [63]–[66], [125]–[127], and [179]. None of the discussion casts doubt on *Bradley*, but the remarks are *obiter* and the analogy is imperfect: see Lord Hughes [157]–[159].

> **Interventions**
>
> It should be obvious that something went wrong in the *Bradley* litigation, from the fact that the Speaker of the House of Commons intervened in the claim for judicial review (on the question of whether the Court should take into account the Ombudsman's evidence to the Public Administration Select Committee), and the Parliamentary Ombudsman intervened in the appeal (to argue that the judge had misunderstood the content of her report, and that the Secretary of State had misrepresented her report in the litigation, and to respond to the 'collateral attack' that she saw the Minister as making against her report [127]). It should all have been fought out in the House of Commons, and in the Public Administration Select Committee of the House.

13.8 Judicial review of ombudsmen

Ombudsmen have legal powers to compel testimony and production of documents, and it would be unlawful for them to try to use those powers for some purpose other than the purpose for which Parliament enacted the powers. A person could lawfully refuse to cooperate with an unlawful demand, or could seek judicial review of a direction from the ombudsman to give evidence (s 8 of the 1967 Act). To resist disclosure successfully, a claimant would have to show bad faith on the part of the ombudsman, or a very strong case that an ombudsman was asking for information that could not possibly help in a legitimate investigation. The High Court will uphold a subpoena (a witness summons) by an ombudsman as long as it is 'bona fide required for the purpose of the investigation', and the ombudsman is willing and able to keep confidential information secure.[20]

Those powers to compel evidence are the ombudsmen's only legal powers. In writing a report they do not exercise legal power. They do not change the legal position of the complainant or the public body. Ombudsmen are not part of the administration of government, either. They are independent investigators of the administration. There ought to be at least one appeal or other form of review from any judicial decision and from many administrative decisions, but an ombudsman is an *investigator* rather than administrator or an adjudicator. No good reason has ever been offered for courts to have any role in controlling the ombudsmen's investigations or reports. But, in fact, people who are disappointed by ombudsmen's decisions have persuaded the courts to assume the role of supervising the work of ombudsmen.

13.8.1 Judicial review of the Parliamentary Ombudsman

Sedley J extended the frontiers of judicial review in *R v Parliamentary Commissioner for Administration, ex p Balchin* [1997] JPL 917, the first judgment to overturn a report

---

[28] *In re a subpoena issued by LCA* (1996) The Times, 4 April (QBD).

of the Parliamentary Ombudsman.[29] The irony of the *Balchin* decision is that it takes the impressive tools that judges developed to oppose unlawful administration, and uses them to control an independent officer who *investigates* complaints of bad administration. It seems that the Ombudsman is now subject to all of the forms of judicial review that courts exercise in respect of administrative bodies. The problem with that approach is the **principle of relativity** (see 1.3): the reasons for judicial interference with other public authorities depend on the functions of the authorities subject to review, and on the capacity of courts to ensure that those functions are better fulfilled than they would be without judicial review. The rule of law does not require judicial scrutiny of the Ombudsman's reports in the way that it requires judicial scrutiny of, for example, decisions of a minister of the Crown to close a school, or to deport an asylum seeker.

Norfolk County Council decided to build a bypass a few metres from Maurice and Audrey Balchin's house, 'Swans Harbour'. The bypass was not even built, but before the plan was abandoned Maurice had lost the equity in the house that he needed to secure his business debts. The County Council had no legal obligation to help out the Balchins by buying their house, although it had a discretion to do so.[30] The Council decided not to help the Balchins.

The Department of Transport (DoT) entered the picture because the Council's road order had to be confirmed by the Secretary of State. The decision letter accompanying the confirmation from the DoT mentioned an inspector's hopes that the Council would look sympathetically on the Balchins' plight. But the letter also pointed out that it was a matter for the Council. In response, the chief executive of the Council wrote to a minister in the DoT to say that the Council knew that it had a legal duty to *consider* buying the blighted property, but that it had no legal duty to buy property out of sympathy, and added: 'I do not wish to sound harsh or bureaucratic but local government is frequently told to act within its powers and to curtail unnecessary expenditure …' (924). The Council's approach *was* harsh and bureaucratic, and Sedley J made it clear that, in his view, the Council could have been held on judicial review to have fettered its discretion unlawfully (929). But how could the Balchins complain to the Parliamentary Ombudsman that the DoT engaged in maladministration that caused them injustice? Their case was that the DoT, if it had engaged in good administration, would not have confirmed the road order without first seeking assurances from the Council that the Balchins would be adequately compensated. The Ombudsman found no maladministration; the Secretary of State could not have made the confirmation order conditional on a sympathetic approach to the Balchins, and whatever the DoT said to Norfolk County Council, 'the council … would have refused such a purchase' (923).

---

[29] See also *R (Cavanagh) v Health Service Commissioner for England* [2005] EWCA Civ 1578 (Sedley, Latham, and Wall LJJ), the first judgment to overturn a report of the Health Services Commissioner (a post held by the Parliamentary Ombudsman). The case marked a significant increment in judicialization of ombudsmen, as the judges held that it is their job to decide what issues are raised by the complaint.

[30] Highways Act 1980 s 246(2A), as amended by the Planning and Compensation Act 1991.

Sedley J held that the Ombudsman's report unlawfully omitted to evaluate a relevant consideration, 'the role and impact of Norfolk County Council's stance' (929). The conclusion seems to be that if the Ombudsman had considered the Council's hostility, he might have found that the Balchins suffered injustice in consequence of the DoT's maladministration in omitting to point out to the Council a power that it already knew it had, and was determined not to use. The effect of the decision was not only to apply to the Ombudsman the same techniques that were developed to prevent arbitrary government; it was also to extend those techniques, by treating it as the task of the judge to decide what facts of a case are relevant to another public authority's decision. That was a departure from the law of judicial review, which only authorizes courts to control another public authority's decision making by quashing *unreasonable* decisions as to the relevance of facts (see 8.2.3).

After the decision in *Balchin (No 1)*, a new Ombudsman reconsidered the complaint in the light of Sedley J's judgment, and like his predecessor he found that the DoT had not engaged in maladministration. In a second application for judicial review, Dyson J quashed the Ombudsman's report on the ground that the Ombudsman had failed to give reasons for finding that the DoT did not overlook the Council's power. The case is authority for the proposition that ombudsmen must give reasons that 'address the principal important controversial issues, but not every single point raised by the parties ...' (*R v PCA, ex p Balchin (No 2)* (2000) 79 P&CR 157, 167). A *third* Ombudsman's report found maladministration in respect of part, but not all, of the complaint, and the Ombudsman concluded that the injustice had found sufficient redress in an apology from the DoT. In a third application for judicial review, the judge once more overruled the Ombudsman on the ground of insufficient reasons (*R v PCA, ex p Balchin (No 3)* [2002] EWHC 1876). The reasons challenges in *Balchin (No 2)* and *(No 3)* reflect the intrusive control that Sedley J had imposed in *Balchin (No 1)*; once it is the court's job to decide the relevance of the facts of the case, the Ombudsman acquires a legal duty to give reasons that enable the court to do that job. And the court treated a lack of adequate reasons as ground for judicial review.

In a *fourth* investigation, the Ombudsman broke new ground by collaborating on a joint report with the Local Government Ombudsman. Finally, in October 2005, thirteen years after the DoT had written to Norfolk County Council to express the hope that it would consider the Balchins' plight 'with the utmost sympathy not to mention urgency', the Ombudsmen reported maladministration by both the Council and the DoT, and recommended a payment of £100,000 from each level of government. The DoT's supposed maladministration was a failure 'to ensure that they did not knowingly allow Councils to mislead themselves as to the intention of any legislation (for which the DoT was responsible) to which the Council were obliged to have regard, and to step in to offer a correct interpretation of the current legislative position if the Council clearly misrepresented that'.[31] But the Council had had regard to the legislation, and

---

[31] Foreword to *Redress in the Round: Remedying Maladministration in Central and Local Government*, 11 October 2005, 5th Report of Session 2005–06 (HC 475), available at http://www.ombudsman.org.uk.

had no duty to compensate. It is hard to see any ground for the Ombudsman's finding of maladministration, except a desire to bring a halt to the extravagant sequence of judicial review decisions. The saga is outlined in Figure 13.2.

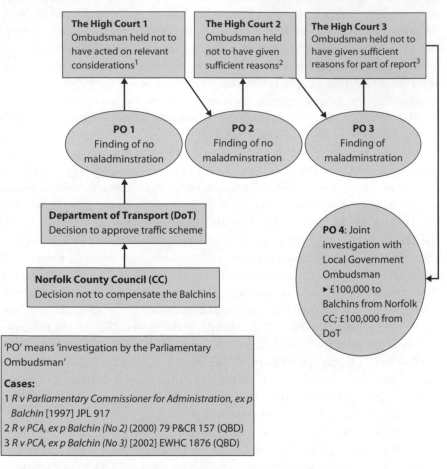

Figure 13.2 The Balchin saga: oversight overkill

Is this level of control of the Ombudsman's work justified? It gives the judge the job of deciding the relevance of facts to the Ombudsman's task of identifying maladministration. Public administration has nothing to gain from the general principle that judges, rather than the Ombudsman, should decide the considerations on which the Ombudsman should base her reports. The doctrine of relevance is a crucial part of the law's opposition to arbitrary government, and the **core rationale** (see 2.8) for judicial review supports the judges' role controlling other public authorities' judgments as to which considerations are relevant to the exercise of a discretionary power, *when doing so can prevent arbitrary government*. The following chain of reasoning seems very attractive:

(1) an ombudsman is a public official with a discretionary power;

(2) the discretionary powers of public officials must be supervised by judges in the interests of the rule of law; and therefore

(3) the reports of an ombudsman should be controlled by judges to impose the rule of law.

But the doctrine of relevance in a case like *Padfield v Minister of Agriculture* [1968] AC 997 is based on the danger that the holder of a discretionary governmental power might use it arbitrarily for his or her improper private or political purposes. Like judges, and unlike government ministers, the Ombudsman is independent. And her task is not to govern; it is to decide whether to make a public criticism of the government. As a result, Sedley J's enhanced doctrine of judicial control over relevance is not necessary to impose the rule of law on government. It will incidentally improve the Ombudsman process, whenever judges happen to make better decisions than she does as to what is relevant to her work. But it would only be justified as a standard of judicial review if judges were generally better at an ombudsman's work than ombudsmen are.

Judicial decisions quashing ombudsmen's reports are still not likely to be common, though: the three in the *Balchin* saga have been the only ones in the Parliamentary Ombudsman's fifty years. Even on the intrusive relevance test, it will ordinarily be difficult to persuade a court to second-guess the Ombudsman.[32] Judicial review should not even happen if it is not a proportionate process for improving the work of ombudsmen. The only argument in favour of any form of judicial review of the ombudsmen is the prospect that it may prevent feeble ombudsmen from unreasonably withholding a valuable investigative facility from complainants who need it. In the *Balchin* case, the Parliamentary Ombudsman had undoubtedly provided that facility to the Balchins at the first step in the long saga.

13.8.2 Judicial review of the Local Government Ombudsmen

The *Balchin* line of reasoning has been applied to Local Government Ombudsmen as well. In *R v Local Government Ombudsman, ex p Turpin* [2001] EWHC 503, (Admin) [36], Collins J held that 'there is nothing in the legislation to exclude the court's usual power to consider whether a discretion, however widely conferred, has been exercised in accordance with law'. But he also emphasized that it is not the court's role to tell the Ombudsman what counts as maladministration.[33] The same point was made very strongly in *R (Doy) v Commissioner for Local Administration* [2001] EWHC 361 (Admin), [16]:

---

[32] And the court will not supervise correspondence by the Parliamentary Ombudsman with potential complainants (*R (Murray) v PCA* [2002] EWCA Civ 1472). *Balchin* did not cite *Re Fletcher's Application* [1970] 2 All ER 527 (CA), in which the Court of Appeal held that there is no judicial jurisdiction to order the Parliamentary Commissioner to investigate a complaint.

[33] Compare also *R v Commissioner for Local Administration, ex p S* [1999] 1 LGLR 633.

> ❛ In essence, the Ombudsman and not the court is the arbiter of what constitutes maladministration. The court's supervisory role is there to ensure that he has acted properly and lawfully. However much the court may disagree with the ultimate conclusion, it must not usurp the Ombudsman's statutory function. ❜

Perhaps one single general improvement in the work of ombudsmen can be attributed to judicial review: although they have discretion over what information to disclose to a complainant, it was held in *Turpin* that procedural fairness requires that they disclose information gathered in their investigation, including interview notes with officials, unless there is some good reason not to do so (such as confidentiality). They cannot withhold any information purely on the basis that it was gathered for the purpose of their investigation.

13.8.3 Judicial review on behalf of a public authority

Can a public authority use judicial review to challenge a report of the *Parliamentary* Ombudsman? It follows directly from the reasoning in *Balchin* that a report adversely criticizing a department must be quashed on judicial review if the judges disagree with the Ombudsman as to what counts as maladministration, or if the judges take a different view from the Ombudsman on the relevance of one of the facts of the case. But allowing judicial review on those grounds at the request of a department would distort the process, and no government agency has ever sought judicial review of a report. Even if an Ombudsman were to make a *Wednesbury*-unreasonable report, the appropriate process is that used by the government in the 'Debt of Honour' case and in the crisis over the *Pensions* report: the department in question should simply reply to the report. Then the Ombudsman can make a special report to Parliament, and the crisis becomes parliamentary business (conducted in the first instance through the Public Administration Select Committee). There is no role for the court to play; the Ombudsman is parliamentary not just in name (and not just in having an 'MP filter'), but also in her capacity both to bring out the facts by her investigation and to put pressure on the department by reporting her assessment of the facts to Parliament. So it seems that if a public body were ever to seek judicial review of a report of the Parliamentary Ombudsman, *Balchin* ought to be distinguished, and permission for judicial review ought to be refused. The only justification for judicial interference on behalf of a complainant such as Maurice Balchin is to ensure that the Ombudsman does not improperly fail to provide the investigative function that Parliament instituted; that rationale does not require any judicial interference at all on behalf of a public body.

By contrast with the Parliamentary Ombudsman, Local Government Ombudsmen have several times been subjected to judicial review on the application of a public authority. In *R v Local Commissioner for Administration, ex p Eastleigh* (1987) 86 LGR 145, Nolan J found that there were defects in the Ombudsman's report, but viewed it as pointless to give a declaration against a report that the local authority simply had to consider, and publicize, and respond to. In the Court of Appeal ([1988] QB 855, 867),

Lord Donaldson rejected that approach: 'The Parliamentary intention was that reports by ombudsmen should be loyally accepted by the local authorities concerned... . in the absence of a successful application for judicial review and the giving of relief by the court, local authorities should not dispute an ombudsman's report and should carry out their statutory duties in relation to it.' But there is no support for the alleged intention of Parliament. Lord Donaldson found it in local authorities' statutory duties to publicize ombudsmen's reports, and to respond. But a local authority has no statutory duty *to implement* a Local Government Ombudsman's report, or even to act on the basis of the findings in a report; the crucial provision in the 1974 Act is that 'it shall be the duty of that authority to consider the report' (s 31(2)). Lord Donaldson's approach reflects an unwillingness to accept the ombudsman principle—that is, the principle that an independent complaints investigator can improve administration without making a legally binding report.

In *Bradley v Work and Pensions Secretary* [2008] EWCA Civ 36, the Court of Appeal backed up Lord Donaldson's approach, but qualified it to make only the finding of maladministration binding. Sir John Chadwick said at [50]:

> ' It is clear to me that Lord Donaldson of Lymington MR, in saying that local authorities should "loyally accept" an LGO's [Local Government Ombudsman's] report, only intended to refer to findings that maladministration and injustice have occurred and not to recommendations. The 1974 Act, like the 1967 Act, gives the ombudsman no power to make mandatory orders. It would be extraordinary if an LGO could do so by the back door in the form of recommendations. Suppose, for example, that the LGO made a recommendation which the local authority declined to carry out for the reason that it was too expensive. It is difficult to see on what established ground for judicial review the court could intervene to quash the recommendation: yet the allocation of budgets and the establishment of spending priorities are classic issues for the elected body's discretion. '

After *Bradley*, a local authority can lawfully decide not to act on a recommendation in an ombudsman's report without seeking judicial review. In *R (Nestwood Homes) v South Holland DC* [2014] EWHC 863, after a dispute about planning permissions, the Local Government Ombudsman recommended compensation of £250,000. The local authority accepted the Ombudsman's findings as to maladministration, and the loss caused by it (as it was bound to do, under *Eastleigh*). But the local authority resolved to pay £50,000 in compensation instead of £250,000 because of financial constraints. Sales J held that the affordability of the compensation payment was a relevant consideration, and that the local authority was entitled to treat it as significant. It is implicit in the decision that the resulting discretion is not unlimited, and that if the compensation had been extremely low, the court might have interfered.

But a report has the effect of a mandatory order (which the local authority can challenge in judicial review) to act on the basis of the ombudsman's finding of maladministration. That judicialization of the ombudsman process was misguided in *Eastleigh*, and the discussion in *Bradley* was *obiter*, as the Court of Appeal in *Bradley* took pains to explain that the Parliamentary Ombudsman differs from the Local Government Ombudsmen because the role of Parliament has no parallel in the local government context.

Ironically, because there is no parliamentary process for resolving disputes between local authorities and Local Government Ombudsmen, there is good ground for applying to local government the rule that *Bradley* applies to central government—that is, a decision by a local authority to reject an ombudsman's report is an exercise of discretionary power that ought to be open to challenge by a dissatisfied complainant on the *Wednesbury* grounds. But there is no basis for judicializing the process by requiring a local authority to go to court to challenge a finding of maladministration. There is good ground to argue that the 1974 Act only imposes the obligations on local authorities that it states—that is, to consider an ombudsman's report, and to publicize the report and its response. And then permission for judicial review should be refused if any public authority seeks to challenge the report of an ombudsman—local or parliamentary—in court. But after *Eastleigh* and *Bradley*, that argument could only be pursued in the Supreme Court.

Learning from Europe?

The decisions of the European Ombudsman (see 13.10) whether to investigate a complaint (and, it seems, his reports) cannot be challenged in court. In Case T 103/99 *Associazione delle Cantine Sociali Venete v Ombudsman and Parliament* [2000] ECR II-4165, [35], the applicant argued that 'an action for failure to act against the Ombudsman would be admissible in order not to deprive his extra-judicial function of all effect'. The Court held, curtly, that the application was inadmissible because 'the Ombudsman is not a Community institution within the meaning of Article 175 [now Art 228] of the Treaty' [46]. An Ombudsman's report does not 'produce legal effects' and is not binding on the European Parliament [50]. It seems unlikely that we will adopt this sensible separation between courts and ombudsmen, because of the English judges' deeply ingrained idea that they are responsible for supervising every other public authority except Parliament.

13.9 Specific ombudsmen

Ombudsman schemes have become increasingly popular techniques for dealing with complaints in specific subject areas: examples include the **Prisons and Probation Ombudsman**,[34] who reports to the Home Secretary; the **Adjudicator's Office**,[35] which investigates complaints about HM Revenue and Customs; and the **Independent Case**

---

[34] http://www.ppo.gov.uk.

[35] http://www.adjudicatorsoffice.gov.uk.

Examiner,[36] who investigates complaints about several government programmes, including the Child Support Agency. They have been created for particular purposes, in contexts in which recourse for people with complaints is not best provided through the tribunals system. As a result, they have varying roles that differ from those of the Parliamentary and Local Government Ombudsmen because of their specializations. They sometimes review the merits of decisions, and sometimes have a conciliation or mediation function. Here, we will look at one particularly interesting specific ombudsman scheme.

13.9.1 The Office of the Independent Adjudicator for Higher Education

For centuries, complaints against universities and colleges were within the jurisdiction of the institution's Visitor—a bishop or other dignitary who would delegate the hearing of a complaint to a judge or lawyer.[37] In 2004, Parliament abolished the jurisdiction of the Visitors over student complaints, and created the Office of the Independent Adjudicator (OIA), a compulsory ombudsman scheme for complaints against higher education institutions.[38]

In spite of the name, the OIA is not an adjudicator, but an ombudsman service. The Adjudicator does not hold a hearing, but writes a report making recommendations on the basis of written submissions and her own investigation. The recommendations in a report are not legally binding, but the institution is expected to go along with whatever is recommended, and is required to report on steps taken as a result of a report. The OIA deals with examinations, disciplinary decisions, decisions about a student's capacity to engage in studies, etc.—every kind of institutional decision affecting a particular student except admissions. In all of these areas, the OIA is not supposed to second-guess academic judgement, but to assess an institution's processes and its adherence to those processes in a particular case. But it can make an adverse report based on a generalized sense that something has gone wrong and that something should be done about it.

In its first year, the OIA received 120 complaints, eighty-six of which were eligible, and found that at least part of the complaint was justified in 50 per cent of cases. The OIA is serious about deferring to a university on questions involving academic judgment (e.g., it will not recommend a change in degree classification even where an examination process has gone wrong, but will only recommend reconsideration). But the OIA will recommend a remedy where the university has used an unfair procedure, or has broken its own rules. The OIA will recommend small sums in compensation for technical failures of an institution to follow its procedures (e.g.,

---

[36] https://www.gov.uk/government/organisations/independent-case-examiner.

[37] At least, in institutions founded before 1992. The Visitor's jurisdiction was well insulated from judicial review (see 9.1.7, p 330).

[38] Higher Education Act 2004. See http://www.oiahe.org.uk.

the OIA has awarded £50 to a student who admitted plagiarism, on the ground that the university had not followed its rules for disciplinary proceedings in the initial handling of the allegation). And substantial sums will be recommended in compensation where studies have to be repeated: one report recommended £9,000 in compensation for each student in a course for which the university failed to arrange professional accreditation promptly; the sum included £2,000 for curriculum failings, £2,000 for 'distress and inconvenience', and £5,000 for loss of opportunity for earnings, caused by the late accreditation. Awards on the latter sort of ground in particular are potentially substantial.

The OIA has had a significant impact on internal complaints processes in universities and colleges. Those institutions need to do what can reasonably be done within a collegiate community to give an impartial decision on issues that affect a student—including an appeal on disciplinary decisions to a decision-making body that has not been involved in earlier decisions, and which adheres strictly to procedural steps announced to students.

13.9.2 The OIA and the courts

The OIA will not investigate a complaint if the student has already gone to court. And the courts may be unwilling to allow litigation against a higher education institution to proceed when the OIA offers a cheaper and simpler alternative.[39] But various forms of litigation could follow an investigation. The OIA is amenable to judicial review (*R (Siborurema) v Office of the Independent Adjudicator* [2007] EWCA Civ 1365). Rejecting the argument of the Adjudicator that judicial review would damage the scheme by making it more formal and legalistic, the Court of Appeal held that: 'For it to become a law unto itself would not achieve the statutory intention' [50]. The Court adopted the same approach that has been applied in judicial review of the Parliamentary Ombudsman (and cited *R v PCA ex p Dyer* [1994] 1 WLR 621, the first judicial review of the Parliamentary Ombudsman).

But there is as little room for judges to improve the operation of the scheme as there is for them to improve the operation of the Parliamentary Ombudsman, and it will be difficult for any claimant to persuade a court to hold that the OIA has acted unlawfully. The courts should not give permission for judicial review unless the claimant has a serious allegation of bad faith or discrimination. But if they follow the *Balchin* reasoning (see 13.8.1), the judges will quash an OIA decision wherever it is based on an interpretation of the legislation that is different from the judges' interpretation.

How is an investigation by the OIA different from a claim that a university has breached its contract with the student, or a claim in judicial review against a university? Like the OIA, a court in judicial review will not second-guess the academic judgment

---

[39] That applies both to applications for judicial review, for which permission to proceed might be refused on the ground that an alternative recourse has not been pursued, and to actions for tort or breach of contract: see *Anufrijeva v Southwark LBC* [2003] EWCA Civ 1406 (an action can be stayed pending alternative forms of recourse, including the OIA).

of the institution,[40] and cannot order the institution to award a degree (*R v Liverpool John Moores University, ex p Hayes* [1998] ELR 261 (QBD)). Ordinary grounds of judicial review apply to universities and colleges, such as the law of due process, including the rule against bias (*R v Leeds Metropolitan University, ex p Manders* [1988] ELR 502 (QBD)). But the courts have deferred to universities in applying them (even where the university did not have a Visitor), at least so long as the university has followed its own procedures.[41] In their deference to academic judgment, the two processes are similar. But the difference is fundamental—the ombudsman is an informal investigator, and the courts will not order the ombudsman to give the same sort of hearing of a claim that the claimant could pursue in court:

> ❛ It is contrary to the whole spirit of a scheme established for the free and informal handling of students' complaints that the outcomes under it should replicate judicial determinations, which continue to be available in civil proceedings in the ordinary courts, for which the OIA is not and was never intended to be a substitute. ❜ [42]

13.10 The European Ombudsman

The European Ombudsman (EO)[43] was introduced by the 1992 Treaty on European Union (TEU). The office was designed to promote the project of closer European integration, by improving direct links between the European institutions and the citizens.

The EO interacts with national ombudsmen, and provides an interesting comparison with the British ombudsmen. Like them, the EO has the task of promoting good standards of administration in general by investigating particular complaints of maladministration. Maladministration is as open-ended in the European Union as in the UK, and overlaps with unlawfulness. In Europe, as in the UK, recommendations of the EO are not legally binding. But compliance of the EU institutions with her reports is very high (82 per cent in 2011).[44] Like the Parliamentary Ombudsman, the EO has a weapon of last resort, which is to lay a special report before the European Parliament.[45]

---

[40] Including on the question of whether examiners are suitably qualified (*R v Cranfield University, ex p Bashir* [1999] ELR 317 (CA)).

[41] *R v University of Portsmouth, ex p Lakareber* [1999] ELR 135 (CA), 140 (Simon Brown LJ).

[42] *R (Maxwell) v OIA* [2011] EWCA Civ 1236 [34].

[43] http://www.ombudsman.europa.eu.

[44] European Ombudsman, *Report on Responses to Proposals for Friendly Solutions and Draft Recommendations: How the EU Institutions Complied with the Ombudsman's Suggestions in 2011* (November 2012), 3, available at http://www.ombudsman.europa.eu/en/cases/followup.faces/en/12376/html.bookmark.

[45] The EU law provisions relating to the Ombudsman were introduced by the Maastricht Treaty and have since been incorporated into the European Ombudsman's Statute: *Decision 94/262 of the European Parliament on the Regulations and General Conditions Governing the Performance of the Ombudsman's Duties*, 9 March 1994, OJ L 113/15, as amended by Decision of 14 March 2002.

(1) **Who** is the EO?

She is an independent official (Art 9 TEU) appointed by the European Parliament (Art 6(1)) (usually after having served as a national ombudsman) and removable by the Court of Justice of the European Union (CJEU) on request from the European Parliament (Art 8).

(2) **Whom** can the EO investigate?

- The EO investigates 'community institutions and bodies, with the exception of the Court of Justice and the Court of First Instance in their judicial role' (Art 2(1)).

- The EO cannot investigate complaints against public authorities of member states, even if the complaint has to do with EU law.

(3) **How** does a complaint get to the EO?

- The complainant can make a complaint either directly or through a member of the European Parliament (MEP) (Art 2(2)).

- The EO can conduct investigations on her own initiative, as well as following a complaint (Art 3(1)).

(4) **What** can the EO **not** investigate?

- If the complaint concerns an employment relationship between an EU body and a member of staff, the internal complaints procedure of the body must be exhausted by the complainant before he or she complains to the EO (Art 2(8)).

- The EO cannot investigate cases before the courts, or question the soundness of a court's ruling (Art 1(3)). Note that the similar restrictions are taken for granted in the UK legislation! They are spelled out in the EU statute because the Finnish and Swedish ombudsmen have responsibility for investigating complaints about judicial decisions.

(5) **When** must a complaint be brought?

The complainant must refer his or her complaint within two years from the date when the facts on which the complaint is based came to his or her attention (Art 2(4)) (twice as long as the twelve-month restriction in ordinary circumstances for the UK ombudsmen).

(6) **How** does the EO **proceed**?

- Institutions and member state authorities must give the EO the information she requests, subject to legally regulated secrecy restrictions.

- Officials must testify at the EO's request (while remaining bound by their duty of professional secrecy) (Art 3(2)).

(7) **What** does the EO look for?

The EO investigates '*instances of maladministration*' (Art 2(2)). There is no requirement of injustice to the claimant.

(8) **What outcome** does the EO give?

- If maladministration is found after an investigation, the EO seeks a 'friendly solution' with the institution to eliminate the maladministration and satisfy the complainant.

- Failing that, the EO may close the file and note a 'critical mark' against the institution. This may be the outcome where the maladministration did not have any serious implications, or where the maladministration cannot be put right.

- Otherwise, the EO will inform the institution of the finding of maladministration and make 'draft recommendations' to which the institution has three months to respond.

- If the institution does not adequately respond or does not accept the draft recommendations, the EO may report to the European Parliament with recommendations.

- The EO also submits annual reports to the European Parliament (Art 3(8)).

There are some important ways in which the EO's remit is more far-reaching than that of ombudsmen in the UK:

- **initiation of investigations**—access of complainants to the EO is direct, and the EO can initiate her own investigations;

- **exclusions and limitations to jurisdiction**:

  - there is no exclusive list of bodies to which the EO's jurisdiction applies—she can investigate all 'Community institutions and bodies';
  - there is no list of matters excluded from the Ombudsman's jurisdiction like that in the British legislation—so, for example, the EO can investigate complaints about commercial and personnel decisions.

There is no injustice requirement: a complainant need not show that he or she was personally adversely affected by the alleged maladministration.

13.11 Administrative audit

An audit is an independent general assessment of an organization's performance. Ombudsmen address particular complaints, but their investigations often yield general conclusions.[46] In her special report to Parliament on the 'Debt of Honour' investigation, the Parliamentary Ombudsman did not simply recommend that Hayward should have an apology. She made three general recommendations about the administration of *ex gratia* schemes: that they should never be announced before eligibility had been worked out; that any change in eligibility should be communicated clearly; and

---

[46] For audits of government finance and expenditure, see 15.4.3.

that it is good administrative practice to review a scheme that generates widespread complaints.[47]

Do those general recommendations reflect an appropriate role for an Ombudsman, or should she stick to recommending a response to a particular complaint? And if she has a more general role to play in promoting good administration, shouldn't she be able to perform administrative inspections on her own initiative (like the EO—see 13.10), rather than merely investigate particular complaints? And shouldn't she have some more general supervisory technique for improving administrative practice in general? Does the requirement of injustice to a complainant, in particular, prevent the Ombudsman from playing a general role?

In fact, the ombudsmen have a very important general role to play in improving administration, but the investigation of particular complaints actually promotes that general function. The Select Committee in 1993 suggested that the Parliamentary Ombudsman should be able to carry out administrative *audits*: general inspections of the administrative practice of departments and agencies. The government rejected the suggestion, on the basis that an audit that approves of a department's administration could prejudice the Ombudsman against those who later complain of maladministration in that department. That point reflects a value of the ombudsmen's role as investigators of particular complaints: the existence of the complaint itself gives a focus and legitimacy to an ombudsman's investigation. The reason for the initiation of an administrative audit would have to be the auditor's own agenda. An ombudsman's investigation has a rationale that arises from the complaint. A general role as an inspector of administration would have some advantages, but it would distort the ombudsman's role in responding to complaints.

Note that the Public Administration Select Committee not only oversees the work of the Ombudsman and examines her reports; it also has a general remit to inquire into the quality and standards of administration provided by civil service departments. So the Committee *does* have a general role. The general effect of the ombudsmen's work arises out of their role as investigators of particular complaints. But there are already several major ways in which the ombudsmen have a general effect on administration.

(1) The Parliamentary Ombudsman **gives general advice** in her reports on particular complaints. There is, at present, no legislative requirement for the government to respond to such advice, but it has the force of the handwriting on the wall: a complainant (and the Ombudsman herself) will be able to refer to the general advice in future investigations.

(2) There is already provision for **annual reports** to Parliament (s 10(4) of the 1967 Act), which give her the opportunity to bring general administrative problems to the attention of the Select Committee.

(3) The Local Government Ombudsmen have the **Commission for Local Administration**, which serves both as a forum for the three Local Government

---

[47]   Parliamentary Ombudsman, 'A Debt of Honour' [223]–[226].

Ombudsmen and the Parliamentary Ombudsman to achieve general consistency, and also gives advice on good administrative practice.

(4) Moves toward **coordination** of Local Government and Parliamentary Ombudsmen's investigations are giving a more general effect to investigations.

(5) The investigation of a single complaint can have **ramifications** for many more people affected by a large-scale administrative scheme. The pensions report, and the Ombudsman's 2005 and 2007 special reports on tax credits,[48] are the most striking examples.

The ombudsmen's role in responding to complaints gives focus to their work and actually enables them to make general contributions to good administration. Unlike the EO, the UK ombudsmen are not likely to develop a role of initiating their own general investigations of success and failure in the administration of public authorities, because the government has found other ways of instituting administrative audits for a wide range of government services (some of which the ombudsmen do not investigate). These new techniques suit the target-based, incentive-led, 'customer'-focused approach to public administration described in Chapter 15.

Four educational inspectorates were unified in **Ofsted** (the Office for Standards in Education, Children's Services and Skills)[49] in 2007. It sets administrative standards and sends inspectors to hundreds of schools every week, publishing its reports on particular schools and reporting to Parliament. The **Quality Assurance Agency** is an independent inspectorate that performs a similar role for nearly 200 universities and colleges, carrying out 'institutional audits' of academic standards and administrative processes in particular institutions.[50] The Health and Social Care Act 2008 has unified the Commission for Social Care Inspection, the Healthcare Commission, and the Mental Health Act Commission into a single **Care Quality Commission**.[51] Police, prisons, and the probation services are regulated by independent inspectorates.[52] These bodies share certain features in regulating very different services: they are independent, they undertake inspections at their own instigation, and they have associated roles in setting standards of good administration. They report on performance to the government or to Parliament. Finally, and perhaps most importantly, they all publicize their findings in forms that allow the public to compare the performance of different schools, universities, hospitals, prisons, and police forces.

---

[48] *Tax Credits: Putting Things Right*, HC 124, 21 June 2005; *Tax Credits: Getting it Wrong?*, HC 1010, 8 October 2007.

[49] https://www.gov.uk/government/organisations/ofsted.

[50] http://www.qaa.ac.uk.

[51] http://www.cqc.org.uk.

[52] http://www.justiceinspectorates.gov.uk/hmicfrs.

13.12 The Equality and Human Rights Commission

Created by the Equality Act 2006, the Equality and Human Rights Commission took over the work of the Commission for Racial Equality, the Equal Opportunities Commission (which dealt with gender discrimination), and the Disability Rights Commission.[53] Like its predecessors, the Equality and Human Rights Commission is an independent agency established by Parliament to fight discrimination by private actors and public bodies. In addition to dealing with race, gender, and disability, the Commission is meant to combat discrimination on the basis of age, sexual orientation, and religion or belief, as well as discrimination that is unlawful under the Human Rights Act 1998.

The Commission has a general responsibility for monitoring and campaigning and producing anti-discrimination publicity. And that general information and publicity role is backed by legal powers. The Commission can:

- issue codes of practice (s 14) (a code takes legal effect if the Secretary of State approves and lays it before Parliament: s 14(7));

- conduct inquiries (into general discrimination questions, such as the causes of inequality) (s 16);

- conduct assessments (of compliance of public bodies with duties not to discriminate) (s 31);

- issue a compliance notice requiring a public body to comply with its legal duties (s 32); and

- conduct investigations into allegations of unlawful discrimination by particular persons.

If an investigation leads to the conclusion that a person has acted unlawfully, the Commission can make an 'unlawful act notice' (against which the person may appeal to a court or tribunal) (s 21). The Commission can enter into a legally binding agreement with the person as to a remedy for the problem, or can require the person to make an action plan.

The Commission's role in litigation is important: it supports the investigation and assessment processes, but goes further, too. The Commission can:

- apply to a court for an injunction if it 'thinks that a person is likely to commit an unlawful act' (s 24);

- apply to a court for an order requiring the person to comply with an action plan (s 22);

- apply to a court for an order requiring a public body to comply with a compliance notice (s 32);

- provide advice and legal representation to private litigants (s 28);

---

53 http://www.equalityhumanrights.com.

- bring judicial review proceedings on grounds of discrimination, in its own name, or intervene in proceedings brought by someone else (s 30); and

- bring Human Rights Act proceedings, even though it does not meet the 'victim' test for standing (see 11.5) in the Human Rights Act (s 30).

The litigation role is inherited from the predecessor discrimination commissions; it was the Equal Opportunities Commission that pioneered this role in dealing with gender discrimination. In *R v Employment Secretary, ex p Equal Opportunities Commission* [1995] 1 AC 1, the House of Lords held that the Commission had standing to seek judicial review, and then went on to demonstrate the potential of such litigation by striking down UK legislation restricting part-time workers' rights as incompatible with the EU Equal Treatment Directive.

The Commission's power to intervene enables it to support claimants who allege discrimination. A notable example of intervention by the Commission for Racial Equality arose in the 'Debt of Honour' saga (see 13.1). The Commission for Racial Equality intervened in *R (Elias) v Defence Secretary* [2006] EWCA Civ 1293 (see 13.5.2, p 491). All three commissions have appeared as intervenors; they all did so in the same case: *Igen et al v Webster; Equal Opportunities Commission, Commission for Racial Equality, and Disability Rights Commission, Intervenors* [2005] EWCA Civ 142. Intervening in litigation has become a significant part of the Equality and Human Rights Commission's work.[54]

The Equality and Human Rights Commission has an investigative role that is significantly different from that of ombudsmen, because it has a general duty to take action on its own initiative to fight a range of forms of discrimination (by private persons, as well as by public authorities). It is a hybrid between an ombudsman, a prosecutor, and an advocacy organization.

13.13 The Inquiries Act 2005

In early July 2011, a scandal over phone hacking by journalists suddenly generated public outrage, when allegations emerged that the *News of the World* had been hacking not only the phones of celebrities, but also the phone of a schoolgirl who was murdered, and the phones of victims of the July 2005 London bombings. The newspaper announced on 7 July 2011 that it would close down, and published its last issue on 10 July. On 6 July, Prime Minister David Cameron announced that he would establish a public inquiry to investigate the culture and ethics of the press, and to make recommendations about regulation of the press. Within two weeks he had appointed Lord Justice Leveson to head the inquiry, and had set out its terms of reference. After hearing from more than 300 witnesses, Lord Justice Leveson issued his 2,000-page report in

---

[54] See, e.g., *Surrey County Council v P* (*Equality and Human Rights Commission & others intervening*) [2014] UKSC 19.

November 2012, recommending—among other things—a new and significantly different form of press regulation to replace the Press Complaints Commission.[55]

Ad hoc public investigations are often set up by the government in this way, as a response to a disaster or a crisis or a public embarrassment. Important examples include the 1999 inquiry into the racist murder of Stephen Lawrence, the BSE Inquiry in 1997, and the Hutton Inquiry concerning the death of the government weapons expert David Kelly in 2003, in the controversy over the Iraq war. The purpose of such an inquiry is to find out what went wrong, and to make a report recommending changes for the better in public policy or public administration.

Setting up an inquiry is a way of saying that a situation needs a serious independent investigation. That can give the government something to do more or less instantly in response to a scandal, without admitting mistakes or taking unpopular decisions. But then the onus is on the government to take the report seriously.

The government can always just ask someone to investigate something. But it has proved useful to create statutory schemes conferring powers on inquiries to compel testimony and production of evidence, and regulating their procedures.[56] As with tribunals, provisions for inquiries had been added to various legislative schemes over decades,[57] with no system. The Inquiries Act 2005 did the same thing for inquiries (but on a much smaller scale) that the Tribunals, Courts and Enforcement Act 2007 (see 12.2) did for tribunals. It replaced dozens of pieces of legislation governing inquiries commissioned by ministers, and created a new framework regulating their establishment, the appointment of people to conduct them, their procedures and their powers, and the submission and publication of reports.

Uniformity is elusive: the Act leaves it to the minister to state the questions the inquiry is to address, to appoint the panel members, to decide the terms of reference (and to change them during an inquiry), to decide whether the inquiry is to make recommendations, and to suspend an inquiry or (after consulting the chairman and giving reasons) to end it. The government will still be able to set up a non-statutory inquiry if it wishes, and specialized schemes will remain for certain areas such as financial services.

The biggest ever inquiry was the Scott Inquiry into the British government's support for the export of high-tech military machine tools to Iraq.[58] Customs officers had prosecuted Matrix Churchill Ltd for violating export restrictions, but the prosecutions broke down when it emerged that the government had encouraged the company to violate the export restrictions. During the prosecutions, ministers asked the courts to keep documents immune from disclosure in the prosecution, on the ground

---

[55] http://www.gov.uk/government/publications/leveson-inquiry-report-into-the-culture-practices-and-ethics-of-the-press.

[56] The first such legislation was the Tribunals of Inquiry (Evidence) Act 1921.

[57] e.g., the Children Act 1989.

[58] Sir Richard Scott, *Report of the Inquiry into the Export of Defence Equipment and Dual-use Goods to Iraq and Related Prosecutions* (HMSO, 1996).

of public interest. In fact, the documents showed that the prosecutions were improper: without telling the customs officers, the government had secretly encouraged Matrix Churchill's exports. Disclosure of the documents was not at all against the public interest; it was against the ministers' personal political interests.

The Scott Inquiry uncovered all of this, and yet its revelations were somewhat obscured in a protracted process and an 1,800-page report, written with such judicious care that the ministers in question were able to keep their jobs and the Prime Minister escaped the embarrassment of resignations. But the inquiry gave the opposition material to portray the government as sleazy, and it played a role in the death throes of the Conservative government; the next year the Conservatives lost the general election to Tony Blair and New Labour. The Hutton Inquiry, by contrast, very largely exonerated the Blair government on the limited issues that were before it. Yet it, too, made secret and embarrassing information available to the public.[59]

Inquiries into governmental scandals are so careful, and they elicit such a volume of complex information, that they are unlikely to inflict the simple political damage that will bring down a government. They are not rapid or decisive; they tend to defuse a crisis and to dissipate political forces by generating mountains of information that can be interpreted in different ways. And even though the decision maker is often a judge, there is a *crucial* difference between inquiries and adjudication: the decision maker does not have to find anyone liable or not liable, and need not decide whether anyone acted lawfully or unlawfully. So the conclusions tend to be complex and qualified, rather than decisive.

In this respect, the Leveson Inquiry was exceptional. The report recommended replacement of the Press Complaints Commission (an industry body that was 'aligned with the interests of the press')[60] by 'a genuinely independent and effective system of self-regulation',[61] with independent appointments, an effective set of sanctions against misconduct, and serious incentives for newspapers to sign up to the scheme. Lord Justice Leveson recommended a legislative framework for assessment of the process and for validation of its code of standards.

The government did not go along with the whole package, and in particular the Prime Minister was not in favour of legislation that would look like regulation of the press. But having set up the inquiry, the Prime Minister had to go most of the way towards acting on its recommendations. And in September 2014 the Press Complaints Commission closed its doors, and the new Independent Press Standards Organisation (IPSO) was launched.[62] IPSO has a royal charter approved by the Privy Council, which the government preferred to legislation. The new body is not what Lord Justice

---

[59] The report, running to only 328 pages, is available at http://webarchive.nationalarchives.gov.uk/20090128221546/http://www.the-hutton-inquiry.org.uk.

[60] The Right Honourable Lord Justice Leveson, *An Inquiry into the Culture, Practices and Ethics of the Press*, HC 779, 29 November 2012, Executive Summary and Recommendations [45].

[61] Leveson Inquiry [47]; see also [52] and [72].

[62] http://www.ipso.co.uk.

Leveson recommended, but it has features—most importantly, considerable independence both from government and from the newspaper industry—that undoubtedly arose from the Leveson Inquiry.

Setting up an inquiry of this kind is a quick way to respond to a scandal; the process may lead in unpredictable directions. As the Leveson Inquiry shows, a report will not dictate government policy. But it will give an independent investigator a powerful opportunity to constrain the government's policy choices.

13.13.1 Legal duties to inquire

The Inquiries Act 2005 did not change the key point: whether to set up an inquiry remains a question for ministers. A minister 'may cause an inquiry to be held' (s 1), which means that the power to hold an inquiry is discretionary.

But the government has no choice, where the law of the European Convention on Human Rights demands an inquiry. The Strasbourg Court has interpreted the right to life (Art 2), the prohibition of torture and inhuman and degrading treatment (Art 3), and the prohibition of slavery and forced labour (Art 4) as imposing positive duties (see 3.6) to investigate allegations of violations of those rights by state officials. The duty is very far-reaching: it reaches, for example, to allegations of unlawful killings by British soldiers in Iraq, where 'as a consequence of lawful or unlawful military action, a Contracting State exercises effective control of an area outside ... national territory' (*Al-Skeini v UK* [2011] 53 EHRR 18 [138]). And the positive duties to inquire extend beyond allegations of wrongdoing by public officials, to situations in which it is possible that a public authority may have failed to protect a person's life, or to protect a person from inhuman treatment, or from forced labour.[63] For example, there is a duty under the ECHR (and therefore, under the Human Rights Act s 6) to investigate suicide or attempted suicide in prison (*R (L) v Secretary of State for Justice* [2008] UKHL 68).

Can the common law be used to compel the government to hold an inquiry? In *R (Keyu) v Foreign Secretary* [2015] UKSC 69, Malaysian citizens, relatives of twenty-four civilians killed by a British Army patrol under colonial rule in 1948, asked the court in judicial review to require the British government to hold a public inquiry into the killings. The Supreme Court held that the ECHR did not apply, because the events in question had happened more than ten years before the ECHR entered into force with respect to the UK. So the claimants also argued that the refusal to hold an inquiry was either *Wednesbury* unreasonable, or failed a proportionality test that ought to be imposed at common law (see 8.3). With a vigorous dissent from Baroness Hale, who thought that it was *Wednesbury* unreasonable not to hold an inquiry [313], the Supreme Court held that the Foreign Secretary's decision was neither disproportionate nor *Wednesbury* unreasonable.

But in *R (Litvinenko) v Home Secretary* [2014] EWHC 194, the Administrative Court held that the Home Secretary had acted unlawfully in refusing to hold an

---

63   See *D v Commissioner of Police of the Metropolis* [2015] EWCA Civ 646, Laws LJ [24].

inquiry. The claimant was the widow of Alexander Litvinenko, who had died in London, apparently as a result of swallowing polonium. The police found that there was enough evidence to charge two Russian citizens with murdering Litvinenko, but Russia would not extradite the suspects. A Coroner's inquest was begun, but the Coroner asked the Lord Chancellor to set up a statutory inquiry under the Inquiries Act 2005 instead, to address the question of whether the Russian government was involved in Litvinenko's death. The Home Secretary wrote to the Coroner, giving extensive reasons why the government did not propose to set up such an inquiry. The three judges of the Divisional Court upheld the claimant's challenge to 'the adequacy or correctness' of the Home Secretary's reasons for refusing to hold an inquiry,[64] and quashed the Home Secretary's decision, and required her to reconsider. There was no real discussion of the ground of review, but the judges plainly thought that the Home Secretary had to give correct reasons. Richards LJ said that 'If she is to maintain her refusal she will need better reasons than those given in the decision letter' [75].[65]

The judges did not mention *Keyu*, and *Litvinenko* is a departure from the Supreme Court's holding in *Keyu*, that a refusal to hold an inquiry is only unlawful if it is *Wednesbury* unreasonable to refuse. So the decision of the Divisional Court in *Litvinenko* cannot stand as a precedent for the proposition that a minister must give correct reasons for not holding an inquiry. But it stands as a reminder of the judges' tendency (in the case of inquiries, as in the case of ombudsmen) to look for a role for judicial review in controlling executive decisions about non-judicial accountability techniques.

Inquiries US style

Parliamentary committees in the UK scrutinize policy and the regular operations of government, but the tradition of using *parliamentary* inquiries to respond to scandals and crises largely broke down nearly a century ago.[66] By contrast, the US tradition of congressional inquiries grew stronger through the twentieth century, and was used to deal with the attack on Pearl Harbor in 1941[67] and the attacks of 9/11.[68]

Conversely, in the United States it is considered to be constitutionally inappropriate for the judges to conduct crisis inquiries:

---

[64] As the Divisional Court had done in *R v PCA, ex p Balchin (No 2)* (2000) 79 P&CR 157 and *R v PCA, ex p Balchin (No 3)* [2002] EWHC 1876; see 13.8.1.

[65] The government relented and set up a statutory inquiry, which concluded that the murder had probably been approved by Russian President Vladimir Putin: http://www.bbc.co.uk/news/uk-35350415.

[66] A turning point came when a committee of the House of Commons split on party lines after its inquiry into allegations of ministerial corruption in the Marconi affair, 1912. But inquiries by parliamentary committees still play an important part in overseeing administration.

[67] http://www.ibiblio.org/pha/pha/congress/part_0.html.

[68] https://9-11commission.gov.

'The legitimacy of the Judicial Branch ultimately depends upon a reputation for impartiality and non-partisanship. That reputation may not be borrowed by the political Branches to cloak their work in the neutral colors of judicial action.'[69]

The separation of the presidency from Congress makes it easier for the legislature to call the executive to give evidence to an inquiry, even though Congress is partisan. So Condoleezza Rice, the (then) National Security Adviser, was an important witness before the 9/11 Congressional Commission. But committee investigations can play a part in partisan politics in the legislature, as they did most flagrantly when Joseph McCarthy used his chairmanship of the Senate Permanent Subcommittee on Investigations to hunt for communists in the government in 1953–54. Opportunities for partisan politics are always available, as committees need majority voting even to subpoena witnesses. When the 9/11 Commission report was issued unanimously by five Democrats and five Republicans, it was a sign of bipartisan solidarity.

13.14 Conclusion: the limits of administrative law

The Parliamentary and Local Government Ombudsmen have become valuable institutions both for securing redress for claimants who have no legal entitlement to a remedy and for improving public administration in general. Their investigative function is in some ways better tailored to promoting just public administration than the application of standards of administrative legality in judicial processes. It is important to remember just how non-legal the ombudsman schemes are: the legislation that establishes them gives no legal effect to their reports (except by imposing a duty on local authorities to consider and to reply),[70] and the only legal powers they have are the powers of access to the information they need in their informal investigations. Ombudsmen ask, in an open-ended fashion, whether something went wrong and what could be improved. The judges, as we have seen, have given legal effect to ombudsmen's reports, by giving judicial review both of the reports, and of public authorities' responses to them. This judicialization of the ombudsman process holds out the prospect of further recourse for a complainant disappointed by the results of the ombudsman process. But the resulting litigation rarely pays off for the complainant, and the judicialization offers nothing of value to a system of independent investigations of complaints that was never designed to be supervised by judges.

What role do the ombudsmen play in the constitution? We tend to think of the rule of law as a constitutional ideal that is imposed by courts on other legal authorities, and which must be respected by the agencies that exercise the executive power of the

---

[69] *Mistretta v United States* 488 US 362, 407 (1989).

[70] Local Government Act 1974 s 31, as amended by Local Government and Housing Act 1989 s 26.

state. Since ombudsmen's reports have no legal authority, and ombudsmen exercise no executive power, it may seem that they contribute to good administrative practice, but not to the rule of law. And in a sense, that is right: the whole point of the ombudsman institution is that we should expect more of the administration of government than just legality. So it may seem that the task of ombudsmen is to promote aspects of good administration that the rule of law (and the constitution) cannot promote.

But remember the unclear announcement of payments to 'British civilians', which was ground for the Ombudsman's recommendations in the 'Debt of Honour' report (see 13.1). Its lack of clarity had no legal consequences; a more definite announcement, by contrast, would have given rise to a legitimate expectation. In criticizing the unclear announcement, the Ombudsman *promoted* (in a way that the law could not do) the values that the rule of law promotes. The ombudsman process offers an obstacle to arbitrary government, because it can expose and criticize a way of administering a scheme that suits a government's political imperative at the cost of ignoring the interests of people affected by the scheme. It is an obstacle to arbitrary government, first, because it enhances accountability: an ombudsman exposes bad government to criticism and requires a response even though the recommendations are not binding. Second, it enhances the representative function of the House of Commons (at national level), and it enhances local democracy. So the ombudsmen actually promote the ideal of responsible government that lies *behind* the rule of law.

Ombudsmen represent a step forward in good administration, and in access to justice. It is an expensive step forward that causes aggravation to public officials, and can lead to the extravagant excess of process that we saw in the *Balchin* case (see 13.8.1). The process creates a risk of recommendations that are themselves arbitrary, in the sense that they reflect the ombudsman's whims, or hasty and over-burdensome judgments swayed by the difficult situation of a complainant. But that risk is minor because of the informal effect of reports, and the risk is worth taking because the ombudsmen offer an effective way in which to hold government accountable for botched programmes like the tax credit scheme and the 'Debt of Honour' scheme—even when nothing unlawful has been done. And it is a process that allows an investigation that neither judges nor MPs are equipped—or authorised—to conduct. So the ombudsmen promote the constitutional ideal of responsible government.

TAKE-HOME MESSAGE ● ● ●

- Both ombudsmen and courts are independent from the administration. Their process and remedies are fundamentally different.

- An ombudsman **investigates**; a court **adjudicates** between two adversaries. A court makes an order with legal effect, to remedy a wrong. An ombudsman does not give a *remedy* at all; he or she makes a report that is not legally binding, and the public agency makes decisions (and may give recompense) in response.

- Equally importantly, a court cannot interfere with lawful acts of administration. An ombudsman can deal with poor administration that is not unlawful. And because of the investigative role, an ombudsman may provide the very useful outcome of discovering what really happened, where a court could not. Note that **tribunals** share the limitations and powers of courts, except that their process is meant to be (and *sometimes* is) less formal than that of a court (see Chapter 12).

- Ombudsmen can make recommendations that extend **beyond the complaint**; the courts must ordinarily make an order that is limited to disposing of the specific dispute.

- The UK ombudsmen have no general role of initiating **audits of administration** to identify shortcomings or successes, or to advise on how to improve services. But that auditing role is filled for a variety of government services by a plethora of specific investigation and scrutiny commissions and, in respect of discrimination, by the Equality and Human Rights Commission.

CRITICAL QUESTIONS • • •

1   What can the ombudsmen do that the courts cannot do?

2   What can the courts do that the ombudsmen cannot do?

3   Why is the Parliamentary Ombudsman parliamentary? Would it be better to have a central government ombudsman, independent of Parliament?

4   Can you explain the relationships among:

   - maladministration;

   - the lawfulness of a decision; and

   - the merits of a decision?

5   If an action is unlawful, does that mean that it should not be identified as maladministration in a report of the Parliamentary Ombudsman?

6   Who should decide what constitutes maladministration—the ombudsmen, or the judges?

7   In *Bradley v Work and Pensions Secretary* [2008] EWCA Civ 36 [63], the Court of Appeal endorsed 'the principle of mutual respect' (Sir John Chadwick)—that is, the constitutional principle of comity (see 1.5.3). Did the decision adhere to that principle?

8   Why is the Parliamentary Commissioner for Administration subject to judicial review if the Parliamentary Commissioner for Standards is not?

9   The European Ombudsman can investigate complaints of maladministration with no requirement that the complainant has suffered injustice as a result. Would a similar regime be an improvement in the role of the UK ombudsmen?

10 The Finnish Parliamentary Ombudsman oversees the legality of actions of the armed forces and government ministers, and oversees the courts. The Swedish

Parliamentary Ombudsmen also oversee courts, as they have done since 1809 (but not ministers). Both can initiate investigations without having received a complaint. Is there any good reason why the UK Parliamentary Ombudsman is more limited in scope?

READING • • •

R v LCA, ex p Bradford City Council [1979] QB 287

R v LCA, ex p Eastleigh Borough Council [1988] QB 855

R v LCA, ex p Croydon LBC [1989] 1 All ER 1033

R v PCA, ex p Balchin [1997] JPL 917

Bradley v Work and Pensions Secretary [2008] EWCA Civ 36

The Ombudsman's report on the 'Debt of Honour' investigation is available at http://www.gov.uk/government/publications/parliamentary-and-health-service-ombudsman-fourth-report-session-2005-to-2006

The Public Administration Select Committee's report on the government's rejection of the Ombudsman's report on pensions: 'Justice Denied? The Government's Response to the Ombudsman's Report on Equitable Life' HC 219, 19 March 2009 is available at http://www.publications.parliament.uk/pa/cm200809/cmselect/cmpubadm/219/219.pdf

A W Bradley, 'The Role of the Ombudsman in Relation to Citizens' Rights' (1980) 39 CLJ 304 —on the relation between ombudsmen and arbitrary government

Roy Gregory and Philip Giddings, The Ombudsman, the Citizen and Parliament (Politico Publishing 2002)—a history of the Parliamentary Ombudsman

Jason Varuhas, 'Governmental Rejections of Ombudsman Findings: What Role for the Courts?' (2009) 72 MLR 102–115

For comment by the Parliamentary Ombudsman on her role:

Ann Abraham, 'The Ombudsman and "Paths to Justice": A Just Alternative, or Just an Alternative?' [2008] PL 1

Trevor Buck, Richard Kirkham, and Brian Thompson, *The Ombudsman Enterprise and Administrative Justice* (Ashgate 2010)

On inquiries:

Jack Beatson, 'Should Judges Conduct Public Inquiries?' (2005) 121 LQR 221

 The following online resources accompany this chapter: **summaries** of key cases and legislation; **updates** on the law; **guidance** for answering the pop quizzes and questions; and **links** to legislation, cases, and useful websites.

Part VI
Private law and public authorities

14 Torts

A claim for damages for loss caused by a public authority may give a court two opportunities: to do justice for the claimant, and also to impose the rule of law on the administration. The challenge is to do both without interfering inappropriately in the administrative pursuit of public goods, and without creating public compensation funds that only a legislature can legitimately create.

LOOK FOR ● ● ●

- The special justification that tort law needs: even if a public authority has acted unlawfully, why should a court order compensation for loss caused by the unlawful action?

- Ways in which rights to compensation can affect public authorities' use of their discretionary powers.

- Special compensation schemes under the European Convention on Human Rights (ECHR) (given effect by the Human Rights Act 1998) and EU law (given effect by the European Communities Act 1972).

> ' It is one thing to provide a service at the public expense. It is another to require the public to pay compensation when a failure to provide the service has resulted in loss. '
> *Stovin v Wise* [1996] AC 923, 954 (Lord Hoffmann)

14.1 Introduction: trespass to property

The common law has rewarded the lawyers who, as Lord Reid put it in a tort case, 'struggled and fought through the centuries to establish the rights of the subject to be protected from arbitrary acts of the King's servants' (*Attorney-General v Nissan* [1970] AC 179, 208). One way in which judges can control arbitrary government is by quashing decisions in judicial review; another way is by holding the act to be a tort, and awarding an injunction or damages.

The law of tort has been especially jealous of property rights.[1] On 11 November 1762, Nathan Carrington and three other men broke into John Entick's house in Stepney. They spent four hours rummaging through papers and breaking open chests, and they carried away hundreds of pamphlets that Entick had printed. So he sued them in trespass. Trespass to property is a tort—that is, unlawful conduct that gives the victim a legal right to a remedy. Not all unlawful actions are torts. A tort gives the victim a right to claim compensation for loss caused by the action, or to ask a court to exercise its discretion to issue an injunction to require the defendant not to continue the tort. But all torts are unlawful. When Entick sued the four men in tort, they claimed that their actions were lawful (and therefore not tortious) because the Earl of Halifax, one of the King's principal secretaries of state, had given them a warrant to search Entick's house and to take his papers. Entick published pamphlets criticizing the Prime Minister, and the government wanted to look for evidence that might support a prosecution for the crime of seditious libel. The defendants in *Entick* claimed that the Secretary of State had 'a jurisdiction' to seize Entick's papers, because the government had to be able to control sedition. In *Entick v Carrington* (1765) 19 Howell's St Tr 1029, 1073, the Chief Justice, Lord Camden, rejected this 'argument of state necessity':

> ' ... the common law does not understand that kind of reasoning, nor do our books take notice of any such distinctions.... If the king himself has no power to declare when the law ought to be violated for reason of state, I am sure we his judges have no such prerogative. '

Lord Camden was able to present his decision as an act of judicial *modesty*, but it was the *judge-made* law of his time that protected people from arbitrary governmental invasions of property.

---

[1] It needn't be ownership: 'The common law protects possession as well as title. A person who is in actual possession of land is entitled to remain in peaceful enjoyment of the property without disturbance by anyone except a person with a better right to possession. It does not matter that he has no title. A squatter can maintain a claim of trespass' (*Harrow v Qazi* [2003] UKHL 43 [87] (Lord Millett)).

The constitutional importance of *Entick* is that the court used the law of tort to control the administration. The case shows the opportunity that the law gives the court to do justice between two persons in private law, and at the same time to impose the rule of law on the government. The courts have faced difficulties reconciling the principles of public law with those of private law. Before we get into the difficulties, it is important to see how deeply private law and public law support each other in a case like *Entick*: the private law of tort demands compensation for loss caused by a trespass to property, and the public law of the constitution demands that the government should not be able to claim a special dispensation to violate a person's private law rights on grounds of state necessity.

Entick v Carrington in the United States

Twenty-five years after *Entick* was decided, the United States adopted a Bill of Rights guaranteeing that 'the right of the people to be secure in their persons, houses, papers, and effects, against unreasonable searches and seizures, shall not be violated' (US Constitution, Fourth Amendment). In *Boyd v United States* 116 US 616, 626 (1886), the US Supreme Court called Lord Camden's decision in *Entick* a 'great judgement', 'one of the permanent monuments of the British Constitution', and a guide to understanding the Fourth Amendment (630):

> ' The principles laid down in this opinion affect the very essence of constitutional liberty and security . . . they apply to all invasions on the part of the government and its employees of the sanctity of a man's home and the privacies of life. '

A government minister cannot give anyone a defence against tort law, but Parliament can do so. If Parliament has authorized an act of a public authority (or of a private person for that matter) that would otherwise be a tort, it is not a tort. The defendant has a defence of statutory authority. But a simple lack of procedural fairness in performing such an act may deprive the public authority of the defence. So *Cooper v Wandsworth Board of Works* (1863) 14 CB (NS) 180 (one of the landmarks of the law of due process—see 4.1) was, like *Entick*, an action in the tort of trespass to property. The alleged trespass was the demolition of Cooper's house by the Board of Works, and the Board's defence was that, because Cooper had not given the required seven days' notice before the beginning of construction, the Metropolis Local Management Act 1855 gave it a statutory power to demolish the house. The defence failed, because even though the Act did not require a hearing, 'the justice of the common law will supply the omission of the legislature' (Byles J, 194). In spite of the statutory power, a demolition is an unlawful interference with property (and therefore a trespass) if a public authority does it without due process.

● *Pop quiz* ●

The trespass in *Cooper* was a tort. Was it also a crime? Can you think of a tort that is not a crime? A crime that is not a tort? An unlawful action that is neither a tort nor a crime? See 14.5.4 on criminal liabilities of public officials.

To do justice in a case like *Cooper* or *Entick*, the law needs to award the claimant compensation for the injury caused by the wrong. A court in judicial review could declare such abuses of power unlawful, and if the claimant got to a judge in time, the court could issue a mandatory order to a public authority not to search Entick's house, or not to demolish Cooper's house without giving him a hearing. But it is easy to see why the law needs to impose liabilities to compensate, and why it is not enough to have processes for quashing unlawful decisions and prohibiting unlawful actions. Cooper and Entick could not get to a judge in time. So they suffered harm that could not be put right with the quashing of a decision, or with a declaration that the public authority had acted unlawfully.

'The justice of the common law' demands not only judicial power to quash unlawful decisions, but also *compensation* to make people in the position of Cooper or Entick as well off (to the extent that an award of damages can do so) as if the wrong had not been done. How does the law decide which unlawful decisions lead to a right to compensation? It is an important rule of public law that the answer to that question is *generally* the same whether the defendant is a public authority or not. But we will see that, by contrast with the law of trespass, it is very difficult to work out how to apply the ordinary law of negligence. It is difficult because of the unique relationships of power and dependency between public authorities and the people for whom they ought to care.

Beyond the general rule that public authorities face the same tort liabilities as other defendants, there is one special public tort: misfeasance in a public office (see 14.5). And Parliament has imposed special duties of compensation on public authorities (see 14.3). Moreover, the Human Rights Act 1998 gives courts a discretion to award damages in compensation for certain losses caused by infringements of Convention rights (see 14.6), and we will need to understand how different that power is from the court's duty in tort law to award compensatory damages. Finally, in respect of EU law, public authorities face something that they do not face in domestic law: a pure duty to compensate for loss caused by action that is unlawful (see 14.7).

14.2 Tort liability of public authorities: four basic principles

Entick and *Cooper* illustrate two basic principles of tort liability of public authorities.

(1) **Administrative authorities are liable for their torts.**

(2) **If Parliament authorizes a public authority to do what would otherwise be a tort, it is not a tort.**

Administrative authorities (unlike judges and MPs) have no common law immunity from liability for torts. If a lorry runs you down in the street because the driver was not paying attention, it *makes no difference* whether the lorry was being driven on behalf of your city council, or on behalf of Tesco. Administrative authorities are liable for torts in the same way as any private person, and are vicariously liable for the torts of their employees in the same way as any employer (*Mersey Docks & Harbour Board Trustees v Gibbs* (1866) LR 1 HL 93).

To the first two basic principles, we should add two principles that restrict tort liability, which you might miss if you read only *Entick* and *Cooper*.

(3) **Acting unlawfully is not in itself a tort. Even acting in a *Wednesbury*-unreasonable way is not in itself a tort.**[2] **There is no general legal right to compensation for loss caused by unlawful administrative action.**

For a public authority to have committed a tort, there must be a reason for the law to give a private person a right to a remedy. The reason may be that the ordinary principles of the common law of tort require a remedy.

(4) **There is no tort where the court would have to pass judgment on unjusticiable questions in order to hold the public authority liable.**

The third and fourth basic principles show why tort law faces a special set of challenges in dealing with losses caused by the conduct of public authorities.

The special position of the Crown

There is one public authority that was immune from torts at common law: the Crown. 'The King can do no wrong' is an old slogan of the common law. And a tort is a wrong. So at common law the Crown was not liable in tort. Of course, 'the King can do no wrong' can mean either 'it is not unlawful if the King did it', or 'if it was unlawful, it was not the King who did it'.[3] So ministers of the Crown were sometimes held liable in tort even when they had the King's authorization (*Earl of Danby's Case* (1679) 11 St Tr 599), and if the defendants in *Entick* had been told by the King himself to ransack Entick's house, they would still have been liable in trespass. There were other techniques, too, for avoiding the injustice that could result from the rule that the Crown was not liable in tort.[4] But the Crown Proceedings Act 1947 abolished the immunity. For most purposes, the Crown is liable in tort and breach of contract in the same way as a private individual.

Acts of the Crown include many acts of ministers and government departments, but not acts of other public authorities such as local authorities, police authorities, or bodies created by statute. Such authorities never benefited from the immunity of the Crown in tort.

---

[2] There is much authority: see, e.g., *Jones v Swansea City Council* [1990] 1 WLR 54.

[3] In *The King v Speyer* [1916] 1 KB 595, 619, Avory J said that the maxim 'only means that His Majesty individually and personally and in his natural capacity is independent of, and not amenable to, any other earthly power or jurisdiction. . . . It is a fundamental general rule that the King cannot sanction any act forbidden by law.'

[4] The 'Petition of Right' was a way of asking for a remedy for loss caused by conduct that would have been a tort or breach of contract if the defendant were not the Crown. It was a plea to the King for justice, which in practice became a form of judicial remedy: see 15.3.1, p 592.

14.3 Statutory liabilities

Parliament can authorize what would otherwise be a tort, and can also impose a liability that a defendant would not otherwise have. Judges and legal scholars say that there is a 'tort of breach of statutory duty'. But the name is misleading, because breaching a statutory duty is not a tort in itself. This so-called tort is a way of talking about a liability to compensate a claimant for loss caused by a breach of statutory duty *for which an Act of Parliament requires a remedy.*

Breaching a statutory duty is not necessarily a tort

In *Meade v Haringey LBC* [1979] 1 WLR 637, 647, Lord Denning tried to change this:

> '…if the public authority flies in the face of the statute, by doing something which the statute expressly prohibits, or otherwise so conducts itself—by omission or commission—as to frustrate or hinder the policy and objects of the Act, then it is doing what it ought not to do—it is going outside its jurisdiction—it is acting ultra vires. Any person who is particularly damnified thereby can bring an action in the courts for damages or an injunction, whichever be the most appropriate.'

Lord Denning's view has never been made the *ratio* of an award of damages, and it was disapproved in *X v Bedfordshire County Council* [1995] 2 AC 633 by Sir Thomas Bingham MR (699) and Lord Browne-Wilkinson (768).

So, for example, the Road Traffic Act 1988 s 39 imposes a duty on local authorities to 'carry out a programme of measures designed to promote road safety'. But a local authority is not liable in tort to a claimant who suffers injury because the authority failed to carry out a programme of measures (*Gorringe v Calderdale MBC* [2004] UKHL 15). The tort that people call 'breach of statutory duty' only arises if:

- the duty was imposed for the benefit of the claimant; and

- the statute gives a right to compensation.

It is obvious that if Parliament confers a right to compensation, that right can be asserted in a claim. So why are statutory liabilities interesting? The answer is that the question of whether a statute confers such a right can be surprisingly controversial. The controversies concern the foundation of the relationship between people and the state.

Yet there is nothing distinctly administrative, or public, about this tort; the classic cases concern the liability of private factory owners to workers injured as a result of failure to follow statutory safety rules, or the liability of drivers to people injured as a result of failure to follow traffic regulations.[5] The especially administrative feature

---

[5]   See *Groves v Lord Wimborne* [1898] 2 QB 402; *London Transport Board v Upson* [1949] AC 155.

of the tort is that claimants have made creative attempts to persuade the judges that liability arises out of public authorities' statutory duties to carry out public functions, even where Parliament does not expressly create a right of action. Those attempts have largely failed. In fact, it may seem that the House of Lords carefully developed more restricted liability for breach of statutory duty by public authorities than by private persons. In the private defendant cases, liability was said to arise, *prima facie,* when the statute imposed a duty for the benefit or protection of a class of persons, and a member of that class suffered injury as a result of a failure to perform the duty. Lord Wright held that the right of action was 'a specific common law right. . . . The statutory right has its origin in the statute, but the particular remedy of an action for damages is given by the common law in order to make effective, for the benefit of the injured plaintiff, his right to the performance by the defendant of the defendant's statutory duty' (*London Transport Board v Upson,* [1949] AC 155, 168).

It seems that another requirement has been added in public authority cases. It was first stated clearly by Lord Jauncey, when a prisoner sued the prison governors for damages for breach of the Prison Rules: 'The fact that a particular provision was intended to protect certain individuals is not of itself sufficient to confer private law rights of action upon them, something more is required to show that the legislature intended such conferment' (*R v Deputy Governor of Parkhurst Prison, ex p Hague* [1992] 1 AC 58, 170–1). That approach seems to add an additional requirement, which a public authority can use to avoid liability for breach of a statutory duty. And Lord Jauncey's remark suggests that the 'tort' is a right of action that Parliament confers, contrary to Lord Wright's claim in the *Upson* case that the tort is a common law right of action.

Have the courts been imposing a common law liability on private defendants, and protecting public authorities from that liability? No. A public authority operating a factory has the same liabilities as a private company. A public authority whose employees operate motor vehicles has the same liabilities as a private company whose employees operate motor vehicles. Lord Browne-Wilkinson explained the requirements imposed in the public authority cases by saying that an action for damages arises only where a statutory duty is 'very limited and specific as opposed to general administrative functions imposed on public bodies' (*X v Bedfordshire County Council* [1995] 2 AC 633, 731–2). The key point is that the purpose of 'general administrative functions', such as the operation of a prison, does not require that the persons affected by the function should have a right to be compensated when the function is not carried out as the law requires. The purpose of factory safety rules and traffic regulations is to protect potential victims, by controlling the special harms that arise from the operation of factories and vehicles. In that context, a right to compensation may promote that statutory purpose of imposing a duty.

In *O'Rourke v Camden* [1998] AC 188, the plaintiff sought compensation for breach of a statutory duty to provide accommodation; his action was struck out because the court was not prepared to supplement the duty to provide accommodation with a duty to provide compensation for a failure to provide accommodation. When Parliament establishes a social welfare scheme, the courts will not add a scheme of compensation.

From the claimant's point of view, you may think that the social welfare scheme is frustrated if there is no remedy for a failure to provide the benefit. But the point of the benefit is *not* to confer a right on the claimant that calls for compensation if it is not delivered. In *Cocks v Thanet District Council* [1983] 2 AC 286, 292–3, Lord Bridge had suggested that once a housing authority decided to exercise its discretion in favour of giving a person housing, that created a private law right enforceable in an ordinary claim:

> Once a decision has been reached by the housing authority which gives rise to [a duty to provide housing], rights and obligations are immediately created in the field of private law. Each of the duties referred to, once established, is capable of being enforced by injunction and the breach of it will give rise to a liability in damages.

But the House of Lords departed from that view: Lord Hoffmann decided in *O'Rourke* that 'the breach of statutory duty of which the plaintiff complains gives rise to no cause of action in private law', whether the housing authority had decided to give temporary housing or not (197).

Striking out

Public authority defendants in tort claims often argue that they have no liability to the claimant *even if* all of the allegations of fact in the claim are proven to be true. The Civil Procedure Rules (CPR) allow a defendant to ask the court before trial to strike out the claim if the statement of case 'discloses no reasonable grounds' for bringing the claim (CPR 3.4(2)). Like *O'Rourke*, many of the cases in this chapter were decided before trial on a motion to strike out a claim (see also *X v Bedfordshire County Council* [1995] 2 AC 633). The court will only strike out a claim if there is no realistic chance that liability will be established if all of the facts alleged in the claim are proven; it has long been established that a claim will not be struck out unless there is no 'real point of difficulty that requires judicial decision' (*Deare v Attorney-General* (1835) 1 Y & C Ex 197, 208 (Lord Abinger CB)), and the judges are especially hesitant to strike out a claim in negligence against a public authority, because it can be especially important to understand the facts (see *Barrett v Enfield* [2001] 2 AC 550, 557).

14.4 Negligence

The 'tort of negligence' is the lawyer's way of referring to a common law liability to compensate a claimant who has suffered loss because the defendant wrongly failed to look out for the claimant's interests. But there is no legal responsibility to look out for all the interests that everyone has. A 'duty of care' is a legal responsibility to take reasonable steps to look out for someone else's interest; failure to do so supports a negligence claim if loss results from the failure. Identifying the duties of care owed by the authority's decision making. This policy of the law puts what I will call an 'inter-ference limit' on negligence liability.

But the interference limit is secondary to another, more basic reason for the decision in *East Suffolk Rivers*. Negligence is not simply careless conduct that leaves the claimant worse off than if the defendant had been careful. A defendant will only be held liable in negligence if loss has been caused by the breach of a *duty of care to the claimant*. The House of Lords in *East Suffolk Rivers* held that the rivers authority had no legal duty to the plaintiff to take care to improve his situation by preventing further flood dam-age. The authority had a duty to the public to use its statutory powers to fight floods, but its only legal duty to the plaintiff was to take reasonable care not to make things worse. Even though the authority's workers were at fault, and the loss would not have been suffered if they had not been at fault, the House of Lords was not prepared to hold the authority responsible for compensating the plaintiff. Parliament had created an agency to help people like the plaintiff; imposing liability for failing to prevent flood damage would have added *another* support: a compensation scheme. 'The justice of the common law', as Justice Byles called it in *Cooper*, does not require such compensation (although, of course, Parliament could create such a scheme). If a helpful neighbour had tried to help and made a ridiculous failure of it, the neighbour would not be liable for the loss caused by the failure. Even though the rivers authority was created to prevent flood damage, it was no more liable to compensate than a neighbour would have been.

The crucial point to keep in mind is that even though it was wrong for the rivers authority to act as it did, justice may not require compensation for the wrong. When negligence liability does arise, the rationale for it is that justice demands not only that a defendant should look out for a person's interests, but also that a defendant should give compensation if it fails to do so. The House of Lords held in *East Suffolk Rivers* that jus-tice required compensation for carelessly injuring the plaintiff, but not compensation for carelessly failing to help the plaintiff. That requirement limits the impact of negli-gence liability on public authorities. I will call it the 'justice ingredient' in negligence liability.

We can state the justice ingredient and the interference limit in the following way:

- **The justice ingredient**: public authorities are only liable in negligence to the extent that the ordinary tort law principles of compensatory justice require it. This means that a public authority is not necessarily liable to compensate a claim-ant for loss caused by carelessness in carrying out a public function; it depends on whether justice requires a remedy for the loss.

- **The interference limit**: the courts will avoid imposing a duty of care in a way that interferes in a damaging way with a public authority's exercise of its public functions (which may happen either if the court could only decide the tort claim by passing judgment on issues on which it ought to defer to the authority's judgment, or else if the fact of liability for careless failures will distort the authority's decision making).

The interference limit is of secondary importance to the justice ingredient. The defendant in *East Suffolk Rivers* would have been liable to compensate the plaintiff if the workers had made the flooding worse by carelessly breaking a wall. In that case, it would have been no defence if the authority said that negligence liability would interfere with the way in which it carried out its public function. The concern not to interfere with the authority's function simply vanishes if a public authority carelessly injures someone; the interference limit is only a reason for the courts to be cautious in imposing liability when a public authority carelessly misses an opportunity to help someone. It is a reason for caution in addressing the difficult task of identifying the justice ingredient.

Both the interference limit on negligence liability and the justice ingredient were controversial in *East Suffolk Rivers*; 14.4.2 and 14.4.3 address the ways in which the law on both issues has developed since.

From the landmark case of *Michael v Chief Constable of South Wales* [2015] UKSC 2, we will see that the principles of *East Suffolk Rivers* still hold—even when the defendant's careless failure to help a claimant has the most drastic consequences. The claimants in *Michael* were the parents and children of a woman who phoned 999, and reported that her ex-boyfriend had come to her home, found her with another man, and assaulted her and bitten her. He had taken the other man away, saying that he would come back to kill her. The police arrived too late. Ms Michael was murdered by the ex-boyfriend. Her family's claim alleged that her death would have been prevented by the police, except that they had breached a duty of care by carelessly mishandling the call. The Supreme Court, in a 5–2 decision, upheld the striking out of the claim in negligence, but allowed the claimants to proceed to trial on their claim that the defendant had breached a positive duty that arises from the guarantee of the right to life Art 2 of the European Convention (see 14.6.2).

Understanding the striking out of the negligence claim in *Michael* will set the scene for understanding the distinctive importance of the tort of misfeasance in public office (14.5), and of damages under the Human Rights Act (14.6).

Differences between a duty of care in negligence and a public law duty:

- A duty of care is *owed to* a particular person or persons, but a duty in public law is not owed to particular persons; it is 'owed to the Crown', as Lord Reid and Lord Diplock put it in *Home Office v Dorset Yacht* [1970] AC 1004, 1030. In our constitution, that is a metaphorical way of saying that it is 'a duty owed to the public at large', as Lord Toulson put it in *Michael v Chief Constable of South Wales* [2015] UKSC 2 [33], as opposed to 'a private law duty to a member of the public' [35].

- The breach of a duty of care gives rise to a right to damages if the breach causes loss: Even when it is unlawful for a public authority to exercise its powers in a way that is *Wednesbury* unreasonable, a person injured does not necessarily have any right to compensation.

14.4.2 The justice ingredient in negligence

It may seem odd that a public authority with a statutory duty to care for people has no 'duty of care' to use its powers to benefit the people in question—as if it were okay for a public authority to be careless in performing its functions. Of course, that is not okay. If an applicant for a housing benefit is entitled to it under a statute, and someone in the office carelessly deletes the application from their computer and forgets about it, the local authority will be in breach of its statutory duties to consider the application and to award the benefit. But a breach of those duties is not the same as the breach of a duty of care to a potential victim that gives rise to liability in negligence. A duty of care is not *simply* a reason for someone to take care for someone else's interests, but also a reason for compensating that person for loss caused by a failure to take care.

Donoghue v Stevenson [1932] AC 562 was the first attempt by an English judge to state the justice ingredient in negligence liability. Lord Atkin offered a 'general conception of relations giving rise to a duty of care' (581):

> ' You must take reasonable care to avoid acts or omissions which you can reasonably foresee would be likely to injure your neighbour. Who, then, in law is my neighbour? The answer seems to be—persons who are so closely and directly affected by my act that I ought reasonably to have them in contemplation as being so affected when I am directing my mind to the acts or omissions which are called in question. '

Lord Atkin warned against making a general rule of liability out of his famous attempt to explain the justice ingredient,[6] and it is easy to see why. Applied to decisions of public authorities, that 'neighbour principle' seems to require compensation whenever a public authority does not take reasonable care to use a statutory power to benefit a claimant who is so directly affected that a reasonable public authority would have him or her in mind. Although he was cautious about the generality of his principle, Lord Atkin certainly meant to create a wide-ranging basis for the duty of care. That is why, in *East Suffolk Rivers* itself, Lord Atkin dissented. He suggested that the decision in *Donoghue v Stevenson* required that the public authority should be liable for its careless failure to help the plaintiff (*East Suffolk Rivers*, 92).

Since *Donoghue v Stevenson*, English courts have made progressive (although uneven) attempts to control and to restrict the reach of Lord Atkin's principle. It does not provide a general guide to negligence liability. Landmark cases on liability of public authorities have helped to shape the development. Lord Atkin's defeat in *East Suffolk Rivers* was the first such case; the second was *Home Office v Dorset Yacht*. The plaintiff brought an action in negligence, alleging that officers from a borstal (a young offenders institution) had carelessly failed to keep custody of seven boys who damaged the plaintiff's yacht. The House of Lords held that if the officers' custody of the boys caused a

---

6   '. . . it is of particular importance to guard against the danger of stating propositions of law in wider terms than is necessary. . . . it is very necessary in considering reported cases in the law of torts that the actual decision alone should carry authority' (*Donoghue v Stevenson*, 583–4).

manifest risk that the boys would damage the plaintiff's property, the officers owed the plaintiff a duty to take reasonable care to prevent the boys from doing so. Lord Diplock held that Lord Atkin's statement of the neighbour principle in *Donoghue v Stevenson* could not apply generally to all allegations of negligence: 'misused as a universal it is manifestly false' (*Home Office*, 1060). But there was no agreement in the House of Lords as to how to contain the principle: Lord Reid held that the neighbour principle ought to be applied unless there is some reason to exclude liability.

The House of Lords took Lord Reid's approach in *Anns v Merton* [1978] AC 728. A homeowner brought a claim in negligence to recover a loss in the value of a house, after the defendant local authority's building inspectors had carelessly failed to spot a mistake by the builder. Lord Wilberforce offered a two-stage test based on *Donoghue v Stevenson* (*Anns*, 751–2):

> ' First one has to ask whether, as between the alleged wrongdoer and the person who has suffered damage there is a sufficient relationship of proximity or neighbourhood such that, in the reasonable contemplation of the former, carelessness on his part may be likely to cause damage to the latter—in which case a prima facie duty of care arises. Secondly, . . . it is necessary to consider whether there are any considerations which ought to negative, or to reduce or limit the scope of the duty or the class of person to whom it is owed or the damages to which a breach of it may give rise. '

As the House of Lords found no special reason *not* to award damages, the *prima facie* liability under Lord Atkin's principle led to an award of damages against the local authority.

The remarkable decision in *Anns* changed the shape of the negligence liability of public authorities for some time. It amounted to a decision that the justice ingredient can be satisfied simply by foreseeability of damage, and proximity between defendant and claimant (and Lord Wilberforce suggested that proximity arose from foreseeability). The defendant in *Anns* was held liable for failing to help the plaintiff, and that is impossible to reconcile with the ruling in *East Suffolk Rivers*. In *Anns*, Lord Wilberforce suggested that the House of Lords in *East Suffolk Rivers* had not yet fully digested the implications of *Donoghue v Stevenson*, so that it had not yet recognized 'the conception of a general duty of care, not limited to particular accepted situations, but extending generally over all relations of sufficient proximity, and even pervading the sphere of statutory functions of public bodies' (*Anns*, 757).

That 'general duty of care' has not survived. Even if the requirements of foreseeability and proximity are met, there needs to be additional reason to impose liability. Lord Keith began to restore the *East Suffolk Rivers* approach in two Privy Council cases on negligence of public authorities: *Rowling v Takaro* [1988] AC 473, 501, in which 'a too literal application' of Lord Wilberforce's two-stage test was not the right way to decide 'whether it is appropriate that a duty of care should be imposed'; and *Yuen Kun Yeu v Attorney-General of Hong Kong* [1988] 1 AC 175, 194, 'the two-stage test in *Anns v*

Merton is not to be regarded as in all circumstances a suitable guide to the existence of a duty of care'. But the idea that foreseeability and proximity create a *prima facie* duty of care was really laid to rest in a case on the liability of auditors: *Caparo v Dickman* [1990] 2 AC 605. After 1990, the House of Lords consistently stood by Lord Bridge's conclusion in *Caparo* that another ingredient was required besides foreseeability of loss and proximity between the claimant and defendant. Even if those requirements are met, no duty of care arises *unless* it is 'fair, just and reasonable that the law should impose a duty of a given scope upon the one party for the benefit of the other' (618). Lord Bridge also insisted on identifying duties of care incrementally, by reference to established situations in which they have been imposed, rather than by applying a general principle.

Is it fair, just, and reasonable to impose a common law duty on a public authority to carry out its statutory role in a way that will benefit a claimant? *Caparo* does not answer the question. The impact of *Anns* on public authorities was evidently put in doubt, but the possibility survived that a public authority might be liable in negligence for a careless failure to help the claimant.

In *Stovin v Wise* [1996] AC 923, though, Lord Hoffmann rejected Lord Wilberforce's reasoning in *Anns*. In *Stovin*, a county council had decided to use its statutory power to cut away a bank from a roadside to improve visibility at a dangerous junction in a highway. But the Council had done nothing to pursue the plan when the plaintiff was injured in an accident on the highway. The defendant driver claimed that the Council breached a duty of care to the plaintiff by failing to follow through on its plan to remove the bank. For the majority, Lord Hoffmann concluded that Lord Wilberforce had offered no rationale for imposing a duty of care, except his argument that the interference limit does not *forbid* liability. So Lord Hoffmann concluded that *Anns* offered no way of meeting the requirement of a justice ingredient (*Stovin*, 950):

> ' Upon what principles can one say of a public authority that not only did it have a duty in public law to consider the exercise of the power but that it would thereupon have been under a duty in private law to act, giving rise to a claim in compensation against public funds for its failure to do so? '

Perhaps Lord Wilberforce thought that proximity itself is the justice ingredient, and that the power to inspect in *Anns* generated a duty of care because it put the inspectors in that relationship of proximity to the homeowners (by giving the inspectors a responsibility to help the homeowners). That is the approach that *Caparo* abandoned. But *Caparo* did not concern public authorities, and *Stovin* represents Lord Hoffmann's solution to the question of the justice ingredient in public authority cases: before a public authority can be liable for carelessly failing to use its statutory power to benefit the claimant, there must be 'exceptional grounds for holding that the policy of the statute requires compensation to be paid to persons who suffer loss because the power was not exercised'. In *East Suffolk Rivers*, the House of Lords was never so explicit, and Lord Hoffmann pushed the reasoning of that case further in *Stovin* (954):

> It is one thing to provide a service at the public expense. It is another to require the public to pay compensation when a failure to provide the service has resulted in loss . . . Before imposing such an additional burden, the courts should be satisfied that this is what Parliament intended.

Lord Hoffmann still distinguished between the tort of breach of statutory duty and a cause of action in negligence for failure to use a statutory power. The distinction is unclear: unlike the former, the latter is 'not exactly a question of construction [of the statute], because the cause of action does not arise out of the statute itself. But the policy of the statute is nevertheless a crucial factor in the decision' (*Stovin*, 952). Yet the policy of the statute can only be identified by construction of the statute. Lord Hoffmann, though, did not apologize for the apparent *lack* of a distinction between the tort of breach of statutory duty, and liability for a careless failure to use a statutory power to benefit a claimant (953): 'If the policy of the Act is not to create a statutory liability to pay compensation, the same policy should ordinarily exclude the existence of a common law duty of care.' The view that emerges is that unless there is some further ground for liability, it is *not* fair, just, and reasonable (as Lord Bridge put it in *Caparo*) to hold a public authority liable to compensate a claimant for carelessly failing to use its powers to benefit the claimant, even where the authority had a duty (in public law) to do so.

In spite of his radical disagreement with Lord Wilberforce's reasoning, Lord Hoffmann did not actually depart from the result in *Anns*. He said that the main ground of that decision was 'general reliance'—a widespread assumption in a community that a power will be exercised with reasonable care. So an assumption that a statutory power of safety inspection will be exercised with reasonable care may ground a duty of care (*Stovin v Wise*, 954). General reliance is *not* reliance—at least, the claimant need not have relied on the public authority taking care. 'General reliance' is best understood as a label for the judges' conclusion that the justice ingredient is supplied by some special responsibility of the public authority to take care in a particular context. And it is limited in its effect: it is implicit in *Stovin* that general reliance does not arise in respect of highway maintenance, and it is implicit in the *Michael* case that, if there is such a doctrine at all (it is not mentioned in *Michael*), general reliance cannot arise in respect of the police response to a 999 call.

Failing such a special responsibility (and it is not clear what is required for a special responsibility), the inexorable logic of *Stovin* is that negligence liability does not arise simply from a careless failure to help the claimant, even where the defendant has a public law duty to help people in the position of the claimant. And the importance of *Michael* is not only that it affirms *Stovin*, but that it establishes that even an especially close proximity (forged by Ms Michael's 999 call) does not in itself generate a duty of care. *Stovin* created a risk to any road user; *Michael* was different because the police had reason to know that there was a particular risk to Ms Michael, so that the facts assumed in *Michael* support a claim that the police had breached the positive duty to her, arising from the guarantee of the right to life under Art 2 of the European Convention on Human Rights (see 14.6.2). *Stovin* involved no such breach. Lord Kerr and Baroness Hale, dissenting in *Michael*, would have held that there was a duty of care because of that special proximity (see *Michael* [175] and [197]). The majority rejected that approach decisively, for reasons that can be put in terms of the justice ingredient and the interference limit:

(1) the **justice ingredient** was missing on the assumed facts ('It does not follow from the setting up of a protective system . . . that if it fails to achieve its purpose, through organisational defects or fault on the part of an individual, the public at large should bear the additional burden of compensating a victim . . .'–*Michael* [114]), and

(2) the **interference limit** was a reason not to extend a duty of care in negligence to the facts of *Michael* ('it is hard to see that it would be in the public interest for the determination of police priorities to be affected by the risk of being sued' [121]).

Yet it is well established that there are *some* situations in which there is just such a liability for careless failure to help someone. Think about the liability of a doctor employed by a public authority. There is no doubt that a doctor who carelessly injures a patient is liable in negligence (and the public authority is vicariously liable). But suppose a doctor attends an emergency and carelessly fails to provide successful treatment, when any reasonable doctor would have healed the patient. It may seem that the doctor is in the same position as the authority in *East Suffolk Rivers*: the doctor has carelessly failed to help the claimant, but has not harmed the claimant. Yet in the case of the careless doctor, it is clear that there was a breach of the duty of care that a doctor owes to a patient. In *Phelps v Hillingdon* [2001] 2 AC 619, the House of Lords held that doctors have such a duty to take reasonable care, and the Law Lords extended it to educational psychologists, and even to teachers. Lord Slynn stated that the *Caparo* 'fair, just and reasonable' criterion was met in *Phelps* because (654):

> ⁶ it is long and well-established, now clementary, that persons exercising a particular skill or profession may owe a duty of care in the performance to people who it can be foreseen will be injured if due skill and care are not exercised. . . . A doctor, an accountant and an engineer are plainly such a person. So in my view is an educational psychologist or psychiatrist and a teacher including a teacher in a specialised area, such as a teacher concerned with children having special educational needs. ⁹

Can that well-established form of liability be reconciled with the basic principle of *East Suffolk Rivers*, as extended by Lord Hoffmann in *Stovin*? Only if the special professional responsibility of a doctor, or psychologist, or teacher means that justice requires compensation for a careless failure to help the claimant (whereas justice does not require compensation for a careless failure to help the claimant by flood prevention workers or highway maintenance workers, or the police). Perhaps the combination of the role of the professional, and the dependence and vulnerability of the claimant, provide the justice ingredient in a way that distinguishes a patient in a medical emergency, or the schoolgirl in *Phelps*, from the plaintiffs in *East Suffolk Rivers* and *Stovin* and the claimant in *Michael*.[7] In any case, the special liability of professionals such as doctors meets Lord Bridge's constraint in *Caparo*, that duties of care should be extended incrementally from established situations of duty. But that approach means that the courts have given up on Lord Atkin's impulse to generalize: the ways of meeting the justice requirement are various and are not explained by a single principle.

A special duty of care to employees

Employers owe their employees a duty to take reasonable steps to protect their health, including their mental health, from being damaged by their employment. This is another reminder of the lack of a single principle determining when justice requires a duty of care. In *Connor v Surrey County Council* [2010] EWCA Civ 286, the Court of Appeal developed the employer's duty of care into an extraordinary control on a public authority's exercise of its public responsibilities. A head teacher suffered from mental illness as the result of bitter disputes caused by a parent at the school, who complained that the head teacher was racist and Islamophobic. The Court held that by calling an inquiry to investigate the parent's complaints, and by delaying a decision to step in and replace the school's governing body, the local authority had breached a duty of care to the claimant. Laws LJ said that: 'The duty is a function of the relationship between employer and employee. It arises quite independently of the impact of action or inaction under statute' [75]. There is no doubt that public authorities, like other employers, owe duties of care to their employees. *Connor* is an extraordinary case because the nature of the duty is stated so widely: it is a duty to take reasonable care to protect the employee's mental health. As we will see in 14.4.3, that very wide duty could (and did in *Connor* itself) turn into a far-reaching control by judges on the ways in which a public authority carries out its public functions.

> **Examples of the justice ingredient—that is, a feature of a case that justifies imposing negligence liability for causing loss by using public powers without reasonable care for the claimant's interests:**
>
> 1. **If the defendant made things worse**: in *East Suffolk Rivers*, justice *would* have required compensation if the authority had carelessly made the flooding worse.
>
> 2. **If the defendant was in control of a third party** and should have foreseen that the third party might cause damage to the claimant, if the defendant did not take reasonable care to control him or her. Thus, in *Dorset Yacht*, justice might require compensation if the borstal officers created a danger to the

---

[7]　See Lord Nicholls in *Phelps*, 666.

yacht by bringing the boys to the island, and then were careless in supervising them. This can be understood as an example of item 1, above.

3. **If the defendant assumed responsibility to safeguard** the defendant (but Lord Toulson said in *Michael* [100]: 'in truth the responsibility has been imposed by the court rather than assumed').

4. **If there was a failure in the role of certain professionals whose role is to safeguard persons in the position of the defendant**, which gives rise to the 'normal professional duty of care' (as Lord Browne-Wilkinson called it in *X v Bedfordshire County Council* [1995] 2 AC 633, 771). In *X* and in *Phelps*, the House of Lords held that justice may require compensation if professionals fail to carry out a special responsibility to provide help to the people they serve.

5. **Reliance**: justice may require compensation if a claimant relied on the public authority to provide protection or help. There was no reliance in *East Suffolk Rivers* or *Anns v Merton*. Suppose that the plaintiffs in those cases could have taken measures of their own, but reasonably decided not to because the authority was dealing with the problem. Then the plaintiff's case in *East Suffolk Rivers* would presumably have had the justice ingredient, and *Anns* would not have been a controversial case.

6. **General reliance**: justice may require compensation if there is a general pattern of reliance on a public authority's role in protecting people from some harm—even if *the claimant* did not rely (*Stovin v Wise*, 954 (Lord Hoffmann)).

7. **Employment**: like other employers, a public authority owes duties not only to take care not to harm its employees, but to take care to protect their interests (*Connor v Surrey County Council* [2010] EWCA Civ 286).

Note on the categories in *Michael*: Lord Toulson, in his speech for the majority, mentioned items 2 and 3 on this list as exceptions to the general rule that a defendant is not liable for carelessly failing to prevent a third party from injuring the claimant ([99]–[100]). He did not mention item 6 (which, he implies, does not apply to the police), and he treated items 4, 5, and 7 as instances of item 3. Item 1 is implicit in his approach: the claimants would have had a right of action, if the police had created a new risk to Ms Michael. Finally, Lord Toulson noted that 'the categories of negligence are never closed', but added that they should only be developed incrementally [102].

14.4.3 The interference limit

In *X v Bedfordshire County Council*, the House of Lords faced a series of unprecedented negligence claims. Several children sought damages in negligence (1) against child protection authorities for carelessly taking a child into care in one case and for carelessly failing to take children into care in five other cases; and (2) against education authorities for failing to assess special educational needs carefully. The question was whether the child protection authorities and the education authorities could owe a duty of care to the children. Lord Browne-Wilkinson approached it by pointing out that they could not be liable for doing what Parliament had authorized. If Parliament has given a discretion—that is, lawful authorization to act one way or another (see 7.2.2)—neither way of acting can be a tort. Since the statutes in X gave the authorities discretion as to how their duties were to be performed, Lord Browne-Wilkinson held that the authorities could not be liable in negligence unless 'the decision complained of is so unreasonable that it falls outside the ambit of the discretion conferred upon the local authority' ([1995] 2 AC 736, relying on Lord Reid's speech in *Dorset Yacht*, 1031). He added that if the issues relevant to the exercise of the discretion were to include 'matters of policy' that are not justiciable, the court would not be able to reach the conclusion that the action was outside the ambit of the discretion (*X*, 738). Finally, he held that even if there is no defence that an action was within a statutory discretion, the court will not impose a common law duty of care on a statutory duty or power if observing the duty of care 'would be inconsistent with, or have a tendency to discourage, the due performance by the local authority of its statutory duties' (*X*, 738). So *X* illustrates the two aspects of the interference limit: (1) deference, to some extent, to the authority's judgment on policy issues; and (2) a concern to avoid distorting the agency's decisions in pursuit of its public purpose, even where the courts do not need to defer to their policy judgments.

Following Lord Browne-Wilkinson's influential speech in *X*, we can say that the courts have three ways of limiting claims that a public authority has negligently exercised a statutory power:

- the rule that discretion gives a defence of statutory authorization;

- the rule that the court will not be able to hold that there is no defence of statutory authorization if the issues are non-justiciable; and

- the rule that the court will not impose a duty of care that puts undue pressure on authority's performance of its functions (*X*, 748–9).

The first two reflect the deference aspect of the interference limit; the third reflects the courts' reluctance to distort decision making by imposing liability, even when no deference is due to the decision maker's judgment. The result of these—the interference limit—is a reason for the courts to be cautious in extending their view as to what satisfies the justice ingredient for negligence.

Discretion

Lord Browne-Wilkinson's idea that a lawful exercise of discretion cannot be a breach of a duty of care was not new. In *Dorset Yacht*, the House of Lords had made it clear that there could be no negligence liability if a boy escaped as a result of 'a system of relaxed control intentionally adopted by the Home Office as conducive to the reformation of trainees' (Lord Diplock, 1068). Similarly, for all of the controversies over *Anns*, it is uncontroversial that the local authority would not have been liable if the faulty foundations had gone undetected because the local authority reduced the number of inspections for reasons of cost. The court would defer to the local authority's decision as to how many inspections it could carry out, rather than being prepared to hold that an insufficient number of inspections was a breach of a duty of care. So the defence of statutory authorization includes deference to a public authority's discretionary decisions.

Yet cases since *X* have cast doubt on the idea. In *Barrett v Enfield LBC* [2001] 2 AC 550, both Lord Slynn and Lord Hutton said that the fact that an action is taken in the exercise of a discretion does not mean that no duty of care can arise. They suggested that it is only when non-justiciable considerations are at stake (see 'Justiciability' below) that a duty of care is excluded. Lord Hutton said that *X* did not preclude 'a ruling in the present case that although the decisions of the defendant were within the ambit of its statutory discretion, nevertheless those decisions did not involve the balancing of the type of policy considerations which renders the decisions non-justiciable' (*Barrett*, 585). And in *Phelps*, Lord Slynn said that he could not accept Lord Browne-Wilkinson's statement that 'an educational authority owes no common law duty of care in the exercise of the powers and discretions relating to children with special educational needs' (657–8).

After *Phelps* and *Barrett*, *X* **can no longer be relied on** for the proposition that educational and social services professionals have no private law duty to take reasonable care in making decisions as to children's special education needs, or in making child welfare decisions. And in *D v East Berkshire NHS Trust* [2005] UKHL 23, the Law Lords were clearly of the view that there can be such a duty of care (although they held that there is no duty of care to the parents). But it is possible to explain the cases after *X* simply as extending what Lord Browne-Wilkinson called the 'normal professional duty of care' (*X*, 771).

Justiciability

Lord Wilberforce in *Anns* distinguished between policy decisions and operational decisions, concluding that: 'It can safely be said that the more "operational" a power or duty may be, the easier it is to superimpose upon it a common law duty of care' (754). Lord Wilberforce said that the courts call questions of 'policy' questions of 'discretion', but Lord Browne-Wilkinson treated 'policy' questions as non-justiciable questions in *X* (737). Similarly, in *Rowling v Takaro* [1988] AC 473, 501, Lord Keith said that Lord Wilberforce's distinction between policy and operation, while not a 'touchstone of liability', was a reminder that the courts should not impose a duty of care in 'cases in which the decision under attack is of such a kind that a question whether it has been made negligently is unsuitable for judicial resolution'.

> ### Can an issue be more or less justiciable?
> 'Non-justiciable' means, as Lord Keith put it, 'unsuitable for judicial resolution'. But a question can be more or less suitable for judicial resolution (see 7.3.1, p 254). The issues that Lord Wilberforce called 'policy' issues are issues on which judges ought to defer to an administrative authority's judgment to some degree. They are not necessarily issues that judges simply must not consider.

The distinction between policy and operation has often been criticized.[8] Sometimes the criticism has been that it is a vague distinction. But the law needs to draw many vague distinctions, and we cannot expect any sharp distinction between acts on which courts should and should not superimpose a duty of care. The more potent criticism, voiced by Lord Hoffmann in *Stovin v Wise*, is that even when a public authority's action is clearly operational, that fact gives no reason in itself to superimpose a duty of care. But in spite of various notes of caution, and Lord Hoffmann's withering attack, the judges have not quite abandoned Lord Wilberforce's distinction as a way of describing acts of public authorities that are challenged in a negligence action.[9] Perhaps the best sense we can make both of *Anns* and of the continuing use of the distinction is simply this: there is reason for judges *not* to impose liability on a public authority for carelessly making a bad decision when judges cannot assess the relevant considerations. That is, the policy/operation distinction is best understood as a way of describing the justiciability rule in *X*. Lord Browne-Wilkinson made something useful of the distinction in *X* by turning it into a way of stating the rule that a duty of care cannot be imposed if doing so would demand judicial assessment of non-justiciable considerations.

Which considerations are non-justiciable? As in *Council of Civil Service Unions v Ministers for the Civil Service* [1985] AC 374 on control of discretion (see 7.3.1, p 254), the judges have given some suggestive examples, but no full explanation. The examples include those of Lord Browne-Wilkinson in *X* (737): '[S]ocial policy, the allocation of finite financial resources between the different calls made upon them or (as in *Dorset Yacht*) the balance between pursuing desirable social aims as against the risk to the public inherent in so doing.' Perhaps the nearest thing to an explanation of the idea of justiciability is Lord Diplock's attempt in *Dorset Yacht* to say why a court should not hold that it is a breach of a duty of care to decide to adopt a system of relaxed control of young offenders in a borstal (1067):

> ' The material relevant to the assessment of the reformative effect upon trainees of release under supervision or of any relaxation of control while still under detention is not of a kind which can be satisfactorily elicited by the adversary procedure and rules of evidence adopted in English courts of law or of which judges (and juries) are suited by their training and experience to assess the probative value. '

When the judges impose a duty on other public authorities to take reasonable care for a claimant's interests, they will breach the requirement of comity if they show no deference to the public authority's view as to what is reasonable. So they should not impose a duty of care at all if doing so will lead inevitably to passing judgment on non-justiciable issues. And in deciding what counts as a breach of a duty of care (that is, in deciding what counts as reasonable care in the use of a public power, when there is a duty to use it with care), the courts must defer, to some extent, to the public authority's view as to

---

[8] See, e.g., Lord Nicholls' speeches in *Stovin v Wise* (938), and in *Phelps* (666).

[9] Lord Slynn said, in *Phelps*, 658, that there was 'some validity' in the distinction.

what is reasonable. The judges should not assume the task of deciding which policies would be reasonable—and they should not take away other public authorities' political responsibility for those decisions.

Interfering with the functions of public authorities

Neither the discretion rule nor the justiciability rule had any application in *East Suffolk Rivers*. The plaintiff's complaint in that case was against sheer incompetence, of a kind that was obvious even to judges. Even so, the court will not impose a duty of care if it would inappropriately interfere with the work of the public authority.

The problem is nicely illustrated by *Alexandrou v Oxford* [1993] 4 All ER 328. The police had invited businesses to connect their burglar alarms to the police station to make it easier for the police to investigate break-ins. When a burglar alarm went off at Alexandrou's computer warehouse, the police investigated, but Alexandrou alleged that they carelessly failed to find the burglars (who finished their burglary after the police left). The claim was struck out. For the striking-out decision, it had to be assumed that the police officers acted carelessly in what Lord Wilberforce would have called a purely operational task. Even then, the courts would not impose a duty of care: if the police were to become liable to provide compensation for the consequences of a failure to respond carefully to an alarm, they would have to abandon the scheme of connecting burglar alarms to the police station unless they could afford to provide crime victims with insurance against carelessness by police officers. An initiative that improves policing might have to be dropped if the courts added a duty in tort to operate the scheme carefully. The same problem affected the decision in *East Suffolk Rivers Catchment Board v Kent* [1941] AC 74. Said Lord Porter (106):

> A local authority faced by such a series of disasters as occurred in the present case might consider that the flooded land was not very valuable, but that they were justified in making an attempt to clear it of water provided the expense was not serious, and think that the expenditure of some small sum would not be too great in an attempt to prevent the damage. . . . If the respondents be right such a decision could never be made safely.

It is expensive even to take steps to avoid purely operational carelessness. So to avoid interfering with good decision making about flood control, the court had to find no liability even for incompetence.

We can put *X* itself in the same category as *East Suffolk Rivers* and *Alexandrou*, because the House of Lords did not strike out any of the claims on the grounds that non-justiciable issues arose, or that it was clear that the plaintiffs would not be able to prove that the public authorities acted outside the ambit of their discretion. The claims[10] were struck out under the *Caparo* doctrine, because it was not reasonable to

---

10 That is, all of the claims in negligence except the claims in the special education cases based on the 'normal professional duty of care'.

impose a duty of care. It would distort the authorities' performance of their statutory functions, and imposing a duty of care would depart from the 'incremental' approach of *Caparo* (*X*, 751). Since *X*, the law has moved forward incrementally, and the 'normal professional duty of care' has been extended in *Phelps* and *Barrett*.

Yet the courts have not abandoned the principle that a duty of care should not be imposed if it will interfere with a public authority's service to the public interest: in *D v East Berkshire NHS Trust* [2005] UKHL 23, in decisions whether to take a child into care, the House of Lords refused to impose on social workers a duty of care *to parents*, on the ground that it would interfere with the critical need for the social workers to attend to the interests of children, where there was reason to think that they might need to be taken into care.

The *D* case has been followed in a line of cases reasserting the interference limit. In *Lawrence v Pembrokeshire County Council* [2007] EWCA Civ 446, the Council suspected the claimant of child abuse, and placed her four children on the child protection register for fourteen months, possibly through a careless mistake. The claimant asked the Court to take a 'small incremental step' [16] beyond the approach of the House of Lords in *D v East Berkshire NHS Trust*, developing the common law so as to give effect to Art 8 of the European Convention on Human Rights. But the Court of Appeal refused to take that step, because of 'the need to provide protection to those who have a duty to enforce the law in good faith from the imposition of a duty in negligence that could or might tend to inhibit them in the effective fulfilment of that duty' (Auld LJ, *Lawrence* [55]).

The long development of this line of cases goes on, but we can now say that the interference limit is a stable and important aspect of the law on claims that negligence in the exercise of public functions has injured the claimant. The chief difficulty in understanding the law is to be able to explain how the exceptional cases—*Phelps* and *Barrett* on duties of professionals, and *Connor v Surrey County Council* [2010] EWCA Civ 286 on a public authority's duty to its employees—can be reconciled with the assertions of the interference limit in cases such as *Lawrence*.

Connor, in particular, poses a difficulty. The Court of Appeal held that the local authority was liable for a breach of its duty to protect the mental health of a head teacher by delaying a decision about replacing the school governors, and by deciding to investigate complaints of racism against the teacher. The remarkable feature of *Connor* lies in the breadth of the duty that was identified: ' . . . to take reasonable steps to safeguard her health, including her mental health' [52]. The liability in *Connor* puts public authorities in a bind: in carrying out their obvious public duty to be prepared to investigate complaints of racism on the part of their employees, they face a risk of negligence liability, because of their duty of care for their employees' mental health.

The interference limit is a reason not to impose a duty of care at all if doing so would interfere with the proper function of the public authority (as in *D v East Berkshire*). And if the law imposes a broad duty to care for employees' mental health, the interference limit ought to be applied in deciding what counts as a breach of the duty. The head teacher in *Connor* certainly had a right to care in her employment, but in the local authority's decision as to whether and when to hold an inquiry into complaints against her, she did not have a right to have her interests cared for in a way that would stand in the way of good operation of the school, or that would hold back the local authority from making a serious response to complaints about her. A good employer cannot legitimately protect an employee against false complaints by refusing to investigate complaints. The law needs to distinguish between the care that a good employer gives to its employees (Ms Connor had a right to that), and the care that a good local authority takes for all of the relevant interests in dealing with a complaint about the conduct of a public official. If the public employer's duty of care is stated as broadly as it was in *Connor*, then the courts should also hold that no breach of the duty can be identified if the judges would need to second-guess the judgment of the local authority on questions of educational policy and operations, in order to identify a breach.

In *Connor* itself, no such restriction on liability was applied. After a detailed review of the line of cases from *X* to *Stovin* to *Phelps* and *Barrett*, Laws LJ held that they were of little relevance because, in *Connor*, there was a 'pre-existing and independent duty of care' [104] (that is, the duty of an employer). And he imposed no interference limit. He held that a public official with a pre-existing duty of care, 'if he is to fulfil his duty of care by means of a public law discretion, must act consistently with the full performance of his public law obligations' [107]. So if it would be unlawful for a local authority to refuse to investigate allegations against a head teacher (e.g., if it would be *Wednesbury* unreasonable to refuse to investigate), then the authority's duty to take reasonable steps to protect her mental health does not prevent it from investigating. But if it would be lawful for the authority either to investigate *or* to decide not to investigate, then, according to *Connor*, its duty of care to the head teacher requires it not to do so. There is no explanation in the case as to how, if the law authorizes the local authority to investigate, it can be a breach of a duty of care for it to do so.

The law on duties of care in negligence towards public employees is unstable, because the decision in *Connor* combined a very broad duty of care and a lack of deference to the public authority on the question of how to exercise its discretion. The result is incompatible with the interference limit established by the House of Lords in *D v East Berkshire*.

14.4.4 The judicialization of war

Negligence liability has been extended to new frontiers as a consequence of the British military involvement in Iraq from 2003 to 2009. Families of soldiers killed by improvised explosive devices, and by friendly fire, have used both the Human Rights Act 1998 (see 14.6.2) and the tort of negligence to seek redress from the Ministry of Defence. In *Smith v Ministry of Defence* [2013] UKSC 41, the Supreme Court allowed the negligence claims to go to trial, and opened the door to litigation over any injury in military operations.

In every aspect of planning and operation, the military should be vividly concerned about the interests of the individual soldier. The military should also be vividly concerned about achieving the objective of the military action. It is obviously the case in the military—although it is shocking to say it—that the second concern takes priority over the first. Military operations are an area of public administration in which it may be right to make decisions that endanger the lives of public servants. The judges should not take upon themselves the job of remedying shortcomings in military planning and operation if doing so will interfere with the complex public pursuit of effective military action, and judges are not well placed to ensure that the action is taken with appropriate concern for the safety (and all the other interests) of military personnel and of others.

The Ministry of Defence had argued that it was not fair, just, and reasonable (under the *Caparo* doctrine) to impose a duty of care in tort to protect soldiers from injury during combat operations. But the Supreme Court refused to strike out the claims. The majority did not hold that it *was* fair, just, and reasonable to impose a duty of care, but that the facts of the case needed to be established at trial in order to establish that. And Lord Hope carefully pointed out the difficulties in establishing a duty of care in the cases, and that the decision maker in question may be constrained by decisions 'taken for reasons of policy at a high level of command' or 'by the effects of contact with the enemy' [99], either of which might mean that it would not be reasonable to impose a duty of care in tort:

> ' Great care needs to be taken not to subject those responsible for decisions at any level that affect what takes place on the battlefield, or in operations of the kind that were being conducted in Iraq after the end of hostilities, to duties that are unrealistic or excessively burdensome. '[11]

The majority in *Smith* did at least pay attention to the interference limit: Lord Hope was quite insistent that the courts should not impose a duty of care in a way that would prevent the Ministry of Justice from forming its own view as to what resources to invest in military equipment, or that would prevent commanders in the field from acting on their own judgment in operations. With those provisos in place, it may seem attractive to allow the claimant to proceed to trial, and to seek to establish facts that make it fair, just, and reasonable to impose a duty of care. But as Lord Mance put it in his dissent: '[T]he approach taken by the majority will . . . make extensive litigation almost inevitable after, as well as quite possibly during and even before, any active service operations undertaken by the British army. It is likely to lead to the judicialisation of war' [150].

Lord Hope himself mentioned the 'risk, which must of course be avoided, of judicialising warfare' [98]. But the Supreme Court has not merely created a risk; it has very deliberately endorsed the judicialization of warfare. In these cases, on deaths caused by roadside bombs, or by friendly fire, it is hard to see how the courts could identify any duty of care (which implies a duty to compensate for loss resulting if reasonable care is not taken) without imposing the unrealistic and excessively burdensome duties that Lord Hope said should not be imposed. Lord Hope concluded his reasons for the

---

[11]   Yet note that Lord Hope very clearly indicates that, in the friendly fire cases, the question is 'not whether a duty was owed but whether, on the facts, it was breached' [98].

majority by saying that 'it is of paramount importance that the work that the armed services do in the national interest should not be impeded by having to prepare for or conduct active operations against the enemy under the threat of litigation if things should go wrong' [100]. Yet the decision invites long and complex litigation after any injury in military operations. The military must now prepare for active operations under the threat of litigation if things should go wrong.

Emergency services

The police, in criminal investigations, have no duty of care in negligence law to people who might be injured by a criminal who is still at large. In *Hill v Chief Constable of West Yorkshire* [1989] AC 53, the House of Lords struck out a claim against the police for negligence in failing to stop the Yorkshire Ripper after they had evidence as to his identity. *Michael v Chief Constable of South Wales* [2015] UKSC 2 established that there is no duty of care in negligence in the police response to a 999 call. But the police have no immunity from negligence liability. It is fair, just, and reasonable to impose a duty of care not to endanger persons in their investigations and other operations (*Knightley v Johns* [1982] 1 WLR 349, *Swinney v Chief Constable of Northumbria Police Force* [1997] QB 464). But even if the police know that a person is in danger, it is not fair, just, and reasonable to impose a duty 'to exercise reasonable care to safeguard victims or potential victims of crime' (*Michael* [115]).

Fire brigades have a statutory duty to provide efficient firefighting services (Fire Services Act 1947), but 'are not under a common law duty to answer the call for help, and are not under a duty to take care to do so. If, therefore, they fail to turn up, or fail to turn up in time, because they have carelessly misunderstood the message, got lost on the way or run into a tree, they are not liable' (*Capital & Counties v Hampshire County Council* [1997] QB 1004 (CA), 1030 (Stuart-Smith LJ)), approved by Lord Hoffmann in *Gorringe v Calderdale MBC* [2004] UKHL 15 [32]).

Ambulance services owe a duty of care in responding to a 999 call: *Kent v Griffiths* [2001] QB 36.

● *Pop quiz* ●
In *Michael* [81], Lord Toulson evidently viewed the different treatment of 999 calls for ambulances as justified by special considerations about ambulance services. Can you reconcile *Michael* and *Capital & Counties* with *Kent v Griffiths*?

14.4.5 Conclusion on negligence

There is no general duty in tort to use public powers with care. But we should return to the easy part of negligence liability: if you are run down because a lorry driver for a public authority was not watching the road, it will do the authority no good at all to argue that negligence liability would create a drain on public funds, or that liability would distort the way in which it carries out its statutory powers. One way of explaining the difference between those easy cases and the controversial cases such as *East Suffolk Rivers* or *Michael* is that a careless driver acting on behalf of a public authority causes harm, whereas the authorities in *East Suffolk Rivers* and *Michael* only failed to provide to a private person a benefit that the authority was responsible for providing to the public. But that distinction (between carelessly causing harm and carelessly failing to help) does not give a rigid division between situations in which public authorities do and do not have a duty of care, because of the 'normal professional duty of care' recognized in *X* and extended in *Phelps* and *Barrett*. In the professional duty-of-care cases, a public authority really is liable for loss caused by a careless failure to help the claimant. And in deciding whether to take a child from its parents, a public authority has no duty to the parents to take care before making a decision that harms them.

The complexity of the law can best be understood if we remember the basic principle of *Caparo*: that negligence liability does not arise unless it is reasonable to impose a duty of care. There needs to be some other ground for establishing a duty of care than that a careful exercise of a public authority's powers could prevent injury or damage to the claimant. There is today no more definite guide to identifying a duty of care than the following.

Summary of public authorities' duties of care

- A duty of care cannot require a public authority not to act in a way in which it has been given **discretion** to act.
- A duty of care cannot arise if identifying it would require a court to pass judgment on **non-justiciable considerations**.
- A duty of care cannot arise unless there is a relation of **proximity**, and it is **foreseeable** that the loss in question will result if reasonable care is not taken.
- Even if there is proximity and the loss is foreseeable, a duty of care cannot arise unless there is a further **justice ingredient**: it must be fair, just, and reasonable to impose the duty of care (the justice ingredient is to be identified 'incrementally' by analogy with previous cases).
- The judges will avoid imposing a duty of care if doing so would inappropriately **interfere with the functions of a public authority**. But imposing ordinary duties of care—for example, to drive carefully and to perform surgery with reasonable care—is never an inappropriate interference.
- Public authorities may be vicariously liable for failures by doctors and certain other professions to meet the '**normal professional duty of care**'.

Because of these principles:

- if a public authority had power to help the claimant, but carelessly failed to do so, that is not enough for it to have breached a duty of care (even if there is, as in *Michael*, a very strong proximity between defendant and claimant); but
- a public authority may breach a duty of care by carelessly failing to use its power to benefit a claimant if it has a relation with the claimant that involves

an **assumption of responsibility** towards the claimant, or if it has induced **reliance by the claimant**, or if there is **general reliance** on the public authority's reasonably careful performance of its functions.

● *Pop quiz* ●

Can you find the authority for the above propositions?

14.5 Misfeasance in public office: the administrative tort

Abuse of power is a ground of judicial review (see 7.1.2). It also forms the basis of the one tort that is specifically public. It may be a tort (a tort of 'misfeasance', sometimes called 'malfeasance') for a public officer to act in a way that causes loss to the claimant, if the conduct is an abuse of power. But abuse of power is not enough. A power may be abused by a very unreasonable decision, and that is not enough to count as a tort. There is a further requirement, which narrowly restricts the tort of misfeasance: the abuse of power must be done in **bad faith**.

If loss is caused by official abuse in bad faith, the claim has the justice ingredient. And no deference is owed to the public officer if the court can identify an abuse (that is why abuse of power is a ground of judicial review of discretionary powers).

For centuries, the courts have held that justice requires compensation for a malicious abuse of public power. In other torts, it really does not matter whether the defendant is exercising public power. But a defendant can only be liable in the tort of misfeasance if the alleged misconduct was *in public office*. Suppose that a private person deliberately decides not to come forward with evidence that would convict an offender, and does so in the hope that the offender will injure you, and the offender is acquitted and does injure you. You have no right of action. But if the defendant is a public officer, the requirements of the tort would be satisfied by such an improper motive unless the alleged tortious conduct were completely independent of the public role of the officer in question (*Racz v Home Office* [1994] 2 AC 45, 53 (Lord Jauncey)). The misfeasance need not be an exercise of a public law power (or even a legal power). The essential thing is that the defendant abused his or her position as a public officer (*Cornelius v Hackney LBC* [2002] EWCA Civ 1073).

Note that although misfeasance is a public tort, it is also a very *personal* tort. It is committed by particular human beings holding public office, not by public authorities. Yet the public authority is vicariously liable, as the result of a landmark decision of the House of Lords in *Racz*. The decision in *Racz* rejected an *obiter dictum* of Lord Bridge in *R v Deputy Governor of Parkhurst Prison, ex p Hague* [1992] 1 AC 58, 164, that the prison governor and the Home Office cannot be vicariously liable for the tort of a prison officer who 'deliberately acts outside the scope of his authority'. That statement would have ruled out vicarious liability for misfeasance altogether, since in every instance of misfeasance the public officer deliberately acts outside the scope of authority. Since *Racz*, it is clear that the public authority is vicariously liable for 'a misguided and unauthorised method of performing [its officers'] authorised duties', although not for 'an unlawful frolic of their own' (*Racz*, 53).

You can see that this tort based on abuse of public office presents a tempting alternative for claimants who cannot succeed in negligence: if only they can persuade the court that the conduct that caused their loss was a malicious abuse of power, they have a right to compensation for loss caused. The claimant does not have to establish that the defendant owed a duty of care. The tort of misfeasance has come under heavy pressure from such claims. A public officer who has acted in bad faith deserves no deference, but the advance of this tort has created difficult questions of what counts as bad faith. So far, however, bad faith (which is, roughly, an attitude towards the claimant that the law condemns as culpable) remains as a restrictive requirement of the tort.

Misfeasance in *Michael*

In *Michael v Chief Constable of South Wales* [2015] UKSC 2, the claimants initially pleaded misfeasance in a public office, as well as negligence and liability under the Human Rights Act. You can see why: if they had succeeded in that claim, they would have received damages in tort even if the police had no duty of care. But the claimants abandoned the misfeasance claim (*Michael* [3]), no doubt because it had become clear that it would be impossible for them to establish the elements of the tort, by showing that the response to Ms Michael's 999 call was deliberately or recklessly sabotaged.

14.5.1 Malice and bad faith

The House of Lords identified two forms of the tort in *Three Rivers District Council v Bank of England* [2003] 2 AC 1, a landmark case based on the collapse of the Bank of Credit and Commerce International (BCCI) in 1991. Investors who had lost billions of pounds wanted compensation from the Bank of England. They claimed that the Bank of England, as the regulatory agency for banks, ought to have closed down BCCI before their money disappeared in massive frauds by BCCI officers. The investors had no claim in negligence: the Bank of England owed them no duty of care, but only a public law duty to use its regulatory powers lawfully. But the amounts at stake made it worth pursuing a difficult, ground-breaking, and ultimately doomed claim in misfeasance in a public office.

The two forms of the tort identified by Lord Steyn in *Three Rivers* have two different 'mental elements'.[12] He calls the first 'targeted malice' (191); the second is

---

[12] The two forms were suggested by Lord Diplock in *Dunlop v Woollahra* [1982] AC 158, 172: '[I]n the absence of malice, passing without knowledge of its invalidity a resolution which is devoid of any legal effect is not conduct that of itself is capable of amounting to such "misfeasance" as is a necessary element in this tort.' The suggestion is that *either* malice *or* knowledge of unlawfulness would satisfy the mental element of the tort.

knowledge that the conduct in question is unlawful (or recklessness as to whether it is unlawful), combined with knowledge that it will probably harm people in the position of the claimant (or recklessness as to whether it will harm such people). The unifying element in the two forms of the tort is, Lord Steyn said, 'abuse of power accompanied by subjective bad faith' (191).

There was no precedent for recklessness as a sufficient mental element for the tort. Lord Steyn added it in *Three Rivers*, saying that this 'organic development' in the law was appropriate because 'reckless indifference to consequences is as blameworthy as deliberately seeking such consequences' (192). That statement is too broad, because some acts, such as murder, are especially blameworthy just because they are deliberate. Yet there is good reason for the decision. Recklessness of the kind Lord Steyn mentions provides the justice ingredient that is needed for tort liability, because there is a special injustice in the use of a public office with such disregard for the interests that the law protects. And judges do not need to defer to a public official who is abusing power in bad faith. Even after *Three Rivers*, the tort requires more than just unlawful action causing harm; it also requires a form of contempt for the people affected. Misfeasance in a public office is *not* a tort of ultra-negligence.

What is subjective and what is objective?

A subjective test requires asking a question about the subject of the test (that is, the person whose conduct is being tested), and an objective test requires asking a question about an object (that is, about what the subject did, or failed to do). The standard of care in negligence law is objective (it is a question of whether the object—what the subject did—was reasonable). The standard of bad faith in misfeasance is subjective (it is a question of whether the subject whose conduct is being tested had a bad attitude). These confusing labels can be left out, by the way: it adds nothing to a mental element in a legal standard to call it 'subjective', because any mental element must be subjective (e.g., if an act is done with malice, the malice is a feature of the subject).

So, in Lord Steyn's phrase 'subjective bad faith', the word 'subjective' (which he could have omitted) should be read as just a reminder that when he says that the tort requires bad faith, he means that it is not enough for the claimant to show that the defendant did something unreasonable (even extremely unreasonable). The defendant is not liable unless he or she had a bad attitude as well.

14.5.2 The scope of the tort: proximity and causation

Suppose that a public officer has engaged in misfeasance (that is, he or she has acted unlawfully with the intention or the reckless attitude that Lord Steyn describes). Which persons qualify as claimants, and which losses will be compensated? In addition to its importance for understanding the mental element of the tort, *Three Rivers* is important for the House of Lords' approach to these questions as to its scope.

The Court of Appeal had held that the tort was limited by a requirement of proximity between defendant and claimant. The House of Lords overturned that holding. As a result, the only limits on the availability of damages (if a public officer has engaged in misfeasance) are:

- that the defendant knew that it was probable that loss of the kind suffered would result, or was reckless as to whether it would result (192); and

- that the claimant's loss was caused by the misfeasance (194).

The causation question is a 'matter of fact' to be decided at trial.

After *Three Rivers*, the Court of Appeal clarified the scope of the tort in *Akenzua v Home Office* [2002] EWCA Civ 1470. Delroy Denton had been arrested in 1994 for possession of drugs and an offensive weapon. He turned out to have entered the UK on a false passport from Jamaica, where he had a record of violent crime. In order to use him as an informer on Yardie gangsters, police and immigration officers decided to let him remain in the UK. His drugs charges and, later, a rape charge, were dropped. Then, in 1995, he raped a woman and stabbed her to death. When her family sued the Home Office and the police for misfeasance, the High Court struck out their claim. But the Court of Appeal reversed that decision, and allowed the case to go to trial. The point in dispute was as to the scope of the tort, not as to the nature of the mental element. That is, the defendants claimed that, under the law as stated in *Three Rivers*, before the second form of the tort could arise, the claimant needed to be a member of an identifiable class of persons towards whose interests the defendant was knowingly or recklessly indifferent. But the Court of Appeal in *Akenzua* decided that the existence of an identifiable class was not essential. Harm to a person arising from Denton's known tendencies would be enough if the other elements of the tort were made out [20]. That result follows naturally from *Three Rivers*.

New law made in *Three Rivers*

- An abusive failure to exercise a power can count as misfeasance (the failure must be deliberate or reckless).

- A defendant who did not know that the conduct in question was unlawful may be liable in misfeasance as long as he or she acted with bad faith—a requirement that is satisfied by recklessness as to whether the conduct is unlawful.

- The tort can be committed without any intention that the loss in question should be caused; it is not enough that the loss is foreseeable, but it *is* enough that the defendant was reckless as to a probable loss.

- There is no requirement of proximity between the claimant and the defendant (confirmed, in the face of some uncertainty about the necessity of an identifiable class of claimants, in *Akenzua*).

14.5.3 Has the tort expanded?

If you read *Three Rivers* and *Akenzua* quickly, it may seem that the tort has been opened up in a way that exposes public authorities to a vast range of new claims in tort. Now a public officer can commit the tort without setting out to hurt anyone, without knowing that the conduct is unlawful, and without even knowing that it will hurt anyone.

Yet, for the present, the tort remains narrowly limited. The House of Lords' decision in *Three Rivers* left the claimants needing to prove not merely that the Bank of England had acted unlawfully, or even that its conduct was *Wednesbury* unreasonable. That would not nearly be enough: in order to succeed, the claimants would have had to prove that the officers of the Bank did not care whether their conduct was lawful, and did not care whether their conduct would harm investors. Even a grossly careless decision is not enough. The test is so demanding that the House of Lords was divided in the decision, not over the ingredients of the tort, but over whether it was an abuse of the process of the court for the case to proceed to a trial, because it was so implausible that the claimants would be able to establish those ingredients. Lord Hobhouse wrote that 'the real grievance of the actual plaintiffs is that they believe that the law ought to allow actions in negligence against regulators but they accept through their counsel that it does not' (289). And Lord Millett thought that there was simply no prospect of success, because the Bank of England would have a defence if its officers honestly believed that there was a reasonable prospect that BCCI would be rescued (294).

The only really significant opening up of misfeasance in public office as a result of *Three Rivers* is that claims will be more likely to proceed to trial. They are not very much more likely to succeed. Speculative allegations of misfeasance will not fail on the question of scope, or on the distinction between intention and recklessness (where *Three Rivers* does change the law, at least by stating what the House of Lords had not determined before). The real hurdle is like the hurdle in sustaining an allegation of fraud in a commercial dispute: without some evidence of corruption or a vendetta, it is very hard to prove an allegation of bad faith in a trial.

Think of the situation in *Akenzua*. If the defendants were reckless in the sense required by *Three Rivers*, they were reckless as to whether the risk of releasing Denton was bad enough that they had a public law duty to keep him in custody—that is, they were reckless as to whether it was so unreasonable to release him because of the risk, that no reasonable police authority would do so. Even if it *was Wednesbury* unreasonable, they would have a defence if they had honestly believed that it was not *Wednesbury* unreasonable. And to succeed the *claimants* would have to prove that they had no honest belief of that kind.

If the police and immigration officers arranged for Denton to be at large for any of the following reasons, they would commit the tort of misfeasance:

- they wanted him to kill a particular person;

- they wanted to see him kill someone, but they did not care who it was;

- they took a bribe to release him, hoping that he would not hurt anyone but knowing that he probably would;

- they did not care whether they were creating a risk so bad (so out of proportion to the protection of the public that they might achieve by using him as an informer) that no reasonable authority would do so.

But they would not commit the tort if they honestly believed the risk was worthwhile, even if the belief was *Wednesbury* unreasonable (because it was extremely unreasonable to assess the risk as they did, or because they were absurdly optimistic about the benefits of using him as an informer). Even a *Wednesbury*-unreasonable decision is not misfeasance, if it is honest. The House of Lords in *Three Rivers* itself insisted that the recklessness required for the tort must be 'advertent',[13] rather than a mere failure to pay attention to a relevant consideration. We might put it that it would not be misfeasance if the public officers were simply to fail to give any thought to the interests of people whom Denton might attack.

But since the courts will not strike out the claim in a case like *Three Rivers*, a claimant can go to trial, and try to persuade the trial judge that bad faith can be inferred from the failure of a public authority to meet a reasonable standard. That will ordinarily be impossible, as *Three Rivers* itself demonstrates: after years of seeking to prove that the Bank of England had acted in bad faith, the claimants' case collapsed and they had to pay 'indemnity costs' (that is, costs that cover a greater-than-usual proportion of the defendant's legal expenses) on the ground that they had made scandalous allegations that they could not substantiate.

After *Three Rivers*, it is much easier for a claimant to force a defendant into an entirely pointless trial. Given the choice, of course, claimants would prefer to proceed to trial and take their chances than to have their claim struck out. And proceeding to trial may give them leverage in negotiating with the public authority defendant, even when there is no serious prospect of success.

Special exemplary damages to punish arbitrary use of government power

In *Muuse v Home Secretary* [2010] EWCA Civ 453, [84], the Court of Appeal held that the claimant, falsely imprisoned on immigration grounds, had been the victim of an 'outrageous and arbitrary exercise of executive power'. A claim for misfeasance in public office could not succeed, because the trial judge had not found that the Home Office officials were recklessly indifferent to the legality of his detention. But for the tort of false imprisonment, which the Home Office admitted, the Court of Appeal awarded £27,500 in exemplary damages (designed to punish the defendant) and £7,500 in aggravated damages (designed to compensate the claimant for the special injury inflicted by cruel conduct), in addition to compensatory damages of £25,000.

---

[13]   See the important discussion of forms of recklessness by Lord Steyn (192–3).

> Exemplary damages are also available in claims for misfeasance in public office. But even though every successful claim in misfeasance involves official misconduct, exemplary damages will not ordinarily be awarded; there must be some additionally oppressive or arbitrary conduct that calls for punishment 'to deter and to vindicate the strength of the law' (*Kuddus v Chief Constable of Leicestershire* [2001] UKHL 29, [91] (Lord Hutton)).

14.5.4 Criminal liability

Just as it is no defence to a claim in tort that the defendant was a public authority, it is no defence to criminal charges for a defendant to claim to have been acting on behalf of a public authority. The difference is that if, for example, a police officer commits an assault while on duty, it is the officer in his or her own personal capacity who can be prosecuted, rather than the police authority. There is no vicarious criminal liability.

In *East Suffolk Rivers*, Lord Atkin said that, in the case of a statutory duty, 'speaking generally, in the absence of special sanctions imposed by the statute the breach of duty amounts to a common law misdemeanour' (88). Lord Atkin was speaking far *too* generally. Not all unlawful acts of public authorities are torts, and they are not all crimes either.

What more does it take for an unlawful act to be a crime? It is enough if the conduct would be a crime if a private person committed it. And there is also one specifically public criminal offence (just as misfeasance in a public office is a specifically public tort): **misconduct in a public office**. It has a very broad reach, but it is not enough that the defendant acted unlawfully. The misconduct in question has to be the sort that justifies a criminal sanction. Corruption is the obvious example. In *R v Bowden* [1996] 1 WLR 98 (CA), the chief building maintenance officer of Stoke City Council was convicted of the offence for sending council employees to do plumbing and electrical work on the home of 'the defendant's lady friend'.

But the offence does not require corruption, and it does not even require that the official take any action; a neglect of a duty is enough, if it is wilful and criminally culpable. In *R v Dytham* [1979] QB 722, a police officer was convicted of misconduct for having done nothing to intervene or to get help as a man was beaten to death outside a club. The same behaviour by a private person would not have been a crime.

In addition to ordinary criminal liabilities, some important offences have been created by statute to control the actions of public officials. Torture, in particular, is a crime if it is done by 'a public official or person acting in an official capacity' (Criminal Justice Act 1988 s 134).

14.6 Just satisfaction: damages under the Human Rights Act 1998

Suppose a man is detained unlawfully and tortured by a public official. If a court were merely to declare that there had been an infringement of his Convention right not to be tortured, that would not be enough to vindicate his right. The state will not really be treating him as a person who has a right not to be tortured, unless he gets some sort of remedy for the harm done as well. In case the state does not give a proper remedy, Art 41 of the Convention provides that the Strasbourg Court:

> ' . . . shall, if necessary, afford just satisfaction to the injured party. '

To enable English courts to give the satisfaction that a claimant can obtain in Strasbourg, the Human Rights Act 1998 s 8 gives the court power to:

> ' . . . grant such relief or remedy, or make such order, within its powers as it considers just and appropriate. '

Courts that have power to award damages may do so, although only if 'the court is satisfied that the award is necessary to afford just satisfaction to the person in whose favour it is made' (s 8(3)). Many ways of infringing a Convention right would be torts. If a claimant suffered torture at the hands of a public official, an award of damages under the Human Rights Act 1998 would not be necessary, because the remedy in the tort of battery will count as 'just satisfaction'. But in addition to tort damages, the claimant would be entitled to a declaration under the Human Rights Act that the Art 3 right not to be subject to torture had been violated. Where an infringement of a Convention right is a tort, separate Human Rights Act damages will only be available if the remedy in tort is insufficient to vindicate the Convention right (see *Dobson v Thames Water* [2007] EWHC 2021).

Human Rights Act damages had the potential to revolutionize the law of compensation for unlawful executive action. Remember the crucial restrictions on damages that arise from the elements of torts: misfeasance in a public office requires bad faith, and negligence requires special reasons for identifying a duty of care. Infringing Convention rights does not require bad faith, and even if there is no common law duty of care, a failure to help someone may be an infringement of a Convention right, where the Strasbourg Court has interpreted the rights as implying positive duties (see 3.6). Art 2 has been interpreted as imposing a positive duty to protect life, Art 3 has been interpreted as imposing duties to prevent degrading treatment, and the Art 8 right to respect for private and family life has been interpreted as imposing duties to provide certain forms of support to persons and families. Any bad administrative decision that affects a claimant (e.g., any failure to provide a social security benefit that a person is entitled to) has the potential to affect his or her private and family life. And maladministration (see 13.5)—which is not otherwise unlawful in English administrative law—may affect people's private and family life severely.

What's more, damages are not available at common law for loss caused by a failure of due process, but since Art 6 of the Convention guarantees many of the same process rights as the common law, the Human Rights Act gives courts power to award damages for failures of due process. The Human Rights Act gave judges tools that they might have used to order compensation for more or less any unlawful action that causes substantial loss to a claimant.

But there has been no such revolution. The English courts have carefully restricted the availability of damages, following strands in the decisions of the Strasbourg Court. Human Rights Act damages have an important, but surprisingly limited, role in the vindication of Convention rights and in the control of administration. Public authorities now need to make good certain losses caused by infringements of Convention rights, but the courts have decided that 'just satisfaction'—which simply means something that ought to satisfy the victim—can often be given without an award of damages, or with the payment of such a modest sum that it would be dwarfed by the cost of the litigation. The reasons for the restrained approach reflect the purpose of the European Convention and of the Human Rights Act; yet we will see that those reasons also turn out to be related to the restrictions on compensation in the law of tort.

14.6.1 Article 8: private and family life

Anufrijeva v Southwark LBC (see 3.6.2, p 101) was the turning point towards the restrained approach to Human Rights Act damages. Several asylum seekers claimed that local authorities had infringed their rights under Art 8 of the Convention. The authorities failed to provide special needs accommodation required by statute for a family member, and maladministration led to delay in deciding two successful asylum applications and in allowing family members to join a refugee in the United Kingdom.

The allegations in *Anufrijeva* would not support a claim for damages in tort. Failing to provide a housing benefit or financial support required by statute is unlawful, and a court could order the benefit to be paid, but the unlawful failure gives a claimant no right to compensation for any resulting loss.[14] Maladministration causing delay is not even unlawful.[15] So the claimants in *Anufrijeva* needed something beyond the law of tort. They argued that unlawful conduct and maladministration by the public authorities had had a detrimental impact on their private and family life, infringing Art 8. The Court of Appeal held that maladministration causing delay and unlawful withholding of benefits do not generally infringe Art 8, even though they do affect private and family life detrimentally. Article 8 is not infringed unless a public authority shows a culpable lack of respect for the claimant's private and family life (which requires, in particular, that the officials involved know that the claimant's private and family life are at risk), and the impact on the claimant is severe [45], [48] and [143]. Carelessness is not enough in itself. So claimants cannot bypass the restrictions on liability in misfeasance and in negligence, by pointing out that administrative failings affect their private and family life.

The law remains uncertain because of the unlimited variety of ways in which administrative failures may affect people, and because of the Strasbourg Court's

....

[14] Except that depriving someone of a benefit in bad faith would be misfeasance: in *Anufrijeva*, there was no claim in misfeasance.

[15] Unless the public authority has acted in a way that is *Wednesbury* unreasonable by delaying. And delay would not support a claim in tort unless it amounted to misfeasance.

unpredictable decisions.[16] In English law, it seems that an unlawful failure to provide social security benefits *may* amount to an infringement of Art 8, if it is bad enough, and in *Bernard v Enfield* [2002] EWHC 2282, the High Court awarded damages of £10,000 for infringement of Art 8 where a local authority had shown 'a singular lack of respect for the claimants' private and family life' [34] by housing a family in a flat that left the severely disabled mother 'lacking privacy in the most undignified of circumstances' [32], so that the claimants had to 'endure deplorable conditions, wholly inimical to private and family life' [61]. As Sullivan J held in *Bernard*: 'Whether the breach of statutory duty has also resulted in an infringement of the claimants' Article 8 rights will depend upon all the circumstances of the case. Just what was the effect of the breach in practical terms on the claimants' family and private life?' [32]. The Court of Appeal in *Anufrijeva* discussed the award in *Bernard* and evidently approved of it. Yet *Anufrijeva* reflects the judges' decision not to use the Human Rights Act to impose any general liability on public authorities to compensate people whom they unlawfully fail to help. A claim that Art 8 has been infringed by an unlawful failure to help is bound to fail, if it was merely careless. Compensation for maladministration or even for unlawful delay in providing a benefit will only be available in the case of grave violations causing severe loss (*Anufrijeva* [67]).

The Court of Appeal found no infringement of Art 8 in *Anufrijeva*, so there was no question of whether an award of damages was necessary for just satisfaction. But the judges took the opportunity to write a guide to the award of damages under the Human Rights Act at [49]–[56], which the House of Lords approved (*R (Greenfield) v Home Secretary* [2005] UKHL 14 [9] and [30]). Here are the highlights.

- The victim of a tort has a right to compensation for loss caused by the tort,[17] but under the Human Rights Act 1998, if a Convention right has been infringed, it does not necessarily follow that the court must award compensation [50].

- The point of litigation in the Strasbourg Court or the English courts is 'to bring the infringement to an end and the question of compensation will be secondary' [53].

- [T]here is a balance to be drawn between the interests of the victim and those of the public as a whole' [55].

- Exemplary damages are not awarded (*Anufrijeva* [55]).[18]

---

[16] So, e.g., for unlawful telephone surveillance, the European Court of Human Rights awarded £10,000 damages with no proof of harm caused by the breach in *Halford v United Kingdom* (1997) 24 EHRR 523, but the declaration of a violation of Art 8 was considered enough for just satisfaction for rather similar tapping of a home phone in *Kopp v Switzerland* (1998) 27 EHRR 93.

[17] Tort damages are nominal, when no real loss has resulted from the tort. There are no nominal damages in negligence, because a right of action arises in negligence only if there was real loss. For an infringement of a Convention right, courts never need to award nominal damages. If there is no real loss, no damages are necessary for just satisfaction.

[18] The European Court of Human Rights rejected a claim for exemplary damages in *Selçuk and Asker v Turkey* (1998) 26 EHRR 477.

- Damages are only awarded as a 'last resort' [56] (although it is a last resort that the court ought to take in the exercise of its discretion, whenever it decides that damages are necessary for just satisfaction).

If a court finds that a Convention right has been infringed, it then asks a further question: whether it is necessary to award compensation for any loss caused by the infringement, in order to vindicate the claimant's Convention right. In a case like *Bernard*, the question will really be whether sending the claimant away with no damages would represent a failure *by the court*, on behalf of the United Kingdom, to show respect for the claimant's right to private and family life. The Human Rights Act does not give damages for all harm caused to private and family life; it empowers judges to award damages if doing so is necessary in order to give just satisfaction, where the defendant showed disrespect for the claimant's private or family life.

14.6.2 Article 2: the right to life

The Convention says that 'Everyone's right to life shall be protected by law', and the Strasbourg Court has gone further, interpreting that provision as conferring a right to certain forms of administrative action to protect life.[19] In *Rabone v Pennine Care NHS Foundation Trust* [2012] UKSC 2 [33], the Supreme Court held that there is a duty under Art 2 'to protect persons from a real and immediate risk of suicide at least where they are under the control of the state', and the justices had no hesitation in extending that duty to a psychiatric patient who was known to be suicidal, even where she was not detained by the defendant.

Claimants have asked the English courts and the Strasbourg Court to extend this liability, as a way of getting around the rule that the police owe no duty of care in negligence to people who might be injured by a potential suspect (see 14.4.4). As we will see, Art 2 has made a great difference in some cases. But the potential for claimants is limited by the Strasbourg Court's approach. It has held that the police only infringe Art 2 through careless investigation in a restricted set of cases:

> ' ... it must be established to [the court's] satisfaction that the authorities knew or ought to have known at the time of the existence of a real and immediate risk to the life of an identified individual or individuals from the criminal acts of a third party and that they failed to take measures within the scope of their powers which, judged reasonably, might have been expected to avoid that risk. '[20]

Interpreted in this way, the right in Art 2 is not a very promising way of getting around the rule in *Hill v Chief Constable of West Yorkshire* [1989] AC 53 that, when investigating crime, the police owe no duty of care to members of the public who might be

---

[19] See 3.6, p 93, on positive duties. The Strasbourg Court established the positive duty to take measures to protect life in *Osman v United Kingdom* (1998) 29 EHRR 245 [115].

[20] *Osman v United Kingdom* (1998) 29 EHRR 245 [116].

injured or killed by a suspect or potential suspect. The claimant in *Hill* itself would not have succeeded under Art 2, for example. And in *Van Colle v Chief Constable of Hertfordshire* [2008] UKHL 50, the House of Lords unanimously held that Art 2 had not been infringed in a case in which the police knew that a suspect had made threats to a witness to a crime, and the suspect then murdered the witness. Even though a disciplinary tribunal had found that a police officer had failed to perform his duties conscientiously in investigating the suspect's attempts to intimidate witnesses, the police had not had reason to perceive a real and immediate risk to the witness's life. The claimant in *Van Colle* persevered and went to Strasbourg, but the European Court of Human Rights held that the Art 2 right had not been violated because there was no 'decisive stage' at which the police ought to have known of a real and immediate risk to the victim's life (*Van Colle v United Kingdom* (2013) 56 EHRR 23 [103]).

The crucial point, demonstrated by *Van Colle*, is that Art 2 is not infringed merely because a person is murdered after the police culpably fail to take steps that might have prevented the murder. But the Strasbourg Court in *Osman* rejected the United Kingdom's argument that a failure of policing only infringes Art 2 if it is 'tantamount to gross negligence or wilful disregard of the duty to protect life' (*Osman* [116]). If the police do know (or ought to know) that there is a real and imminent threat to someone's life, Lord Bingham held in *Van Colle* that they would infringe the right to life if they 'did not do all that could reasonably be expected of them' to avoid the risk [30].

And that aspect of the courts' interpretation of the ECHR means that liability for breach of Art 2 really does extend to one situation in which there is no negligence liability: in *Michael v Chief Constable of South Wales* [2015] UKSC 2 (see 14.4.1), the police ought to have known that there was a real and imminent threat to Ms Michael's life, after she had phoned 999 and told them so. For this reason, although the Supreme Court upheld the striking out of the claim in negligence, the claim of a breach of the positive duty in Art 2 was allowed to go to trial. Here we see where Art 2 really does make a difference. *Michael* was a textbook case in which the *Osman* test is met. There was a breach of Art 2 if the authorities knew or ought to have known of a real and immediate risk to Ms Michael's life, and failed to take measures that they could have taken to prevent it.

The difference the Human Rights Act makes

Michael's case is a striking illustration of the role of claims for damages under the Human Rights Act.

On the one hand, it was a major setback for the claimants when the claim in negligence was struck out. If they succeeded in negligence, the court could be expected to make a very large award of damages; as we will see below, an award of damages under the Human Rights Act in respect of the very same loss could be expected to be very modest. Lord Toulson, writing for the majority in *Michael*, said that if the Court fashioned a duty of care in tort that had the same scope as Art 2, it would be 'gold plating the claimant's Convention rights by providing compensation on a different basis from the claim under the Human Rights Act 1998' [125].

On the other hand, the claim under the Human Rights Act gave the *Michael* claimants something valuable that the law of tort did not give them: an opportunity to go to trial, which is a way of holding the defendant accountable for their loss, and the prospect of a relatively modest award of damages that would signify that accountability. And the prospect of going to trial gave them an opportunity to negotiate with the defendant over compensation.

Art 2 has not only affected policing; the decision in *Smith v Ministry of Defence* [2013] UKSC 41 raised the prospect of litigation over Art 2 in every case of injury in military operations. Along with the holding that a claim in negligence could proceed to trial where soldiers had been killed by roadside bombs or in friendly fire incidents (see 14.4.4), the Supreme Court held that the claimants' claims under the Human Rights Act, based on Art 2 of the Convention, could proceed to trial. Lord Hope for the majority wrote that Art 2 'is not violated simply by deploying servicemen and women on active service overseas as part of an organised military force which is properly equipped and capable of defending itself' [62]. That suggests that the judges have taken it upon themselves to decide whether a military force is properly equipped and capable of defending itself. But the majority decision did not go that far. Just as he had done in respect of duties of care in negligence (see 14.4.4), Lord Hope insisted that positive obligations under Art 2 should not be 'unrealistic or disproportionate' [76]. If the allegations relate to decisions on procurement or operations 'at a high level of command and closely linked to the exercise of political judgment and issues of policy', or if they relate to decisions made while 'actively engaged in direct contact with the enemy', then they will be 'beyond the reach of article 2' [76]. But a claim might fall in 'the middle ground'. In the middle ground, Lord Hope said, 'No hard and fast rules can be laid down. It will require the exercise of judgment. This can only be done in the light of the facts of each case' [76].

The result, just as in the negligence aspect of the *Smith* case, is to generate a prospect of litigation if anything goes wrong, which military commanders must take into account in planning military operations.

Self-restraint in Strasbourg

In *Hirst v UK (No 2)* (2006) 42 EHRR 41, the Strasbourg Court held that it is contrary to the Convention for the UK to have a blanket ban on voting by prisoners (see 3.10). Years and years later, the British government has not acted to comply with the decision. So in *Firth v UK* [2014] ECHR 874, a group of claimants who had been denied the vote while in prison asked the Strasbourg Court to order the UK to pay compensation. There had been speculation that the judges would feel that they had to award compensation to give 'just satisfaction' (Art 41), since the claimants were getting no satisfaction at all from the British government. But, in a very terse judgment, the Strasbourg Court concluded 'the finding of a violation constitutes sufficient just satisfaction for any non-pecuniary damage sustained by the applicants' [18]. It is a reminder that the Strasbourg Court does not treat compensation as a default setting. There has to be some reason for compensation other than the fact that a Convention right has been violated.

14.6.3 Article 6: due process

It is very, very hard to get damages for infringement of the right in Art 6 to a fair hearing within a reasonable time. In *R (Greenfield) v Secretary of State for the Home Department* [2005] UKHL 14, a prisoner was given twenty-one additional days of imprisonment by the prison management, as a penalty for an alleged drugs offence, after a hearing that infringed Art 6 (the decision maker was not independent, and the prisoner was wrongly denied legal representation). If that failure of due process had been a tort, then the court would have had to assess damages by asking what would have happened if due process had been given, awarding a figure designed to make the claimant as well off as if that had happened. But it was not a tort, and under the Human Rights Act Lord Bingham, with whom all of the Law Lords agreed, held that no damages should be awarded. He approved the view of the Court of Appeal in *Anufrijeva* that, in Human Rights Act cases, 'the concern will usually be to bring the infringement to an end and any question of compensation will be of secondary, if any, importance' (cited in *Greenfield*, at [9]). He said that 'the pursuit of damages should rarely, if ever, be an end in itself in an Article 6 case', and approved the *Anufrijeva* warning that claimants should not seek damages that are bound to be much smaller than the cost of pursuing them (*Greenfield* [30]). The difference between damages in tort and under the Human Rights Act started to emerge in *Anufrijeva*. But in *Greenfield*, Lord Bingham went further. The Court of Appeal in *Anufrijeva*, at [74], had held that, although 'the discretionary exercise' of awarding Human Rights Act damages is different from the remedial decision in tort law, 'the levels of damages awarded in respect of torts' may 'provide some rough guidance' in exercising the s 8 discretion. Lord Bingham said in *Greenfield*, at [19], that 'this approach should not be followed' and held that the Human Rights Act 'is not a tort statute', and that its purpose 'was not to give victims better remedies at home than they could recover in Strasbourg', so that the English courts should not award damages by analogy to tort damages.

In *Osman v United Kingdom* (1998) 29 EHRR 245 [164], the Strasbourg Court awarded damages for infringement of Art 6 'on an equitable basis' of £10,000, holding that 'the Court cannot speculate as to the outcome' that would result from proceedings conforming to Art 6. 'On an equitable basis' means that the damages are meant to treat the claimant fairly without actually reflecting the magnitude of the loss that was suffered.

The 'equitable' approach

The Strasbourg Court sometimes presumes that a loss has occurred and awards equitable damages, and has made awards without even taking evidence on what the actual loss is.[21] This approach adds to the inconsistency of the Court's compensation decisions. Yet there can be good reasons for taking the equitable approach: the Strasbourg Court is not well equipped to assess losses, its compensatory role is not central, and its awards are modest. A modest figure plucked

---

21 See, e.g., *Öneryildiz v Turkey* (2005) 41 EHRR 20 [159].

out of the air is its way of vindicating a claimant's Convention rights, through an award that is largely symbolic.

Lord Bingham held in *Greenfield*, at [19], that the English courts should follow the Strasbourg Court's equitable approach: 'The court routinely describes its awards as equitable, which I take to mean that they are not precisely calculated but are judged by the court to be fair in the individual case. Judges in England and Wales must also make a similar judgment in the case before them.'

In *Greenfield*, Lord Bingham saw no need even for the modest damages that can be awarded on the equitable approach. The remedy of a declaration itself gave just satisfaction. It has been accepted in the Strasbourg Court that financial compensation is not generally necessary to give just satisfaction for an infringement of Art 6 (*Kingsley v United Kingdom* (2002) 35 EHRR 177). But it has not been uncontroversial: two dissenting judges in *Kingsley* said: '[A] mere finding of a violation cannot constitute in itself adequate just satisfaction. Applicants are entitled to something more than a mere moral victory or the satisfaction of having contributed to enriching the Court's case law' [O-III2].

14.6.4 The puzzle about Human Rights Act damages: what are they for?

In tort, the question of whether compensation should be awarded is packed into the question of liability. Once the defendant is held liable in tort, the defendant must compensate the claimant for loss caused by the tort. Under the Convention, however, the court (in Strasbourg or in England) finds an infringement and *then* asks a separate question: whether a remedy in damages is needed to do justice. As Lord Hoffmann put it in *R (Wilkinson) v Inland Revenue Commissioners* [2005] UKHL 30 [25], the Human Rights Act 1998 'did not create a statutory duty for which damages could be recovered as if the breach of Convention rights was a tort in English law. And the jurisprudence of the Strasbourg court shows that it is more concerned with upholding human rights in member States than with awarding damages'. The Supreme Court held in *R (Sturnham) v Parole Board* [2013] UKSC 23, reaffirming *Greenfield*, that 'the quantum of awards under section 8 should broadly reflect the level of awards made by the European court in comparable cases' (Lord Reed [13]). If Human Rights Act damages and compensation awarded by the Strasbourg Court are not like tort damages, and are not the courts' central concern, what are they for?

Strasbourg decisions often say that the point is to put the claimant in the same position as if the right had not been infringed: in *Piersack v Belgium* (1984) 7 EHRR 251, [12], 'the applicant should as far as possible be put in the position he would have been in had the requirements of Art. 6 not been disregarded'.[22] This principle was adopted

---

[22] Compare *Hobbs v United Kingdom* (2007) 44 EHRR 54 [67]: '[T]he principle underlying the provision of just satisfaction is that the applicant should as far as possible be put in the position he would have enjoyed had the violation found by the Court not occurred.'

by the Court of Appeal in *Anufrijeva* [59] and by the House of Lords in *Greenfield* [10] and *Wilkinson* [26]. Yet that idea is simply incompatible with the decisions that the Strasbourg Court has made. Putting a claimant in the same position as if a wrong had not been committed is the underlying principle of *tort* damages (*Livingstone v Rawyards Coal Co* (1880) 5 App Cas 25, 39 (Lord Blackburn)). And the courts' practice, both in Strasbourg and England, regularly defies the supposed principle.

First of all, the Strasbourg Court's 'equitable' approach is a rejection of the attempt to put the claimant in the same position as if the right had not been infringed. Instead of putting a figure on the amount of the loss and awarding that amount in compensation, the Court offers a token amount, which is meant to be a fair response to the infringement of a right. Token awards are in fact quite standard, where damages are necessary for just satisfaction (e.g., see *Bernard v Enfield* [2002] EWHC 2282—£10,000 for infringement of Art 8; *R (KB) v Mental Health Review Tribunal* [2003] EWHC 193—amounts ranging from £750 to £4,000 to six claimants for delays in tribunal hearings). In *R (Lee-Hirons) v Secretary of State for Justice* [2016] UKSC 46 [46], damages were held to be unnecessary for a failure for twelve days to give reasons for returning the claimant to detention in a secure hospital, and Lord Wilson held that the effect on a claimant would have to be 'grave', before a court would award damages for breach of the duty to give reasons under Art 5.2 of the Convention.

Second—and this is really another aspect of the equitable approach—the claimant's own conduct is relevant to an award of just satisfaction in Strasbourg, so that the purpose of an award is not really compensatory at all. In *McCann v United Kingdom* (1996) 21 EHRR 97, three IRA members went to Gibraltar to carry out a terrorist attack. SAS soldiers who planned to arrest them shot them dead, thinking that they were about to set off car bombs. By a narrow 10–9 majority, the European Court of Human Rights held that the bombers' right to life had been infringed because the soldiers' instructions gave them a misguided impression that the bombers had to be shot to prevent explosions. If the Court had really set out to put the victims in the same position as if their Art 2 right had not been infringed, it would presumably have awarded the damages that the victims' families sought—a huge sum designed to put the claimants in the same position (so far as money could do it) as if the bombers had not been killed. But the Court dismissed the claim with little discussion: 'having regard to the fact that the three terrorist suspects who were killed had been intending to plant a bomb in Gibraltar, the Court does not consider it appropriate to make an award under this head' [219].

Here is the secret to these puzzles: awarding damages is a technique that judges can use to achieve the purpose of the Convention, which is to enforce the member state's commitment to respect the Convention rights. They are not to be awarded at all unless they are *necessary* for that purpose. Damages in tort are focused on the claimant, and designed to put the claimant in the same position as if their right had not been infringed.

Providing financial redress for loss caused by a violation of a right *can* be an essential step in vindicating the right; it depends on the nature of the violation. We should note that, in cases of identifiable pecuniary loss inflicted through the breach of a Convention right, the courts may make huge compensation awards under the Human

Rights Act. In *R (Infinis Plc) v Gas and Electricity Markets Authority* [2013] EWCA Civ 70, the defendant Authority refused accreditation for two power stations; the decision was held to have violated the right to protection of property in Art 1 of Protocol 1. Compensation of over £2 million was upheld by the Court of Appeal. The Authority had argued that the Court should not order payment of the full amount that had been lost as a result of the decision, because of the difference between the role of compensation in human rights cases and in tort cases. But the Court of Appeal held that 'the basic principle when deciding whether to award damages and the amount of any award is restitutio in integrum' [26]—that is, putting the claimant in the same position as if the loss had not been inflicted. Where the amount of the loss 'can readily be calculated' [27], the court may simply award it. The Court did not resolve the standing puzzle of Human Rights Act damages: how can *'restitutio in integrum'* be the principle of those damages, if the Strasbourg Court takes an equitable approach, and no effort is made to put an amount on the claimant's loss, when it is intangible? In fact, there ought to be no principle that a loss should be compensated, even if it can readily be calculated.

But at least we know that substantial compensation is not limited to identifiable pecuniary loss. Remember that many violations of Convention rights *are torts*. English law would fail to respect the right not to be tortured if torture were not a tort. Substantial damages are available, and that is the only adequate way of responding to the fact that the victim's right not to be tortured has been violated. But in other cases (such as *McCann*, or *Greenfield*), damages that aim to put the claimant in the position in which he or she would have been had the infringement not happened are not necessary for the purpose of treating the victim as a person whose Convention rights are respected, and making the UK a country that respects Convention rights. The question is whether, *after the court's decision*, the victim of a violation of a Convention right is in a position to complain that the UK does not uphold the rights guaranteed in the Convention. As Laws LJ put it in *D v Commissioner of Police of the Metropolis* [2015] EWCA 646, 'The focus is on the state's compliance, not the claimants loss' [66].

14.7 European Union law: a unique liability to compensate for unlawful conduct

There is *one* context in which public authorities are liable to compensate a claimant for loss caused by unlawful government conduct. In Case C-6/90 *Francovich v Italy* [1991] ECR I-5357, the European Court of Justice (ECJ) held that a claimant could get compensation in the court of a member state for loss caused by a failure to implement EU law. Italy had failed to implement an EU directive to protect workers from losing back pay when their employer went bankrupt. The ECJ awarded compensation against the Italian state to workers affected by a bankruptcy. The ECJ set requirements for liability for failure to implement a directive: the directive must have been intended to require the state to create identifiable rights for individuals, and the particular claimant's loss must have been caused by the failure to implement. The liability extends to any state action that violates EU law; it applies to state decisions that infringe directly effective rights. Later cases have required that the breach of EU law must be *serious*: '[T]he decisive test for finding that a breach of Community law is sufficiently serious is whether the member state or the Community institution concerned manifestly and gravely disregarded the limits on its discretion' (Case C-46/93 *Brasserie du Pêcheur* [1996] ECR I-1029 [55]).

That requirement of seriousness indicates what is going on in these EU cases: they are concerned with the relation between the European Union and its member states. *Francovich* compensation is targeted against disregard by member states of their legal obligations under EU law (including directives). The decision in *Francovich* was one of the ECJ's very inventive exercises in giving effect to EU law within the legal systems of member states, by giving 400 million people the opportunity to sue their government for damages if the state was refusing or failing to comply with EU law. The ECJ was trying to take a unique international agreement and make it into a legal order. State liability for loss caused by unlawful government action is an extraordinary technique for making EU law effective.

Administrative action contrary to EU law: liability to compensate, and *fines too*

In Case C-64/88 *Commission v France (Fisheries)* [1991] ECR I-2727, the ECJ held that France was not enforcing fishing quotas adequately. After giving France warnings, the Commission went back to the ECJ. In Case C-304/02 *Commission v France* [2005] ECR I-6263, the ECJ held that the sale of undersized fish, which France was failing to control, was enough 'to prejudice seriously . . . the Community system for conservation'. The ECJ imposed a lump sum fine of €20 million, plus a €58 million penalty payment for each six months of continued infringement. This liability for an administrative failure to implement EU law is part of the general liability of member states for violation of EU law. In domestic administrative law, there is nothing like this legal technique of enforcing public authorities' compliance with the law by fining them. That is partly because there is no equivalent in domestic law to the Commission (a body committed on behalf of the European Union to seeing that EU decisions have effect).

The decision invented a power in the ECJ to impose *both* a lump sum fine and a penalty payment (and to do so when the Commission had not asked for a lump sum fine). Like the liability to compensate in *Francovich*, it is another in the long line of creative ECJ moves to enhance the uniform effectiveness of EU law.

14.8 Conclusion: tort and the rule of law

Why has no such imperative been felt to make *English* law effective, by awarding compensation for loss caused by unlawful action? The common law judges have not been less inventive than the ECJ judges. Since the 1200s, they have been more or less actively intent on subjecting public authorities to the rule of law. But the simple point is that although the rule of law requires that public officials abide by the law, it does not require that loss caused by unlawful conduct of officials should always be compensated.

It is an important constitutional principle that reasons for compensation for wrongs by a private defendant are also reasons for compensation for wrongs by a public authority. That rule creates an important control on the exercise of discretionary powers, just by compensating a claimant for loss caused when the executive branch of government violates the respect for property and persons that we are entitled to from each other. Apart from that, compensation for wrongs requires some special legislative basis, such as the European Communities Act 1972 (giving effect in English law to *Francovich* compensation for breaches of EU law) or the Human Rights Act 1998.

But we should remember the one very important exception: a malicious abuse of public power leads to liability at common law to compensate, and may be a crime. Malicious abuses of power by private persons give no right to compensation, and are not in themselves criminal. The common law does not just declare abuses of power unlawful; it also remedies the harm done, where justice between persons and government demands it.

TAKE-HOME MESSAGE • • •

- There is **no general right to compensation** for a person who has been harmed by unlawful administrative action, or even for a person whose Convention rights have been violated.

- But there is **no general immunity** from liability in tort for public authorities.

- The **Human Rights Act 1998** authorizes damages for an unlawful violation of a Convention right if that is necessary in order to give the victim **just satisfaction**.

- The courts have refused to use common law **duties of care** to impose liability on a public authority that could and should have used its power to benefit a member of the public.

- Public authorities can be vicariously liable for a breach of the special duties of care that certain **professionals**, including doctors, educational psychologists, and teachers, owe to the persons for whom they care.

- A claimant is entitled to compensation from the UK government for loss caused by a serious failure to implement **EU directives** that were designed to lead to the conferment of identifiable rights on the claimant.

CRITICAL QUESTIONS • • •

1 **Should there be compensation for all loss caused by unlawful acts of public authorities?**

2   Should compensation depend on the wrongfulness of the official action? Why not on a principle that the public should pay for losses by a private individual that are incurred in achieving benefits for the public?

3   If it is not a tort for a public authority to cause you harm by acting unlawfully, why is misfeasance in public office a tort?

4   Do Human Rights Act damages make any real difference to the availability of compensation for unlawful administrative conduct?

5   Can a public authority be liable in negligence for carelessly misinterpreting a statute?

6   Does an action of a public authority have to be *ultra vires*, before it can be a tort? Is a driver or a surgeon working for a public authority acting *ultra vires*, if he or she drives carelessly or operates carelessly?

7   In *R v Minister of Agriculture, ex p Padfield* [1968] AC 997 (see 2.3, p 50), the House of Lords held that the Minister had used his statutory power for an improper purpose. Could the applicants for judicial review have succeeded in a claim for the tort of misfeasance in public office?

8   The claimants in *Three Rivers District Council v Bank of England* [2003] 2 AC 1 thought that they had lost their money because the regulator, the Bank of England, had not shut down the Bank of Credit and Commerce International when it should have. Why couldn't they just claim that the Bank of England had been negligent?

READING • • •

Entick v Carrington (1765) 19 Howell's St Tr 1029
East Suffolk Rivers Catchment Board v Kent [1941] AC 74
Case C-6/90 *Francovich v Italy* [1991] ECR I–5357
X v Bedfordshire [1995] 2 AC 633
Case C-46/93 *Brasserie du Pêcheur* [1996] ECR I–1029
Stovin v Wise [1996] AC 923
Phelps v Hillingdon [2001] 2 AC 619
Three Rivers District Council v Bank of England [2003] 2 AC 1
Anufrijeva v Southwark LBC [2003] EWCA Civ 1406
Michael v Chief Constable of South Wales [2015] UKSC 2

On tort liability of public authorities in general:
Tom Cornford, *Towards a Public Law of Tort* (Routledge 2008)
On negligence:
Donal Nolan, 'The Liability of Public Authorities for Failing to Confer Benefits' (2011) 127 LQR 260

Stelios Tofaris and Sandy Steel, 'Negligence Liability for Omissions and the Police' (2016) 75 CLJ 128

On misfeasance in a public office:

Donal Nolan, 'A Public Law Tort' in K Barker et al, eds, *Private Law and Power* (Hart 2016)

On the judicialization of war:

Jonathan Morgan, 'Negligence into Battle' [2013] CLJ 14

On the *Three Rivers* litigation:

Adrian Zuckerman, 'A Colossal Wreck: The *BCCI-Three Rivers* Litigation' [2006] Civil Justice Quarterly 287

On Human Rights Act damages:

Richard Clayton, 'HRA Damages after *Greenfield*: Where Are We Now?' (2006) 11 Judicial Review 230

Should there be monetary remedies against unlawful conduct in general?

Roderick Bagshaw, 'Monetary Remedies in Public Law: Misdiagnosis and Misprescription' (2006) 26 Legal Studies 4

Tom Cornford, 'Administrative Redress: The Law Commission's Consultation Paper' [2009] PL 70—arguing that the monetary remedy contemplated in the Consultation Paper would replace much of negligence law with an unprincipled remedy

Michael Fordham, 'Monetary Awards in Judicial Review' [2009] PL 1 —in favour of compensation for loss caused by unlawful conduct in general

The following online resources accompany this chapter: **summaries** of key cases and legislation; **updates** on the law; **guidance** for answering the pop quizzes and questions; and **links** to legislation, cases, and useful websites.

15 Contracts

Contracts are used to structure the legal relationship between government and private service providers. And contract forms a new model both for relationships among public agencies and for the overall relationship between government and the people it serves. For the government, the challenge is to deliver services with integrity, equity, and efficiency. For administrative law, the challenge is to provide forms of accountability that do what the law can do to promote those goals.

LOOK FOR • • •

- The ways in which, for the purpose of contracting, public bodies are the same as *and* different from private parties.

- The potential for government by contract to provide:
  - better government services, with
  - more transparency, and
  - less waste.

- The risk that government by contract will, on the contrary, damage each of those values.

- The role of courts in supervising contracting decisions of public authorities.

- The scope of legal control over private bodies that ought to be accountable for acting in the public interest.

> ' ... the role of the State is not to control, but to enable. Making modern public services the cornerstone of the enabling state—where the State provides strategic direction not micro-management—requires a transformation of how we deliver our services. '
>
> *Tony Blair, Foreword to Capability Reviews,* **Cabinet Office, July 2006**

15.1 Government by contract and proportionate administration

For centuries, governments have been using contracts to enable and to empower— and to pursue their own agendas. Modern England was shaped by the move from the medieval feudal system to a system in which the government got things done through contracts. The importance of contracts grew, evolved, and was then eclipsed after World War II, when Britain's welfare system and state industries were built on direct administration of huge government projects by government departments. But the role of contracts as an instrument of government has massively increased since the 1980s, as they have become the basis for new kinds of partnership between government and private companies. And the really new development since the 1980s is that contracts have become the model for agreements *within* government, between departments and the wide range of new agencies created to provide services.

Just as dispute resolution is not just a job for judges (see 12.7, p 475), administration is not just a job for government departments. The move toward **proportionate process** (see 12.1) means that there is no presumption that a legal dispute is to be resolved in a court (although courts have very far-reaching supervisory jurisdiction over institutions that resolve legal disputes).

This chapter explains the parallel development of a principle of **proportionate administration**—that is, delivery of public services through techniques of service provision and with techniques of accountability that are in proportion to the public interests at stake. There is now no presumption that public administration is to be conducted by a government department (although departments have a very far-reaching role in making and overseeing arrangements with private companies and with a variety of public agencies).

So we have undergone a third constitutional shift in public administration, which is more recent than the shift to proportionate process, or the judicial adventure of the twentieth century (see 2.6), and which is still under way. Like those shifts, the move to proportionate administration has ancient roots.

It was presumed in the mid-twentieth century that administration of public projects and programmes was a job for government officials. The idea was that public administration was to be done by servants of the Crown, exercising powers and carrying out duties assigned to them by Parliament, with funding appropriated by Parliament. They were to act under direction by ministers of the Crown. The ministers and the civil servants were accountable to the courts for the lawfulness of their conduct. The civil servants were accountable to the minister leading their department for all aspects of their conduct. The ministers were accountable to Parliament for all aspects of their departments' work. That was the **command model** of public administration.

Since the 1980s, the United Kingdom has been shaking off the command model. Some major government functions have been privatized. Others are delivered by public agencies that are partly independent from government departments, or by private companies under contracts with government departments. Departments retain very far-reaching control—in a variety of forms—over the delivery of public services. Civil servants have a new role of advising ministers on how to secure value for money from private service providers. The government is committed to deliver services through techniques tailored for efficiency, and tailored to provide accountability in forms that are **proportionate** to the need for accountability.

The obvious potential benefit is an enhancement of public services, and the obvious potential danger is loss of public accountability in the push for efficient service provision by companies that are accountable only to their private shareholders. But we should not take it for granted that government by contract will either enhance services or destroy accountability.

15.1.1 Privatization and regulation

Since the 1970s, the following great government projects have all been privatized:

- coal mining (nationalized 1946, privatized 1994);

- railways (nationalized 1948, privatized 1982–93);

- telephone service (largely nationalized 1912, privatized 1984);

- Royal Mail (established 1516 through private monopolies, nationalized 1660, privatized 2013–2015);[1]

- utilities:
  - water (nationalized from local authorities in 1973, privatized 1989);
  - gas (nationalized 1948, privatized 1986); and
  - electricity (nationalized 1947, privatized 1991).

Privatization means that the government has got out of administering the enterprise altogether, having sold its coal mines and railways and utilities to private enterprise, subject to regulation by government agencies. Privatization reflects a decision that an industry should not be administered by the government.

Robocop (1987): a US administrative law classic
In a world of rampant crime and disorder, Omni Consumer Products runs the Detroit police force. The corporation plans to replace the police officers with robots. After Model ED-209 goes on a killing spree, a young executive introduces Robocop as a safer alternative: a robot built from the remains of a police officer killed on duty. A crooked rival has Robocop's inventor killed by drug traffickers,

---

[1] http://www.royalmailgroup.com/500-years-history-delivered-your-doorstep; http://researchbriefings. files.parliament.uk/documents/SN06668/SN06668.pdf

and orders ED-209 to destroy Robocop. Robocop seeks revenge. The moral is, don't sell the police force to a crooked multinational corporation.

Robocop is the story of a failure of **proportionality** in public administration. Detroit privatized the police to achieve effective public service delivery. The resulting loss of accountability meant that Detroit lost the rule of law. The movie is a satire on government by contract.

The UK has not sold off the police. But much of the business of government (the postal service, the health service, schools, nursing homes, the prison service...) has been transformed by the impulse that went out of control in *Robocop*. The challenge for public administration in the real world is to achieve accountability techniques that are proportionate to the need for accountability, in a particular field of public service.

Privatization actually *eliminates* problems of administrative law, by taking an industry out of public administration. It generates new problems that call for new legal regimes of regulation. The privatization of the government's monopoly industries changed accountability problems within the public sector into problems of how to regulate parts of the private sector. A whole range of new **non-departmental public bodies** (NDPBs), independent of government, was created to prevent abuses of market position, and to protect the public from other sorts of service failure. Other similar agencies have been created to regulate industries that had never been nationalized (such as agriculture and legal services), and the Competition and Markets Authority investigates concerns referred from other regulators or from government, with powers to stop companies from merging, or to require a company to sell off part of its business. The most important regulatory bodies are the following.

Major regulatory agencies

Care Quality Commission
Charity Commission for England and Wales
Competition and Markets Authority
Financial Conduct Authority (independent regulator for financial services)
Food Standards Agency
General Medical Council
Legal Services Board
NHS Improvement (independent regulator of NHS foundation trusts)
Gambling Commission
Ofcom (independent regulator for communications industries)
Office of Rail and Road
Ofgem (Office of Gas and Electricity Markets)
Ofqual (Office of the qualifications and examinations regulator)
Ofsted (Office for Standards in Education)
Ofwat (Water Services Regulation Authority)

Independent regulation of industries by these bodies is a new development since the 1980s. It has now become a stable structural feature of government in the UK, although successive governments tend to respond to problems in particular industries by rearranging them. The Conservative–Liberal Democrat coalition government established in May 2010 set out to reform public bodies and to abolish many of them, but none of the major regulatory bodies were abolished. That reflects a reliance on technical expertise, and trust in the capacity of regulators with job security and independence from government to pursue the public good. The regulatory agencies are subject to judicial review, and the courts will impose due process. But agencies' independence, their expertise, and their familiarity with the industry in question mean that it will be very difficult to persuade a court to intervene on matters of substance.[2] The legislation setting them up gives them very open-ended roles in setting standards that are generally very technical, which means that the judges will not substitute their judgment for that of the regulator on the substance of the standards.

The industries they regulate (especially communications, utilities, and food) are so vast that these regulators have substantial power over the nation's economy. Are they accountable for their exercise of that power? Deferential judicial review is really only a guard against process failures. Several of the agencies make reports to Parliament; this process provides a form of accountability. The regulators have transparent processes and their decisions are public, which also subjects them to a form of accountability (see 15.2). But no one regulates the regulators. Regulators, like judges, ombudsmen, and auditors, are not chiefly controlled by processes to resolve disputes about their decisions. Instead, the system relies on the openness of their work, on good appointments, and on the independence of the regulators.

15.1.2 Public–private partnerships

Many aspects of the business of government that have not been privatized have been contracted out. For any organization, contracting out means taking a function that has been done in-house and hiring someone else to do it (and, ideally, to do it better and/or at lower cost). It was invented by large companies in the 1980s, and applied to government by the Conservatives and then Labour. When the resulting deal involves an ongoing relationship, the government calls it a **'public–private partnership'** (PPP). New public enterprises such as the National Lottery have been constructed from the start on the basis that:

- the government decides what service is to be provided (and typically presents legislation to Parliament to structure the scheme, and to authorize expenditure);

- companies bid for the contract to provide the service;

- an NDPB awards a licence or licences to one or more providers; and

- the NDPB regulates the work of the private service provider (with the sanction of withdrawing the provider's licence or deciding not to renew it).

----

2   See, e.g., *R (Grierson) v Ofcom* [2005] EWHC 1899.

The crucial feature of an NDPB is that it is not part of a department. So it is not directly responsible to a minister in the way that a department is, and the relationship with the government can be set out in an agreement that puts the NDPB more or less at arm's length from the ministers. The idea is that government should decide what public goods need to be secured, but that 'delivery' can best be achieved by involving private companies that are seeking profits. It will work if the incentives of a marketplace can be brought to bear so that the profit seeker will avoid waste in supplying the service, and at the same time address the requirements of the people who receive the service (the 'consumers' or 'customers'). It remains the role of the public authority in the partnership to set standards, and to see that they are met.

Delegation of powers and contracting out

In *Carltona v Commissioners of Works* [1943] 2 All ER 560 (CA), Lord Greene said that the act of an official in a department can count as the act of the minister. The functions given to ministers are 'so multifarious that no minister could ever attend to them . . . . Constitutionally, the decision of such an official is, of course, the decision of the Minister. The Minister is responsible. It is he who must answer before Parliament for anything that his officials have done under his authority . . . ' (563). As a result, if officials in a department make a decision on behalf of a minister, it is not an *ultra vires* delegation of a statutory power that Parliament conferred on the minister, and it is not a violation of the **genuine exercise** rule (see 8.1.2). The *Carltona* principle was extended to NDPBs in *Castle v Crown Prosecution Service* [2014] EWHC 587.

But conversely, the *Carltona* principle does not apply if the allocation of the power to a minister was intended to provide a 'safeguard' for a claimant, 'which can only be meaningful' if the power is exercised personally by the minister. So in *R (Bourgass) v Secretary of State for Justice* [2015] UKSC 54, the Supreme Court held that a requirement that a prisoner could not be segregated for more than seventy-two hours 'without the authority of the Secretary of State' could not be satisfied by a decision by a prison governor [88]–[90].[3]

The Deregulation and Contracting Out Act 1994 allows a minister to delegate discretions to a **private body** in the same way as discretions can be exercised by civil servants under *Carltona*. It does that in one of the most remarkable pieces of opaque drafting in the statute books (s 69(2)): 'If a Minister by order so provides, a function to which this section applies may be exercised by, or by employees of, such person (if any) as may be authorised in that behalf by the office-holder or Minister whose function it is.' Under this provision, the difference between private companies and departmental officials is that the acts of departmental officials can count as acts of the minister without the minister having issued an order.

---

[3] The government promptly changed the prison rules after the Supreme Court's decision, to allow a prison governor to make the decision: Prison and Young Offender Institution (Amendment) Rules 2015/1638 rule 2(3).

> The provision applies to any function of a minister conferred by 'any enactment' (s 69(1)(a)), but with exclusions: functions that interfere with the liberty of an individual, powers of search or seizure and entry to property, and powers to make subordinate legislation must still be exercised by the minister or civil servants.

15.1.3 Internal contracting

Public–private partnerships and the privatization of some industries have served as a model for new ways of regulating relations *within* government, through techniques that mimic the market-based, incentive-driven operations of private companies. **Internal contracting** is the practice of regulating public administration through agreements between government agencies. **Executive agencies** operate under arrangements with government departments that are like contracts with private bodies. Unlike an NDPB, an executive agency is part of a department and carries out ministerial policy, but with a degree of independence that depends on the agency's purpose. There are hundreds of these agencies, including Her Majesty's Courts and Tribunals Service, the Prison Service, UK Visas and Immigration, and the Child Maintenance Service. Three-quarters of central government employees work in them. The traditional accountability to the minister is kept in principle (with the minister in turn accountable to Parliament for oversight of the agency). To oversee the agency, the department formulates an agreement that sets out the agency's budget, and procedures for the department to set and monitor performance targets. It is a strange sort of agreement: it is not a contract, because the agency has no separate legal personality from the department. And it is not really a deal negotiated between two parties who could each take their business elsewhere. But the 'agreement' is symbolically important as a government-by-contract technique that aims at the business-like creation of incentives and setting of standards for delivery of a service.

Executive agencies can be investigated (and their chief executives can be grilled) by parliamentary select committees. But since the theory was that an agency would operate within a policy framework set by the department, the ideal is that accountability should be secured through the agreement. With the agency restricted to delivering a service, and with the department setting targets and regulating the agency through the framework agreement, what could go wrong?

In fact, executive agencies have been faced with some of the most massive administrative challenges in the country. The Child Support Agency, the Rural Payments Agency, and the Prison Service, for example, operate controversial and difficult schemes in which the policy formation aspects of 'service provision' cannot be picked apart from implementation. It might seem that the internal contracting model would enable a department to make policy in the public interest, and then to contract with an agency for the implementation of its policy. But implementation inevitably involves elaborating the policy. It would be a mistake to think that an executive agency can be a good service provider because delivery does not engage controversial issues of the public interest. The question is, instead, whether the public interest can best be promoted by an organization that has a form of independence and distance from the parent department, or whether the independence and distance destroy an important form of accountability.

Non-ministerial departments: the ultimate in executive independence

Some government agencies need to be completely independent of ministerial oversight. The important examples are the Crown Prosecution Service, the Serious Fraud Office, HM Revenue and Customs, and the major regulatory agencies listed in 15.1.1. They are 'non-ministerial departments', because they are run by civil servants, but are not responsible to ministers.

15.1.4 Citizens as customers

Finally, the relationship between all of these organizations and the people they serve has been reconceived on the contract model: the citizen has become a '**customer**', whose choices are meant to drive public service delivery in the way that customer choices drive pizza delivery.

'Choose and Book': patients as customers in the NHS

On the 'NHS Choices' webpage[4]—which serves as the front page for the whole National Health Service—you can find facilities and services offered at different hospitals, performance ratings, patient feedback, waiting times, and even patient survival rates for some operations. Then, if you need a hip replacement, you can go to 'Choose and Book'.[5] You can get advice from your GP, but you can make your own choice of a hospital for your operation with a location that suits you, a convenient time slot, good facilities, and an attractive survival rate.

The point is both to give patients a new form of control over their own lives, and to improve service delivery by creating a market: NHS service providers are subjected to an economic imperative to compete with each other for the funding that flows from patient choices. The dangers include the potential market failures that may arise from faulty information in any market: inefficient choices will distort service delivery if the customer has limited information, or is misled by it. And the service providers only indirectly face incentives to improve services; their direct incentives are to improve customer perceptions through advertising, public relations, and finding ways to raise their ratings on the NHS Choices site. The dangers also include the risk of damaging the public service ethos of the health service.

---

4 http://www.nhs.uk.

5 http://www.chooseandbook.nhs.uk/.

15.1.5 New public management

These things go together: privatization, PPPs, new executive agencies with arrangements modelled on PPPs, and a wide-ranging commitment to 'customer' choice. The whole array of business-like attitudes to public service provision has been called **'new public management'** for so long that it really isn't new anymore.[6] Introduced by the Thatcher government in the 1980s, it became standard practice in the UK when New Labour came into power in 1997 and took the agenda forward in new, more sophisticated ways. Today, the new public management agenda involves:

> '... a focus on management, performance appraisal and efficiency; the use of agencies which deal with each other on a user-pay basis; the use of quasi-markets and contracting out to foster competition; cost-cutting; and a style of management which emphasises, among other things, output targets, limited term contracts, monetary incentives and freedom to manage.'[7]

Consider Figure 15.1, a flow chart for administrative structuring. In 1998, the Cabinet Office under New Labour directed public bodies to ask these questions every five years, regarding every activity that they do.

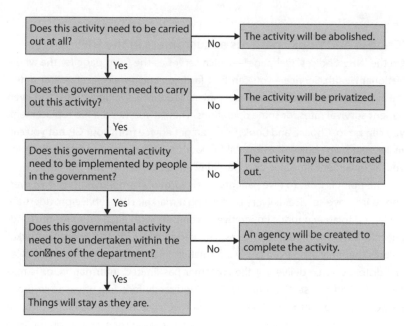

Figure 15.1 New public management: the flow chart

. . . .
6   See, e.g., Christopher Pollitt, *Managerialism and the Public Services* (2nd edn, Blackwell, 1993).

7   *Public Service*, Report of the House of Lords Select Committee on the Public Service (chaired by Lord Slynn), 19 January 1998, available at http://www.publications.parliament.uk/pa/ld199798/ldselect/ldpubsrv/055/psrep01.htm.

The 2010 Conservative–Liberal Democrat coalition government brought a change of emphasis. Its reforms of public administration inclined against creating an agency to undertake an activity, except where technical expertise or political impartiality and independence from ministers are essential. But the structure of the reasoning remains the same, and it shows the durability of new public management. **Proportionality** (see 1.5.6, p 27) provides the pattern: the first question is what is needed, and then the government's involvement in the relevant activity should be proportionate to the need.

It seems to be the right approach in principle: why would we want more government activity than is required for accomplishing something worthwhile? But the right approach in principle can lead in practice to decisions that damage the public interest—either by abandoning valuable governmental functions, or by damaging accountability for their performance. Those two results will come about if economy and efficiency come to be seen as the purposes of government action, when in fact they are only crucial requirements in carrying out functions whose purpose is public service.

So the basic model for achieving proportionality in twenty-first-century British public administration—accepted by every government since the 1980s—is to privatize services that can be privatized, to contract out what cannot be privatized, and to create internal analogues of contracts for provision of services that cannot be contracted out. The common strand in all of these aspects of government by contract needs to be appreciated: they divide the public decision as to what public services should be provided from the provision of the service. Contract is the central device in the still-evolving management of public services. The core management technique is a deal between the policy maker and the service provider (between government and a private service provider, or between government agencies).

Government by contract has the potential to achieve proportionality in public service by enabling people to make choices as consumers. And it has the potential to damage the ethos of public service, and to abandon administrative accountability in favour of service provision by companies seeking to profit by taking public money and cutting corners. This chapter focuses on the challenges that the political choices raise for the law, and on the ways in which legal accountability can be secured under government by contract. But the legal and the political are intertwined. We will see that the search for proportionate administration requires further political choices to be made—by the courts, and by the government, and by Parliament—in the development of legal accountability measures.

Robocop blows up genuine proportionality dangers into a thriller. But now think of every other police movie you have seen, in which the bad cops are public servants working under the command model. The accountability disaster in *Robocop* arises from privatization, but accountability can be fragile in traditional public administration, too. It would be simplistic to think that the new model, which is still in flux, simply represents a loss of public accountability for the sake of efficient public services. Accountability and efficiency are both more complicated than that.

FROM THE MISTS OF TIME

If only by hiring private persons to do jobs, governments have always used contracts (*except* those governments that have not accepted that anything is private). In England, government by contract emerged in the fourteenth century, when the feudal techniques for raising armies broke down. As Lord Sumption has written,

> 'The last English King to make extensive use of the feudal military obligation was Edward I, who died in 1307. The last summons of feudal host was in 1327. From the middle of the fourteenth century, the wars of the Kings of England were fought by volunteers who served for honour and wages. Their obligations were based on contract and on money payment, and not on the tenure of land.'[8]

To pay those volunteer soldiers for extended campaigns, the King needed to make deals with the nobles who were in theory obliged to provide troops. Parliament was a forum for working out the deals between King and country that were needed for fighting the French: Parliament started in the late Middle Ages as the first public–private partnership, and evolved into a general political accountability mechanism.

In early modern times, Britain's imperial policy emerged through deals between the Crown and private companies of investors and adventurers in North America (the Hudson's Bay Company) and India: with a massive private army and a huge bureaucracy, ruling a fifth of the world's population, the East India Company had wider powers than Omni Consumer Products had in the fictional Detroit of *Robocop*.

15.2 Accountability and efficiency

In any public project, there are various ways in which different actors may be held accountable **through** different processes, **for** different aspects of their conduct, **to** different institutions or to the public.

In principle, the media and voters in an election and the people's representatives in the House of Commons can hold the government to account to the public for any aspect of public service provision. But those general forms of accountability are not effective at achieving good administration in particular cases. Particular cases come to the attention of the media and Parliament only when there is a scandal. Even when a scandal leads to questions in the House of Commons, Parliament is likely to be an ineffective forum for achieving justice.

---

[8] 'Magna Carta Then and Now', 9 March 2015: http://www.supremecourt.uk/docs/speech-150309.pdf.

Table 15.1 Examples of accountability

		To	Through	For
Ministers		Parliament	Questions in the House of Commons[9]	Their department's work
MPs		Electors	An election	Their conduct in office and their policies
A private company in a PPP	are accountable	The partner department or agency	An action in the High Court[10]	Compliance with the contract
Civil servants		Ministers	Managerial control	Implementing government policy
Courts		The parties, and the public	Openness in their process, and the giving of reasons	Just and lawful decisions
All of the above		The public	The media	Anything that interests the media and cannot be kept secret

Legal accountability techniques should hold government accountable in ways that cannot be secured through parliamentary politics or the force of public opinion. Legal accountability is essential for providing good public services with integrity. The challenge in this chapter is to work out how accountability for particular decisions can best be secured through law, when the government uses contract as a technique of administration.

A contract itself is an accountability structure. It identifies what a party is accountable **for**, and identifies (or takes for granted) processes **through** which the party may be held accountable **to** the other party (see Table 15.1). Here is the promise for achieving economy and efficiency through contractual techniques: competition for business can stimulate higher quality in the provision of public services, with less waste. Several companies competing for customers can provide some services better and more cheaply than a government department can. The profit pressure motivates the company both to provide what the customers really want, and to do so without wasting money. If the company faces competition from other companies, it will be under

....

9   There are other accountability mechanisms in Parliament, including the National Audit Office, select committees and Public Bill committees, and the Parliamentary Commissioner for Standards. All of these techniques are backed by the government's need for the confidence of the House of Commons.

10   An action for breach of contract is *not* the main accountability mechanism for contracting out, although it forms a backstop that can give force to the department's ability to hold a contractor to targets set out in the agreement and to demand a remedy. Commercial pressure on contractors to perform well in order to secure further government contracts can also enhance the effectiveness of the contract as an accountability technique.

pressure to provide a good service at a low cost to the user. It is really difficult to organize government departments so that they provide good services at low cost.

Also, and equally importantly, the career advancement pressure on individual employees will operate differently in a private organization, where it will be tied to the profit pressure on the company. Private companies can be wasteful, but they tend to be better at tying the criteria for their employees' rewards and advancement to success in delivering valued services at low cost.

15.2.1 Accountability illustrated: care for the disabled

In the UK, as part of the creation of a welfare state after World War II, the National Assistance Act 1948 required local authorities to provide housing for elderly or disabled people who needed care that was not otherwise available to them. The local authorities could operate nursing homes of their own or provide housing by arrangement with a charity. As part of the shift to government by contract, the Conservatives' National Health Service and Community Care Act 1990 (s 42) amended the 1948 Act to allow local authorities to contract out to bodies providing housing 'professionally or by way of trade or business'. How can accountability be secured if provision of care in nursing homes is contracted out?

The service should be provided in a way that achieves a good public purpose without waste, and with integrity (that is, honest, faithful application of a scheme) and with equity (that is, substantive fairness). In the provision of housing for disabled people in nursing homes, do those purposes require accountability to the resident in the nursing home? Or accountability to Parliament? Or accountability to the taxpayer? Or to a court or tribunal? It's obvious: those purposes require all of these forms of accountability, and more. Accountability to Parliament will help to ensure the accomplishment of Parliament's purposes in creating the scheme. Accountability to the taxpayer will put pressure on the government to achieve those purposes without waste. Accountability to the resident in the nursing home will protect the integrity of the scheme by helping to ensure that it is not operated in a way that abuses anyone or withholds benefits from anyone arbitrarily. And accountability to the resident will also help to ensure that the purpose of the scheme is accomplished; if the scheme itself is a good one, that result will promote equity.

Legal accountability may offer ways of enhancing accountability to the resident, for example through a claim *by* the resident for breach of contract (if he or she has a contract with the nursing home). Judicial review of the conduct of the nursing home (as in *R v North and East Devon Health Authority, ex p Coughlan* [2001] QB 213— see 8.4.4, p 303) enhances the nursing home's accountability to the resident, with the authority of an independent court with a supervisory jurisdiction to impose the rule of law on the administration. And accountability of staff in the nursing home to a court through a criminal prosecution for murder or assault is essential for the protection of vulnerable people.

Accountability techniques carry dangers and costs. Accountability to the taxpayer may put pressure on the government not only to avoid waste, but also to favour the wealthy by cutting support for the destitute. Accountability to the patient through a court will subject the scheme's operators to expensive litigation that can be pursued by people who have no legitimate complaint (**process cost**—see 4.2, p 125), and may lead to distorted decision making that privileges the particular complainant in a way that damages the ability of a home to benefit other residents or potential residents (**process danger**—see 4.2, p 125). Process danger and process cost are instances of accountability danger and accountability cost.

Accountability is not necessarily a good thing

It depends on the form of accountability, and whether it promotes good government without creating disproportionate costs or dangers. Judges, for example, are accountable to the public and the parties because they have to hear cases in open court and give reasons for many of their decisions. But it would be an abandonment of the rule of law if courts could be held to account **to** any other institution for the justice or lawfulness of their decisions **through** any technique for interfering with the judges' decision, or for interfering with their employment as judges. And Parliament must not be held to account **to** courts **through** judicial review for the wisdom of its enactments.

The government could build and operate nursing homes, or contract the work out to a private nursing home operator, or privatize and give funding to the disabled to buy services from private homes. The potential benefit from privatizing or contracting out public services is that private companies may be able to provide them more efficiently, with less waste than a government department. Efficiency will mean better services, or lower cost to the public, or both. The potential drawback is loss of accountability for integrity and equity and quality of service. But the challenge is not to choose whether to have unaccountable, but efficient, private delivery, or inefficient, but accountable, public delivery. The choices are extremely complex because private agencies are not necessarily more efficient *or* less accountable than public agencies, and accountability and efficiency are not always opposed to each other. Accountability is not simply opposed to efficiency; in fact, some forms of accountability are necessary for securing efficiency.

Accountability in public administration (in all of its forms) is a way of securing some public good. Here are three public goods that a scheme of social care should aim for:

(1) the social provision of places in good nursing homes for those who need them;

(2) efficiency in provision; and

(3) responsible application of the scheme.

The first good requires good strategy and funding. And (since the first good is the provision of good **homes**) it requires that residents be treated with respect, as people who should be involved in decisions about their home. Market mechanisms may help to secure the second good, but they may put pressure on the application of the scheme. The third good requires sound decisions as to whether a particular person needs care, and whether he or she is able to pay for it. Legal accountability techniques should provide redress against failures in the application of the scheme. But such techniques should be developed in a way that does not impair efficient provision (by subjecting the scheme to overly expensive processes, or by requiring the provision of services that will not promote the first good, for example by privileging a complainant over other residents).

What about equity? It is the form of social justice that justifies the whole scheme. It can only be achieved through the political construction of a scheme that sets out to provide homes to meet real needs, *and* efficient implementation, *and* application that not only has integrity, but also involves the exercise of discretions with concern to meet the needs that justify the scheme.

The question of how, if at all, legal accountability techniques can help to secure equity in nursing home provision is one of the most challenging in public law, and we will come to grips with it (15.5), after dealing with the capacity of public authorities to enter into contracts (15.3) and surveying legal techniques for controlling public authorities' decisions whether to enter into contracts (15.4).

15.3 Capacity to contract

15.3.1 The Crown

The Crown has an inherent (see 7.2.1, p 248) general power to contract, exercised on its behalf by departments. The capacity to contract is not a prerogative of the Crown, because the Crown has it in the same way as most public authorities. It is *not exactly* the same as private persons' legal power to contract, because the law gives private persons the power to contract for the purpose of enabling them to exercise the autonomy that an individual or a private commercial association ought to have in a civil society. Public authorities have power to contract because it is useful for the fulfilment of their roles, and because there is nothing unjust or contrary to constitutional principle in their capacity to contract.

Yet the law finds something awkward about the Crown's liability in contract. At common law, the only remedy for breach of contract was a 'petition of right'. In legal terms, it was merely a request, although the practice was for the Crown to ask the High Court to advise whether the petition should be granted, and to accept the advice. It worked because the government found it useful to establish a practice of acting as if it were legally bound by its agreements. Now, under the Crown Proceedings Act 1947 s 1, a contracting party can bring an ordinary claim against the Crown. But even today, injunctions and orders for specific performance cannot be made against the Crown (Crown Proceedings Act 1947 s 21).[11] And damages awards cannot be enforced against the Crown by ordinary processes of execution.

---

[11] Except that the Public Contracts Regulations 2006, SI 2006/5, implementing the EU procurement rules (see 15.4.4), give the court power to grant an injunction (reg 47(10)).

It may seem that being bound by contract would limit the freedom of decision that the Crown needs to have in the public interest. In fact, the truth is almost the reverse: being capable of entering into a binding agreement is extremely valuable. If you cannot bind yourself, it is hard to get people to deal with you. The Crown Proceedings Act 1947 overturned a legal immunity of the Crown for good constitutional reason: it is in the public interest for the Crown to be able to bind itself in the same effective, transparent manner as other contracting parties, and persons who contract with the government ought to have the same recourse as they have against other contracting parties.

But ministers cannot bind the Crown in a way that will obstruct the future use of the prerogative. During World War I, the government gave an undertaking to a Swedish shipping company not to detain its ship in Britain. But, once it arrived, the government refused to let the ship leave. The company sought damages for breach of contract (through a petition of right against the Crown). The judge advising on the petition held that there was no contract (*The Amphitrite* [1921] 3 KB 500).

How can that be reconciled with the Crown's general capacity to contract? In *The Amphitrite*, Rowlatt J held that the government can bind itself by a **commercial** contract, and if it does so, it must perform it or pay damages for breach like any other contracting party. But this was not a commercial contract; it was an arrangement as to future 'executive action' (503):

> ' . . . it is not competent for the Government to fetter its future executive action, which must necessarily be determined by the needs of the community when the question arises. It cannot by contract hamper its freedom of action in matters which concern the welfare of the State. '

Of course, commercial transactions are executive, too. So we have to read Rowlatt J's phrase 'executive action' as a technical term for, roughly, 'executive action that must, in the public interest, be unhindered by commitments that the government has purported to make'. The interesting thing about *The Amphitrite* doctrine is that it is a court that must decide when the public interest requires the government to have that freedom.

A contractor may find that an agreement with the government is unenforceable in matters which concern the welfare of the state. And the government's freedom means that the government lacks the power that comes with contractual competence: the inability to enter a binding contract can be very inconvenient. That potential inconvenience has not seriously hampered the government—or it would have put legislation before Parliament in the decades since *The Amphitrite* was decided.

15.3.2 Statutory bodies

The functions of other public authorities tend to be more specific than those of the Crown; when those functions require the power to contract, a public authority ought to have it—unless the power to contract creates a special risk of abuse.

But the traditional common law rule is that they have no general power to contract. Whether they can make contracts depends on whether the statute establishing the body empowers them to do so. And if the statute gives a limited power, a contract will be invalid if it is outside the power.

Consider a body with very specific powers—a railway company. Lord Blackburn held in *Attorney General v Great Eastern Railway* (1880) 5 App Cas 473, 481, that, 'where there is an Act of Parliament creating a corporation for a particular purpose, and giving it powers for that particular purpose, what it does not expressly or impliedly authorize is to be taken to be prohibited'. Local authorities have much wider functions, but Lord Templeman applied the traditional approach in *Hazell v Hammersmith LBC* [1992] 2 AC 1, 22: 'A local authority, although democratically elected and representative of the area, is not a sovereign body and can only do such things as are expressly or impliedly authorized by Parliament.'

This rule would be damaging, except that the courts are prepared to hold that the power to contract is impliedly authorized where the statutory body needs it. As Lord Selborne LC said in the *Great Eastern Railway* case: '[W]hatever may fairly be regarded as incidental to, or consequential upon, those things which the legislature has authorized, ought not (unless expressly prohibited) to be held, by judicial construction, to be ultra vires' (478). The result (although the courts have not put it this way) is the same as if there were a general doctrine that public authorities have inherent power to make contracts that they need to be able to make, if they are to carry out their responsibilities well.

Of course, it is not generally the judges' job to decide what public authorities need to do their job well. Parliament can always specify the powers of a public body if it sees fit, but if it does not do so, the courts have to decide what specification of those powers is necessary to accomplish what Parliament set the body up to do. The courts must decide the public interest here, just as they must decide whether the public interest requires that the Crown should not be bound by an agreement.

Although their ability to raise money is very tightly controlled, local authorities are the best example of a public authority with an unspecific statutory grant of power to contract, given to them in the Local Government Act 1972 s 111:

> '. . . a local authority shall have power to do any thing (whether or not involving the expenditure, borrowing or lending of money or the acquisition or disposal of any property or rights) which is calculated to facilitate, or is conducive or incidental to, the discharge of any of their functions.'

It is exactly right that local authorities should have the power to contract when it facilitates the discharge of their functions. But uncertainty as to what sorts of contracts are authorized by this broad provision makes it harder for local authorities to contract, where it is unclear whether a particular sort of contract is within an authority's power. If the contract is in the end held to be outside the authority's powers, one party or the other will be able to escape from a bargain that the local authority made with the intention of binding itself.

In *Crédit Suisse v Allerdale Borough Council* [1997] QB 306, a local council added a time-share complex to a recreation centre, to help pay for the swimming pool. The time-share operation was set up as a company, whose directors were council members and officers. The time-share units did not sell well and the company went bankrupt. The bank tried to cash in on a guarantee that the Council had given for the company's debts, but the Court of Appeal held that the guarantee was *ultra vires* (that is, outside the local authority's legal power), because the Council lacked statutory authority to set up the company and enter into the guarantee. As Neill LJ put it, far from being necessary to its functions, the setting up of the company and the giving of the guarantee were actually designed to *escape* the controls placed on borrowing by local authorities in the 1972 Act.

The *Crédit Suisse* case created a serious problem for local authorities, since banks had to expect that if any clever financing arrangement ran into difficulty, the council's agreement with the bank might be held to be *ultra vires*. And it wouldn't even matter if the council wanted to honour its agreement, because the council's auditors can take issue (as they did in *Crédit Suisse*) with payments under a contract that may be *ultra vires*.

Parliament addressed the problem in the Local Government (Contracts) Act 1997, which allows a local authority to enter into a 'certified' contract, which will have effect *as if* the local authority had power to enter into it even if it was actually *ultra vires* (s 2). So a local authority will not be able to get out of a certified contract, and that enables local authorities to deal with banks in spite of *Crédit Suisse*. A certified contract can still be challenged in judicial review (s 5); if the contract is held to be unlawful, the Act gives the court wide discretionary power (which the court would in any case have had under the ordinary law of judicial review remedies—see 10.4.6) to do justice to anyone who entered into the 'contract'.

● *Pop quiz* ●
A breach of contract is unlawful. Does that mean that a breach of contract is a ground of judicial review?

15.4 How does the law control government contracts?

From the late 1980s, the Conservative government introduced contracting out as standard practice in central government, and imposed it on local authorities as compulsory competitive tendering (CCT).[12] The goal was to get better value for money by bringing competition into public projects. The practice did not merely require local authorities to seek competitive bids when they contracted out; it required them to put internal operations up for tender—to contract the services out if a private company made the best bid, and to contract the services *in* if the best bid came from within the public body.

----

[12] Local Government, Planning and Land Act 1980; Local Government Acts 1988 and 1992.

In CCT, if a bid from a private contractor is successful, the private contractor carries out the project and the resulting PPP is governed by a real contract. If the in-house department wins the competitive tendering, the work is carried out under a so-called 'contract' between the local authority and one of its own departments. That forced the works departments and education departments of local authorities to compete, as 'direct service organizations' (DSOs), with private contractors, for provision of services such as housing maintenance and school meals.

The courts gave little help to council workers who resented the contracting out of housing services through CCT. For example, the Court of Appeal held that a resolution of a council to accept an internal tender gave the workers no legitimate expectation (see 8.4) that the council would continue to provide them with work (*R v Walsall, ex p Yapp* [1994] ICR 528). The council accepted an internal tender for housing maintenance and repair, and then decided to seek new tenders for the work, using its power to vary its resolutions. Nolan LJ held that: 'The only legitimate expectation of the applicants and their fellow employees under public law, as it seems to me, was that the council would not vary the resolutions . . . save on rational grounds, and after due consultation with those affected' (537). The courts will not superimpose a requirement of substantive fairness on the council's tendering decisions.

On the other hand, the courts have upheld a council's ability to choose its own internal works department over the bids of private contractors: councils have no general duty to choose a cheaper private bid over an internal bid (*R v Portsmouth City Council* [1997] CLC 407 (CA)).

Local authorities resented the compulsory programme, and after 1997 the Labour government set out to achieve the same benefits in a less rigid scheme called '**Best Value**'. The Local Government Act 1999 designated English local authorities (and other bodies such as police authorities) as 'best value authorities' (s 1), and required that: 'A best value authority must make arrangements to secure continuous improvement in the way [in] which its functions are exercised, having regard to a combination of economy, efficiency, and effectiveness' (s 3(1)). That duty is backed by duties to consult council taxpayers and service users, and to publish 'Best Value Performance Plans'. The Secretary of State has a very wide power to require an authority to exercise its functions with economy, efficiency, and effectiveness, and can even take over a function of the authority (s 15). The Best Value regime provides just as important a role for competition and contracting out, while adding more flexible central ministerial control than the CCT regime.

Contracting out under CCT or the Best Value regime creates a PPP between a public authority and private companies that provide services. And when a local authority decides that 'economy, efficiency and effectiveness' are best served by choosing to have the service provided by an internal department after competitive tendering, it makes the organization of government more business-like through internal contracting. Either way, the government moves away from the command model toward a deals model of administration. The Localism Act 2011 added a policy of decentralization, in which the government seeks to achieve value for money by imposing transparency on local authorities, rather than through the central control over decisions that the Best Value regime enabled.

15.4.1 The private finance initiative

Compulsory competitive tendering is a form of contracting out in which the finance is provided by the government. In 1992, John Major's Conservative government developed a model in which funding for public infrastructure projects would come from private investors. In opposition in the 1990s, Labour opposed the resulting **private finance initiative** (PFI), but New Labour expanded it in government under Tony Blair, and the Conservative–Liberal Democrat coalition government extended it further after 2010 by encouraging local councils to use it for home building. By 2011, the value of the obligations owed to private partners under PFI contracts was £145 billion.[13] A review of the programme led in 2013 to the establishment of 'PF2', an initiative to shorten negotiation periods, improve flexibility, and involve government agencies as co-investors in projects.[14] The PFI has become a major source of funding for new projects such as prisons and hospitals, and has delivered hundreds of new schools and dozens of major transport projects, including the Channel Tunnel Rail Link.[15] In March 2016, there were 716 PFI and PF2 projects, with a total value of £59.4 billion.[16]

The PFI is a variety of PPP in which the private partner brings a financial investment to the partnership. The private partner or partners ordinarily design, build, finance, and operate an 'asset' such as a hospital, a bridge, a prison, or a school, under a contract that gives the private partner a return over the lifetime of the project (typically twenty-five or thirty years). It is different from privatizing a hospital, for example, because even though the private partner owns the building, a public authority, rather than the market, decides what services the hospital is to provide, and funding to the private partner is determined through a contract with the public authority (which may be an agency of central government or of a local authority). Both the private partner and the public partner have a stake in the financial success of the initiative.

The partners in a PFI deal may agree that the public authority will take a share in the ownership of the asset, or the asset may belong to the private partner. In the contract, the public authority will insist that the private partner take at least some of the risk of cost overruns, but the private partner will insist that the public authority take at least some of the risk that public demand for the project will dry up. The private partner gets the promise of a stream of revenue either in payments from the public authority for provision of services, or through payments made directly by the public (such as tolls on the Skye Bridge).

13 HM Treasury, *A New Approach to Public–private Partnerships* (December 2012), 15.

14 HM Treasury, *A New Approach to Public–private Partnerships* (December 2012), 11.

15 For the list of PFI projects current in 2016, see http://www.gov.uk/government/publications/private-finance-initiative-and-private-finance-2-projects-2016-summary-data.

16 HM Treasury, 'Private Finance Initiative and Private Finance 2 projects: 2016 summary data', December 2016, p 5.

A PFI deal is meant to transfer to private companies some of the risks associated with the project, and enables the government to set performance standards in the contract, backed up with financial penalties. So the prospect is more efficient delivery of, for example, the Transport for London Tube renewal programme, with the public paying only for the services actually received, when it receives them.

But it isn't magic: it all has to be paid for eventually, through a substantial stream of revenue to the private partner over many years (from the government, or from users of the service, or both). The spreading of risk and the public authority's ability to penalize poor performance only work if the private partner stays solvent. Which, of course, means that the risk isn't altogether transferred: the public authority will still have to meet the need for the service if the private partner goes bankrupt.

And the transaction costs of a good PFI are substantial: public authorities will be fleeced by private partners if they do not invest skill and resources in forecasting the risks and costs and benefits of the project. The cost of the work that needs to be done before entering into a PFI (and of monitoring work as the project proceeds) means that PFI is only feasible for large projects.

The public benefit of getting projects built sooner, at reduced risk, comes at a cost. Along with the accountability risks of other PPPs, the PFI imposes a financial burden: the burden of promising the private partner a stream of income. So the government is committed to entering into PFIs only when the benefit (through accelerated, economical investment, or through sharing of risk) makes it worthwhile for a public authority to take on the commitment.

The 'factors' the Treasury looks for to decide whether a PFI project would give value for money ('VfM')

- 'a major capital investment programme, requiring effective management of risks . . .;
- the structure of the service is appropriate, allowing the public sector to define its needs as service outputs that can be adequately contracted for in a way that ensures effective, equitable, and accountable delivery of public services . . .;
- the nature of the assets and services . . ., as well as the associated risks, are capable of being costed on a whole-of-life, long-term basis;
- the value of the project is sufficiently large to ensure that procurement costs are not disproportionate;
- the technology and other aspects of the sector are stable . . .;
- . . . confidence that the assets and services provided are intended to be used over long periods into the future; and
- the private sector has the expertise to deliver, there is good reason to think it will offer VfM, and robust performance incentives can be put in place[.]'[17]

---

[17]   HM Treasury, *Value for Money Assessment Guidance* (November 2006), 6.

Notice that **accountability** is in that list of factors, and so is **equity**. The list shows how those two fundamental principles of any good public service can get lost in a welter of other considerations of risk, demand, cost, and return on investment, which involve financial guesswork. The accountability risk is that the fragile link between policy formation and implementation will be disrupted altogether. A school or a prison or a hospital can only be run well by people who are committed to the good of the community, and of the individuals at school, or in prison, or in hospital. And their commitment needs to be supported by the management of the operation.

One of the risks of pursuing efficiency through various forms of PPP, including PFI, arises from the fact that work is done by employees of a private service provider, rather than by public employees. That can be very attractive to the public partner, as it offers a way of operating a project with low wages without the public authority having to pay a political price for paying low wages. It is politically easier for a private employer than a public employer to treat employees poorly. The government's approach to PFI does not treat equity and accountability as requirements of justice or of constitutional principle. It treats them as factors to be considered alongside value for money and financial risk management. And it puts a distance between government and the people who guard prisoners and make school meals, giving those people an indirect, commercial relationship with the community they serve.

15.4.2 Parliamentary control

Parliamentary control is available in principle over all governmental contracting (including the PFI), because the government has *no inherent power to raise money, or to spend it.*

FROM THE MISTS OF TIME

In the late Middle Ages, the King could spend his own private wealth as he saw fit, but the wealth of the country was not his to deal with except by the consent of those in the country (the wealthy barons) from whom he wanted it. This principle should have been obvious right from the Norman Conquest in 1066, but the barons had to force the King to admit it in Magna Carta, and to assemble a council—a precursor of Parliament—to negotiate taxes (Magna Carta 1215 cl 12, 14). In Magna Carta, the King promised to consult the bishops and nobles about taxation; the principle that he could not raise taxes without approval of Parliament was not securely established until the Bill of Rights 1689 enacted 'That levying Money for or to the Use of the Crowne by pretence of Prerogative without Grant of Parlyament for longer time or in other manner then the same is or shall be granted is Illegall' (art 4). That is the law today.

The control of Parliament over government by contract should not be underestimated, but it operates at a very abstract level, and in a way that is only a part of parliamentary politics in general. The government needs an Act of Parliament to raise taxes, but the House of Commons has statutory power to authorize the expenditure that is needed for government by contract.[18] Because of the complexity of government expenditure today, we cannot expect MPs to have the time or expertise to scrutinize the expenditure they are authorizing, without help. Parliament needs a much better-focused technique in order to do its job of scrutinizing expenditure; the National Audit Office is the technique.

15.4.3 Audits

The Comptroller and Auditor General, the head of the National Audit Office (NAO), is an independent officer of the House of Commons; he has to confirm to Parliament that government spending transactions have parliamentary authority. The NAO audits the accounts of all government departments and most NDPBs. And the NAO carries out value-for-money audits designed to pursue 'three Es': **economy** ('spending less'); **efficiency** ('spending well'); and **effectiveness** ('spending wisely').[19] That role is *far* more intrusive than judicial review. As creative as the judges have been, lack of efficiency or wisdom is not a ground of judicial review. So, for example, the NAO's report on the Iraq war passed judgment on the military success of the campaign (favourably) and on the government's planning for reconstruction after the war (unfavourably).[20]

The role of providing accountability *for efficiency* is crucial to the government-by-contract agenda. The NAO is the watchdog, and serves as the chief technique for securing accountability for efficiency in central government.[21] The role of auditors today is not simply to check the accounts for accuracy; it is similar to the role of management consultants in private industry. They are prepared to take an overall view of how an organization can pursue its purposes better. While it is not their job to identify the purposes,[22] they *do* pass judgment as to what counts as success in the organization's work, and not just on how to cut costs.

But a VfM audit report makes no legally binding decision. The role of the NAO is simply to make a criticism of government's workings after an independent investigation. Its role is like that of an **ombudsman** (see Chapter 13), because it is to investigate

---

[18] Exchequer and Audit Departments Act 1866 s 14.

[19] http://www.nao.org.uk/what_we_do/value_for_money_audit.aspx. The National Audit Act 1983 s 6 authorizes the NAO to 'carry out examinations into the economy, efficiency and effectiveness with which any department . . . . has used its resources in discharging its functions'.

[20] *Operation TELIC: United Kingdom Military Operations in Iraq*, Session 2003–04, HC 60 (11 December 2003) [6.4].

[21] The European Court of Auditors has the same role in the European Union. It has an auditing function and a general mandate to improve financial management: http://eca.europa.eu.

[22] The NAO cannot 'question the merits of the policy objectives of any department, authority or body in respect of which an examination is carried out' (National Audit Act 1983 s 6).

and report. But there are at least three important differences between the NAO and ombudsmen:

- the NAO does not resolve particular complaints about administration;

- conversely, unlike an ombudsman, it can start its own investigation of general issues; and

- unlike the ombudsmen, its role has not been judicialized (see 13.8.1).

It is simply clearer in the case of the NAO than in the case of ombudsmen that the role is purely to make a report on an investigation. The reports of the Auditor General have never been judicially reviewed. If anyone were ever to seek judicial review, there would be a strong argument that permission (see 10.3.2) should be refused. Anyone with a complaint about a value-for-money report from the NAO (whether a government department, or a member of the public) ought to look to Parliament and not to a court for a remedy, if any remedy is needed.

The work of the NAO is overseen by the Public Accounts Commission, which is really a committee of MPs (consisting of the chairman of the Committee of Public Accounts, the Leader of the House, and seven other MPs appointed by the House who are not ministers) (National Audit Act 1983 s 2). The Commission examines the NAO's work and reports to the House of Commons.

The NAO's investigative role also provides information for the Public Accounts Committee, a select committee of the House of Commons that has been responsible since 1861 for examining the accounts of expenditure of funds granted by Parliament. Both the NAO and the Public Accounts Committee support the constitutional responsibility of Parliament to scrutinize public expenditure.

15.4.4 Control over contracting in EU law

The control of government procurement is one of the most creative ways in which the European Union has pursued its purpose of creating a single market. Public procurement was an obvious target for EU law because it has enormous economic importance, and member states tended to buy goods and services from private suppliers in their own countries. The EU rules start with the Treaty, because the single market provisions on free movement of goods and services imply that governments must open up their procurement processes to suppliers and service providers from other member states. A variety of directives have been issued to require member states to secure open procurement by public authorities in general.

The rules do two very important things, both of which have been implemented in English law by the Public Contracts Regulations 2006, SI 2006/5. First, a contracting authority must award a public contract to the **lowest price or the most economically advantageous** bid—which means that the lowest price bid wins unless there is reason to think that there will be economic advantage in paying more. Second, 'economic operators' interested in tendering for public contracts get **process rights**, including the right to know the criteria for a successful bid ahead of time. Criteria for economically advantageous tenders must be specified in advance. The process for the award of the contract must be transparent, and there is a duty to give reasons.

These rules create an opportunity for a disappointed bidder to argue that the public authority has not followed its criteria, or has not considered a bid fairly. Companies bidding for a public contract would have no such procedural rights under the ordinary law of due process. The change creates a technique for a disappointed tenderer to challenge a decision to award a contract to one of its competitors, by catching the public authority in a breach of the process rules.[23] And once a bidder has won a public contract covered by the regulations, the public authority cannot amend the contract so as to make it substantially more attractive to the private contractor; a 'material variation' will be treated as a whole new contract requiring open bidding, and a competitor of the private contractor can seek judicial review to quash a variation of the contract.[24]

These controls on government contracting were designed to reduce trade barriers between EU member states, but you do not have to come from outside the UK to challenge a contracting decision by a public authority. The effect of the rules is to give English judges a jurisdiction to impose standards of good procedure on public authority contracting decisions in general.

15.4.5 Common law judicial control over contracting

Apart from the EU procurement rules, it is difficult to get judicial review of a government decision not to make a contract with you. It seems to be contrary to the idea of contract, which is a legal device for parties to decide their own rights and obligations. If you are disappointed that Tesco will not enter into a contract with you, you have no legal recourse. Why should you have any recourse if a public authority will not enter into a contract with you?

The reason is really just the **core rationale** for judicial review (see 2.8). The considerations are the same as with *any* duty that the law imposes on a public authority, but not on Tesco. It is not so remarkable to impose duties of due process, and for the courts to have jurisdiction to prevent abuse of power in contracting. The law allows private contractors to decide their own purposes, as long as they do not commit a crime or a tort, or breach a regulatory requirement. But on the *Padfield* doctrine (see 2.3, p 50), public authorities do not have an altogether free hand in deciding their purposes. A public authority cannot do something by contracting that it has no power to do directly. A contract designed to achieve that would be *ultra vires*.

But if a contract is not a way of evading limits on the powers of a public authority, the courts are very restrained in judicial review of contracting. If an authority has the power to enter into an agreement, the courts will defer massively on the content of the

---

[23] See, e.g., *Lettings International Ltd v Newham* [2007] EWCA Civ 1522 [20]. But an opponent of a project or a policy has no such rights under the regulation, and no standing to seek judicial review on the ground that the public authority has breached the rules: *R (Chandler) v Secretary of State for Children, Schools and Families* [2009] EWCA Civ 1011.

[24] See *Edenred Ltd v HM Treasury* [2015] UKSC 45.

contract, and will even defer to some extent on the process that ought to be pursued in negotiations.

In the early days of contracting out, Glidewell LJ suggested that judicial review was only available for certain sorts of contract decisions: those in which there is a 'public law element' in the decision itself (*Mass Energy Ltd v Birmingham City Council* [1994] ELR 298, 306). And Waller J held in *R v Lord Chancellor's Dept, ex p Hibbit & Saunders* [1993] COD 326, 328, that 'it would need something additional to the simple fact that the governmental body was negotiating the contract to impose on that authority any public law obligation in addition to any private law obligations or duties there might be . . .'.

That additional public law element is unnecessary. All the law needs is to hold onto the right grounds of judicial review. If a public authority agrees to buy paperclips from Company A, the courts should refuse permission for judicial review if Company B wants to argue that their paperclips were a better buy, or that the public authority had not given them a fair hearing as to whether it should buy their paperclips. But even in a purely commercial matter, courts should be prepared to hear a claim that a public authority has abused its power. *Every* governmental decision to buy something has a public law element *if* it is an abuse of power. And in negotiating any contract, the law imposes on a public authority an obligation to use its contracting power for proper purposes and not, for example, for a private vendetta or for private profit. In *Cookson & Clegg v Ministry of Defence* [2005] EWCA Civ 811 [18], the Court of Appeal held that judicial review will be available 'if there were bribery, corruption or the implementation of a policy unlawful in itself, either because it was *ultra vires* or for other reasons'. Those grounds of review should apply to any contracting decision. And if a refusal to contract with a particular supplier or service provider in a purely commercial matter were discriminatory or malicious, the commercial party ought to have a remedy in the tort of misfeasance in public office (14.5).

Real abuses of power are rare. It is much more common, though, for a company to invest substantial resources on a good bid for a multimillion-pound contract, and to complain, on coming second in the competition, that the process was unfair or that the substance of the decision was irrational. In *Cookson & Clegg*, a disappointed bidder for a large clothing contract for the military claimed that the Ministry had broken the regulations that implemented the EU directive. The company *also* sought judicial review, asking the Court to strike down the decision to award the contract to a rival for 'irrationality' (see 7.1.3). The company wanted the Court to apply standards of public law reasonableness in addition to the regulation requirements. The Court of Appeal refused to allow judicial review to proceed alongside an ordinary claim based on the regulations, because of the **last resort rule** (see 2.7): judicial review is *not* available to hear every allegation that a public authority has acted unlawfully, but is only available where it is necessary in the public interest for the court to impose the rule of law on administration. An ordinary claim based on the regulations gave the claimants fair recourse against the decision they were challenging.

And consider a case that was not subject to the EU procurement rules, brought by the second-place contestant in a very close competition for a contract to provide bailiff services to the Court Service in Wales and Cheshire. In *R (Menai Collect) v Department for Constitutional Affairs* [2006] EWHC 724 [47], the unsuccessful bidder claimed that the decision was unlawful because the panel that evaluated the bids did not pass all of the information on to the board that took the final decision:

> ‘ It is not every wandering from the precise paths of best practice that lends fuel to a claim for judicial review. It is, I think, for this reason that the examples given of cases where commercial processes such as these are likely to be subject to review are such as they are in the reported cases, namely bribery, corruption, implementation of unlawful policy and the like. ’

A court will refuse to enter into 'a quasi-regulatory scrutiny' [49] designed to check whether a contracting public authority assessed the bids in the right way. The core rationale for judicial review does not require a court to impose its decision on how to assess the bids in place of the decision made by the contracting public authority.

The result of *Cookson & Clegg* and *Menai Collect* is that permission to bring a claim for judicial review of a decision not to award a contract to a claimant should be refused, unless the claim alleges a serious abuse of power. So if you are angry that a public authority turned you down and accepted a bid from a competitor, you cannot seek judicial review on the ground that it was unreasonable for the public authority to reject your bid. This is why the EU procurement rules are important: they impose much closer judicial control on the contract process than common law judicial review does.

15.4.6 The public-sector equality duty

The Equality Act 2010 s 149 controls government by contract—and spending decisions in general—by requiring public authorities to have due regard to the need to advance equality of opportunity for people who might otherwise suffer disadvantage on account of 'protected characteristics' (race, sex, disability, age, gender reassignment, pregnancy and maternity, religion or belief, and sexual orientation). Since it is very difficult to persuade a court to interfere with public spending decisions, the public-sector equality duty (PSED) has created a new avenue for litigation by persons and groups with complaints against the substance of such decisions (see 8.3.2). The more important impact of the Equality Act 2010 is that it mandates a process of 'equality impact assessment', which has become part of the policy-making process for government by contract, and for all kinds of public decisions over finance.

15.5 Contracting out of administrative law?

Who can be subjected to judicial review, for which sorts of decisions? We can ask similar questions about who can be charged with the crime of misconduct in a public office (for which sorts of actions), or sued in the tort of misfeasance in a public office, or investigated by an ombudsman or an auditor, or taken to a tribunal, or who can be required to respond to a freedom of information request. Most controversially, the law needs to determine who can be held to have acted unlawfully under the Human Rights Act 1998 s 6, by infringing a Convention right.

This set of questions is important quite apart from contracting. People with grievances have made varied, more or less successful attempts to bring legal controls on abuse of public power to bear on actors that are not part of government and that have no contract of any kind with government, but are carrying out a role that has a relation to the public interest that, according to the complainant, calls for the controls of administrative law. We will look at those various attempts, starting in this section with a special challenge that arises in determining the scope of judicial review and other administrative law controls: **can the government escape from the controls on its conduct imposed by administrative law by contracting services out to private actors?**

The important points to start with are that the law must:

(1) decide the scope of the process in question by reference to the **purpose of the standards** to which the process gives effect; and

(2) look at the **kind of decision** being made, and not simply at the **kind of decision maker**.

In addressing those two points, keep in mind the danger that may arise from government by contract: if, for example, a public authority nursing home is controlled by judicial review, but a private nursing home providing places under a contract with the public authority is not controlled, then it seems that the authority can escape the rule of law by contracting out. In *R v Servite Houses, ex p Goldsmith* (2001) 33 HLR 35 [105], Moses J held that when a local authority contracted out the provision of nursing home care to a private service provider, judicial review was not available against the private company: 'If I am right in my reasoning, it demonstrates an inadequacy of response to the plight of these applicants now that Parliament has permitted public law obligations to be discharged by entering into private law arrangements.' This section concerns what it would take for the law to make an adequate response when public bodies use contracts to provide services.

15.5.1 The scope of judicial review

It is essential for the law to protect people against abuse of power by a private person or a private company, but the law's techniques for doing so are found in the law of crime, tort, property, and contract, along with any regulatory regimes that Parliament may impose (for environmental protection, land use planning, food safety, fair competition, truth in advertising, fire safety, decent working hours, a minimum wage, etc.). And as Coulson J said in *TH v Worcester Cathedral* [2016] EWHC 1117 [76], 'the administrative court is not there simply to fill in the gaps left by statute or the common law'.

The Civil Procedure Rules (CPR) limit the scope of judicial review to controlling 'the exercise of a public function' (CPR 54.1). The rules do not say what that means. In *R v Panel on Take-overs and Mergers, ex p Datafin Plc* [1987] QB 815, the Court of Appeal allowed an application for judicial review to proceed against a body that was not a government agency. Lord Donaldson MR said that the Panel was not even a legal person (824), yet the Court treated it as a legal person by subjecting its conduct to judicial review. The leading investment banks in the City of London had organized a form of self-regulation over the conduct of company takeovers; the Panel is a committee of people they appoint to oversee the 'City Code', and to decide whether the Code has been infringed.[25] Lord Donaldson asked (at 827): 'What is to happen if the panel goes off the rails? Suppose, perish the thought, that it were to use its powers in a way which was manifestly unfair. What then?' His answer was that the courts would then give judicial review, on the same grounds of lack of natural justice and abuse of power that apply to the conduct of public authorities.

● *Pop quiz* ●
Is the Panel on Take-overs and Mergers a public authority?

An abuse of power would go unremedied without the judicial willingness to interfere, and it would be the abuse of a kind of power (a regulatory power over commercial trading) that the Panel had for the public good, so that there is a public interest in preventing its abuse. And the Court could effectively impose a legal requirement of procedural fairness, and legal protection against abuse of power, without damaging the Panel's pursuit of its legitimate purposes. The capacity of the Court to impose the rule of law on the Panel, without interfering inappropriately, justifies the availability of judicial review; it is an application of the core rationale for judicial review, which does not require that the defendant should be an agency of the state.

Unfortunately, Lord Donaldson did not stop there. He went on to emphasize the ways in which the government had relied on the industry's self-regulation through the Panel, rather than imposing legal regulation. 'As an act of government', he said, 'it was decided' that the Panel should carry on the regulation of takeovers (835). The suggestion is that it was the government's relations with the Panel that justified judicial review. But the core rationale for judicial review applies regardless of any relation between the Panel and government, because of the Panel's function (the nature of the issues at stake, the reasons for which it is the Panel that is addressing them, and the implications of the decision for the people affected). The real task for the Court in *Datafin* was not to ask (as it seemed to), 'Is this body closely enough connected to government that we can review it?', but to ask the following set of questions: 'Does this Panel's power need controlling in the public interest, to prevent it from being abused? If so, are the courts capable of forming the judgments that would be needed to provide that control? And would the Panel's functioning be unduly damaged by subjecting it to the judicial review process?' For certain unusual bodies like the Panel, which are on the borderlines of public administration, the courts should be prepared to ask those questions. But we will see that there is a prospect that the same questions can be addressed *not* through judicial review, but in an ordinary claim for a declaration, with no requirement of any connection between the government and the defendant.

....
[25] See http://www.thetakeoverpanel.org.uk.

15.5.2 Judicial supervision of private bodies: 'the common law abhors all monopolies'

In the 2002 Gold Cup, *Be My Royal* crossed the finishing line first, but the Jockey Club's disciplinary committee disqualified the horse for failing a drugs test. The Jockey Club's Appeal Board upheld the decision. William Mullins, the horse's trainer, sought judicial review on the ground that the decision was arbitrary and capricious, and was based on a misconstruction of the rules on horse doping.

The Administrative Court refused permission for judicial review (*R (Mullins) v Jockey Club (No 1)* [2005] EWHC 2197). That was unsurprising, given the landmark decision in *R v Jockey Club, ex p Aga Khan* [1993] 1 WLR 909 (CA). The *Aga Khan* case had decided that there was no jurisdiction to give judicial review of Jockey Club disciplinary decisions, because the Club was not a government agency, and because there were adequate remedies for any abuse of power in an action for breach of contract.

Meanwhile, a string of decisions before and after *Aga Khan* held that judicial review was unavailable against the National Greyhound Racing Club, the Chief Rabbi, and the Football Association[26]—although the Advertising Standards Association and a pharmaceutical industry committee were subjected to judicial review as instruments for the same sort of commercial self-regulation of an industry as in *Datafin*.[27]

It may seem that these cases represent an arbitrary judicial refusal to control a potential abuse of power. If the government had regulated horse racing, and a tribunal applied the rules against doping horses, then William Mullins would definitely have had access to all of the controls of judicial review (although judicial review would be unavailable if a claim in contract would provide an adequate remedy—see 15.2, p 588). And it makes no difference, from Mullins' point of view, whether the committee allegedly abusing its power was a government agency regulating horse racing, or a private club regulating horse racing. The test of governmental connection from the *Aga Khan* case does not reflect the nature of the power, which is what ought to determine whether the courts are prepared to impose the rule of law on its exercise.

But the refusal of permission for judicial review was not the end of the road for the *Be My Royal* litigation. After he had refused judicial review in *R (Mullins) v Jockey Club*, Stanley Burnton J transferred the claim from the Administrative Court to the Queen's Bench Division, to proceed under CPR 8 as a claim for a declaration that the horse's disqualification was unlawful. And the decision in that case, *Mullins v McFarlane* [2006] EWHC 986 [38], suggests that the court 'has a supervisory jurisdiction over

26 *Law v National Greyhound Racing Club* [1983] 3 All ER 300 (CA) (in which the *defendant* claimed that it was subject to judicial review, to try to get the court to strike out an ordinary action); *R v Chief Rabbi, ex p Wachmann* [1992] 1 WLR 1036; *R v Football Association, ex p Football League* [1993] 2 All ER 833.

27 *R v Advertising Standards Authority, ex p Insurance Service* (1989) 2 Admin LR 77 (DC); *R v Code of Practice Committee of the British Pharmaceutical Industry, ex p Professional Counselling Aids* (1990) 3 Admin LR 697. And the Law Society and the General Council of the Bar are subject to judicial review of their exercise of power in the public interest: *Swain v Law Society* [1983] 1 AC 598 (HL), 618; *R v General Council of the Bar, ex p Percival* [1991] 1 QB 212 (DC).

tribunals such as the Appeal Board, irrespective of the existence of a contract between the claimant and the tribunal or the body appointing it'. *Mullins* represents the rediscovery of a form of control over the private use of power that the courts had forgotten. In *Nagle v Feilden* [1966] 2 QB 633, the Court of Appeal allowed a trial to go ahead on a claim that the Jockey Club's rule against women trainers was arbitrary and capricious. Lord Denning held that the rule against women horse trainers 'may well be said to be arbitrary and capricious. It is not as if the training of horses could be regarded as an unsuitable occupation for a woman, like that of a jockey or speedway-rider' (647).[28]

What was the legal basis for this action for a declaration that a private organization was acting arbitrarily? Lord Denning excavated the ancient law on the right to work from Sir Edward Coke's judgment in the famous case of the *Tailors of Ipswich* (1614) 11 Co Rep 53a, 53b:

> '... at the common law, no man could be prohibited from working in any lawful trade, for the law abhors idleness, the mother of all evil, ... and especially in young men, who ought in their youth, (which is their seed time) to learn lawful sciences and trades, which are profitable to the commonwealth, and whereof they might reap the fruit in their old age, for idle in youth, poor in age; and therefore the common law abhors all monopolies, which prohibit any from working in any lawful trade. '

This rule has three crucial features: (1) the justification Coke offered was the public interest (although the rule also benefited individuals); (2) yet it was a common law rule; and (3) the rule was imposed on private organizations for the benefit of persons who had no other argument of private right (such as a contract) against the organization.

The result is judicial control of private power based on just the same **core rationale** as judicial control of public power: the mere capacity of the judges to prevent certain forms of injustice in a way that is itself ruled by law. So Salmon LJ said in *Nagle*: 'One of the principal functions of our courts is, whenever possible, to protect the individual from injustice and oppression. It is important, perhaps today more than ever, that we should not abdicate that function' (654).

In *Mullins*, at [39], Stanley Burnton J moved the law beyond the common law right to work, at least tentatively: 'My provisional view is that there is no jurisdictional (in the narrow sense of the word) boundary to the power of the Court to grant declaratory relief in this context: the jurisdiction of the Court under CPR Part 40.20[29] to grant declaratory relief is unrestricted.' So can the courts control arbitrary private decisions in general? No: the power is restricted to 'this context'. The context includes the fact, as Lord Denning put it, that the Jockey Club has 'a virtual monopoly in an important field of human activity' (*Nagle v Feilden*, 644).

---

28 It would take the Sex Discrimination Act 1975 to change the law on access to those professions that Lord Denning considered to be unsuitable for a woman.

29 CPR 40.20:'The court may make binding declarations whether or not any other remedy is claimed.'

The 'provisional' approach of *Mullins* is to use the procedural flexibility of the CPR to broaden the ancient doctrine of the *Tailors of Ipswich* case into a wide jurisdiction to control *some* arbitrary decision making by private bodies.

The *Mullins* move does not promise a wide-ranging overhaul of English law, because the instances will be rare in which the issues at stake are justiciable, *and* an injustice by a private body cannot be remedied by the law of contract, tort, property, trusts, or criminal law, or any regulatory scheme. But within its limits, it simply circumvents the suggestions in earlier cases, such as *Aga Khan* and *Datafin*, that judicial review is not available unless the defendant has a connection with government. In a claim for a declaration under CPR 8, it gives courts the same supervisory role as in judicial review. While showing deference (just as they should in judicial review of public authorities) to 'the decision of an impartial qualified tribunal whose knowledge and experience of the subject matter in question is likely to exceed those of the Court' (*Mullins v McFarlane* [39]), the courts have the opportunity to apply the familiar grounds in deciding whether to declare that a decision of the private body was unlawful:

- *Wednesbury* unreasonableness—'The court's role, in the exercise of its supervisory jurisdiction, is to determine whether the decision reached falls within the limits of the decision-maker's discretionary area of judgment' (*Bradley v Jockey Club* [2004] EWHC 2164 [43]);[30]

- legal error in applying the Rules (*Mullins v McFarlane* [48]); and

- bias[31] and other forms of procedural unfairness (*Mullins v McFarlane* [38]).

It is all there, just as in judicial review of public authorities. As it was put in a case following *Bradley*: 'It is well established that a decision of a body such as the Horseracing Regulatory Authority cannot be challenged by judicial review proceedings. But it is equally well established that the High Court retains a supervisory jurisdiction over such decisions, and the approach to be adopted is essentially that which the Administrative Court would adopt in public law cases' (*Fallon v Horseracing Regulatory Authority* [2006] EWHC 2030, [12]). It seems that if the defendant is not a public authority, you simply need to bring a claim for a declaration under CPR 40.20, rather than a claim for judicial review under CPR Part 54.

That process has the potential to right wrongs that are more serious than arbitrarily disqualifying a racehorse. People housed in a care home by a private company acting under a contract with a local authority have no recourse in judicial review if the private agency unfairly closes their home after promising that they can stay there (*R v Servite Houses, ex p Goldsmith* [2001] LGR 55).[32] Moses J felt constrained to that outcome by

---

30 And the Court of Appeal held in *Nagle v Feilden* that arbitrariness or capriciousness in the Jockey Club's rules would be unlawful.

31 See *Modahl v British Athletic Federation Ltd (No 2)* [2001] EWCA Civ 1447.

32 Contrast the availability of judicial review of decisions of public bodies providing nursing care: *R v North and East Devon Health Authority, ex p Coughlan* [2001] QB 213—see 8.4.4, pp 303–7.

Datafin and *Aga Khan*, because Servite Houses' relationship with the local authority was 'purely commercial', and the courts 'cannot impose public law standards upon a body the source of whose power is contractual and absent sufficient statutory penetration' (*Servite Homes*, 81). In order to do a responsible job of extending the common law's historic protection against abuse of private power to the *Servite Homes* situation, the courts would have to keep to a test of *abuse* of the power that private housing agencies have over the residents of a care home (rather than taking over the general management of private care homes). That requires a combination of comity with the public authority that commissioned the service, and respect for the private agency's ability to enter into a commercial arrangement without having undue obligations superimposed for the public good. Then the judges have the opportunity to right an injustice without interfering in the commercial arrangement between the housing agency and the local authority. Control *on abuse of power* would not damage the commercial arrangement inappropriately.

In public administration, the potential is incomparably greater than in private administration for injustices that can only be remedied by a supervisory jurisdiction (permission for judicial review against public authorities is given in thousands of cases every year; *Bradley* and *Mullins and Fallon* are rarities). And the judicial review *process* is still restricted to the control of *public* functions. That is a relatively new development; *R v Master of the Company of Surgeons* (1759) 2 Burr 892, argued on the very same legal basis as the *Tailors of Ipswich* case, was an application for a *mandamus* (the predecessor of the mandatory order) against a private body.[33] In the eighteenth century, *the prerogative writs (certiorari* [quashing order], *mandamus* [mandatory order], prohibition [prohibiting order]) *were not restricted to claims against public authorities*. The great case of *R v Barker* (1762) 3 Burr 1265 (see 11.1.1, p 410), after all, was a *mandamus* against the trustees of a Presbyterian meeting house. In the nineteenth century, this aspect of the prerogative writs withered, so that, by the twentieth century (when English judges started to think about 'public law' as the law controlling the state), they were thought to be available only against public authorities. The CPR keep that twentieth-century doctrine (CPR 54.1). But it seems that the courts' old capacity to control private abuse of power is returning, by way of the summary process for seeking a declaration in CPR 8, and the power to give a declaration in CPR 40.20. If the courts have that power, then the law can control private decision makers in the same context-sensitive way as it controls public authorities, where there is a public interest in the prevention of arbitrary decision making.

15.5.3 'Public authorities' under the Human Rights Act 1998

The European Convention on Human Rights binds the 'contracting parties'—the states—that agreed to it. So a claim in the Strasbourg Court is a claim against 'one of the High Contracting Parties' (e.g., the United Kingdom), alleging that the state has violated

---

[33] The Company of Surgeons required that even an apprentice should know Latin; Lord Mansfield thought that the justification of that restriction on employment was 'too plain to argue'.

a Convention right. All legal responsibility under the Convention lies on the state. But Art 1 of the Convention says that 'the High Contracting Parties shall secure to everyone within their jurisdiction the rights' in the Convention. And the Strasbourg Court has taken a very broad view of what counts as a violation of a right *by the state*: 'The State cannot completely absolve itself from its responsibility by delegating its obligation . . . to private bodies or individuals' (*Storck v Germany* (2005) 43 EHRR 96 [103]).

Because of the positive obligations (see 3.6, p 93) that the Strasbourg Court has imposed on states under Art 2 (right to life), Art 3 (prohibition on torture), and Art 8 (right to respect for private and family life), it will often be the case that a private act against an interest protected by the Convention will reflect the violation of a right by the state: for example, if the UK does not prevent excessive corporal punishment in a private school, the victim can complain in the Strasbourg Court (*Costello-Roberts v United Kingdom* [1993] ECHR 16). But the private school will not have violated the Convention, because it is not a contracting party. The defendant in the *Costello-Roberts* case was, of course, the UK. If a private school were to torture you, the UK would have violated your Convention right (1) if it failed to carry out a positive duty to protect you from abuses by private persons;[34] or (2) if the school was, in effect, a way in which the UK provided education, so that the state's responsibility to conform to Convention rights ought to be seen as having been delegated to the school. That sort of delegation would take a close institutional connection between the UK government and the school, and the Strasbourg Court would not find that a school is part of the British state just because education is of public importance. The school would have to be, in effect, *an agency of* the state.

Within the UK, the Human Rights Act 1998 s 6 makes it unlawful for a 'public authority' to act in a way that is incompatible with a Convention right. Section 6 defines the phrase 'public authorities', confusingly, to include any person certain of whose functions are 'functions of a public nature' (s 6(3)(b)).[35] It is the same in effect as if the Act made it unlawful for *anyone* to infringe a Convention right in carrying out a function that has a public nature.[36] The judges call public authorities under s 6 'core public authorities', and they call other people or bodies 'hybrid'[37] or 'functional'[38] public authorities if their functions are public for the purposes of s 6(3)(b).

What gives a function a 'public nature'? The question creates a conundrum for the courts when public authorities contract with private agencies for the provision of public services—especially housing provided under local authorities' statutory duty to arrange nursing home provision for people who need care because of age, illness, or disability (National Assistance Act 1948 s 21). The local authority is, of course, carrying

---

[34] *X and Y v The Netherlands* (1985) 8 EHRR 235; *Z v United Kingdom* (2001) 34 EHRR 97.

[35] A person that has some public functions for s 6(3)(b) is not a public authority in respect of a particular act, 'if the nature of the act is private' (s 6(5)).

[36] Unless that person is acting in a way required by primary legislation: see 3.3, p 78.

[37] *Aston Cantlow v Wallbank* [2003] UKHL 37 [7]–[9].

[38] *Coombs v North Dorset NHS Primary Care Trust* [2013] EWCA Civ 471 [27].

out a public function—a function paid for and organized by government on behalf of the public, giving effect to a decision by Parliament on behalf of the state that doing so is in the public interest. If the local authority carries out that duty by operating its own nursing home, and a resident is evicted or a home is closed down, then he or she can complain that the decision infringed the Art 8 right to respect for private and family life, and since the decision certainly affected his or her private life, the local authority will have to show that the impact was not disproportionate to the value of pursuing a legitimate purpose recognized by Art 8 as justifying interference with someone's privacy.[39]

What if the local authority carries out its statutory duty to provide housing by contracting out its housing provision to a private operator of nursing homes? If the private housing association were to abuse a resident (e.g., by evicting him or her or shutting down the nursing home arbitrarily), then the local authority would need to take new steps to carry out its duty to provide housing, and if the debacle came about because of a failure by the local authority to take the steps that it ought to take in those circumstances out of respect for the resident's private and family life (e.g., by regulating nursing homes, and by entering into a responsible agreement with the nursing home), then local authority would have infringed the resident's Convention right, and he or she would have a remedy against the local authority under the Human Rights Act 1998, and a remedy in Strasbourg against the United Kingdom.

But there is a remedial gap when a private operator is trying to evict a resident (*Poplar Housing v Donoghue* [2001] EWCA Civ 595), or when the private operator proposes to close the resident's home and the resident wants to stay there (*R (Heather) v Leonard Cheshire Foundation* [2002] EWCA Civ 366). In those situations, seeking damages from the local authority for any violation of the housing statute or a Convention right would be a distant second-best. For a resident who doesn't want to be thrown out of his or her home, Convention rights against the local authority and the UK won't stop the company from evicting him or her or closing the home.

Residents in that predicament have asked the courts to hold a private nursing home company to be a 'functional' public authority. In both *Poplar Housing* and *Heather*, the Court of Appeal accepted that carrying out what would certainly be a public function for a public authority does *not* necessarily count (for a private body) as performing a public function. But the housing association in *Poplar Housing* was held to be a 'functional public authority' because its role was 'enmeshed' with the activities of the local authority. Its role was 'so closely assimilated to that of Tower Hamlets [the local authority] that it was performing public and not private functions' (70). The local authority itself set up Poplar Housing to operate homes, and transferred housing stock to it, including the defendant's flat; Poplar Housing was subject to guidance from the local authority.

The housing provider in the *Heather* case was not enmeshed with the public authority, and was held *not* to be subject to the Human Rights Act 1998 s 6. The Court found that, on the facts, there was 'no black hole into which [the residents] would sink' [31]. The result in *Heather* gives every local authority a financial incentive to contract out its

---

[39] See *Sims v Dacorum Borough Council* [2014] UKSC 63.

care provision to private concerns that will be able to do it more cheaply than the local authority could do it, if the Convention rights put expensive constraints on building management. And the availability of Human Rights Act *proceedings* itself means that, as a result of *Heather*, local authorities face an expense that private operators would not face when they want to close a home or move a resident.

The House of Lords' first opportunity to deal with functional public authorities came in *Aston Cantlow Parochial Church Council v Wallbank* [2003] UKHL 37, which held that a 'core' public authority is a governmental organization of the kind that the UK is answerable for in the Strasbourg Court. The House of Lords gave a list of factors to be considered, including 'the extent to which in carrying out the relevant function the body is publicly funded, or is exercising statutory powers, or is taking the place of central government or local authorities, or is providing a public service' [12]. That list has become the accepted guide to 'functions of a public nature' in s 6(3)(b) of the Human Rights Act.[40] Only the 'public service' factor moves beyond the *Poplar Housing* approach of focusing on relations with government. And that factor did not help to resolve the question in *Heather* of whether a private nursing home operator is providing a public function when it provides housing under a contracting-out agreement with a local authority.

Here is the conundrum the courts face. The function of the private nursing home in *Heather* is clearly a public function in one sense: the resident is receiving social housing at state expense for a public purpose adopted on behalf of the public by authority of Parliament. And the function is clearly *not* a public function in another sense: the provider is providing housing and nursing care in exchange for money. It is carrying out just the same function as if the resident were paying for his or her own care. If the company provides the same services to customers who pay their own way, it is not providing a public function, and its function does not change its nature when the cheque for housing a particular resident comes from a local authority. 'Function of a public nature' is ambiguous, because a single function can be public in one sense and private in another sense. And the Human Rights Act 1998 s 6 cannot be applied without a resolution to the ambiguity. It ought to be resolved in a way that gives effect to the purpose of treating a private body as a 'public authority' under s 6. But even that purpose is unclear. It was extraordinary for the drafters of the Human Rights Act to put such a strain on the words 'public function': those words leave it to the judges to decide this aspect of the reach of the Human Rights Act.

As regards the contracting out of accommodation along with nursing care, Parliament decided *not* to leave it to judges, and enacted that, when a local authority contracts out nursing care, private care homes that provide accommodation with nursing care are to be taken to be exercising a function of a public nature for the purposes of the Human Rights Act.[41] But before the legislation came into effect, the House of Lords took on the conundrum of social care in *YL v Birmingham City Council* [2007] UKHL 27. It is the landmark case for the interpretation of 'functions of a public nature'

---

[40] See, e.g., *R (Weaver) v London & Quadrant Housing Trust* [2009] EWCA Civ 587 [35].

[41] First in the Health and Social Care Act 2008 s 145(1), and then in the Care Act 2014 s 73.

in s 6 of the Human Rights Act. And the Law Lords were sharply divided. The claimant, an eighty-four-year-old woman with Alzheimer's disease, was placed in a private nursing home under a three-way agreement between the local council, her family, and the home. The home threatened to evict her because of the conduct of her daughter and husband during visits. If the nursing home company, Southern Cross, were carrying out functions of a public nature under that agreement, then she could use Art 8 of the Convention to challenge her eviction. The matter was not resolved by the list of factors offered in *Aston Cantlow*. A public function was obviously being fulfilled (social care, which the Council had a statutory duty to provide to YL). But the Law Lords could not agree on whether it was a *function of Southern Cross*. To Baroness Hale and Lord Bingham, it was obvious that Southern Cross was fulfilling a public function (Lord Bingham [20]): 'The performance by private body A by arrangement with public body B, and perhaps at the expense of B, of what would undoubtedly be a public function if carried out by B is, in my opinion, precisely the case which section 6(3)(b) was intended to embrace.' But to the majority, it was obvious that Southern Cross was *not* fulfilling a public function (Lord Scott [26]): 'Southern Cross is a company carrying on a socially useful business for profit. It is neither a charity nor a philanthropist. It enters into private law contracts with the residents in its care homes and with the local authorities with whom it does business.'

The tantalizing feature of the judges' reasoning is that both sides are right, in a sense. Southern Cross was, of course, carrying out a public function in a sense, because the arrangement was a public authority's way of carrying out a public function (state provision of housing for vulnerable people who don't have the money to pay for themselves), and it is a function that is at the heart of the welfare state. Described another way, Southern Cross was obviously *not* carrying out a public function: it was acting for the private purpose of making a profit for its private owners.

Imagine that Alice, Beatrice, and Candice live on Care Street (see Figure 15.2). In Number 1, Southern Cross houses Alice, who is paying for her own care. In

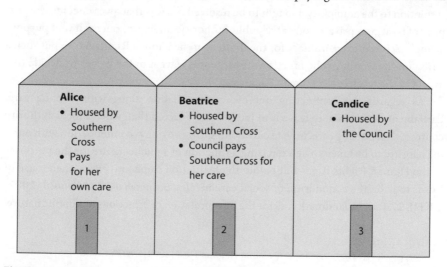

Figure 15.2 Public and private functions on Care Street

Number 2, Southern Cross houses Beatrice, under an agreement with the council in which the council pays for her care. Beatrice is in the position of the claimant in *YL*. In Number 3, the council houses Candice in a home that it owns and operates.[42]

Candice can bring proceedings against the Council under the Human Rights Act, to vindicate her Art 8 rights. Alice cannot bring proceedings against Southern Cross under the Human Rights Act. The dissenters in *YL* thought that it would be arbitrary to deprive Beatrice of legal protection that Candice has, just because the council contracted out Beatrice's housing. The majority in *YL* thought that it would be arbitrary for Beatrice to have legal protection against the home's decisions that Alice did not have, just because the council is paying for Beatrice and Alice is paying for herself.

The solution to the practical problem is obvious: Alice ought to be protected from abuses as well as Candice is.[43] That would erase the conundrum about how to treat Beatrice under the Human Rights Act 1998 s 6(3)(b), because it wouldn't matter anymore. Justice demands that the law protect Alice from abuse when she pays her private nursing home for her care, and there is nothing about the community's relationship with Beatrice and Candice (through the local authority, with or without Southern Cross helping out) that requires that the law protect them better than it protects Alice.

The care conundrum

The question of whether the private nursing home is carrying out a public function in caring for people on behalf of a local authority *only* matters if the Human Rights Act 1998 gives Candice more protection than Alice has. If that is the case, either Alice is not properly protected from abuse in her private relationship with the nursing home company, or Candice is getting more protection than she needs (that is, the combination of the substance of the Convention rights and the Human Rights Act processes impose too great a burden on the operation of nursing homes).

How should the judges resolve the conundrum? Given what amounts to an extraordinary delegation of power to the judges through the ambiguity of s 6(3)(b), they ought to impose the protections of the Human Rights Act if that is what it takes to prevent an abuse of public power through the contracting-out process. The majority decision

---

[42] If Denise in Number 4 is housed by a 'registered social landlord' (RSL), she can use the Human Rights Act 1998, because RSLs *are* functional public authorities: *R (Weaver) v London & Quadrant Housing Trust* [2009] EWCA Civ 587. That decision is compatible with *YL* because, although they are private bodies, RSLs are subsidized by the state and play a role in policy implementation; they are 'enmeshed' in the work of local authority.

[43] Note that the statutory solution mentioned above, n 41, gives Beatrice the same rights against Southern Cross that Candice has against the Council, but does nothing for Alice.

in *YL* does an injustice *if* it merely hands to local authorities a technique for evading protections that residents of nursing homes need. But that is only the case if Beatrice is exposed to genuine abuse as a result. And if Alice is exposed to genuine abuse by her private nursing home, then the failing is just as bad. So the problem *ought* to be immaterial (because Alice ought to have good protection from abuse), and if it is immaterial, then the majority decision was right in *YL*, and the claimant only lost a legal technique for fighting the nursing home that she did not need to protect her from a genuine abuse.

The majority decision does no injustice to Beatrice, if Alice has protection from abuse of private power. On the other hand, if Alice is not protected from abuse of private power, then the decision in *YL* allows a council, by contracting out, to leave Beatrice in the same vulnerable position as Alice. But then, the problem is not that *YL* allows the public authority to contract out of the Human Rights Act. The problem is that residents of private nursing homes in general need protection that the law is not providing. Either way, the decision in *YL* was justified.

● *Pop quiz* ●
Can and should the judges do anything for Alice [hint: see 15.5.2]?

15.5.4 Public authorities in EU law

Directives of the European Union bind the member states, but not private parties. So the Court of Justice of the European Union (CJEU) has had to decide how to draw the line around the bodies whose acts count as acts of a member state. It did so first in Case 152/84 *Marshall v Southampton and South West Hampshire Area Health Authority* [1986] QB 401, 413, in which the decisive principle was that no body should be able to act incompatibly with a directive if its doing so would represent a way for the member state to avoid the effect of the directive. So 'the "state" must be taken broadly, as including all the organs of the state'. Which organs are those? In Case C-188/89 *Foster v British Gas* [1991] 2 WLR 258 [20], the Court endorsed two criteria offered by the Commission: '[B]oth the criterion "exercise of a public function" and that of "real control" can bring a person, in this case an employer, within the concept of "the state".' The 'public function' criterion was meant to catch bodies such as police services that act independently of the government; the point in *Foster* was that the Court also wanted to catch any body controlled by the member state: '[T]he state may not benefit from its default in respect of anything that lies within the sphere of responsibility which by its own free choice it has taken upon itself, irrespective of the person through whom that responsibility is exercised' [21].

This problem is different from the domestic problems of identifying public authorities for the sake of judicial review, or even under the Human Rights Act. The difference is that the Court's purpose is to hold *member states* to their obligations under directives. So in this context, the connection with government really matters.

Table 15.2 summarizes the availability of administrative law processes.

Table 15.2 Summary: who or what is subject to administrative law processes

The following process	Is available against a body or person that:
A claim for judicial review:	—exercises a 'public function' (CPR 54.1); the defendant must meet the ambiguous criteria in *Datafin*[44] of public function, and/or connection (of some kind) to government.[45]
An ordinary claim for a declaration or injunction:	—interferes with the right to carry on a trade (*Tailors of Ipswich*[46]) or has a virtual monopoly in an important field of human activity (*Nagle*,[47] *Mullins*[48]).
A claim in tort:	—is alleged to be the tortfeasor.
A criminal prosecution for misconduct in a public office:	—has an 'office of trust concerning the public'.[49]
Proceedings under the Human Rights Act 1998:	—has functions of a public nature, in an unexplained sense that the courts have been left to work out[50] (but each House of Parliament is excluded).
Proceedings in the Strasbourg Court for infringement of the Convention rights:	—is a contracting party to the Convention (i.e., the United Kingdom or one of the other nations that have signed the Convention).
Proceedings for breach of an EU directive:	is an organ (very broadly construed) of the member state.
Proceedings in an English court for breach of the EU's procurement rules:	—is on a long list of 'contracting operators' that includes central government departments, local authorities, fire and police authorities, and NDPBs.[51]
A complaint to the Parliamentary Ombudsman:	—is on the list in the Parliamentary Commissioner Act 1967 covering government departments, executive agencies, and other bodies fulfilling public functions.[52]
A request for information under the Freedom of Information Act 2000:	—is a 'public authority', defined by a very long list, with the addition of publicly owned companies.[53]

[44] *R v Panel on Take-overs and Mergers, ex p Datafin Plc* [1987] QB 815 (CA).

[45] *R v Jockey Club, ex p Aga Khan* [1993] 1 WLR 909 (CA).

[46] *In re Tailors & Co of Ipswich* (1614) 11 Co Rep 53a.

[47] *Nagle v Feilden* [1966] 2 QB 633.

[48] *Mullins v McFarlane* [2006] EWHC 986 (QB).

[49] *R v Bembridge* (1783) 3 Doug 327, 332.

[50] Human Rights Act 1998 s 6(3)(b). See *YL v Birmingham City Council* [2007] UKHL 27.

[51] Public Contracts Regulations 2006, SI 2006/5, reg 3(1).

[52] Parliamentary Commissioner Act 1967 Sch 2.

[53] Freedom of Information Act 2000 s 3.

15.6 Conclusion: private law and public law

Accountability is crucial for good government, and yet accountability is not automatically a good thing. The right kinds of accountability do not simply mean more control of public decision making. As regards the role of courts in holding administrative authorities to account, it is a remarkable fact that unfair, unreasonable, arbitrary uses of power are *not necessarily* subject to judicial control. Claimants may quite rightly face all sorts of potential obstacles to using the impressive grounds of judicial review to secure redress against an arbitrary use of power. We have seen the obstacles in Chapter 10 on how to sue the government (time limits, the discretions of the courts, and the problems created by *O'Reilly v Mackman* [1983] 2 AC 237), and in Chapter 11 on standing, and in this chapter on the need to establish that the defendant (or its decision) is 'public' in the relevant sense. And a claimant needs to use other processes and remedies *instead of* judicial review, if doing so will secure a just result (see 2.7).

In achieving the right sorts of accountability for government by contract, non-judicial forms of accountability are, in some ways, for some purposes, more useful than judicial review. Specification of criteria and the imposition of procedural transparency in contracting-out processes, with oversight by auditors, give a more impressive set of accountability techniques than is provided by the rather hands-off judicial review that is available to control contracting-out decisions. And public information as to whether policy is being carried out in practice doesn't just reduce costs; it can also enhance responsibility in delivering services.

Judges still have a role in controlling government by contract, but it is largely the role of preventing abuse of power. If government is accountable to courts for abuse of power in service provision, and accountable to auditors for the efficiency of its spending decisions, *and that's all*, then there is a dangerous lack of accountability for integrity and accountability for equity. There is still an inescapable role for political accountability for good public service provision, both in central and local government.

15.6.1 What is public law?

The rule of law does not require judges to control everything; can we say that it does require them to control all abuse of public power? In the 1980s and 1990s, it seemed crucial to distinguish between public law and private law. Lord Diplock in *O'Reilly v Mackman*, 275, Lord Bridge in *Cocks v Thanet District Council* [1983] 2 AC 286, 292, and Lord Wilberforce in *Davy v Spelthorne* [1984] 1 AC 262, 276, started talking about 'public law' as a new thing; Lord Scarman said that there was a 'newly fledged distinction in English law between public and private law' (*Gillick v West Norfolk and Wisbech Area Health Authority* [1986] 1 AC 112, 178). But the distinction between public law and private law is ancient.[54] And, in fact, the Law Lords did not really mean 'public law' when they started talking about 'public law' as something new in the 1980s.

----

[54] e.g., it is an ancient rule of the common law that 'all kinds of crimes of a public nature, all misdemeanors whatsoever of a public evil example against the common law, may be indicted; but no injuries of a private nature, unless they some way concern the King' (*R v Bembridge* (1783) 3 Doug 327, 332, Lord Mansfield).

Law in general is public, in one sense: it is available for members of the community to know (at least, it ought to be, and in England it is). It is enforced (and disputes are adjudicated) by public officials. What's more, law is (or at least it ought to be) made for the public good. That includes the law of contract, which benefits the public (that is, the people of the community) by enabling persons to enter into binding agreements on reasonable terms, and by providing public techniques for enforcement and dispute resolution. So if all law is public in these respects, what is the sense of distinguishing public law from private law?

People call the law of contract 'private law' because it regulates a private transaction (such as the purchase of a car). A type of transaction is private if it does not necessarily impose on the parties to the transaction any legal duty to the community. Tort law is private law, because even though it serves the public good, and public bodies are subject to it, the duties it imposes are duties owed by one person to another, and not necessarily[55] to the community, and the rights that it provides are rights held by one person against another, and not necessarily against the community. So, for example, if you demolish my house unlawfully, you are liable in tort law to compensate me, whether you are acting for a public authority or not, and whether I am a public authority or not. Tort law regulates the relation between the tortfeasor and the victim, and their duties to each other (which may involve no duties to the community). Lawyers use the term 'private law' for legal standards that regulate types of transaction and relationship that may not involve any duties owed to the public. A legal dispute is a dispute over private law if neither party has any legal duty to the public that is relevant to the dispute.

In the Court of Appeal in *O'Reilly v Mackman*, Lord Denning said that: 'Private law regulates the affairs of subjects as between themselves. Public law regulates the affairs of subjects vis-à-vis public authorities' (255). But that is wildly inaccurate because, as Lord Denning knew very well, private law regulates the affairs of subjects vis-à-vis public authorities whenever the public authority has a contract or alleges a tort by a private person, or a private person alleges that a public body is liable in tort. If you buy a used car from a car dealer, and you buy a used car from a government agency, it makes no difference at all that one transaction is an affair between subjects and the other is an affair vis-à-vis a public authority. Your legal rights are just the same in the two cases. And we saw in Chapter 14 that tort law is *generally the same* whether the defendant is private or public, with the exception of the tort of misfeasance in a public office.

The courts emerged from Lord Diplock's era with an artificial view of judicial review as the unique and exclusive forum for 'public law'. By 'public law', Lord Diplock roughly meant the judicially administered aspects of administrative law: the legal standards for the use of the power of public authorities that are applied in claims for the prerogative remedies. After the *Roy*[56] and *Mercury*[57] cases (see 10.2.1, pp 376), it seemed fiendishly difficult to distinguish public from private. Largely because of

---

[55] Tort law protects bodies too, incidentally, since a public body may make a claim in tort.

[56] *Roy v Kensington & Chelsea* [1992] 1 AC 624.

[57] *Mercury Communications v Director General of Telecommunications* [1996] 1 WLR 48.

the *O'Reilly* fiasco (see 10.2.1, pp 370), the courts thought that they had to draw a boundary in the twilight zone between the public and the private. But if a claimant alleges that a public authority has abused its power to determine a contract term, the issue is not *in between* the public and the private. Those cases involve *both* public law and private law at the same time: the parties in *Roy* and *Mercury* had contracts *and* the content of that private law relationship was determined by a public authority's decision (which was controlled by the standards of lawful administration that have been developed in judicial review). It was the combination that made the distinction between public law and private law seem mysterious in those cases.

In fact, the distinction is simple and clear. Public law *authorizes* and *requires persons and agencies to act in the public interest*. Criminal law is public law (it imposes duties to the community, and if they are breached, the community can bring legal proceedings for the imposition of sanctions to enforce the duties). So is the law of contempt of court (see 10.4.5), and the law of taxation, and the law of planning, and the law of building regulations, and environmental protection law.

> ### Public law and private law
> It is sometimes said that private actors are not subject to **public law**. But Tesco is subject to all sorts of public law: tax law, criminal law, health and safety regulations, planning law, etc. Tesco is subject to **public law**, but is not subject to **administrative law**, which is the law of public administration.

Public law imposes duties to serve the public interest; *administrative law* creates institutions and processes through which one public authority may exercise legal authority to control another public authority. Administrative law requires the courts to oversee the integrity of decision making by persons and bodies that the law ought to require to act on behalf of the public.

But although the distinction between private and public is *simple*, it is also *vague*. And, in one respect, there actually is a twilight zone between public and private, and the courts must be prepared to draw the line: it concerns the *Datafin* question (see 15.5.1) of whether the standards imposed on public authorities in judicial review are to be imposed on non-governmental organizations. As we have seen, the practical effects of this boundary-drawing exercise are less important than they seemed to be twenty years ago, when the courts had decided that judicial review was 'public', and had not yet developed the scope of the action for a declaration as a tool for imposing justice in private administration. The courts had lost track of the heritage of Lord Mansfield, who was prepared to use *mandamus*—an instrument of administrative law, in which the courts take responsibility for the integrity of decision making—without reckoning whether the defendant was a public authority.[58]

---

[58]   *R v Barker* (1762) 3 Burr 1265 (see 15.5.2, p 610).

The government-by-contract model has become a structural feature of public administration. The model needs to be reconciled with the principle of proportionate administration—the principle that administrative structures and techniques should be crafted in a way that provides sufficient accountability and efficiency for the purpose at hand.

To achieve good government, the state needs partnerships with private service providers. And PPPs do not need to result in an accountability disaster. But they *will* do so whenever accountability for some particular public interest (say, efficiency) is given priority over accountability for equity.

TAKE-HOME MESSAGE • • •

- Government may be able to serve the community better and at less cost by contracting with private companies for a service than by delivering a service itself. Or it may end up damaging the community by treating the people it serves as if they were customers.

- If political accountability is damaged through government by contract, the courts cannot make up for it. But they can do some basic tasks that provide **legal accountability**:
  - controlling government by just decisions as to whether a particular agency has **capacity** to enter into a particular contract;
  - providing judicial review against contracting decisions that judges can identify as an **abuse of power**; and
  - providing a check on the unjust avoidance of public law obligations through contracting out.

- The law of the **European Union** gives judges a remarkable role in controlling spending decisions. It does so because of the distinctive EU project of creating and sustaining a single market for goods and services, and not because judges should generally be controlling government expenditure.

- **Auditors** are generally better equipped to investigate the effectiveness of government spending than judges are.

- It is difficult for judges to decide to what extent private organizations are subject to their forms of control over public power through judicial review and the Human Rights Act. But courts should also control **purely private uses of power**.

- **Public law** imposes legal obligations to serve the public interest.

CRITICAL QUESTIONS • • •

1 Would you be able to get judicial review of a decision by the government to privatize the British Army by selling it to a company and paying the company for security services?

2   How is an auditor different from an ombudsman?

3   No public authority should be able to expand its powers by making an *ultra vires* contract. No public authority should be able to get out of a contract by claiming that it had no power to make the contract. Can you reconcile these two ideas?

4   Does the common law of due process require courts to decide the process by which public authorities decide whether to enter into a contract?

5   Is a private nursing home carrying out a public function when it houses a resident whose accommodation is paid for by a public authority?

READING • • •

Nagle v Feilden [1966] 2 QB 633

R v Panel on Take-overs and Mergers, ex p Datafin Plc [1987] QB 815 (CA)

R v Jockey Club, ex p Aga Khan [1993] 1 WLR *909* (CA)

Crédit Suisse v Allerdale Borough Council [1997] QB 306

Poplar Housing v Donoghue [2001] EWCA Civ 595

R v Servite Houses, ex p Goldsmith [2001] LGR 55

R (Heather) v Leonard Cheshire Foundation [2002] EWCA Civ 366

Aston Cantlow Parochial Church Council v Wallbank [2003] UKHL 37

Mullins v McFarlane [2006] EWHC 986

YL v Birmingham City Council [2007] UKHL 27

Essential viewing:
Robocop (1987)
On government by contract:
Anne Davies, *The Public Law of Government Contracts* (OUP 2008)
Mark Freedland, 'Government by Contract and Private Law' [1994] PL 86
Peter Cane, *Controlling Administrative Power, An Historical Comparison* (CUP 2016)
On accountability:
Anne Davies, *Accountability: A Public Law Analysis of Government by Contract* (OUP 2001), ch 4, 'Accountability Mechanisms'
On government by contract in the United States of America:
Jody Freeman and Martha Minow, eds, *Government by Contract: Outsourcing and American Democracy* (Harvard University Press 2009)
On public procurement:
Christopher McCrudden, *Buying Social Justice* (OUP 2007)
Eleanor Aspey, 'The Search for the True Public Law Element: Judicial Review of Procurement Decisions' [2016] Public Law 35
On which functions are 'public' for the purpose of judicial review:
Colin Campbell, 'Monopoly Power as Public Power for the Purposes of Judicial Review' (2009) 125 LQR 491
Alexander Williams, 'Judicial Review and Monopoly Power: Some Sceptical Thoughts' (2017) 133 LQR 656–82

On the applicability of judicial review to private actors:
Neil Duxbury, 'The Outer Limits of English Judicial Review' [2017] Public Law 235–48
On common law judicial control over contracts:
Stephen Bailey, 'Judicial Review of Contracting Decisions' [2007] PL 444
On what counts as a 'public authority' under the Human Rights Act 1998:
Stephanie Palmer, 'Public, Private and the Human Rights Act 1998: An Ideological
  Divide' (2007) 66 CLJ 559

 The following online resources accompany this chapter: **summaries** of key
cases and legislation; **updates** on the law; **guidance** for answering the pop
quizzes and questions; and **links** to legislation, cases, and useful websites.

Glossary

The Index shows where you can find further explanation of these terms.

Abuse of power: A use of public power that is blameworthy (either because it oppresses some person, or is very damaging to the public interest). Abusing a power is different from merely using it wrongly. Abuse of power is generally a ground of **judicial review**; using a power wrongly is generally not a ground of judicial review.

Access to justice: A requirement of the rule of law. Persons must be able to pursue a legal complaint before a court or tribunal (which means not only that the court or tribunal has to be open and provide due process, but also that the party seeking to bring proceedings must have the means to do so, and legal representation if it is necessary).

Action: The old term (before the Civil Procedure Rules 1998) for a claim in which a party asserts a legal right to a remedy in a civil court (now called an 'ordinary claim').

Administration: The operation of the executive branch of government. Administration includes both the formation and the implementation of policies, so far as it can be done without primary legislation or judicial decision. 'The administration' is a general term for the institutions and officers that carry out administration (see 1.2).

Administration of justice: The conduct of administrative and judicial processes that are designed to do justice (whether criminal or civil) according to law (whether **public law or private law**).

Administrative justice: A general term for processes designed to do justice between **complainants** and the administration. It is used in this book in the more particular sense of processes outside the courts (such as internal complaints processes, and the processes of ombudsmen, tribunals, and auditors) for securing just administration.

Administrative law: An array of legal processes and techniques for empowering public authorities (not only administrators, but also many others) and controlling their conduct. Administrative law is reflexive: it controls the conduct of institutions such as tribunals and ombudsmen that were themselves designed to control the administration.

Alternative dispute resolution (ADR): A way of resolving a dispute without taking it to a court or tribunal for a binding determination.

Appeal: A proceeding in which a higher tribunal or court re-examines the decision of a lower tribunal or court, or of an administrative authority. The point is not to repeat the initial proceeding, but to determine whether there is ground for reversing it. Appeal processes are created by statute; the **judicial review** process has been developed through the common law.

Application for judicial review: The term that was used for a claim for **judicial review** (see **claim**) before the Civil Procedure Rules 1998.

Arbitrariness: A decision is arbitrary if it is unresponsive to reason—that is, if the decision maker does not base the decision on relevant reasons (see 1.1.3).

Bias: The attitude of a decision maker who is hostile towards one side in a process or proceeding in which the decision maker ought to be impartial.

Cause of action: Right of action.

Certiorari **('to be certified'):** A prerogative writ developed at common law, which has been replaced by the 'quashing order' in the Civil Procedure Rules 1998.

Civil servant: A servant of the **Crown** employed by a department of central government ('public servant' is the term for anyone who works for a **public authority**, including civil servants, police, local authority employees, employees of executive agencies, and non-departmental public bodies, employees of the Armed Forces, etc.).

Claim: A judicial proceeding in which a claimant seeks a remedy. In an ordinary claim, the claimant must establish a right to a remedy; the claimant has no right to proceed with the claim if he or she does not assert grounds on which such a right to a remedy could be established (a **right of action**).

In a **claim for judicial review**, the claimant asks the court for permission to commence a proceeding in which the court will review the lawfulness of a decision 'in relation to the exercise of a public function' (CPR 54.1). The claimant must have standing (which requires a 'sufficient interest' in the matter—see 11.1.2), and must show that there is a ground for judicial review, but need not show any right to a remedy.

Comity: Respect that one **public authority** ought to show for the good functioning of another (see 1.5.3).

Complainant: A person who has a complaint against a **public authority**.

Compound decision making: Decision making in which an initial decision is subject to review or appeal (see 5.3.2), so that a lack of independence or impartiality in the initial decision may potentially be cured by the availability of review or appeal. Most administrative decision making is compound in this sense.

Court of specific jurisdiction: A court with a **jurisdiction** that is limited to a particular size or type of claim. These are also called 'inferior courts' (a term at least as old as *R v Cowle* (1759) 2 Burr 834, 861 (Lord Mansfield)), because their decisions are normally subject to appeal or review in a superior court.

Council of Europe (http://www.coe.int): The treaty organization, set up in 1949, that is responsible for the European Convention on Human Rights. The Council of Europe and the European Union are independent of each other, although they cooperate on joint programmes.

CPR: The Civil Procedure Rules 1998, available at http://www.justice.gov.uk/courts/ procedure-rules/civil/rules.

Crown: Until the eighteenth century, the Crown was a symbol for the power of the state, which the monarch wielded. Today, the Queen herself is a symbol for the power of the state, which is wielded by the **government**. 'The Crown' is a name for the government of the United Kingdom as a legal person.

Deference: A reviewing decision maker defers to an initial decision maker if the reviewing decision maker can interfere with a decision, but will only do so if there are special grounds (that is, grounds *other* than merely that the reviewing decision maker would have taken a different decision) (see 7.2.4).

Derogate: To suspend the effect of a law in a specific situation or class of situations (see 1.1.2, p 9).

Discretion: A **public authority** has discretion to the extent that the law authorizes or requires it to choose a course of action without determining what course of action is to be chosen.

District judge: A judge in the county courts.

Due process: The decision-making procedures that are required to be followed in making a decision. They may be required by legislation, or by the decision maker's own rules or practice, or by **natural justice**.

European Union (http://europa.eu/index_en.htm): In 1950, Belgium, France, Germany, Italy, Luxembourg, and the Netherlands set up a free-trade arrangement for coal and steel, which has since evolved into a unique interstate political and legal system. In 1957, the Treaty of Rome created the European Economic Community. Britain joined in 1973. The single market was really completed in the 1990s, and the term 'European Union' was adopted in 1993. Today, there are twenty-seven member states. The major EU institutions are the European Parliament, the Council of the European Union, the Commission, the Court of Justice of the European Union, the European Court of Auditors, and the European Ombudsman. The UK is negotiating a withdrawal from the European Union, which is scheduled to take effect on 29 March 2019, unless a different timetable is agreed (See 'Note on Brexit', p xxi).

Executive agency: An agency that provides a public service, typically under a framework agreement setting out its responsibilities and its accountability within a department. Unlike a **non-departmental public body**, it is part of a department, but it has a greater or lesser degree of managerial independence from the departmental structure.

Ex gratia: As a favour (that is, even though the law does not require it).

Fairness: A **public authority** acts unfairly if it wrongly neglects an interest of a person affected by the decision. The neglected interest may be an interest in the outcome (in which case the unfairness is substantive), or an interest in participation in the making of the decision (in which case the unfairness is procedural—see **natural justice**).

Procedural unfairness is a ground of **judicial review**. Substantive unfairness is not a ground of judicial review *in itself*, but certain forms of substantive unfairness ground judicial review.

Fundamental freedoms: A term for freedom of thought, conscience and religion, freedom of expression, freedom of assembly and association, which are protected by Articles 9–11 of the European Convention on Human Rights.

Government: In the *traditional English sense*, 'the government' means the ministers of the **Crown** and the departments that they administer. The word can also be used *in the broad sense* for all public authorities including the courts and Parliament. 'The government' in the traditional English sense is the central leadership of the executive branch of 'government' in the broad sense. The word 'Government' is sometimes capitalized when it refers to a particular Prime Minister and his or her administration.

Grounds for judicial review: Features of a decision that courts treat as reasons (subject to the court's **discretion**) for interfering with the decision in **judicial review**.

Habeas corpus ('get the body'): Early prerogative writ from a court of common law or equity, requiring a person to be brought to the court. The courts developed it into a technique for inquiring into the lawfulness of detention, and Parliament extended it in 1640 to apply to detention ordered by the King.

Human right: A right that persons have because they are human. The European Convention on Human Rights uses the term to mean, roughly, rights that are so fundamental to a civilized community that the contracting states have assumed a duty under the Convention to protect them in law (see 3.4). According to the **Council of Europe**: 'Human rights are inalienable rights which guarantee the fundamental dignity of the human being. The European Convention on Human Rights guarantees civil and political human rights. The European Social Charter, its natural complement, guarantees social and economic human rights.'[1]

Inferior court: Court of specific jurisdiction

Inherent jurisdiction: The power of the High Court to hear new kinds of claim, and to create new remedies, or processes, or doctrines to do justice between the parties before it. The power is limited in various ways by common law and statute; it is not a power to ignore the law, but a power to develop the law in the interest of the good administration of justice. The development of *habeas corpus* is one dramatic and important instance of the exercise of inherent jurisdiction. Its constitutional source is delegation from the **Crown** to the Queen's judges of the sovereign power to administer justice.

Irrationality: An action is irrational if it cannot be understood as the action of someone acting for an intelligible purpose. But in **administrative law** the term is given a special meaning, which is, roughly, 'extremely unreasonable'. 'Irrationality' in that technical sense is often (but not always—see 7.3.2) a ground of **judicial review**.

----

[1] http://www.coe.int/t/dghl/monitoring/socialcharter/presentation/aboutcharter_EN.asp.

Issue: A disputed question that a court must answer in order to decide a **claim**.

Judicial review: Consideration by a court of the lawfulness of administrative conduct. But the phrase is sometimes used as a term for the act of interfering with a decision, or as a term for a claim for judicial review.

Jurisdiction: Legal power of decision (as in *Anisminic v Foreign Compensation Commission* [1969] 2 AC 147) or action (as in *Entick v Carrington* (1765) 19 Howell's St Tr 1029, concerning whether the **Secretary of State** had 'a jurisdiction' to seize Entick's papers). Courts, tribunals, and administrative decision makers all have jurisdiction to make legally binding decisions, although the doctrine of review for error of law (see 9.1, p 319) has made English lawyers hesitate to talk about the jurisdiction of administrative decision makers. Lord Reid used the term in a 'narrow sense' (for power to address an issue) and in a 'broad sense' (for power not only to address an issue, but to reach a particular decision on it) (see 9.1.7).

Justice: Respect for rights. Just administrative action promotes the public good (which includes the overriding public good of respecting the rights not only of citizens, but also of people in general). Justice is not, in itself, a ground of **judicial review** (see 1.5.6), because the rule of law often requires that a **public authority** abide by rules that may prevent it from acting justly, and the rule of law may prevent a court from quashing an unjust decision. But the rule of law itself is valuable only insofar as it serves justice. So justice is, indirectly, the main point of the grounds of judicial review, and of law in general.

Justiciability: An issue is justiciable if it is suitable for resolution by judges, through a judicial process.

Legitimate expectation: An expectation that deserves legal protection. The form of protection can vary. The reason for giving legal protection may be that it is procedurally unfair for an administrative authority to disappoint your expectation without giving you a hearing, or that disappointing your expectation would involve substantive unfairness that a court ought to prevent.

Locus standi: **Standing**.

Maladministration: Bad administration. It is not generally a ground of **judicial review**, although some forms of bad administration give **grounds for judicial review**. Ombudsmen have the task of investigating complaints of maladministration.

Mandamus **('we command'):** A prerogative writ developed at common law, which has been replaced by the 'mandatory order' in the Civil Procedure Rules 1998.

Margin of appreciation: The doctrine developed in the European Court of Human Rights in Strasbourg, that it should give national authorities some leeway in the application of the Convention rights, because those authorities 'are in principle better placed than an international court to evaluate local needs and conditions' *Sahin v Turkey* (2005) 41 EHRR 8 [100].

Misfeasance: An **abuse of power** that is carried out in bad faith. Misfeasance in a public office is the only tort that can be committed only by public officials.

Natural justice: Legal jargon for procedures that the common law requires. Usually interchangeable with **procedural fairness** (see 4.2).

New public management: Management of public projects and government programmes through techniques learned from the management of private enterprise.

Non-departmental public body (NDPB): A **public authority** that is somewhat independent of government. An **executive agency** is set up to implement policy set by a department under a framework agreement. An NDPB is typically more independent than an executive agency, and sets policy at arm's length from a department (but some NDPBs are called 'executive NDPBs' because they provide government services—the Environment Agency is an example).

Non-justiciable: *See* justiciability.

Obiter dicta: *See* ratio.

Ombudsman: An officer who investigates a complaint of bad administration, and then issues a report on what happened and what, if anything, should be done about it. The Parliamentary Ombudsman, also referred to as the Parliamentary Commissioner for Administration, serves as an ombudsman for central government, and also as the Health Service Ombudsman (http://www.ombudsman.org.uk). Local Government Ombudsmen (http://www.lgo.org.uk) investigate complaints about administration by local government.

Order in Council: A legislative instrument made by the **Privy Council**. The Privy Council's role is to rubber-stamp legislation drafted by government departments and presented by ministers. An Order in Council can be an exercise of the prerogative, or it can be a statutory instrument (where a statute provides that delegated legislation under the statute is to be made by Order in Council). An Order in Council made in the exercise of the prerogative counts as primary legislation under the Human Rights Act 1998 s 21.

Ouster clause: A statutory provision purporting to prevent the courts from interfering with a decision of a **public authority**.

Parliamentary sovereignty: A rule of the UK constitution, which imposes no legal limits on Parliament's power to make laws. Acts of Parliament cannot be overruled by any other institution, and Parliament cannot bind its successors as to the content of legislation.

Plaintiff: The term used for a **claimant** in an action before the changes in the Civil Procedure Rules 1998.

Policy: A course of action adopted by a **public authority**, or a reason for a course of action. The term is commonly used for the sort of governmental purpose on which judges, tribunals, and (or ombudsmen ought to defer (to some extent) to administrative officials.

Prerogative powers: Powers that belong exclusively to the **Crown**, and which are exercised by the government. They allow ministers to make certain decisions without an Act of Parliament.

> 'Prerogative is nothing but the power of doing public good without a rule.'
> **John Locke,** *Of Civil Government* **(1689) Chapter XIV [166]**
> 'Prerogative: A sovereign's right to do wrong.' **Ambrose Bierce,** *The Devil's Dictionary* **(1911)**

Presumption of non-interference: The principle that a decision of a public body should have effect, and should be interfered with only if there is ground for judicial review.

Prima facie: 'At first glance' or presumptively. A ruling is *prima facie* valid, or a *prima facie* right or duty exists, if the ruling is valid or the right or duty exists *unless* some special reason defeats the presumption that it is valid or exists.

Principle of relativity: The principle that the requirements of constitutional principles depend on the context in which they are applied.

Principles: Starting points for reasoning about what is to be done. The principles of **administrative law** are basic starting points for reasoning about how the law ought to control public action for the good of the public and to give effect to claims of right (see 1.5 and 1.6).

Private finance initiative (PFI): A form of **public–private partnership** in which the private partner invests in a large building project, such as a school or a hospital. The private partner typically owns the facility that is built, and the public partner agrees to provide the private partner with a stream of future income from the service that the facility will be used to provide.

Private law: Law designed to protect and to promote the interests of particular persons. It includes the law that gives rights to public authorities and private persons in contract and the law of property, and the rules of tort law that impose duties to respect interests of private persons and of public authorities, and the rules and processes for giving judicial remedies for breach of private law rights and duties. There are, of course, reasons of public policy for making such laws.

Privatization: The sale of a public enterprise to private owners, accompanied by (1) a government decision not to carry on a public enterprise in the industry in question; and (2) (typically) new forms of licensing and regulation of the resulting enterprise.

Privy Council: A council that advises the **Crown**. Cabinet ministers and some other ministers are appointed to the Privy Council for life. There are hundreds of Privy Councillors, but the advice of the Privy Council is given by the members who currently hold ministerial office. Judicial decisions are made on behalf of the Privy Council by a committee of Supreme Court justices and senior Commonwealth judges; that committee serves as the court of final appeal for overseas territories and for those Commonwealth countries that have not abolished appeals to the Privy Council. See http://jcpc.uk.

Procedural fairness: A decision is procedurally unfair if it is biased, or if the process by which it is made wrongly disregards the interest that an affected person has in participating in the decision. **Fairness** is the primary requirement of **due process**.

Procedure: A step that a decision maker takes to get information for making a decision, or to hear argument as to what decision it ought to make, or to communicate its decision, or to reconsider its decision, or to entertain an appeal from a decision of another decision maker.

Proceeding: The process by which a case is heard by a **tribunal** or court.

Process: The set of procedures by which a decision is made (and, potentially, communicated, and explained, and reconsidered, or made subject to appeal …).

Prohibition: A prerogative writ developed at common law, which has been replaced by the 'prohibiting order' in the Civil Procedure Rules 1998.

Proportionality: A just relation between legitimate ends that a public authority pursues and the means by which it pursues them. Ordinarily, it means not damaging a protected interest of a person in a way that is out of proportion to the value of the **public authority**'s action.

Public authority: A person or institution with a power that is exercised on behalf of the community, and subject to controls for the good of the community. The question of who or what counts as a public authority may have different answers in different contexts, depending on the purposes of a particular doctrine of **public law** (see 15.6.1).

Public law: Law designed to serve the public interest directly (**private law** promotes the public interest indirectly, by enabling members of the community to make just legal arrangements with each other, and to seek vindication of their rights against each other). Public law gives legal powers for the administration of government and for the making of law, and controls the use of those powers, and imposes duties on private persons and public bodies to serve the public interest. It therefore includes, for example, tax law, criminal law, and constitutional law (cf. **administrative law**).

Public–private partnership (PPP): An ongoing arrangement between a **public authority** (often a government department or **executive agency**) and a private company for the provision of a public service.

Quasi-judicial: A decision or function of a **public authority** is quasi-judicial if it is similar to the decision or function of a judge, so that it requires the public authority to act similarly to the way in which a judge would act. The term has not been used very much since *Ridge v Baldwin* [1964] AC 40 restored the ancient rule that an administrative decision does not need to be quasi-judicial in order to be subject to the law of **due process**.

***Ratio* or *ratio decidendi* ('reasoning' or 'reason for decision'):** In the common law, the legal basis on which a court decides a case. It determines the effect of the decision as a precedent. A decision binds future courts only as to the *ratio* (and does so subject to powers such as that of the Supreme Court to overrule its own earlier decisions).

Common law courts have **jurisdiction** only to adjudicate claims, and not to make general enactments, so the *ratio* is restricted to the statements of law made by a judge or judges in order to explain the court's decision in the case. Any further statements of law made by the judges are *obiter dicta* ('things said along the way').

Reasonableness: It is unreasonable to act in a way that is not guided by the appropriate reasons. The public authorities to which a decision-making responsibility was assigned are often better able to assess those reasons than the judges (who are responsible for the rule of law, but not for good decision making in general). For that reason, unreasonableness is not a general ground of **judicial review**. An action is unreasonable in the special, restricted sense that does provide a ground of judicial review if it is not guided by reasons on which the law requires judges to insist. A decision should be quashed as unreasonable on judicial review when it is inconsistent with reasons that it is right for judges to impose on other decision makers.

Relator proceeding: A claim brought by the Attorney General at the request of a person. These proceedings reflect the general **standing** of the **Crown** to ask its courts to determine the lawfulness of official conduct. But they have become obsolete because the courts have become willing to give **standing** to private litigants to seek **judicial review** in (it seems) all circumstances in which they might have asked the Attorney General to bring a claim.

Res judicata: The rule that judicial decisions are final (subject to appeal). There is no such general rule for administrative decisions; a **public authority** generally has authority to reconsider an administrative decision, subject to the doctrine of **legitimate expectations**.

Right: An entitlement of a person that must be respected regardless of benefits that could be achieved by acting contrary to the person's interest. A legal right is a legal entitlement that the law protects by imposing duties on other persons. See **human right**.

Right of action: The right that a claimant has to a remedy in an ordinary claim *if* the alleged facts are proved. In an ordinary claim, the claimant's statement of case must assert a right of action; if it 'discloses no reasonable grounds for bringing or defending the claim', the court may strike out the statement (CPR 3.4(2)). A claimant for **judicial review** need not assert a right of action.

Rule of law: A country has the rule of law if law (that is, a systematic scheme of open, prospective, stable, general rules) controls those aspects of the life of the community that ought to be controlled by law. The rule of law requires independent courts that can determine legal rights and obligations. It does *not* require that judges make all public decisions. One central challenge for administrative law is working out the extent to which the rule of law requires judicial control over decisions by other public officials (see 1.5.4 and Chapter 2). But the rule of law is not only a matter of judicial control over decision making; it also makes a variety of demands on good administration—chiefly, faithful adherence to the law by public officials, but also independence within the administration for certain decision makers, such as prosecutors, and transparency in the adoption of rules and policies.

Secretary of State: A secretary of state really was a secretary under Elizabeth I; today, they are Cabinet ministers who head the major departments. At time of writing, there are Secretaries of State for: the Home Department; Foreign and Commonwealth Affairs; Energy and Climate Change; Health; Culture, Media and Sport; International Development; Education; Justice; Business, Energy, and Industrial Strategy; Housing, Communities and Local Government; Work and Pensions; Environment, Food, and Rural Affairs; Defence; Transport; International Trade; Northern Ireland; Scotland; Wales; and Exiting the European Union. The phrase 'the Secretary of State' is a common term in legislation for whatever minister heads the department in question. So, for example, legislation saying 'the Secretary of State may . . . ' gives a power to the department.

Separation of powers: The constitutional principle that governmental power should be allocated to separate institutions in ways that promote the rule of law, democracy, and the effective formation and implementation of public policy, and that the separate institutions should interfere with each other only in ways that protect responsible government.

Standing: The right to bring proceedings, formerly known as '*locus standi*'. To have standing to bring a claim for **judicial review**, the claimant must have a 'sufficient interest' in the matter.

Strasbourg Court: The European Court of Human Rights in Strasbourg.

Subsidiarity: Allocation of power to the level of government (e.g. a local council, a regional assembly, a national legislature, or the institutions of the European Union) at which it can be exercised most effectively and responsibly.

Substance: The content of a decision (that is, *what is decided*; see 6.9.1); cf. **process**.

Tariff: The period of time that a prisoner must spend in prison for punitive purposes, before being considered for parole. (Parole is then to be granted if release would not be dangerous to the community or to particular people.)

Tribunal: Any adjudicative forum is a tribunal (courts are tribunals). But the word 'tribunal' is used in a special sense in English **administrative law** to refer to an independent, or quasi-independent, adjudicative authority that is separate from the courts, and which hears a legal dispute between two parties (so it is different from an **ombudsman**, who investigates a complaint).

Ultra vires: Latin for 'outside [someone's] lawful powers'. In **administrative law**, English lawyers and judges sometimes talk as if acting *ultra vires* means acting in a way that *Parliament intended to be* outside the **public authority**'s powers. But no public authority has lawful power to act contrary to law, so an action of a public authority is *ultra vires* if it is unlawful for any reason (e.g. because Parliament has prohibited such action, or because some other rule of law prohibits it).

Upper Tribunal: The appellate and **judicial review** body for the tribunal system, set up by the Tribunals, Courts and Enforcement Act 2007.

***Wednesbury* grounds (or *Wednesbury* principles):** Lord Greene's explanation, in *Associated Provincial Picture Houses v Wednesbury* [1948] 1 KB 223, of some of the restricted grounds on which a court will quash an unreasonable decision of a **public authority**.

***Wednesbury* unreasonableness:** A decision is *Wednesbury* unreasonable if it is 'so unreasonable that no reasonable authority could ever have come to it' (*Associated Provincial Picture Houses v Wednesbury Corporation* [1948] 1 KB 223, 230, 234 (Lord Greene)). It is essential to remember that Lord Greene mentioned other grounds of control of **discretion** too, besides *Wednesbury* unreasonableness: they are often called the *Wednesbury* principles.

White Paper: A document produced by the government or a parliamentary committee outlining a policy or a legislative proposal.

Index